Business Ethics and Corporate Governance

C.S.V. MURTHY

B.Sc., B.E., MIE., Chartered Engineer,
Industrial Consultant,
Visiting Faculty at Various Management Colleges,
Bangalore.

ISO 9001:2015 CERTIFIED

First Edition : 2009
Edition : 2011, 2012, 2013,
Edition 2014, 2015, 2018
Edition : 2019, 2021, 2022
Edition : 2023
Edition : 2024

Published by : Mrs. Meena Pandey
for **HIMALAYA PUBLISHING HOUSE PVT. LTD.,**
"Ramdoot", Dr. Bhalerao Marg, Girgaon, Mumbai - 400 004.
Phone: 022-23860170, 23863863; **Fax:** 022-23877178
E-mail: himpub@bharatmail.co.in; **Website:** www.himpub.com

Branch Offices :

New Delhi : "Pooja Apartments", 4-B, Murari Lal Street, Ansari Road, Darya Ganj, New Delhi - 110 002. Phone: 011-23270392, 23278631; Fax: 011-23256286

Nagpur : Kundanlal Chandak Industrial Estate, Ghat Road, Nagpur - 440 018. Phone: 0712-2721215, 2721216

Bengaluru : Plot No. 91-33, 2nd Main Road, Seshadripuram, Behind Nataraja Theatre, Bengaluru - 560 020. Phone: 080-41138821; Mobile: 09379847017, 09379847005

Hyderabad : No. 3-4-184, Lingampally, Besides Raghavendra Swamy Matham, Kachiguda, Hyderabad - 500 027. Phone: 040-27560041, 27550139

Chennai : No. 34/44, Motilal Street, T. Nagar, Chennai - 600 017. Mobile: 09380460419

Pune : "Laksha" Apartment, First Floor, No. 527, Mehunpura, Shaniwarpeth (Near Prabhat Theatre), Pune - 411 030. Phone: 020-24496323, 24496333; Mobile: 09370579333

Cuttack : Plot No 5F-755/4, Sector-9, CDA Markat Nagar, Cuttack - 753 014, Odisha. Mobile: 09338746007

Kolkata : 3, S.M. Bose Road, Near Gate No. 5, Agarpara Railway Station, North 24 Parganas, West Bengal - 700109. Mobile: 09674536325

DTP by : Sri Siddhi Softtek, Bengaluru.

Printed at : M/s. Charita Impressions, Hyderabad on behalf of HPH.

PREFACE

Ethical behaviour is the best long-term business strategy for a company – a view that has become increasingly accepted in the recent years. This does not mean that occasions never arise when doing what is ethical will prove costly to a company. Such occasions occur many a times in the life of a company. When we ask the business people to define the word 'ethical' 50 per cent defines it as 'what my feelings tell me is right?' Another 25 per cent defines it in religions terms as what is in accordance with my religious beliefs. Next 18 per cent define it as what 'conforms to the golden rule". The dictionary says ethics as 'the principles of conduct governing an individual or a group. Business ethics is a specialised study of moral right and wrong. It is a study of moral standards and how these apply to the systems and organisations through which modern societies produce. We have a good array of eminent Indian scholars on this subject.

The main aim of the text is to introduce the readers to the ethical concepts, which are vital to resolve moral issues in business to improve certain reasoning and analytical skills needed to apply ethical concepts during business decisions and to give short introductions to the moral issues involved in the management of specific problem areas.

I hope this book will be useful to the VTU MBA students to understand the basic principles of the ethics as it is written to their syllabus. Important and fundamental topics are covered in this book. This book would provide fundamental concepts to enable the students to understand this subject.

The book has been organised in 6 modules with a vast number of illustrations and a few case studies.

The modules covered are:

Module 1: An Overview of Business Ethics

Module 2: Individual and Organisational Factors

Module 3: External Context

Module 4: Internal Context - Employee

Module 5: Business Ethics in a Global Economy

Module 6: Corporate Governance

I am deeply indebted to the excellent DTP work undertaken by Mr. S.Madhu and his father, in bringing out this book in a limited time.

I also thank Shri.Niraj Pandey and Shri.Vijay Pandey of Himalaya Publishing House who took keen interest at every step in publishing this book. On the home front, I want to thank all my family members and close relatives for the help rendered to me at times in numerous ways.

I welcome from readers, suggestions and improvements.

C.S.V.MURTHY

Contents

MODULE 1

An Overview of Business Ethics

1.1 Definition and Nature of Business Ethics

An Understanding of Ethics

In any organisation, from top management to employees at all levels, **ethics** is considered as everybody's business. It is not just only achieving high levels of economic performance, but also to conduct one of business's most important social challenges, ethically, at the same time simultaneously. What are the ethical problems which arise in business and how to solve them or what can be done about them are explained in this module.

The problems in a business are multifold. Many of the vendors offer kickbacks to the buyers, for the purchase of their goods. These bribes are many a times hefty and within a short period, the buyers make plenty of money.

'**Money laundering**' is another example. In USA, the Bank of Boston Corporation shipped over $1 billion in cash to Swiss banks and the banks of other European nations, without reporting these transactions to US bank regulators. Twenty-one other banks also failed to file the required forms for big cash transactions. After investigation, it is learnt that drug enforcement officials suspected that such large cash flows make possible cloak secret drug sales, gambling earnings, or other illicit gains that are hidden in banks and "cleaned up" or "laundered" so as to appear the they were made honestly (Ref.:Money laundering, Business Week, March 18, 1985, pp.74-82).

Ethical Problems, What We Face?

A number of **ethical problems** are available. Ethical problems in business can arise also in a very personal, human way as stated below:

(i) When orders dropped in any manufacturing company, the supervisor is asked to terminate a few employees to save cost. The supervisor knows that some of them though loyal, hard working, they have to be terminated to save his skin. He knows it is unfair to terminate the employees and still he is helpless. Even if he is given two months termination time by the company, he will not reveal his plans of termination to the employees to be terminated with a fear that employees would quit while still needed or not work as hard as they usually did after being told. The supervisor had to enforce all company rules and policies. For him, the ethical dilemma relates to two dimensions:

- Personal
- Professional

(ii) In another case, a senior librarian who was very casual and negligent in his attitude, had to make one of his weak assistants a scapegoat at the end of the year when library inventory was checked and nearly 500 books were short. The senior librarian knew very well that his assistant is highly loyal, sincere and honest in his work and such a thing would not have happened from him. However, the reason of the books lost could not be found out by him and he had to put the blame on his junior who is mentally weak and innocent. Otherwise, he had to take the full blame. He took the decision of putting the blame on his junior rather than on himself.

There would be many episodes like this, raising ethical questions for a number of reasons. Sometimes society is harmed. At other times, the individual makes profit in an unfair way at the expense of others. We all know the story of the clever monkey that ate the curd rice and smeared it on to the face of the goat. The goat was punished severely by his master who thought that it had eaten the same.

A business firm suffers many a times with higher costs when money is '**embezzled**' or when the firm has to pay hidden costs for its supplies. (**Embezzlement** is fraudulent appropriation of another's property by the person to whom it was entrusted). Thus it can be noticed that 'money laundering' cloaks illegal activities and protects lawbreakers like the monkey-goat episode.

Meaning of Ethics

Ethics in Latin language is called 'Ethicus' and in Greek, it is called 'Ethicos'. In fact, this word has originated from 'ethos', meaning character or manners.

Ethics is thus said to be the source of morals; a treatise on this; moral principles; recognised rules of conduct.

The character of a man is expressed in terms of his conduct (ref. Fig. 1.1).

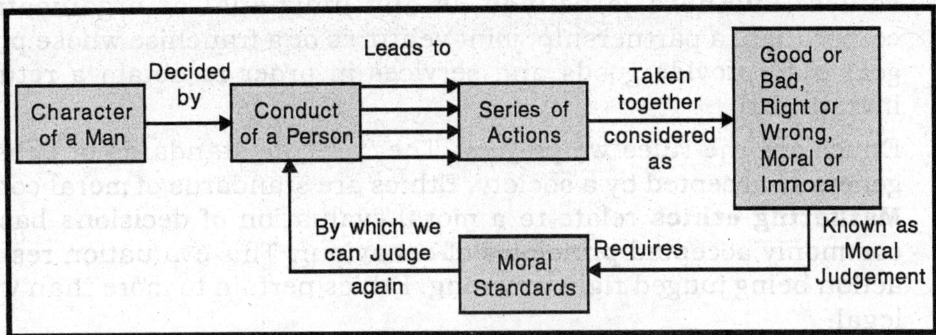

Fig. 1.1 Meaning of Ethics

Ethics thus can be considered as the source of character of a person expressed as right or wrong conduct or action.

Definition of Ethics and Business Ethics

We will examine different definitions given for **ethics** in the dictionaries as well as in books.

- According to Concise Oxford Dictionary, 'ethics' is relating to morals; treating of moral questions; morally correct; honourable.
- It is the study of morals and moral choices. It focuses on standards, rules and codes of conduct that govern the behaviour of individuals and groups.

- In the simplest terms, **business ethics** are moral principles that define right and wrong behaviour in the world of business. What constitutes right and wrong behaviour in business is determined by the public interest groups, and business organisations, as well as an individual's personal morals and values.
- The other dictionary meaning of 'ethics' is that it is the 'science of morals'; it is that branch of philosophy, which is concerned with human character and conduct. It is a treatise on morals (capable of knowing right and wrong).
- 'Ethics' refer to the code of conduct that guides an individual while dealing in a situation. It relates to the social rules that influence people to be honest in dealing with the other people.
- Ethics are the principles of behaviour that distinguish between the right from the wrong. **Business ethics** is the evaluation of business activities and behaviour as right or wrong. **Ethical conduct** conforms with what a group or society, as a whole considers right behaviour.
- Ethics can be defined as the study of what makes up good and bad conduct inclusive of related actions and values. Business ethics, which is a subject of the study of Ethics and is defined as the study of what makes up good and bad conduct as related to business activities and values (**Business** is defined as any individual or organisation, a corporation, a partnership, joint ventures or a franchise whose primary goal is to provide goods and services in order to obtain a return on investment).
- Ethics are the rules we play by. They are the standards of behaviour generally accepted by a society. Ethics are standards of moral conduct. **Marketing ethics** relate to a moral evaluation of decisions based on commonly accepted principles of behaviour. This evaluation results in action being judged right or wrong. Ethics pertain to more than what is legal.
- According to R.Wayne Mondy, 'Ethics is the discipline dealing with what is good and bad, or right and wrong, or with moral duty and obligation.'
- Ethics is that branch of philosophy, which is concerned with the rightness or wrongness, goodness or badness of human conduct. Ethics provides the basis for deciding that a particular action is morally good or bad.
- Ethics describes what is 'right' and what is 'wrong' in human behaviour, and what 'ought to be'. Business ethics are the desired norms of behaviour exclusively dealing with commercial transactions. Ethics is a description of 'observed' as well as 'desirable behaviour' and 'conduct' that attempts to articulate moral values.
- Ethics concern the rightness or wrongness of human conduct.
- According to John Donaldson, **Business ethics**, in short can be described as the systematic study of moral (ethical) matters pertaining

to business, industry or related activities, institutions, or practices and beliefs. It can also refer to the actual standards, values or practices or beliefs (An example of the latter use is seen in the title of Max Weber's book, 'The Protestant Ethic and the Spirit of Capitalism'). Business Ethics is the systematic handling of values in business and industry.

- The word 'ethics' is derived from the Greek word 'ethos' which refers specifically to the "character" and "sentiment of the community."
- Shea, in 1988 defines ethics as the principles of conduct governing an individual or a profession and "standards of behaviour."
- Ethics are the 'rules or standards that govern behaviours.' As per Brian Harvey, ethics stands for a practice as well as a reflection on that practice. As a practice, it can be described as the conscious appeal to norms and values, to which, on reasonable grounds, we hold ourselves obliged, as, reciprocally, we hold others obliged to the same norms and values. As a reflection, ethics is the methodical and systematic elaboration of the norms and values, we appeal to in our daily activities.
- Ethics are about norms and values of a certain seriousness, about standards and ideals, i.e., ones that people cannot easily neglect without harming others, or without being looked at disdainfully by significant others. It is about keeping your promises, respecting sentiment of beings, and distributing benefits and burdens in a fair and equitable way.
- **Business ethics** are the application of general ethical rules to business behaviour.
- According to Keith Davis and associates, ethics are a set of rules that define right and wrong conduct. These rules tell us when our behaviour is acceptable and when it is disapproved and considered to be wrong. **Business ethics** are the application of general ethical rules to business behaviour.
- **Business ethics** concentrate on moral standards as they apply to business policies, institutions and behaviour. It is a specialised study of moral right or wrong. It is a form of applied ethics. It includes not only the analysis of moral norms and moral values, but also attempts to apply the conclusions of the analysis to that assortment of institutions, technologies, transactions, activities and pursuits that we call business.
- **Business ethics** are nothing but the application of ethics in business. It proves that businesses can be, and have been ethical and still make profits. Today, more and more interest is being given to the application of ethical practices in business dealings and the ethical implications of business.
- **Business ethics** are rules of business conduct, by which the proprietary of business activities may be judged. It also relates to the behaviour of managers.

Introduction to Business Ethics

Ethics is commonly defined as a set of principles prescribing a behaviour code, explains what is good and right, or bad and wrong. It may even outline moral duties and obligations. There is a combination of two familiar words, namely business and ethics in 'Business ethics'. **Business ethics** are concerned with **moral issues in business** just as medical ethics are concerned with morality of medical practices and policies, or political ethics are concerned with the morality of political affairs. In business ethics, we arrive at two things:

- Looking at the problems which raises moral issues in business.
- Critically examining the various problems for solving them.

By what method do we decide on answers to questions of moral right and wrong in business? There is no special or unique process to do this, nothing more or less than is involved in any disciplined enquiry into complex problems, whether in business or anywhere else.

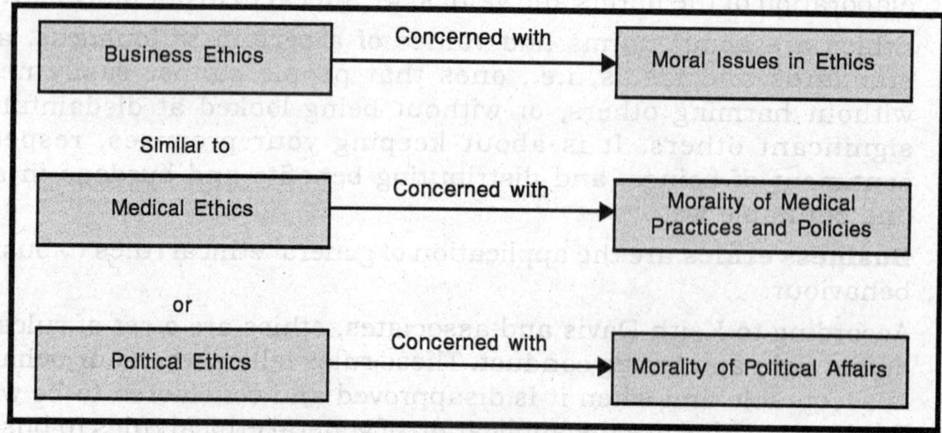

Fig. 1.2 Understanding of Business Ethics

We can subject this to three different kinds of tests.

- **Test of agreement with the evidence:** Does the evidence support or deny the explanation we have put forward? Example, we are arguing for the benefits of greater worker participation in the running of companies, what is the evidence that employees actually want such involvement?
- **Test of internal coherence:** Are all the parts of the explanation in agreement with each other or is itself contradictory in some way? Does it say things which are somehow in opposition and so cannot be or are unlikely to be, equally true at the same time?

Example: We cannot accept the workers who are exclusively interested in maximising wages and argue for the importance to them of an enhanced self esteem that would come from participation in decision making.

- Test of its compatibility (with our more general system in belief): Does it fit in with what we generally take to be true in this area or does it somehow contradict our assumptions, or at least test uncomfortably with them? How well, for example, does the claim that the workers are exclusively interested in maximising wages, fit in with what we generally accept about human motivation?

We attempt to solve ethical problems in much the same way as we would solve any other complex and contentious questions. There is the same range of test available and the same kind of critical relationship to theory.

Nature of Ethics

- The concept of ethics **deals with human beings only**. Only human beings are endorsed with the freedom of choice.
- The study of ethics has become a set of systematic knowledge about moral behaviour and conduct; study is a science - a field of social science.
- The science of ethics is a **normative science**. Normative sciences judge the value of the facts in terms of an idea; concerned with judgements of 'what ought to be,' but not with factual judgements.
- Ethics **deals with human conduct** which is voluntary and not forced or coerced by persons or circumstances. Eg. Injuring or even killing a person who has come to kill you is not considered a moral or legal offence, but a cold blooded murder is considered to be the highest kind of moral or legal crime. Ethics is basically an area **dealing with moral judgement** regarding voluntary human conduct.
- Business ethics is nothing, but the application of ethics in business.
- Business ethics can be, and has been, ethical and can still make profits.
- More interests shown today in the application of ethical practices in business dealings and the ethical implications.
- Profit maximisation and discharging of social responsibilities at the maximum limit cannot be done simultaneously as they are at opposite ends. (eg. concern for task i.e., productivity and concern of workers).
- By introducting advanced technology to replace occupations of ageold inhabitants is an ethical dilemma. Many managerial decisions have ethical implications and these decisions give rise to managerial dilemmas.

The nature of ethics is shown in fig. 1.3 which is self explanatory.

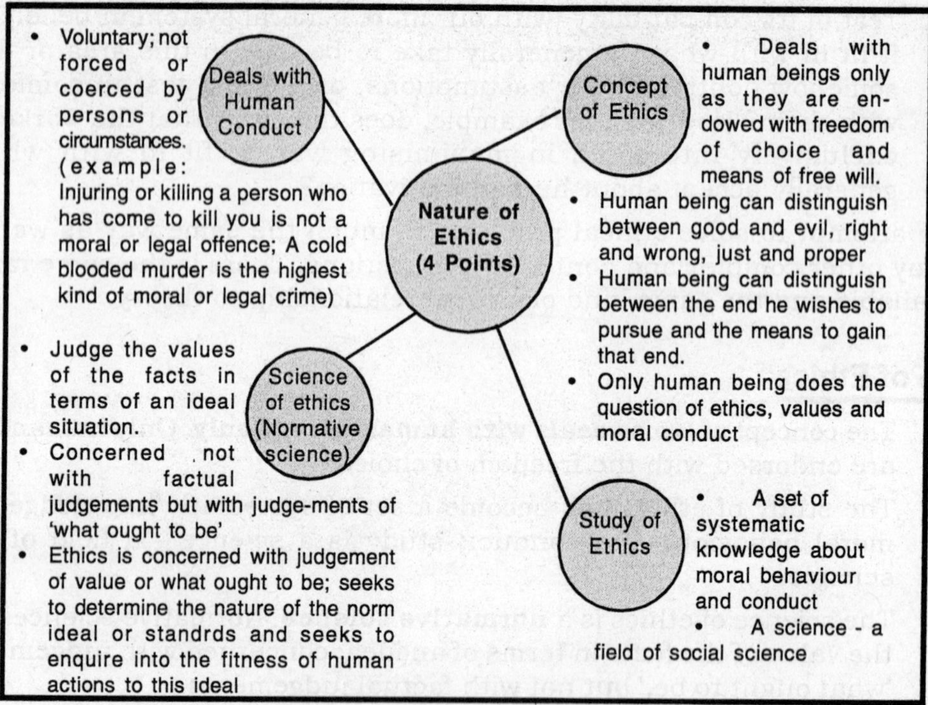

Fig. 1.3 Nature of Ethics

Nature of Business Ethics

(i) Most ethical questions could be of two types Overt and Covert: Eg. bribery, theft, sabotage, collusion etc.

(ii) Ethical issues commonly occur in management. It goes many a times for beyond the commonly discussed problems of bribery, collusion and theft, reaching into areas of corporate acquisitions, merger of firms, marketing policies and capital investments.

For example, if two firms are merged, ethical question arises with regard to demoting or firing the employees of those who have been serving honestly for many years.

(iii) Ethics want a manager to be honest within himself and also in the society. The manager has to perform his jobs well and his quality reflects in the success of a business. Ethical issues may be sometimes occur as managerial dilemmas, measured by revenues, cost and profits and the stated performance (in terms of obligation to persons both inside and outside the organisation).

(iv) Following characteristics for a decision to be ethical are needed:

(v) Ethics is unstructured (does not have standard format or framework; abstract in concept; does not have universal concept) as shown in fig. 1.5:

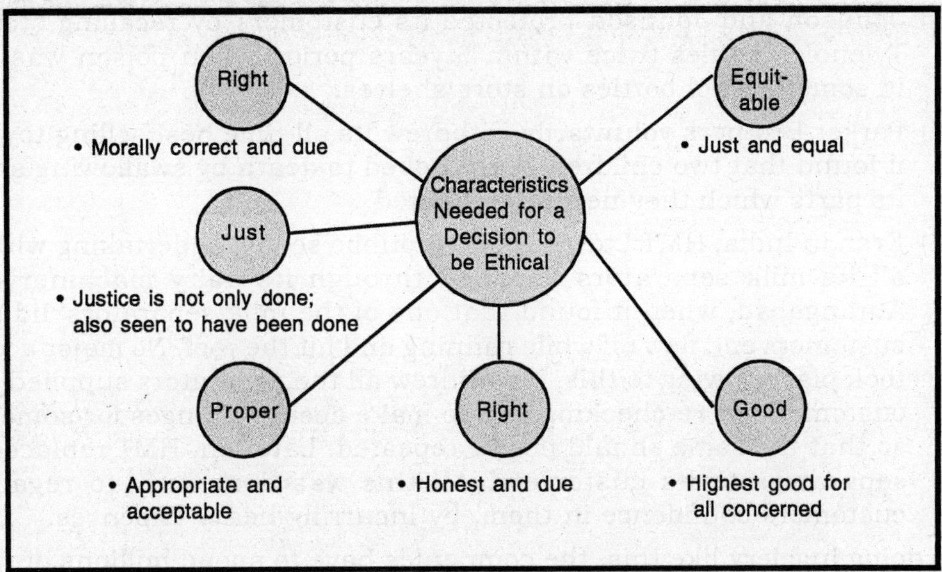

Fig. 1.4 Characteristics of an Ethical Decision

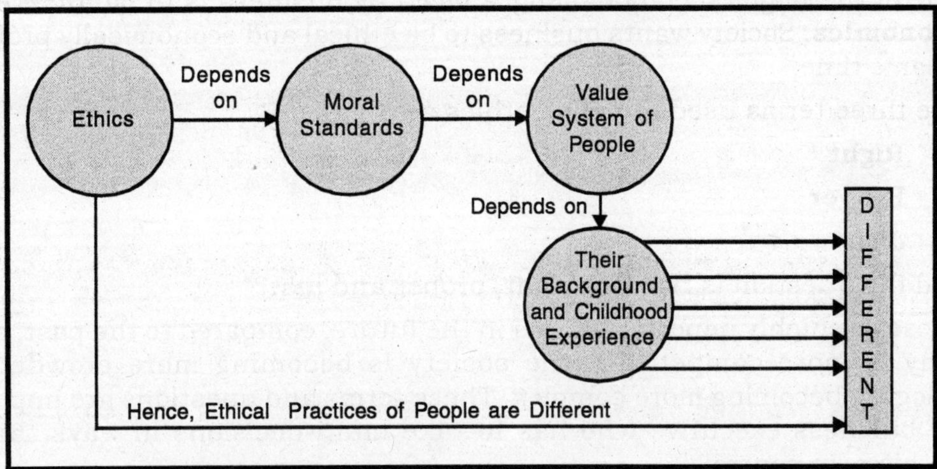

Fig. 1.5 Different Ethical Practices of People

(vi) Ethical decisions should express some obligations to others. If a decision helps in benefitting only to oneself, then that is not an ethical decision. The very concept of being ethical means that results in some good for the larger society and not just for oneself.

Ethical Performance

Business frequently demonstrates a high level of ethical performance too. **Ethical business performance** means adhering to society's basic rules that define right and wrong behaviour. The following examples reveal the same.

(i) Johnson and Johnson protected its customers by recalling stocks of Tylenol capsules twice within 5 years period when poison was found in some Tylenol bottles on store shelves.

(ii) Parker Brothers voluntarily withdrew its all time best selling toy when it found that two children were choked to death by swallowing some of its parts which they never anticipated.

(iii) Even in India, HMT Ltd., a reputed public sector undertaking withdrew all its milk separators supplied through its dairy machinery unit, Aurangabad, when it found that one of the milk separators' lid at the customers end flew off while running and hit the roof. No major accident took place. Owing to this, it withdrew all the separators supplied to the customers for re-checking and to make design changes for some time, so that the same should not be repeated. Later on, HMT replaced new separators to its customers. All this was done only to regain the customers confidence in them, by incurring heavy expenses.

By doing jugglery like this, the companies have to spend millions of rupees or dollars on recalls/resupply etc.

One of the major social challenges faced by business is to **balance ethics and economics**. Society wants business to be ethical and economically profitable at the same time.

The three terms used to define ethics are:

- **Right**
- **Proper**
- **Just**

and the question is "what is right, proper and just?"

These are highly important terms in the future, compared to the past, as our economy is more competitive, the society is becoming more crowded and technology is becoming more complex. These terms and questions are important for any business executive who has to take multi-decisions in ways that are beyond his own control.

The ethics of management is coined with the above three terms and the determination of what is 'right,' 'proper' and 'just' in the decisions and actions that affect other people - goes far beyond simple questions of bribery, theft and collusion. **Collusion** is a secret agreement to deceive.

The Common Domain of Business Ethics

Majority of the business practitioners and ethicists alike show a good and clear competence in handling more dilemmas. Experience and reflection have taught them how to spot the ethical implications of a given situation and how to approach them in an orderly way. 'Moral point of view' is to be adopted to track moral elements, adequately. This involves that one tries to determine the specific interests and rights of all parties involved. Taking the moral point of view as the first moral decision, one makes in a process of forming a moral judgement.

As an example, a young girl is suffering from neuro-blastom, the parties concerned are her parents, family doctor on one hand and the insurance company on the other. All insurance companies might have excluded from their policies willingly or inadvertently, cases facing lethal illness of clients, similar to the one of the young girl. If equity is the basic moral concept, one cannot accept a moral obligation in one case, and reject it in another that, in all relevant respects is similar to the first.

The moral core issue is to be determined in addition to two or three possible core issues in a given situation. Once the core issue has been identified, however, it is another thing to come up with a well argued position to give good reasons, that is for a moral preference in the case. The real hard work of ethical analysis takes place with the joint effort of the concerned (preferably) who are in a position to influence the decision and with some support of ethical expertise if required.

Objectives of Ethics

The **objectives of ethics** are as shown in figure 1.6 below:

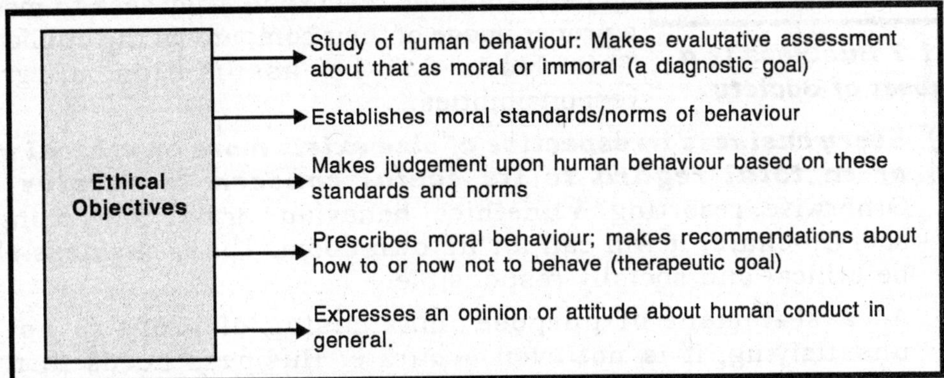

Fig. 1.6 Ethical Objectives

(i) The primary objective is to define the highest good of man and set a standard for the same. Here we have to consider ethics to deal with several interrelated and complex problems which may be of psychological, legal, commercial, philosophical, sociological and political in nature.

(ii) The other objectives are many. These are

- Study of human behaviour; making evaluative assessment about them as moral or immoral (a diagnostic goal).
- Establishing moral standards and norms of behaviour.
- Making judgement upon human behaviour based on these standards/norms.
- Prescribing moral behaviour and making recommendations about how to behave or vice versa (therapeutic goal).
- Expressing an opinion or attitude about human conduct in general.

1.2 Need and Benefit of Business Ethics

Need for Business Ethics

Some of the experts in business ethics have stated the following

(i) ***Business Operates within the Society:*** It is a part or subsystem of society. Business's functioning must contribute to the welfare of the society. In order to survive, develop and excel, business must earn social sanction of the society where it exists and functions. Without earning social sanctions, business cannot get loyal customers, cannot operate in the market place. It will soon collapse and die away.

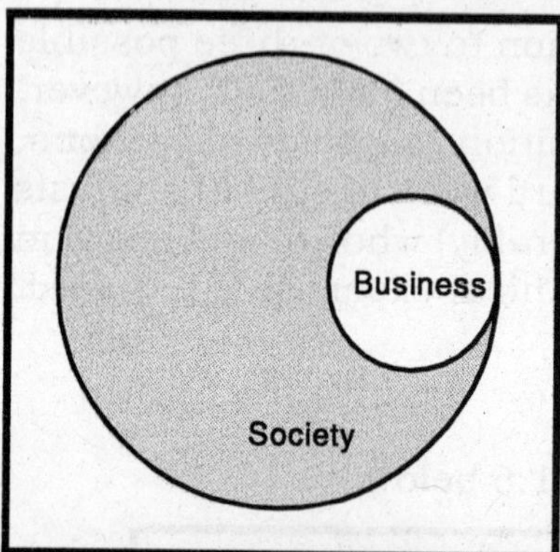

Fig. 1.7 Business is a Subset of Society

If business grows larger, the public takes more interest in it, since this will lead to a greater impact on the community. Managers are tuned to public opinion and they react to it. They seek to maintain a proper image of their company in the public mind. This leads to the assumption of greater responsibilities.

(ii) ***Every business irrespective of size exists more on ethical means or in total regard to its social concern to survive long:*** Otherwise, resorting to unethical behaviour or not concerning with social welfare, it will call for its own doom. Thus, business should be ethical and socially responsible.

As a statement of purpose, maximising of profit is not only unsatisfying, it is not even accurate. Business needs to remain ethical for its own good. Unethical actions and taking decisions will shorten the life of the business like a flash in the pan, quickly growing and even more quickly dying and forgotten.

(iii) ***Business needs to function as responsible corporate citizens in the country:*** It is that organ of the society which creates wealth for the country. Hence, narrow mentality and narrower goals and motives are to be avoided.

Importance of Business Ethics

Business ethics has already been defined earlier. However, it is the application of general ethical rules to business behaviour. It is not a special set of ethical rules different from ethics in general and applicable only to business. For example: If a society's ethical rule says that dishonesty is unethical and immoral, then anyone in business, who is dishonest with employees, customers, creditors, stockholders or competitors is acting unethically and immorally. Similarly, if protecting people from harm is considered ethical, then business firm that recall a defective and dangerous product is acting in an ethical way.

In most cases, the general public expects business to exhibit high levels of ethical performance and social responsibility. Business firms and their employees are encouraged to act ethically is to prevent harm to society. "Do no harm" is one of the strongest ethical principles. Next is to protect business firms from abuse by unethical competitors. Bribery and kickback schemes have become very common and penalise honest business firms. High ethical performance protects the individual who work in business.

Businesses that treat their employees with dignity and integrity reap many rewards in the form of high morale and improved productivity. People feel good about working in an ethical company since they are protected along with the general public.

In spite of the positive benefits of good ethical practices, ethical problems occur for the following reasons:

- Personal gain/dubious character
- Individual values widely differ with organisational goals
- Managers values and attitudes
- Competitive pressures
- Cross-cultural contradictions

(i) Personal gain

Business who employs people sometimes wrongly whose personal values are less than desirable. This will cause ethical problems. People will be sometimes greedy, and put down their own welfare ahead of all others, not bothered about the welfare of the fellow employees, the company or society. Since ethical qualities are difficult to anticipate and measure at the time of recruiting employees, many people of the above mentioned type will creep in, though an effort to weedout ethically undesirable applicants are made. The embezzler, the expense account paddler, the chronic sick leaver and the bribe taker slip in. Since perfect screening system is lacking, business is not likely to eliminate this kind of unethical behaviour entirely. Business has to proceed carefully in screening applicants, taking care not to trample individual rights in the search for potentially unethical employees. Contrary to popular opinion, personal gain is not the most important reason why unethical practices occur in business.

One of the marketing officers of a company in Bangalore, with the above mentioned qualities of personal gain is making lot of money apart from his highest salary. The proprietor of the company knows and tolerates this, pretending as though he does not know what is going on. The reason being, is that this marketing officer is very good in his work and support many a times the proprietor on critical issues.

(ii) Individual values vis a vis organisational goals

A company if it pursues goals or uses methods that are not acceptable to some of its employees will create ethical conflicts in business. **'Whistle blowing'** would be the outcome if an employee 'goes public' with a complaint which results after he fails to convince the company to correct the alleged abuse.

In one of the machine tool manufacturing companies in India, an officer posted abroad had good qualifications and vast experience in foreign countries was recalled suddenly and asked to work under one of the directors of the company who was not much qualified. The methods, procedures, followed in the department by the director was not accepted by the officer and there used to be heated arguments even though many good suggestions were made with his experience. All these were in vain and the director was so furious about the officer and made the officer to work in an isolated place without any responsibility assigned to him. Eventually, the officer was forced to resign on his own.

As could be seen from the above, the protesting employees in these companies were not trouble makers. Instead, they wanted to correct the internal company procedures. They felt that the company's goals, methods etc. which employers were following would harm everyone including themselves as well as customers and the general public. On the contrary, the people at the helm felt that they are right and the protesting employees are wrong and unethical. This was a **ethical dilemma**. The protesters or the employees who do not like the company's practices 'Blow whistle' by revealing the situation to the general public.

(iii) Managers values and attitudes

As decision makers, managers have more opportunities than others to set an ethical tone for the company. They are the key people to act ethically or unethically. Ethical guidance usually will be provided by the top levels to the employees down below. The values held by the top managers are important in promoting ethical activities.

Managers ask three key questions when making a decision:

- Will it work? (**Pragmatic approach**) Major decision making orientations of managers from five nations referred that pragmatic approach and ethical approach contributes the major approaches.
- Is it right? (Ethical approach)
- Is it pleasant? (Affective approach)

Values most likely to influence managers at work are:

- Service to customers
- Ability
- Company loyalty
- Achievement
- Organisational efficiency
- High productivity

A 1982 report on a group of over 1400 corporation executives rated values are important as under:

- Responsibility and honesty 88%
- Capable 66%
- Imaginative 55%
- Logical 49%
- Ambitions 37%

The above value preferences are due to the influence of their companies have on the managers. Another reason is the professional responsibility that managers feel concerning their jobs.

Organisational effectiveness is their central goal while at work. If the organisation is to be made effective, good management is required. Then other goals are:

- Organisational efficiency
- Organisation reputation
- High morale
- Organisational leadership
- High productivity

Similarly,

- Organisational growth
- Organisational stability
- Profit maximisation - also would follow

Lastly,

- Organisational value to community
- Service to public - are also necessary

The factors which might cause the managers to make unethical decisions as per an article in Harvard Business Review, (January-February 1997, p.66) are as under:

Behaviour of the supervisors in the company is most important.

Followed by this are:

- Behaviours of one's equals in company
- Industry's ethical climate
- Society's moral climate
- Formal company policy (or lack there of)
- Personal financial need

These research findings show that the values and attitudes of managers are a critical element in a company's ethical performance.

The idea behind competitive bidding is that the bayer can get a product at the best price by setting up competion between the various suppliers. Especially with large contracts, the temptation to cheat on the bidding is great. Newspapers frequently report stories of deblerate underbidding to with contracts followed by cost over runs that are unavoidable; Theft of information on other bids in order to be able to underbid them etc. Problems also exist with buyers who make purchase decisions based on elements other than the advertised bid criteria, who leak information to a perferred bidder or who give advance notices or detailed knowledge of evaluation procedures to preferred bidders.

(iv) Competitive pressures

When companies compete for a similar product, they sometimes engage in unethical activities in order to wipe out a competitor from the market. Rivalry between employees for advancement can motivate some kind of unethical behaviour.

In one of the cases, a private company, was there from a long time making certain machinery. This company had a very good collaborator from Europe to back up them for those products. The design of the product was good, products were light and liked by its customers. The private company after collaboration had enjoyed nearly 50 years solid foot holding and doing very well by marketing the products with less competition and making high profits with high prices for their products. However, the performance of the products were good and it was well established in the market since a long time and they could sustain even without business for certain years. A well established public sector at the same time was forced by the government to take up the manufacture of similar products of the private company and to compete with them.

The public sector company could not compete with the private company for the following reasons:

Public sector company collaborated with a firm abroad of less repute which was not popular in the market. The products of that company was very robust, performance wise not so good. Added to this, adequate back up support was not there.

Further, the private company had amassed high profits every year and monopolised more or less from a long time. They were able to go down to any price and compete. The price of their products when competition developed was always kept 10% lesser than public sector and was supplying better products to customers.

The public sector could not compete due to its high overheads, high collaboration fees, uncompetitable products, poor backup service from collaborator, high cost of machinery installed, high salary of people etc.

Further, the private sector was able to secure orders through discounts, presentations, gifts, etc., which the public sector could not afford to do it. The main intention of private sector was to wipe out the public sector and it succeeded to the major extent and is sitting pretty even today making the public sector, almost in the verge of closing. This subject has also been dealt in para 1.5.

(v) Cross-cultural Contradictions

Ethical problems occur when certain corporations cannot do business at home, would try to enter other societies where ethical standards differ. At home, if it is difficult to follow the ethical standards, then such unsafe products (their countries doesn't permit) are sold where and there is demand in other countries and where ethical standards permit to use such products. Acceptable safety standards differ among nations and that honest differences of opinion exist among scientists and safety experts. There are some companies who have built factories in nations whose pollution control laws are less stringent than a particular country regulations. They are charged with "**exporting pollution**".

What is thought to be ethically acceptable by one nation is considered unethical by another. The resultant ethical dilemmas can be difficult ones for business firms and their managers to solve.

Four groups to which business has a responsibility. Companies have a responsibility to:

- **Society**
- **Employees**
- **Customers** (Consumers)
- **Investors**

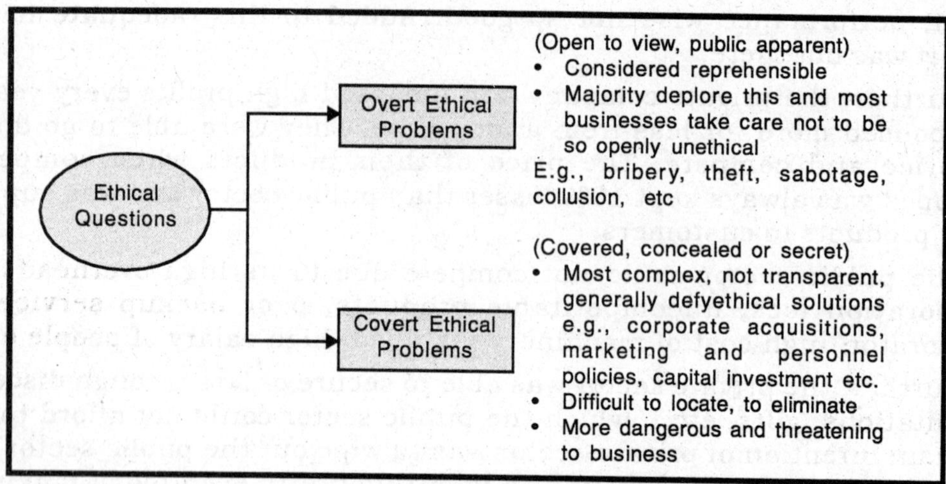

Fig. 1.8 Ethical Questions

1.3 History of the Development of Business Ethics

Engineering ethics is young:

Earlier Books Showed: Engineering Ethics is regarded as encompassing little more than the drafting and promulgating by professional societies (in the form of codes, guidelines and options).

After World War II: Organisations and journals which emerged addressed the responsibilities of scientists and engineers for the consequences of their professional work regarding war, mass destruction weapons, fashioning gas chambers etc.

Mid 1970s: Engineering periodicals mentioned very commonly about ethics in engineering.

Late 1970s: Systematic attention devoted by engineers and members of schorarly disciplines.

1978-1980: Robert Baum's National project on philosophy and engineering ethics defined the concept of Engineering Ethics; Sponsored by the National Science Foundation (NSF) and National Endowment for the Humanities (NEH).

1980: First interdisciplinary conference at Rensselaer polytechnic Institute.

1981: Business and Professional Ethics journal was created.

Late 19th century: Newly emerging professional societies for engineers formally expressed this (writing codes of ethics).

1.4 Arguments for and against Business Ethics

Ethics in Business

All over the world, there is a growing realisation that ethics is important for any business and to achieve the progress of any society. Ethics give rise to efficient economy. It is not the government or law which will protect the society. But ethics alone can protect it. Ethics are good in itself. Ethics and profits go together in the long run. An ethically responsible company is one which has developed a culture of caring for people and environment, a culture which flows downwards from the top managers and leaders. **Ethics** can be described as the conscious appeal to norms and values to which, on reasonable grounds, we hold ourselves obliged, as reciprocally, we hold others obliged to the same norms and values. As a reflection, **ethics** are the methodical and systematic elaboration of the norms and values we appeal to in our daily activities. Where these activities are organised under business issues, we face ethics in the practical and reflective variety of business ethics.

On innumerable occasions, people in business are facing ethical questions in which a balance has to be found between the different and often conflicting rights and interests of the parties involved. One may even say that the weighing of rights and interests, at stake in determinate circumstances, constitutes the common domain of business ethics.

Ethical rules are guides to moral behaviour. For example: All societies have ethical rules forbidding, lying, stealing, deceiving and harming others, similar to the other ethical rules that approve of honesty, keeping promises, helping others and respecting the right of others. These are the basic rules of behaviour which are of much use for the preservation and continuation of organised life.

Most of the people find major source of ethical guidance and moral meaning in religious beliefs and organisations. The family institution is equally important as it imparts a sense of right and wrong in children when they grow up, as schools and other similar institutions like cultural associations and television etc. The totality of these exposures will create in them a concept of ethics, morality and socially desirable behaviour.

Ethical rules are present in all societies, all organisations and all individuals, though they may vary greatly from one to another. What is considered ethical by one society may be forbidden by another society. One particular religious notion of morality may differ with others. Still ethics is a universal human trait. All people wherever they are, need rules to govern their conduct, rules that tell them whether their actions are right or wrong, moral or immoral, approved or disapproved.

Business and Ethical Responsibility

As many agree Business has an ethical responsibility to become a more active partner in dealing with social concerns. Business must creatively find ways to become a part of solutions, rather than being a part of problems. Corporations should not isolate themselves from participation in solving our environmental problems, leaving it up to others to find the answers and to tell them what not to do. There are example of corporations demonstrating such leadership, even when this has been a risk to their self interest. Though Bowie admits that business has a responsibility to educate the public and promote environmentally responsible behaviour, it is to be understood that corporate moral leadership goes far beyond public educational campaigns, needing moral vision, commitment and courage, risk and sacrifice. Business is capable of such a challenge. Business ethics movement should do nothing short of encouraging such leadership demanded by morality.

Good ethics may be good business in majority of the cases. When the crunch comes, when ethics conflicts with the firm's interests, any ethics program that has not already faced up to this possibility is doomed to fail because it will undercut the rationale of the program itself. In business, as in all other human endeavours, we must be prepared to pay the costs of ethical behaviour. So also in the environmental movement, a similar danger occurs with corporations choosing or being wooed to be environmentally friendly on the grounds that it will be in their self interest. There is the risk of participating in the movement for the wrong reasons. The frequent strategy of the new environmentalists is a business to help solve environmental problems by finding pure or virtually costless ways for them to participate. They feel that compromise, not confrontation, is the only way to save the earth.

Business Ethics is a Management Discipline

The field of business ethics has grown in recent years into an inter- disciplinary area of study that has found a secure niche in the fields of liberal arts and business education. On this, credit goes to many individuals - both philosophers and business scholars - who have succeded in relating ethical theory to the various problems of ethics that arise in business. Business is a fruitful subject for philosophical exploration and practicing managers in the world of business can benefit from the results.

There was a time, say about 50 to 60 years back, when it was thought that business ethics are a contradiction of terms.

The concept was: If it is business, it cannot be ethical and if it is ethical at all, it does not represent business.

Fortunalty, at that time, there were significant people who disagreed with the philosophy and demonstrated that it is a false statement eg. JRD Tata, Birla etc.

(i) McNamara says that business ethics has come to be considered a management discipline, especially since the birth of the social responsibility of business. Business owned responsibility to work to improve society; E.g. environmental protection, equal right, public health, education improvement etc. Business has replaced the word 'stock holder' with 'stakeholder' (employees, customers, suppliers and the wider community).

(ii) As per Robert Kreitner in his book "Management" says "Highly publicised accounts of corporate misconduct in recent years have led widespread cynicism about Business Ethics."

(iii) Gallup poll asked in 1992 Americans to rate the ethical standards of various professions.

The professional ratings are given in the figure shown below:

Various Professions	*Rating*	*On honesty and ethical standards*
Business executives	18%	High/very high
Druggists/Pharmacists	66%	"
Medical Doctors	52%	"
Police Officers	42%	"
Funeral Directors	35%^	"
Journalists	27%	"
Stock Brokers	13%	"
Members of Congress	11%	"
Car Sales people	5%	"

Fig. 1.9 Professional Ratings on Various Professions

Now, the subject of ethics is receiving serious attention in management circles.

Arguments For and Against Business Ethics

Business ethics is the process of rationally evaluating our moral standards and applying them to business situations. Many people have objected to the very idea of applying moral standards to business activities. They have also looked at what can be said in favour of bringing ethics into business.

Three Objections of bringing Ethics into Business

Occasionally, people object to the view that ethical standards should be applied to the behaviour of people in organisations. Business persons claim that they should single mindedly pursue the financial interests of their firm and not sidetrack their energies or their firm's resources into "doing good works." Three arguments advanced in support of this are as wider:

(a) In perfectly competitive free markets, the pursuit of profit will by itself ensure that the members of society are served in the most socially beneficial ways. To be profitable, each firm has to produce what the members of society want and has to do this by the most efficient means available.

(b) Business managers should single mindedly pursue the interests of their firms and should ignore ethical considerations is embodied in what Alex C.Michaels (called as 'Loyal agents' argument) "As a loyal agent of his/her employer, the manager has a duty to serve his/her employer as the employer would want to be served (if the employer had the agents' expertise)".

An employer would want to be served in whatever ways will advance his/her self interests.

Therefore, in loyal agent of his/her employer, the manager has a duty to serve his/her employer in whatever ways will advance the employer's self interests.

the argument can be, and often has been used to justify a manager's unethical or illegal conduct (Nazi officers used after world war II to defend their involvement in Hitler's morally corrupt government).

(c) Objection is sometimes made against bringing ethics into business. This is the objection that to be ethical it is enough for business people merely to obey the law. Business ethics is essentially obeying the law. It is wrong, however to see law and ethics as identical. It is true that some laws require behaviour that is the same as the behaviour required by our moral standards.

Our moral standards are sometimes incorporated into the law when enough of us feel that a moral standard should be enforced by the pressures of a legal system. In contrast, laws are sometimes criticised and eliminated when it becomes clear that they blatantly violate our moral standards. Most ethicists agree that all citizens have a moral obligation to obey the law so long as the law does not require clearly unjust behaviour. In most cases, it is immoral to break the law.

Points for bringing Ethics into Business

As explained earlier, several arguments are found that ethics should not be brought into business. We found them all wanting. Why ethics should be brought into business-opposite claim to be judged.

(i) Ethics should govern all voluntary human activities and because business is a voluntary human activity, ethics should also govern business.

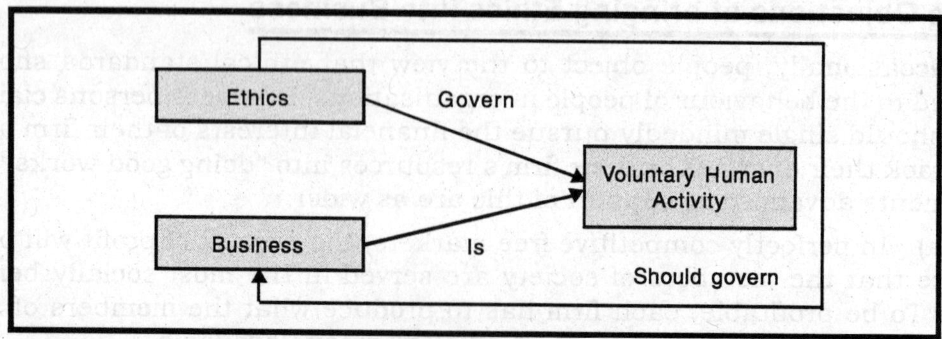

Fig. 1.9 Ethics, Business, Human Activity Relationship

(ii) Ethics should be part of business, points out that business activities, like any other human activities cannot exist unless the people involved in the business and its surrounding community adhere to some minimal standards of ethics. "Business is a cooperative activity whose very existence requires ethical behaviour."

All businesses require a stable society in which to carry on their business dealings. No business can exist entirely without ethics, the pursuit of business requires at least a minimal adherence to ethics on the part of those involved in business. A great western philosopher Hobbies wrote that distrust and unrestrained self interest would create "a war of every man against every man" and in such a situation, life become "nasty, brutish and short," in a society without ethics.

(iii) Ethics should be brought into business by showing that ethical considerations are consistent with business pursuits, in particular with the pursuit of profit. Examples seen are good companies where a history of good ethics has existed side by side with a history of profitable operations. Merck long standing ethical culture-one of the most spectacularly profitable companies of all time. Others are Xerox, Home depot, HP, Silicon graphics, Johnson and JOhnson, Starbacks Coffee etc. In India Tatas, Hindustan Lever, Wipro etc. Many chance factors also affect profitability like recessions, weather patterns, changing consumer tastes etc. These companies are not many in which ethics by chance happened to coincide with profits for a period of time.

Many difficulties also arise in trying to study whether ethical companies are more profitable than unethical ones. There are many different ways of:

- measuring profit
- factors that can affect a company's profits
- along which companies can be compared in dimensions.

Prisoner A with Prisoner B	Prisoner B with Prisoner A: Cooperates	Prisoner B with Prisoner A: Not Cooperates
Cooperates	A gets 1 year B gets	A gets 3 years B Nil
Not Cooperates	A gets Nil B gets 3 years	A gets 2 years B gets 2 years

Two men who are arrested for robbing a store secretly agree that neither will confess that they committed the crime. ?The police commissioner separates the two men and tells each prisoner the same thing.

If neither admits - Jail for 1 year; If both prisoners confess - 2 years jail
If one keeps quiet - 3 years jail and the other confesses - goes free

Fig. 1.10 Prisoner's Dilemma (as an ethical issue example)

Despite the above difficulties, several studies have been made regarding correlation of profitability with ethical behaviour. The results have been mixed.

(iv) Consider an argument based on the prisoner's dilemma. A prisoners dilemma is a situation in which two parties are each faced with a choice between two options: Either cooperate with the other party or do not cooperate.

(i) Mutual cooperation → Only 1 year in jail (Both gain some benefit)

(ii) Both do not cooperate → 2 years in jail (neither gets the benefit)

(iii) Either cooperate with the other party or do not cooperate (If one cooperates and the other not - 1st suffers a loss and the 2nd benefits)

Single prisoner's dilemma:

(a) Rational and self interested (they will inevitably choose not to cooperate)

(b) the other party has only two choices: to cooperate or not to cooperate;

Suppose if he cooperates, I will be better if I do not cooperate

Suppose if he does not cooperate, it is clearly better for me not to cooperate

Both the parties will reason this way, and end up in not cooperating.

1.5 Economic Issues, Competitive Issues Legal and Regulatory Philonthriphic Issues

The concept of corporate social responsibility originated in the 1950s when American corporations rapidly revealed their activities in size and power. During 1960s and 1970s, the nation confronted pressing problems such as poverty, unemployment, race relations, urban blight and pollution. In the last two decades of 20th century, corporate social responsibility became a cry everywhere recognising a responsibility to society, but the responsibility was weighed against the demands of being competitive in a rapidly changing global economy. Corporate social responsibility recognise that business firms have not one but many different kinds of responsibility including:

— Economic issues,

— Competitive issues,

— Legal and regulatory issues, and

— Philonthrophic issues

The concepts of ethics and social responsibility are often interchangeable. Both have a distinct meaning. Social responsibility is to maximise its positive impact on stakeholders and to minimise its negative impact as an organisation's obligation.

The four levels of social responsibility are as shown in the figure below in an hierarchy as a pyramid.

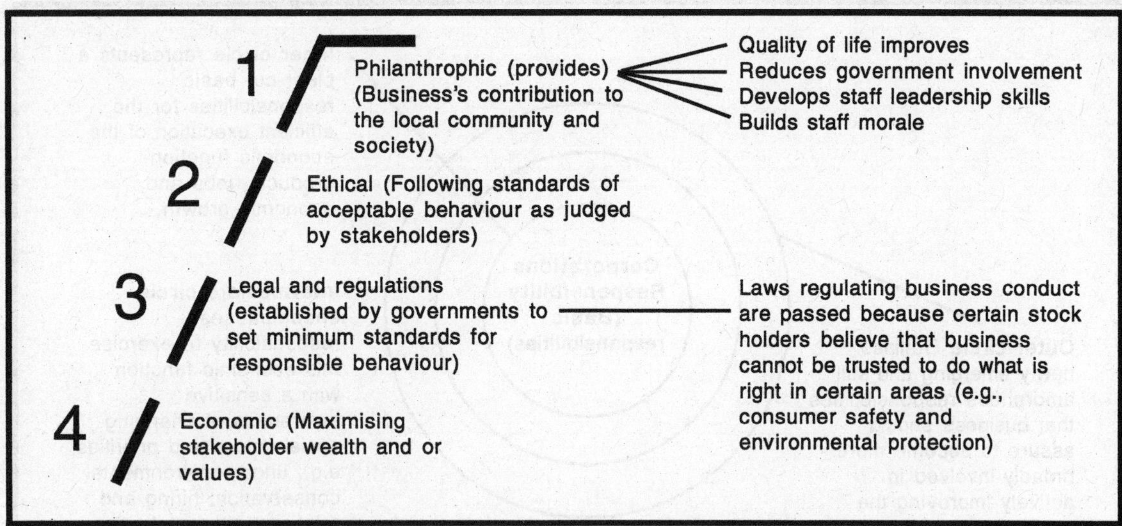

Fig. 1.11 Four Levels of Social Responsibility

Corporations have an economic responsibility to produce goods and services and to provide jobs and good wages to the work force while earning a profit. It also includes the obligation to seek out supplies of raw materials, to discover new resources and technological improvements and to develop new products.

Business firms have legal and regulatory responsibilities. One of these is to act as a judiciary, managing the assets of the corporation in the interests of shareholders. They also have numerous legal responsibilities to employees, customers, suppliers and other parties. The vast body of business law is constantly increasing as legislatures, regulatory agencies, and the courts respond to greater social expectations and impose new legal obligations on business.

The concept of corporate social responsibility is often expressed as the voluntary assumption of responsibilities that go beyond the purely economic and legal responsibilities of business firms. Social responsibility is the selection of corporate goals and the evaluation of outcomes not solely by the criteria of profitability and organisational well-being but by ethical standards or judgements of social desirability. The corporate objective of earning a satisfactory level of profit and a willingness to forego a certain measure of profit in order to achieve non-economic end in a consistent way should be the motto.

Competitive bidding is a well established practice in purchasing. It can lead to many ethical problems associated with deception on the part of the vendor or with unfairness on the part of the buyer in choosing a vendor.

The competitive pressures in businesses has already been dealt in para 1.2, (page 16).

Laws and regulations are established by governments to set minimum standards for responsible behaviour. These are for society's codification of what is right and wrong. Two types of laws which are in vogue are civil and criminal laws. These regulate business conduct and are passed as society needs it, which includes:

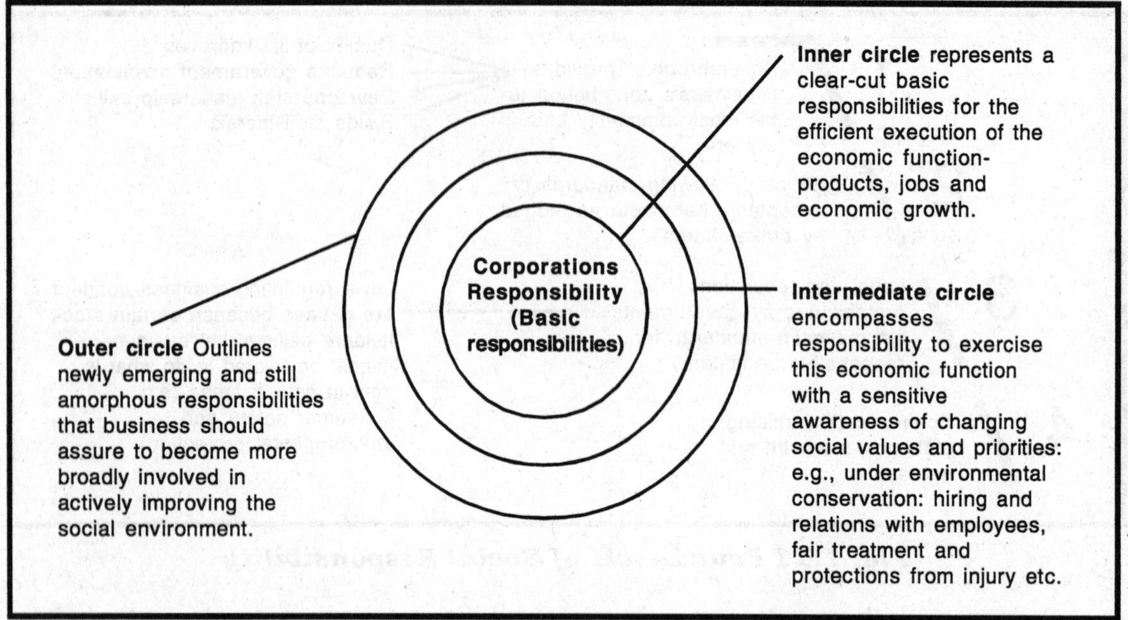

Fig. 1.12 Corporations Responsibility

- Consumers
- Interest groups
- Competitors
- Legislators

The above group of people believes that business must comply with society's standards. Such laws regulate competition, protect consumers and the environment, promote safety and equity and in the work place, provide incentives for promoting good conduct.

Businesses contribute to the local community and society and as such philanthropic issues touch on business's social responsibility. Companies contribute significant amounts of money to education, the arts, environmental causes and the disadvantaged by supporting local and national charitable organisations.

The ethical aspects of business competition would be severe from the rivalry among businesses for customers and profits. If the competition is not fair enough or do not adhere to legal and socially accepted methods of gaining advantage, stakeholders, other competitors may be adversely affected. Size of some firms may be helpful in taking advantage over others to exploit the detriment not only of competing firms but also consumers and communities.

On the whole, business ethics embodies standards, norms and expectations which reflects a concern on major stockholders, consumers, employees, suppliers, shareholders, competitors and also the community. Firms should take care of ethical concerns in their foundation values. They should incorporate ethics in their business strategy considering social responsibility as a value to be embedded in daily decision making.

1.6 Framework for Ethical Decision Making

Ethical Decisions, How Are They Made?

The structure of such decision making has classically involved the determination and weighing of four factors; as mentioned in para 3.1.

- The end - the outcome sought
- The means - the methods employed
- The motive - the urge makes the decision necessary in the first place
- The foreseeable consequences

If any of these factors was wrong, the entire action was immoral.

Example: If any garment manufacturer selects a small place in India where their is no industry and make improvements in the place through:

- Bringing a higher standard of living to the local people
- Providing opportunities
- Providing skill
- Producing quality products at a competitive price
- Products used by local people also to meet their requirements

But paid kickback to the local state government officials for operation.

The Ten Commandments of legal and ethical intelligence gathering by Fuld and company (published its own guide lines) are as under:

1. Thou shalt not lie when representing thyself.
2. Thou shalt observe thy company's legal guidelines as set forth by the Legal Department.
3. Thou shalt not tape record a conversation.
4. Thou shalt not bribe.
5. Thou shalt not plant eaves dropping devices.
6. Thou shalt not deliberately mislead anyone in interview.
7. Thou shalt neither obtain from nor give thy competitor any price information.
8. Thou shalt not swap misinformation.
9. Thou shalt not steal a trade secret (or steal employees away in hopes of learning a trade secret).
10. Thou shalt not knowingly press someone for information if it may jeopardise that persons job or reputation.

Ethical Decision Making

Ethical issues arise out of every day business decisions. An individual's personal beliefs and the moral atmosphere of the organisation in which one works significantly after the behaviour one exhibits. Many philosophers, organisational relationships, and opportunity influence behaviour, as does the organisational environment.

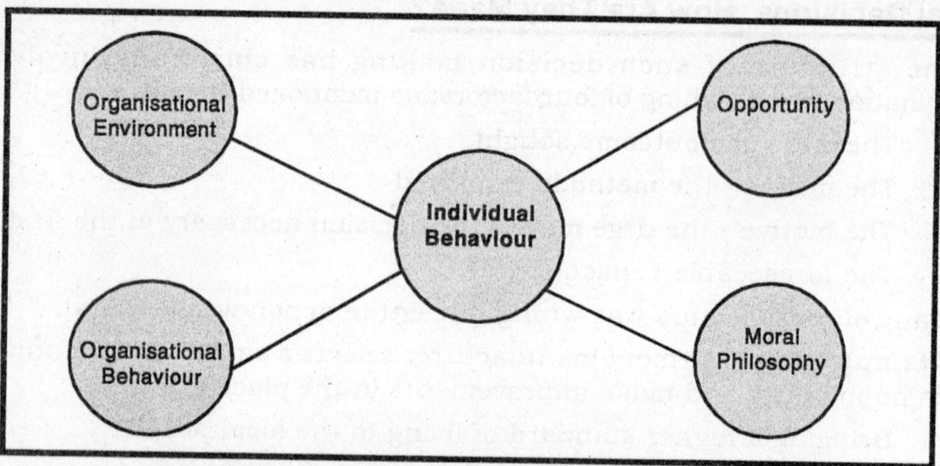

Fig. 1.13 Individual Behaviour Components (Factors Influencing Behaviour)

Ethical Decisions, How Are They Made?

The structure of such decision making has classically involved the determination and weighing of four factors:

- The end - the outcome sought
- The means - the methods employed
- The motive - the urge makes the decision necessary in the first place
- The foreseeable consequences

If any of these factors was wrong, the entire action was immoral.

Example: If any garment manufacturer selects a small place in India where their is no industry and make improvements in the place through:

- Brought a higher standard of living to the local people
- Provided with opportunities
- Provided skill
- Produced quality products at a competitive price
- Products used by local people also to meet their requirements

But paid kickback to the local state government officials for operation.

The Ten Commandments of legal and ethical intelligence gathering by Fuld and company (published its own guide lines) are as under:

1. Thou shalt not lie when representing thyself.

2. Thou shalt observe thy company's legal guidelines as set forth by the Legal Department.
3. Thou shalt not tape record a conversation.
4. Thou shalt not bribe.
5. Thou shalt not plant eavesdropping devices.
6. Thou shalt not deliberately mislead anyone in interview.
7. Thou shalt neither obtain from nor give thy competitor any price information.
8. Thou shalt not swap misinformation.
9. Thou shalt not steal a trade secret (or steal employees away in hopes of learning a trade secret).
10. Thou shalt not knowingly press someone for information if it may jeopardise that persons job or reputation.

The Ethical Organisation

An organisation is by definition, organised. It is not just a group or mass of people. It has structure which enables it to make collective decisions and act on those decisions.

People are generally moral agents. Their actions are governed by rules, explicit or implicit, which can be subjected to ethical appraisal.

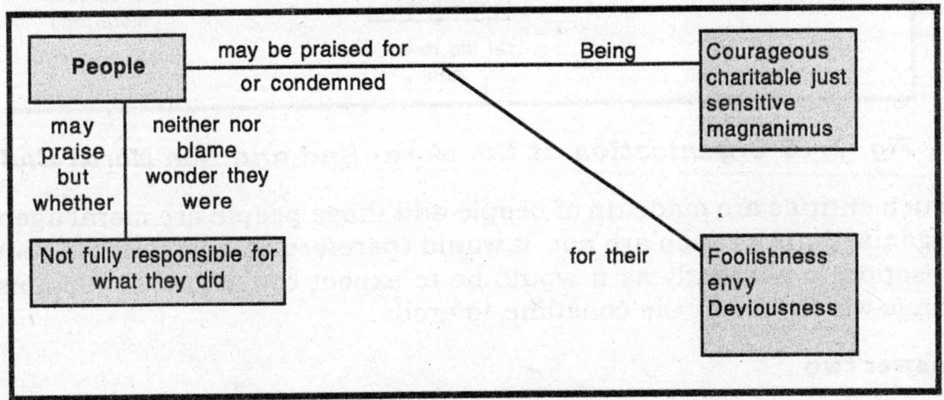

Fig. 1.14 People as Moral Agents

Exception is children who may be selfish or act unfairly. We accept that they would gradually acquire full moral responsibility for their actions.

Animals on the other hand may be courageous or altrustic. We suspect in them a degree of anthromorphism in extending moral language too far in their direction.

Rocks, Stones, Trees etc. do not have moral responsibilities.

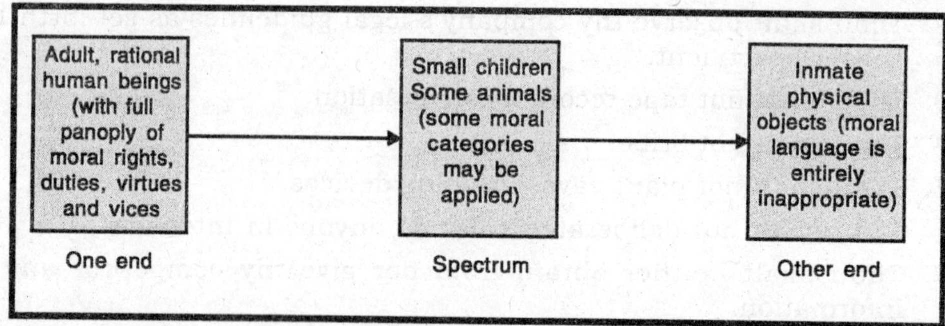

Fig. 1.15 Spectrum showing Moral Rights of Different Individuals, Animals, Objects

The question is now where does the organisations fall in the spectrum? Let us analyse the organisations and give three answers.

(i) Answer one

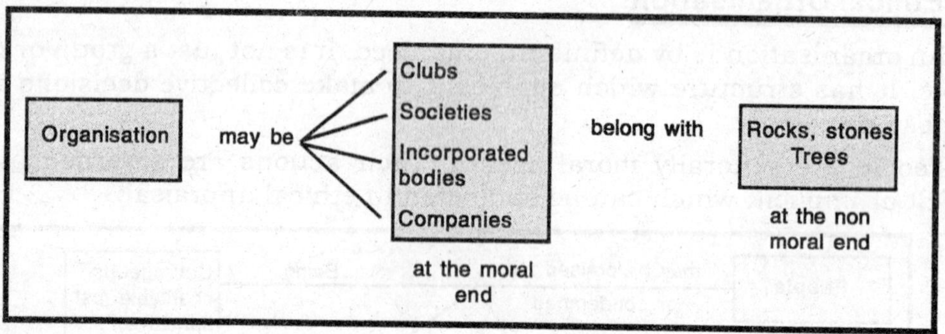

Fig. 1.16 Organisation at the Moral End and Non-Moral End

Such entities are made up of people and those people are moral agents, but the organisations as such are not. It would therefore be an absurd to require an organisation to act justly as it would be to expect the sea to be responsible in decidings which bits of the coastline to erode.

(ii) Answer two

Organisations may well be agents of a kind which it makes sense to praise or blame for their actions, even though they are not agents in exactly the same way as human beings are obligations cannot be laid on organisations because they are not very effective or efficient entities for carrying them out. A bank should operate according to the financial principles and not impose its political or social values on the community.

(iii) Answer three

Organisations have sufficient structural complexity to be agents whom it makes sense to call to account for their actions and the consequences of those actions. Some organisations have flat, relatively informal and open structures whilst others may be rigid, hierarchical and formal. This variation may be relevant to the questions of:

- whether organisations can take decisions readily or with extreme difficulty?
- whether they do so with the full consent of all involved or in the teeth of opposition and dissent?

It may not be relevant to the question of:

Whether they can take decisions at all?

If a body can take decisions and implement them, then it must be responsible for those decisions and the consequences. It may not be possible for such organisations to be responsible in the way that people can be, but they can be responsible in a way appropriate to organisations.

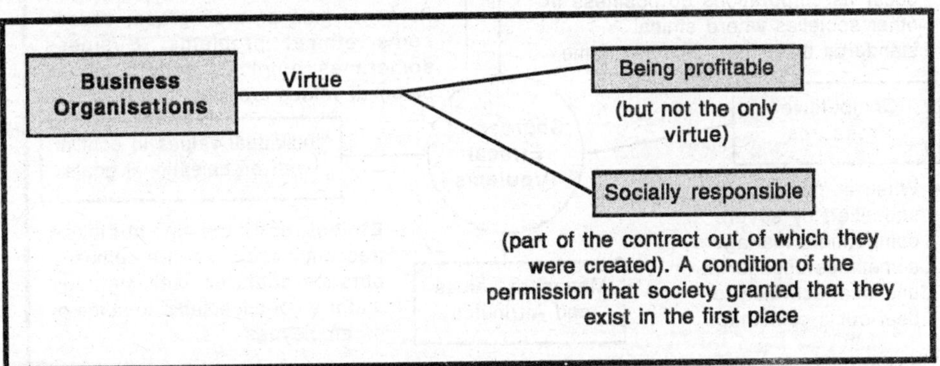

Fig. 1.17 Business Organisation's Structural Complexity

There are no such things as organisations, there are only individuals

Organisations cannot have moral or social responsibilities sometimes seems to take as its premise assertion, that there are no such things as organisations, there are only individuals. Such an assertion cannot be as simple as it seems. We must read the premise as asserting something more sophisticated namely that organisations are made up of people and that they have no real existence of their own apart from the people, out of which they are constituted. This is like saying that rainbows do not (really) exist. Rainbows were made out of the sunlight refracted through raindrops, and that were it not for the existence of raindrops and sunlight there would not be rainbows.

Ethical Issues that Arise for Managers

The ethical issues that arise for managers are indeed for all people, including employees, customers, consumers and members of the public. Corporate activities affect us all, and so the conduct of business is a matter of concern for everyone with a stake in ethical management. The ethical issues we will be examining are those considered by managers in the ordinary course of their work, but they also major issues debated in the parliament and scrutinised by courts. this is because ethical issues in business are closely tied to important matters of public policy and to the legislative and judicial processes of the government.

Difficulties in Decision Making

In spite of the positive benefits of good ethical practices, ethical problems do occur in business. Some of the main reasons are:

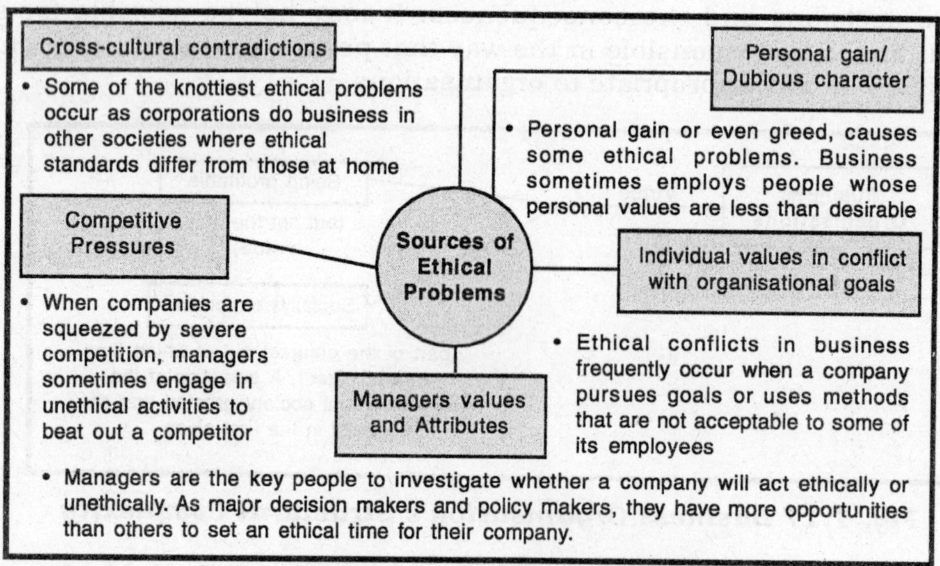

Fig. 1.18 Sources of Ethical Problems

How to use Ethical Reasoning

What business needs is a set of guidelines for thinking about ethics. The guidelines should help corporate managers and employees.

- Identify the nature of the ethical problem
- Decide which course of action is likely to produce the most ethical results

Three methods of ethical reasoning are:

- Utilitarian
- Rights
- Justice

Method	Critical Determining Factor	An action is ethical when	Limitations
Utilitarian	Comparing benefits and costs	Net benefits exceed net costs	Difficult to measure some human and social costs. Majority may disregard rights of minority
Rights	Respecting rights	Basic human rights are respected	Difficult to balance conflicting rights
Justice	Distributing Fair Shares	Benefits and costs are fairly distributed	Difficult to measure benefits and costs. Lack of agreement on fair shares

Fig. 1.19 Critical Determining Factors of Ethical Action of Different Methods

Levels of Decision Making

Decision making occurs in several distinct levels:

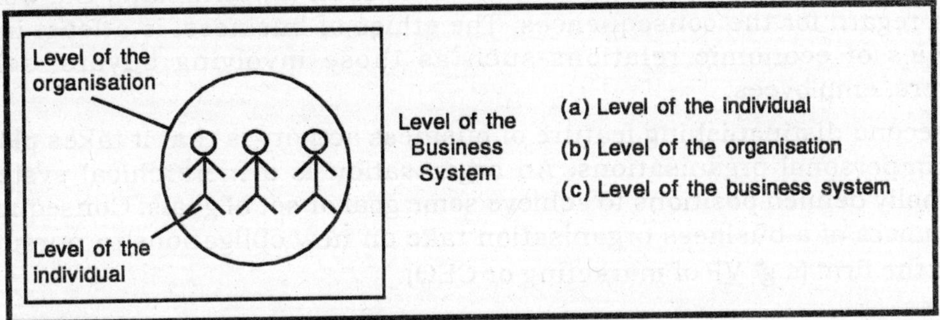

Fig. 1.20 Levels of Decision making

- Individuals in the work place and require them to make a decision about their own response → Individual decision making. e.g. Whether to live with the difficult boss or to blow the whistle on the padding?
- Problems at the level of the organisation (Individual decision maker is acting on behalf of the organisation to bring out some organisational change). e.g. Sexual harassment (an individual matter for the person suffering the abuse).

  But a manager in an office must take steps to rectify and ensure non-occurrence of such a situation in future.
- Problems resulting from accepted business practices or from features of the economic system cannot effectively be addressed by any single organisation, much less a line individual.

Examples: Sales practices - one company cannot change single handedly because of competition with possibly less ethical competitors.

Business Decision Making

The individuals are faced with questions about ethics in their relations with customers, employees and members of the larger society. Frequently the ethically correct course of action is clear, and people in business act as per that. Exceptions occur, when there is uncertainty about ethical obligations in particular situations or when considerations of ethics come into conflict with the practical demands of business. e.g. Sales representative not sure about the extent to which he is obligated to provide information about possible delays in delivery to customers.

In deciding on an ethical course of action, we can rely to some extent on the rules of right conduct that we employ in everyday life. Deception is wrong (e.g., whether we deceive a friend or a customer).

One of the features that distinguishes business activity is an economic character. In the world of business, we interact with each other not as family members, friends or neighbours but as buyers and sellers, employers and employees and the like. Employment is also recognised as a special relation with its own standard of right and wrong. Employers are generally entitled to hire and promote whomever they wish and to layoff (or terminate) the workers without regard for the consequences. The ethics of business, is atleast in part the ethics of economic relations-such as those involving buyers, sellers, employers, employees.

A second distinguishing feature of business activity is that it takes place in larger, impersonal organisations. An organisation is a hierarchical system of functionally defined positions to achieve some goal or set of goals. Consequently, the members of a business organisation take on new obligations to pursue the goals of the firm (e.g. VP of marketing or CEO).

Business Ethics and Technology

Technology consists of all methods, processes and tools that human invent to manipulate their environment. Contemporary business is being continuously and radically transformed by the rapid evolution of new technologies that raise new ethical issues for business.

New technologies always from time to time have had a revolutionary impact on business and society. Long back, we had agricultural revolution. Favouring technologies developed. In 18th century, Industrial revolution transformed western society and business through electromechanical machines powered by fossil fuels such as the steam engine, automobile, rail road and cotton gin. Before industrial revolution, most businesses were small organisations that operated in local markets. After industrial revolution, new forms of machine production enabled businesses to become big and large organisations.

New technologies developed in the end of 20th Century are again transforming society and business and creating the potential for new ethical problems. The developments are the revolution in biotechnology, information technology developing extremely powerful and compact computers, but also the development of the Internet, Wireless Communication, digitisation and numerous other technologies. To cope with these rapid changes, business organisations have had to become smaller, flatter, nimble; they have had to deal with a host of intriguing new ethical issues.

All ethical issues raised by new technologies are related to risk someway. Are these risks predictable? How large are the risks and are they reversible? Are the benefits worth potential risks? Who should decide? Do the people on whom the risk will fall know about the risk etc.

New technologies like IT (say computers) have created are related to piracy-regarding ethical issues. ITs have also raised difficult ethical issues about the nature of the right to property (computer software, computer code or any other kind of data-text, numbers, pictures, sounds etc.) or computer services. Computerised information like software programmes or digitised pictures can be copied perfectly count less times without in anyway changing the original.

Biotechnology has also created another host of **ethical issues**. Example, Genetic Engineering in new techniques that let us change the genes in the cells of humans, animals and plants to create and market has varieties of vegetables, grains, sheep, cows, rabbits, bacteria, viruses etc. Genes composed of DNA contain the blue prints that determine what characteristics an organism will have. The consequences of releasing genetically modified organisms into the world cannot be predicted. Engineered animals may drive out natural species; Engineered plants may poison wild organisms. Is it ethical for businesses to market and distribute such unpredictable engineered organisms throughout the world?

Power and Political Action in Organisations

Government level politicians often receive low marks of approval from the general public political standards regularly hit the front pages of daily newspapers. But politics and politicians exist in all forms of organised society, not just government. And political action can be positive when it promotes cooperation among individuals and groups with different interests and objectives.

Politics is a network of interactions by which power is acquired, transferred, and exercised on others. Individuals and orgnaisational units use power to take political action. Politicians work with and through many people (hence the term networking). Thus politics transcends traditional organisational boundaries. Power is the medium of exchange in politics, just as the dollar is the medium of exchange in economics. Shrewed politicians acquire power and transfer it to others when it can purchase something of value. Just like a banker, a politician can keep a balance sheet. When power is transferred, something is expected in return. To the politician, a favour given now is often power to be extracted in the future.

Managers must at least recognise the political forces in their organisations. Some may choose to behave essentially as politicians. In fact, some management theorists apply political science techniques to their analysis of organisations.

The degree of politicking a manager does is limited not only by formal organisational restrictions but also by the managers personal code of ethics and conscience. The fact that at times politics may be unethical should not prelude studying the subject. And politicking cannot be condemned per se. Some politically based accommodations are constructive; others perhaps are destructive, both of organised activity and of individual morals.

It is apparent that some degree of politicking is a fact of organised life, regardless of the caliber of people involved or the degree of formalisation of organisational rules and regulations. No doubt, some political maneuvering can make contributions toward an organisations effectiveness. When there is a head on conflict and where interdependence make some degree of cooperation essential, concessions worked out between parties involve often some bending or reinterpretation of rules. On many occasions, the conflicting interests are all legitimate and rest on solid ground. In the late 1980s USX Corporation (formerly United States Steel Corporation) used politics to begin solving its productivity problems.

Corporate Governance

Corporate means legally united into a body so as to act as an individual. **Governance** is control or direction. The two put together it gives a meaning that it brings together many different groups for the purpose of conducting business.

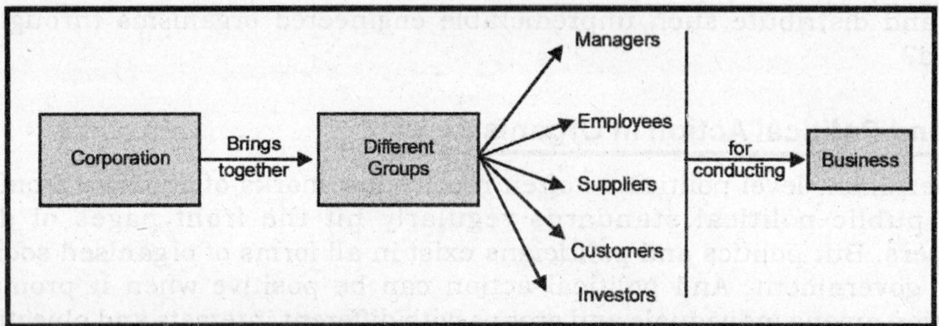

Fig. 1.21 Relationship between Corporation and Business

Companies develop certain formal systems of;

— Accountability

— Oversight

— Control etc.

With a main view to provide an opportunity for employees not to make unethical decisions and these are known as **corporate Governance**.

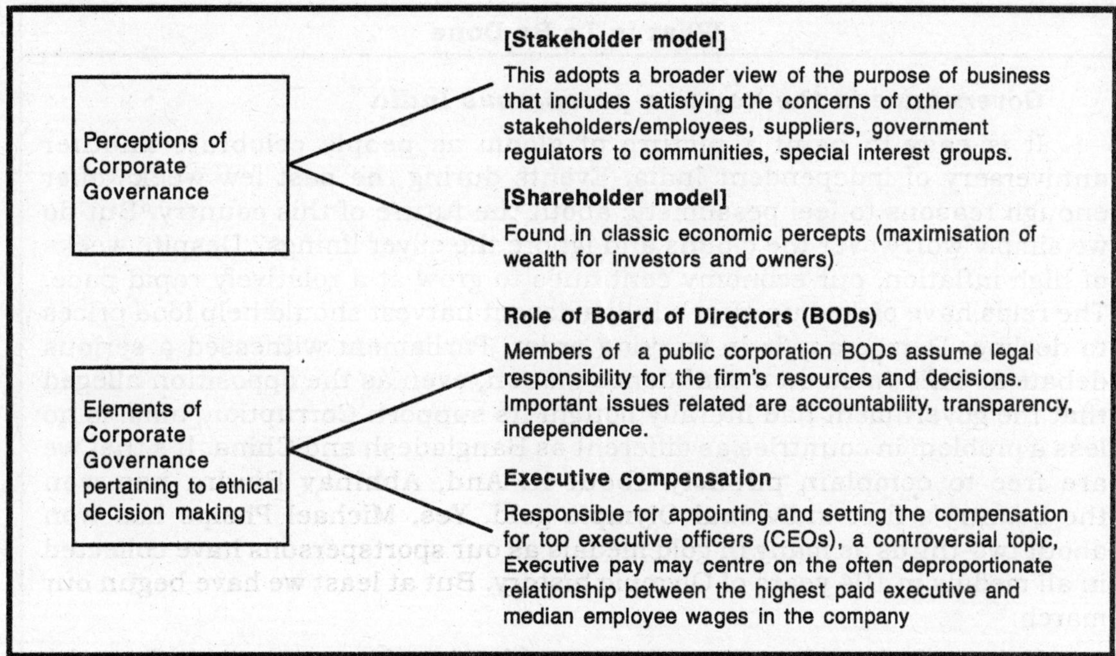

Fig.1.22 Perceptions and Elements of Corporate Governance pertaining to Ethical Decision Making.

Fig.1.22 shows the perceptions and elements of corporate governance pertaining to the ethical decisionmaking.

The organisational ethical decision making does not rely strictly on the personal values and moral values of employees. Organisations have their own culture and if this is combined with corporate governance mechanisms, it may significantly influence business ethics.

Nature of the Corporations

The three theories involved are:

The below mentioned corporate constituencies have different and sometimes conflicting interests. Question is in whose interest should the corporation be run?

Corporation if analysed, the question raises again. Is it

- the **private property** of the stockholders who wants the business to be done in the corporate form? This becomes **Property rights theory** (an extension of the property rights and the right of contract that belongs to all persons).
- the corporation-a public institution sanctioned by the government for some social good? This would be **Social institution theory**. **Corporate property** has an inherent public aspect and the privilege is granted by the government.

What Is To Be Done

Governance is the key to a prosperous India

It is easy to paint a picture of gloom as people celebrate another anniversary of independent India. Events during the past few weeks offer enough reasons to feel pessimistic about the future of this country. But do we simply worry over the clouds and ignore the silver linings? Despite weeks of high inflation, our economy continues to grow at a relatively rapid pace. The rains have picked up after a lull; a decent harvest should help food prices to decline. Democracy is in working order. Parliament witnessed a serious debate as MPs voted on a confidence motion, even as the opposition alleged that the government had literally bought its support. Corruption, alas, is no less a problem in countries as different as Bangladesh and China. It's that we are free to complain publicly about it. And, Abhinav Bindra has won the country's first individual Olympic gold. Yes, Michael Phelps has won about two-thirds as many in gold medals as our sportspersons have collected in all medals in 104 years of Olympic history. But at least we have begun our march.

However, when the prime minister addresses the nation today from the ramparts of the Red Fort, he should be worried. Specifically, about the state of our national security. The country is facing a continuous low-intensity war. The enemies of the Indian state are of many ideological hues and some operate with covert financial and logistical assistance from other countries. The national security adviser recently said 800 terror cells are operating in the country. Thank you for the information, but how do you plan to deal with them? Is it just a case of an underpaid, poorly-equipped force incapable of dealing with new forms of terrorism? Is there a failure on the part of successive governments, which have created monsters that now threaten to rip the country apart? Many questions, few answers. But, surely, the near-collapse of governance in much of the country has helped extremists-Maoists in central India to insurgents in J&K and the north-east-to thrive. How exactly are we dealing with this low-intensity malaise?

Governance is perhaps the single-most important issue that needs attention. It is not merely about building modern institutions; it is about ensuring that these institutions are accountable to the people, while they uphold the rule of law. That's possible only if the state climbs down from its commanding heights and revamps itself in the role of a facilitator and a servant of the people instead of being seen only as a ruling authority.

Respect for the rule of law is possible only when people see themselves as both the masters and beneficiaries of the state. Our rumbustious democracy has focused too much on elections. It is time it restructures radically its state of governance and the quality of relations between the state and the people.

(Ref: The Times of India, Bangalore, 15th August 2008).

- shareholders, along with other investors, employees etc. each own assets that they make available to the firm? This becomes the **Contractual theory** of the firm.

The firm results from the property rights and the right of contract of every constituency and not from those of shareholders alone.

Another important question is whether corporations are needed to serve the interests of shareholders alone or the interests of a wider range of constituencies?

The answer to this question, depends on the theory of the firm it accepts. All the above three theories conclude that the interests of shareholders are primary. But the arguments that they provide are different and need to be understood properly.

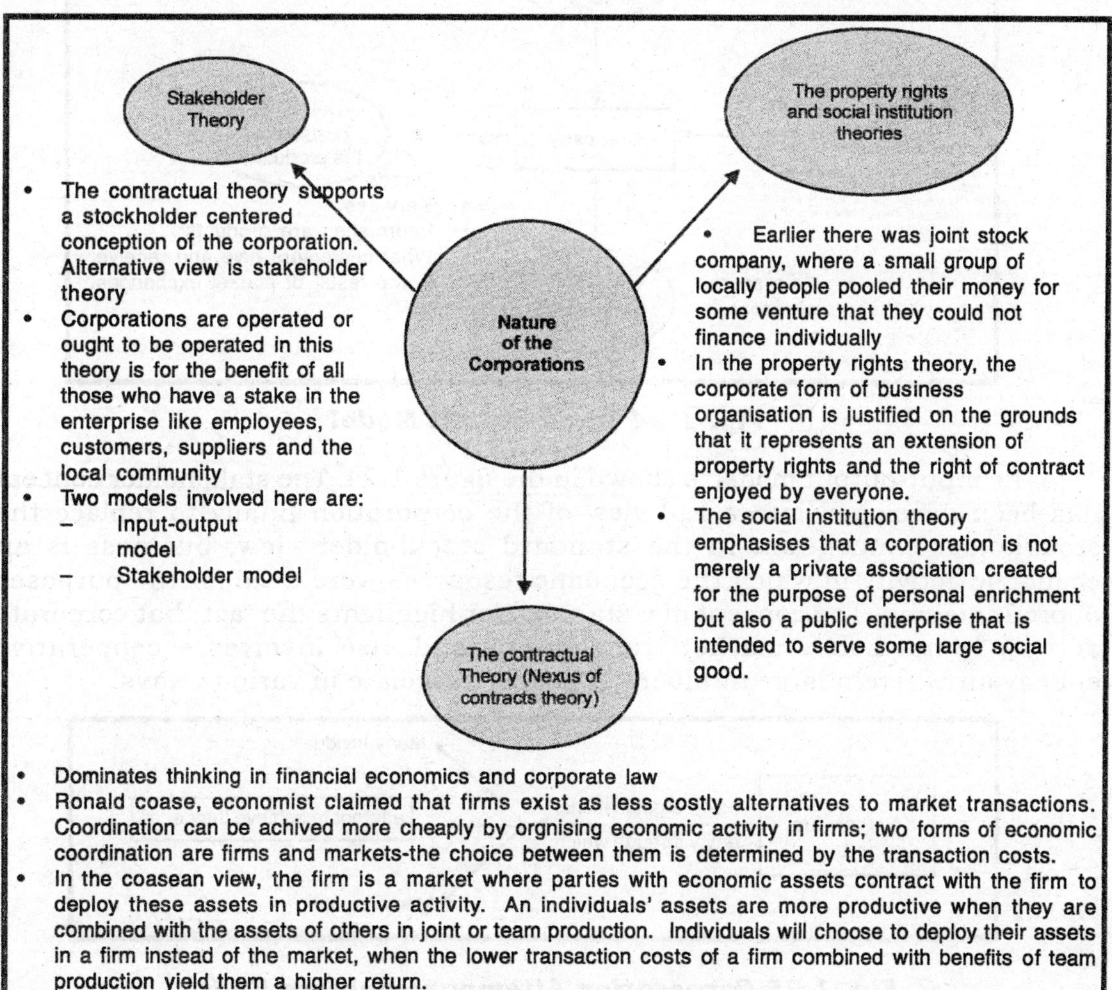

Fig. 1.23 Theories based on the Nature of the Corporation

Definition of Stakeholders

Stakeholders are groups who are vital to the survival and success of the corporation; or

Groups or individual who can affect or are affected by the achievements of the organisations objectives.

Relation of each stockholder group is different; each of these constituencies is integral to the operation of a corporation; role is taken into account by managers.

Input-Output Model under Stakeholder Theory

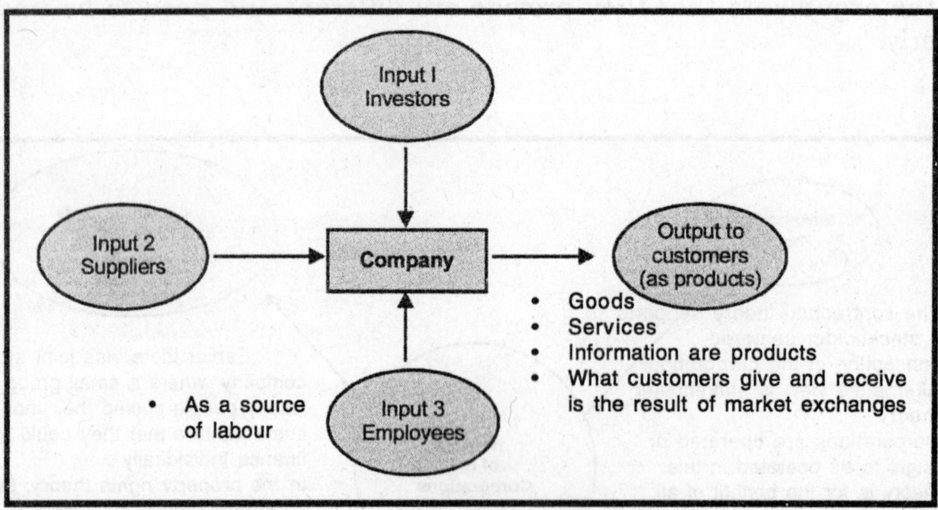

Fig. 1.24 Input-output Model

The input-output model is shown in the figure 1.24. The stakeholder concept has been developed into a full view of the corporation finally to replace the stockholder conception. In the standard stockholder view, business is an economic activity in which the economic resources were used for the purposes of profit making. The concept of a stakeholder highlights the fact that corporate activity is not solely market transactions and also involves a cooperative endeavour wherein large numbers of people associate in various ways.

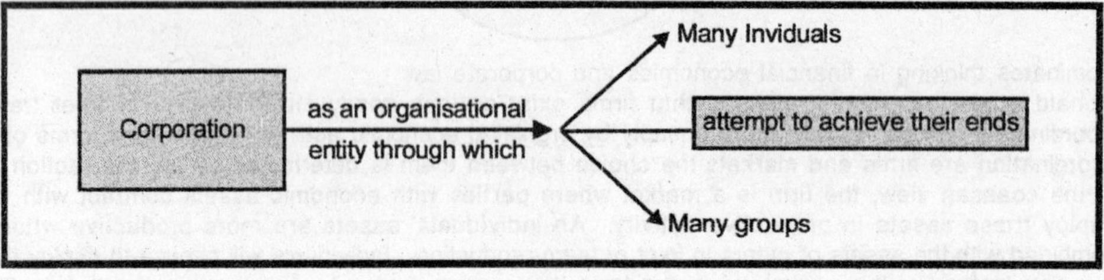

Fig. 1.25 Corporation Attempt to Achieve Ends

A firm reacts continuously with its stakeholder groups and the success of a firm depends on how the relations are organised.

Uses of the Stakeholder Model

Thomas Donaldson and Lee E-Preston have distinguished three uses of the above model:

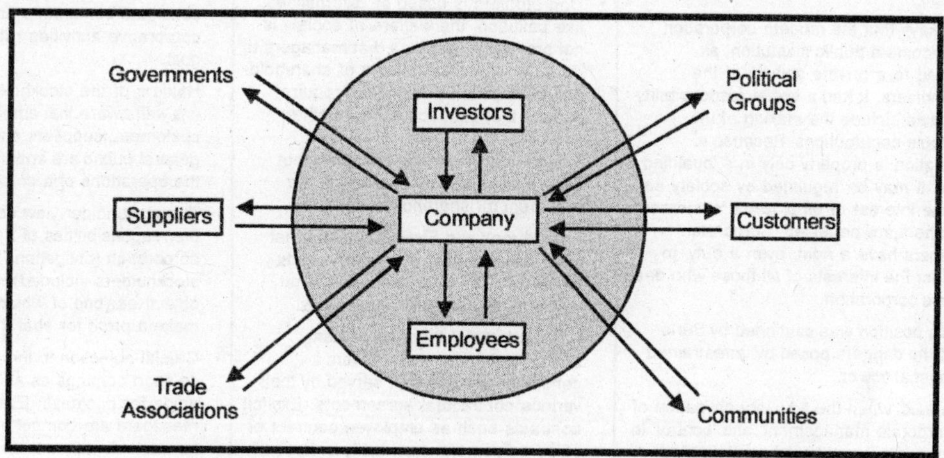

Fig. 1.26 The Stake Holder Model

- Descriptive-instrumental and normative
- The model can be used as description of the corporation to understand the corporation by all the concerned
- The model can be used instrumentally as a tool for managers. Any ultimate goal of the company does not provide much help in the daily conduct of business. eg. profit making. Instead, telling managers to handle the stakehold relations in the right way is a more practical action guide that may lead ultimately to the ultimate goals. The companies which care stakeholders are highly profitable
- The model can be used as a normative account of how corporations ought to break their various stakeholder groups. The earlier two uses of the model suggests that corporations must deal with their stakeholders as a matter of practical necessity. This use as a normative recognised the interests of employees, customers and others as worth furthering for their own sakes. The interests of all stakeholders are of intrinsic value.

Criticisms on various theories:

The property rights and social institution theories	*Contractual theory*	*Stakeholder theory*
• Berle argued that the corporation is an 'economic institution which has a social service as well as a profit making function'. • Dodd says that the modern corporation had become a public institution, as opposed to a private activity of the shareholders. It had a social responsibility that could include the making of the charitable contributions. Because a corporation is property only in a 'qualified sense' it may be regulated by society so that the interest of employees, customers and others are protected. Corporate managers have a right, even a duty, to consider the interests of all those who deal with the corporation. • Dodd's position was cautioned by Berle about the dangers posed by unrestrained managerial power. • Berle said 'when the fiduciary obligation of the corporate management' and 'control' to stockholders is weakened or eliminated, the management and control become for all practical purposes absolute. Berles estimation says, for the law to release managers from a strict accountability to shareholders, not out of respect for their property rights as owners of a corporation but as a matter of sound public policy. • Berle described the role of corporate managers as a 'seizure of power without recognition of responsibility-ambition without courage. But without the absence of effective restraints on managerial power, Berle concludes:....''we had best be protecting the inte-rests we know, being no less swift to provide for the new interests as they successively appear." • Although the separation of ownership and control documented by Berle and means undermined the properties theory, a fully developed social institution theory did not replace it. Alternatively, a conception of the corporation as a quasipublic institution emerged, in which managers have limited discretion to use the resources at their com-mand for the good of employees, customers, and the larger society.	• Argument for shareholder control is similar to Adam Smiths famous invisible hand argument. • One problem is posed by externalities, like pollution. the welfare of society is not promoted. The idea that managers to consider only the interests of sharehold-ers appears to invite, indeed require, actions that impose harms on other constituencies. Easter brook and Fischel recognise this possibility but deny that it has any bearing on the argument for shareholder control. • Easterbrook and Fischel contend that clear assignments of property rights would force firms to internalise what would otherwise be external costs. • The contractual theory argument assumes that nonshareholders constituencies are well served by their various contractual agreements. Explicit contracts such as employee contract or sales agreement, are legally enforce-able. • Many contracts are implicit. They depend on the goodwill of the manage-ment. • Implicit contracts are a kind of promise, and it seems unfair for shareholders to benefit by, in effect, going back on their word. • The contractual theory assumes that shareholders bear all residual risk, but other constituencies, most notably employees and suppliers bear some. When other groups besides shareholders bear residual risk, they are sometimes accorded a seat on the board of directors. • Lastly the contractual theory takes no account of the fact that the contracting groups have unequal bargaining power; this imbalance results in correspond-ingly unequal distribution of the wealth created by a firm.	• Some reject this model in its normative use on the ground that the interests of all groups other than shareholders constitute constraints on corporative activities rather than goal. • Holders of the stockholder view are well aware that employers, customers, suppliers and the general public are important to the operations of a corporation. • The stakeholder view confuses the responsibilities of a corporation (obligations of stockholders included) with its objectives (one of which is to make a profit for shareholders). • Crucial objection to this model is its short comings as an action guide for business. Even managers are committed to honour obligations to all stakeholders will find that many questions are unanswered. Many difficult corporate decisions involve trade offs in which a benefit to one group must be balanced against a loss to another. • The implications of stakeholder theory for corporate governance are unclear. • In keeping with the Berle's concern about the dangers of unrestrained managerial power, a stakeholder corporation would need to be structured so as to ensure the well being of corporate constituencies. Till to day no stakeholder theorist has offered a detailed proposal for changes in corporate gover-nance that would result in a stakeholder corporation.

Fig. 1.27 Criticisims on Three Theories

Codes of Ethics - Individual, Corporate, Industry

Individual Codes of Conduct

When examining business ethics, it is important to realise that the corporations, partnerships, and other entities that make up the business community are a composite of individuals. If the readers of this book are asked wetter they obtained their ethical values; they might respond from:

- Parents
- Teachers
- Temples
- Brothers/Sisters
- Peers
- Environment, in which they live.

In any event, corporations and the culture of a corporation, are greatly influenced by that ethical values individuals bring to it. Often business managers are faced with a conflict between their individual ethic values and those of the corporation.

Corporate Ethical Conduct

The sum, total of individual employees ethical values influences corporate conduct, especially in a corporation's early years. The activities of these years, in turn form the basis of what constitutes a 'corporate culture' or an environment for doing business. In a free market society, values of productivity, efficiency and profits become part of the culture of all companies. Approximately, 90% of all major corporations in USA have adopted codes of conduct since the mid 1960s.

A study of corporate codes reveals that the actions most typically forbidden are:

- Paying bribes to foreign government officials
- Price fixing
- Giving gifts to customers or accepting gifts from suppliers
- Using insider information
- Revealing trade secrets

Industry Ethical Codes

In addition to corporate ethical codes, industry codes exist such as those of the National Association of Broadcasters or the National Association of used car Dealers. These codes are rather general and contain either affirmative inspirational guidelines or a list of shall not's. A "hybrid model" including 'dos' and 'don'ts' generally addresses itself to subjects such as:

- Honest and fair dealings with customers
- Acceptable level of safety, efficacy or cleanliness of limen

- Nondeceptive advertising
- Maintenance of experienced and trained personnel, performance of competent services and furnishing of quality products.

Professional Codes of Ethics

Within a corporation, managers often interact with individual employees who have professional codes of conduct that may supersede corporate or industry wide codes in terms of what activities they can participate in and still remain licensed 'professionals.'

Professional is an often overused term referring to every thing from persons to hair stylists to engineers, lawyers and doctors. When discussing professions or professionals, the authors mean a group that has the following characteristics.

1. Prelicensing mandatory university educational training, as well as continuing education requirements.
2. Licensing exam requirements.
3. A set of written ethical standards that are recognised and continually enforced by the group.
4. A formal association or group that meets regularly.
5. An independent commitment to the public interest.
6. Formal recognition by the public as a professional group.

Kohlberg's Moral Development Model

Ethics is the study of morality. A person involves in ethics if he turns to look at the moral standards. These moral standards have been absorbed from family; all religious places like churches, mosques, temples; friends and society. Further questions will be asked whether these standards are reasonable or unreasonable and what these standards imply for situations and issues. The process of examining one's moral standards and of applying them to concrete situations and issues is important. This includes:

- A person's ability to use and critically evaluate his/her moral standard which develops in the course of a person's life.
- Reasoning processes through which these moral standards are employed and evaluated.

Moral Development

The general belief is that a person's values are formed during his childhood and do not change subsequently. The psychological research conducted on this and as well as with one's own personal experience, it is seen that as people mature, they change their values in very deep and profound ways. This is similar to changes found in people's physical, emotional and cognitive abilities develop as they grew. The ability to deal with moral issues develops as they move though their lives. As seen in a human, identifiable stages of growth in physical development, so also the ability to make reasoned moral judgements also develops in identifiable stages.

The children are told what is might and what is wrong by parents and other elders. they obey the same to avoid punishment. The adherence of these by the children is essentially based on a self absorbed avoidance of pain. When they grew up, these conventional moral standards gets internalised and is then based on living upto the expectations of family, friends, and surrounding society. As rational and experienced adults, we acquire the capacity to critically reflect on the conventional moral standards bequeathed to us by our families, peers, culture, or religion. The next step by us is rationally evaluate these moral standards and the consequences, and to revise them, if we find them inadequate, inconsistent or unreasonable.

In short, we thus do ethics. Our morality now increasingly consists of moral standards that are more impartial and we do paropakar with taking care of ourselves.

The psychologist Lawrence Kohlberg who conducted extensive research in this field for 20 years concluded that is a sequence of six identifiable stages in the development of a person's ability to deal with moral issues.

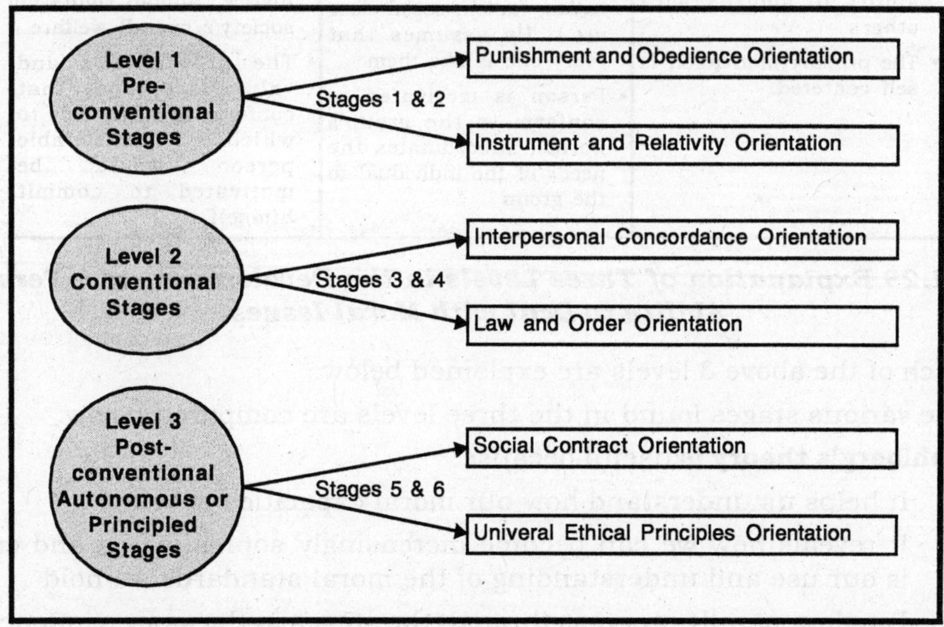

Fig. 1.28 Six Stages in the Development of a Person's Ability to Deal with Moral Issues

Preconventional stages Stages 1&2	*Conventional stages Stages 3&4*	*Post-conventional stages Stages 5&6*
• Child is able to respond to rules and social expectations • Can apply the labels good, bad, right, wrong • Rules are externally imposed on the self; may be pleasant or painful consequences of actions or in terms of the physical power of those who set the rules eg. Ask a child of 5 to 6 years whether stealing is wrong. It says yes. Why it is wrong? It doesn't have the answer. Even if it says 'Mummy will punish me, if I steal' the child will only see the situation from its point of view. It doesn't have the ability to identify with others • The primary motivation is self centered.	• Maintaining the expectations of one's own family, peer group, or nation as valuable in its own right • Exhibits loyalty to the group and its norms • The adolescent at this level asked 'why wrong? why right?' he replies what my family has taught me? What my friends think? What our law says? What we Indians hold? • Adolescent is now able to see situations from the view point of others • Adolescent takes up are-the familiar view points of the people who belong to his level social groups (family, peers, organi-sation, nation, social class etc.). He assumes that every one is like them • Person is motivated to conform to the group's norms; subordinates the needs of the individual to the group	• The person do not accept the values and norms of the groups to which he belongs • He sees situations from a point of view that impart-ially takes everyone's interests into account • He questions the laws and values that society has adopted • Redefines them in terms of self-chosen moral principles that can be justified in rational terms. If the same question is put to him, the person will respond in terms of what it has been decided through processes that are fair to everyone or in terms of justice, human rights or society's overall welfare • The proper laws and values are those that conform to principles to which any reasonable person would be motivated to commit himself.

Fig. 1.29 Explanation of Three Levels in the Development of a Person's Ability to Deal with Moral Issues

Each of the above 3 levels are explained below:

The various stages found in the three levels are compared below:

Kohlberg's theory is useful because:

- It helps us understand how our moral capacities develop
- It reveals how we can become increasingly sophisticated and critical is our use and understanding of the moral standards we hold
- People generally progress through the stages in the same sequence and not every one progresses through all the stages
- Implies that the moral reasoning of people at the later stages of the moral development are better than the reasoning of those at earlier steps

Stage 1 *Punishment and obedience orientation*	*Stage 2* *Instrument and relativity orientation*	*Stage 3* *Interpersonal concordance orientation*
• The physical consequences of an act wholly determine the goodness or badness of that act • The child's reasons for doing the right thing are to avoid punishment or defer to the superior physical power of authorities; there is little awareness that others have needs and desires similar to one's own	• Right actions become those that can serve as instruments for satisfying the child's own needs or the needs of those for whom the child cares • The child is now aware that others have needs and desires similar to his own and begins to defer to them to get them to do what he wants	• Good behaviour at this stage is living to the expectations of those for whom one feels loyalty, affection and trust such as family and friends • Right action is conformity to what is generally expected in one's role as a good son, brother, friend etc. • Doing what is right is motivated by the need to be seen as a good performer in one's own eyes and in the eyes of others
Stage 1 *Law and Order orientation*	*Stage 2* *Social contact orientation*	*Stage 3* *Universal ethical principles orientation*
• Right and wrong now come to be determined by loyalty to one's own larger nation or surrounding society • Laws are to be upheld except where they conflict with other fixed social duties • The person is now able to see other people as parts of a larger social system that defines individual roles and obligations • He can separate the norms generated by this system from his interpersonal relationships and motives	• The person becomes aware that people hold a variety of conflicting personal views and opinions • Emphasises fair ways of reaching consensus by agreement, contract and due process • The person believes that all values and norms are relative and that apart from this democratic consensus, all should be tolerated	• Right action defined in terms of moral principles chosen because of their logical comprehensiveness, universality and consistency • These ethical principles are not concrete like ten commandments • Abstract general principles dealing with justice society's welfare, the equality of human right's respect for dignity of individual human beings and the idea that persons are ends in themselves and must be treated as such. The persons reasons for doing what is right are based on a commitment to these moral principles and the person sees them as criteria for evaluating all other moral rules and arrangements including democratic consensus.

Fig. 1.30 Comparison of Various Stages Found in Three Levels in the Development of a Person's Ability to Deal with Moral Issues

Kohlberg's theory however, has been subjected to a number of criticises as under:

– For cleaning that the higher stages are morally preferable to the lower stages. No doubt, higher stages incorporate broader perspectives and widely acceptable justifications, it does not follow that these perspectives are morally better than the lower ones.

– Second criticism is one that arises from the work of Carol **Gilligan**, a psychologist. Although the Kohlberg's theory correctly identifies the stages through which men pass as they develop, it fails to adequately trace out the pattern of development of women.

Gilligan claimed two different ways to approach moral issues:

(i) **Male approach:** According to Gillign, males tend to deal with moral issues in terms of impersonal, impartial and abstract moral rules-exactly the kind of approach that is exemplified by the principles of justice and rights that Kohlberg says are characteristic of post conventional thinking.

(ii) **Female approach:** Kohlbeg does not recognise this. Females Gilligan claimed tend to see themselves as a part of a 'web' of relationships with family and friends; when females encounter moral issues, they are concerned with sustaining these relationships, avoiding hurt to others in these relationships, and earing for their wellbeing.

However, both Kohlberg and Gilligan agreed that there are stages of growth in our moral development. Both also agreed that moral development moves from a preconventional stage focused on the self, though a conventional stage in which we uncritically accept the conventional moral standards of the groups to which we belong and on a mature stage in which we learn to critically and reflectively examine the adequacy of the conventional moral standards of the groups to which we belong, and once mature stage in which we learn to critically and reflectively examine the adequacy of the conventional moral standards.

Moral Reasoning

Moral reasoning is a more intentional form of decision making where the actor considers the basis for and implications of the decision before acting. The decision maker considers evidence and reaches conclusions or judgements, about the right and wrong way to act. Moral reasoning, suffer from being too absolute or from being too relativistic. Absolute is where one believes that the same rule applies, no matter the circumstances; Relativistic is where the answer always seems to depend entirely on circumstances.

To avoid these two extremes, one might look to a model of reasoning such as the stakeholder model of decision making.

Stakeholder Model

This model has already been explained in page Nos 41. **Stakeholders** include all of the groups and/or individuals affected by a decision, policy or operation of a firm or individual.

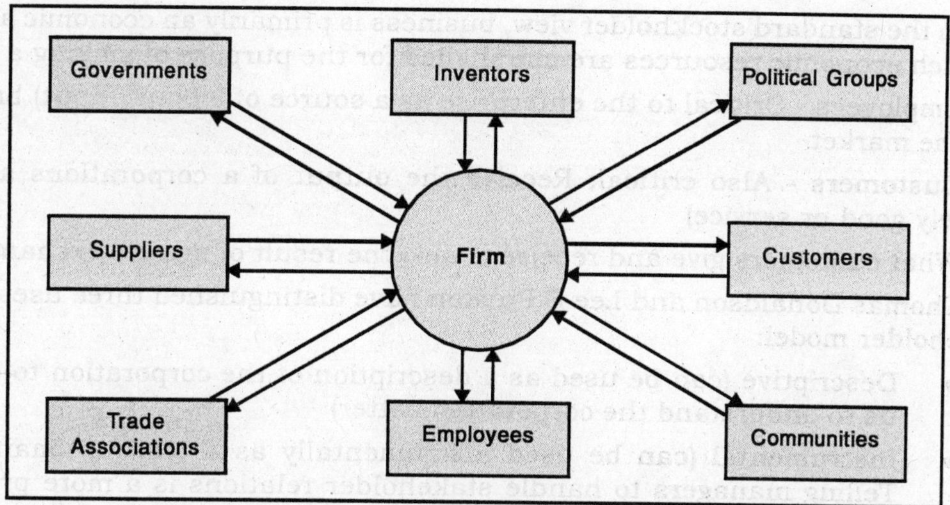

Fig. 1.31 The Stakeholder Model

The **contractual theory** generally supports a stockholder centered conception of the corporation. An alternative is **stakeholder theory**. The central claim of the stakeholder approach is that corporations are operated or ought to be operated for the benefit of all those who have a stake in the enterprise as shown above in the figure. A stable holder is variously defined as those groups who are vital to the survival and success of the corporation and as any group or individual who can affect or is affected by the achievement of the organisations objectives. Although the relation of each stakeholder group to the corporation is different each of the constituencies is integral to the operation of a corporation, and its role must be taken into account by managers.

Serious attempts have been made to develop the stakeholder concept into a full blown view of the corporation that might replace the stock holder central conception.

The Input-Output Model

The input-output model is shown below:

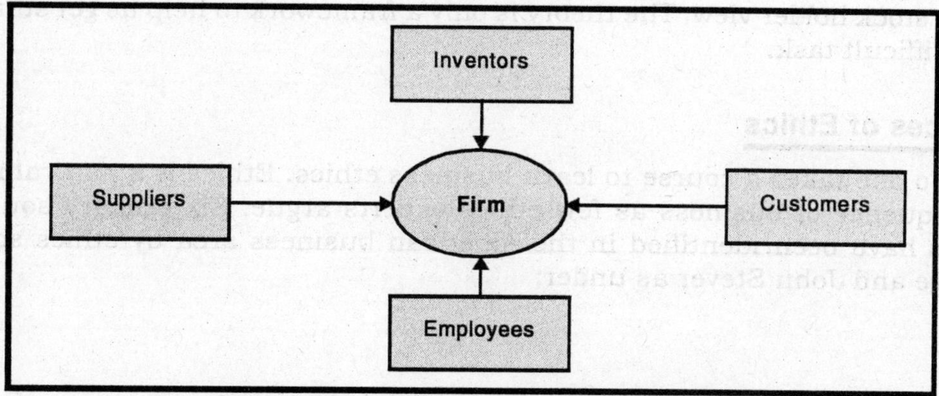

Fig. 1.32 The Input-Output Model

In the standard stockholder view, business is primarily an economic activity in which economic resources are marshalled for the purpose of making a profit.

Employees - Critical to the enterprise as a source of labour (Input) brought into the market

Customers - Also critical; Receive the output of a corporations activity (namely good or service)

What customers give and receive is also the result of market exchanges.

Thomas Donaldson and Lee E.Preston have distinguished three uses of the stakeholder model:

- Descriptive (can be used as a description of the corporation to enable us to understand the corporation better)
- Instrumental (can be used instrumentally as a tool for managers. Telling managers to handle stakeholder relations is a more practical action guide e.g., making profit as a goal)
- Normative (How corporations ought to treat their various stakeholder groups).

Descriptive and Instrumental uses of the stakeholder model suggest that corporations must deal with their stakeholder as a matter of practical necessity.

Used normatively, managers recognise the interest of employees, customers and others as worth furthering for their own sakes.

According to Donaldson an Preston 'The interests of all stakeholders are of "intrinsic value."

Criticisms on this theory are:

- On normative use, the interests of all groups other than shareholders constitute constraints or corporate activities rather than goals.
- Shortcomings as an action guide for business.
- The implications of stakeholder theory for corporate governance are unclear.

Despite these objections, the above model remains a promising alternative to the stock holder view. The theory is only a framework to help us get started on that difficult task.

Sources of Ethics

No one takes a course to learn business ethics. Ethics is a natural market consequence of business as few ethics experts argue. Six primary sources of ethics have been identified in the American business area by ethics scholars George and John Stever as under:

(i) Genetic Inheritance

In recent years, socio-biologists have lots of evidence and arguments to suggest that the evolutionary forces of natural selection influence the development of traits such as cooperation and alteration that lie at the core of our ethical systems.

(ii) Religion

The great world religions as we have seen are:

- Judaism
- Christianity
- Islam

The business people in these religions believe that their religion provides them with ethical principles/standards, which can be applied in business. The Jewish tradition and the Christian tradition refer the religious ethical teaching as the 'Ten Commandments' which are believed to have been divinely revealed as the will of God.

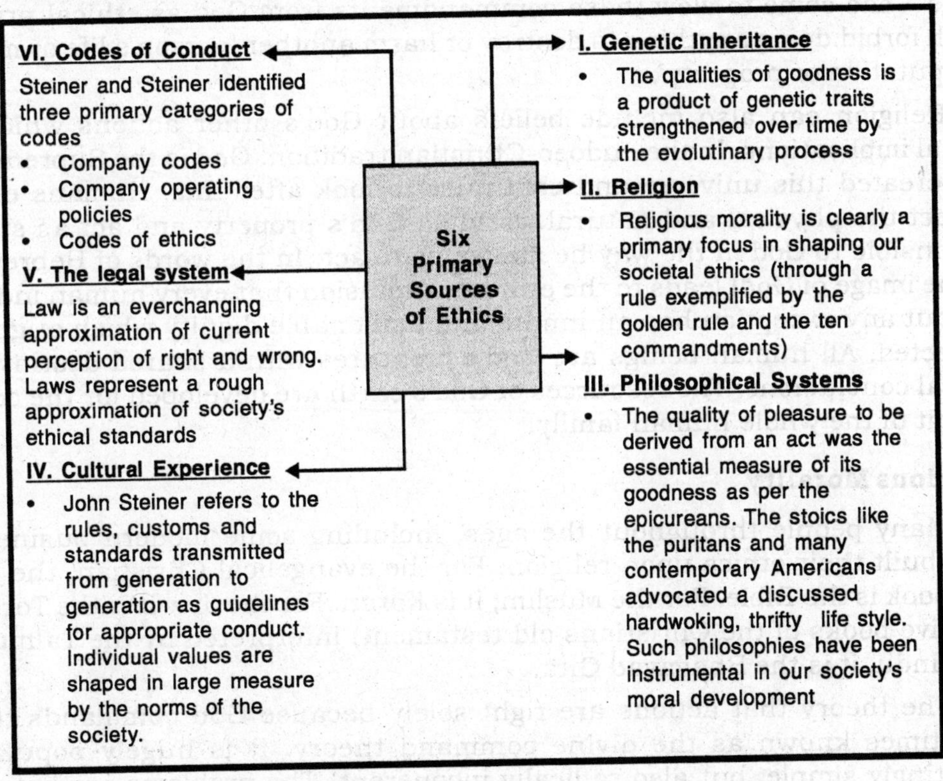

Fig. 1.33 Six Primary Sources of Ethics

The Ten Commandments

These are one of the earliest recorded codes of conduct as found in the Bible.

The ethical commands in this are:

- Honour your father and your mother, that you may have a long life in the land which the Lord, your God, is giving you.
- You shall not kill
- You shall not commit adultery
- You shall not steal
- You shall not bear false witness against your neighbours
- You shall not covet your neighbour's house. You shall not covet your neighbour's wife, nor his male or female slave, nor his ox or ass, nor anything else that belongs to him.

Tradition in both cases - and reinforced for Christians by the teaching of Jesus - has come to view these commandments from God as ethical principles which forbid doing anything to destroy or harm another 'person's life or marriage or reputation or property'.

Religion can also include beliefs about God's other actions which have ethical implications. In the Judoeo-Christian tradition, God is the Supreme being who created this universe and continues to look after this. Humans ethically respect the physical and natural world as God's property and act as stewards responsible to God in the way he makes us to act. In the words of Hebrew Bible (in the image of God) leads to the ethical conclusion that every human individual without any exception has an innate and inalienable dignity which ought to be respected. All human beings are God's creatures with a shared destiny in the ethical conclusions. The resources of God's earth are developed for the common benefit of the whole human family.

Religious Morality

Many people throughout the ages, including some modern businessmen have built their ethics upon religion. For the evangelical Christian, the ethical rule book is the Bible. For the Muslim, it is Koran. For the Jew it is the Torah (the first five books of the Christians old testament) interpreted by the Talmud. For the Hindu, it is the Bhagavad Gita.

The theory that actions are right solely because God commands them is sometimes known as the divine command theory. It is hugely popular and temptingly simple, but also radically incoherent. The problems are not merely about proving the God's existence or demonstrating that we know He will. The deeper problem is that even God is the final arbiter on ethical matters, how does He Himself decide what is right or wrong?

Some religious believers opine that God, being ruler of the universe, not only has the power to make laws on behalf of humanity and also able to back them up by sanctions. According to classical Christian and Islamic teaching, God will reward the righteous with the joys of heaven, and push the wicked to the torments of hell. It may be argued that what makes actions right and wrong is the fact (if it is a fact) of divine reward and retribution. The fact of reward or punishment will not make actions right or wrong that they should be rewarded or punished, rather it is because actions are right or wrong that they should be rewarded or punished. We are still unaware of reasons independent of God's will to explain why an action is right or wrong. Being religious is to be equated with believing in God was the argument so far, is not necessarily the case. Buddhists and Jains are religions and their religions have very clearly defined codes of ethics. A creator God does not feature in their scheme of things. Morality can exist without religion, whereas religion cannot usually exist without morality. Few religions have moral codes. Does a religion add to a moral code? Religious morality might extend beyond a secular morality is that religion typically holds that there are dimensions of reality beyond the purely physical world.

Hindus not only seek for peace, well being of humanity, but also for moksha. The Christian does not merely seek for the secular well being of humanity, but for the 'kingdom of heaven'. The Jew may seek for the messaic age of peace, justice and harmony. Believers in a religious morality will often claim that the actions they are prescribed will help to bring about that supernatural goal.

The follower of a religion has freedom to practice the religion of one's choice is generally regarded as a fundamental human right. Those involved in international business are therefore ill advised to ride rough shodover the religious convictions of their trade partners, who may well believe that their entire eternity could be at stake.

In Latin, religion is termed as religion which means, 'I bind'. Religion binds people together. A religion can also enable its followers to experience a sense of belonging to a tradition or a community. The Muslims undertaking of the Haj (Pilgrimage to Mecca), Hindus to Benares and Tirupathi and the Christians coming together for the sacrament are always in which these respective communities are bound together in a brotherhood or a fellowship (a word often employed by the Christian). Belonging to a community entails having distinctive characteristics. One way of ensuring that a community is distinctive is by imposing special obligations upon its members.

In Hindu Philosophy, the schooling starts for the children in the house. Morals are taught in the house by the parents specially by the mother. Then they will be sent to the school where they will be refined. 'Matru devo Bhava', Pitru devo Bhava', 'Acharya devo Bhava'. Mother is given first preference, then father, then the teacher, that is Guru or Acharya.

A religion can provide its followers with a distinctive means of achieving a desired end. Many religions in fact deplore extremes of wealth and poverty and aim for an age where there will be compassion and justice (This need not entail absolute equality. Most religions explicitly rejected this). Contemporary Islam prescribes that a certain proportion of one's wealth should be given as alms for the poor (Zakat), and that unearned interest may not be gained for monies lent. Similarly, the Jews in ancient times suggested methods by which inequalities of wealth could be levelled down. They even followed, on the institutions jubilee year, all debts automatically gets cancelled. Roman Catholic church, has propagated the doctrines of the just wage and just price, from a long time. The Jain religion recommended that the people in the business world should decide, in advance on achieving their fortune, what standard of wealth they hope to achieve and when such fortune is exceeded, the surplus should be made available for worthy causes. Even without belonging to a religion, such good practices can be made. Individual resolutions are easier to break (in the period of new year or during a period such as Lent) than obligations. Rich Hindus donate lot of wealth to the temples where free food is offered every day for the needy people. Example: Dharmastala in Karnataka, Tirupati in Andhra Pradesh, Mantralaya, Horanadu, etc.

When we examine the relationship between morality and religion, we see that different religions seem to generate different moral codes. A society in which there is a dominant religion or ideology can be expected to produce a reasonably uniform set of values. Capitalism flourishes generally with its emphasis on private ownership, competition and the profit motive. A nation's success is measured in terms of its GNP (Gross National Product) and consumption is encouraged by means of an advertising industry which attempts to stimulate wants and boost demand.

As business has become increasingly internationalised, there is an increasing likelihood of people of different countries encountering business partners from very different cultures, from different religions, who subscribe to radically different ethical systems. If an Hindu wants to start a business in Middle East, he has to join with a local person who is from a different culture and from a different religion. European communion countries have migrant workers from India, Africa, Middle East, Far East etc. and as these people settle, a cosmopolitan new generation of business people emerges. Likewise when Japanese start new business outside their country, their stuff gets mingled with the locals and their distinctive methods are used.

It might be questioned whether international variations amongst managers are any more diverse than the differences between managers in the same single country or the same continent. In India itself, we find diverse religions, varied cultures in businesses. The view can some times be labelled as **universalism**. According to this school of thought there is only one fundamental '**World Management Culture**' with minor variations in attitudes and values amongst different managers.

An alternative view is that international differences in attitudes and values amongst managers can be attributed to the political and economic difference which exist between different countries. This view can be labelled as the '**economic clusters**' view.

Lot of reservations are there about cultural relativism. Haire et al. mentioned in general, world management styles could be classified into five broad cultural clusters as under:

- Nordic European (Scandinavian countries like Denmark, Norway, Sweden and Germany)
- Latin-European (Belgium, France, Spain and Italy)
- Anglo-American
- Developing countries (Argentina, Chile, India)
- Japan

According to a study of International managerial values made by George England in his book, "The Manager and his values" (Cambridge, Mass: Ballinger, 1975) Personal values of 2500 managers in five countries were examined USA, Japan, Korea, India and Australia.

Japan and Korea, though they have historical hostility and apparent cultural classes, fell next to USA and Australia with similarities. Not much differences were found between India and Japan. In the case of international culture and moral diversity, British business managers often underrate or ignore it (Religious affiliation is weak in UK). There are no easy solutions in ethical dilemmas in international business or in dealing with ethnic minorities within a culture.

- Wearing of a turban instead of a safety helmet by a sikh cannot be insisted by a British supervisor.
- Europeans to be obliged to go without alcohol in an Arab country.
- Seeking planning permission in India should a Westerner resort to giving bribes to officials, especially when most other business people do?

Cultural relativist motto would be 'when in Rome, do as the Romans do'.

There is one serious problem when it entails in the context of International business. If it is desirable for western managers abroad to conform to prevailing norms in the countries in which they do business, equally the same would have to apply in reverse. Immigrant workers in USA and Europe ought, to be expected to conform to the norms of western society. The cultural relativist would probably make no concessions to the Sikh who insisted on the importance of the turban, the practising Jew who wished to observe the Sabbath, the Muslim who finished to set aside time for prayer on Friday at noon, and so on such conclusions would certainly be unpalatable to most people; not only do they reflect an inherent intolerance to cultural diversity; implementation would be disastrous for industrial relations. This would be counter to principles of religious freedom, inherently bound up with respecting the individual.

The **golden rule** is 'Act in a way you would expect others to act towards you' or 'Do unto others as you would have them do unto you.'

The great world religions as we have seen are:

- Judaism
- Christianity
- Islam

The business people in these religions believe that their religion provides them with ethical principles/standards, which can be applied in business. The Jewish tradition and the Christian tradition refer the religious ethical teaching as the '**Ten Commandments**' which are believed to have been divinely revealed as the will of God.

The ethical commands in this are:

- You shall not kill
- You shall not commit adultery
- You shall not steal
- You shall not bear false witness against your neighbours
- You shall not covet your neighbour's house.

Tradition in both cases - and reinforced for Christians by the teaching of Jesus - has come to view these commandments from God as ethical principles which forbid doing anything to destroy or harm another 'persons life or marriage or reputation or property'.

Religion can also include beliefs about God's other actions which have ethical implications. In the Judoeo-Christian tradition, God is the supreme being who created this universe and continues to look after this. Humans ethically respect the physical and natural world as God's property and act as stewards responsible to God in the way he makes us to act. In the words of Hebrew bible (in the image of God) leads to the ethical conclusion that every human individual without any exception has an innate and inalienable dignity which ought to be respected. All human beings are God's creatures with a shared destiny in the ethical conclusions. The resources of God's earth are developed for the common benefit of the whole human family.

(iii) Philosophical Systems

Epicure means a follower of Epicures (341-270 BC), a Greek follower who taught that pleasure was the chief good; Epicurean is a follower of Epicures. **Stoic** is a disciple of the philosopher Zeno (340-260BC) who opened his school in a collonnado called the Stoa Poikite (Painted p-orch) at Athens-later Roman stoics were Cato the younger Seneca, Makas Aurelius; one indifferent to pleasure or pain; stoicism, the doctrine of the stoics, a school of ancient philosophy strongly opposed to **Epicurianism** in its views of life and duty.

(iv) The Legal System

The law serves to educate us about the ethical course in life. The law does not, and most would agree, should not be treated as a vehicle for expressing all of society's ethical preferences.

(v) Codes of Conduct

Following are the three primary categories:

- **Company Codes:** These are generally brief; highly generalised, expressed broad expectations about fit conduct.
- **Company Operating Policies:** Contains an ethical dimension, express policies as to gifts, customer complaints, hiring and other decisions serve as a guide to conduct and as a shield by which the employee can protect against unethical advances from those outside the firm.
- **Code of Ethics:** (Professional and Industry Associations have developed code of ethics, such as Affirmative Ethical Principles of the American Institute of Certified Public Accountants). It is a growing expression of the business community's sincere concern about ethics.

Six Primary sources of Ethics in the American Business are

George and John Steiner, noted scholars have identified six primary sources of ethics in the American business arena. These are already explained in fig. 1.34.

Six Primary Sources of Ethics
• The Legal System • Religion • Genetic Inheritance • Philosophical Systems • Code of Conduct • Cultural Experience

Fig. 1.34 Six Primary sources of Ethics

Religion

The religion is as explained in page 11-19.

- Via a rule exemplified by the Golden Rule (or its variations in many religions) and the Ten Commandments, religious morality is clearly a primary force in shaping our societal ethics
- The applicability of religious ethics to the business community is the concern
- The question is all the more relevant since the Golden Rule is not limited to western thought.

- Could the Golden Rule serve as a universal, practical, helpful standard for the business persons conduct?

Philosophical Systems

- To the Epicureans, the quality of pleasure to be derived from an act was the essential measure of its goodness. The stoics, like the puritans and many contemporary Americans advocated a disciplined, hardworking, thrifty life style. These philosophers like other philosophers, have been instrumental in our society's moral development

The Legal System

- **Laws** represent a rough approximation of society's ethical standards. Thus, the law serves to educate about the ethical causes in life. The law should not be treated as a vehicle for expressing all of society's ethical preferences.

Codes of Conduct

Steiner and Steiner identified three primary categories of such codes:

- **Company codes**, ordinarily brief and highly generalised express broad expectations about its conduct.
- **Company operating policies** often contain an ethical dimension. Express policies as to gifts, customer complaints, hiring and other decisions serve as a guide to conduct and as a shield by which the employee can protect against unethical advances from those outside the firm.
- **Affirmative ethical principles of the American Institute of Certified Public Accountants:** Many professional and Industry Associations have developed codes of ethics as above. Codes of conduct seem to be a growing expression of the business community's sincere concern about ethics. However the utility of such codes remains unsettled.

Genetic Inheritance

- As already said in page 11, Socio-biologists in the modern age have amassed persuasive evidence and arguments suggested the evolutionary forces of natural selection influence the development of traits such as cooperation and altruism that lie in the core of our ethical systems.
- Those qualities of goodness often associated with ethical conduct may in some measure be a product of genetic traits strengthened over time by evolutionary process.

Cultural Experience

- Steiners refer to the rules, customs and standards transmitted from generation to generation as guide lines for appropriate conduct.

Individual values are shaped in large measure by the norms of the society.

A Model of Ethics

A **model of ethics** is presented below in Fig. 1.35. Ethics consists of mainly two relationships as indicated in the figure. A person or organisation is ethical, if these relationships (combined together) are strong and positive.

The Time magazine article has said "large sections of the ethical roofing has been sagging badly from the White house to churches, schools, industries, medical centres, law firms and stock brokers - pressing down on the institutions and enterprises that make up the body and blood of America."

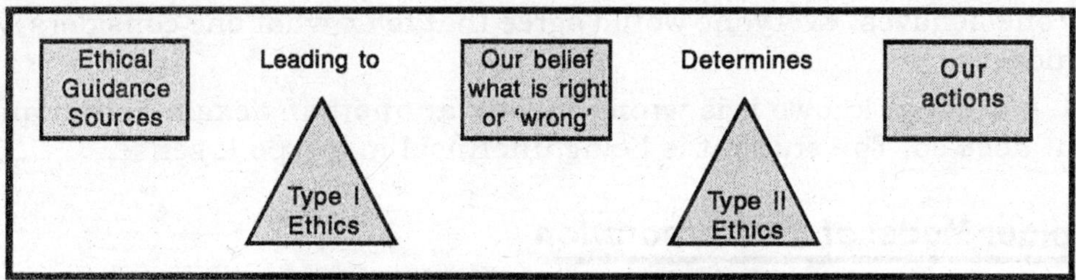

Fig. 1.35 A Model of Ethics

Everyone makes ethical decisions or unethical decisions everyday.

Example

- Too many changes in the work - you may not tell your assistant all the changes.
- Professors may err in your favour in computing your grade.
- CEO may favour one of his assistants who is less experienced, with only one time contact and on the impression he gets and sends him abroad on an important assignment, neglecting other experienced capable personnel.

Minor private decisions are unimportant. But decisions in small matters tend to set a pattern for the more important ones you may make as managers.

A multi-industry survey conducted at USA indicated that 40% of the managers said that their superiors had at some time told them to do certain things unethical. Despite the ambiguity, ethics appears to be moving up in the corporate priority list. Many of the companies have introduced codes of ethics. Industry associations adopt such codes, then recommend to members.

Refer figure 1.7. The sources of ethical guidance should lead to our beliefs or convictions about what is right or wrong. People have a responsibility to avail themselves of these sources of ethical guidance. Individuals should care about what is right and wrong and not just be concerned with what is expedient. The strength of the relationship should be between what is right and wrong and not just be concerned with what is expedient.

The strength of the relationship between what an individual or an organisation believes to be moral and correct and what available sources of guidance suggest is morally correct is **"Type I Ethics."**

E.g., A student copies in the examination, though every one condemns this practice. This student is unethical, but perhaps only in a type I sense (Here the student believes it is acceptable to copy another student's paper in the examination).

Simply having strong beliefs about what is right and wrong and basing them on the proper sources may have little relationship to what one does.

Type II Ethics is the strength of the relationship between what one believes and how one behaves. Everyone would agree that to do what one considers wrong is unethical.

E.G. A student knows it is wrong to look at another's examination answer sheet but does so. The student is being unethical in a type II sense.

Stakeholder Model of the Corporation

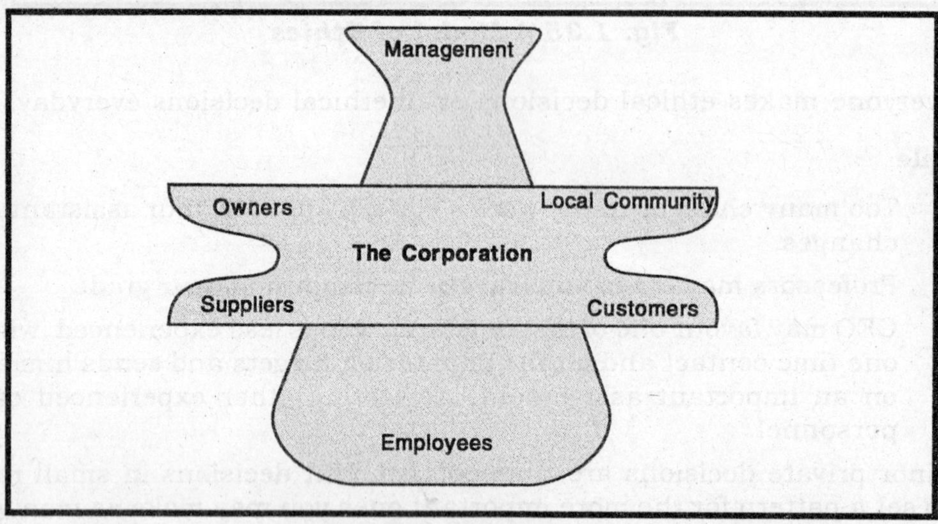

Fig. 1.36 A Stakeholder Model of the Corporation

Figure 1.36 above depicts the stakeholders in a typical large corporation. Corporations consist of stakeholders, that is, groups and individuals who benefit or harmed by, and whose rights are violated or respected by corporate actions. The concept of stakeholders is a generalisation of the notion of stock holders, who themselves have some special claim on the firm. Similar to stock holders have a right to demand certain actions by management, so do other stakeholders have a right to make claims. The stakes of each are reciprocal, since each can affect the other in terms of harms and benefits as well as rights and duties.

Ethics and Business

We shall analyse the relationship between Ethics and Business:

- Ethics conflicts with profits, whereas
- Business always choose profits over ethics

There are companies which suggest a somewhat different perspective - a perspective that many companies are increasingly taking. The management of such companies spend millions of dollars developing products that they knew had little chance of ever being profitable because they felt that had an ethical obligation to make its potential benefits available to people. In such cases, at least, companies choose ethics over profits. Ethical behaviour creates the kind of goodwill and reputation that will expand opportunities for profit according to some of the Ethicists.

Many of the companies will not invest in Research and Development projects since they have good reason to suspect that they will prove unprofitable. We find different type of companies operating differently with regard to ethics and profits.

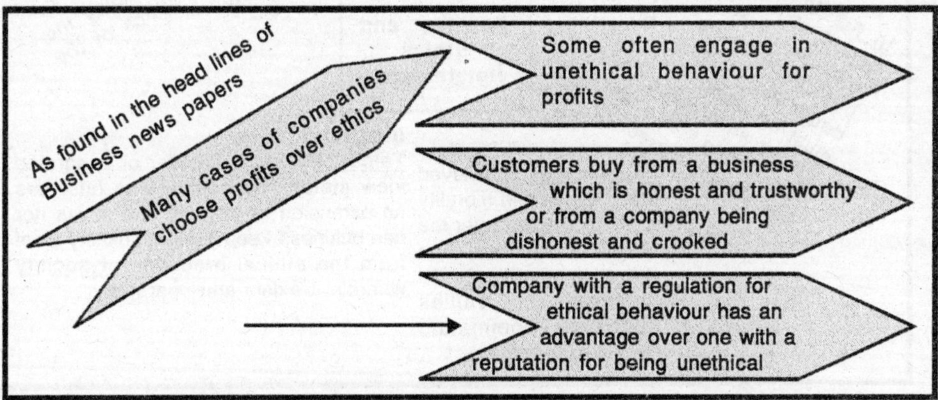

Fig. 1.37 Profits and Ethics in Business

Some argue that it is unethical, to make profit in companies. Even our Ex-Prime Minister Jawaharlal Nehru has said in 1950, profit is a dirty work, referring to public sector companies. Even private companies making profits were viewed with disclaim. In today's meaning, every company is expected to justify its existence in the market place and hence the profit making is a must. A sick and loss making company is a liability and a burden to the society. It cannot discharge its responsibilities to the society; cannot meets its welfare commitment to its employees. A company which makes losses, misutilises scarce natural resources, cannot pay creditors, does not earn for its shareholders, make huge liabilities, upsets the economy, promotes inefficiency, disliked by all, and the most important ones is it cannot at any cost discharge its social responsibility, cannot meet its welfare commitments and jeopardises the future of its employees. Such companies are a nuissance and a burden to the economy. It has

- no right to exist
- no business to force its employees into economic insecurity.

Hence those are highly unethical.

It is therefore ethical for the companies to make profits. The first and the most important ethical obligation is to make profits for the company shareholders, for its employees; for creditors and for the company to discharge its social responsibilities and welfare commitments.

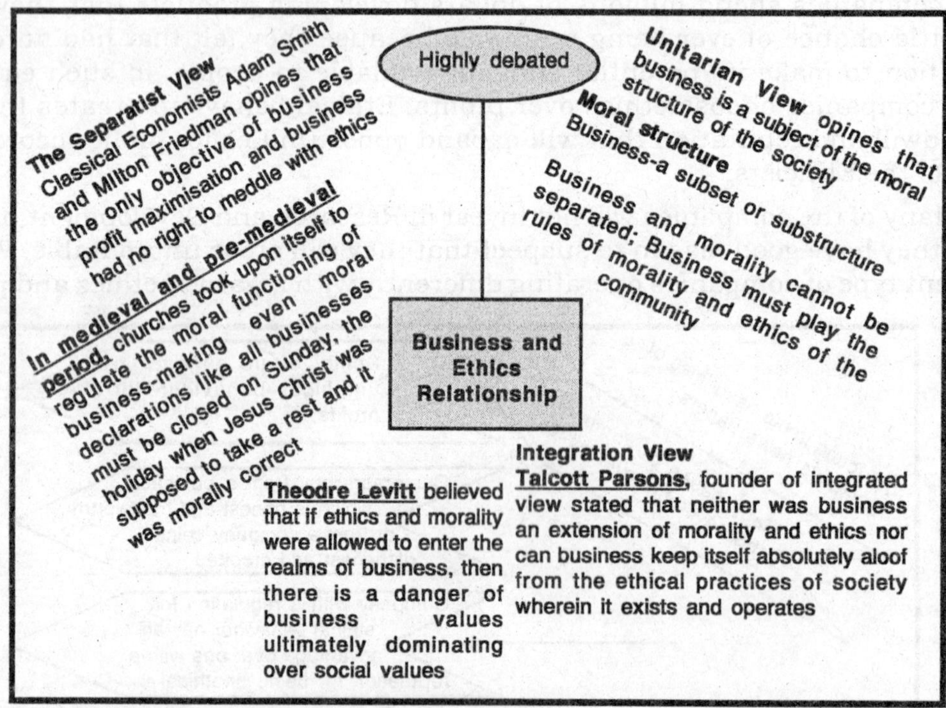

Fig. 1.38 Business and Ethics Relationship

Types of Ethics

Following three different types of ethics are explained below:

Transactional Ethics

Asymmetrical relations of unequal claims and conflicting interests do not exhaust the arsenal of possible action patterns. The concept of common interests needs to be specified because of different types of common interests can be distinguished. Common is used in the sense of occurring simultaneously. Their communality is that they occur at one and the same time and place, without, however, dependent on one another. All parties involved in the action pattern have interests that happens to coincide in time but that do not affect each other. "I am pursuing my affairs, as he pursue his affairs". We both are aware of each others existence, but that is all the relationship we have - a very thin relationship.

There is morality involved in this relation. In order to let each party's transaction run smoothly, all parties have to accept the principle of equality, implying that every agent should allow every other the same amount of freedom or action he claims for himself. The moral principle of equality tells us where to refrain from intrusions in the freedom of action of others while following one's own affairs, which is negative principle, as well as basic.

Interests can also be common in the stronger sense of being connected. It can also be noted that if connected interests are at stake, the interests of both cannot be realised (without the interest of the other being satisfied as well). Both parties are needed to arrive at the intended result (a cooperative arrangement for mutual benefit). Every party is indispensable, every party is equally entitled to an appropriate share in the outcome of the arrangement. All market transactions fall within this category.

Example: I need vegetables from vegetable vendor. The vendor want customers like me for survival, so we both are dependent on each other, as long as we both contribute appropriately, together we generate a surplus that none of us on his own is able to produce.

In order to let things run smoothly, again adherence to two specific moral principles is required.

- Principle of honesty, i.e., one should operate in good faith fairly and equitably, not betraying the confidence received.
- Principle of reciprocity ie. one should avoid free riding on somebody else's efforts.

The domain of ethics covering transactions that are performed on the basis of simultaneous or connected interests and that are general by the principles of equality, honesty and reciprocity is indicated as the domain of transactional ethics.

Participatory Ethics

Participatory Ethics is a privileged part of business ethics. Within the category of other including actions, guided by common interests, we find another type of actions (not by simultaneous or connected interests) but by shared interests. Parties cooperate in order produce a more distant common good that has three characteristic features.

- The good can only be realised through the participation of all parties.
- Participation cannot be enforced (no explicit moral obligation to take part in the project).
- Though participation may be profitable by participating parties as well as the community at large, none of the parties have to participate in order to survive (every possible participant can obtain without risking a lasting damage for himself).

The important thing is that parties join the alliance voluntarily, committing themselves to a self imposed and non-enforceable obligation. This entails a specific type of social relations that is guided, once more, by two particular moral principles.

- Principle of decency (a specimen of moral aesthetics) where a real opportunity to contribute to the general welfare presents itself and no insurmountable obstacles arise, one should have solid moral reasons not to go for it.
- Principle of emancipation (specific groups deserve the space and means for development that history has unwarrantedly denied them up to now). Special attention is given to the least powerful in order to defend those, who, by themselves, are defenceless. On the basis of principle of decency, corporations voluntarily contribute to a city development project that aims at an optimal distribution of space (devoted to different kinds of housing, to offices, to traffic, cultural and shopping facilities, and to open spaces) preferred for the benefit of all.
- Participatory ethics is about the shape of solidarity in an age of individualisation. It is the ethics of the civil society, recently rediscovered as a solid ground for collective arrangements where both the marked and the state fail. By participating on a regular basis, in common projects on behalf of general welfare, a corporation demonstrates that it can take seriously its corporate citizenship.

Recognitional Ethics

To a certain extent, the same is true with regard to self directed actions. As long as the actor is his own beneficiary, and no legitimate claims are raised by others, no specific moral qualifications are due. We face here an ethics of self development guided by the principle of fidelity to ones basic self. Things change, however and dramatically sometimes, as soon as legitimate rights and interest of other intervene in the pattern of an intendedly self directed action. Serious claims are at stake that require recognition on the part of the actor creating a moral asymmetry between the actor and the party affected by self directed action. From a moral point of view, on such situations, the positions of the parties involved would be claimant on one side and that of a duty bound actor on the other, the former being morally entitled to the recognition of his claims and interests, whereas the latter is obliged to recognise these claims (implying one party's moral rights vis-a-vis the other party's corresponding moral duty). In terms of interest we face a situation of conflicting interests and unequal claims. The rights of the partly affected have a great moral weight than the freedom to act of the acting party. The domain of ethics will be at stake here as the domain of '**recognitional ethics**'.

Basic moral principles which characterise the field of recognitional ethics is the principle of recognition itself the formal and conscious recognition (one may get involved in situations of moral asymmetry and then will have to react accordingly). Basic also is what traditionally called the principle of beneficence or the principle of nonmalificence (no harm should be done to others, that harm done should be compensated. Everybody to a reasonable extent has the moral duty to avoid harm being done by others).

The domain of recognitional ethics covers a large part of traditional ethical interventions. Ethics in fact is about asymmetrical relations about the rights of interests of the one generating a duty for another.

E.g. The employees aged 57 to 60 years morally obliged to retire to give way to some younger colleagues, who, being in the midst of their careers can raise a more weighty claim to a job?

Recognitional ethics clarifies and support this type of discussions applying the two principles mentioned above and other moral convictions that are considered appropriate.

Code of Ethics, American Marketing Association

Members of the American Marketing Association (AMA) are committed to ethical professional conduct. They have joined together in subscribing to this Code of Ethics embracing the following topics:

Responsibilities of the Marketer

Marketers must accept responsibility for the consequences of their activities and make every effort to ensure that their decisions, recommendations, and actions function to identify, serve, and satisfy all relevant publics: consumers, organizations and society. Marketers' professional conduct must be guided by

1. The basic rule of professional ethics: not knowingly to do harm;
2. The adherence to all applicable laws and regulations;
3. The accurate representation of their education, training and experience; and
4. The active support, practice and promotion of this Code or Ethics.

Honesty and Fairness

Marketers shall uphold and advance the integrity, honor, and dignity of the marketing profession by:

1. Being honest in serving consumers, clients, employees, suppliers, distributors and the public;
2. No knowingly participating in conflict of interest without prior notice to all parties involved; and
3. Establishing equitable fee schedules including the payment or receipt of usual, customary and/or legal compensation for marketing exchanges.

Rights and Duties of Parties

Participants in the marketing exchange process should be able to expect that:

1. Products and services offered are safe and fit for their intended uses;
2. Communications about offered products and services are not deceptive;
3. All parties intend to discharge their obligations, financial and otherwise, in good faith; and
4. Approximate internal methods exist for equitable adjustment and/or redress of grievances concerning purchases.

It is understood that the above would include, but is not limited to the following responsibilities of the marketer:

In the area of product development management:

Disclosure of all substantial risks associated with product or service usage.

Identification of any product component substitution that might materially change the product or impact on the buyer's purchase decision.

Identification of extra-cost added features.

Questions

1. Define ethics.
2. Define business ethics.
3. What are the factors influencing behaviour?
4. How are ethics and law related to one another? If the law a substitute for ethics?
5. 'Ethics is considered as everybody's Justice'. Do you agree? Comment.
6. What do you mean by Money Laundering?
7. Have you faced any ethical problems in your life? Explain with examples any two of them.
8. What do you mean by Ethics?
9. What are the three tests you conduct to solve ethical problems. Is it in the same way as you would solve any other complex and contentious questions?
10. Mention the three items used to define ethics. Explain each one of them in brief.
11. Mention the various objectives of Ethics.
12. Explain the nature of Ethics.
13. Mention the six primary sources of ethics. Explain each one of them.
14. Define universalisability? What is the criteria for universalisability?
15. What do you mean by ethical codes? How does this help business organisations?
16. What is meant by 'Greatest good for the greatest number?'
17. What are the six primary sources of ethics in the American business? Explain.

18. Explain a stakeholder model of the corporation.
19. What is the relationship between Ethics and Business. Explain with a sketch.
20. 'Business is a subset of society'. Comment.
21. What is the need for Business Ethics?
22. State the importance of Business Ethics. Explain each one of them.
23. Explain a model of Ethics with a sketch. Give an example.
24. Mention two results derived from the concept being ethical.
25. Explain the nature of business ethics. Mention the characteristics needed for a decision to be ethical.
26. Why do ethical practices of people are different?
27. Explain the factors influencing business ethics.
28. How can the quality of ethical performance can be improved in a business firm?
29. What do you mean by corporate culture?
30. Mention the various objectives of business ethics?
31. Explain how business ethics is considered as a Management discipline?
32. 'Subject of ethics is receiving serious attention in management circles, in the recent days'. Comment.
33. Ethics cover wide areas. Which are the areas according to you? In what ways?
34. What is the relationship between morality and ethics? Explain what do you mean by moral judgements.
35. Compare and contrast Ethics with morals and values.
36. Explain Kohlbergs Theory of model regarding Ethical Judgement.
37. Explain Carol Gilligan's Theory or Model regarding conception of Moral development.
38. Mention the characteristics of Business Ethics.
39. Do the ten commandments represent a moral code or an ethical code? Why?
40. What are the different types of ethics? Compare and contrast them.
41. What do you mean by transactional ethics? Explain.
42. What do you mean by participatory ethics? Explain.
43. What is recognitional ethics? Explain.
44. Explain the various factos influencing individual behaviour.
45. 'Ethical issues arise out of everyday business decision.' Comment. If you agree, give an example.
46. How are the ethical decisions made? Which are the four factors involved? Give an example.
47. Explain the role of moral philosophies in decision making.

48. Mention a few suggestions for ethical decision making. Explain them.
49. 'People are generally moral agents in an ethical organisation' Substantiate.
50. Mention the ethical issues that arise for managers.
51. In spite of the positive benefits of good ethical practices, ethical problems do occur in business. Give reasons.
52. Comment on the guidelines to be followed by the corporate managers and employes needed in business. Discuss the various methods of ethical reasoning and how to use them?
53. Discuss on the three levels of decision making.
54. How do you decide on an ethical course of action during business decision making? Explain with suitable examples.
55. What are the arguments for and against business ethics?
56. Mention three objections of brining ethics into business.
57. Whar are your arguments in bringing ethics into business?
58. Do you think that new technologies will bring in host of ethical issues? If so, explain with examples.
59. Explain the relationship between business ethics and technology.
60. Explain code of ethics in regard to individual, corporate, industry and professional classification.
61. Explain the Kohlberg's moral development model.
62. What are the six stages in the development of a person's ability to deal with moral issues? Explain and compare them.
63. How did Gilligan differed from Kohlenberg and what are the common points between them?
64. Explain a stake holder model with a sketch.
65. Explain the input-output model with a sketch.
66. What are the responsibilities of corporations?
67. Work out a comparison between corporation and business. What is the corporate governance?
68. Define stake holder. What are the three theories found in the nature of the corporations?
69. Explain an Input-Output Model under stakeholder theory.
70. Explain the stake holder model.

MODULE 2

Individual and Organisational Factors

2.1 The Role of Moral Philosophies in Decision Making

The Key Components of Decision Making

The Key components of ethical decision making are shown in Fig. 2.1 **Ethical issues intensity** is defined as the importance of the ethical issue in the eyes of the individual, work group, organisation. It reflects the ethical sensitivity of the latter that faces the ethical decision-making process.

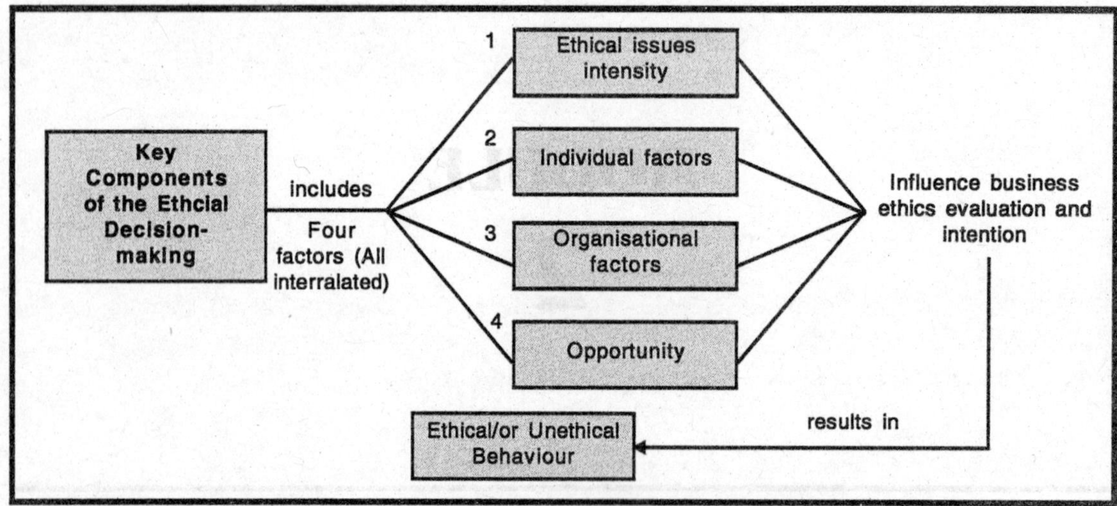

Fig. 2.1 Key Components of Ethical Decision Making

(i) The first step is to recognise that an ethical issue requires that an individual or workgroup choose among several actions that will be evaluated as ethical or unethical by various stakeholders.

Ethical issues are perceived differently by different individuals. Their decisions are based on their own values and principles of right or wrong. These values and principles are learned through the socialisation process with other family members, social groups, religious place and by formal education.

(ii) In the work place, an orgnaisation's values often have greater influence on individuals decisions than that person's own values. Decisions are made jointly in work groups and committees (through conversations, discussions with co-workers). Organisational culture and structure operate through the individual relationships of the organisation's members to influence other members' ethical decisions. **Corporate culture** plays a vital role. It involves norms that prescribe a wide range of behaviour for the organisation's members.

(iii) Ethical opportunity results from certain conditions. These

— provide rewards (internal or external)

— limit barriers to ethical or unethical behaviour.

It includes a person's immediate job context (includes the motivational techniques used by their bosses to influence employee behaviour). In the case of unethical behaviour, it can be eliminated through formal codes, policies and rules that are adequately enforced by management.

Moral philosophy is a set of principles setting forth what is believed to be the right way to behave. **Role** is something that is moral conforms to a standard of acceptability. A **philosophy** is a study of the general principles of a subject, such as morality. Individuals learn the principles through socialisation by family members, social groups, and formal education.

- Believers in this philosophy seeks the greatest satisfaction for the largest number of individuals.

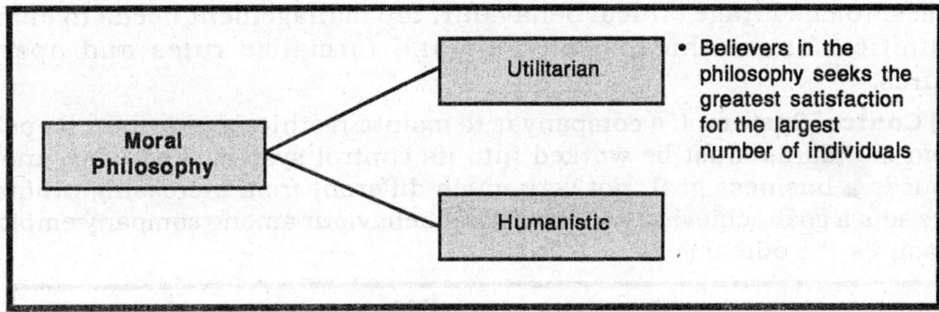

Fig. 2.2 Moral Philosophy

Utilitarian philosophy as per Mr.Speck said in the Wrath of Khan "The needs of the many outweigh the needs of the few...or the one." This philosophy is illustrated by actions.

Suggestions for Ethical Decision Making

(i) Top Management can improve behaviour: Businesses are beginning to set standards and establish ethical principles to be implemented within the organisations. One reason businesses have been slow to consider ethical principles in their decision making is the lack of understanding of how managers develop their moral philosophies. Robert Lomon once said "I never thought ethics was something that could be formally taught. It was something you learned growing up at home, in school, and in temple, church."

Lomon, learned the hard way that ethics is something that top management must be concerned about on a daily basis. In 1985, his company pleaded guilty to two thousand counts of fraud as a result of cheque overdrafts. Some executives thought they were doing Lomon a favour by increasing profits through the overdraft scheme.

(ii) Codes of ethics improves decision making: Businesses establish codes of ethics and corporate policies on ethics to foster ethical decision making by reducing the opportunity for unethical activity. Enforcement of corporate policies is a common way of dealing with ethical problems. The establishment of corporate policies and codes of ethics helps employees understand what is expected of them. Understanding how individuals choose their standards of ethics, and what prompt a person to engage in unethical behaviour may reverse the current trend towards unethical activity in business.

(iii) Interaction with peers and other colleagues: People, learn ethical behaviour from interacting with individuals in social, business and other groups. Thus businesses, should examine their structure to see how policies, rewards and punishments affect ethical behaviour. Without company wide standards for behaviour, employees generally base ethical decisions on their observation of peers and management.

Codes of ethics are formal statements of what the company expects from its employees. to encourage ethical behaviour, top management needs to eliminate opportunities for unethical behaviour and formalize rules and operating procedures.

(iv) Control System: If a company is to maintain ethical behaviour, its policies, rules and standards must be worked into its control system. Reducing unethical behaviour is a business goal, not very much different from increasing profits. The business sets a goal-achieving greater ethical behaviour among company employees-and measures the outcome.

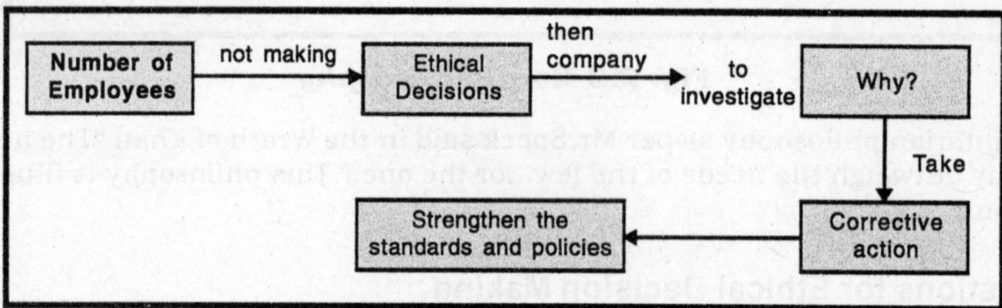

Fig. 2.3 Control System

- Ethical behaviour occurs only when a plan is developed and successfully implemented.
- Through stronger reinforcement of current standards and policies.

2.2 Ethical Theories - Teleology

Introduction

In the earlier chapters, we described the role of values in business and mentioned how business ethics are important parts of the professionalism of business. What exactly are ethical judgements and how do we justify them?

In the case of **ethical judgements**, the situation becomes difficult. A product say, if one calls it with green colour, he will have little difficulty in understanding and explaining what is meant. Green is a colour and is a physical property which can be seen only with the eyes. Ethical judgements seem to be different.

It is one thing to engage in an activity, but alter quite another to state what exactly is going on when we do it. We can make moral judgements, but finds difficulty in explaining the same exactly in the manner it is taking place when we do so. If we describe something as good or bad, right or wrong, we do not seem to be talking about a property we can see, touch, hear or experience in any obvious way with our senses. The question arises; What are we doing when we make an ethical judgement?

Are we making a statement about the physical world in which we live, which can be true or false? Are we doing something totally different? Are there moral truths, known like empirical statements about our saying?

Cognitivism and Non-cognitivism

In ethical theory, the first and most profound division is between the claim that it is possible to know moral right from wrong and the denial of that claim. The claim and counter claim about that we can and cannot know, the position which declares we can know is called '**cognitivism**' and vice versa is '**non-cognitivism**'. 'Cognitive' is capable of using certain knowledge; apprehension.

There are objective moral truths which can be known, just as we can know other truths about the world under '**cognitivism**'. Statements of moral belief, on this view, can be true or false.

Under non-cognitivism, object assessment of moral belief is not possible. It is all subjective. There is no truth or falsity to be discovered. There is only belief, attitude, emotional reaction, and the like.

Analytical approach to Ethical Problems

It is true that until fairly recently, religion was seen at the starting point, the well spring, of right behaviour. Those who subscribed to the Juedeo Christian tradition could fall back on the Torah, the Ten Commandments and the Sermon on the mount for ethical precepts. Though these are subject to vast amounts of interpretation, these moral standards were often considered not far short of absolute.

After the two horribly destructive world wars took place, with the threat of global annihilation arising out of spread of atomic weaponry, disillusion, and cynicism have led some prominent theologists and philosophers to devise a different ethical base. Since the Judeo Christian ethic did not prevent the holocaust, the search for some more 'workable' foundation for morality started.

Categories of Ethical Theories

Three important aspects that could form a basis for an ideal business house are:

- The human values
- Business ethics
- Market Karmas

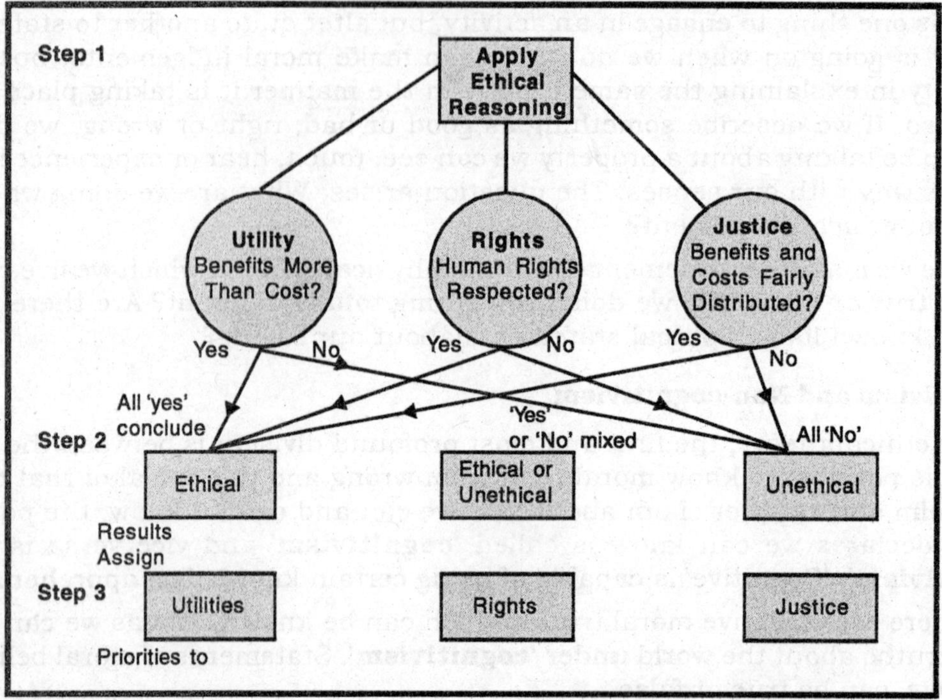

Fig. 2.4 Analytical Approach to Ethical Problems

The philosophical rules of these concepts lie in means-ends approach, theory of ethical management and positive competition. In corporate or organisational contexts, when managerial decisions and actions are taken within the bounds set by the above indicated aspects of decision making: Total Quality of Management (TQOM) improves. The profit earned by the organisation can in true sense be referred to as **'Subh-labh'**, when the organisation gives due consideration to above indicated dimensions (three aspects indicated).

Figure 2.5 represents house of 'Subh-labh', with business ethics as its foundation, market karmas as its interior space and human values as its roof. This house of 'Subh-labh' metaphorically represent a new theory or a new approach to business ethics. This theory implicitly takes a balanced view of Dharma, Arta, Kama, Moksha, building a house of 'Subh-labh' metaphorically represents the Indian dream.

Ethical theories are broadly divided into two categories:

- **Teleological** (example:Utilitarianism)
- **Deontological** (example: Kantianism)

Teleology means the doctrine of the final causes of things (**Tele** means distance or final); **Teleological** is related to probable outcome or consequences, whereas **Deontology** is the science of duty or ethics.

This can be divided into four theories as under, including Hybrid and concept of virtue.

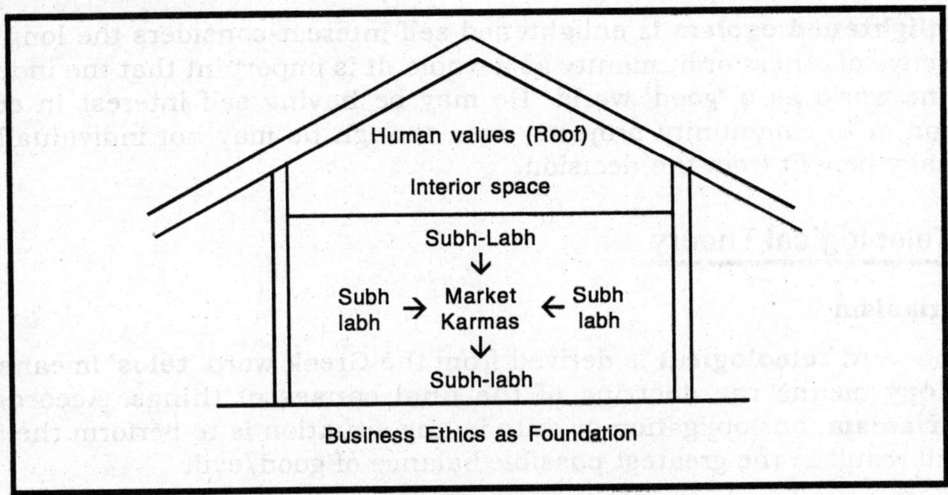

Fig. 2.5 The House of Subh-Labh
(Basis for an ideal business house)

(i) Teleological Theory: Determine the ethics of an act by looking to the consequences of the decision (The Ends); Rightness of actions is determined solely by the good consequences they produce.

(ii) Deontological Theory: Determine the ethics of an act by looking at the process of the decision (The means).

Does not appeal to consequences (Kantian ethics).

(iii) Hybrid Theory: Ethical egoism identifies a means for decision making.

Do what you want, while also identifying the greatest good as that which is the greatest good for the decision maker; hence a hybrid.

(iv) Concept of Virtue: Does not appeal to consequences e.g., Aristole's Ethics.

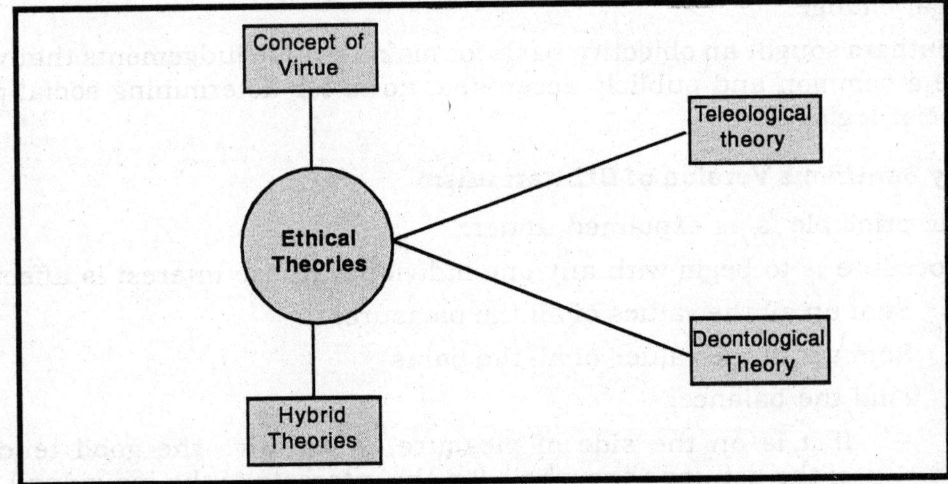

Fig. 2.6 Ethical Theories Types

Enlightened egoism is enlightened self interest-considers the long range perspective of others or humanity as a whole. It is important that the individual treat the world as a 'good' world. He may be having self interest in curbing pollution or in community projects, even though he may not individually and personally benefit from the decision.

2.2.1 Teleological Theory

Utilitarianism

The word **teleological** is derived from the Greek word **'telos'** (means end). **Teleology** means the doctrine of the final causes of things. According to **utilitarianism**, our obligation or duty in any situation is to perform the action that will result in the greatest possible balance of good/evil.

Classical Utilitarianism

In **Classical Utilitarianism**, pleasure is taken to be ultimately the only good and evil is the opposite of pleasure or pain; **Goodness** here is human well being. Whatever makes human beings generally better off or provides some benefit is **good**. Whatever makes them worse off or harm them is **evil**. Utilitarianism does not attempt to resolve these differences but accepts each person's own conception of what being better off means for him or her.

Utilitarianism is a powerful and widely accepted ethical theory that has specific relevance to problems in business. It fits easily, with the concept of value in economics and the use of cost benefit analysis in business.

Traditional Utilitarianism

The creators of Traditional utilitarianism were Jeremy Bentham (1748-1832) and John Stuart Mill (1806-1873). Under them, utilitarianism was not an ivory tower philosophy but a powerful instrument for social, political, economic and legal change.

Bentham sought an objective basis for making value judgements that would provide a common and publicly acceptable norm for determining social policy and social legislation.

Jeremy Benthams Version of Utilitarianism

The principle is as explained under:

Procedure is to begin with any one individual whose interest is affected:

- Sum up all the values of all the pleasures
- Sum up all the values of all the pains
- Find the balance:
  - If it is on the side of pleasure, it will give the good tendency of the act upon the whole (on the interests of the individual)
  - Vice versa.

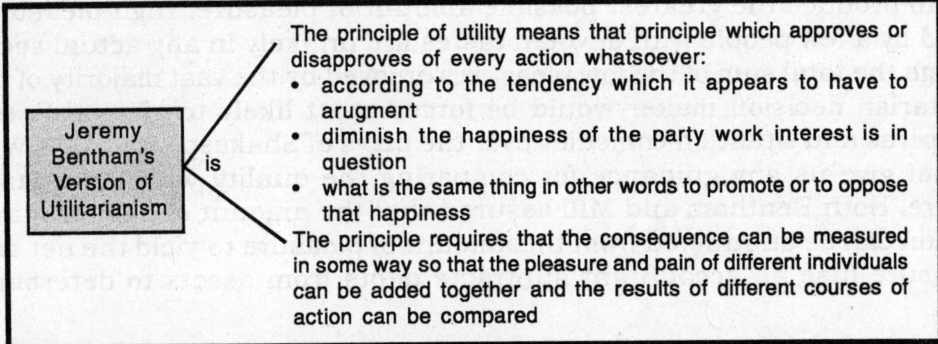

Fig. 2.7 Principle as per Jeremy Benthams version of Utilitarianism

- Repeat for all other individuals whose interests are affected.
- Resulting sums will show the good or bad tendency of the action for the whole community.

This theory is open to some obvious objections like long-standing opposition of many philosophers to the thesis of hedonism. Even pigs are capable of pleasure. Utilitarianism is a 'pig philosophy' according to critics, fit only for swine. One observed consequence of Bentham's view as per critics is that it would be better to live the life of a satisfied pig than that of a dissatisfied human being such as Socrates. **Hedonics** is the doctrine of pleasure. It is the doctrine considering the happiness as the highest good. Utilitarianism does not require the thesis of hedonism. However, and many things besides pleasure have been regarded as good by their theorists including friendship and aesthetic enjoyment.

John Stuart Mill's version of Utilitarianism

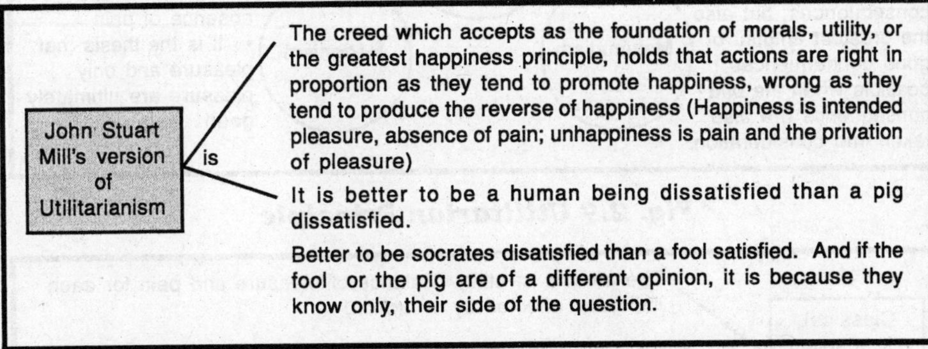

Fig. 2.8 John Stuart Mill's version of Utilitarianism

Mill was aware of the objections to Bentham's theory and in his work on Utilitarianism in 1863, he attempted to develop a more defensible version of the utilitarian position.

In spite of some pleasures are better than others, this insight does not succeed in saving the thesis of hedonism or the utilitarian principle that we ought to produce the greatest possible amount of pleasure. High pleasures are enjoyed by a few people with devoted tastes are unlikely in any actual society to outweigh the total sum of the low pleasures enjoyed by the vast majority of people. A utilitarian decision maker would be forced most likely to give preference to soap operas and situation comedies over the plays of Shakespeare Mill's Writings does not give us any guidance for comparing the quality with the quantity of pleasure. Both Bentham and MIll assured that the amount of pain produced by an action can be subtracted from the amount of pleasure to yield the net amount of pleasure (use an accountant subtracts debts from assets to determine net worth).

Classical Utilitarianism

It is stated as "An action is right if and only if it produces the greatest balance of pleasure over pain for everyone."

This may be a concern of not only of philosophers, but also of economists (since utility has been generally accepted as a basis for economic theory). Need in economics is for precise calculations of utility and misgivings about Bentham's simplistic hedonistic calculus.

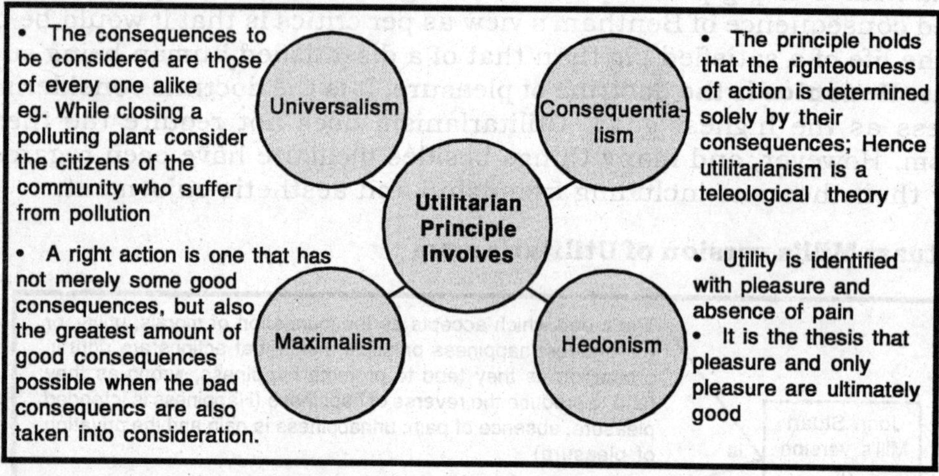

Fig. 2.9 Utilitarian Principle

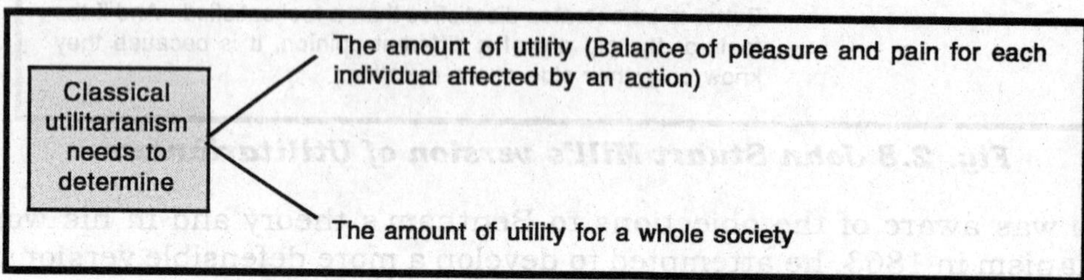

Fig. 2.10 Classical Utilitarianism

A problem arises, however, we attempt to determine exactly how much pleasure each course of action will produce (pleasure cannot be measured precisely in terms of quantity). E.g. In order to buy a gift (action) for a friend that will produce the greatest amount of pleasure, we need to know something about that person's desire and tastes.

Comparing the pleasure and pain of different people bring a problem about the interpersonal comparison of utility. Imagine two people who each insist after attending a concert that he or she enjoyed it more. There seems to be no way in principle to settle this dispute. Rough comparisons are sufficient for utilitarian calculations.

Though bribery is morally wrong in most situations, Carl Kotchian contended that it is an accepted practice in many parts of the world. It is also a necessity in a competitive climate since majority of the companies follow this.

Both are having merits, but no consensus among philosophers which is more apt.

The principle of rule-utilitarianism would have to consider the consequences of a general practice of bribery. Bribery usually results in higher prices and reduced quality decline in efficiency, because people are led by personal advantage to make decisions on considerations other than the value of the goods and services being offered. On rule utilitarian grounds, bribery is properly regarded as morally wrong.

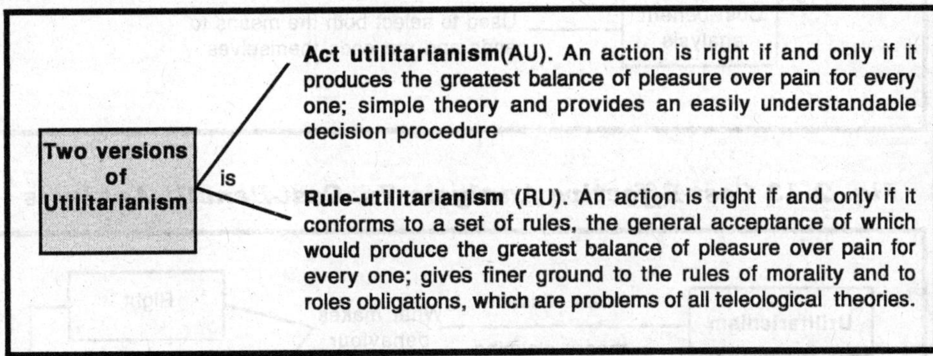

Fig. 2.11 Two Versions of Utilitarianism

Bentham's ideal of a precise quantitative method for decision making is most fully realised in cost benefit analysis. This method differs from his hedonistic calculus primarily in the use of monetary limits to express the benefits and drawbacks of various alternatives.

From the economic point of view, **cost-benefit analysis** is simply a means for achieving an efficient allocation of resources. The chief advantage of cost benefit analysis is that the price of many goods is let by the market, so that the need to have knowledge of people's pleasures or preference ranking is largely eliminated. It is not used as a basis for personal morality but as a means for making major investment decisions and decisions on broad matters of public policy.

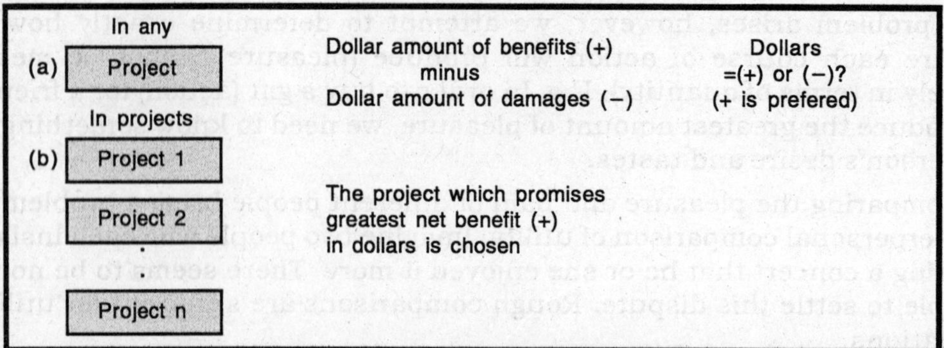

Fig. 2.12 Bentham's Precise Quantitative Method for Decision-Making

The dictionary meaning of **Utilitarianism** is the ethical theory which finds the basis of moral distinctions in the utility of actions (their fitness to produce happiness).

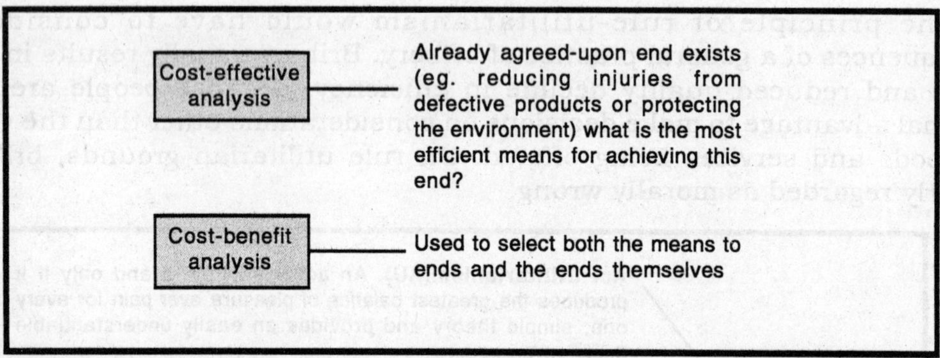

Fig. 2.13 Cost-Effective Analysis Vs. Cost-Benefit Analysis

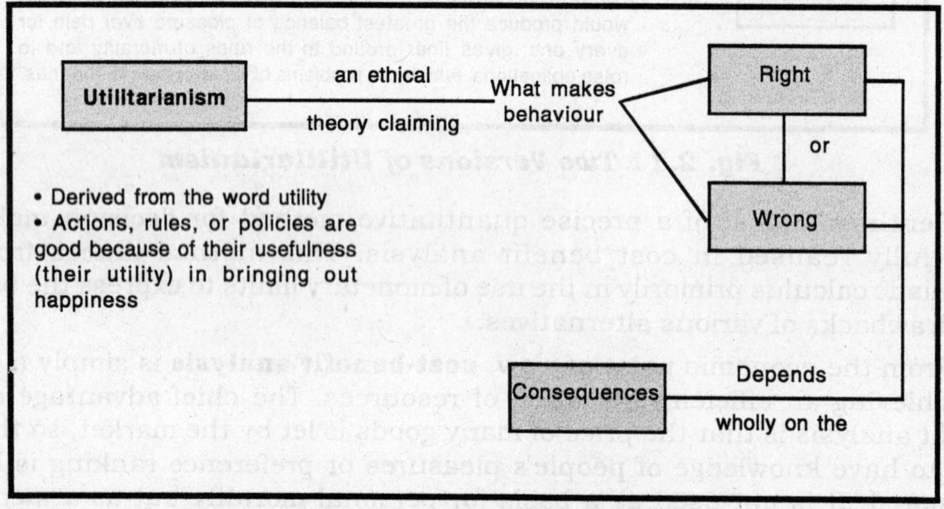

Fig. 2.14 Meaning of Utilitarianism

In putting the emphasis on consequences, **utilitarianism** affirms that what is important about human behaviour is the outcome or results of the behaviour and the intention a person has when he or she acts. On one version of utilitarianism, what is all important is happiness producing consequences according to Becker and Becker (1992).

Credely put, actions are:

- good when they produce happiness
- bad when they produce unhappiness.

Utilitarianism and Consequentialism

Philosophers are not consistent in using these two terms:

(i) Sometimes **consequentialism** is seen as the broadest term referring to ethical theories that claims that what makes an action right or wrong is the consequences - not the internal character of action.

(ii) Utilitarianism in this case is a particular version of this theory with the emphasis specifically on happiness producing consequences.

Sometimes, the distinction is made in the opposite way., **Utilitarianism is seen as the broadest theory** and **consequentialism as a particular form of utilitarianism**.

However, individuals should follow a basic principle.

"Every one ought to act so as to bring about the greatest amount of happiness for the greatest number of people."

Then the questions would be:

What is the proof of this theory?

What should each one of us act to bring about the greatest amount of happiness?

Why shouldn't we each seek our own interest?

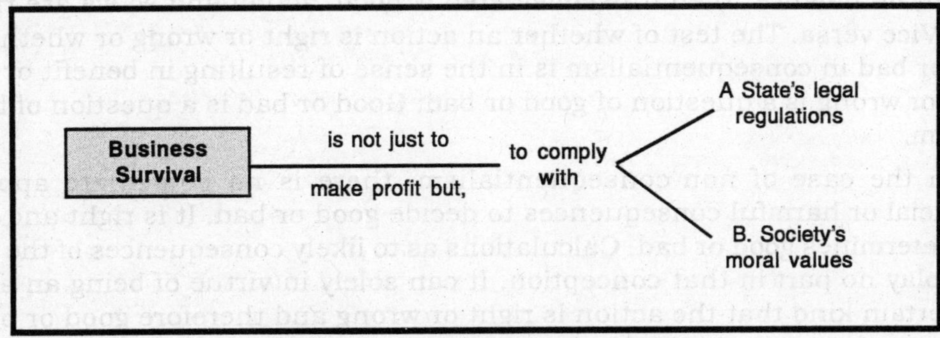

Fig. 2.16 Business Survival

Failure in A or B will prevent the business from continuing to trade. It may be noted that most businesses, like most people do not wish to simply to survive, but would like to prosper. Vast literature exists to identify factors which distinguish success in business. From the point of business ethics, values which in other contexts would be seen as indisputably moral ones are evidently important.

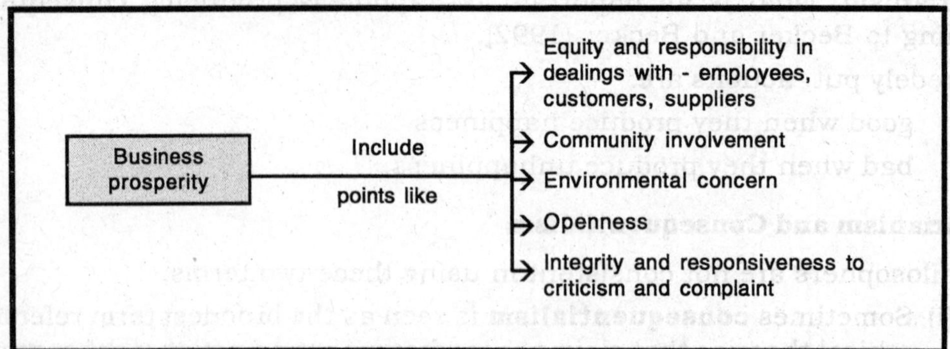

Fig. 2.17 Business Prosperity

These are not just the qualities we expect in businesses if things were ideal, but are increasingly being recognised as qualities actually possessed by some of the world's most successful business corporations.

Consequentialism versus Non-consequentialism

As we have seen in the earlier subject, the divide in cognitivist thinking is between theories which assess moral right and wrong in terms of the consequences of actions and those which do not. These theories are termed as 'consequentialist theories' and 'non-consequentialist theories'. This distinction is to be treated with some caution. It is doubtful if non-consequentialist theories, even the most extreme, can or do totally ignore consequences in assessing right and wrong. Consequentialist theories are the most exclusive.

With conquentialist theories, we look to the results of actions to determine the truth or falsity of moral judgements about them. The action resulting in benefit, on balance, then it is considered a 'good' action and so we are right to do it. Vice versa. The test of whether an action is right or wrong or whether it is good or bad in consequentialism is in the sense of resulting in benefit or harm. Right or wrong is a question of good or bad; Good or bad is a question of benefit or harm.

In the case of non-consequentialism, there is no immediate appeal to beneficial or harmful consequences to decide good or bad. It is right and wrong that determines good or bad. Calculations as to likely consequences of the action need play no part in that conception. It can solely in virtue of being an activity of a certain kind that the action is right or wrong and therefore good or bad.

Non-consequentialist theories:

In his book 'Morality', the great philosopher Bernard best provides a list of ten moral rules that he believes express our considered judgements about the basis norms governing the moral life.

GERT'S TEN MORAL RULES	
1. Don't Kill	2. Don't cause pain
3. Don't disable	4. Don't deprive of freedom
5. Don't deprive of pleasure	6. Don't deceive
7. Keep your promise	8. Don't cheat
9. Obey the law	10. Do your duty.

Ethics and morality are terms we use to identify the norms governing human conduct in society that have a significant impact on human welfare. Ethics are like law, but society upholds legal norms by imposing severe penalties when they are violated, whereas it does not always do this where morality is concerned.

Ethics egoism, ethics relativism, the view that right is what my religion teaches me, and the position that defines right conduct simply in terms of the dictates of conscience are attractive because they contain important elements of moral truth. But none of these positions by itself qualifies as a complete or acceptable theory of right conduct.

Deontology defines an action as right if it respects the moral rules and wrong if it violates them. There are different kinds of deontology. Deontology reflects important features of our moral common sense, but it usually breaks down as a guide to conflict when lists of rules differ or when rules conflict.

Teleology sees right conduct as what produces most of certain types of basic values in the world. The best known form of teleology is utilitarianism. It defines an action is right if it produces the greatest amount of happiness for the greatest number of persons. Utilitarianism is very useful in resolving conflicts about moral questions because of its decision rule.

Ethical theories typically address questions of value, right conduct and personal moral character (called sometimes as the question of "Virtue"). The question of right conduct takes precedence in our thinking because the answer to its shapers our answers to the questions of value and moral character.

One of the most initially plausible moral theories is **utilitarianism**. It says that when we have a choice the right thing to do is that which brings the "greatest happiness of the greatest number." Nothing is wrong which does this and nothing is right which fails to do it. The first difficulty with this is what counts as happiness.

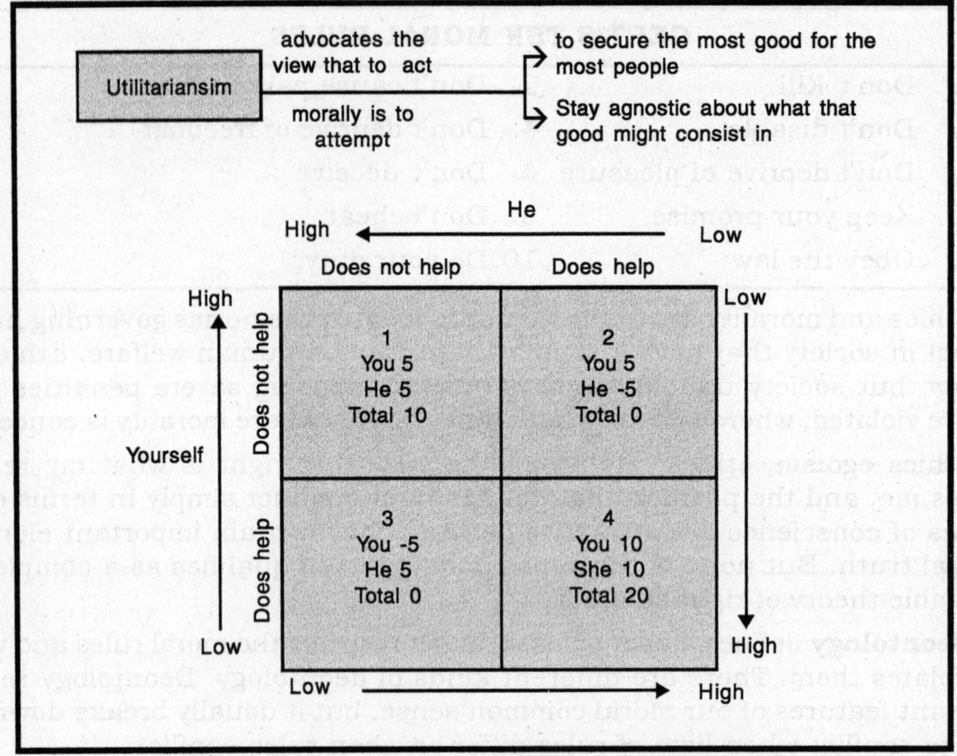

Fig. 2.18 The Collaborator's Dilemma

The choices open to you, together with both the outcomes are shown in figure.

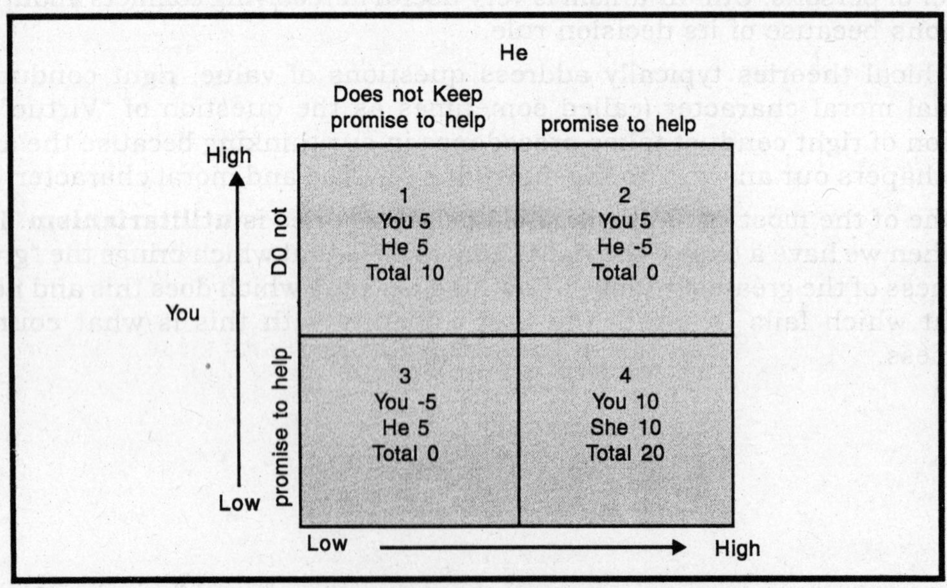

Fig. 2.19 The Promise Keepers Dilemma

In the collaborator's dilemma	*In the promise keepers dilemma*
Assumption: The extra time needed for the project would cost you five points each in effort, lost opportunities etc. (+5 and -5). **See Quadrant 2 and Quadrant 3** Either of you acting (DO and DOES not in both the cases)- individually without the benefit of the other would generate nothing in compensation Total Zero (0) Similarly, **Quadrant 1 and Quadrant 4** Generates 10 and 20 points respectively. However, acting together, you will probably generate outcomes worth 15 points each in terms of enhanced reputation, promotion, bonuses etc. (Disregard at the moment, losses and benefits that might accrue to the people). Optimum outcome (Quadrant 4) cannot be secured by yourself. Collaboration helps to reach optimum.	Similar things happen as in the collaborators dilemma.

If you were reasonably sure that you knew what the other man does, then it is clear what would make sense for you to do. If you choose to collaborate, you gamble on securing 10 points for yourself and a total of 20 for overall, but you risk achieving nothing and suffering a personal loss of 5. There is no risk at all, if you decide not to probably, the other person will be sensible too and there will, overall, be a net gain to you both compared to what you might have lost.

Utilitarianism is the ethical theory which finds the basis of moral distinctions in the utility of actions ie., their fitness to produce happiness.

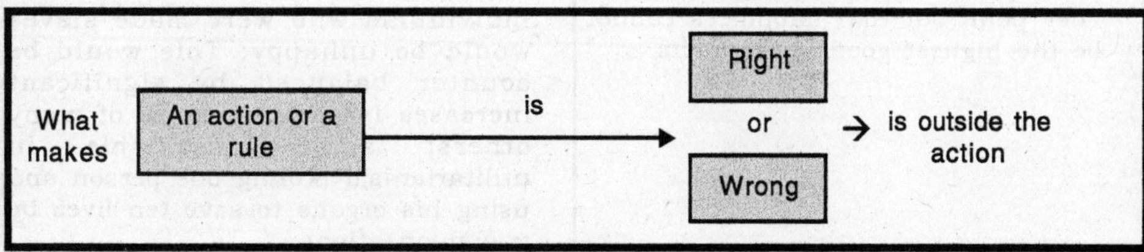

Fig. 2.20 Utilitarian Theory

Deontological Theory

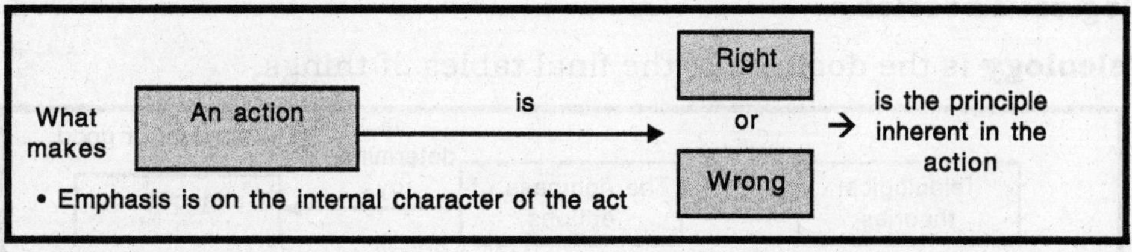

Fig. 2.21 Difference between Utilitarian Theory and Deontological

Theory

If an action is done from a sense of duty, and If the principle of the action can be universalised → Action is right

eg. If I tell the truth, because I recognise that I must respect the other person → Action is right (I act from duty)

Alternatively,
If I tell the truth, because I fear being caught or because I believe I will be rewarded on this → Action is wrong (My act is not morally worthy)

Deontology	*Utilitarianism*
• Principle inherent in the action. • Individuals are valuable in themselves (not because of their social value). • Theory asserts that there are some actions that are always wrong, no matter what the consequences. • Often recognise self-defense and other special circumstances as excusing killing, but these are cases when it is argued, the killing is not exactly intentional (The person attacks me. I would not otherwise aim at harm to the person, but I have no other choice but to defend myself). • According to deontologists, the utilitarians go wrong when they fix on happiness as the highest good. They point out that happiness cannot be the highest good for humans.	• Outside the action. • Criticised because it appears to tolerate sacrificing some people for the sake of others. • Right or wrong are dependent on the consequences-vary with the circumstances. • Every person is counted equally. No one person's unhappiness/happiness is more important than another. • Concerned with total amount of happiness; we can imagine situations where great overall happiness might result from sacrificing the happiness of a few. eg. Having a small number of slaves would create great happiness for a large number of individuals. The individuals who were made slaves would be unhappy; This would be counter balanced by significant increases in the happiness of many others; seems justifiable in utilitarianism (killing one person and using his organs to save ten lives by transplantation).

Fig. 2.22 Deontology Vs Utilitarianism

Teleological Theories

Teleology is the doctrine of the final tables of things.

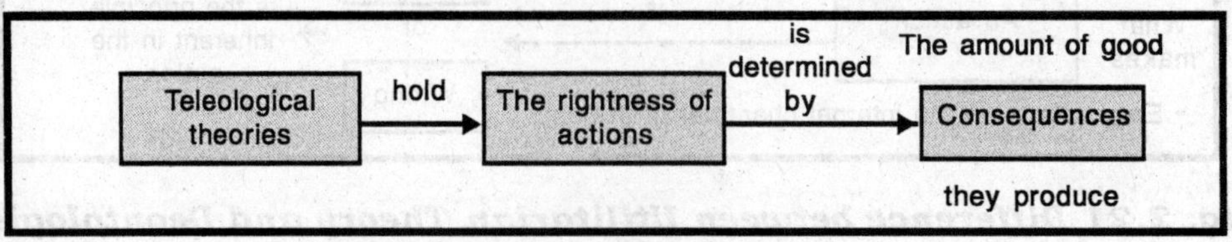

Fig. 2.23 Teleological Theories

'Teleogical' word is derived from the greak word **Telos** (means end). **Teleological ethics** focuses on the end results and then relating the end results to the process of achieving the autonomy of the individual.

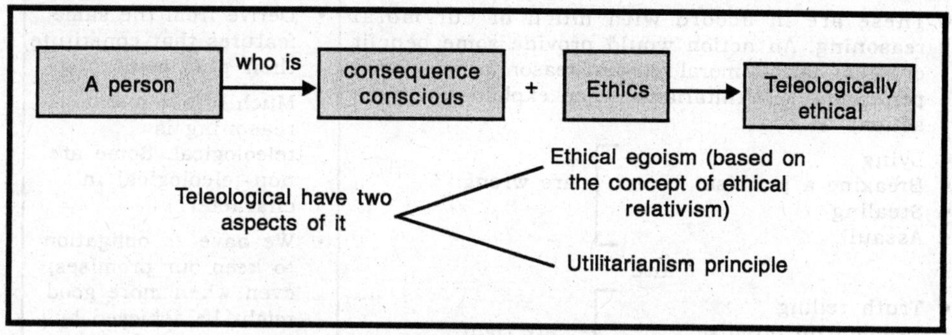

Fig. 2.24 Teleological Ethics

- **Teleological** is normally connected with consequences.
- **Deontological** is concerned about the quality of one's intention towards that.

In teleological theory, actions are justified on technological theories by virtue of the end they achieve rather than feature of the actions themselves. The concept of goodness is fundamental in teleological theories and the concepts of rightness, obligation or duty are defined in terms of goodness.

As per utilitarianism, our obligation, or duty is to perform the action in any situation that will result in the greatest possible balance of good or evil. In **classical utilitarianism**, pleasure is taken as the only good, and evil is the opposite of pleasure, or pain. Utilitarianism in broader terms is human well being (providing some benefit). If it makes worse off or harms, it is evil. Differences of opening exist about the constituents of benefits and harms. Utilitarianism does not attempt to resolve these differences. It accepts each person's own conception of what is better for him or her.

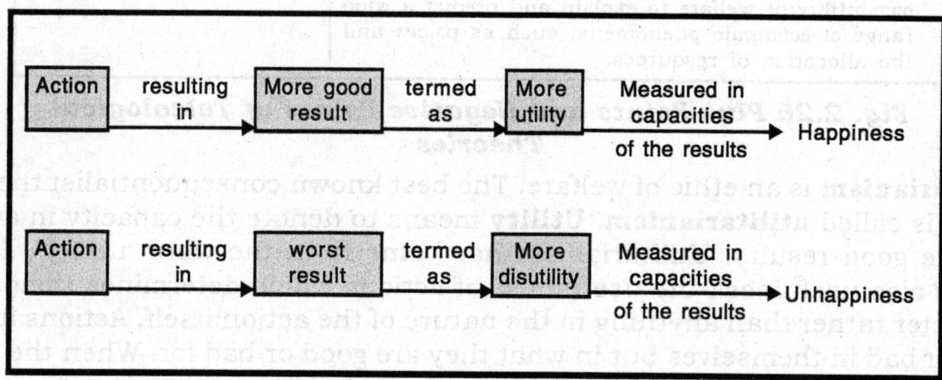

Fig. 2.25 Actions Resulting in Happiness or Unhappiness

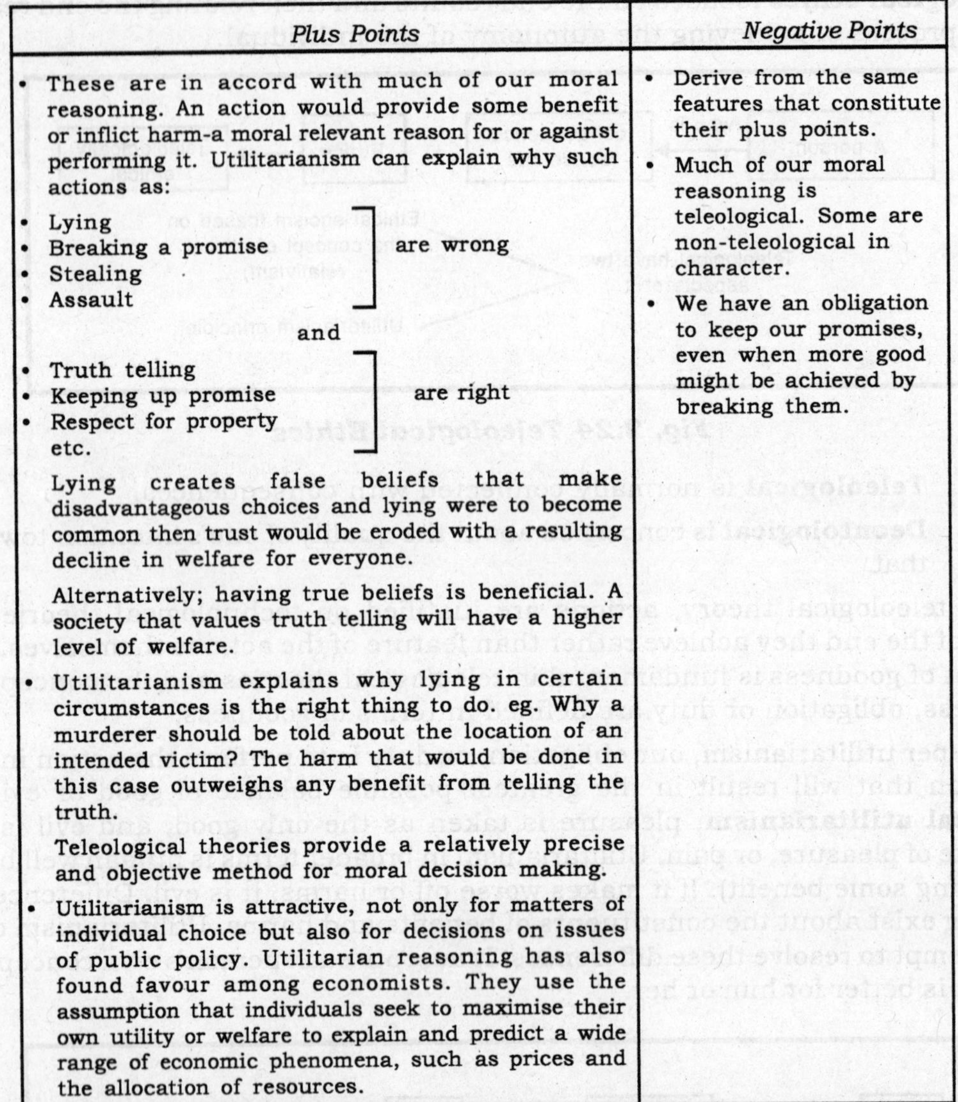

Plus Points	*Negative Points*
• These are in accord with much of our moral reasoning. An action would provide some benefit or inflict harm-a moral relevant reason for or against performing it. Utilitarianism can explain why such actions as: • Lying • Breaking a promise • Stealing • Assault } are wrong and • Truth telling • Keeping up promise • Respect for property etc. } are right Lying creates false beliefs that make disadvantageous choices and lying were to become common then trust would be eroded with a resulting decline in welfare for everyone. Alternatively; having true beliefs is beneficial. A society that values truth telling will have a higher level of welfare. • Utilitarianism explains why lying in certain circumstances is the right thing to do. eg. Why a murderer should be told about the location of an intended victim? The harm that would be done in this case outweighs any benefit from telling the truth. Teleological theories provide a relatively precise and objective method for moral decision making. • Utilitarianism is attractive, not only for matters of individual choice but also for decisions on issues of public policy. Utilitarian reasoning has also found favour among economists. They use the assumption that individuals seek to maximise their own utility or welfare to explain and predict a wide range of economic phenomena, such as prices and the allocation of resources.	• Derive from the same features that constitute their plus points. • Much of our moral reasoning is teleological. Some are non-teleological in character. • We have an obligation to keep our promises, even when more good might be achieved by breaking them.

Fig. 2.26 Plus Points and Negative Points of Teleological Theories

Utilitarianism is an ethic of welfare. The best known consequentialist theory of ethics is called **utilitarianism**. **Utility** means to denote the capacity in actions to have good results. Utilitarianism has come from the word 'utility'. **Utility** means also usefulness-the usefulness of actions which determines their moral character rather than anything in the nature of the action itself. Actions are not good or bad in themselves but in what they are good or bad for. When the result is bad, it is termed as disutility.

As early as in 1800, Jeremy Bentham (1748-1832) a British philosopher and social reformer is remembered for his classic formulation, earliest thinker of ethical matters, utilitarianism in the earlier stage. The formulation he offered was characteristically bold and unequivocal. 'Utility' is one thing and the only thing, he said, it is happiness. Vice versa for 'Disutility'. Actions are right to the extent they maximise happiness or at least minimise unhappiness, wrong to the extent they maximise unhappiness or minimise happiness. The obvious choice between happiness and unhappiness is happiness; We would select between the choices of producing happiness, an action which produces most happiness. Similarly, the choice between the choices of producing unhappiness, an action which produces least happiness i.e., lesser of the two evils.

When asked Bentham, regarding identification of utility with happiness, the answer was that it is the only thing desirable as an end in itself. All other things are only desirable as a means to the end of happiness. Fame, fortune, sanctity, serenity, knowledge, power, love, friendship or whatever others-are of value only in so far as they are conducive to happiness. They are good only in so far as they lead to that single ultimate good. Happiness is the only good thing in itself. Conversely, unhappiness is the only thing bad in itself the only ultimate good.

The objection was how happiness could be measured? Bentham hoped for a precise, scientific measure. In this, he was clearly being unrealistic-what is perfectly possible, though, is a set of crude but effective calculations. We make consequentialistic assessments of the rightness or wrongness of actions, and this involves some sort of rough and ready calculation of the impact on human happiness of the actions.

Happiness plays a peculiarly fundamental role in human conduct. It shares in a commitment to a doctrine known as "hedonism" (from the Greek for 'pleasure'). This is a theoretical perspective and can be broadly divided into two sorts of claims;

- Psychological hedonism (idea of happiness as the ultimate goal of human behaviour)
- Ethical hedonism (idea that moral good is identical with happiness - very basis of Benthamite utilitarianism. Happiness was the ultimate measure of moral right and wrong).

Had Bentham accepted some purely individualistic interpretations of psychological and ethical hedonism, his would be the kind of hedonism known as 'egoism'. He is very clear, however that the good we must seek is the common good. It is the total of sum of human happiness which must be maximised and not simply our own individual happiness-termed as '**Greatest Happiness Principle**', greatest happiness for the greatest number. Our own happiness, should have no priority. It should simply be part of the sum.

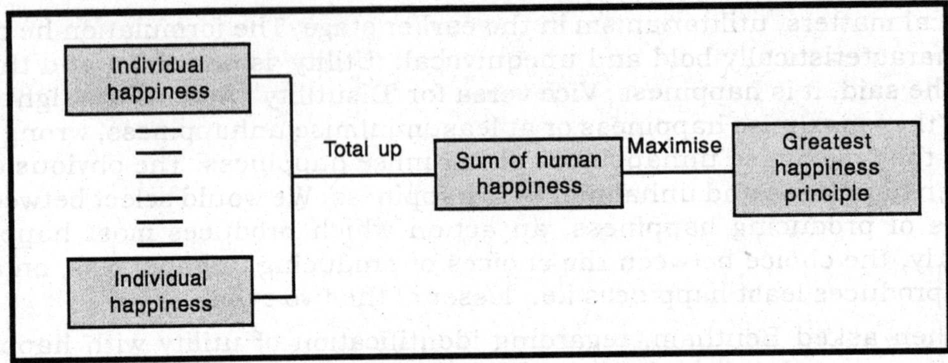

Fig. 2.27 Greatest Happiness Principle

Bentham's **ethical hedonism** is therefore explicitly and diametrically opposed to egoism. He rejects an egoistical interpretation of the psychological hedonism also, for in requiring us to sometimes sacrifice our own happiness for the greater happiness. Otherwise, we would not be capable of following the greatest happiness principle and there would be no point in proposing it as a guide to conduct.

The Utilitarian Method of Reasoning is:
1. Accurately state the action to be evaluated. 2. Identify all those who are directly and indirectly affected by it. 3. Specially all the pertinent good and bad consequences of the action for all those directly affected - as far into the future as appears appropriate and imaginatively consider various possible outcomes and the likelihood of their occurrence. 4. Weigh the total good results (the degree of happiness produced) against the total bad results, considering such matters as the quantity and duration of the harms and benefits involved. 5. Carry out a similar analysis, if necessary, for those indirectly affected, and for society as a whole. 6. Sum up all the good and bad consequences. If the action produces more good than bad, the action is morally right (✓); if it produces more bad than good, the action is morally wrong (X). 7. Consider, imaginatively, whether there are various alternatives other than simply performing or not performing the action and carry out a similar analysis for each of the other alternate actions. 8. Compare the results of the various actions. The action that produces the most good (or the least bad, if none produces more good than bad) among those available is the morally proper thing to do.

Fig. 2.28 Utilitarian Method of Reasoning

(**Source:** The Ethical Manager, Ronald M.Green, *Macmillan Publishing Company*, New York, 1993, pp.75.)

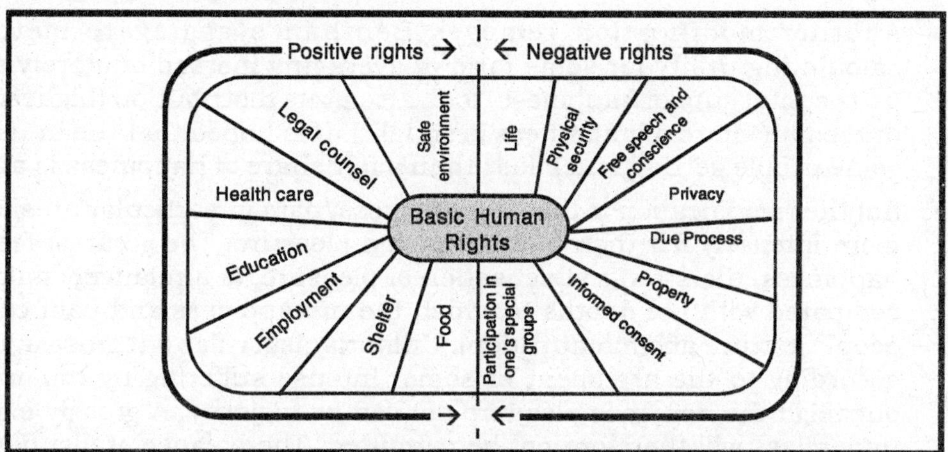

Fig. 2.29 Basic Human Rights

Modifications Done to the Greatest Happiness of People

Let us consider a situation where 20% of the population is under class, weaker section. They are in that state of no fault of their own, suffers from low wages, high unemployment, limited access to educational and welfare provision, no or little political influence. They are unhappy with their lot but cannot do much about it. The other 80% gain from this underclass by exploiting them through cheap labour (specially in times of economic recession). They have all other benefits which the under class do not have. They are very happy with their lot. When the total sum of happiness is added, it is found that this arrangement gives maximum happiness, with the total available resources. Alternatively, if 20% minority is increased with little happiness, this would not be enough to offset a marginal decrease in the happiness of the 80% majority. What is wrong with this situation is that it is unjust. Why should a minority suffer to keep the majority in a better position? Bentham has made the common good the sole arbiter of right and wrong. He has made as an aggregate in the form of the sum of human happiness. The sacrifice of the rights and interests of individuals and minorities to the common good is therefore possible.

Several modifications to traditional Benthamite utilitarianism have been suggested.

- What moral rule will maximise human happiness, if it were to be universally followed? Is the crucial question instead of 'what will happen if this is done?' The aim is to arrive at general rules of conduct rather than decisions about the rights and wrongs of particular acts and hence known as 'Rule utilitarianism'.
- Alternatively, 'Act utilitarianism' can deal with problems of justice. Is this moral rule conducive to the greatest human happiness? We cannot be permitted to disadvantage others simply because it will benefit us. If everyone did so, everyone would suffer. The overall outcome in the long term would be disutility.

- Another modification removes Bentham's aggregate method of calculating utility for some form of averaging instead of merely adding up the total sum of happiness, look also at its distribution (highest mean or median share of happiness is sought). It is hoped that the injustice of some people getting much less than a fair share of happiness is avoided.
- Another modification is that unhappiness/pain in particular area usually more intensely felt than happiness and pleasure. The greatest feeling of happiness, the strongest sensation of pleasure, is a relatively mild affair compared with the depths to which the unhappiness and pain can take people (torture and malnutrition). Utilitarianism rules out gross injustices according to the argument of some. Intense suffering by minority will outweigh the immense pleasure derived by majority. A grossly exploited underclass will therefore not be permitted. The balance of disutility over utility would make the things worsen.
- Lastly, instead of happiness or unhappiness as the only objective, it advocates to adopt a broadly consequentialist approach in which the maximisation of benefits and the minimisation of harm remains the aim. Instead of a pluralist, nonhedonistic approach is adopted, in which happiness and unhappiness simply take their place in an indefinite list of harmful and beneficial things. E.g. Freedom, friendship, knowledge, love, honesty and so on, are seen as good things in their own right and not merely for the happiness they promote. Similarly, tyranny, enmity, ignorance, hate, deceit and so, are seen as bad in their own right. This goes for justice and injustice also. If a minority is exploited simply for the enhanced benefit of the majority, the increased happiness of that majority is just part of that equation. It must be balanced not only against the unhappiness of the minority but also against the harm of injustice. However, it can be argued that more enhanced happiness will not be sufficient to justify gross injustice.

Strengths and Weaknesses of Teleological Theory

Strengths:

- They are in accord with much of our ordinary moral reasoning; An action would provide some benefit or inflict some harm. This is a morally relevant reason for or against performing it. Utilitarianism explains why such actions as lying, breaking a promise, stealing and assault are wrong, whereas truth telling, promise keeping, respect for property etc. are right.
- It provides a relatively precise and objective method for moral decision making. Assuming that the goodness of consequences can easily be measured and compared, a teleological decision maker need only determine the possible courses of action and calculate the consequences of each one.

Weaknesses: This derives from the same features that constitute their strengths. Though much of our ordinary moral reasoning is teleological, some are decidedly non-teleological in character. We have an obligation to keep our promises, even when more good might be achieved by breaking them.

2.2.2 Deontology

- Deontology has been already explained in Para 2.2.1.

Kantianism

Kantianism is an ethic of duty. Non-consequentialism in ethics is an approach labelled **'deontological'** (for duty in Greek). Its classic, indeed definitive formulation, is that provided by the German philosopher Immanuel Kant (1724-1804). This is in many ways diametrically opposite to that of Benthams utilitarianism. It clears one thing and only one thing is good in itself. For Bentham one thing is happiness, for Kant, it is a 'goodwill'. An action is morally right as per Kant, only if the person performing it is motivated by a 'Good will'. Vice versa. The possession of such a will alone makes the action right; the absence makes it wrong.

A good will according to Kant means the action done for reasons of principle from a sense of duty, nothing else. Self interest is certainly not be the motive, but neither can kindness, loyalty, sympathy or any other laudable sentiment. These thought can be admired, do not constitute a specifically moral motivation for acting. A sense of duty can alone provide that (Hence title 'Deontological' for this theory).

The next question arises, how can we know that when an act is done from a sense of duty? Kant says, it is done in accordance with what he calls the **Categorical Imperative**. Kant expresses the categorical imperative in several ways, all of which are, equivalent. Two definitions centered on this are:

- I ought never to act except in such a way that I can also will that my maxim should become a universal law.
- Act on such a way that you always treat humanity never simply, **as a means**, but always at the same time **as an end**.

These two are certainly complementary, Kant's claim that they are equivalent is unconvincing. They are seen as two separate but mutually supportive formulations of what constitutes the categorical imperative.

In the first formulation, the **maxim** which Kant mentions is the principle on which I act, which may be either a good or bad principle.

For example, A personnel officer decides to break an employees confidentiality, he might be acting on a maxim like.

Whenever it is convenient to break a promise in circumstances such as this, I shall do so!

When I am asked to disclose 'personal information, I will disclose what is non-confidential'.

Secondly maxim is expressed when a more responsible decision on confidentiality might be expressed.

In reality, maxims may be more complicated than the above example. The personnel officer may wish to qualify circumstances in which he might exceptionally reveal confidential information for example; if the police asks for it.

Universalising is a maxim means that the principle upon which we act (the maxim) should be one wish we can, with consistency, wish all other people to act upon. Some maxims can be universalised, while others cannot be done. Actions performed under it are in accordance with the categorical imperative and are therefore morally right.

In the second formulation of the Kant's categorical imperative is based on idea 'respect' for persons. It contracts human beings with objects;' vegetables, fruits, chairs, tables. The worth of the objects lies simply in the use to which human beings can put them. Human beings are persons of intrinsic value, not of instrumental value like objects. They are feeling, purposeful, rational, capable of having aims of their own which they can care for deeply. To act morally, one should respect the personhood of people (unlike the objects) and never treat them simply as a means to end but always, and primarily as an end in themselves.

In both the above formulations, Kantianism is distinguished from utilitarianism by the absence of any explicit and direct appeal to consequences in determining right and wrong. The sole importance is the motive for the action with utilitarianism, in contrast, motives are incidental.

Details	***Kantianism***	***Utilitarianism***
1. Explicit and direct appeal to consequences in determining right and wrong	Absent	Yes
2. Motive for the action	Sole importance	Incidental
3. Good in themselves	Yes	Only as a means to the end of maximising utility
4. Matter only in so far as they are conducive to performing actions which maximise utility	No	Yes
5. Consequentialist flexibility and non-consequentialist inflexibility	Strong	Weak (where uitilitarianism is weak, kantianism is strong)
6. Permit the sacrificing of individuals or minorities to collective self interest	No	Yes
7. Common good must have priority over every thing else	Yes	-
8. Disallowed all lying:	Yes	-
9. Theory:	Non-consequentialism (Deontological)	Consequentialism
10. Ethics of:	Duty	Welfare
11. Formulations on:	Sense of duty, categorical imperative maxim, universalizing	Utility, more good, maximise happiness, hedonism

Fig. 2.30 Kantianism Vs Utilitariansim

Deontological Theories

Deontology is the science of duty. **Deontological theories** unlike teleological theories such as utilitarianism, deny that sequences are relevant to determining what we ought to do. They take it for granted that certain actions are right not because of some benefit to themselves or others but because of the nature of these actions or the rules from which they follow.

Example Bribery is wrong, some people say by its very nature, regardless of its consequences.

Non-consequentialist reasoning in ethics include arguments:

- Based on principles (example Golden Rale, Do unto others as you would have them do unto you).
- Those that appeal to basic notions of human dignity and respect for others.

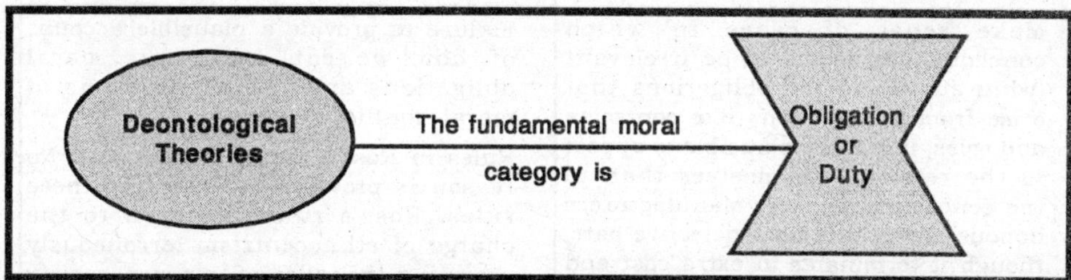

Fig. 2.31 Fundamental Moral Category of Deontological Theory

Goodness and other concepts are to be defined in terms of duty.

W.D.Ross, a British Philosopher talked out deontological theory consisting of a set of 'absolute moral rules'.

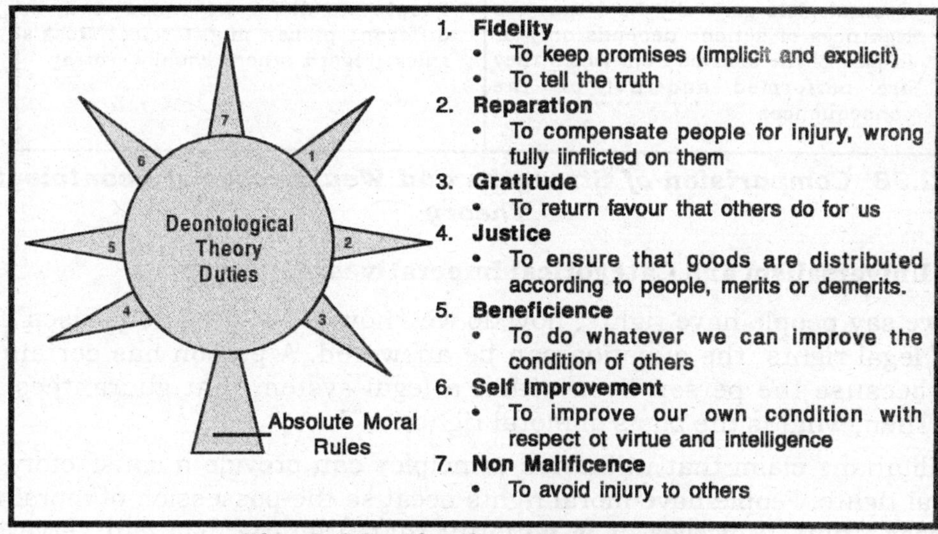

Fig. 2.32 Absolute Moral Rules
(Seven rules suggested by W.D. Ross)

While Teleological concepts allow the rigour of the brain, Deontological concepts – promotes that of the heart.

– pertains to the duty orientation.

As per Deontological theory, people behave ethically as they find it their solemn duty towards that.

For example: It is the duty of the parents to protect the life and interests of their children whatever may be the consequences for that.

The concern in this theory has been primarily for the duties and not for any other motives.

This theory considers factors other than consequences, while examining the ethical judgements and actions. It is based on the concept and belief of duty.

Strengths and Weaknesses of deontological theories are given below:

Strengths	***Weaknesses***
• Make sense of cases in which consequences seems to be irrelevant (while justifying the obligations that arise from the relations like contracts and roles, it is more plausible to appeal to the relations themselves than to the consequences). e.g. Manufacturers honour a warranty on a defective part, though it terminates in extra cost and affecting the customer in satisfaction. • The way they account for the role of motives in evaluating actions; one giving charity out of genuine concern. Other, out of friends compulsion. No doubt, both will bring good. • Deontologists generally hold that the rightness of actions depends only or in part of the motives from which they are performed and not on the consequences.	• Failure to provide a plausible account of how we can know our moral obligations and resolve problems of moral conflict. • Rules in Ross's theory is plausible; No reason is provided in accepting these rules. Ross's rules are open to the charge of ethnocentrism (erroneously accepting the rules of our own society as though they were universal); Further no order of priority among the rules; we have no guidance in cases where they conflict (whether we have to tell the truth when doing so, will harm some one? • People at different times and in different places might reject Ross's rules; regard others equally worthy.

Fig. 2.33 Comparision of Strengths and Weaknesses of Deontological Theory

Kant's Universalism and Categorical Imperatives

If we say people have rights, how do we know is the question arises. In the case of legal rights, the question can be answered. A person has certain legal rights, because the person lives within a legal system that guarantees those rights. Then, what is the basis of moral rights?

Utilitarians claim that utilitarian principles can provide a satisfactory basis for moral rights. People have moral rights because the possession of moral rights maximises utility. However, it is doubtful that utilitarianism can serve as an adequate basis for moral rights. To say that someone has a moral right to do something is to say that he is entitled to do it regardless of the utilitarian benefits it provides for others. Utilitarianism cannot easily support such a nonutilitarian concept.

A more satisfactory foundation for moral rights is provided by the ethical theory developed by Emmanuel Kant. Kant in fact attempts to show that there are certain moral rights and duties that all human beings possess regardless of any utilitarian benefits that the exercise of rights and duties may provide for others.

Kant's theory is based on a moral principle that he calls the categorical imperative and that requires everyone should be treated as a free person equal to everyone else. Every one has a moral right to such treatment, and every one has the correlative duty to treat others in this way. Kant provides at least two ways of formulating this basic moral principle; each formulation serves as an explanation of the meaning of this basic moral right and correlative duty.

First formulation principle: An action is morally right for a person in a certain situation if, and only if, the person's reason for carryingout the action is a reason that he or she would be willing to have every person act on, in any similar situation.

Second formulation principle: An action is morally right for a person if, and only if, in performing the action, the person does not use others merely as a means for advancing his own interests, but also both respects and develops their capacity to choose freely for themselves.

Kant denies that time and space are the product of experience, but shows them to be categories-conceptions in which our minds wear the same perceptions. Ethical implications of Kant's categorical imperatives in this terms runs as:

Act only according to the maxim by which you can at the same time will that it should become a universal law. Or, in simple terms:

I am never to act unless I am acting on a principle that I am willing to have everyone act upon: Kant formulated four laws regarding the categorisation of objects.

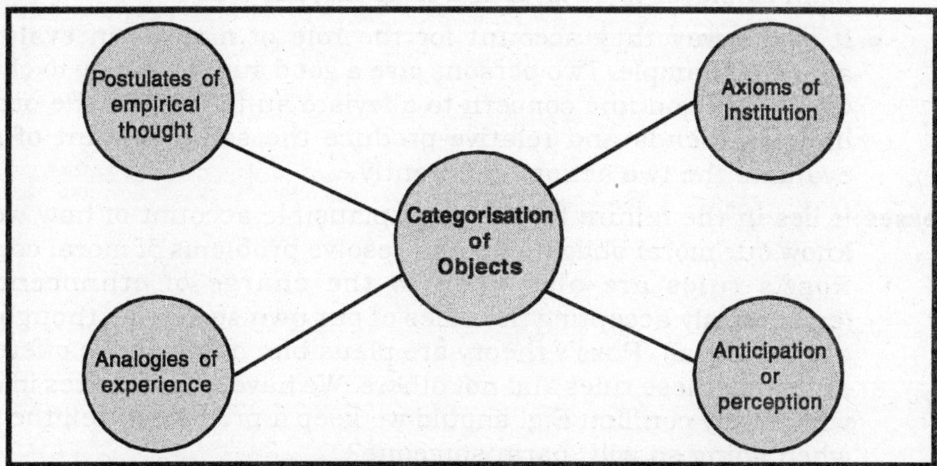

Fig. 2.34 Categorisation of Objects

These form the basis of judgement and related directly to the:

- Transcendental aesthetic
- Transcendental analytic and
- Transcendental dialectic.

The basic difference between hypothetical imperative and categorical imperative is that:

Hypothetical imperative uses 'ifs' and 'buts' - thereby tendering one act as the causative to another. Example: You can expect a good harvest if you seed the soil properly and timely.

Categorical imperative is defective and unconditional.

Main Weakness of Deontological Theory

It is in the failure to provide a plausible account of how we can know our moral obligations and resolve problems of moral conflict. Though the rules in Ross's theory are pleasable, no reason is offered for accepting these rules and not others. Ross's rules are also open to the charge of ethnocentrism (erroneously accepting the rules of our own society as though they were universal). People might accept other rules as worthy, rejecting Ross's rules at different times and in different places.

Strengths and Weaknesses of Deontological Theories

Strengths:

- According to W.D.Ross's (British Philosopher in 20th century) theory is that they make sense of cases in which consequences seem to be irrelevant. Example: A manufacturer has an obligation to honour a warranty on a defective product even if the cost of doing so exceeds the benefit of satisfying a consumer. An employee has an obligation to an employer to be loyal and to do his/her job.
- It is the way they account for the role of motives in evaluating actions. Example. Two persons give a good sum of money to charity. One out of genuine concern to alleviate suffering and the other to impress friends and relative-produce the same amount of good; evaluate the two actions differently.

Weaknesses: It lies in the failure to provide a plausible account of how we can know our moral obligations and resolve problems of moral conflict. Ross's rules are also open to the charge of ethnocentrism (erroneously accepting the rules of our own society as though they are universal). Ross's theory are plausible, no reason is offered for accepting these rules and not others. We have no guidances in cases where they conflict. E.g. should we keep a promise or tell the truth when doing so will harm someone?

2.2.3 Virtue Ethics (Aristotle's Nicomachien Ethics)

Utilitarian and Kantian ethics both address the question (inspite of their differences).

- What actions are right?

  Virtue ethics asks instead:

- What kind of person should we be?

Moral character rather than right action is fundamental in this ethical tradition which originated with the ancient Greeks and received its fullest expression in Aristotle's Nicomachean ethics.

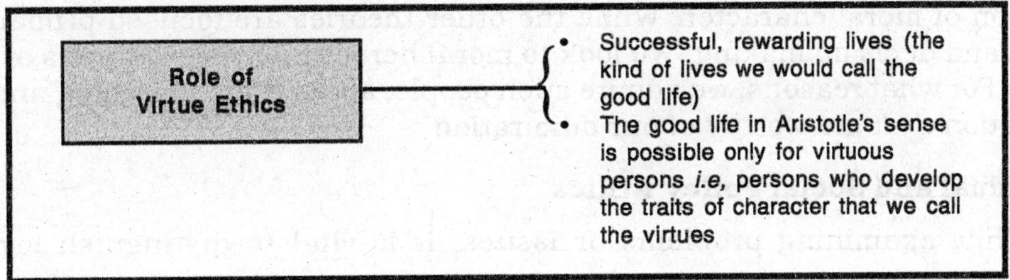

Fig. 2.35 Role of Virtue Ethics

Aristotle not only made the case for the necessity of virtue for good living but also described particular virtues in illuminating detail.

Virtue ethics theory does three things:

- It defines the concept of a virtue.
- It must offer some list of the virtues-and a list of their corresponding virtues.
- It offers some justification of that list and explain how we define what are virtues and vices.

E.g. Honesty is in the list of the virtues.

What is it about honesty that makes it a virtue? How honesty can be defined as a virtue to someone who disagreed?

Aristotle defines **virtue** as a character trait that manifests itself in habitual action. Honesty for example cannot consist in telling the truth once. It is the tract of a person who tells the truth as a general practice.

For the Greeks, **virtue** means excellence and ethics was concerned with excellences of human character.

Virtue ethics = Excellences of human character

A person possessing such qualities exhibited the excellences of human character. A tradition going all the way back to Plato and Aristotle. The qualities are to function well as a human being.

The list of possible virtues is long. There is no general agreement on which are most important. The possibilities include:

- Courage
- Benevolence
- Generosity
- Honesty
- Tolerance
- Self-control etc.

Virtue theorists try to identify the list of virtues and to give an account of each. They give an account of why the virtues are important. What is courage? What is honesty?

Virtue theory seems to fill a gap left by other theories, since it addresses the question of moral character. While the other theories are focused primarily on action and decision making. We look to moral heroes e.g., as exemplars of moral virtue. For what reasons, we admire such people, about their character, and their motivation that are worthy of our admiration.

Individual and Social Policy Ethics

While examining problems or issues, it is vital to distinguish levels of analysis.

Approaches

Levels ↓ / Approaches →	Social practices	Public policy	Individual choice
Macro Level			
Micro Level			

Macro Level Problems	*Micro Level Problems*
• Pertaining to groups of people; a community, a state, a country. • A solution is sought in the form of a law or policy that specifies how people in that group or society ought to behave, rules of that group ought to be. • Macro level questions are asked. eg. should software engineers be held liable for errors in the software they design?	• Pertaining to individuals (in the presence or absence of law or policy). eg. - should I lie to my friend. – Should I work on a project making military weapons? – Should I make a copy of this piece of software)

Virtue Ethics Theory

Philosophers find it difficult to define virtue as they are not in agreement. Aristotle described virtue as a character trait that manifests itself in habitual action.

Both utilitarian and Kantian ethics both put the same question, in spite of their differences, what actions are right?

Virtue, for Aristotle, is integrally related to what he calls practical wisdom which may be described roughly as the whole of a what a person needs in order to do well. Most lists of the virtues contain few surprises. Such traits benevolence, compassion, courage, courtisey, dependability, friendliness, honesty, loyalty, moderation, self control and toleration are most talked about.

Virtues are acquired traits. Mere feelings like hanger, are not virtues according to Aristotle. Honesty on the other hand cannot consist in telling the truth once. It is rather trait of a person who tells the truth as a general practice. A virtue is also something we actually practice. Honesty involves habitually telling the truth; It is not knowing how to tell the truth.

Aristotle classified **virtue** as a state of character, which is different from a feeling or a skill. A **virtue** is something that we admire in a person; a **virtue** is an excellence of some kind that is worth having its own sake. **Honesty** is a trait that everyone needs for a good life. **Virtues** are those traits that everyone needs for the good ones no matter his or her specific situation.

The virtues, moreover are not merely means to happiness but are themselves constituents of it.

Defending a list of the virtues requires both that we determine the character traits that are essential to a good life and we give some content to the idea of a good life itself.

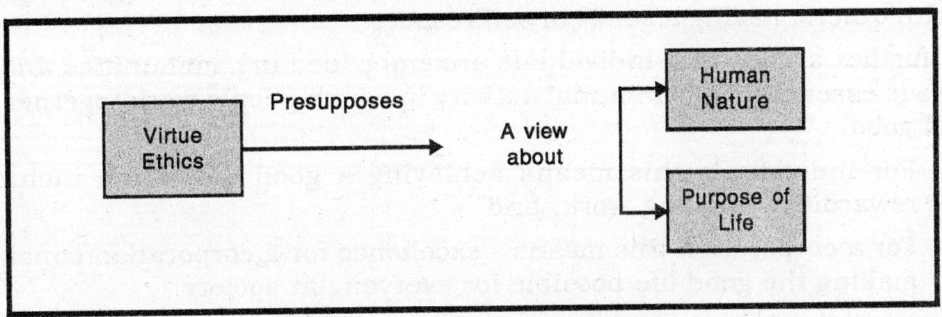

Fig. 2.36 Virtue Ethics

The possibility of applying virtue ethics to business depends on a context that includes:

- Some conception of the nature
- Purpose of business.

Virtue Ethics in Business

Virtue ethics could be applied to business, if the virtues of a good business person are the same as those of a good person. A **moral virtue** is an acquired disposition that is valued as part of the character of a morally good human being and that is exhibited in the person's habitual behaviour. A person is said to have moral value when the person is disposed to behave habitually in the way and with the reasons, feelings and desires that are characteristic of a morally good person. A moral virtue must be acquired, and not merely a natural characteristic such as intelligence, beauty or natural strength. It is praiseworthy in part because it is an achievement. Its development requires effort.

Virtual ethics looks at moral issues from a very different perspective than action based ethics, it does not follow that the conclusions of virtue ethics will differ radically from the conclusions of an action-based ethic.

The four classical virtues on which Aristotle and Aquinas both agreed are: courage, temperance, justice and prudence. However, the three theological virtues-faith, hope and charity-that Aquinas added because of their special importance for a Christian life would not count as moral virtues because they are desirable only with a special kind of life devoted to the pursuit of special religious objectives.

Applying virtue ethics to business would require, to determine the end at which business activity aims. If the business purpose is merely to create as much health as possible then we get one set of virtues.

Roberts C.Solomon says that more wealth creation is not the purpose. Solomon has developed a virtue ethics based view and his book Ethics and Excellence mentions that "The bottom line of the Aristotelian approach to business ethics is that we have to get away from 'bottom line' thinking and conceive of business as an essential part of the good life, living well, getting along with others, having a sense of self respect.

He further argues that individuals are embedded in communities and that business is essentially a communal activity in which people work together for a common good.

- For individuals this means achieving a good life which includes - rewarding, fulfilling work, and
- For a corporation this means - excellence for a corporation consists of making the good life possible for everyone in society.

Honesty in business is not necessarily the same as honesty in other spheres.

Strengths and Weaknesses of Virtue Ethics

The main strengths of this derive from a better fit with our own moral experience:

- Utilitarianism and Kantian ethics provide universal moral principles that can be applied to specific cases.

  The proponents of a virtue ethics approach respond that people generally do not reason in that way. With regard to a complex ethical dilemma, most people is to ask what they feel comfortable with or what a person they admire would do. Codes of ethics generally offer abstract principles and sometimes specific rules. They stress that a professional should be a person of integrity. This conception of the character of a professional may be a more effective guide than principles and rules.

- Utilitarianism and Kantian ethics expects treating the interests of everyone impartially. We consider the interests of family members, friends, members of a local community to be of greater moral importance.

  The virtue ethics view individuals as embedded in a community and holds that a web of close relationships is essential for a good life (Its proponents claim, to give an account of the importance of relations in morality).

  However the well known weaknesses of virtue ethics afflict both Aristotle' theory and modern attempts to restore the Aristotelian tradition.

- A virtuous character can take us only so far in dealing with genuine ethical dilemmas. Some of these involve the limits of rules (when not revealing information become a lie or conflicts between rules). Merely relying on the virtues of honesty and compassion does not give us much guidance in such situations. Some difficult ethical situations exist where the virtues do not readily apply (Bribing a foreign official, drug testing of employees etc.). Importance of dilemmas in ethics has been overstated and questions of rights and justice should not be the central concerns of ethics according to some virtue ethics theorists.
- Aristotle is accused of over looking the fact that our interests often conflict.

Finally, we can say that the idea of virtue business is not hopelessly out of place. There are certain character traits that will lead to success in business and also elevate the tone of business. The world of business contains leaders and ordinary workers with exemplary character.

All the three theories agree that certain virtues are important to have, though only virtuous ethics makes being virtuous the essential element in leading a moral life.

2.3 Justice and Fairness

(i) Justice, like rights, is an important moral concept with a wide range of applications. We use it to evaluate not only the actions of individuals but also social, legal, political, and economic practices and institutions. Though the word 'just' is sometimes used interchangeably with right and good, it generally has a more restricted meaning that is closer to fair. Questions of Justice often arise, when there is something to distribute.

Four theories of justice are shown by Aristotle, Mill, Rawls and Zozick. The purpose of these theories is primarily to provide a means for reevaluating existing and proposed institutional arrangements.

As per Nicomachean Ethics, the word justice has a double meaning. In one sense, it applies to the whole of virtue. A just or morally upright person is one who always does what is morally right and obeys the law. Justice in this sense is

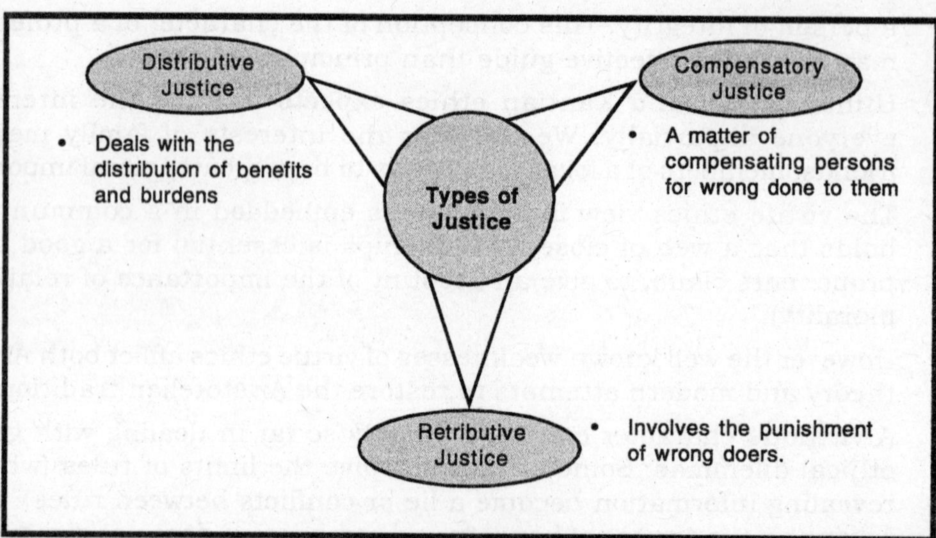

Fig. 2.37 Types of Justice

called **Universal Justice** by Aristotle. The other sense of justice which he called **particular justice** is concerned with virtue in specific situations.

Distributive Justice

Distributive justice arises mostly in the evaluation of our social, political and economic institutions, where the benefits and burdens of engaging in cooperative activities must be spread over a group. A **just distribution** is one in which each person shares equally, but in others, unequal sharing is just if the inequality is in accord with some principle of distribution. In the politics, Aristotle observed that "all men think justice to be a sort of equality." But what sort of equality justice remains is a source of controversy to the present day. Aristotle expressed the idea of treating like cases alike in an arithmetical equation that represents justice as an equality of ratios.

Compensatory Justice and Retributive Justice

Compensatory Justice and Retributive Justice are concerned with correcting wrongs. Generally compensating the victims is the just way of correcting wrongs in private dealings such as losses resulting from accidents and the failure to fulfill contracts; whereas retribution-that is, punishment-is the just response to criminal acts, such as assault or theft.

Ethical issues in finance are important because they bear on our financial well being. Ethical misconduct as everyone knows, may be by individuals acting alone or by financial institutions has the potential to rob people of their life savings. As huge money is involved in financial dealings, there must be well-developed and effective safeguards in place to ensure personal and organisational ethics. Though the law governs much financial activity, strong emphasis must be placed on the integrity of the finance professionals and on ethical leadership in our financial institutions. Certain principles in finance ethics are common to the other aspects of business:

- Duties of fiduciaries (held in trust)
- Fairness in sales practices
- Securities markets

Activities like **insider trading** and **hostile takeover** raise unique issues that require special consideration.

(ii) Fairness It means the quality of being just, equitable and impartical. Honest is truth fulness integrity and trustworthiness. Both honesty and fairness relate to the general moral attributes of decision makers. They should not harm the related parties like customers, clients, employees and even competitors. Through deception, misrepresentation or coercison.

Fairness is the desposition to deal equitably with the perceived injustices of others. Fairness often relates to doing the right thing with respect to small matters in order to cultivate a long-term business relationship.

(b) Fair Labour Association: A non profit whose members include manufacturers, universities and groups promoting human, consumers, religious, shareholder and labour rights. Participating firms agree to have their facilities and those of their contractors monitored by both internal and independent external organisations.

Is Capitalism Just?

Justice is a particular but pervasive crucial aspect of morality. It is the morally proper treatment of people, ensuring that what is done to the people is what ought to be done to them. It is about giving people what is 'fair' and what they have a 'right' to and whatever it is that, to their advantage or disadvantage they 'deserve'.

The different types of justice depends on exactly what it is that people are morally entitled to:

- **Procedural justice** - concerned with the fair and impartial administering of rules of procedure in trials and the like.
- **Corrective justice** - concerned with giving proper recompense for wrongs suffered.
- **Retributive justice** - concerned with dealing out morally appropriate punishments for wrongs committed.
- **Distributive justice** - concerning about the questions on the justice of capitalism are raised.
- **Social justice** - concerning about the large society. The people concerned can be members of a particular group, society at large, or even humanity in general.

Social justice is often the term used when the justice of capitalism is discussed.

The point for discussion here is the unequal distribution of wealth and income in capitalist societies. It is true that no one pattern of distribution precisely fits every capitalist society.

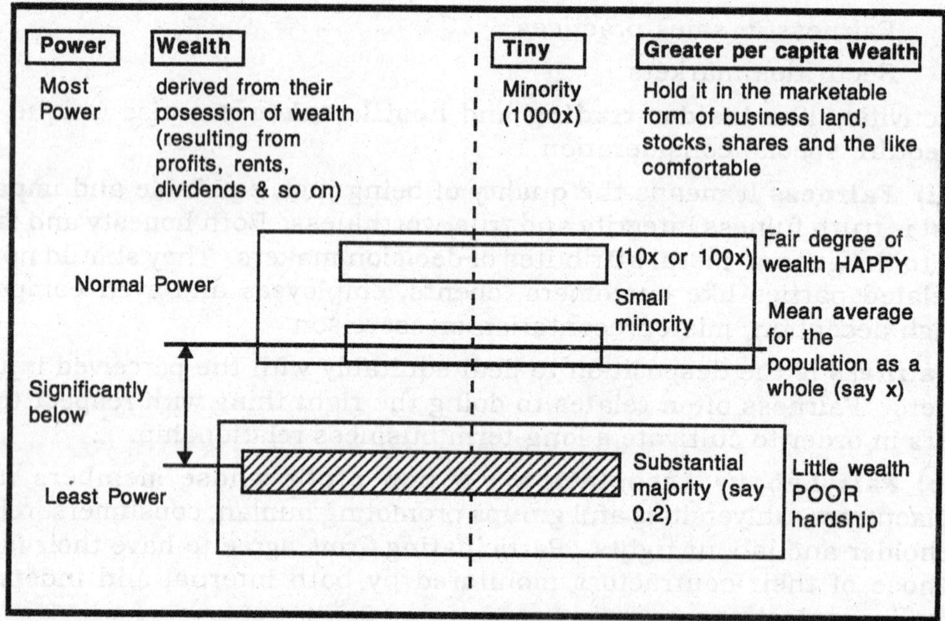

Fig. 2.38 Inequalities in the Distribution of Wealth and Income in Capitalist Societies.

Note:

1. Wealth will be in the form of housing and pensions.
2. Inequality depends on how much more it relates to the top than the bottom.
3. There is also the specifically capitalist arrangement of vesting control of enterprises in suppliers of capital. This provides a peculiarly direct correlation between wealth and power. It grants to the rich influence over people's working lives, over their economic fortunes and even, through purchase or ownership of the media of mass communication, their opinions. An unequal distribution of power is also at issue.
4. Many argue that there ought to be a totally equal distribution of wealth and power, since their concern is invariably limited to the extremes; a sizeable minority being poor and mostly powerless; a small minority being very rich and powerful. Nor are they even all concerned to redress every extreme, of riches as well as poverty of power as well as wealth. Inequality of wealth at the bottom end is a problem for welfare capitalism. To reduce the inequality of wealth at the top end through the use of progressive taxation to fund welfare programmes a means to an end of reducing poverty rather than a deliberate policy. Also aims at reducing those inequalities of work place power that are specific to capitalism. For market socialism,

there is not only a concern with power and wealth, but with extremes of wealth at top and bottom. It seeks to transfer ownership as well as control from capital to labour as part of a general policy of aiming at the widest possible dispersal of both wealth and power.

Unfairness in Markets

What does this mean? Fairness is not a matter to prevent losses. Markets produce winners and losers. Most of the cases, the gain of one may equal loss to other, though market exchanges are advantageous to both the parties. Involvement in a stock market is like playing a sport. The aim is not to prevent losses but to ensure that the game is fair. The regulation of financial markets protects the general public apart from the individual investors. The latter can be treated unfairly by the operations of financial markets in many ways.

The main kinds of unfairness are:

- Fraud and Manipulation
- Equal Information
- Equal bargaining power
- Efficient pricing

(a) Arguments against insider trading

The difficulty lies while defining insider trading is because of the disagreement over the moral wrong as shown in Fig. 2.38 below.

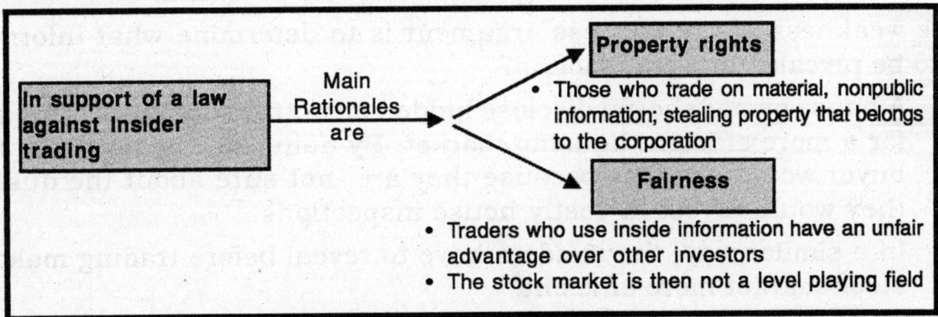

Fig. 2.39 In Support of a Law Against Insider Trading

Definitions are different based on the above two rationales: (i) Narrow (ii) Broad.

Narrow: On the property rights or misappropriation theory, only corporate insiders or outsiders who bribe, steal, or otherwise acquire wrongfully corporate secret materials/information can be guilty of insider trading.

Broad: The fairness argument applies to any one who trades on material, nonpublic information, no matter how it has been acquired.

(b) The Fairness Argument

All traders need not have the same information as per fairness in the stock market. With different information, generally trades take place between buyers and sellers of a stock leading them to different conclusions about the stock. A shrewd investor who has spent great time and money after studying the prospects of a company tries to exploit his acquired knowledge. Otherwise, we do not find any incentive to seek out new information.

For other traders, the information is unavailable not for lack of effort but for lack of access.

- We have seen many a times, the seller of a home fails to reveal hidden structural damage. One principle of stock market regulation is that both buyers and sellers of stock should have sufficient information to make rational choices. The companies publish annual reports and disclose important developments in a timely manner.
- The top executive who hides any vital news from the investing public can be sued for fraud. Alternatively for good news such as an innovation, need not be announced until the company buy the rights. But to trade on that information before it is publicly announced, might also be described as a kind of fraud.
- Insider trading is generally prosecuted which prohibits fraud in securities transactions. In fraudulent transactions, one party such as the buyer of the house with structural damaged is wrongfully damaged because of lack of knowledge that the other party hid.

The weakness of the fairness argument is to determine what information ought to be revealed in a transaction?

- A house owner should disclose hidden structural damages. This makes for a more efficient housing market. By doing so, the potential house buyer would pay less because they are not sure about the quality or they would invest in costly house inspections.
- In a similar way, the insiders have to reveal before trading makes the stock market more efficient.

Some economists argue without a law against insider training, the stock market would be more efficient. If insider trading were permitted, information would be registered more quickly in the market and at less cost than the research task done by stock analysts. The main beneficiaries in this are not individual investors but market professionals (gather news on the street and act fast).

- Law also preserves the illusion that there is a level playing field and individual investors have a chance against market professionals.
- Cost of registering information can be considered under economic argument and will not look at adversed consequences of legalised insider trading which are many. Employees interest may be in information that they can use is stock market; they may be less

concerned with information that is useful to the employer and the company. The company itself might provide information for maximum benefit to insiders.

The strongest argument against legalisation might be the breach of fiduciary duty that would result. This is the harm that legalised insider trading could do. Serving as a fiduciary for personal gain is a violation of duty. This is shown below:

The argument that insider trading constitutes a breach of fiduciary duty accords with recent court decisions in USA that have limited the prosecution of insider trading to true insiders who have a fiduciary duty. The drawbacks of the argument are:

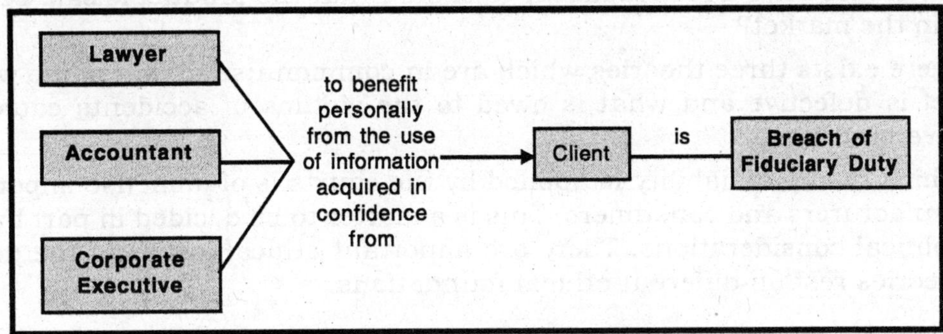

Fig. 2.40 Breach of Fiduciary Duty

- Outsiders, whom prosecutors have sought to convict of insider trading, would be free of any restrictions
- Insider trading is no longer an offense against the market, but the violation of a duty to another party.

The duty would be violated by a fiduciary who buys and sells the property or undertakes some other business dealing on the basis of confidential information.

(c) Fair Value

Merger accounting calls for the assets and liabilities of a target business to be brought into the buyers consolidated accounts at their previous book values, subject only to adjustments to achieve consistency with the buyers accounting policies.

Acquisition accounting is different and requires adjustments to ensure that the consolidated balance sheet at the end of the acquisition reflects the fair values of the targets separable assets and liabilities. The concept of fair value can be illustrated by looking at fixed assets and provisions.

The **fair value** of a fixed asset is represented by the cost of replacing it with an asset which would give the same service. Because of inflation, an assets fair value is usually greater than to its net book value.

Ideas of justice as applied in business relate to evaluations of fairness. Justice is fair treatment and due reward in accordance with ethical or legal standards.

2.4 Theory of Due Care

The right of consumers to be protected from harmful products raises a number of problems for manufactures as products can injure, and even kill people (if products are used improperly).

Every dangerous product can be made safer at some cost. Is there any limit to the safety improvements that a manufacturer ought to provide? Do manufacturers have a responsibility to ensure that the product is safe before it is put in the market?

There exists three theories which are in common use to determine when a product is defective and what is owed to the victims of accidents caused by defective products.

Which theory of liability is applied by the courts is of immense importance to manufacturers and consumers. This is a matter to be decided in part by legal and political considerations. There are important ethical issues in the debate. The theories rest on different ethical foundations.

The Due Care standard

The standard of due care for manufacturers or other persons involved in the sale of a product to a consumer including wholesalers and retailers, covers a wide range of activities. Among them are:

- **Design** - Designed in accordance with government and industry standards to be safe.
- **Materials** - Materials specified in the design; should meet government and industry standards.
- **Production** - Due care should be taken in fabricating parts to specifications and assembling them correctly.,
- **Quality control** - A systematic programme to inspect products between operations at the end to ensure that they are of sufficient quality.
- **Packaging, labeling and warnings** - Product should be packaged so as to avoid any damage in transit.
- **Notification** - The manufacturers of some products should have a system of notifying consumers of hazards that only become apparent later.

One question arises that in due care theory is whether manufacturers have an obligation to ensure that a product is safe to use as intended or to anticipate all the conditions under which injury could occur.

The Problem of Misuse: This duty also extends to foreseeable misuse by the consumer.

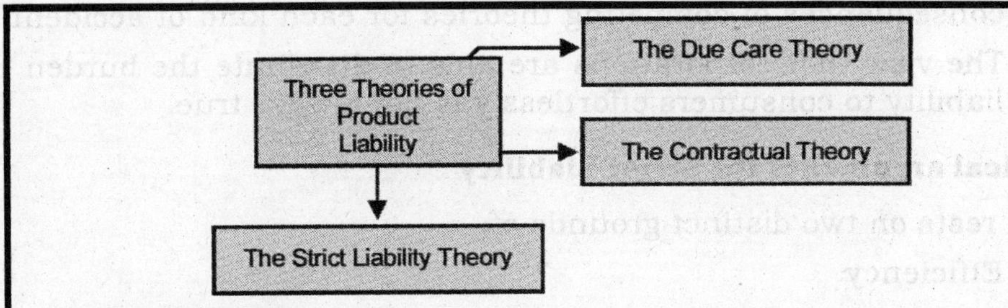

The Due Care Theory

- Manufacturers ought to exercise due care. Their obligation is to take all reasonable precautions to ensure that products they put on the market are free of defects likely to cause harm. It is based on the Aristotelian principle of compensatory justice, the contractual theory, on freedom of contract and strict liability, largely on utilitarian considerations. The disadvantage of this theory is the difficulty of deciding what constitutes due care and whether it was exercised.

The Contractual Theory

- The responsibility of manufacturers for harm resulting from defective products is that specified in a sales contract. The seller and buyer relation is viewed here as a contractual relation, which is subject to the terms of a contract. Even in the absence of an explicit, written contract, there may be an implicit, understood contract between the two parties that is established by their behaviour. It is the least satisfactory because of the power of manufacturers to write warranties and other agreements to their own advantage and to offer them to consumers on a 'take it or leave it' basis.

The Strict Liability Theory

- Manufacturers are responsible for all harm resulting from a dangerously defective product even when due care has been exercised and all contracts observed; Now gaining wider acceptance in the courts. Here, Law is strict liability, a manufacture need not be negligent nor be bounded by any implied or express warranty to have responsibility. Despite the absence of fault, is arguably the best theory. It provides a powerful incentive for manufacturers to take extreme precautions and creates a workable legal framework for compensating consumers who are injured by defective products. To be just, the costs have to be properly distributed so that they are fair to all parties.

Fig. 2.41 Three Theories of Product Liability

The Concept of Negligence: The major difficulty with the due care theory is establishing what constitutes due care.

Objections to the Contractual Theory: The objections are:

- The understandings in a sales agreement, which are the basis for implied and express warranties, are not very precise.
- A sales agreement may consist of a written contract with language that sharply limits the right of an injured consumer to be compensated. If buyers and sellers are both free to contract on mutually agreeable terms, then the sales agreement can explicitly disclaim all warranties express or implied.

Objections to the Strict Liability

- Product liability covers many different kinds of accidents and the most efficient or equitable system for one kind may not be efficient or equitable for another. Careful studies need to be made of the consequences of competing theories for each kind of accident.

- The view that corporations are able to distribute the burden of strict liability to consumers effortlessly is not always true.

The Ethical arguments for Strict Liability

This rests on two distinct grounds of:

- Efficiency
- Equality

One argument is purely utilitarian and justifies strict liability for securing the greatest amount of protection for consumers at the lowest cost. The second argument is that strict liability is the farthest way of distributing the costs involved in the manufacture and use of products. Both of these arguments recognise that there is a certain cost in attempting to prevent accidents and in dealing with the consequences of accidents that do on product safety. Preventing accidents requires that manufacturers expend greater resources on product safety. The efficient argument hold by one advocate that responsibility be fixed wherever it will most effectively reduce the hazards to life and health inherent in defective parts that reach the market.

The equity argument principle holds as expressed by Richard A.Epstein as follows:

'The defendant who captures the entire benefit of his own activities should....also bear its entire costs.' In so far as manufacturers are the beneficiaries of their profit making activity, it is only fair, according to this principle, that they be forced to bear the cost, which includes the cost of the injuries to consumers as a result of defective products. Much of the benefit of a manufacturer's activity is shared by consumers, however. But they also share the cost of compensating the victims of accidents through higher prices. It is also just that they do so insofar as they reap some benefit.

2.5 Integration of the Various Perspectives

Moral philosophy and the role of moral philosophies in decision making is explained.

Many moral philosophies exist. Each one is complexly described. This is a very vast subject and is not explained in this book. The most basic concepts needed to understand the ethical decision making in business is given as under. There is no one particular moral philosophy, since there is no one correct way to resolve ethical issues in business.

The philosophies that are used in business decisions are:

- Teleology (acts are morally right or acceptable if they produce some desired result, such as realisation of self interest or utility)
- Utilitarianism (right or acceptable actions as those that maximise total utility, or the greatest good for the greatest number of people)

- Deontology (the preservation on individual rights and one the intentions associated with a particular behaviour rather than on its consequences)
- Egoism (right or acceptable actions as those that maximise a particular person's self interest as defined by the individual)
- Relativism (ethicalness subjectively on the basis of individual and group experiences)
- Virtue Ethics (what is moral in a given situation is not only what conventional morality requires, and what the person with a good moral character would deem appropriate)
- Justice (ethicalness on the basis of fairness; distributive, procedural and interactional)

The decision maker would have more factors to consider in making his/her choice. Those might reach a different decision. Business people are guided by moral philosophies as they formulate business strategies on these and resolve specific ethical issues.

2.6 Cognitive Moral Development

Individuals make different decisions in similar critical situations, since they are in different stages of moral development. They advance through stages of moral development as their knowledge and socialisation continue over time. Kohlberg's Moral development model indicates that people make different decisions in similar ethical situations because they are in different stages of six cognitive moral development stages:

In Kohlberg's model, people progress through six stages of moral development as shown in Fig..... These six stages can be further reduced to three levels of ethical concern:

(i) Immediate self interest (pre-conventional states)

(ii) Social expectations (conventional stages)

(iii) General ethical principles (post-conventional autonomous or principled stages)

This model helps us to know why people change their beliefs or moral values? People continue to change their decision priorities after their formative years. People progress through the stages of moral development, and with time, education, and experience. They may change their values and ethical behaviour. An individual's moral development can be influenced by corporate culture, especially ethics training in the context of business.

2.7 Moral Reasoning

Moral Reasoning

Moral reasoning is a more intentional form of decision making where the actor considers the basis for and implications of the decision before acting. The decision maker considers evidence and reaches conclusions or judgements, about the right and wrong way to act. Moral reasoning, suffer from being too absolute or from being too relativistic. Absolute is where one believes that the same rule applies, no matter the circumstances; Relativistic is where the answer always seems to depend entirely on circumstances.

To avoid these two extremes, one might look to a model of reasoning such as the stakeholder model of decision making.

Stakeholder Model

This model has already been explained in page Nos 21 and 376. **Stakeholders** include all of the groups and/or individuals affected by a decision, policy or operation of a firm or individual.

The **contractual theory** generally supports a stockholder centered conception of the corporation. An alternative is **stakeholder theory**. The central claim of the stakeholder approach is that corporations are operated or ought to be operated for the benefit of all those who have a stake in the enterprise as shown above in the figure. A stable holder is variously defined as those groups who are vital to the survival and success of the corporation and as any group or individual who can affect or is affected by the achievement of the organisations objectives. Although the relation of each stakeholder group to the corporation is different each of the constituencies is integral to the operation of a corporation, and its role must be taken into account by managers.

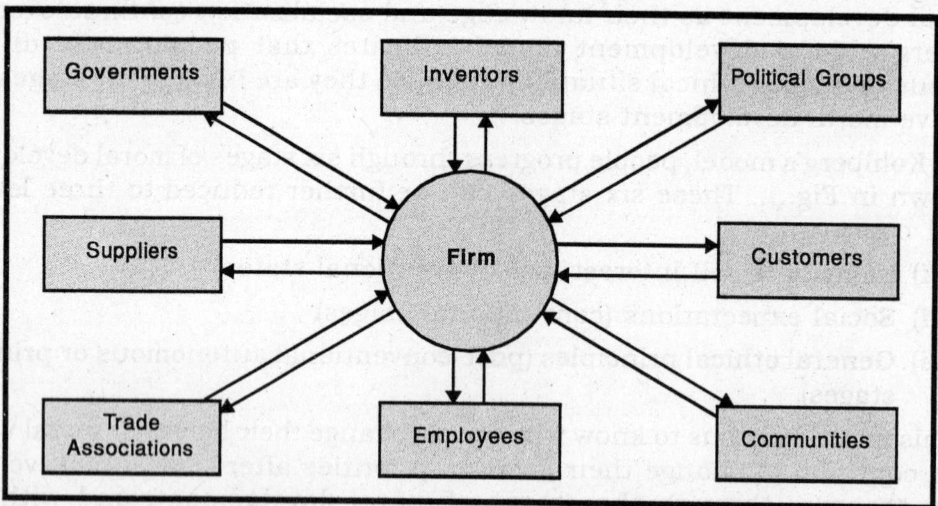

Fig. 2.42 The Stakeholder Model

The concept of moral philosophy is not exact. Moral philosophies can only be assessed on a continuum. Individuals use different moral philosophies depending on whether they are making a personal decision or a work place decision.

The **contractual theory** generally supports a stockholder centered conception of the corporation. An alternative is **stakeholder theory**. The central claim of the stakeholder approach is that corporations are operated or ought to be operated for the benefit of all those who have a stake in the enterprise as shown above in the figure. A stable holder is variously defined as those groups who are vital to the survival and success of the corporation and as any group or individual who can affect or is affected by the achievement of the organisations objectives. Although the relation of each stakeholder group to the corporation is different each of the constituencies is integral to the operation of a corporation, and its role must be taken into account by managers.

Serious attempts have been made to develop the stakeholder concept into a full blown view of the corporation that might replace the stock holder central conception.

2.8 The Role of Corporate Culture and Leadership

Executive and Supervisory Leadership

The crucial role of top management is a prime business asset. To achieve results, CEO need to be openly and strongly committed to ethical conduct and give constant leadership intending and renewing the values of the organisation. Executives play a crucial role in creating, maintaining and changing ethical culture. Leaders at every level serve as role models and employees have more daily contact with their supervisors than they do with executive leaders. Supervisors are responsible for rewards and punishments and they carry the message of how things are really done in the organisation. In view of this, separate sets of questions were asked to employees for their perceptions of executive and supervisory ethical leadership. Perceptions of these two groups were highly related (correlation=0.78). This suggests that employees think similarly about supervisors and executive leaders with regard to their attention to ethics, so do supervisory leaders.

Leadership is a key ethical culture factor employees paint all leaders with the same broad ethical brush. When it comes to ethics, leaders are leaders, and the level may be supervisory or executive doesn't seem to matter much to employees.

Ethics managing in organisations is not just managing **formal ethics or compliance programmes. Ethical climate or culture** which is the broader ethical context in an organisation is more important than specific ethics compliance programme goals or characteristics. The elements of ethical culture that guide employee thought and action covers:

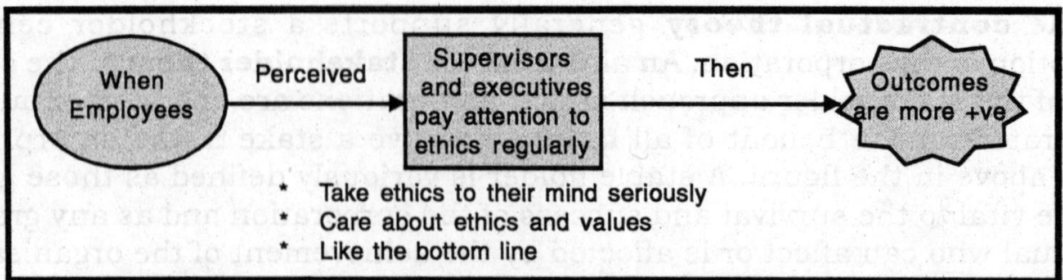

Fig. 2.43 Positive Outcomes achieved when Employees Perceive Supervisors and Executive pay attention to Ethics

- Leadership
- Perceived/fairness
- Employee authority structure
- Reward systems
- Ethics as a topic of conversation in the organisation
- Organisal focus that communicates care for the employees and the community.

Culture is defined as the way we do things around here. It is the shared beliefs top managers have

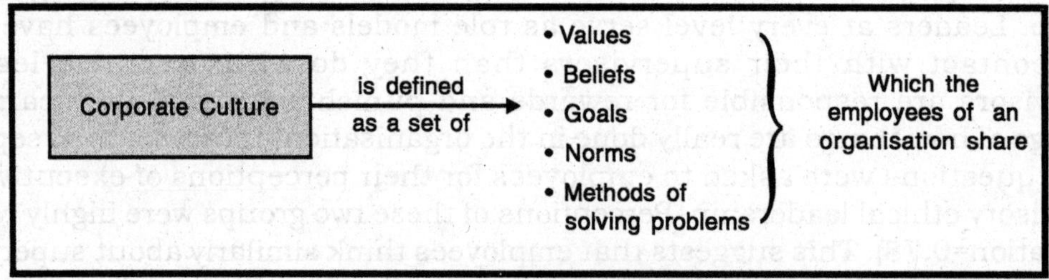

Fig. 2.44 Corporate Culture

Generally organisational culture and corporate cultures are interchanged. Corporate culture refers to the set of values, beliefs, goals, norms and ways of solving members which is shared in the organisation by employees. There may be formally expressed or unspoken. Corporate culture can be classified in many ways and a cultural audit can be conducted to identify organisations culture.

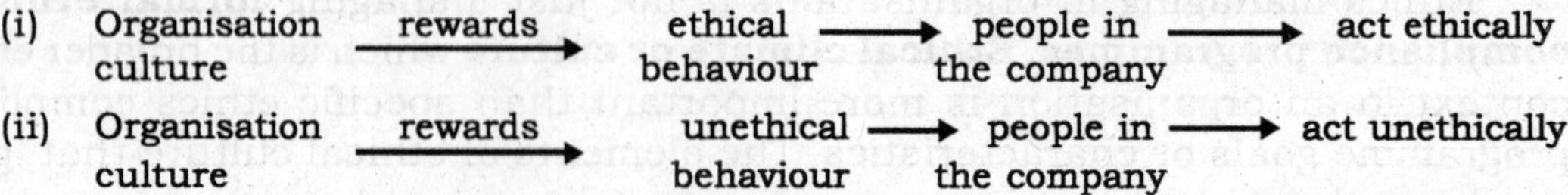

Corporate culture involves values and rules that prescribe a wide range of behaviour for organisational members, **the ethical climate** reflects whether the firm has an ethical conscience.

Corporate culture's important component is the company's ethical climate.

The ethical climate is a function of:

- Corporate policies on ethics
- Top management's leadership on ethical issues
- Influence of coworkers
- Opportunity for unethical behaviour.

In para 1.4, Factors influencing business ethics have been discussed. These include **corporate culture** and **leadership**. The other factors are individual characteristics, strategy and performance and environment.

Leadership

It is the ability or authority to guide others towards achieving goals. This has an effective impact on the ethical decision making process because leaders have the power to motivate others and enforce both the organisation's rules and policies and their own view points. A leader must not only gain the respect of his or her followers but also provide a standard of ethical conduct.

People are a major focus of Organisational Change Management

This includes activities such as developing innovative ways to:

- measure
- motivate
- reward performance

It is the people who will ultimately cause the change to be a success or a failure. The implications of change on individuals are important without which we can never really hope to manage large scale change effectively.

Most of today's work is done by forming teams. This needs team collaboration and team working for its to succeed.

Another important thing needed in change management is the crucial role of leadership.

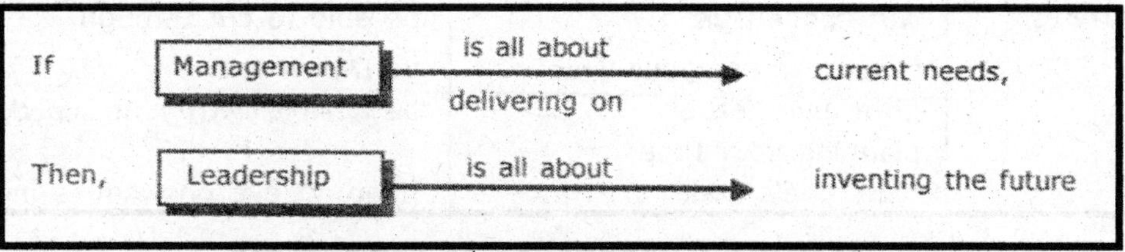

Fig. 2.45 Management vs. Leadership

Leadership of Changes in the 21st Century

Leadership to organise changes is not simple; It is to be taken as a balancing act as per Paul Evans, an expert in this field. There is an absolute need for leaders to accept the challenge of navigating between opposites.

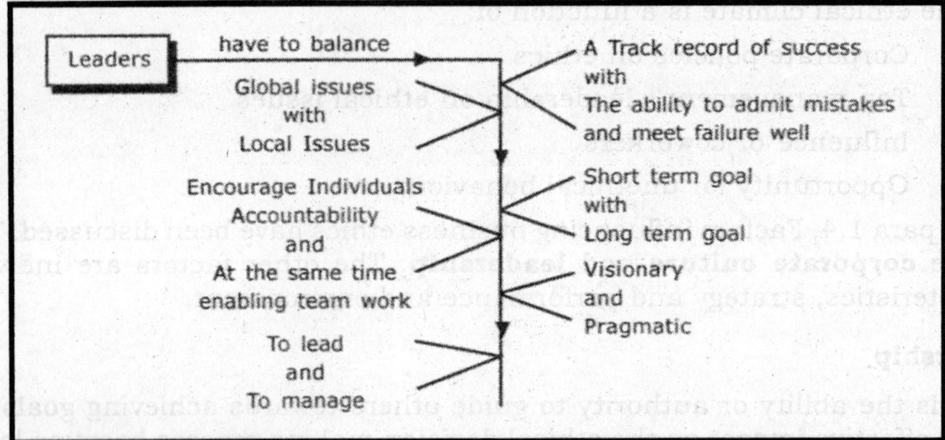

Fig. 2.46 Leaders have to Balance between Opposites

Paul Evans is emphasising the need for leaders to pay attention to both managment and Leadership.

Paradoxes of Leadership

These are found as under:

(i) To be able	to build a close relationship with one's staff	to Keep the staff at a suitable distance
	to Lead	to hold oneself in the background
(ii) To	be tolerant	Know how you want things to function
	be a visionary	Keep one's feet on the ground
	be dynamic	be reflective
	be sure of yourself	be humble
(iii) To keep	the goals of one's department in mind	at the same time be loyal to the whole firm.
(iv) To try to	win consensus	be able to cut through
(v) To	freely express your view;	be Diplomatic
	do a good job of planning your time;	be flexible with your schedule
	trust one's staff	Keep an eye on what is happening

Fig. 2.47 Paradoxes of Leadership

(Source: By Evans, 2000)

Three dimensions of leadership

Leaders of change need to balance their efforts across all three dimensions of an organisational change.

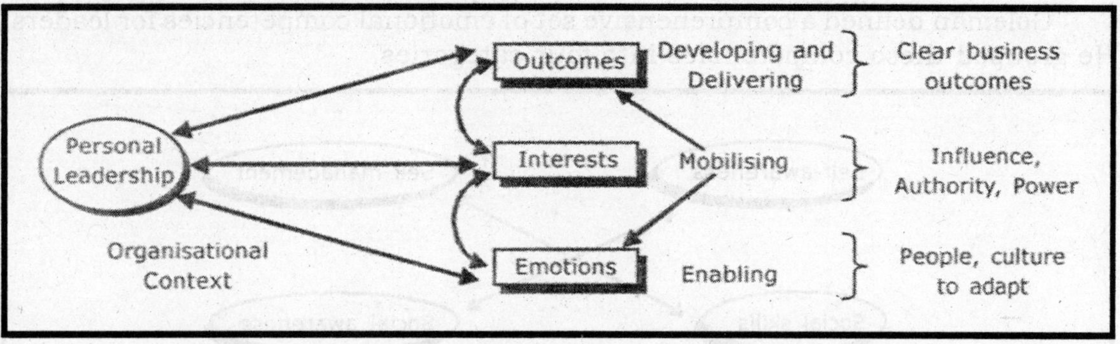

Fig. 2.48 Dimensions of Personal Leadership

Personal Characteristics of Leadership

Cammoek identifies six personal characteristics of leadership. These are:

- Passion
- Courage
- Faith
- Concern of others
- Sense of **self**
- Integrity

Under sense of self, leaders are enabled to be secure and confident. They feel

secure in their position-and develop presence.

'Self' which we are thinking are listed below:

- Self confidence
- **Self analysis**
- Self development
- Self discipline
- Self regulation
- **Self efficacy**
- **Self esteem**
- Self interest
- **Self awareness**

Integrity is the most important attribute of change leader. Integrity means consistency in thought, word and deed. Change leaders have to be people who are consistent in their thoughts, words and behaviour; practise what you preach is the motto. They must live with the values that they want their organisations to embrace. While qualities of character and integrity cannot be taught, they can be acquired by discipline of self analysis and self development. One needs to work on oneself to develop these qualities.

Self Awareness

Self awareness is knowing one's internal states, preferences, resources and intuitions:

- Emotional awareness:- Recognising one's emotions and their effects
- Accurate self-assessment:- Knowing one's strengths and limits.
- Self-confidence:- A strong sense of one's self worth and capabilities

Goleman defined a comprehensive set of emotional competencies for leaders. He grouped these competencies into four categories.

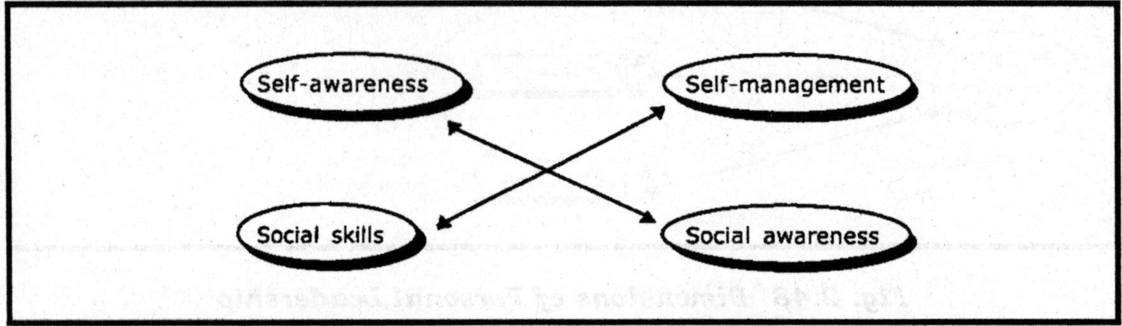

Fig. 2.49 Self-awareness as one of the Important Categories of Emotional Competencies for Leaders

Self awareness as per Goleman is at the heart of emotional intelligence. To back this up, Goieman's research shows that if self-awareness is not present in a leader, the chance of that person bei'1g competent in the other three categories is much reduced.

The leader of change has to be courageous and self aware. He has to choose:

- The right action at the right time.
- To keep a steady eye on the ball.

However, the leader cannot make change happen alone. A team needs to be in place, with well-thought-out roles; and committed people who are in for the duration, not just for the kick-off.

For years, we have been told that the world of organisations is one that is ruled by the rational mind. Recent studies such as Daniel Goleman's (1998) on emotional intelligence and management competence, suggest that what makes for more effective managers is their degree of emotional self awareness and ability to engage with others on an emotional level.

If we want to know the meaning of awareness alone, it is data generation, seeking information, sharing information, requiring past performance, environment scanning.

Self Analysis

In order to have a long survival, the company should have the ability to fit with the changing business environment and be at the ,cutting edge of competition.

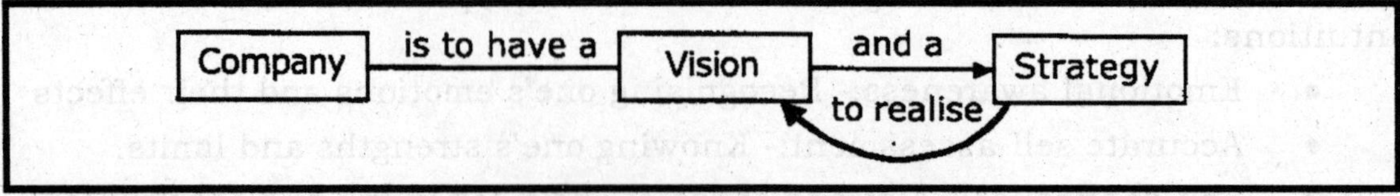

Fig. 2.50 Self Analysis

To plan strategically, a company needs to undertake a comprehensive analysis of:-

- What it presently is?
- What it should be?
- How it must change in the context of the business environment in which it operates?

The organisation should have to:

- Develop a futuristic perspective (With a vision leading to a specific mission)
- Conduct a competitive analysis of the industry and its strategic segments
- Examine its core competencies in the context of competitors, market segments, technology advancements, time and resources.

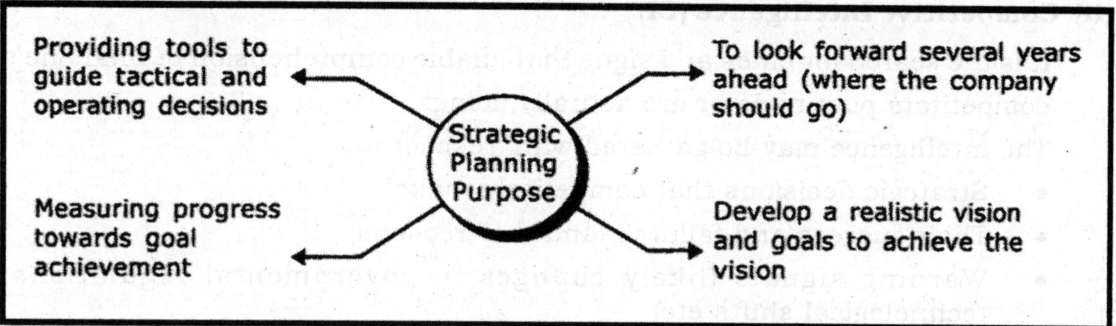

Fig. 2.51 Strategic Planning Purpose

To plan strategically, a company has to examine the business and industry environment in which it operates; At the same time, it has to obtain the competitive field of vision.

(i) Competitive Analysis
(ii) Competitive Intelligence
(iii) Self analysis
(iv) Future scenarios

(i) Competitive Analysis

The competitive field of vision is the strategic map permitting an organisation to:

- plot all the players in the arena (including suppliers, vendors, distributors, retailers etc)
- predict the moves of the other players. (anticipating changes that are likely to occur; see how they impact on its core businesses)

The competitive analysis focuses on:

— Each competitors unique position in respect to:

- its maturity in the context of the industry
- its past experience
- its product/company image
- the market segment in which it operates
- the extent of its market share
- the market forces and barriers (entry and exit) determining competition

— Gathering information about competitors (current, new and emerging)

In order to decipher the competitive map, a company has to gather the necessary . intelligence.

(ii) Competitive Intelligence (CI)

It is the search for clues and signs that enable comprehension of what one's competitors plan to do or are actually doing:

The intelligence may be gathered with' respect to:

- Strategic decisions that competitors make'
- Their success and failures (and the" reasons)
- Warning signals (likely changes in governmental regulations, technological shifts etc)
- Any significant changes in the business scenario (changes at the top management level of the competing enterprises, changes in government that may call for policy changes at the industry level)

CI Assists in:

- Determining the needs of current and potential customers.
- Identifying opportunities before they become evident.
- Enabling an organisation to implement its strategy ahead of its customers.

Gathering competitive intelligence can succeed if CI is considered an organisational competency

(iii) Self analysis

Self analysis has already been explained under strategic planning purpose. A company should work on self analysis to determine on the basis of what its core capabilities are? such as IT technology, R &D, innovativeness, good customer/supplier relations etc. Capabilities are broader in many perspectives.

Competencies are generally technological and production skills, that enable companies to adapt quickly to changing markets. These are specific. e.g., Honda's expertise in 'dealer management and product realisation'. Such companies adapt quickly to changing market or specific skills to suit customer needs. The core competencies emerge from:-

- An interaction of a few key players in the company
- A series of experimental successes in the market place

Based on the core competencies the company can diversify quickly. Honda's competency in the design of engines made the company diversify into various products such as:

- Cars
- Lawn movers
- Boat engines etc
- Snow
- Blowers
- Lawn tools

Similarly other companies like Sony, Canon etc also worked in a similar way.

The capabilities/competencies in the company can be examined considering the following seven aspects:

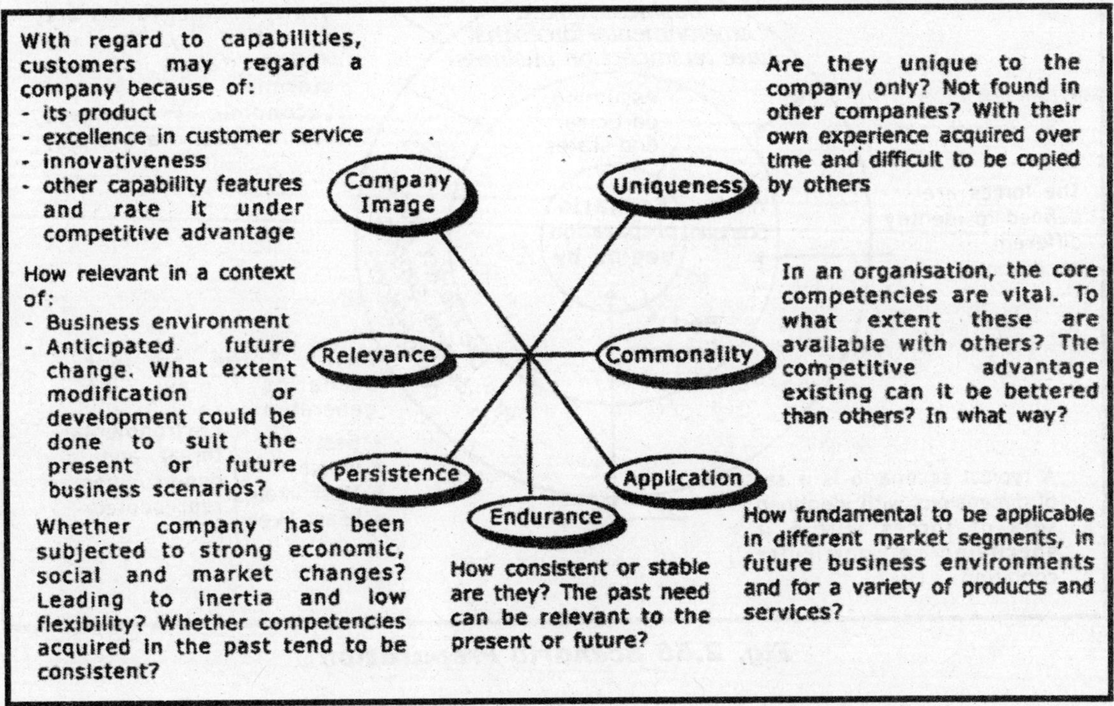

Fig. 2.52 Capabilities/Competencies in the Company

(iv) Future scenarios

On the basis of competitive intelligence and self analysis, an organization may identify its scenarios to help assist in its strategic planning. A **scenario** can be defined as speculative, detailed, well thought out narratives of future business environment based on short term, medium term, long term (of 5 years, 10 years, 15 years) future circumstances. The idea is to map out a wide range. of possible futures. This helps to manage organizational change by foresight. The companies which are following the above are Shell Oil, AT&T, Xerox, Motorola etc. Scenarios may be developed or built around a framework with the following factors:

- Time frame
- Scope
- Environmental Fluctuation

A characteristic of the future is unknownability. (The performance/success of the companies is subject to environmental forces. These could change suddenly or in fundamental ways. Major uncertainities like highly primitive competition or sudden discontinuation would find future scenario preparation as an useful tool in strategic planning.)

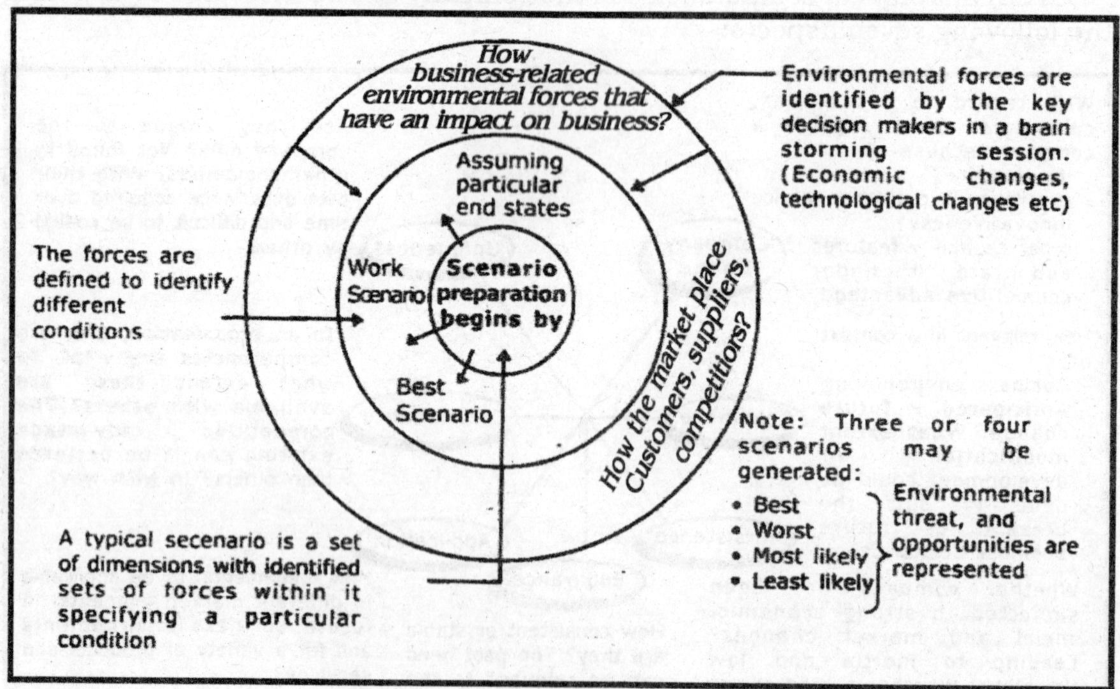

Fig. 2.53 Scenario Preparation

Preparation of scenario is a team effort utilizing the experience of individual managers, their industry experience/knowledge, their intuition and imaginative projections into the future.

Advantages of Scenario preparation includes

- A more fundamental- way of analyzing a future business environment than traditional methods (scanning, trend analysis)
- Assists in mapping a broad range of business environments (provides insight into the opportunities, as well as the threats and key uncertainties that fail in the organization and its current strategy)
- Assists in planning change tactics (if a business scenario suddenly changes)
- Helps develop a futuristic perspective in managers, challenging their conventional approach or current mental models
- Helps develop team work, awareness of other's perceptions and ideas
- Assists in training managers for corporate leadership

Computer based system dynamic models can be used for alternative policies and complex issues in testing their assumptions.

Self Efficacy

The dictionary meaning of **efficacy** is virtue or energy. **Self efficacy** is the ability of the individual to produce the result intended. It refers to the confidence individual has in his or her ability to achieve challenging goals. This also can be taken as a belief that one has the capability to deal with any type of difficult task.

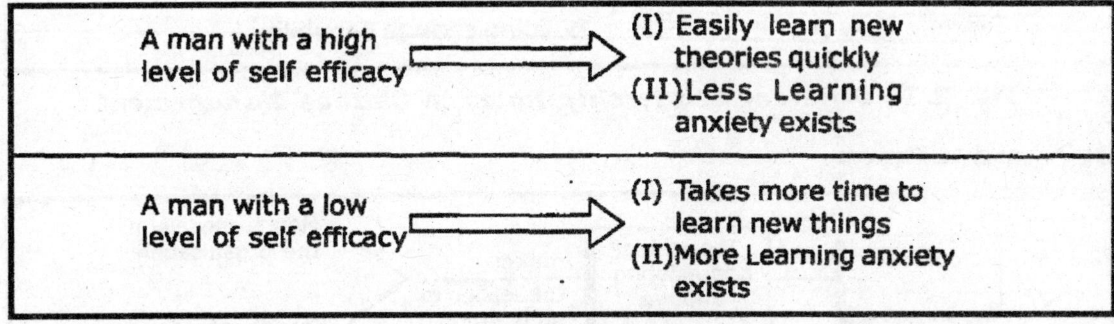

Fig. 2.54 Self Efficacy

A critical role for change managers as well as leaders is to devise ways of enhancing the self efficacy in their organisation.

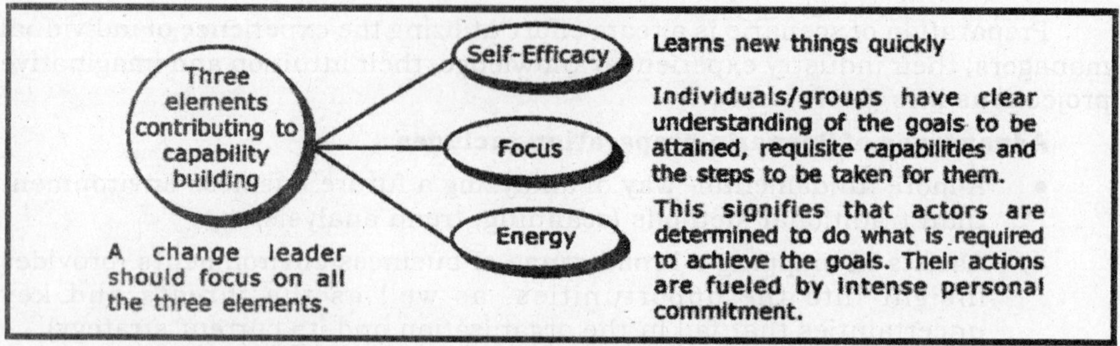

Fig. 2.55 Elements Contributing to Capacity Building

Aimless pursuit of learning has little value.

Most managers and organisations do not pay attention to the above three capability building critical tasks.

The importance of leadership in change management cannot be over-emphasized. Change programmers often fail because of lack of commitment and support from the top management. Credibile and visible leadership is needed in all the phases.

Leadership Roles needed in Change Management

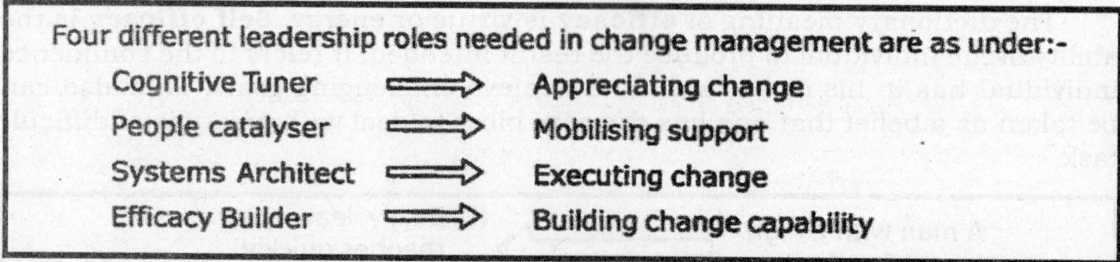

Fig. 2.56 Different Leadership Roles in Change Management

(i) Cognitive Tuner:

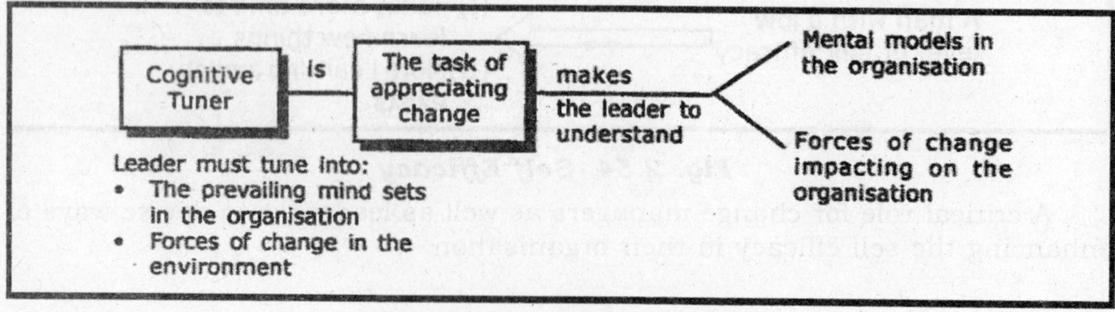

Fig. 2.57 Cognitive Tuner

Cognitive tuning means, it is a process undertaken with largely a process of reflection, analysis and thinking, occurring through the medium of dialogue and conversations. It is paying attention to mental models both inside and outside the organisaiton. It is not merely about understanding the need for change. The very act of it, initiates change in an organisation.

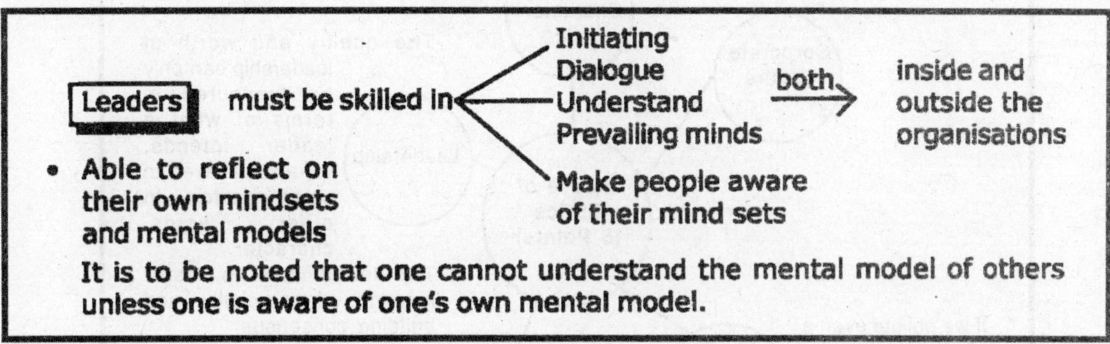

Fig. 2.58 Needed Leader Skills

(ii) People Catalyser

He has to mobile the support of people.

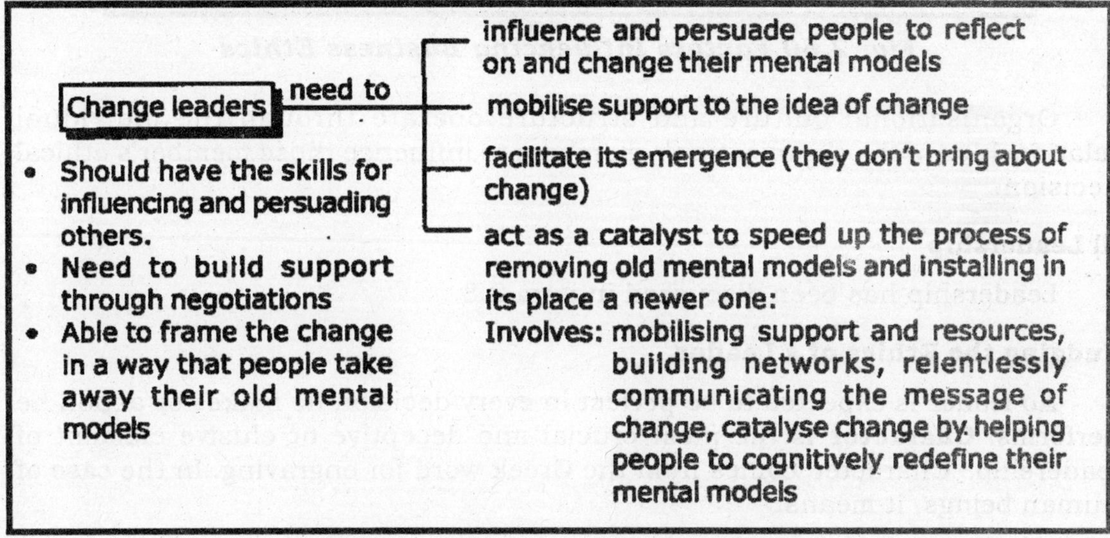

Fig. 2.59 Needs of Change Leaders

2.9 Structure and Business Ethics

Following are the factors which influence Business Ethics:

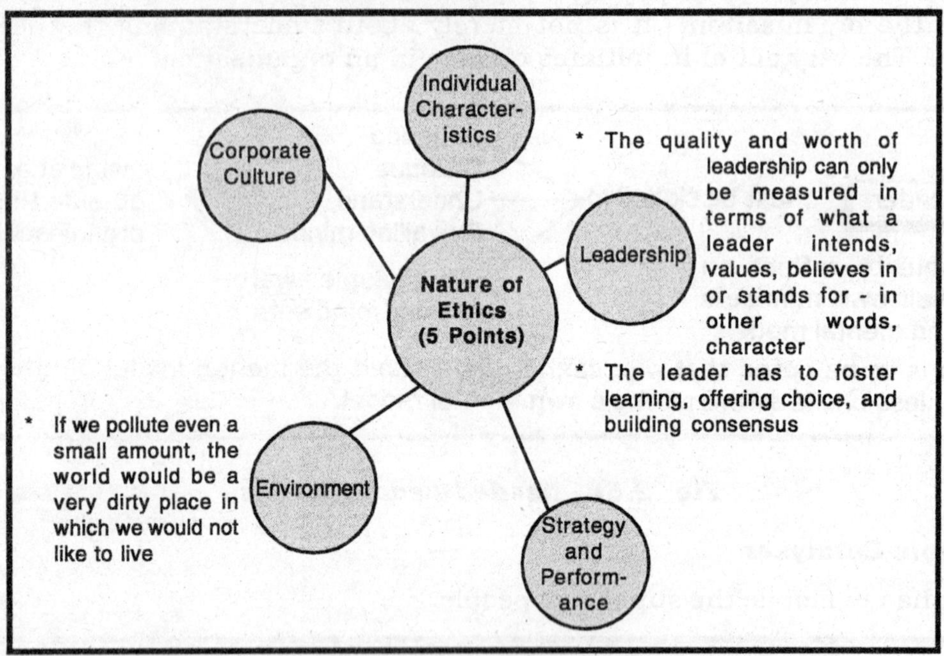

Fig. 2.60 Factors Influencing Business Ethics

Organisational culture and structure operate through the individual relationships of the organisation's members to influence those member's ethical decision.

(i) Leadership

Leadership has been discussed in para 2.8.

Judging the Ethics of a Leader

No leader is expected to be perfect in every decision he makes or action he performs. **Character** is the most crucial and deceptive or elusive element of leadership. 'Character' comes from the Greek word for engraving. In the case of human beings, it means:

- The enduring masks
- Etched-in factors in our personality.

which include our inborn talents, the learned and acquired traits imposed upon us by life and experience.

As per Gail Sheehy, character is fundamental and prophetic as expressed in his book 'America's Search for Leadership' New York, Bantam Books 1990, p.311) in regard to leadership and the issues of leadership are those of today and will change in line. Character is what was yesterday and will be tomorrow. It establishes both our day-to-day demeanor (conduct). It is not only useful but essential to examine the character of those who lead us. e.g. Watergate affair of the early 1970s of the links between character and leadership.

Leaders rule us, run things, wield power. Hence we must be careful whom we choose as leaders. Whom we choose is what we shall be. Heraclitus wrote "character is fate," the fate our leaders reap will also be our own.

Leaders good or bad, great or small, high or low, arise out of the needs and opportunities of a specific time and place. It may devise plans, establish an agenda, bring new and often radical changes to the table, but all of them are a response to the millieu and membership of which they are a part. The character, goals and aspirations of a leader are not developed in a vacuum leadership, even in the hands of a strong, confident, charismatic leader remains, at bottom, relational. Leaders require causes, issues and primarily, a hungry and wiling constituency.

Power is a Latin word derived from posse (to do, to change, to influence, to be able etc.). To have the power is to possess the capacity to control or direct change. The central issue of power in leadership is that whether it can be used wisely and well? **Leadership** assumes competition, conflict and debate where brute power denies it. 'Leadership mobilises' says Burns. Leaders must engage followers, not merely direct them. Leaders serve as models and mentors, not martinets (a strict disciplinarian). Novelist James Baldwin says 'Power without morality is no longer power.'

Teaching is one of the primary jobs of leadership as per Peter Senge in his "The fifth discipline" book. He said the primary tasks of leadership are:

- Leader as steward
- Leader as designer
- Leader as teacher.

Hewlett Packard's motto is the achievement of an organisation are the results of the combined efforts of an individual. A moral leader is someone who supposedly tells people the difference between right and wrong from on high. There is much more to moral leadership than merely telling others what to do.

The vision and value of leadership must have their origins and resolutions in the community of followers, of whom they are a part and whom they wish to serve. Leaders must drive, lead, orchestrate and cajole, but they cannot force, dictate or demand. Leaders may offer a vision, but followers must buy into it.

Abraham Zaleznick says that leadership is based on a compact that binds those that lead with those who follow in the same moral, intellectual and emotional commitment.

Leadership is hard to define and moral leadership is even harder. We only recognise moral leadership when we see it. It is mandatory that an organisation as a whole from top to bottom - make a commitment to ethical behaviour to actually achieve it, the model for that commitment has to originate from the top.

Strategy and Performance

In order to act with integrity, a firm must articulate its values, its priorities. The most prevalent form of values articulates and communication would occur is:

- **Corporate mission**
- **Code of conduct**
- **Code of ethics**

If the firm has defined its individual value structure, individual decision makers within the firm have guidance in connection with difficult dilemmas.

Codes may refer to general areas of business conduct or may apply to a specific area of the firm's business.

E.g. Reebok has human rights production standards in ensuring that the factories it uses have humane working conditions. Other strategies exist like (i) to communicate corporate values (ii) to continually update corporate programmes to work effectively. Some firms have used corporate ombud persons. An **ombudperson** is someone who is neither an advocate for the firm nor for an employee; Instead he administers a general reporting structure that holds fairness to all as an important goal.

Ethics officers association can also serve which allows representatives to continually explore developing issues that face the firm. Three types of strategies found in firms are:

(a) **Corporate strategy**

(b) **Business strategy**

(c) **Functional strategy.**

Strategy at the corporate level is termed as **corporate strategy**. Corporate level strategy represents the pattern of entrepreneurial actions and intents underlying the organisations strategic interests in different business, divisions, product lines, technologies, customer groups and customer needs.

Business Strategy is the managerial plan for directing and running a particular business unit. Such strategy defines the product market posture of its individual business units. Business strategy deals specifically with the issues of (i) how the organisation intends to compete in that specific business (ii) what the role/thrust of each key functional area will be in contributing to the success of the business in the market place (iii) how resources will be allocated within the business unit.

Like Corporate strategy, business strategy has also two aspects-external and internal.

Functional strategy is the plan to manage a principal subordinate activity within a business.

Improvement of Ethical Performance in Business

The quality of ethical performance can be improved in a business firm, if it wishes to do so, for which it needs the following:

- Top management attitudes.
- Opening up corporate culture to broad ethical standards.
- Organisational changes that help employees at all levels.
- Building ethical safeguards into the company.
  - – Codes of ethics
  - – Ethics committees
  - – Ethics training programs
  - – Ethics audits

Ethical business performance means 'adhering to society's basic rules that define right and wrong behaviour.'

Business meets:

- Public expectations.
- Prevents social harm.
- Protects itself from abuses by employees and other firms.
- Preserves the dignity and integrity of individuals who work in business.

Law and ethics are not identical. Ethical rules tend to be broader and more basic than laws, and general public wants business to act ethically as well as lawfully.

Corporate Culture

The corporate response to public demands for ethical behaviour and concern for the 'appearance of propriety' is the corporate reputation. The question is why do firms engage in ethical behaviour? May be profit motives. An ethical decision does not always lead to the highest profits possible. Perhaps the firm engages in ethical decision making because 'it is the right thing to do' as per Sears Roebuck and Co. Engaging in ethical behaviour, implementing ethics programs or instituting codes of conduct all contribute both to the internal culture of the firm as well as to the external stakeholders perception of the firm.

Environment

Every human being is concerned about the environment. It is as early as in 1960s, warmings came in the form of burning rivers, dying lakes and oil fouled oceans. Our food is contaminated with radioactivity, mother's milk with DDT traces, water we drink contains lead and mercury. Our breath of air is highly contaminated. Many says these are warmings from planet earth of eco-catastrophe, unless we could find limits to our growth and changes in our life style. Our Planet Earth is more loudly reminding us than before about all such mishappenings and we began to listen more than before.

2.10 Interpersonal Relationships in Organisation

The life inside the organisations are of varied types. Organisational life touches on many of the most problematic characteristics of business organisations:

- The alienation experienced by workers doing repetitive work.
- The feelings of oppression created by the exercise of authority.
- The responsibilities heaped on the shoulders of managers.
- The power tactics employed by managers who are anxious to advance their career ambitions.
- The pressures felt by subordinates and superiors as they both try to get their jobs done.

Some other problems which could be added are:

- Health problems created by unsafe working conditions.
- Conflicts of interest created by an employee's allegiance to other causes.
- The absence of due process (complex system intended to ascertain whether the conduct of employees was really such as to merit dismissal or some other penalty-penalising an employee on the basis of flimsy or incomplete evidence is rightly considered as injustice) for non-unionised employees.
- Invasion of privacy by a management's legitimate concern to know its own worker.

The traditional model of the organisation can be divided into 3 parts as shown under. Only part I is explained.

First main part describing:

- The traditional model of the organisation, the organisation as a rational structure.
- Employee's duties to the firm as defined by the above model.
- Employer's duties to employee as defined by the above model.

Second main part describing:

- A more recent view of the organisation.
- The organisation as a 'political' structure.

The ethical issues raised here are (i) Political analysis of the firm, (ii) Employee rights and organisational politics.

Third main part discusses:

- New view of the organisation.
- The organisation as a network of personal relations focussed on caring.

We have covered in this chapter only part I of figure 2.60.

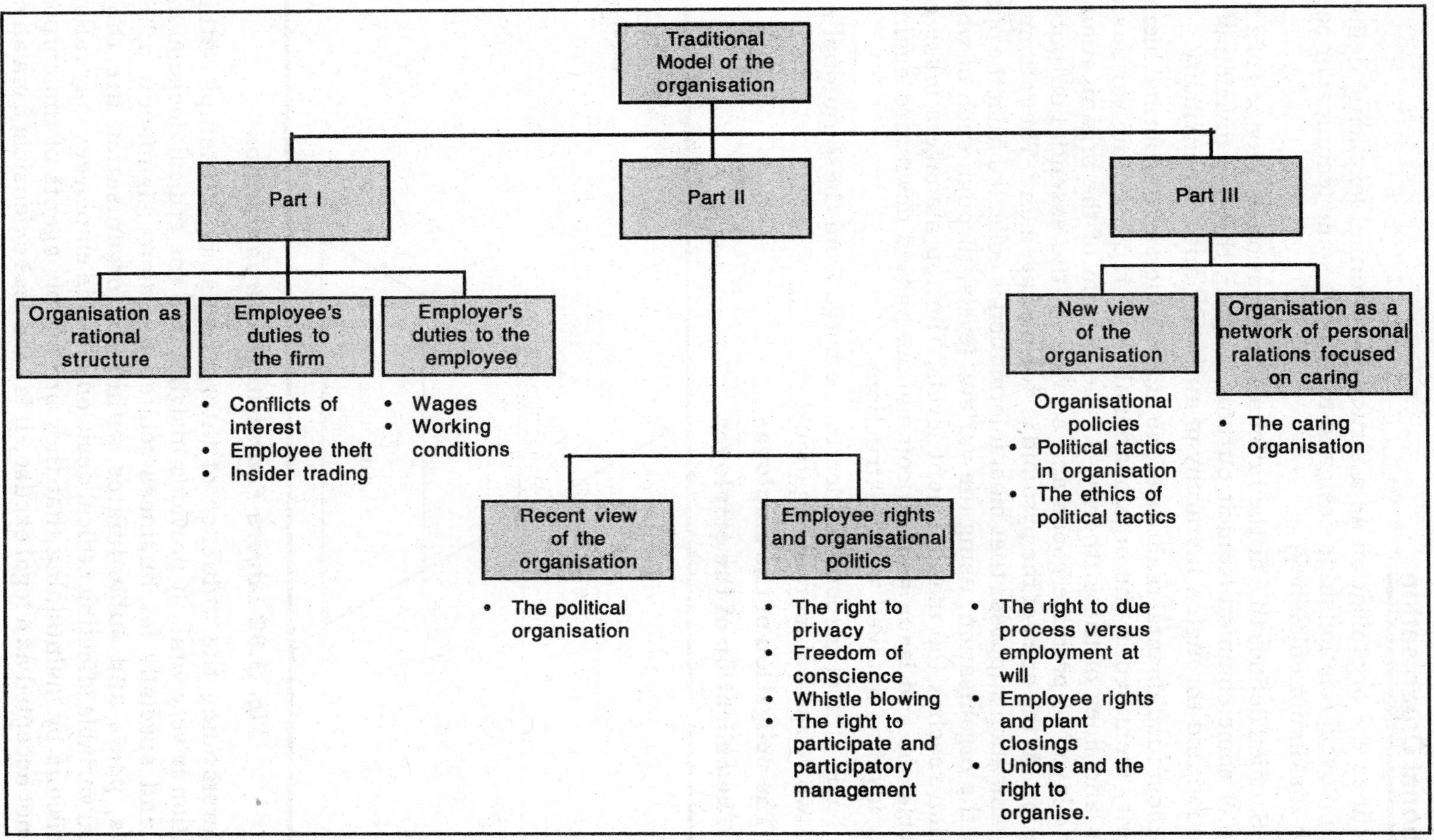

Fig. 2.61 Traditional Model of the Organisation

The Rational Organisation

It defines the organisation as a structure of formal (explicitly defined and openly employed) relationships designed to achieve some technical or economic goal with maximum efficiency.

E.H.Sachien defines this as the rational coordination of activities of a number of people of some common explicit purpose or goal, through division of labour and function and through a hierarchy of authority and responsibility.

The most fundamental realities of the organisation are the formal hierarchies of authority identified in the organisational chart representing various official positions and lines of the authority. At the bottom of the organisation is the 'operating layer' to produce goods and services – the essential outputs of the organisation. At the apex of the pyramid is 'top management'. The rational model of the organisation supposes that most information is collected from the operating layers of the organisation, using the various levels, through each of which the information reaches top management levels. The top managers make general policy decisions and issue general commands, passed downward again to the operating layer as detailed work instructions.

The basic ethical responsibilities that emerge from these rational aspects focus on two reciprocal moral obligations:

- **The obligation of the employee.**
- **The obligation of the employer.**

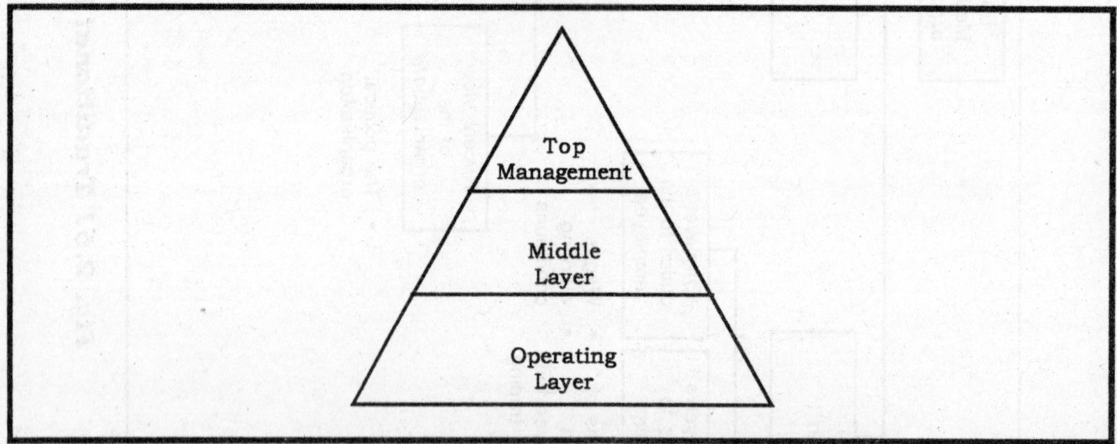

Fig. 2.62 Layers Found in the Organisation

Understanding the influence of interpersonal relationships within the organisation is very vital. It provides insights into the ethical decision making process and specially for business-related decisions significant other like superiors, peers and subordinates within the organisation are the most influential variable affecting ethical decisions. Some employees may rationalise their decisions by maintaining that they are supply agents of the corporation which is not accepted as a legal excuse. It is even less defensible from an ethical perspective.

2.11 The Role of Opportunity and Conflict

Employees main moral duty is to work:

- Towards the goal of the firm.
- To avoid any activities which might cause harm to those goals.
- To obey organisational superiors.

To be unethical, basically is to deviate from the above in order to serve one's own interests in ways that, if illegal, are counted as a form of **'white collar crime'**.

Conflicts of Interest

Conflicts of interest in business arise when an employee or officer of a company is engaged in carrying out a task on behalf of the company and the employee has private interest in the outcome of the task.

- Possibly antagonistic to the best interests of the company.
- Substantial enough that it does or reasonably might affect.
- The independent judgement the company expects the employee to exercise on its behalf.

Conflicts of interest need not be financial. It can also arise when officers or employees of company hold another job or consulting position in an outside firm with which their own company deals or competes with. It may be actual or potential. Conflicts of interest can be created by a variety of different kinds of situations and activities. Two kinds of situations and activities demand further attention:

- Bribes
- Gifts

A **commercial bribe** is a consideration given or offered to an employee by a person outside the firm with the understanding that when the employee transacts business for his own firm, the employee will deal favourably with that person or with that person's firm. The consideration may consist of money, tangible goods, the 'kickback' as part of an official payment, preferential payment, or any other kind of benefit. Accepting gifts may or may not be ethical. The purchasing agent for example, who accepts gifts from the sales person with whom he or she deals without asking for the gifts and without making said gifts a condition of doing business with them, may be doing nothing unethical. The employee of a firm has a contractual agreement to accept only certain specified benefits in exchange for his labour and to use the resources and goods of the firm in pursuit only of the legitimate aims of the firm.

Employee theft is often petty involving the theft of small tools, office supplies or clothing. It occurs at the managerial level through:

- Padding of expense accounts
- White collar crime (embezzlement, larceny, fraud in the handling of trusts, or receiverships, and forgery)

Enbezzlement is the fradulent approapriation of anothers properity by the person to whom it was entrusted.

Larceny is the legal term in England and Ireland for stealing; theft.

The ethics of these forms of theft are not clear. Modern kinds of theft are thefts of various forms of information.

The ethics of using a computer to gain entry into a company's data bank for copying company's computer programs.

Trade secrets: 'Proprietary information' or 'trade secrets' consist of nonpublic information concerning:

- Company's own activities, technologies, future plans, policies or records, if known by competitors affect the company's ability to compete.
- Owned by the company might not be patented or copyrighted since it was developed by the company for its private use from resources it owns or purchased for its private use with its own funds.
- The company indicates through explicit directives through security measures or through contractual agreements with employees that it does not want anyone outside the company to have that information.

Firm's Duties to the Employee

The basic moral obligation of the employer to the employees according to the rational view of the firm is to:

- Provide them with the compensation they have freely and knowingly agreed to receive in exchange for their services.

Two main issues related to this obligation are:

– The fairness of wages

– The fairness of employee working conditions.

Working conditions inadequacy, inadequate wages will make the work contract unfair.

Under working conditions, two major things are:

- Job satisfaction (job specialisation is essential at all levels. Jobs must be expended in five dimensions: Skill variety, Task identity, Task significance, Autonomy, Feedback)
- Health and safety (Job accidents are due to work place hazards and hazardous occupations, safety programs are to be implemented).

Ethical opportunity results from conditions that either provide rewards, whether internal or external, or limit barriers to ethical or unethical behaviour. It includes a person's immediate job context. This includes the motivational techniques, superiors use to influence employee behaviour. The opportunity employees have for unethical behaviour in an organisation can be eliminated through formal codes, policies, and rules that are adequately enforced by management. To control opportunities for unethical decisions, most companies have developed formal corporate governance systems of:

— accountability
— overnight
— control of organisational decisions and resources.

Ethical dilemmas pertaining to problem solving situations in which decision rules are often vague or in conflict. There is no substitute for the employee's own critical thinking and ability to accept responsibility for their decision.

Ethical Conflict and Ethical Congruence

Theophane A Mathais characterises the above motivation in an interesting way. These are the motivation behind **"feeding the hog"** and being the **"silent saboteurs"** as various forms of ethical conflict. This is the term used for the condition where the values of the organisation, the values of the employees and the perceived criteria of success are misaligned. This misalignment results in employees believing. They must protect themselves from the organisation and/ or gives them the reason to believe it, is appropriate to strike back at the organisation.

THEN he would, by the classical system defined above, be 'immoral'.

THOUGH his motive, his end, foreseeable consequences were good.

DECLARED his means involved are 'immoral/illegal act'.

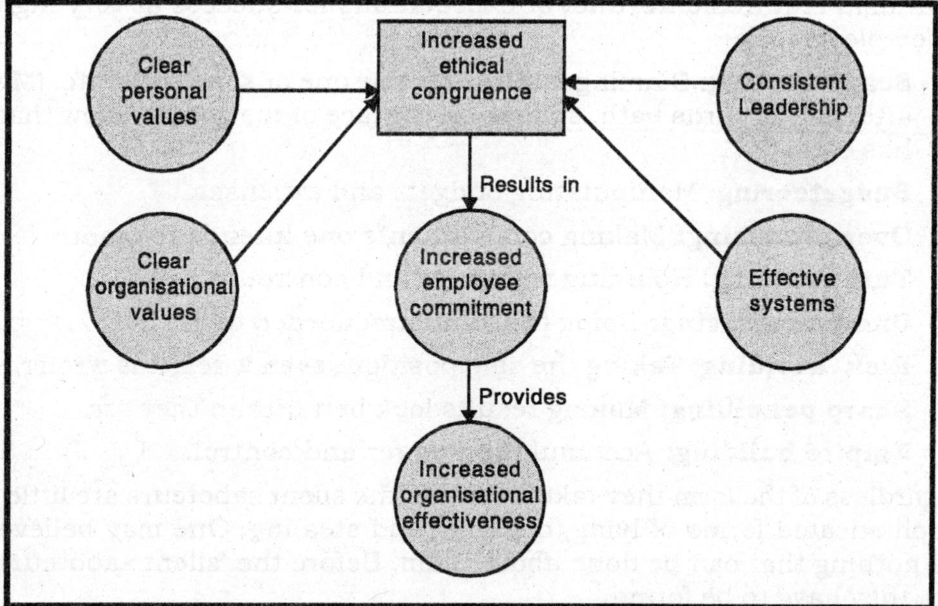

Fig. 2.63 Steps to achieve Increased Organisational Effectiveness

The organisational state where values, behaviours and perceptions are aligned is called '**Ethical congruence**'.

In Tangible systems of ethical, conflict: Symptoms are there during discussions about lying, cheating and stealing.

When we talk about finding and fixing ethical conflict, we are discussing ways to increase total ethical congruence. That means we reduce indirect tangible and intangible costs as well. **Congruence** in dictionary term is agreeing or conceding exactly when super imposed.

'**Feeding the hog**' is a retaliatory response; '**Salient saboteurs**' is a defensive response. **Feeding the hog** is a unique way of punishing their employees for perceived wrongs. It is one of the two most powerful drives that cause good people to do bad things. It is how people strike back when they believe the organisation is being unfair. People in all fields and at all levels feed the hog. This name has come from a sick lumber company. A consultant invited and found from one of the employees, than when the later frustrated or angry at the employer used to feed the hog (hog was a big mechanical wood chipper on the back of the plant to feed all unusable scrap) out of frustration. But this employee was using finished lumber and feeding the hog.

Another intentional, counter productive behaviour of employees is '**Silent saboteurs**', 'Silent because nobody talks about them and 'saboteurs' because they undermine the organisations business plans, creating failures, ... eating at its effectiveness from the inside like a cancer. Often they are clever, but never funny. this is self preservation. The common practices which individuals employ to meet organisational requirements/and/or expectations for success at very high cost to their employers are:

- **Scape goating:** Blaming failure on some one or something etc. (Monkey after eating curds bath, smears on the face of the goat to show that goat has eaten).
- **Budgeteering:** Manipulating budgets and expenses.
- **Over promising:** Making commitments one intends to ignore.
- **Turf guarding:** Hoarding resources and control.
- **Under archieving:** Doing the minimum needed to get by.
- **Risk avoiding:** Taking the safe position, even when it is wrong.
- **Sharp pencilling:** Making results look better than they are.
- **Empire building:** Accumulating power and control.

Regardless of the form they take as above, the silent saboteurs are little more than sophisticated forms of lying, cheating and stealing. One may believe that there is nothing that can be done about them. Before the 'silent saboteurs' can be fixed, they have to be found.

Employees in organisations often feel compelled to engage themselves as above in counter - productive and unethical actions as the result of conflict between their perceptions of the organisations requirements, expectations, or actions, and their (the employees) personal values. These employee behaviours are often ignored by management because of the belief that nothing can be done to prevent them. But they are dangerous.

Employees in every segment of business, industry and government have developed their own unique responses to these ethical conflicts. Those responses negatively impact, both, the organisation effectiveness and the employees' satisfaction.

Conflict occurs when employees think they know the right course of action, yet their work group or company requires or promotes unethical decisions. Here they may participate out of unwillingness or even go outside the organisation to publicise and correct a harmful situation. **Whistle blowing** involves exposing an employer's wrong doing to outsiders, such as the media or government regulatory agencies.

A company if it pursues goals or uses methods that are not acceptable to some of its employees will create ethical conflicts in business. **Whistle blowing** would be the outcome if an employee goes public with a complaint which results after he fails to convince the company to correct the alleged abuse.

Both opportunity and conflict affect ethical decision making in interpersonal relations. **Opportunity** is a set of conditions that limit unfavourable behaviour or reward favourable behaviour which are internal or external.

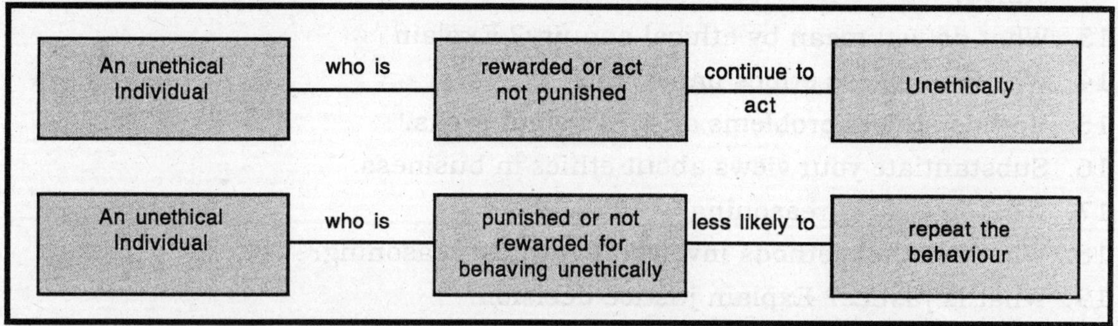

Fig. 2.64 Behaviour of an Unethical Individual

Conflict occurs when there is a question as to which goals or values take precedence in a situation (individual, organisation or society) persons with certain values not coinciding with the same values of others may fight or leave the organisation. Personal-societal conflict develops when an individuals values differ from those of society. When society feels that a particular activity is unethical and legal, new laws may be enacted to help redefine the minimum level of ethical behaviour e.g., marketing of new products may bring business into conflict with society, when those products rack moral issues for certain groups.

Questions

1. Explain the role of moral philosophies in decision making.
2. Mention a few suggestions for ethical decision making. Explain them.
3. Mention the ethical issues that arise for managers.
4. In spite of the positive benefits of good ethical practices, ethical problems do occur in business. Give reasons.
5. What are the arguments for and against business ethics?
6. Mention three objections of bringing ethics into business.
7. What are your arguments in bringing ethics into business?
8. Do you think that new technologies will bring in host of ethical issues? If so, explain with examples.
9. Explain the relationship between business ethics and technology.
10. Explain code of ethics in regard to individual, corporate, industry and professional classification.
11. In what way the ethical theories are divided into different categories? Discuss each one of them.
12. What is business ethics? What are the moral issues concerned with business ethics?
13. What do you mean by ethical enquiry? Explain.
14. Why is business ethics important?
15. How do ethical problems arise? In what areas?
16. Substantiate your views about ethics in business.
17. What is ethical reasoning?
18. What are the methods involved in ethical reasoning?
19. What is justice? Explain justice decision.
20. What are individual rights involved in ethical decisions?
21. What do you mean by utilitarianism?
22. Discuss the analytical approach involved in ethical problems.
23. What is meant by ethical relativism?
24. How are ethical decisions made?
25. Explain ethical conflict and ethical congruence.
26. What are the steps involved to achieve increased organisational effectiveness?
27. Explain the terms:
    - Scape goating
    - Turf guarding

- Sharp pencilling
- Budgeteering
- Under archieving
- Empire building
- Over promising
- Risk avoiding

28. What do you mean by:
    - Feeding the hog
    - Silent saboteurs.
29. Mention how the ethical theories are broadly divided? Explain each one of them.
30. Explain how analytical approach to ethical problems are undertaken?
31. Explain Teleological theory briefly. What are its strengths and weaknesses?
32. What do you mean by classical utilitarianism? Explain its principles.
33. Explain the principle behind Jeremy Bentham's version of utilitarianism.
34. Explain the principle behind John Stuart Mill's version of utilitarianism.
35. 'An action is right if and only it produces the greatest balance of pleasure or pain for every one'. What is the type of utilitarianism involved here? Examine the various points considered here?
36. Mention the two versions of utilitarianism.
37. Explain the Benthams Precise quantitative method for decision making with a sketch.
38. Compare and contrast cost effective analysis and cost benefit analysis.
39. Explain Deontological theory briefly. Compare its strengths and weaknesses.
40. Compare Deontology with utilitarianism.
41. Explain the actions resulting in happiness or unhappiness.
42. Explain the greatest happiness principle? What are the modifications done to it?
43. Explain the positive and negative rights of basic human rights.
44. What do you mean by Kantianism? Explain Kant's universalism and categorical imperative.
45. Compare and contrast Kantianism with Utilitarianism.
46. List down the ten commandments briefly.
47. Write down the employer-employee relationships in ethics.
48. Explain virtue Ethics or Aristotle's Nicomachien Ethics?
49. Explain the virtue ethics theory and virtue ethics in business. What are its strengths and weaknesses?

50. Explain Cognitivism.
51. Explain Non-cognitivism.
52. Compare and contrast cognitivism with non-cognitivism.
53. Define utilitarianism. Explain.
54. What do you understand by Ethical Hedonism?
55. Discuss on Benthamite Utilitarianism.
56. Explain greatest happiness principle.
57. What do different religions say about the ethicality of business?
58. What do religions have a bearing on business?
59. Compare and contrast Kantianism and Utilitarianism.
60. What is Kantianism and what are its principles?
61. What do different religions say about the ethicality of business?
62. What are the benefits and limitations of a written code of corporate ethics?
63. Define code of ethics, explain.
64. Explain the meaning of ethics in business.
65. Explain how business can improve its ethical performance?
66. What is the responsibility of an individual who believes that the strategy of his organisation is unethical? Should the individual report on the organisation or should he leave the employment of the company on the ground of a mismatch of values?
67. What are the differences between consequential, deontological and relativistic ethical systems? If you had to combine these systems, how would you do it?
68. It has been persuasively argued that, by and large, government should not place major restrictions on the activities of corporations in capitalistic societies. The use of voluntary industry codes of conduct are sufficient to handle any problems that might occur. What are your reactions on this argument?
69. Compare and contrast consequential, deontological and relativistic ethical systems?
70. Explain Kant's universalim.
71. Explain categorical inperatives.
72. Define justice. What are the different types of justices. Explain each one of them.
73. What is fair value? Explain.
74. Discuss the theory of Due care.
75. Which are the theories of product liability? Explain each one of them.

76. Discuss on the integration of the various perspectives.
77. Explain cognitive moral development with the help of a model.
78. Discuss on the Kohlberg's moral development model with a sketch indicating the stages involved. What do you conclude from this model?
79. What are the six stages in the development of a person's ability to deal with moral issues? Explain and compare them.
80. How did Gilligan differed from Kohlenberg and what are the common points between them?
81. Explain a stake holder model with a sketch.
82. Explain the input-output model with a sketch.
83. What is the role of corporate culture in ethical decision making?
84. How is corporate culture is classified.
85. In general, explain how the ethics work in an organisation?
86. What is a traditional model of the organisation? What are its constituents?
87. Explain organisation as a rational structure.
88. Explain all aspects about employee's duties to the firm.
89. What do you mean by conflicts of interest? Explain.
90. What is insider trading? What are the unethical aspects involved in insider trading?
91. Do you find insider trading ethical? Justify.
92. What are the employer's obligations to an employee?
93. Explain the political organisation.
94. What are the employee rights and organisational policies in an organisation?
95. What do you mean by organisational politics?
96. 'Organisation is a network of personal relations.' Give your views.
97. Define conflict. When does this occur?
98. What is whistle blowing? Explain.
99. Explain the factors influencing business ethics.
100. What do you mean by corporate culture?
101. Discuss on leadership citing your own examples whenever possible.
102. Discuss on the interpersonal relationships in an organisation.
103. What is conflicts of interest? Mention its types. How do you manage conflicts of interest in an organisation?

❖❖❖

MODULE
3

External Context Ecology

3.1 The Dimensions of Pollution and Resource Depletion

Definition of environmental study

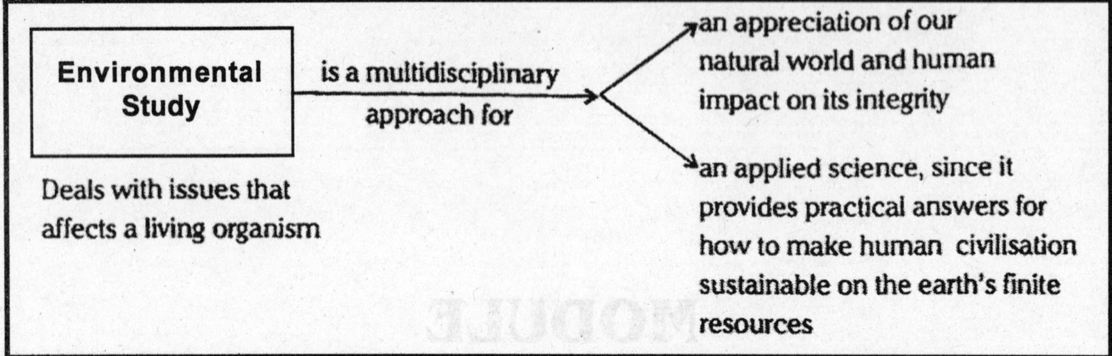

Fig. 3.1 Environmental Studies as a Multi-disciplinary Approach

The **Components of environmental study** are the following:

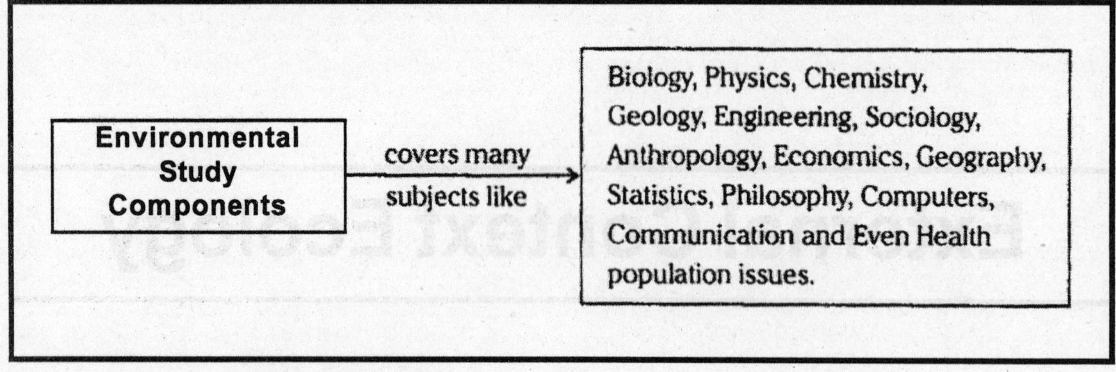

Fig. 3.2 Coverage of Environment Study

Scope of environmental study

Let us look at the place where we live. When man first started living, he had originally God gift landscape such as:

- Rivers and seas
- Rocks and mountains
- Forests covered with dense trees, shrubs etc.
- Deserts where heaps of sands found
- A combination of several things as mentioned above.

As years passed, human beings modified some of these landscapes to his/her convenience and for his/her comfort. They built houses, and lived along with other people forming villages, towns and cities. Now we find modern cities. These cities get food from villages. Rice, wheat, corns, vegetables, fruits etc. are all supplied from nearby villages to towns and cities which again in turn depend on natural landscape such as forests, grasslands, rivers, seas for resources such as water for agriculture, fishing, fuel wood, fodder and fish. So our daily activities are all associated with the environment where we are living and they are also affected by us.

The above explanation shows that human beings have to depend on nature so much that if they do not protect the environmental resources available on the earth, they are bound to suffer and cannot continue to live. For these reasons, humans treat the environment as 'Mother Nature' and respect it to a great extent in order to protect their own livelihoods. This has resulted in several cultural practices that have helped traditional societies to protect and preserve natural resources in every part of the world. It is also true that traditions are based on such values.

Technology is changing very fast in the modern days. In several millions of man's existence, he could only bring fire and gun in the 1st 2 million years. But in the last 200 years, man in the hunt of producing more resources have moved into the vast application of technological innovations. An example in this direction could be given with the help of a clock metaphor:

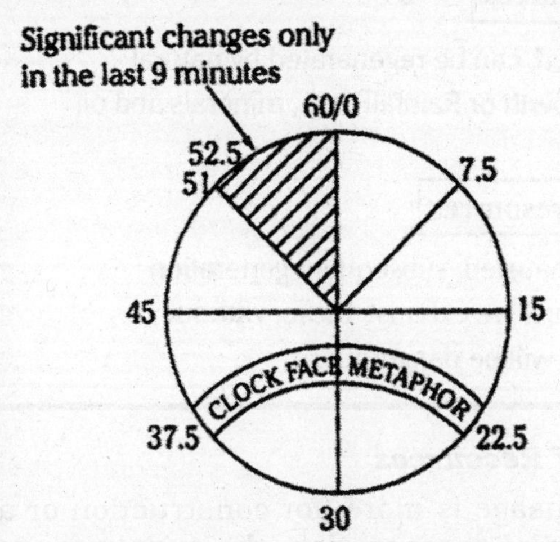

Imagine a clock face and 60 minutes on it. Imagine each minute on clock as 50 years (1 minute = 50 years) The clock now represents, 60 × 50 years = 3000 years.

Any area of life on the above clock face can be placed and get roughly the same measurements.

- 51-60 minutes (Last 9 minutes ago) significant media changes have taken place. The printing press came into use in western culture.
- Above 3 minutes ago, (57-60 minutes on the clock) the telegraph, photograph, locomotive arrived. (150 years back)
- About two minutes ago, telephone, rotary press, motion pictures, automobile and radio arrived. (100 years back)
- About one minute ago, the talking picture, one and half minutes ago computers. (50-75 years back)
- Televisions appeared in last one minute. (50 years back)
- Communications satellites in the last 18 seconds.
- The laser beam-perhaps the most patent medium of communication of all appeared only a fraction of a second ago

Fig.3.3 Clock - Face Metaphor

At '0' minute on the clock (3000 years ago i.e., 1000 B.C.), there were no scientific/technology development. Agriculture was the only predominant activity of man. It is only7 in the last 9 minutes, significant changes have taken place in science and technology.

As shown in figure 3.2, **the scope of environmental studies is wide and covers many topics.** In the recent days man has increased the growth of varieties of food with the help of fertilisers and pesticides. He has developed fishing and rearing of animals in a better way for the production of meat. He has irrigated farmland by constructing megadams to rivers, which otherwise would have flowed into the ocean as a waste, developed industries for varieties of products to meet the people's needs. Though all these helped for man's development on one side but these have inevitably led to environmental degradation. We have observed the customer-oriented society. By doing so, we have used up large amount of natural resources like water, minerals, petroleum products, wood etc.

The **resources** can be grouped as under:

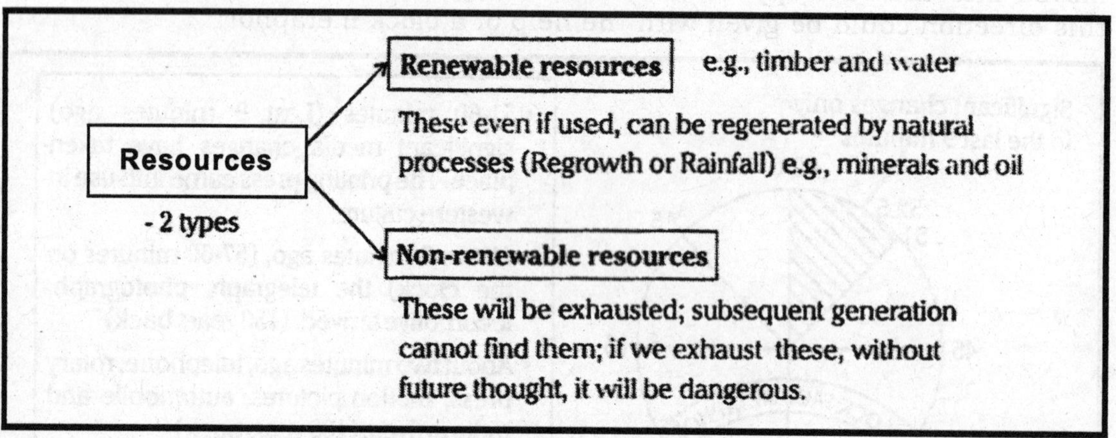

Fig.3.4 Types of Resources

However in the case of timber, if the usage is more (for construction or as firewood from a forest) than the regrowth and regeneration, the supply cannot be replenished. Deforestation leads to floods in the monsoon and dry rivers, once the rains are over. Natural resource is something like money in our bank. Only if the interest is used for our expenses, then the money will be intact.

It has to be well understood by everyone who uses resource that these are required in the future also in the long term. Hence the multiple effects on the environment resulting from routine human activities are to be well thought of. It should not go as a waste. Unsustainable utilisation results from overuse of resources:

- may be with population increase
- improper use of resources (using more than needed)

- wasteful behaviour patterns (without thinking of future about environmental impacts)

Hence everyone of us should be concerned about our environmental assets and change our ways of wastage if any.

Think Tank 1

- Value of the resource we are using.
- Source of resource.
- Who uses this resource? How expensive is it?
- Is this usage an improper one?
- Who is responsible for improper usage?
- How we could help in conserving this?
- Prevention for unsustainable use.
- Methodology adopted to reduce, reuse and recycle.
- Are you the person who is more fortunate in using it more? Who uses less? i.e., unequal distribution.

Ask series of questions and change your lifestyle to live and to become more sustainable in order to support our environment.

Importance of environmental study

The coverage of environmental study has been shown in figure 3.2. As already said, environmental managements cover wide topics and most of the disciplines.

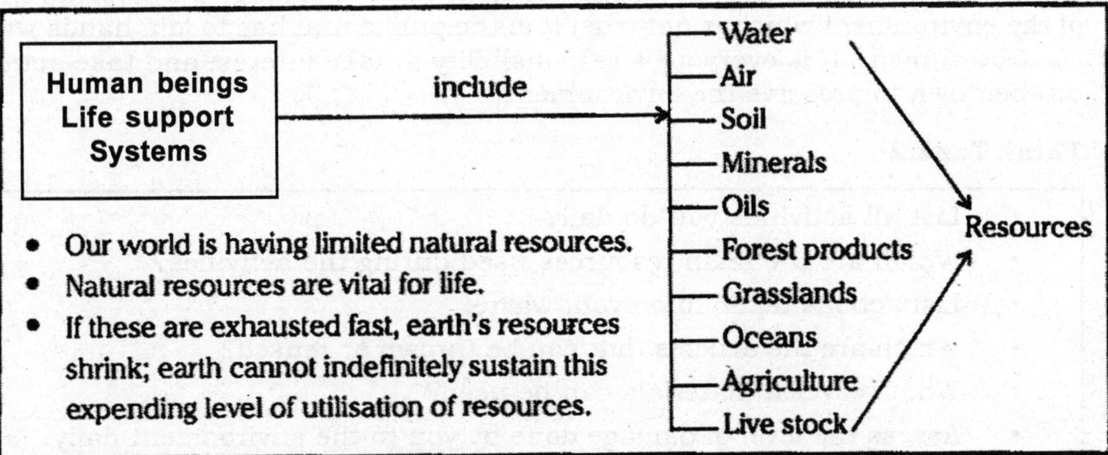

Fig.3.5 Life Support Systems of Human beings

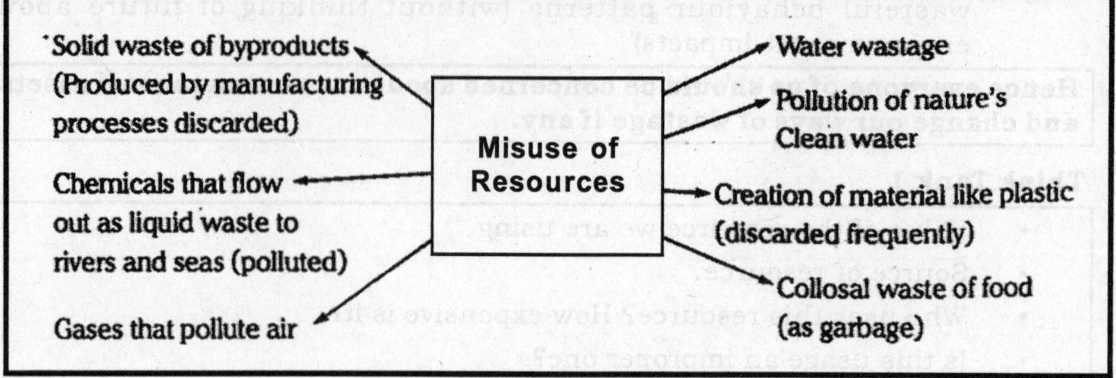

Fig.3.6 Misuse of Resources

Increasing amounts of waste cannot be managed by natural processes.

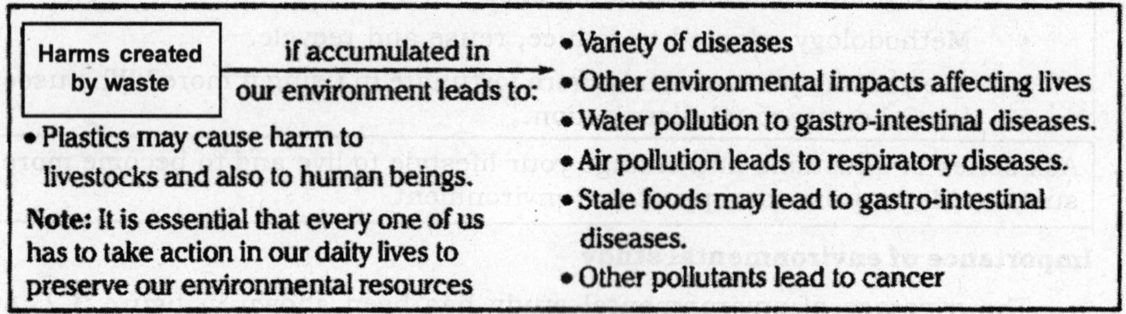

Fig.3.7 Harms Created by Waste

Everyone expects that Governments alone have to manage the safeguarding of the environment which is not true. It is the public that has to join hands with the Government. It is everyone's responsibility to take interest and take action on their own to preserve the environment.

Think Tank 2

- List all activities you do daily.
- Which are the main resources used during the activities?
- List actions taken to prevent waste.
- Which are the articles that can be thrown or reused?
- What recycled materials can be used?
- Assess the level of damage done by you to the environment daily.
- Overall assessment of the damage done by you in the year.
- Analyse items like all plastic items (bags, pens etc.), fossil fuels (petrol, diesel, natural gas)
- How much water you waste everyday (during brushing, toilet, washing clothes, washing scooter/car etc.)?

- Analyse source of water and finally where it leads to?
- Any improvements you can adopt in your ways to use water?
- Food source, chemicals used, transportation, cooking methods, daily wastage, how wastage disposed?
- How much energy you use daily? Source, wastage done everyday. How can you conserve energy?
- How paper is made? Source, how manufactured, how much you use daily? How much wasted? How to prevent this wastage?

Multidisciplinary nature of environmental studies.

The value of nature

This can be studied in three types:

- Productive value of nature
- Aesthetic/recreational value of nature
- Option value of nature.

(i) Productive value of nature: Scientists do extensive research and make new advances in fields like biotechnology.

- World's species contain an incredible and varieties of complex chemicals which can be acted for developing new medicines and industrial products. These can be further used to develop innumerable number of new products in the future.
- For the development of man, flowering plants and insects are important (most species are of rich groups of living organisms); If we degrade and destroy their very existence, these3 species will be destroyed. **Man is only a destroyer of species, but he cannot create them.** Valuable resources, if man starts destroying them, they cannot be created by him. Future generations cannot have the advantages of such valuable resources.
- Following points need urgent attention of everyone:

— Protect all living species; everyone should understand that the world is not for only human existence. Every creature should exist. This concept would help every living species to support each other. Human being intellectual, cannot prevent the extinction of certain species. We have to protect the national parks and wild sanctuaries, where the wild species live. This is an important aspect of a sustainable living.

— Agriculture and Forest should have a close link. If crops are to be successful, the flowers of trees and plants must be pollinated by insects and birds. These need forests.

(ii) Aesthetic (Recreational value of nature): These values of nature enliven human's existence on earth. National parks and wild life sanctuaries, if created at ideal places provide recreational value. The beauty of nature is so great and is enjoyable by every human. It encompasses every aspect of the living and nonliving part of our earth. Everyone is thrilled by seeing a huge mountain, the powerful waves of the sea, the giant trees in a forest and the vast expanse of the desert filled with sand everywhere. The incredible diversity of plant and animal life that has brought into the development of several philosophies of life. On these, several thesies have been worked out. Lot of artists, writers and poets work on these to vitalise their as well as our lives.

Exceptional recreational values can be experienced by seeing nature or hearing the nature's sound or even tasting some of the products during our nature tourism/wildlife tourism/ecotourism. This can also be considered as an aspect of adventure tourism. The recreational facilities offer:

- Pleasurable experience
- Respect for love and nature
- Serve as key tools in educating people (on fagility of the environment and the need for sustainable life styles).

In urban areas, it may be difficult to create certain wilderness experience.

However following can be created as they are vital to the psychological and physical health of urban dwellers.

— Green spaces like parks, gardens.

— Even in tall buildings, some facilities can be created for plants, trees and birds.

— Zoological parks and aquariums.

— Zoos, Museums.

— Botanical garden.

The above helps young children to know more about the nature and to love wild life. In future days, they would become conservationists.

In small places like district, taluk levels, the small nature aware can be created by developing:

— mimic-small-scale natural ecosystems, which are helpful for the people for instituting conservation, education and awareness. These things can be developed in a small wood lot, a patch of grass-land, a pond ecosystem or situated along an undisturbed river or coastal area.

(iii) The option value of nature:

Option Value —is→ How we utilise nature's goods and services?

- One can use goods indiscriminately and waste a lot and destroy its integrity and long-term values.

  OR

- One can use its resources sustainably and reduce our impact on the environment and preserve its goods/services for the future.

The second is preferable in the interest of all considering the future generation.

Nature has given us several goods and services. These, we use recklessly and enjoy its benefits. We do not think properly about its availability in the future. Every activity that we do in our daily lives has an adverse impact on nature's integrity. If we go on using all these resources in an unlimited way, we find the following effects:

- We kill all species of plants and animals. Finally, they will become extint on earth.
- Pollute air, water.
- Degrade land.
- Create enormous quantities of waste.
- Finally leave nothing for future generations.

Our present generation has developed its economies and life styles on unsustainable patterns of life.

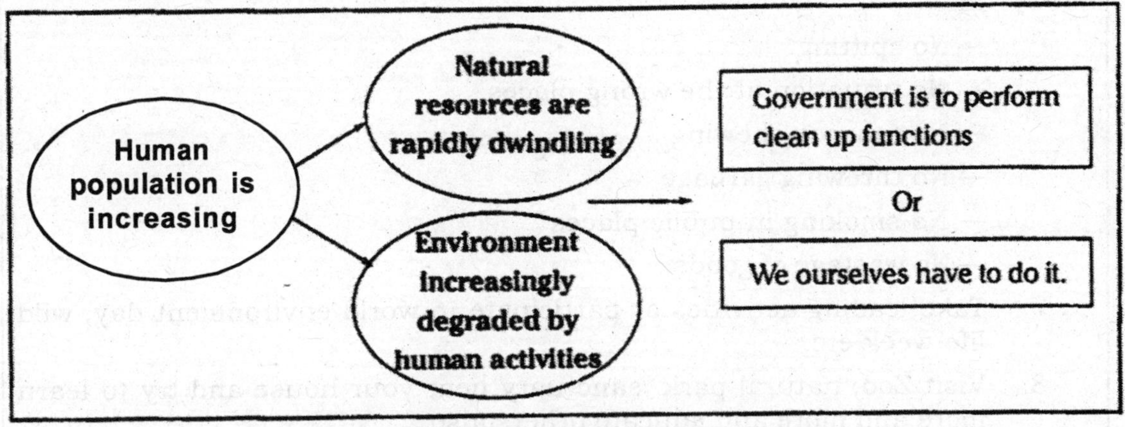

Fig. 3.8 Need for Public Awareness

As individuals, people have to take a major part in the prevention of environmental degradation.

This should come as a part of our life. Prevention is better than cure. We cannot clean up or rebuild the environment once it is damaged. We can contribute more and inform the Government wherever the damage is taking place (the source that lead to pollution and degradation of the environment). In order to do this, **public awareness** is essential. News papers, magazines, radio, television, educate people which would influence public opinion. Press and media will add to the peoples efforts. It is the responsibility of politicians to consider seriously about the complaints made by public to act immediately. People have to join together and influence politicians to bring about green policies. Earth has a limited supply of resources. It should not be destroyed and it is to be conserved. This message has to be spread to each and everyone.

Think Tank 3

1. Read Newspaper articles, technical magazines on environment and natural resources available to you and learn more on the subject - You can also visit websites and learn more about current topics on the natural resources.
2. Join a group if any, nearby to your place on this subject and exchange your views along with your group and share your views with other groups.
3. Discuss matter with friends and relatives. Educate others who are not aware of such conservations.
4. Learn the principles of 3 R_S; Reduce, Reuse, Recycle and finally waste disposal; save paper, water, electricity; Reduce use of plastics.
5. Support local activities in saving trees, waste recycling etc. Know the usage of environmentally-friendly products.
6. Practice and introduce good hygienic activities in your living area like:

   — No spitting

   — No urination at the wrong places

   — No tobacco chewing

   — No throwing garbage

   — No smoking in public places

   — No wastage of goods.
7. Take leading activities or participate in world environment day, wild life week etc.
8. Visit Zoo, natural park, sanctuary near your house and try to learn more and more and educate others also.

Various institutions involved in the study of environment Government organisations

- BSI (Botanical Survey of India - established in 1890 at Calcutta)
- ZSI (Zoological Survey of India - established in 1916 at Calcutta)
- WWF (World Wide Fund for Nature - India, New Delhi) First initiated in 1969 in Mumbai.

Other organisations

These are -

- CSE (Centre for Science and Environment, New Delhi)
- CPR - EEC (Set up in Madras in 1988) Centre for Programs/ Environmental Education Centre

- CEE (Centre for Environment Education, Ahmedabad in 1989)
- BVIEER, Pune (Bharati Vidyapeeth Institute of Environment Education and Research)
- UKSN (Uttarkhand Seva Nidhi, Almora)
- Kalpavriksh, Pune
- SACON (The Salim Ali Centre for Ornithology and Natural History, Coimbatore)
- WII (The Wildlife Institute of India, Dehradoon in 1982)
- MCBT (The Madras Crocodile Bank Trust in 1976)
- ANET (The Andaman and Nicobar Islands Environmental Team in 1992)
- Atmosphere is to provide oxygen as a part of carbon dioxide used for the growth of plants (in turn what is left out by plants in earth are used by men)

(i) Troposphere is the only part warm enough for us to survive in, is about 12 kms thick. Tropos is a Greek word means, 'Turning'.

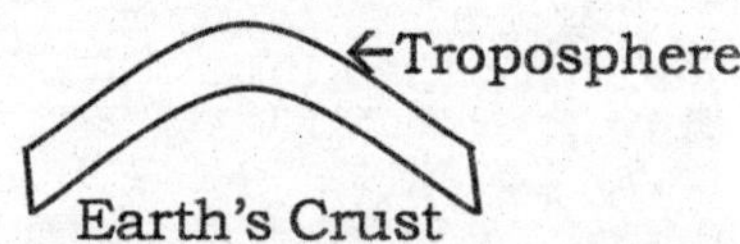

Stratosphere is 50 km thick and contains a layer of sulphates which is important for the formation of rain. It also contains a layer of ozone, which absorbs ultraviolet light (UV) known to cause cancer, without which no life could exist on earth. The atmosphere is not uniformly warmed by the sun. This leads to air flows and variations in climate, temperature and rainfall in different parts of the earth. This happens to be a very complex dynamic system and should not be disrupted as this affects all mankind. Most air pollutants created by man have both global and regional effects.

All living beings need air for survival without which it cannot exist even for a span of few minutes. In order to support life, air should be clean. The pollutants of air created by industrial units release various gases like carbon monoxide, carbon dioxide and toxic fumes, into the air. Burning fossil fuels would also pollute air, Fossil fuels are the natural fuel such as coal or gas formed from the remains of living organisms. The build up of carbon dioxide (known as the **'green house effect'** in the atmosphere has lead to the current **'global warming'**).

Green house effect is the trapping of the sun's warmth in the lower atmosphere caused by higher levels of carbon dioxide and other gases (causes **global warming**).

Green house is a light structure with the sides and roof mainly of glass, for repairing plants. A green house is valuable for over wintering frost tenders in cool climates. In addition, plants may be raised from seed or from cuttings in open trays or in heated propagators. In summer, blinds can be used to shade plants from direct sun, and automatic vents fitted to control air circulation and humidity. In winter, a fan is useful for maintaining suitable temperature levels.

Greenhouse gas may be any of various gases, especially carbon dioxide that contribute to the greenhouse effect. The growing number of scooters, motor cycles, cars, buses, lorries, trucks which all run on fossil fuel (petrol and diesel) is a major cause of **air pollution**.

Air pollution is very bad. It affects man's health leading to acute and chronic respiratory diseases like infections in the lung, asthma and even cancer.

(ii) Hydrosphere is the waters of the earth's surface. It covers three quarters of the earth's surface. A major part of the hydrosphere is the marine ecosystem in the ocean, while only a small part forms fresh water e.g., in rivers, lakes and glaciers (renewed by a process of rainfall and evaporation). Some of these are stored in underground aquifyers. Humans are the main causes for changes in the hydrosphere e.g., deforestation, by cutting the trees, the land is denuded of vegetation, the rain erodes the soil and the sea takes away the major part of it.

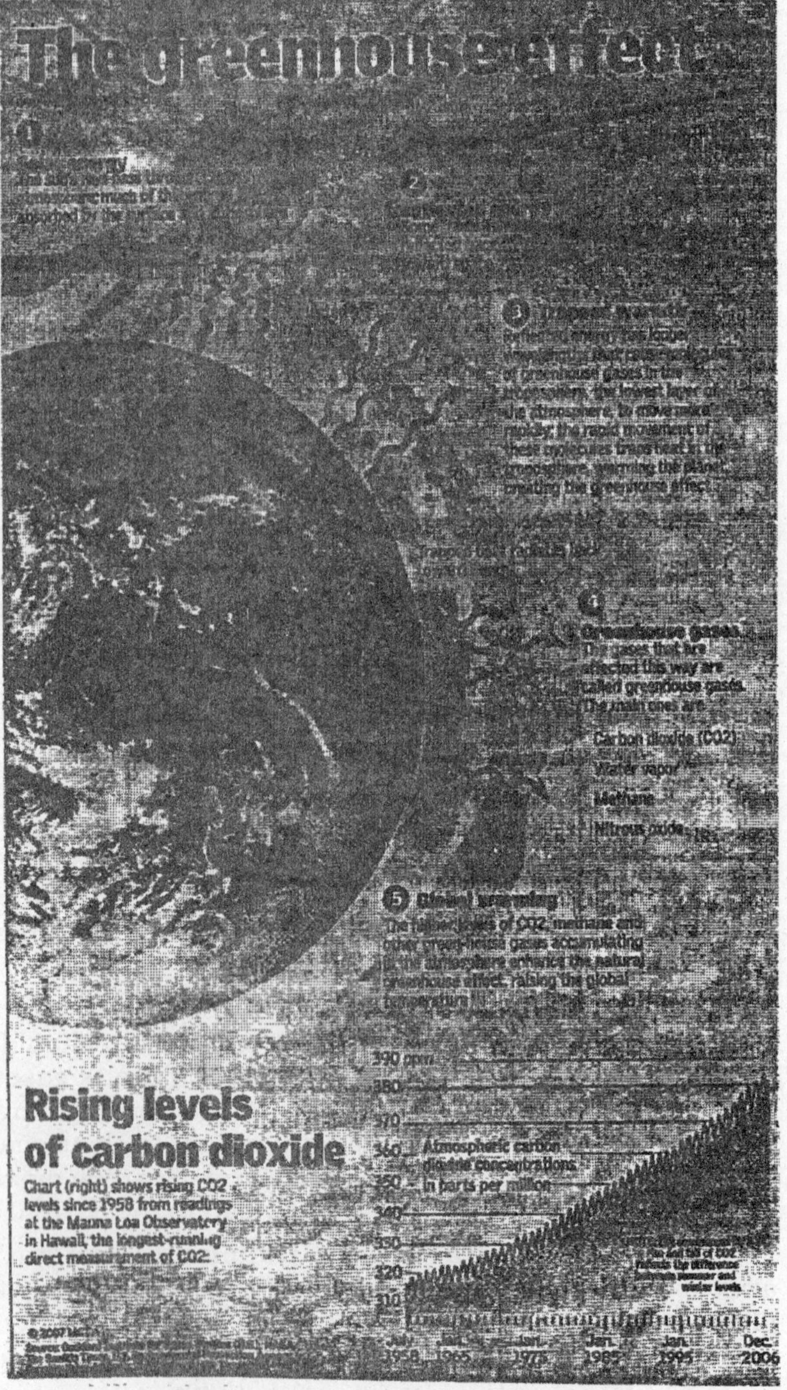

Fig. 3.9 The Greenhouse Effect

Added to this, chemicals from industry and sewage make way into rivers and then to sea.

Water pollution creates problems to the health of mankind as we cannot get clean water. Because of pollution, water has become unhygienic now-a-days.

(iii) Lithosphere

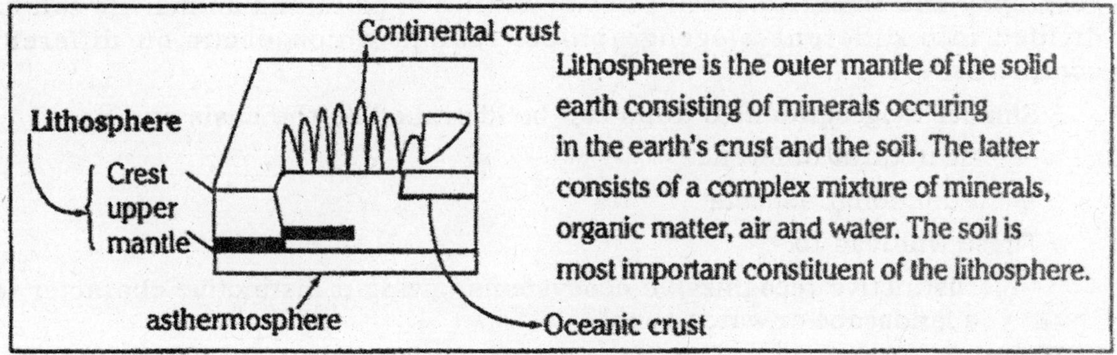

Fig. 3.10 Lithosphere

It is outer mantle of the solid earth consisting of minerals occurring in the earth's crust and the soil. The latter consists of a complex mixture minerals, organic matter, air and water. The soil is most important constituent of the Lithosphere. It is the original part of the earth consisting of the crust and upper mantle. The lithosphere involves soil, the basis for agriculture to provide us food, stone, sand and gravel used for construction, micro nutrients in soil.

It is the rigid outer part of the earth consisting of the crust and upper mantle. The lithosphere involves soil, the basis for agriculture to provide us food; stone, sand and gravel used for construction; micronutrients in soil essential for plant growth; microscopic flora, small soil fauna and fungi in soil, important living organisms of the lithosphere which break down plant litter as well as animal wastes to provide nutrients for plants; a large number of minerals on which our industries are based; oil, coal and gas, extracted from underground resources which provide power for vehicles, agricultural machinery, industry, and for our homes.

- The lithosphere began as a hot ball of matter which formed the earth about 4.6 billion years ago.
- About 3.2 billion years back, the earth cooled down considerably; life began on our planet.
- The crust of the earth is 6-7 km thick and lies under the continents.
- Lithosphere has 92 elements; only 8 are common constituents of crystal rocks. Rocks when broken down form soil on which man is dependent for agriculture.
- Of these constituents, 47% is oxygen, 28% is silicon, 8% is alluminium, 5% iron, sodium magnesium, calcium, potassium 4% each; together a total of 200 common mineral compounds are there.

(iv) Biosphere is the regions of the Earth's crust and atmosphere occupied by living organisms (Taken from the German word Bio sphare).

This is the relatively thin layer on the earth where the life exists. The air, water, rocks and soil, and the living creatures are within it. These form structural and functional ecological units, which together can be considered as one giant global living system. Under this framework those characterised by broadly similar geography and climate, as well as communities of plant and animal life can be divided into different biogeographical realms which occur on different continents.

Smaller biogeographical units can be identified on the basis of:

— Structural difference

— Functional aspects

These will lead to:

— Distinctive recognizable ecosystems (giving a distinctive character to a landscape or waterscape)

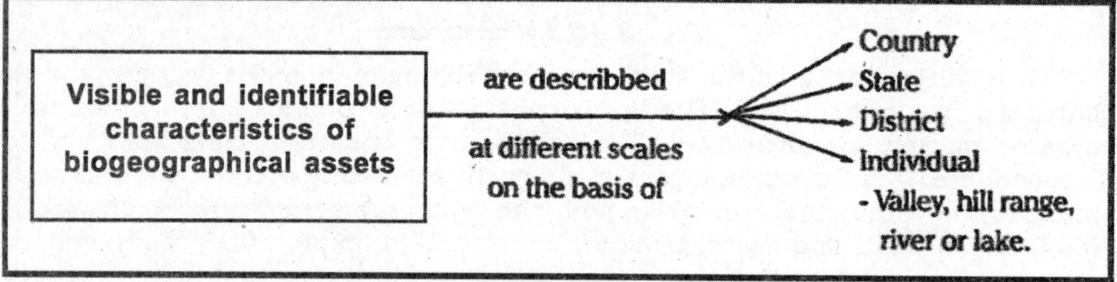

Fig. 3.11 Characteristics of Biogeographical Assets

E.g., A lake. The structural features include:

— Size

— Depth

— Quality of its water

The specific conditions for different plant and animal communities include:

— Periphery

— Shallow part

— Deep part

The functional aspects are:

— A variety of cycles like the amount of water within the lake at different times of the year.

— The quantity of nutrients flowing into the lake from the terrestrial ecosystem.

This example can be used as a model to understand the nature of any other ecosystem and the changes take place over the time in any of the ecosystems.

We have explained the four spheres above atmosphere, troposphere, stratosphere, hydrosphere, biosphere. These are closely interlinked systems. This atmosphere, hydrosphere, lithosphere are all connected through the hydrological cycle as shown in figure 3.12.

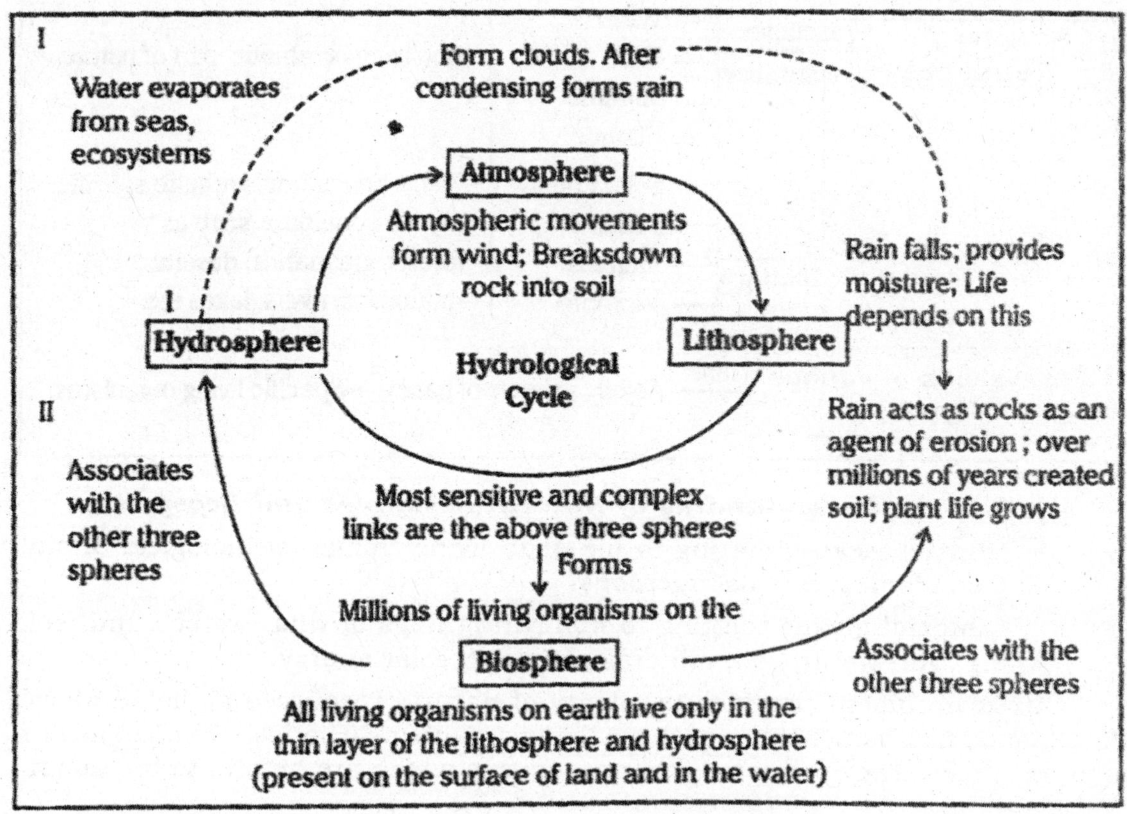

Fig. 3.12 Hydrological Cycle

With the above interrelated connections of the above spheres we can understand the inter-relationships of the separate entities like

- Soil
- Water
- Air
- Living organisms

Natural Resources and Associated Problems

Introduction

Natural resources are materials or conditions occurring in nature and capable of economic exploitation. **Natural history** is the study of animals or plants especially as set forth for popular use. These are the facts concerning the flaura and fauna etc., of a particular place or class.

Fauna is the animal life of a region or geological period. Natural resources include many things as under:

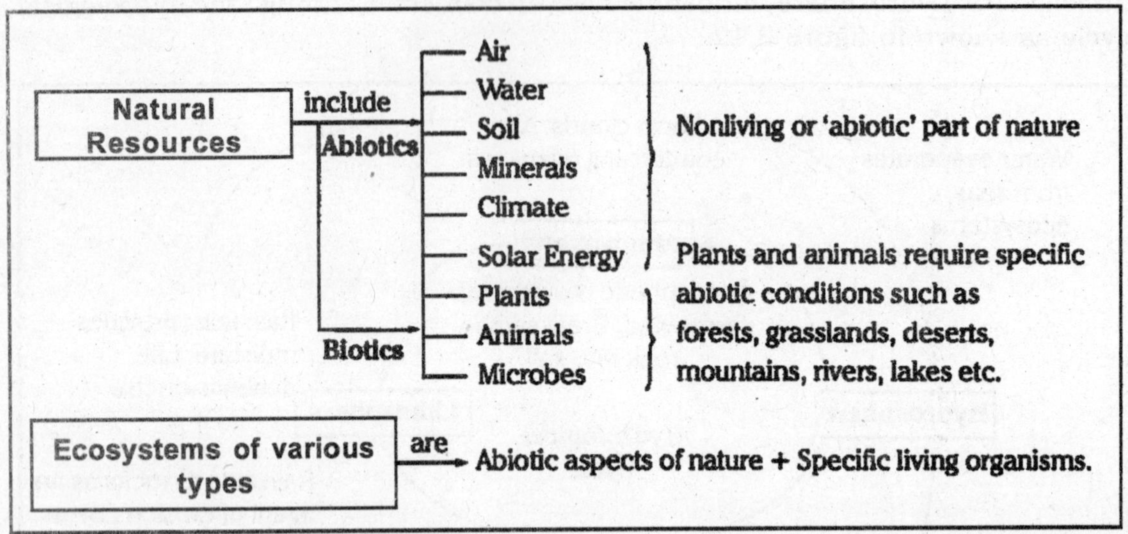

Fig. 3.13 An Understanding of Natural Resources and Ecosystems

- **'Biotic'** means relating to life or to living things (of biological origin) e.g., plants, animals, microbes.
- **'Abiotic'** means relating to nonliving things of what we see and feel. e.g., Air, water, soil, minerals, climate, solar energy.

Our environment provides us plenty of natural resources as listed above both biotic and abiotic. Many of these living organisms (Biotics) are used as our food resources. They are some other organisms which are helpful to be human and plants like:

- Bees as pollinators, dispensers of plants.
- Earth worms inside the soil for recycling nutrients for plant growth.
- Fungi/termites break dead plant materials which helps replenishing of soil nutrients.

Man depends on resources which are provided by various sources or spheres.

(1) Atmosphere of the Earth: It forms a protective shell over the earth. The Earth's atmosphere is about 700 km (430 miles deep) and is divided into 5 main layers according to the way the temperature changes as the height varies. The layers are as under:

(i) Troposphere: The lowest layer contains 75% of all the gas in the atmosphere and water in large quantities. Air movement within this layer produces the earth's weather.

(ii) Stratosphere: The next higher level is Ozone layer lies within this providing protection from the Sun's harmful ultra violet rays.

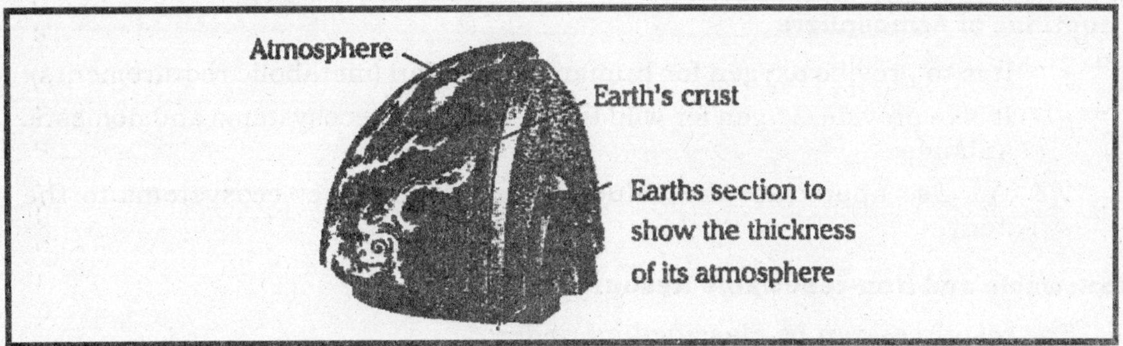

Fig. 3.14 Atmosphere above Earth

(iii) Next is Mesosphere which is the region of the atmosphere above stratosphere.

(iv) Next hyper level is **thermosphere** where the bottom of this called ionosphere. Radio signals transmitted by bouncing off the ionosphere, a layer within the thermosphere that is made-up of electrically charged (ionized) gas particles. Thermo denotes heat (from the Greek word therme).

(v) The highest layer is exosphere, farthest from earth in the atmosphere.

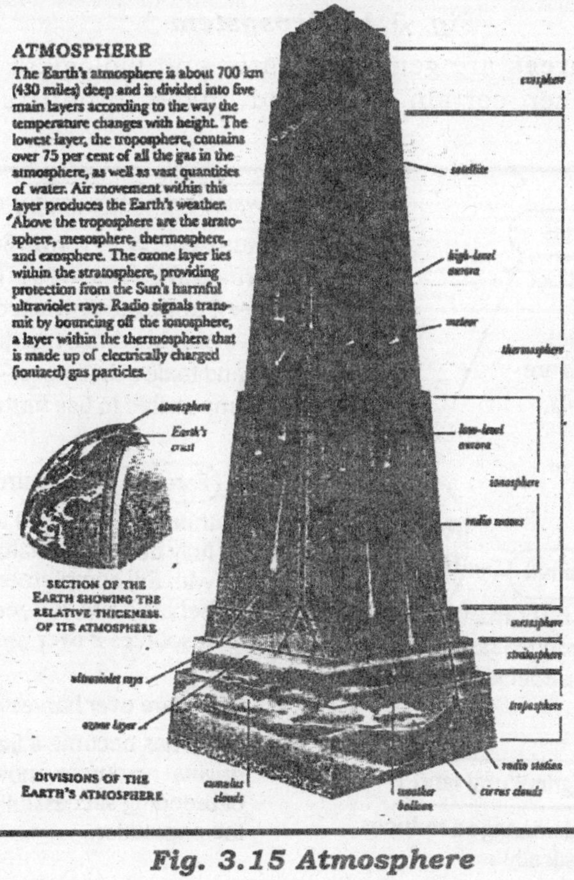

Fig. 3.15 Atmosphere

Functions of Atmosphere

- It is to provide oxygen for human respiration (metabolic requirements).
- It is to provide oxygen for wild fauna in natural ecosystems and domestic animals.

We can also appreciate the value of preserving intact ecosystems to the fullest extent.

Renewable and Non-renewable Resources

The resources can be classified as under:

- **Renewable resources** (renewable only within certain limits)
- **Non-renewable resources** (cannot be reconstituted as a resource. e.g., Fossil fuels such as oil and coal)

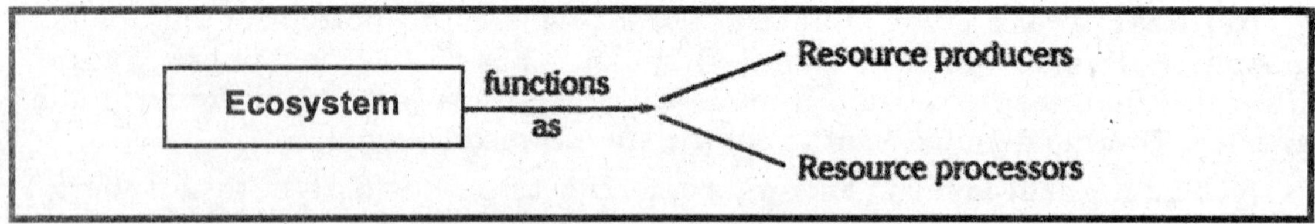

Fig. 3.16 Ecosystem

Renewable resources are generally water and biological living resources, but renewable only when certain limits and linked to natural cycles such as water cycle.

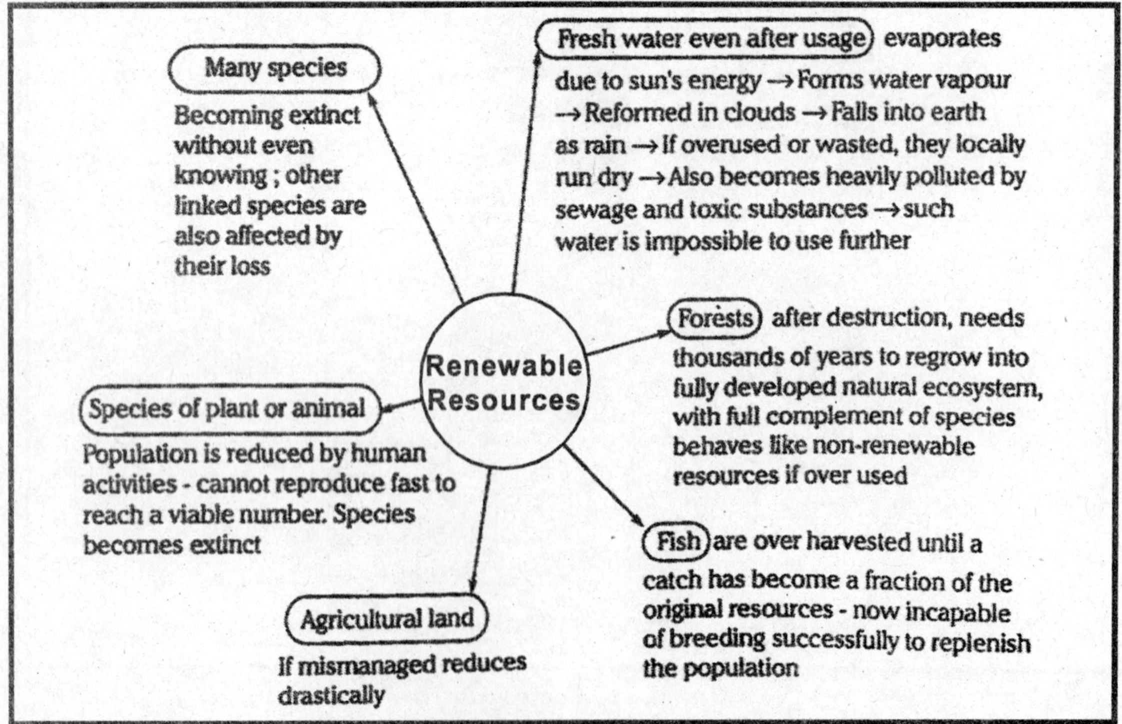

Fig. 3.17 Renewable Resources

The above resources can be classified as under:

- Forest resources
- Water resources
- Mineral resources
- Food resources
- Energy resources
- Land resources.

(a) Forest Resources

In the olden days, forests were situated in large tracts of our country. People used them for their living. As agriculture became main occupation in the latter years, the forests were left with patches and controlled mostly by tribal people. These people hunted animals and gathered plants and lived from them. Deforestation started subsequently for getting timber used for building ships. The Government created and protected forests which curtailed access to the resources. This happened during the British period. Immediately after independence, over utilisation and forest degradation occurred again as restrictions by Government were not as strict as found earlier. Hence forest wealth dwindled. Timber extraction continued till 1970s. Big trees were felled. It was a serious loss for everyone as the concentration was only on the sources of revenue from timber.

— Estimation of land in India under forests should be around	..... 33%
— As on today the save is only	..... 12%
Deficiency	..... 21%

Hence we have to increase forest cover in addition to protecting our forests.

The controls needed in this direction are:

Watershed protection

- Rate of surface run-off water is to be reduced
- Flash floods and soil erosion are to be presented
- The run off should be gradual and prolonged to safe guard against drought.

Erosion control

- This happens when rain directly washes our soil away.
- To prevent this, we have to hold soil.

Maintaining soil nutrients and structure (also termed as Land Bank)

Atmospheric regulation

This is absorption of solar heat during evapotranspiration and by maintaining carbon dioxide levels for plant growth and local climatic conditions.

Consumptive use

Consumption of forest produce by local people who collect it for their subsistence.

(a) Food used now-a-days is only by gathering plants, fishing, hunting from the forest. In the earlier days, wild life was plentiful. People used after killing them for food. As a result, their population have diminished. If hunting is still continued, there may be extinction of some of the species.

(b) Fodder for cattle.

(c) Fuel wood and charcoal for cooking and heating.

(d) Timber and Bamboos for household articles and construction.

(e) Poles for building homes.

(f) Fibre for weaving baskets, ropes, nets, string etc.

(g) Sericulture for silk.

(h) Agriculture for rearing bees for honey; forest bees also pollinate crops.

(i) Medicinal plants for traditional medicines.

(j) Productive and selling of forest resource in urban areas as well as for exports.

— As a source of income for supporting forest people.

— Forest produce such as fuel wood, fruit, gum, honey, fibre, bamboos etc., collected and sold in markets as a source of income.

— Major timber extraction for construction, industrial uses, paper, pulp etc.

— Sugarcane for sugar production.

— Sandalwood.

Though some of the tree cutting are banned by the forest department, illegal logging continues in many of the forests of India and the World.

Forest people know to value of forest resources as they live on these resources. We also to a certain extent know the value of forest resources. Water we are using is dependent on the existence of forests on the watersheds around river valleys. As we are all aware, many useful products which we use comes from forests such as furniture, sandlewood, paper, honey, medicines from herbs and plants. We depend on plants as they emit plenty of oxygen which we use for breathing available in the air.

Indias serious environmental problems are:

— Forest degradation due to timber extraction.

— People's dependence on fuel wood to cook meals and heat their homes.

Not enough trees have been planted at a sufficient rate for the above two problems.

MOEF formulated the National Forest Policy of 1988 to give added importance to Joint Forest Management (JFM) to sustainably manage our forests to enable the local village communities and the forest department to work together.

Village Forest Committees were formed; New JFM guidelines were issued in 2000. As per this, atleast 25% of the income from the area must go to the community.

In 2002 there were 63,618 JFM committees; Managed 1,40,953 sq.km. of forest in 27 states in India.

In many states, nontimber forest products are available to the people free of costs. Rotational grazing schemes were introduced in some states in forest regeneration.

(b) Water Resources

The biggest challenge involved in this century in the world is the need to rethink about the overall management of world resources.

— World population has passed to 6 billion mark.

— India's population is about 1/5th of the world's population.

— Young people in developing countries would increase including India.

— Enormous demand for fresh water would increase, but world has limited fresh water supply.

— Fresh water withdrawals are estimated at 3800 cubic kilo litres - twice to that of the figure 50 years back in India.

— A person needs a minimum of 20 to 40 liters of water daily for drinking and sanitation on an average.

— More than one billion people world wide have no access to clean water. Water supplies are unreliable.

— Water conflicts are increasing between state to state and also in country to country.

— By 2025, shortage of water is bound to happen.

— At the global level 31 countries are already having short of water.

— Another 48 countries face serious water shortages.

— 20 major cities in India are expected to face chronic or interrupted water shortages.

— 100 countries share the waters of 13 large rivers and lakes.

— The upstream countries have upper hand.

— India and Bangladesh have an agreement on the water use of Ganges river.

— If the basic needs are to be fulfilled, the need for water plays an important role. In some of the areas, this is not fulfilled. There are overutilisation of water at some places. The wastage of water is also there. River water is left top sea at some places because of the danger it might create. Waste of water is found during bath by using shower, even while brushing our teeth, or while washing clothes. Water is wasted recklessly.

— Agriculturists use sometimes more water than normal to grow crops for the same yield (use of drip irrigation systems).

— Pollution of surface water and underground water resources by the excessive use of chemical fertilizers and pesticides.

— Industry not bothered about its liquid waste by releasing it into rivers and the sea and polluting the same.

— The polluting industry do not use efficient treatment plants by bribing the corrupted people. Drastic action is needed to punish them.

— Public awareness is to be increased to produce only ecofriendly products to make them popular.

— Health hazards caused by pesticides should be known by the people affecting their food and in other products of their daily living.

— Pressures on farmers should be put to reduce the use of chemicals as it is injurious for health.

(c) Mineral Resources

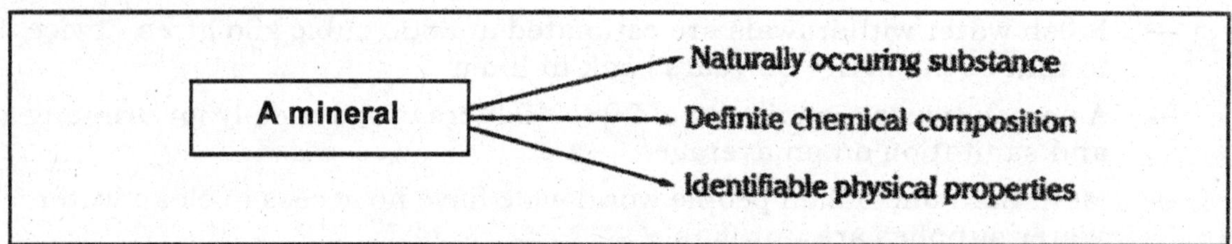

Fig. 3.19 Mineral Characteristics

An **Ore** is a mineral or combination on minerals from which a useful substance, such as a metal can be extracted. This metal is useful to manufacture useful products.

Millions of years are needed to form minerals in the earth's crust like iron, alluminium, zinc, copper and manganese. These are raw materials used in industries. Important non-metallic resources include coal, salt, clay, cement and silica. Stone is used for building material such as granite, marble, limestone. These are another category of minerals.

Diamonds, emeralds and rubies have aesthetic and ornamental value. Minerals with such values and special properties are used by people as ornaments. Oil, gas and coals are also minerals formed in different ways when ancient plants and animals were converted into underground fossil fuels.

Mining is a process wherein minerals and their ores need to be extracted from the earth's interior, so that they can be used. Mining operations are done as under:

- **Prospecting:** Searching for minerals.
- **Exploration:** Assess the size, shape, location and economic value of the deposit.
- **Development:** The work of preparing access to the deposit.
- **Exploitation:** Extracting minerals from the mines.

Geologists, mining engineers, geophysicists and geochemists work together to discover new deposits. Now-a-days GIS (Geological information system) is extentively used to survey and study the geology of the area. Method of mining depends on the location of the ore or mineral deposit and its closeness to the surface or deep within the earth. Topography of the region and the physical nature of the ore deposit are also important.

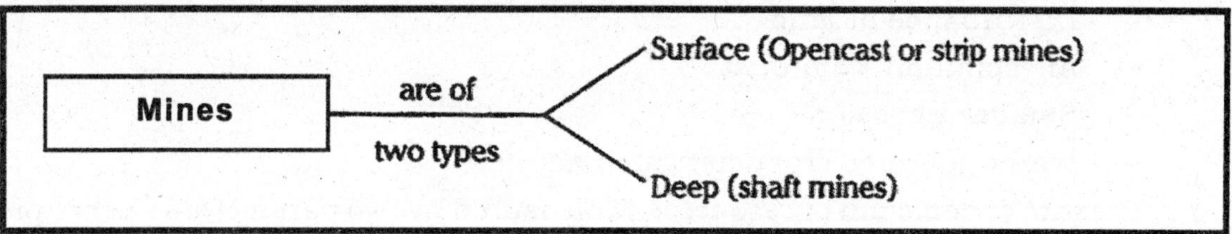

Fig. 3.20 Mines

Minerals are mined differently on the basis of the above. The method chosen for mining depends on the maximum yield to be obtained at cost under the existing conditions and with the least danger to the personnel involved.

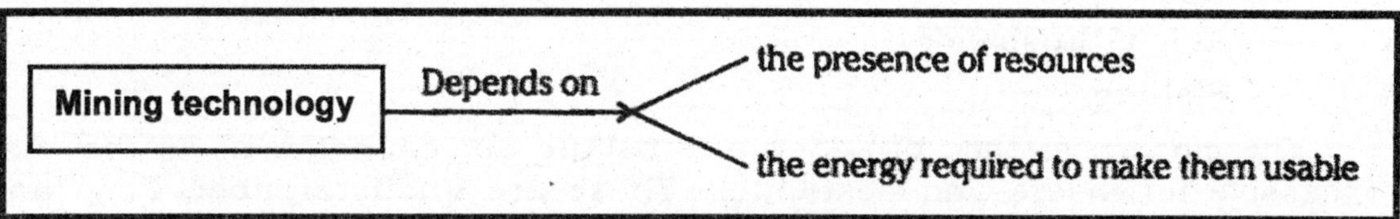

Fig. 3.21 Mining Technology

- Mining is a very hazardous occupation; as such safety of workers is important.
- Underground mining is more hazardous than surface mining.
- Metal mining is less hazardous than coal mining; the hazards in underground mines are rock/roof falls, flooding, inadequate ventilation.
- Coal mines have more large explosions and the deaths are more.
- Occupational hazards are of long term in mining. Dust hazards are high and is injurious to health causing a lung disease. Certain fumes generated are poisonous.
- Methane gas, emanating from coal strata is health hazardous.
- Uranium mines have radiation hazard which is life threatening.

- Mining operations affect the environment and is mainly responsible for environmental degradation, leading to a variety of side effects like:
  — Depletion of available land
  — Waste from industries
  — Conversion of land to industry and pollution of land, water and air by industrial wastes.

Government has created global public awareness and has taken action in several cases to stem the damage to the natural environment. Numerous international agreements and laws exist to prevent the activities and events affecting the environment.

Mining and processing of minerals involve major environmental concerns:

— Disturbance of land

— Air pollution from dust

— Smaller emission

— Water pollution from disrupted aquifers

The rate of depletion of resources is measured by two parameters - per capita mining and per capita consumption.

(d) Food Resources

India as on today is self sufficient in food production. This comes entirely from:

— Agriculture

— Animal husbandry

— Fishing

The modern method of agriculture pollute our environment as they use excessive fertilisers and pesticides. These are unsustainable. Food and Agriculturals Organisation thinks about sustainable agriculture which conserves land, water, plant and animal genetic resources. This will not degrade the environment and is economically viable and socially acceptable. Large farms generally adopt single crops (monoculture). If this crop is affected by a pest, the entire crop is affected. The farmer will have no income and suffers a loss. As such the farmer uses traditional varieties and grows several different crops. The chance of complete failure is eliminated or lowered. Inorganic fertilizers and pesticides can be avoided using alternatives which is known as **Integrated Crop Management**.

The highly populous countries like India and China which are also developing though these countries produce plenty, they are unable to keep pace with the growing demand.

Out of 105 developing countries, in 64 countries food production is considered poor and is unable to go in line with the population growth levels. They do not have financial means to import the food. India is little safer to produce enough food by cultivating a large portion of its arable land through irrigation. The green revolution we adopted in 1960s reduced starvation. Still many of the technologies are being questioned.

- Forests, grass lands, wetland are converted for agricultural use - serious ecological questions are being asked.
- Fish resources (Marine and Inland) show evidence of exhaustion.
- Fertile soils are being exploited faster.
- Availability of nutritious food to all. Tribal people are under malnutrition (more in the case of women and children).

On the other hand, if we look at the other developed countries, we observe the following:

- A changing trend in dietary habits.
- Living standards are ignoring.
- People are shifting more towards vegetarian food (eating more grain than meat).
- Feed for live stock based on agriculture increases (more land per unit of food produced); world's poor suffers in food.

(e) Land Resources

Land is one of the man resources and supports life. The uses of land are:

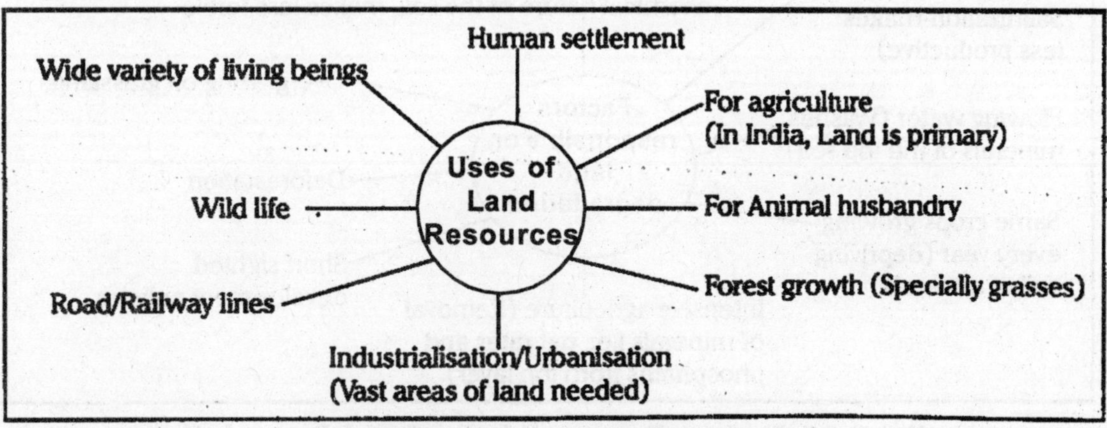

Fig. 3.22 Uses of Land Resources

Land is over-used and misused in many countries. India is also one among them. This has resulted in desertification, land slide, soil erosion. The adverse consequences of the above are harmful. Land is to be checked for proper use in a planned and wise manner.

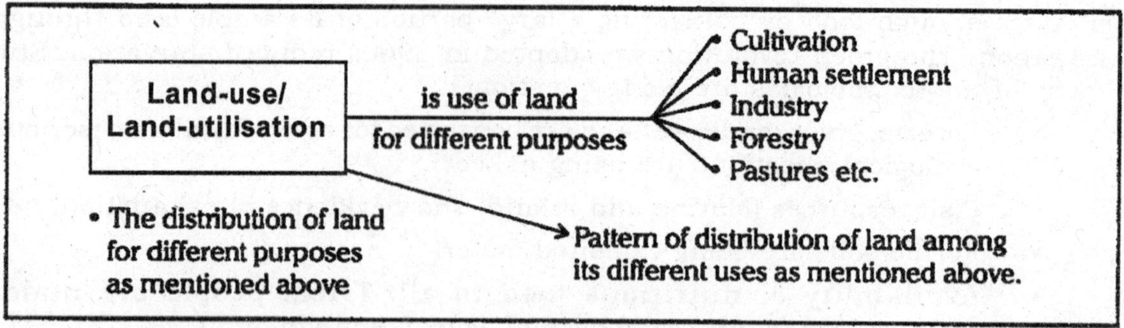

Fig. 3.23 Land-use/Land-utilisation

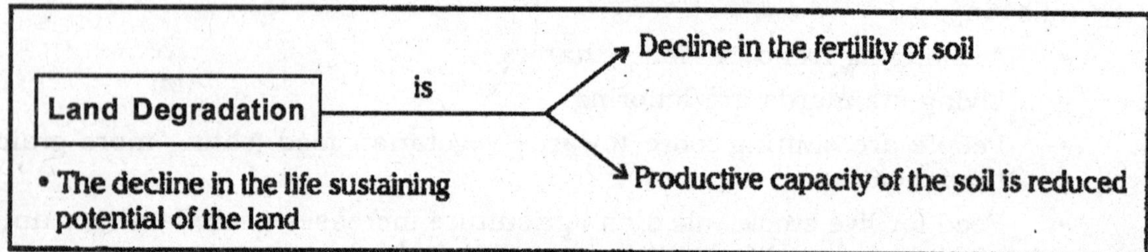

Fig. 3.24 Land Degradation

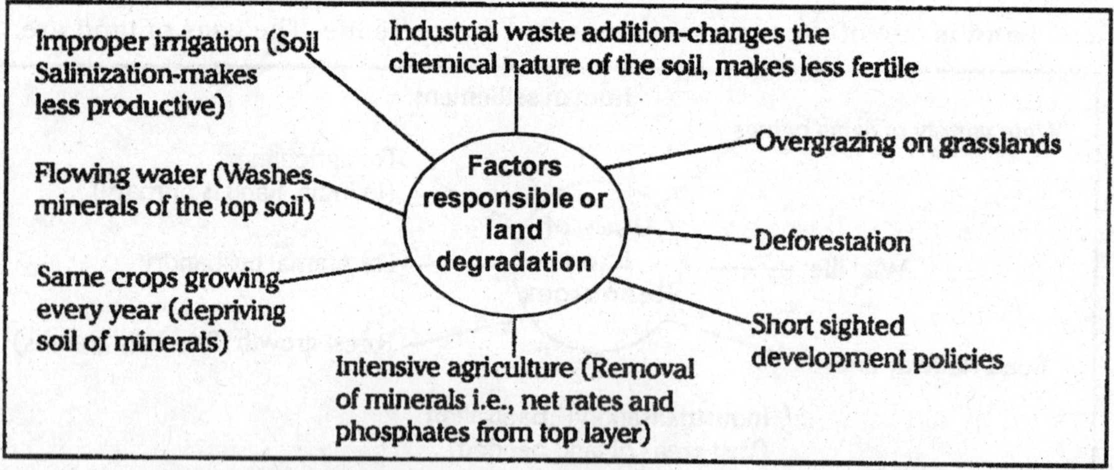

Fig. 3.25 Factors Responsible for Land Degradation

India's Land use pattern (1990-2000 statistics)

- Total geographical land ... 329 million hectares
  - Survey and classified ... 306 million hectares
  - Not surveyed (mountains, deserts, forests) ... 23 million hectares
- Surveyed and classified (thick) ... 306 million hectares
  - Under forests ... 23% (69 million hectares)

- Not available for cultivation ... 14% (Villages, towns, transport development and barren land)

42 million hectares

- Out of cultivation 1-5 years ... 8% (25 million hectares)
- Permanent pastures and grazing ... 3% (11 million hectares)
- Culturable with some efforts ... 6% (18 million hectares)
- Culturable ... 46% (141 million hectares)

Waste land should be reclaimed and put to productive use.

The National Wasteland Development Board was established in 1985 to formulate action plans for arresting land degradation and deforestation, regeneration of degraded forest areas, reclamation of ravines, wetlands and tracts, mine spoils, brings wastelands into sustainable use, increase miobass availability, check land degradation, restore ecological balance.

(f) Energy Resources

Energy Resources in India is as under:

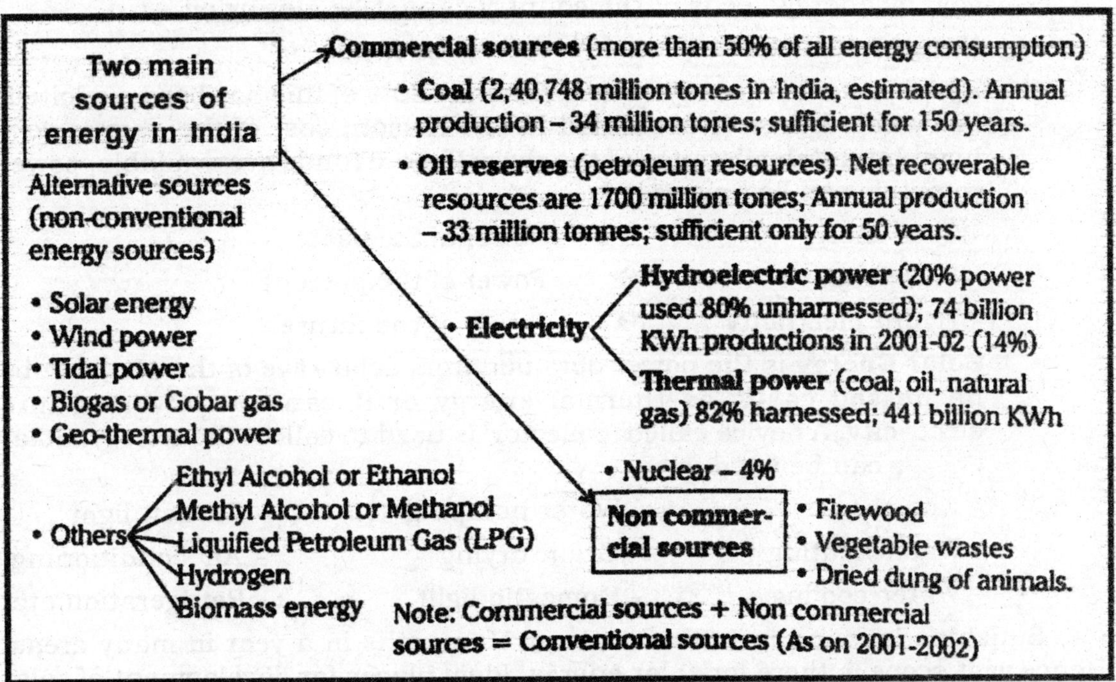

Fig. 3.26 Sources of Energy in India (in a nutshell)

Fuel wood (Fire wood) From the past, it is an important source of power, even in industries (big or small) e.g., tile and brick industries, steel industries (VISW) Visveswaraiah Iron and Steel Works, Badravati, used as a kitchen full both in rural and urban areas; 65% of the rural energy is met by this fuel.

Agricultural waste (Straw or Vegetable waste) Used for cooking in rural areas; consumption of agricultural waste for power; 65 million tonnes a year.

Dried Dung of Animals A source of power (both in rural and urban area) 73 million tonnes of dried dung are used as energy resource every year.

Non conventional energy resource (Alternative energy resources)	These sources →	Not used conventionally or generally (Solar, Biogas, Gobar gas, wind energy or Wind power, Tidal power, Geothermal power.)

Fig. 3.27 Non-conventional Energy Resources

Why there is a need for non-conventional source of energy?

The reasons are:

- Reserves of coal are insufficient to meet country's demand; not of good quality; coal fields are concentrated in Gondawana coal fields; too deep and costly for extraction.
- Oil reserves are also very poor; demand has increased because of transportation means; world oil prices have increased; imports of oil cost by energy needs of the country cannot be met by oil.
- Natural gas is inadequate to meet the needs.
- Hydel power is the only option. But only 20% of this has been exploited. Seasonal character of rainfall is one reason; cost of the dam is very high. Interstate disputes of the river; If more funds are available, power from this can be harnessed.

  - Coal energy → Power of the past
  - Petroleum → Power of the present
  - Hydro electricity → Power of the future

- **Solar Energy** is the power obtained from solar rays of the sun; can be harnessed easily as thermal energy or it can be converted into electricity. A device called 'collector' is used to collect the energy. Solar energy can be used for:

- Cooking	- Water pumping	- Garden light
- Water heating	- Grain drying	- Air conditioning
- Water cooling	- Domestic light	- Refrigeration etc.

Sunshine is found in India for about 10 months in a year in many areas. Hence vast scope is there for solar energy. Ideal places for development of solar energy are:

- Jodhpur
- Barmes

- Jai salmer
- Bikaner

are places where sun's rays are there throughout the year.

Many research stations in the country exist to conduct research in harnessing solar energy for cooking, heating and lighting. This may be soon an important source of power in India.

- **Wind power** This is for many purposes:

— Pumping water from wells for irrigation, threshing, winnowing and grinding.

— Generating power on a small scale (unsteady and uncertain, low velocity wind) Coastal and hilly regions are ideal for setting up wind mills.

- Mandovi (Kutch in Gujarat)
- Tuticorn (in Tamil Nadu)

Tidal power (Energy generated from tides)

Several agencies investigated to get energy from tides. IT can be developed in the gulf of Cambay and Kutch (West Coast), estuary of the Mooghly (East coast). This power is not ideal because of: (i) uncertainty (ii) huge investments (iii) large scale development needed to make it economical.

Biogas (Gobar gas): It is a methane gas produced by fermenting cattle dung, small plants are needed (Gobar gas plants); This gas is used for cooking, heating and lighting, energizing pump sets in rural areas. The slurry left over can be used as compost manure. These are antipollution agents, maintain economical balance. These provide employment in rural areas. India is having highest cattle (more than 300 million and 480 million tones of wet dung is available every year). Gobar gas plants are available in plenty at low costs (Rs.7000-8000); gestation period is one month. Plants are developed in different states of India. Since 1961, these plants have become popular in the rural areas as the work of publicizing and propagation work was entrusted this to Khadi and Village Industries Commission.

Geo-thermal power: It is the power developed from the heat generated by the earth, which can be used for multipurpose like cooking, heating etc. This was first initiated in Italy in the beginning of 20th century. Not so popular because of the difficulties that control the development of the power. In India, the exploration of this power started in 1960 under the geological survey of India at places where hot springs were found in the country (Jammu & Kashmir, Madhya Pradesh, Narmada Valley, West Coast, Damodar Valley etc.).

Alcohols as fuels

Ethyl Alcohol /Ethanol	Methyl Alcohol (Methanol)	LPG	Hydrogen	Biomass
• Ethanol burns in air; produces heat, gives CO_2 and water.	• Burns at a lower temperature than diesel and petrol.	• Used in vehicles.	• Hydrogen burns in air gives heat.	• Organic matter of plants and animals includes wood, crop residue, agricultural waste, poultry, piggery waste produces energy by burning.
• Ethanol obtained by fermenting plant sugar with yeast. • Ethanol's calorific value is low. • Cheaper than petrol; water soluble, biodegradable. • Eco-friendly; used as alternative fuel for petrol.	• Highly advantageous as an alternative.	• Can reduce pollution and emission in air.	• High calorific value. Used as a fuel in rocket for launching space craft. • Produces electricity in fuel cells. • Non-polluting.	• Renewable.

Hurdles to switching to Biofuels

In less than a year now, all cars on Indian roads are expected to run on ethanol - blended fuel. Ethanol, which is made from molasses, a by product in sugar manufacturing, as seen as one of the ways to cut down of costly oil imports. It is also regarded as a green fuel. The Government has set a deadline of October 2008 for oil firms to begin selling 10% blended fuel known as E10. But, are we ready for it?

There are several road blocks to meet the government dead line.

(i) Oil firms are unlikely to have an adequate supply of ethanol. They have been struggling to meet the blending requirements for 5% ethanol which is now mandated in some states. Though oil firms floated tenders for 560 million liters of ethanol, so far they have managed to procure less than a third of their target. When E10 becomes mandatory in October, the situation will further worsen with demand for ethanol is expected to jump to 1,130 mln litres.

(ii) Two Indian car manufacturers and the automobile industry are not yet ready for E10. Some of the latest car models are geared for the higher content of ethanol - blended fuel. A majority of the cars on Indian roads would probably have to be modified if they are to run on E10. This is likely to cause chaos.

(iii) The supply side of ethanol is very bad since the sugar companies say that they have the capacity to meet the increased requirement of ethanol. However they are worried about ram;ping up production of ethanol since they are not sure of the government road map to introduce blended fuel. Increasing production requires major investment by sugar companies, which cannot happen overnight.

(iv) October 2008 deadline for E10 seems like a pipe dream. Questions have been raised about the viability of ethanol blended fuel. In America, government subsidies have ensured that nearly 30 mln tonnes, of maize is diverted to the production of ethanol. Many American farmers are growing more maize by switching over to maize from other crops. Sugar based ethanol poses more problems in Indian context. Sugarcane is a water intensive crop and increased production is going to deplete ground water. Other alternative material for producing biofuels is Jatropha and agricultural waste (These are in a nascent stage). The government needs to dramatically speed up research in these areas if it hopes to switch on to biofules.

Conservation of Energy Resources

A great need for conservation is absolutely necessary. Following may be adopted:

- Proper estimation of all available energy resources to be undertaken.
- Exhaustive surveys needed to find reserves of coal, petroleum and natural gas.
- Improve the methods of extraction of coal for productivity and quality. Adopt better methods of transportation of coal to reduce losses. Have restrictions on the use of good quality coal; Also have better use of secondary coal products.
- Adopt new techniques of oil drilling and refining; Develop methodology to increase productivity and avoid losses of oil in refining. Exploitation of oil reserves from ocean floors to be undertaken to increase production.
- Adopt distribution of oil overlong distances to reduce the losses. Conservation of petroleum reserves is needed (Reserves are limited) develop proper engines for vehicles to reduce the consumption of oil. Try and develop alternative sources of energy for vehicles. The consumption of petroleum for military purposes is to be reduced.
- Minimise environmental effects of coal, petroleum and natural gas.
- Hydel power is to be developed more and more.
- Try for increased use of renewable sources of energy (solar, wind, tidal, geothermal etc.).
- Use of biogas should be advocated to a large extent.

Soil Erosion

Soil is a loose maternal on the earth's surface. It is a thin layer of loose powdery material which we see on the earth's surface. It is formed due to the disintegration and decaying of rocks by the weathering process; It is weathered, worn out rock materials and decomposed (decanted) vegetable and animal matters.

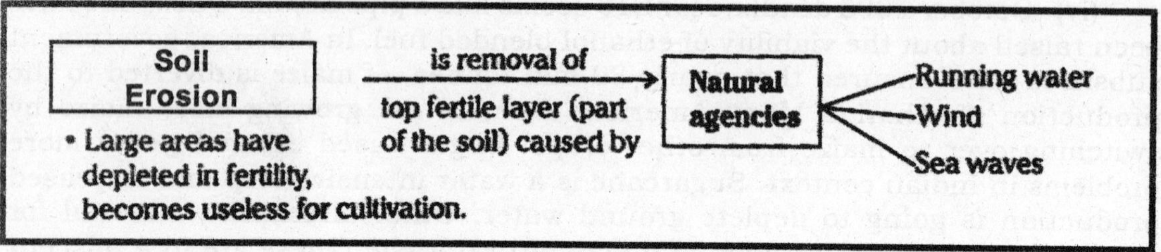

Fig. 3.28 Soil Erosion

Causes of soil erosion

There are many causes. Important ones are:

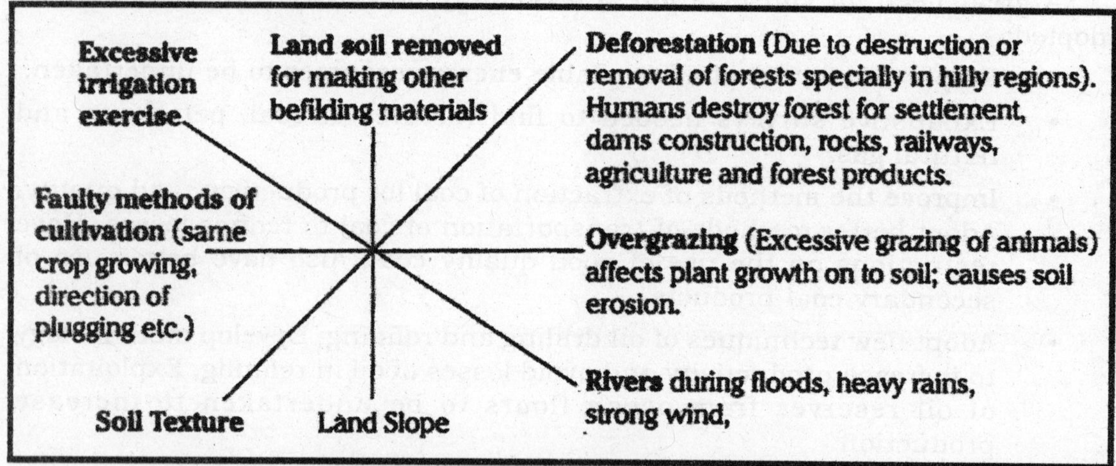

Fig. 3.29 Causes of Soil Erosion

Effects of soil erosion: The negative effects of soil erosion are:

- Reduces subsoil water, results in desertification, results in blocking of navigable channels, causes changes in the course of rivers; limits percolation of water and as a result, the natural springs dry up.
- Reduces the fertility of the soil, rivers are filled and floods are caused.
- Makes cultivable land unfit for cultivation.
- Limits percolation of water and as a result, the natural springs dry up.

How do you conserve soil?

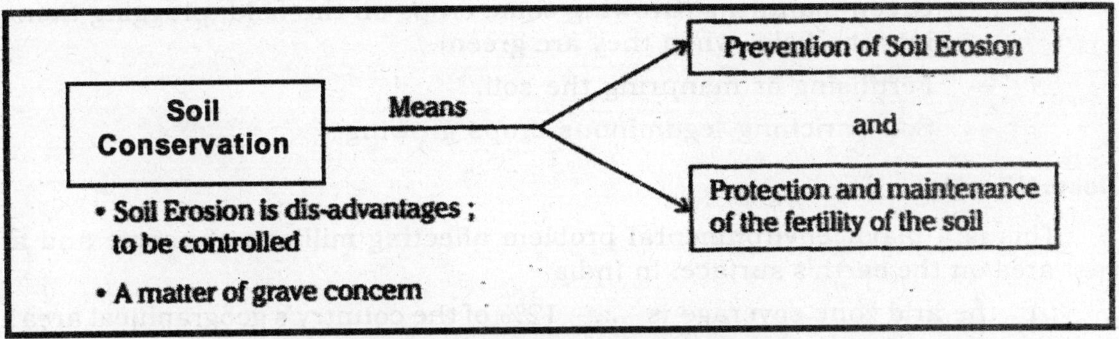

Fig. 3.30 Soil Conservation

Techniques of soil conservation

The techniques of soil conservation are as shown below in the figure 1.31.

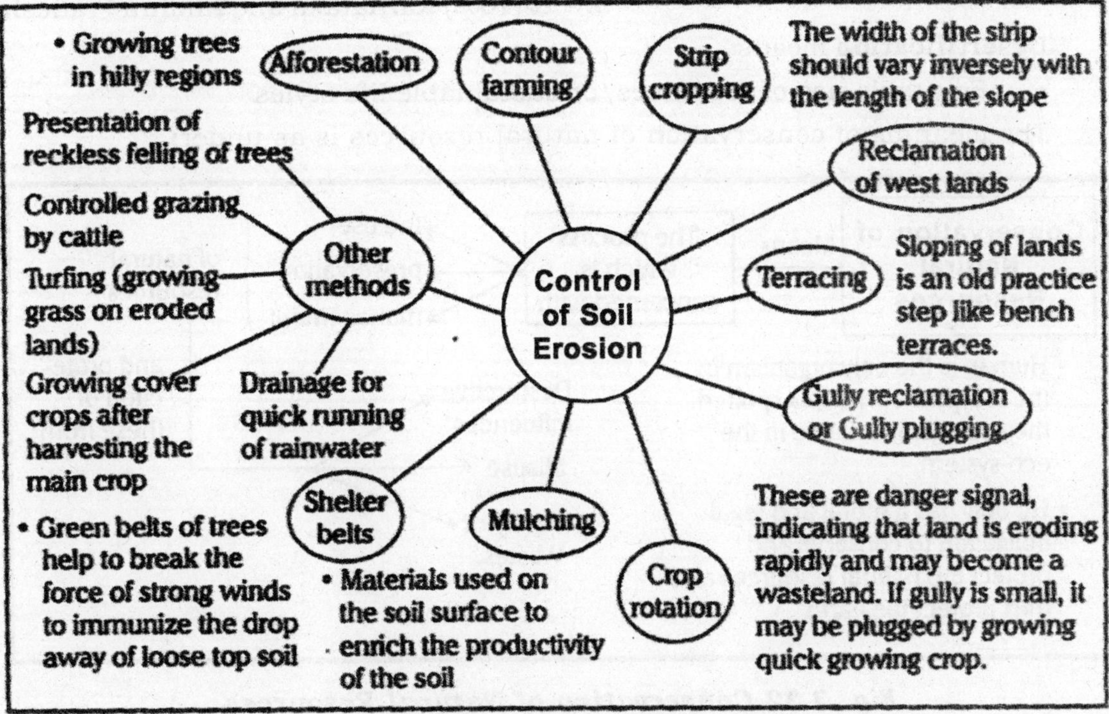

Fig. 3.31 Control of Soil Erosion

- Wastelands can be reclaimed and used for cultivation.
- Control of soil exhaustion and improvement of soil fertility.
  - — **Rotation of crops** (growing of different crops at different seasons to avoid exhaustion of soil in respect of nutrition at any point of time.

— Adding animal refuse (dung) to agricultural lands.

— Green manuring (Growing some crops on the field, plugging them into the field, when they are green)./

— Fertilising or manuring the soil.

— Soil enriching leguminous crops growing.

Desertification

This is a major environmental problem affecting millions of people and a vast area on the earth's surface. In India

(i) the arid zone coverage is ... 12% of the country's geographical area.

(ii) the arid zone occupies ... 3,20,000 sq.km (62%) of hot deserts (Rajasthan)

... (19%) Haryana

... (9%) Punjab

... & (10%) Karnataka and Andhra Pradesh

Desertification means:

• Equitable use of resources/or sustainable life styles

The meaning of conservation of natural resources is as under:

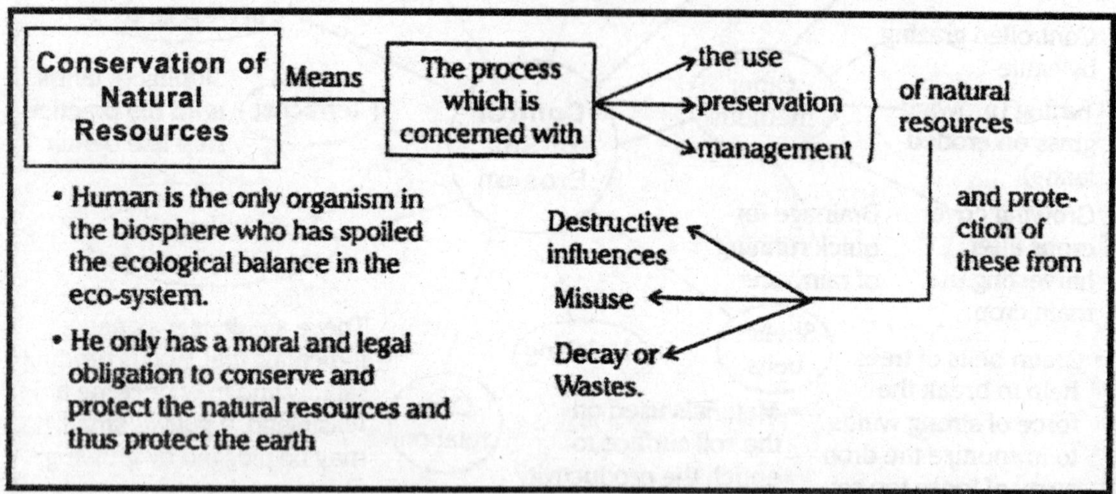

Fig. 3.32 Conservation of Natural Resources

Every individual in the society has to conserve and protect the natural resources by considering it as his duty.

Role of an individual in conservation and protection of Natural Resources: Following points need attention.

Proper exploitation, proper application of natural resources	Create resource consciousness
Use alternative energy resources rather than fuel resources.	- Proper education
Avoid reckless felling of trees in forest	- Create awareness of resources
Ensure pollution free environment (Use green manure instead of chemical fertilizers, minimize the fertilizers, pesticides, insecticides etc., arrest water, air, soil pollutions)	- Proper resource development
	- Exploitation of resources only in the right direction, not recklessly.
	- Resources for only proper use
	- Consider future needs of people and act accordingly to conserve
	- Widen the uses of natural resources

Fig. 3.33 Individuals Role in Conservation and Protection of Natural Resources

Equitable use of resources for sustainable style

As the human population increased, man through technological and scientific developments developed his activities fast to meet the needs of human. Otherwise greater problems would have occurred. He did not think at that time the consequences of the methods he adopted seriously, as it has now posed a threat to environment. The developmental activities were so fast and these became a great concern for conservation of natural resources. The exhaustion of biological systems and deterioration of the quality of environment cannot be continued forever. At certain point of time in the future, our activities in the same direction would collapse. Mankind may find scarcity even for the basic necessities. Threat to environment and to man himself is to be arrested and sustainable development is to be ensured. This is possible only when there is:

- No damage to environment
- Everyone should be assured of at least basic requirements to lead a happy life.

Sustainable development should ensure	***Sustainable development attained ensure among measures (considering ecologically)***
• Equity amongst: - All nations (rich or poor)	• Development ecological efficient methods of handling industrial, commercial and domestic wastes
• Equity between: - All religions, social classes genders within the same nation	• Encourage - Pollution free non-conventional sources of energy - Production and use of environmentally friendly products - Afforestation
- Generations (present and future)	• Discourage - Deforestation
- Economics, social science ecology, spirituality (guided by economic, environmental, culture, social and ethical considerations)	• Improve by educating people about environmental awareness • Sensitization, socialization and humanitisation of environmental issues

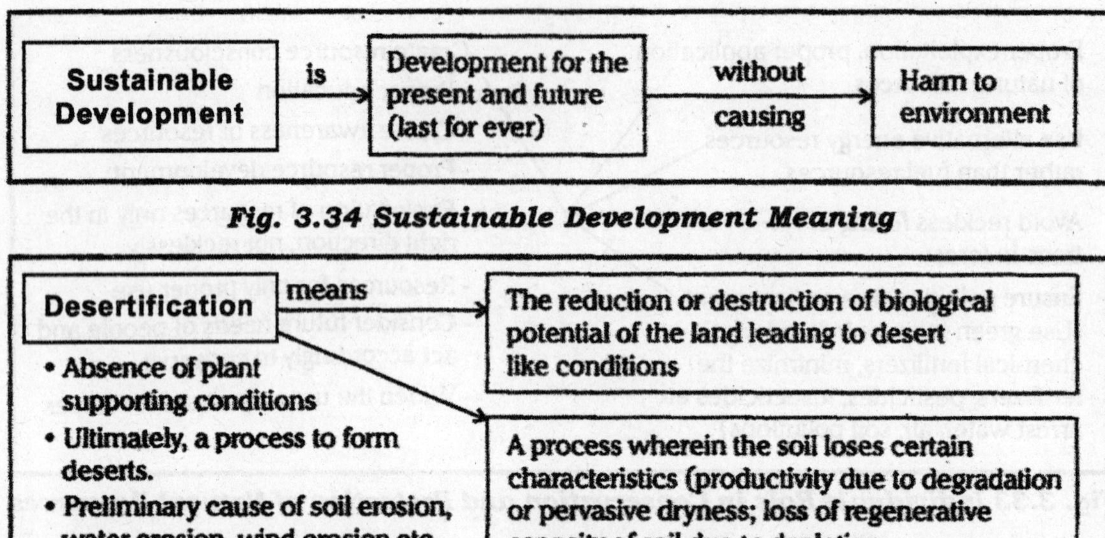

Fig. 3.34 Sustainable Development Meaning

Fig. 3.35 Desertification Meaning

Causes of Desertification: These are:

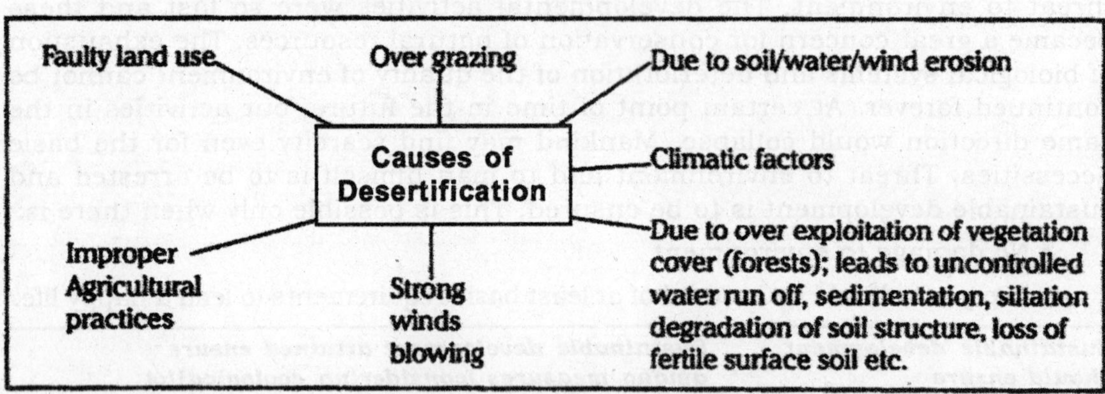

Fig. 3.36 Causes of Desertification

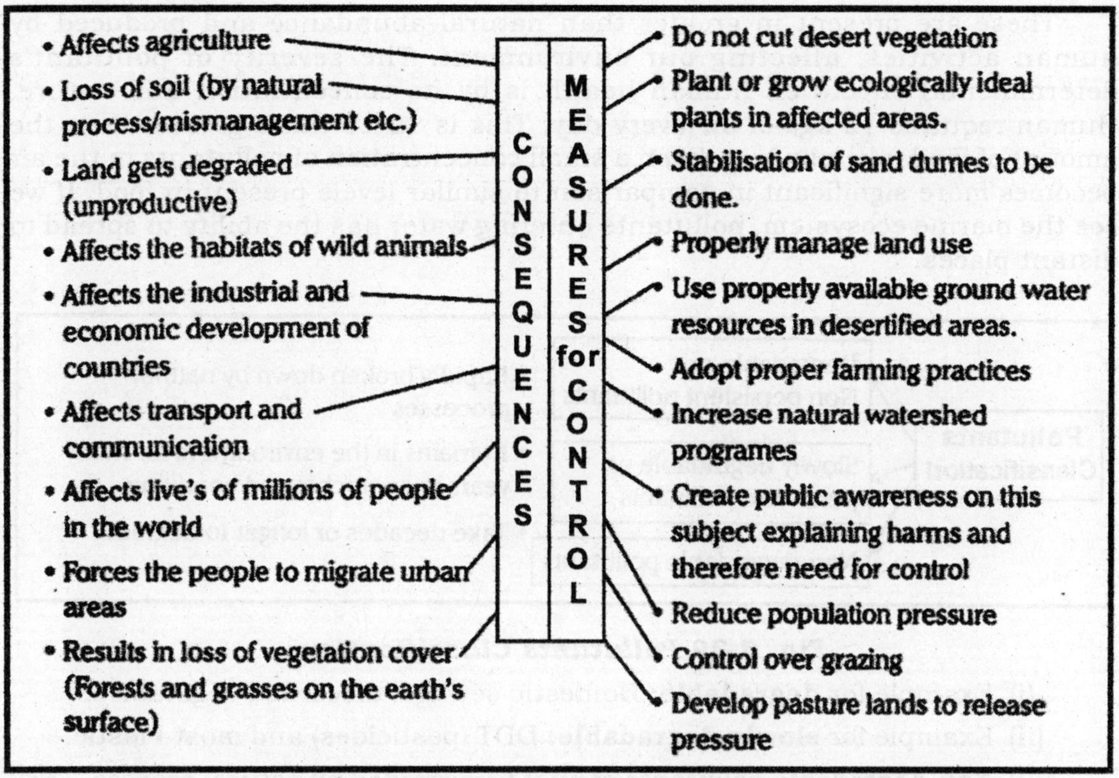

• Affects agriculture
• Loss of soil (by natural process/mismanagement etc.)
• Land gets degraded (unproductive)
• Affects the habitats of wild animals
• Affects the industrial and economic development of countries
• Affects transport and communication
• Affects live's of millions of people in the world
• Forces the people to migrate urban areas
• Results in loss of vegetation cover (Forests and grasses on the earth's surface)
CONSEQUENCES
MEASURES for CONTROL
Do not cut desert vegetation
Plant or grow ecologically ideal plants in affected areas.
Stabilisation of sand dumes to be done.
Properly manage land use
Use properly available ground water resources in desertified areas.
Adopt proper farming practices
Increase natural watershed programes
Create public awareness on this subject explaining harms and therefore need for control
Reduce population pressure
Control over grazing
Develop pasture lands to release pressure

Fig. 3.37 Consequences and Measures of Desertification

3.2 The Ethics of Control

ENVIRONMENT POLLUTION

Definition of Pollution and Classification of Pollutants

Pollution
is the effect of unwanted changes
in our surroundings
Creating harmful effects on
Plants
Animals
Human beings

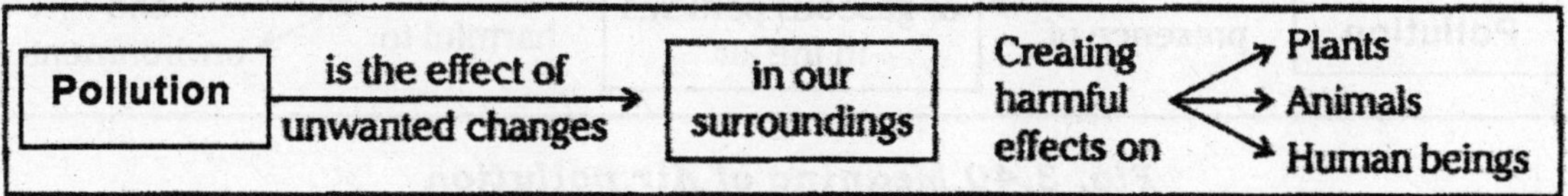

Fig. 3.38 Meaning of Pollution

Major ecological changes have taken place by mankind.

Man is the most dangerous in contaminating air, water and land in the recent days.

Pollutants include following substances:

- Solid
- Liquid
- Gaseous

These are present in greater than natural abundance and produced by human activities, affecting our environment. The severity of pollutant's determinental effects on human health is by its concentration and nature. Human requires 12 kgs of air every day. This is 12-15 times greater than the amount of food taken by him. Even a small concentration of pollutants in the air becomes more significant in comparison to similar levels present in food. If we see the marine ecosystem, pollutants entering water has the ability to spread to distant places.

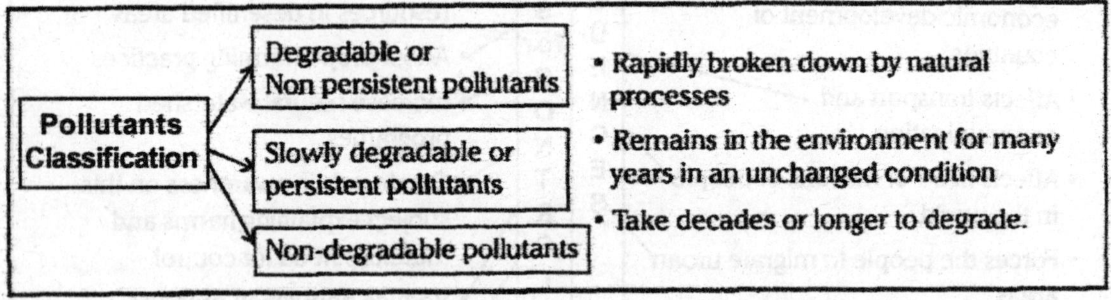

Fig. 3.39 Pollutants Classification

(i) Example for **degradable:** Domestic sewage, discarded vegetables.

(ii) Example for **slowly degradable:** DDT (pesticides) and most Plastic.

(iii) **Non-degradable** pollutants cannot be degraded by natural process. They are difficult to eradicate in the environment and continue to accumulate. E.g., Toxic elements (lead or mercury); nuclearwastes.

Causes, Effects and Control Measures of Pollution

Air pollution

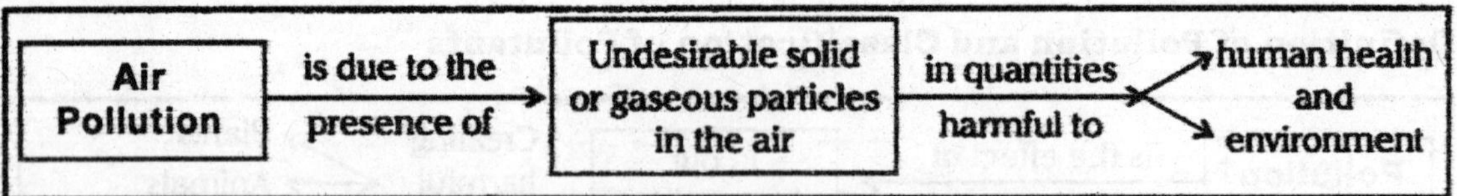

Fig. 3.40 Meaning of Air pollution

How is the air polluted?

It is by natural causes such as:

- Volcanoes releasing ash, dust, sulpher and innumerable gases.
- Forest fibres that are occasionally caused by lightening.

As compared to pollutants created from human activity, naturally occurring pollutants remains in the atmosphere for a short time and do not lead to permanent atmospheric change.

Pollutants emitted from identifiable sources are produced by:

Primary pollutants

- Natural events (Dust storms and volcanic eruptions etc.)
- Human activities (emission from industries and vehicles etc.)

Secondary pollutants

- Certain chemical reactions in the atmosphere takes place among the primary pollutants (Sulfuric acid, Nitric acid, Carbonic acid etc.)

It is to be noted that the primary pollutants form 90% of the global air pollution. The five major pollutants together contribute in this are CO and CO_2, nitrogen oxide, sulphur oxides, volatile organic compounds (mostly hydrocarbons) and lastly suspended particulate matter.

What is a particulate?

Particulate is a small piece of solid material of various constituents dispersed into the atmosphere e.g., smoke particles from fires, asbestos tiny bits, dust particles, industries ash. The effects of these range from formation of soot to the carcinogenic (cancer-causing). Repeated exposure of the above affect man to accumulate the same in the lungs and interfere with the ability of the lungs to exchange gases.

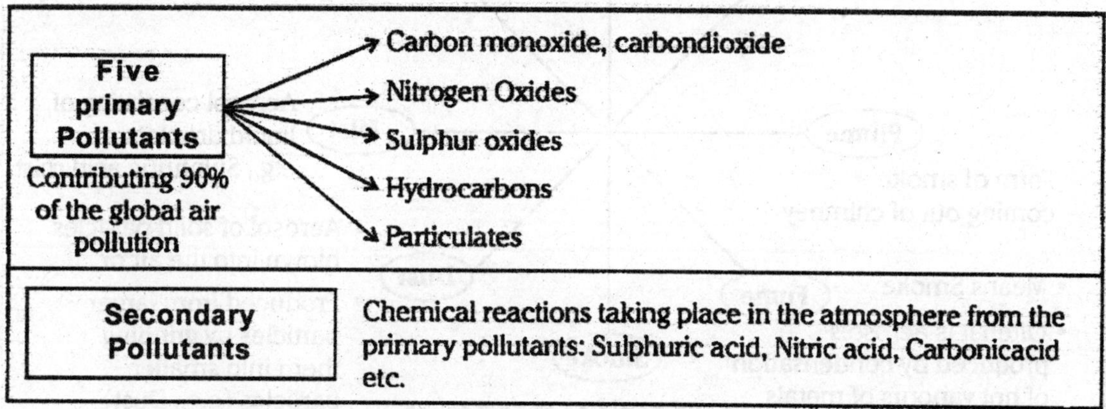

Fig. 3.41 Pollutants (primary and secondary)

(i) Carbon monoxide: Colourless, odourless, toxic gas. This is produced when organic materials (like natural gas, coal or wood) are incompletely burnt. Many of recently increasing vehicles are poorly maintained and with inadequate pollution control equipment, which releases CO. It is not a persistent pollutant. Natural processes can convert this to other harmless compounds. If no new carbon monoxide is introduced into the atmosphere, the old carbon monoxide is removed.

(ii) Nitrogen oxides are significant since it produces secondary air pollutant such as ozone and found in vehicular exhausts.

(iii) Sulphur oxides are produced when sulphur containing fossil fuels are burnt.

(iv) Hydrocarbons: These are a group of compounds consisting of carbon and hydrogen atoms. These are evaporated from fuel supplies and are remnants of insufficient burning of fuel. When rain comes, hydro-carbons are washed out of the air and run into surface water found as only film on the surface. These do not cause a serious issue until they react to form secondary pollutants.

To reduce the release of hydrocarbons into the atmosphere:

- Use higher oxygen concentrations in the fuel-air mixture.
- Use valves to prevent the escape of gases.
- Fit catalytic converts in automobiles.

(v) Particulates: Already explained earlier.

The types of particulates are many:

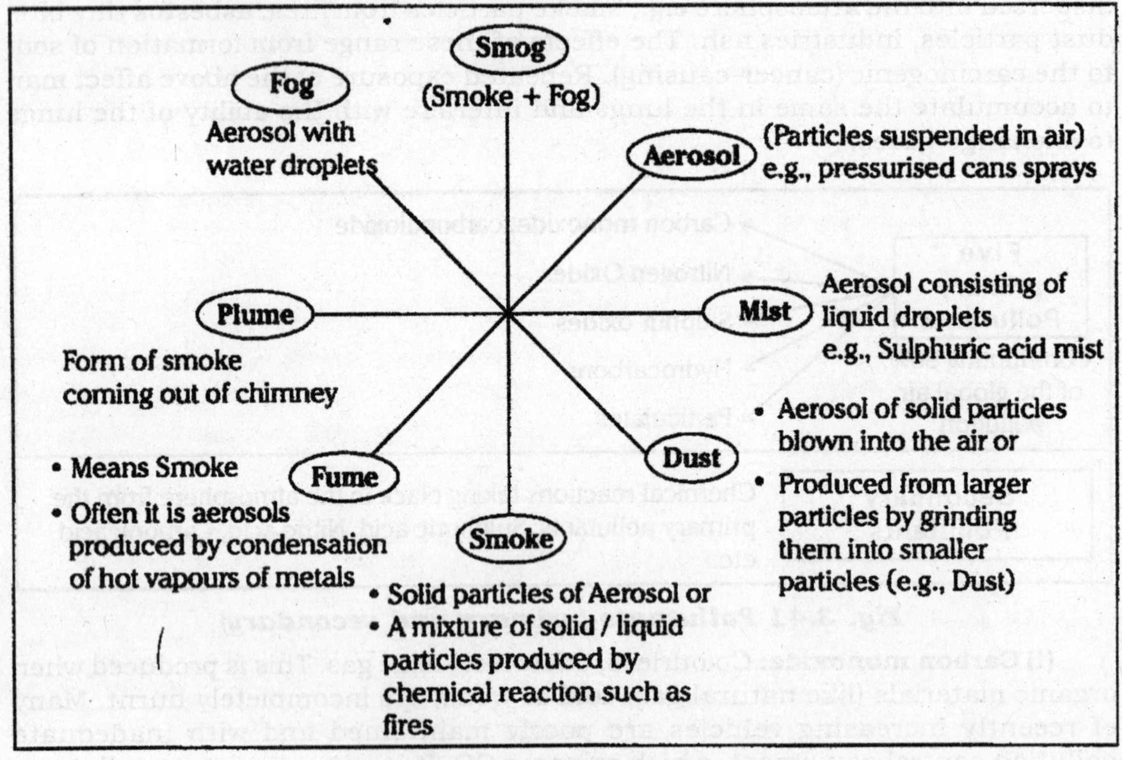

Fig. 3.42 Types of Particulates

Pollutants can also be classified as under:

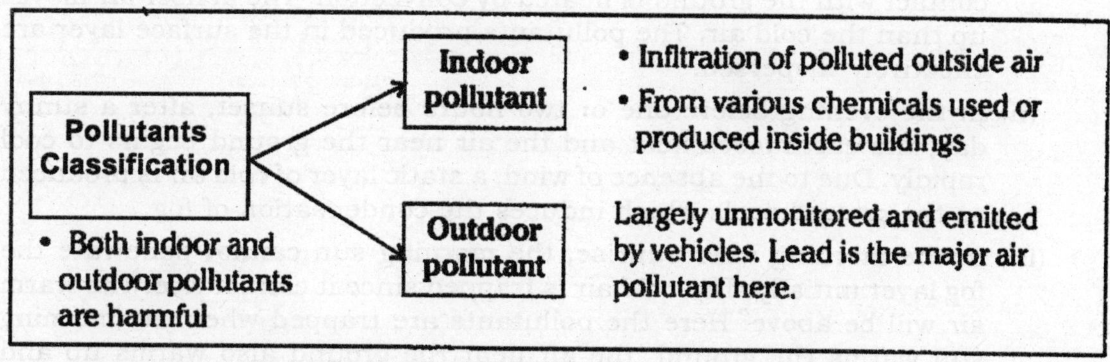

Fig. 3.43 Pollutants (Indoor and Outdoor)

Lead is the most dangerous air pollutant emitted by vehicles. High lead levels are found in metropolitan cities. Unleaded petrol is used in vehicles to avoid the source of air borne lead emissions in India.

Pollutants in the atmosphere

Pollutants when entered into the troposphere, they are:

- Transported downward, diluted by large volume of air, transformed through physical or chemical changes.
- Removed from the atmosphere by rain or attached to water vapour that subsequently forms rain or snow, falls on the earth surface.

The atmosphere disperses pollutants by mixing them with large volume of air that covers the earth and dilutes the pollutants to acceptable levels.

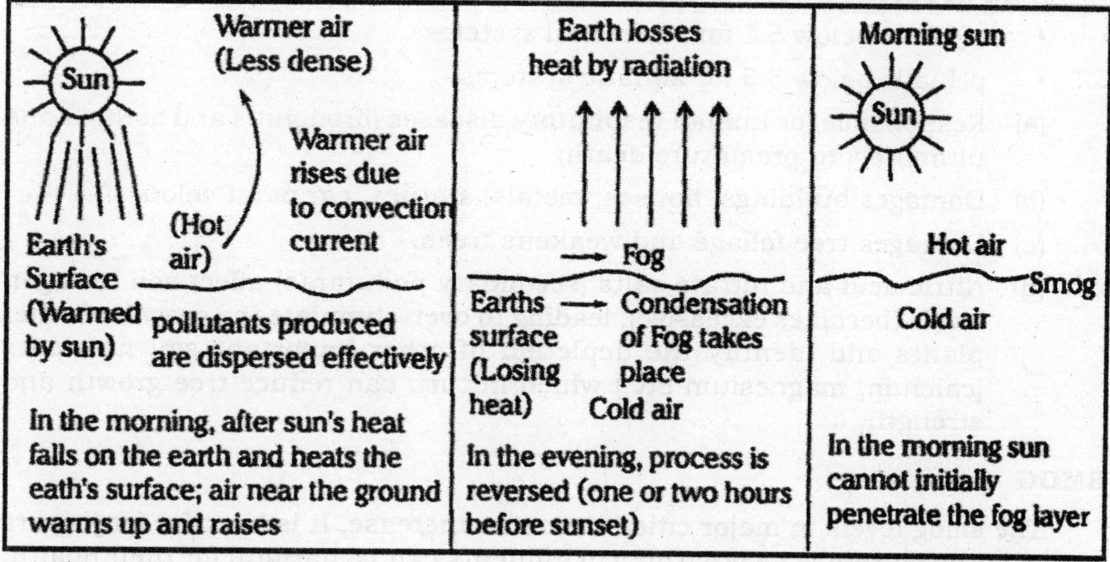

Fig. 3.44 Pollutants in the Air (during different timings of the day)

(i) In the day time after the sun warms the earth's surface, layer of air in contact with the ground is heated by convection. The denser air moves up than the cold air. The pollutants produced in the surface layer are effectively dispersed.

(ii) In the evening before one or two hours before sunset, after a sunny day, the earth loses heat and the air near the ground begins to cool rapidly. Due to the absence of wind, a static layer of cold air is produced as the ground cools which induces the condensation of fog.

(iii) In the morning after sunrise, the morning sun cannot penetrate the fog layer initially. The cold air is trapped since it cannot rise. The warm air will be above. Here the pollutants are trapped when the morning sun warms the ground, the air near the ground also warms up and rises. This may be broken strong winds. In cold regions, this situation persists for several days leading to smog (smoke + fog).

The velocity of the wind affects the dispersal of pollutants. Strong winds dilute the pollutants rapidly, vice versa with the low velocity winds, concentration of pollutants remains high.

As already said, if sulphurdioxide and nitrogen oxides are transported by winds, they form secondary pollutants (nitric acid vapour and sulphuric acid droplets and particles of sulphate and nitrate salts). These chemicals come down on earth's surface in two ways:

- Wet (Acidic rain, snow, fog and cloud vapour)
- Dry (As aciding particles)

If both are combined, the mixture is called **acid deposition**; called as **acid rain.**

Acid deposition has harmful effects as under:

- pH falls below 5.1 for terrestrial systems
- pH falls below 5.5 for aquatic systems.

(a) Responsible for human respiratory diseases (bronchitis and asthma and ultimately to premature death).

(b) Damages buildings, houses, metals, statues, car paint colours.

(c) Damages tree foliage and weakens trees.

(d) Nitric acid and nitrate salts (secondary pollutants) affect soil nitrogen levels (becomes excessive), leading to over-stimulate the growth of other plants and identify the depletion of other important soil nutrients (calcium, magnesium etc.) which in turn can reduce tree growth and strength.

SMOG

The smog levels in major cities are on an increase. It is harmful for joggers to run in the mornings as breathing in affluents can be harmful for their health. Now if you are thinking what really is smog, then here is a clue:

Smog refers to hazy air that causes difficult breathing conditions.

Smog = Smoke + Fog (combination of words)

A large part of the gases that form smog is produced when fuels are burnt. Smog forms when heat sunlight reacts with these gases and find particles in the air. Its occurrences are often linked to heavy traffic, high temperatures and calm winds. During the winter wind speeds are low and cause the smoke and fog to stagnate. Hence pollution levels can increase near ground level. This keeps the pollution close to the ground, right where people are breathing. It hampers visibility and harms the environment. Heavy smog greatly decreases ultraviolet radiation. In fact, in the early part of the 20th century, heavy smog in some parts of Europe resulted in a decrease in the production of natural vitamin D leading to a rise in the cases of rickets.

Smog causes a misty haze similar to fog, but very different in composition. So during winters, you can exercise indoors in air conditioning when air quantity is good.

Plant lots of shrubbery in your yard as it is a good deterrent of pollution and dirt from the street.

Effects of air pollution

(i) On living organisms

We have natural defense systems in our respiratory system. The mechanisms involved help in protecting humans from air pollution.

- The hair in our nose, filters out large particles.
- The sticky mucus captures small particles, dissolves gaseous pollutants.
- When irritated by pollutants, sneezing and coughing takes place and expels the contaminated air and mucus.

Air pollution affects

- The people who smoke continuously, breaks down these natural defenses causing/contributing to diseases like lung cancer, asthma, chronic bronchitis and emphysema.
- Old people, infants, pregnant ladies, with heart disease, asthma or other respiratory diseases.
- Cigarette smokers responsible for exposure to carbon monoxide. Even 0.001% of carbon monoxide exposure for several hours causes collapse, coma and even death. Carbon monoxide remains attached to the hemoglobin in the blood for a long time and reduces the oxygen carrying capacity of blood; perception and thinking, slows reflexes, causes headaches, drowsiness, dizziness and nausea. Carbon monoxide in heavy traffic causes some of the above, and blurred vision. In large doses it can cause death by poisoning.

- Sulphur dioxide irritates the respiratory issues; causes a condition similar to bronchitis. It reacts with water, oxygen and other material in the air to form sulphur containing acids. In makes corrosive to the lungs when inhaled.
- Nitrogen oxides and NO_2 can irritate the lungs, increases asthma and chronic bronchitis, respiratory infections (influenza, common colds etc.).
- Suspended articles in the air increases our respiratory tract, leading to asthma and bronchitis. With exposure to a long period, it damages lung tissue and leads to the development of chronic respiratory disease and cancer.
- Volatile organic compounds like benzene and formaldehyde, particulates like lead and cadmium can cause mutations, reproductive problems or cancer. If ozone is inhaled for a long period, it causes coughing, chest pain, breathlessness and irritation of the eye, nose and throat.

(ii) On plants	**On materials**
• Gaseous pollutants damage the leaves of crop plants.	• Air pollutants cause damage worth crores of rupees.
• Air pollutants break down the heavy coating that helps prevent excessive water loss and leads to damage from diseases, pests, drought and frost; interferes with photosynthesis, plant growth, reduces nutrient uptakes and causes the leaves to turn yellow, brown or drop off; flower buds become stiff and hard. Fall off and unable to flower.	• Air pollutants break down the external paint of cars and houses.
• Air pollutants from smelters, coal burning power plants, industrial units, vehicles, damage trees and other plants.	• These have discoloured, disfigured irreplaceable movements, historic buildings, marble statues, heritage and natural beauty sites.

(iii) On the stratosphere

Ozone layer is in the upper stratosphere consisting of considerable mounts of ozone and works as an effective screen for ultra violet light. This layer is up to 60 KM and it is densest in the region between 20-25 KM from the earth's surface. This layer also has a mixture of other atmosphere gases. In the densest ozone layer, the ratio of ozone to other gas molecules is 1:1,00,000. Hence ozone is so important and any small changes in ozone would produce dramatic effects on the life on earth.

The ozone is recorded in Dobson units (DU). It is from the earth's surface up to an attitude of 50 KMs known as total column ozone. It is a measure of the thickness of the ozone layer by an equivalent layer of pure ozone gas at normal temperature and pressure at sea level (100 DU=1 mm of pure ozone at normal temperature and pressure at sea level).

Ozone is O_3 (3 atoms of oxygen instead of two). It can be produced naturally from the photodisassociation of oxygen gas molecules in the atmosphere. The ozone formed in this way is constantly broken down by naturally occurring processes that maintain its balance in the ozone layer. If the pollutants are not there, the creation and breakdown of ozone are governed by natural forces, but its presence of certain pollutants can accelerate the breakdown of ozone.

Ozone Hole

In 1985, a large scale destruction of the ozone came into light when some British researchers published measurements about the ozone layer. It was known earlier that ozone shows fluctuations in its concentrations, accompanied sometimes by a little ozone depletion. CFCs were established leading to ozone depletion. CFCs are chlorofluero carbons which are stable, non-flammable, non-toxic and harmless to handle. This is ideal for many industrial applications like:

- aerosols
- foam for mattresses and cushions
- air-conditioners
- disposable styrofoam cups
- refrigerators
- glasses
- fire-extinguishers
- packaging material for insulation, cold storage etc.
- many cans which give out foams and sprays (perfumes, room fresheners etc.)

CFCs give a long life span in the atmosphere due to their stability.

Similarly halons have structure containing bromine atoms instead of chlorine and is more dangerous to the ozone layer than CFCs; used in fire-extinguishing agents as they do not harm the people and equipment during fire-fighting. CFCs and halons migrate in the atmosphere (upper) after release. They are heavier than air; to be carried by air currents upto a point just above the lower atmosphere and diffuses slowly into the upper atmosphere. This is a slow process and can take 5-15 years. In the stratosphere, unfiltered UV radiation severs the chemical bonds releasing chlorine (CI) from the rest of CFCs an oxygen molecule (O_2) and an oxygen (O) atom.

CFCs are evenly distributed over the globe. The ozone depletion is pronounced over the south pole due to the extreme weather conditions (Antartic). The presence of ice crystals make the CI-O bonding easier.

India has signed Montreal protocol in 1992; aimed at controlling the production and consumption of ozone depleting substances.

How to solve ozone depletion problem?

Ozone layer changes, affect many things and the following problems are bound to happen:

Effects on human health	*Effects on food production*	*Effects on plant and animals*	*Effects on materials*	*Effects on climate*
• Sunburn, cataract due to increased UV Radiation, Aging of the skin, Skin cancer due to radiation.	• Affects the ability of plants to capture light energy during photosynthesis due to UV.	• Damaged by UV.	• UV radiation damages paints, fabrics.	• Atmospheric changes induced by pollution contribute to global warming.
• Weakens the immune system by reducing the body's resistance to certain infections	• Reduces the nutrient content of plants, growth of plants.	• Zooplanktons (microscopic animals) the breeding period is shortened.	• Fades faster.	• Green house effect is found.
- Measles - Chicken pox - Viral diseases that elicit rash and parasitic diseases like Malaria.	Eg: as seen in the case of cabbage and legumes.	• Plkanktons form the basis of the marine food chain, any shortage in number and species influences fish and selfish production.		

Green House Effect: Atmospheric constituents like water vapour, CO_2, methane, nitrogen oxides and CFCs trap heat in the form of infrared radiation (IR) near the earth's surface. This phenomenon is similar to what we observe in a green house. The heat is trapped in the green house increasing the temperature inside and ensuring the luxuriant growth of plants.

Global warming: It is a phenomenon caused due to the increase in the concentration of gases like carbon-di-oxide, nitrogen oxides, methane and CFCs.

Adverse effects of global warming

- With earth warming, the polar ice caps melt causing a rise in ocean levels and flooding of coastal areas.
- Countries like Bangladesh and Maldives have more effect. 3 meters more height would sunk maldives island.
- Rise in temperature results in a fall in agricultural produce.

- Changes in the distribution of solar energy brings changes in habitats (agricultural area will have droughts, rains in desert, changes in species of natural plants, agricultural crops, insects, livestock and microorganisms). Temperature rise in polar regions by global warming cause disastrous effects. Large quantities of methane released after permafrost melts, accelerate the process of global warming.

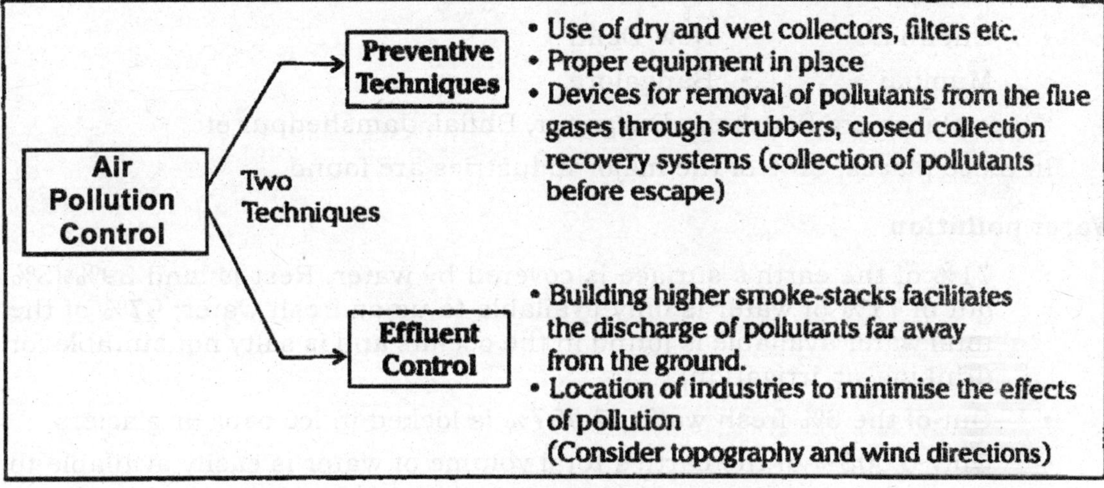

Fig. 3.45 Air Pollution Control

Atomspheric Radioactivity: This originates from two sources:

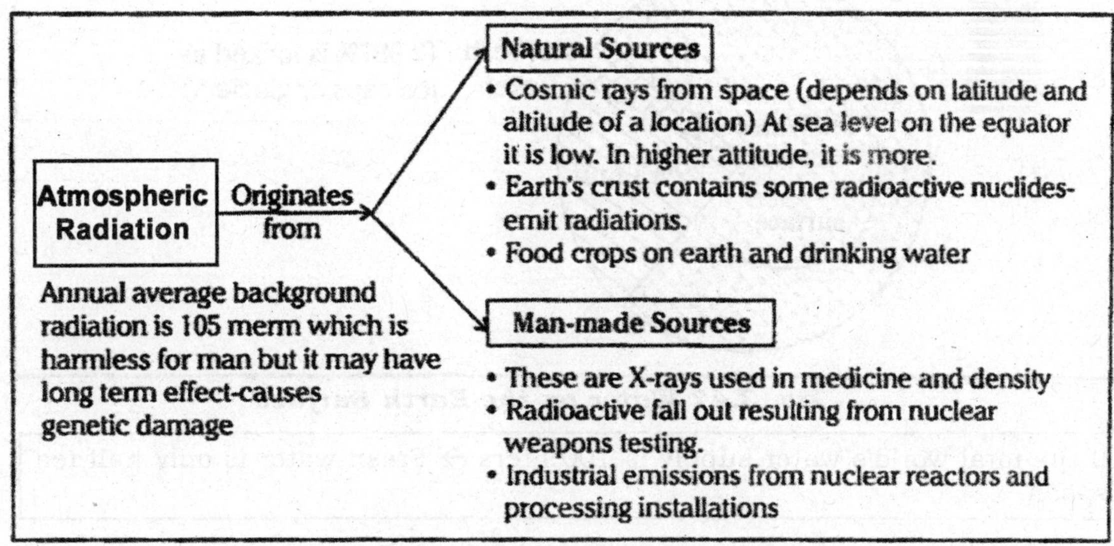

Fig. 3.46 Air Atmospheric Radiation

Most polluted city is Mumbai, followed by other cities like New Delhi, Kolkata and Chennai. Auto exhaust is also responsible for air pollution in India.

Air pollution in India

Important industrial belts in India are mostly centred around big cities like:

- Kolkata
- Chennai
- Mumbai
- Hyderabad
- New Delhi
- Bangalore

Other places are Rourkela, Durgapur, Bhilai, Jamshedpur etc.

In these places, 80% of the major industries are found.

Water pollution

- 71% of the earth's surface is covered by water. Rest is land 39% (3% out of 71% of water is only available to us as fresh water; 97% of the total water available is found in the oceans and is salty not suitable for drinking or irrigation).
- Out of the 3% fresh water, 2.997% is locked in ice caps or glaciers.
- Only 0.003% of the earth's total volume of water is easily available to us as soil moisture, ground water, water vapour and water in rivers, lakes, streams and wet lands.

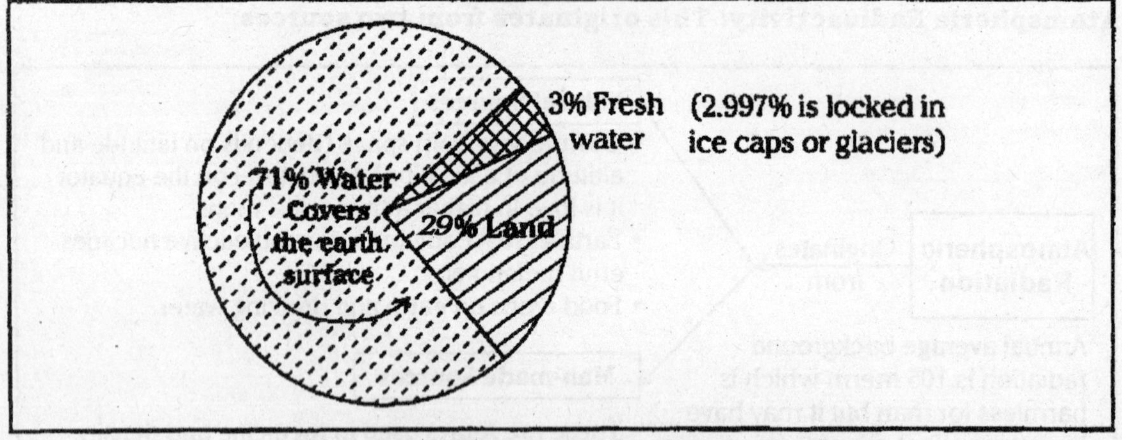

Fig. 3.47 Water on the Earth Surface

If the total world's water supply is 100 liters → Fresh water is only half tea spoon.

Hence the water is a very precious resource.

There is a fear that the countries may fight in future for fresh water.

By 2050, people might get only 50% of the fresh water what man uses today. The fresh water becomes scarce. The access to water resources will be a major factor for countries to determine the economic growth.

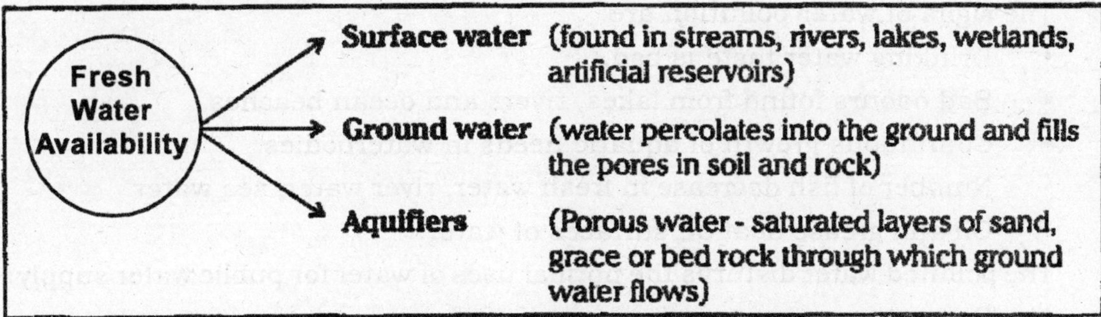

Fig. 3.48 Fresh Water Availability

Aquifiers are replenished naturally by rainfall. The water particulates downward through the soil and rock known as **'natural recharge'**.

The quantity of water as said earlier is of vital concern for mankind. It is directly linked with human welfare. Pollution of drinking water causes water-borne diseases, sometimes wipeout entire populations of cities of developing countries. The major sources of water pollution are:

- Domestic waste from urban and rural areas.
- Industrial wastes which are discharged into natural waterbodies.

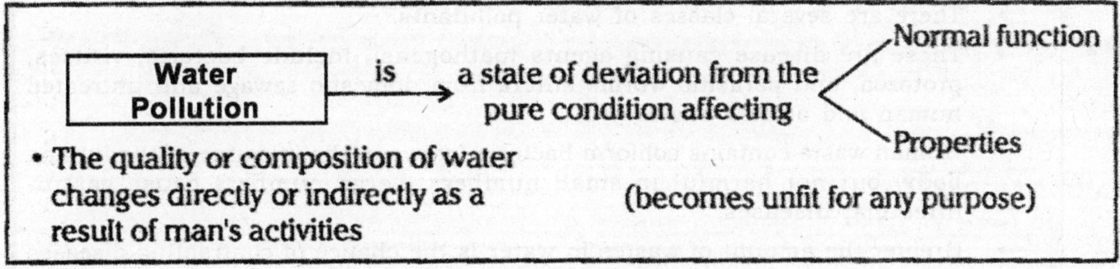

Fig. 3.49 Water Pollution

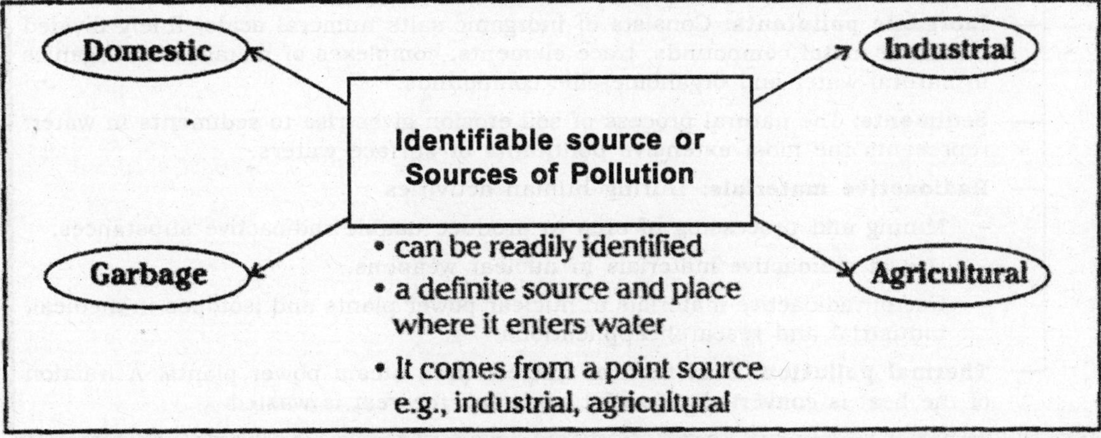

Fig. 3.50 Sources of Pollution

The signs of water pollution are:

- Drinking water taste is bad.
- Bad odours found from lakes, rivers and ocean beaches.
- Continuous growth of aquatic needs in waterbodies.
- Number of fish decrease in fresh water, river water, sea water.
- Oil and grease float on surfaces of water.

The polluted water disturbs the normal uses of water for public water supply.

- Recreation
- Aesthetics
- Fish, other aquatic life and wild life
- Agriculture
- Industry

Water pollutants

The broad classification of water pollutants can be described as under:

WATER POLLUTANTS

- There are several classes of water pollutants.
- These are disease causing agents (pathogens), include bacteria, viruses, protozoa, and parasitic worms enters from domestic sewage and untreated human and animal wastes.
- Human waste contains coliform bacteria (grows in the intestine of the human body) but not harmful in small numbers. Large numbers cause gastro-intestinal diseases.
- Greater the amount of wastes in water is the chance of contracting diseases from them.

— **Organic pollutants:** Include oxygen-demanding wastes, disease causingagents, plant nutrients, sewage, synthetic organic compounds and oil.

— **Inorganic pollutants:** Consists of inorganic salts numeral acids, finely divided metals or metal compounds, trace elements, complexes of metals with organics in natural water and organometallic compounds.

— **Sediments:** The natural process of soil erosion gives rise to sediments in water; represents the most extensive pollutants of surface waters.

— **Radioactive materials:** During human activities

- Mining and processing of ores to produce usable radioactive substances.
- Use of radioactive materials in nuclear weapons.
- Use of radioactive materials in nuclear power plants and isotopes in medical, industrial and research applications.

— **Thermal pollution:** Coal fired or nuclear fired steam power plants. A fraction of the heat is converted to useful work and the rest is wasted.

Fig. 3.51 Water Pollutants

The reasons for the above may be from any of the following:

- **Anaerobic bacteria** (do not require oxygen) begin to break down wastes. Their respiration produces chemicals that have a foul odour and an unpleasant taste, which are harmful to human health.
- The water soluble nitrates and phosphates that cause the excessive growth of Algae and other aquatic plants. (Eutrophication) with the use of the water by clogging up water-intake pipes, changing the taste and smell of the water, causing a build up of organic matter. The fish and other aquatic species die if the organic matter decays and the oxygen levels decrease.
- If the quantity of fertilisers applied in a field is more than actually required by the plants, the chemicals pollute the soil and water. Excess fertilisers cause **eutrophication**, pesticides cause **bioaccumulation** and **biomagnification**. The pesticides that enter water bodies are introduced into:
  - — Water-soluble inorganic chemicals like mercury and lead can make the water unfit to drink, harm fish and other aquatic life, reduce crop yields, accelerate the corrosion of equipment.
- Under thermal pollution, the hot water released by power plants and industries use large volumes of water to cool the plant, results in a rise in temperature of the local water bodies. This warm water after discharged not only decreases the solubility of oxygen but changes the breeding cycles of various aquatic organisms.
- Oil washed into the surface water in the run-off from roads and parking lots also creates havoc with ground water.

Water pollution prevention through control measures

This can be done as under:

- **Setting up effluent treatment plants** to treat waste which can reduce the pollution load. Treated effluent can be reused for gardening or cooling purpose.
- **Root zone process,** a new technology involves running contaminated water through the root zones of specially reed beds, the plants of which can absorb oxygen from the surrounding air. The oxygen is pushed through the porus stem of the reeds into the hollow roots. This creates conditions for the growth of numerous bacteria and fungi which oxidise impurities in the waste waters and the water becomes clean.

Soil pollution

The soil is a good resource for which there is no substitute. The fertilisers are also not a substitute for fertile soil. The soil is a thin covering of land consists of:

- Minerals
- Organic material
- Living organisms
- Air and water

All these would support the growth of plant life.

Climate and time are important factors in the development of soil. Soils development is slow in extremely dry and cold climates and fast in humid and warm climate soils. A soft parent material develops into 1 cm of soil within 15 years under ideal climatic conditions. Under poor climatic conditions, it may require hundreds of years.

Soil Horizons

Mature soils are arranged in a series of zones called **soil horizons**. Each horizon has a texture and composition varying with different types of soils. Soil profile is a cross-sectional view of the horizons in a soil.

- Top layer/surface litter layer ..... 'O' Horizon
- Uppermost layer of the soil ..... 'A' Horizon

These two top layers also contain:

— a large amount of bacteria, fungi, earthworms.

— small insects,

which form complex food webs in the soil, help recycle soil nutrients and contribute to soil fertility.

- Sub soil ..... 'B' Horizon
- Area below the sub soil ..... 'C' Horizon

'B' Horizon contains less organic material and fewer organisms than the **'A' Horizon. 'C' Horizon** consists of weathered parent material; helps to determine the pH of the soil, influences the soil's rate of water absorption and retention.

Soils vary in their content of:

- Clay........ Very fine particles
- Silt........ Fine particles
- Soil........ Medium sized particles
- Gravel...... Coarse to very coarse particles

The relative amount of different size and types of mineral particles determine the soil texture.

Soils with same quantity of mixture of clay, sand, silt and humus are called **loams**.

Why soil degrades?

This may be due to:

- Erosion
  - Continuous contour trenches
  - Gradonies
  - Excess use of fertilisers
- Problems with pesticide use
- Excess salts and water

(1) Soil Erosion

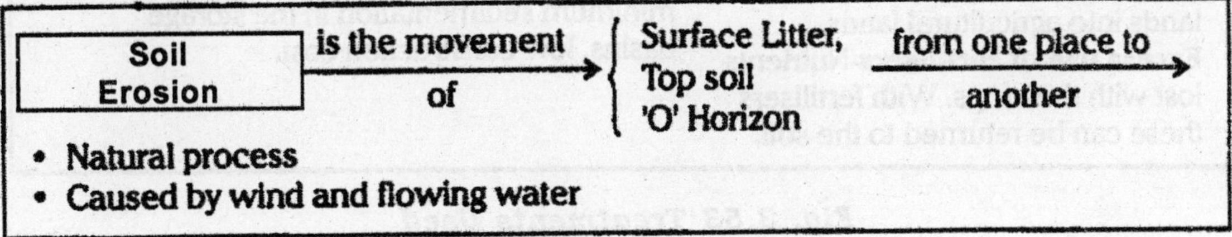

Fig. 3.52 Soil Erosion

Soil erosion is accelerated by human activities such as:

- Farming
- Over grazing (by live stock)
- Deforestation
- Construction
- Burning of grass cover

The loss of the top soil makes it less fertile and its water holding capacity is reduced. This clog lakes and increases the turbidity of the water, ultimately leading to the loss of aquatic life. One inch of top soil to be formed normally requires 200-1000 years depending upon the climate and soil type. If the topsoil erodes faster than its formation, the soil becomes a **non-renewable resource**.

Soil conversation measures

This is needed to minimise the loss of the top soil.

The techniques that protect the soil from erosion are many.

Both water and soil are conserved through integrated treatment methods.

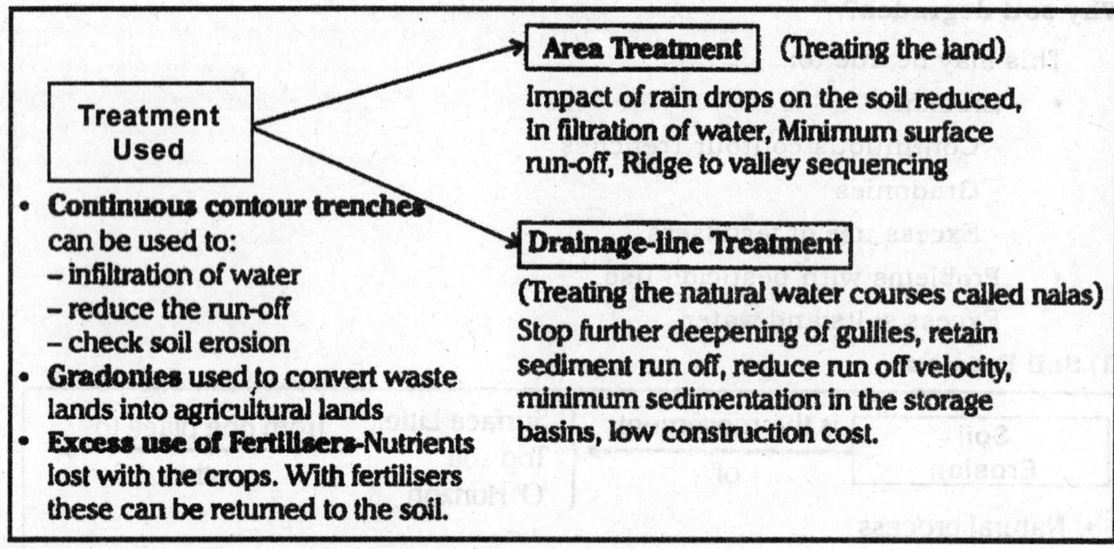

Fig. 3.53 Treatments Used

Problems with pesticide use

Pesticides kill the pests and a large variety of living things, including humans.

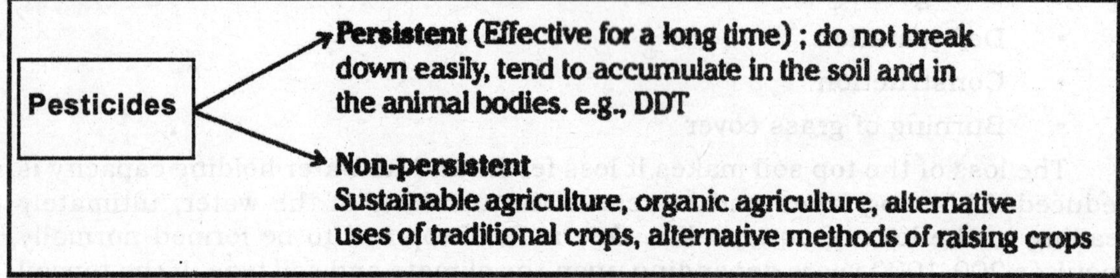

Fig. 3.54 Pesticides

Integrated pest management (IPM) is a technique that uses a complete understanding of all the ecological aspects of a crop and the particular pests to which it is susceptible to establish pest control strategies that uses no or few pesticides.

Persistent pesticides may

- become attached to small soil particles (easily moved by wind and water affecting soils everywhere).
- accumulate in the bodies of animals leading to **bio-accumulation;** transferred to other animals by eating the former.

- ability of insect populations to become resistant to them (useless in a couple of generations).
- Bio-magnification takes place (acquiring increasing levels of a substance in the bodies).

Excess salts and water

Irrigated lands can produce higher crop yields than rain water. Irrigation water contains dissolved salts and in dry climates, water evaporates leaving its salts (Sodium chloride in the top soil). Accumulation of salts is called **salinisation**. From this,

- Plant growth reduces
- Yield low
- Kills the crop
- Render the land useless for agriculture.

Salts are to be flushed out by using more water. Cost increases for crop production.

Water logging is another problem during irrigation. Large amounts of water used will reach the salts deeper into the soil. If water table is raised because of the poor drainage, the roots of the plant will be flooded with saline water and dies. Best way is to adopt sustainable farming practices to avoid the degradation of soil.

Marine pollution

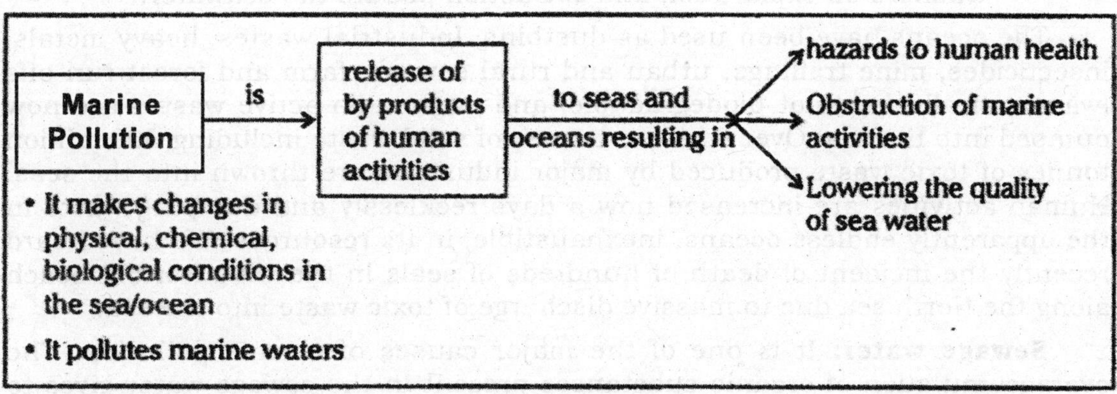

Fig. 3.55 Meaning of Marine Pollution

The pollutants of marine pollution are several like sewage, garbage municipal waste, farm waste, oil spill etc.

Causes that pollute marine waters

The causes are attributed to the following activities:

- Waste through pipes directly discharged into the sea e.g., Municipal water and sewages from residences and hotels, in coastal towns (by high coastal population).
- Organic pollutants.
- Pesticides and fertilisers from agriculture (washed off by the rain from land to the sea).
- Petroleum and oils washed off from roads-reaches the sewage system; storm water overflows and carries the material into rivers and finally to the seas.
- Radio-active waste.
- Off shored oil exploration and extraction.
- Ships carrying toxic substances like:
  - Oil
  - Liquefied natural gas
  - Pesticides
  - Industrial chemicals etc.
- Ship accidents and accidental spillages at sea might happen and damage the marine environment. The dredged material at the channels and entrances to ports may contain heavy metals and other contaminants. Spillages from oil rigs, oil pipe lines, oil tankers also occur.
- Offshore oil exploration and extraction pollute the seawater.

The oceans have been used as dustbins. Industrial wastes, heavy metals, insecticides, mine trailings, urban and rural sewage, farm and forest run offs (wastes of all kinds not biodegradable) and even radio active wastes are now dumped into the sea. Over 9 billion tonnes of solid waste including 300 million tonnes of toxic waste produced by major industries are thrown into the seas. Human activities are increased now a days recklessly and dumping waste in the apparently endless oceans, inexhaustible, in its resources. We have heard recently the incident of death of hundreds of seals in the UK's Norfolk beach along the North sea due to massive discharge of toxic waste into the sea.

Sewage water: It is one of the major causes of marine pollution. The overaccumulation of organic substances present in the sewage water gives to **eutrophication**. The excess nutrients contribute to the growth of minute plants near the sea surface. This prevents the sun rays from reaching deep into the sea. It also reduces or even stops the photo-synthetic activities and takes oxygen and gives out carbon dioxide. Scarcity of oxygen concentration in water may lead to the death of other organisms.

Organic wastes: Pollution due to organic wastes is vital. The amount of oxygen dissolved in the water is important for the plants and animals. Wastes affect the oxygen concentration and thereby the quality of water. The greatest volume of water discharged to water course and the sea is sewage, which is organic in nature and degraded by bacterial activity. The oxygen in the water breaks down the waste into stable inorganic compounds. The oxygen concentration is reduced. If it comes down below 1.5 mg/l, the rate of aerobic oxidation is reduced. It is replaced by the anaerobic bacteria that can oxidise the organic molecules without oxygen. End products like hydrogen sulphide, ammonia and methane are formed. These are toxic to many organisms. This will result in the formation of an anoxic zone (low in oxygen content). This results in disappearance of lives except for anaerobic bacteria, fungi, yeasts and protozoa. As a result, the water will have a foul smell.

Control measures to reduce the pollution load on marine waters

This is done by:

- Introduction of sewage plants to reduce the biological oxygen demand (BOD) of the final product before it is discharged to water.

Three types of treatment are: Primary, Secondary and Advanced.

Primary	Secondary
• It uses physical processes. • Screening and sedimentation to remove pollutants that settles, float, too large to pass through screening devices like stones, sticks, rags, that clog pipes. The disposal of materials are through a device 'communiter' which grinds the material into small pieces and left in the waste water. It passes then through a grit chamber. • The detention time here is for organic material to settle. It then passes into a primary settling tank (sedimentation tank) where the flow speed is reduced to allow for settling the suspended solids by gravity. • If the waste is to undergo only primary treatment, it is chlorinated to destroy bacteria and control odors. • Primary treatment removes 35% of BOD and 60% of the suspended solids.	• Main objective is to remove most of BOD (biological oxygen demand). • Three commonly used approaches are: - Trickling filters - Activated sludge process - Oxidation ponds. In the trickling filter, a rotating distribution arm sprays liquid waste water over a circular bed of first size rocks or other coarse materials. In the activated sludge process, the sewage is pumped into a large tank and mixed for several hours with bacteria rich sludge and air bubbles to facilitate degradation by micro-organisms. Oxidation ponds are large shallow ponds 1-2 mm deep where raw or partially-treated sewage is decomposed by microorganisms.

Advanced sewage treatment involves a series of chemical and physical processes. It removes specific pollutants left in the water, after primary and secondary treatment.

Oil pollution: Oil pollution of the sea normally is important because it can be seen. There are several sources through which the oil can reach the sea as under:

- **Tanker operations** (Nearly 3 bln tonnes crude oil a year is transported by sea) - This is half the world's population.
- **Dry Docking:** All ships need periodic dry docking for servicing, repairs, cleaning the hull etc. Residual oil, finds its way into the sea.
- **Bilge and Fuel oils:** Ballast tanks take up valuable space. Additional ballast is sometimes carried in empty fuel tanks. While being pumped, it carries oil into the sea.
- **Tanker accidents.**
- **Off-shore oil production.**

Control measures for oil pollution

A time-consuming and labour-intensive process is to be adopted in cleaning the oil from surface waters and beaches. Chemical dispersants can be used to accelerate the process which can be sprayed on the oil.

Slick lickers of various types (a continuous belt of absorbant material dips through the oil slick and is passed through rollers to extract the oil slick and is passed through rollers to extract the oil) have been designed.

Rocks, harbor walls can be cleared with pressure steam or dispersants.

Effects of marine pollution	*Controls of marine pollution*
Many adverse effects as under: • **Eutrophication** is caused. • Develops **red tides** (phytoplankton blooms of such intensity that the whole area is discoloured) Marine species are killed due to clogging of gills or other structures. • **Oil slick** is formed. Oil slick is caused, when liquid oil is spilled on the sea and spreading over the surface of the water to form a thin film. Sea temperature, winds, currents and the nature of the oil causes the rate of spreading and the thickness of the film. • Oil slicks damage marine life. • Oil slicks can affect the flowering, fruiting and germination for salt-marsh plants.	• Harmful in someways and it is to be controlled through certain measures. - Domestic and industrial waste water to be treated before discharging into sea or ocean. - Measures are to be taken to prevent oil spill through leakage and breakage. • Ecofriendly way of reducing the effect of oil spill (use of bacteria capable of eating up of the oil) is to be undertaken. • Skimming of oil off the surface with suction device can be undertaken. • Floating of oil is removed with suitable absorbents e.g., sawdust, polymethane foam, chopped straw, chalk with sand.

- Salt marshes and mass grove swamps are likely to trap oil and the plants which form the basis of ecosystems.
- Oil slicks affect fish and selfish production facilities.
- Commercial damage can come from tainting (an unpleasant flavour to fish and sea food happens). This is detectable even at extremely low levels of contamination, thereby reduces the market value of food.
- Birds often clean their plumage by preening and in the process consume the oil which depending upon its toxity, leads to intestinal, renal or lever failure. If liquid oil contaminates a birds plumage its water repellent properties are lost.
- Oil slicker can be removed from chemical additives which can solidify oil from water surface.
- Overfishing of a single species should be controlled (conserve marine bio-diversity).
- Disturbances (Deforestation along a river as example) can lead to the degradation of coral reef should be controlled.
- Pressures on marine resources can be regulated through establishment of:
  - marine protected areas
  - bio regional management approach
  - international agreements.
- **Integrated farming systems** with recycling and use of biological control to reduce reliance on antibiotics would help pollution from agricultural and aquacultural practices.

Noise pollution

Noise is undesirable and nobody wants unwanted sound. Not all sound is noise e.g., Music to one person may be a noise to another. Noise is not so harmful as compared to the contamination of air or water, but it is a pollution problem that affects human health. It contributes to a general deterioration of environmental quality.

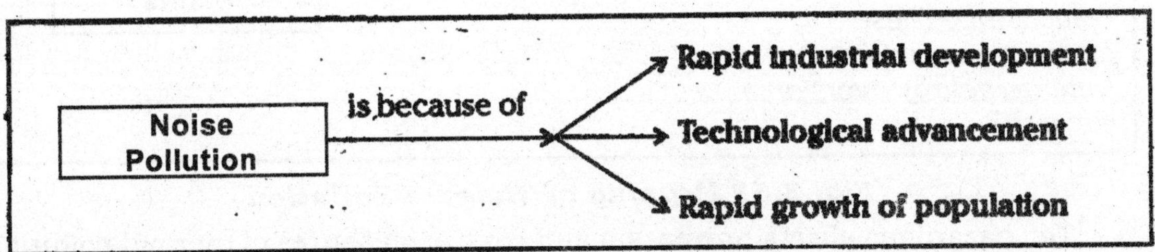

Fig. 3.56 Noise Pollution

We use machinery, technology in our industry and as a result the noise would increase and in some cases beyond limits.

Fig. 3.57 Noise

Sound is measured in a unit called the decibel (dB)

Noise emanates from:

- Factories
- Vehicles
- Loud speakers (during festivals, election times)
- Electronic gadgets
- Functions
- Radio or music systems
- Fire crackers.

The difference between sound and noise is:

- subjective

- a matter of personal opinion

Harmful effects of noise

- When exposed to high sound levels.
- Can range in severity from being extremely annoying to extremely painful and hazardous.

Thermal Pollution

The meaning of thermal pollution is as under:

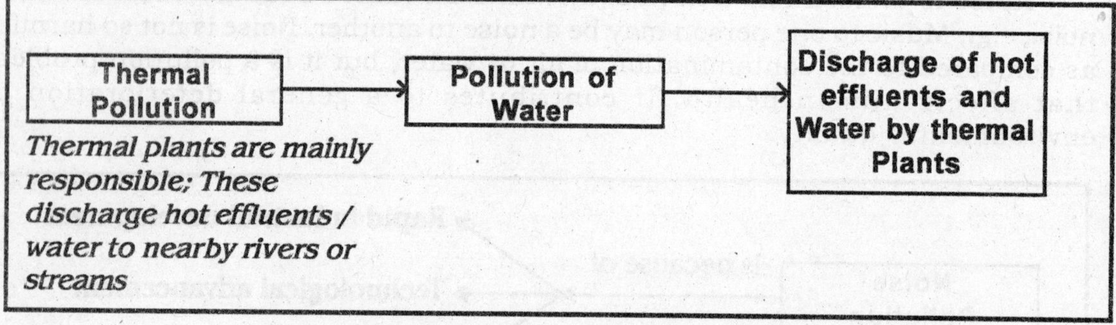

Fig. 3.58 Meaning of Thermal Pollution

The hazardous effects prevention and control measures of thermal pollution are shown in figure 3.59.

Reduction in Emissions to cost India $2.53 trillion

- To reduce greenhouse gas emissions by 9.7% by 2036 would cost $2.53 trillion, if 1990 emission levels are taken as the baseline.
- Worse still, undertaking technological changes that help increase efficiency in the way India uses its fossil fuels (like petroleum which emit Greenhouse gases (GHGs) will become extremely exorbitant.
- If India undertakes any kind of commitments under the UNB Frame work on climate change, it is bound to hit Indian economy.
- Developed countries have begun a loud campaign demanding that India and China too undertake some kind of binding targets to cut emissions just like the developed countries do under the existing regime.

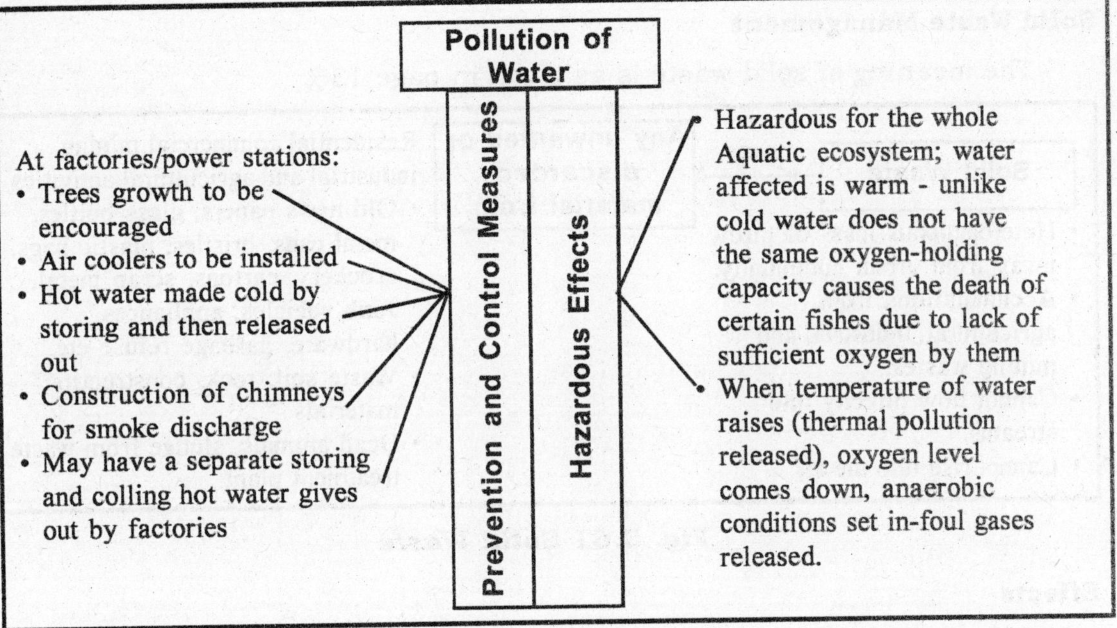

Fig. 3.59 Effects, Prevention and Control of Thermal Pollution

Nuclear Hazards (Nuclear or Radioactive Pollution)

It is a clean energy. But the waste resulting from nuclear reaction is a form of pollution known as **Radioactivity**.

Sources, Effects and Control of Radioactive Pollution

Sources	*Effects*	*Control Measures*
• Nuclear power plants, Nuclear bombing, Nuclear weapon tests. • During transportation of nuclear wastes from place to place. • Disposal of nuclear wastes (use in mining, medical etc.). • Uranium mining (uranium is used in nuclear power plants).	• High penetration power of radiations-Hence harmful. • Distinguishing a normal isotope with a radioactive isotope through a biological system is difficult; Radioactive isotope absorbed and incorporated in bodies of lying organisms. • Dumping of radioactive wastes in sea-Marine life is affected. • Radiation affects organisms through damage to DNA. • Small radiation exposure creates serious biological consequences and remains toxic for long time. • The problem of radioactive pollution is compounded by the difficulty in assembling its effects.	• Nuclear devices should be exploited underground only. • Proper disposal methods of radioactive wastes without affecting humans, plants and animals to be considered. • Nuclear medicines and radiation therapy-only when needed and in small proportions.

Fig. 3.60 Sources, Effects and Control of Radioactive Pollution

Solid Waste Management

The meaning of solid waste is as given in page 136.

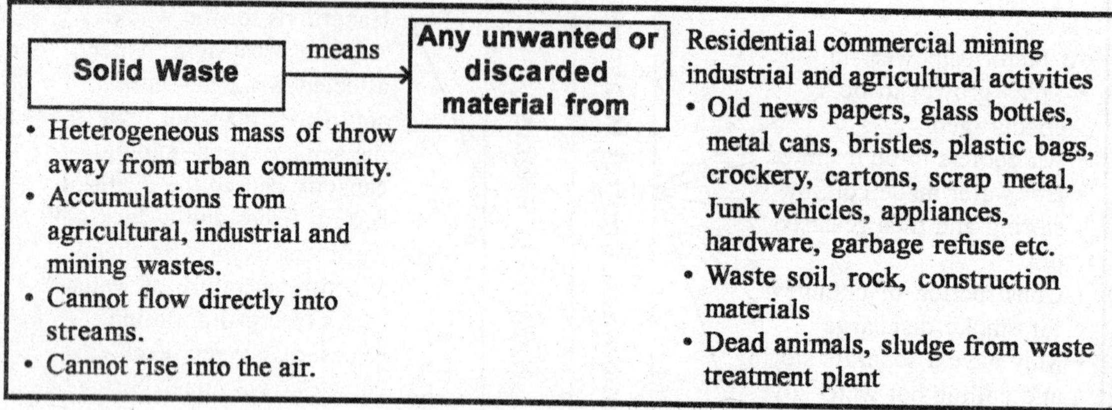

Fig. 3.61 Solid Waste

Effects

Because of solid wastes, certain adverse effects are found:

- Industrial, agricultural, construction, mining wastes result in air and pollution mainly because of dust and chemicals.
- Ground water contamination by certain wastes.
- Surface water contamination by run off.
- Solid wastes affect aesthetic value of environment (disfiguring colours, etc.); health rises.
- Bad odour, pests, rodents, etc.; generation of inflammable gas by methane within waste dumps.
- Bird menace above the waste dwarfs like eagles, crows causing aircrafts failures or delays.
- Food for rats, flies, cockroaches, mosquitoes causing diseases like, malaria, plague, fever, cough and cold viral infections.
- Erosion and stability problems relating to slopes of the waste dump.

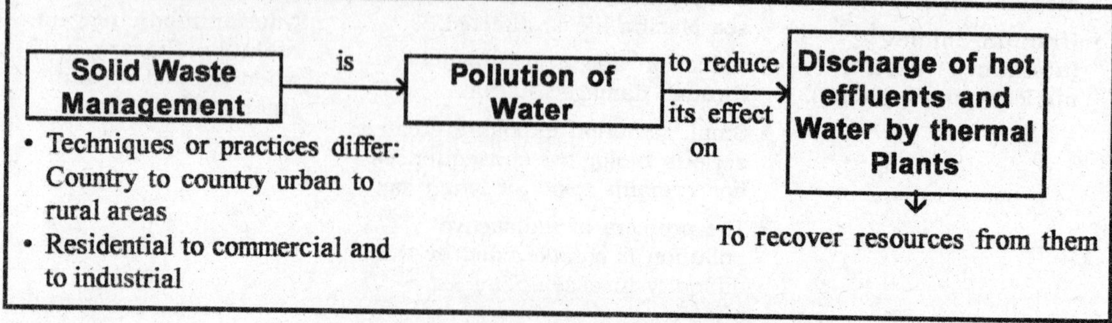

Fig. 3.62 Solid Waste Management

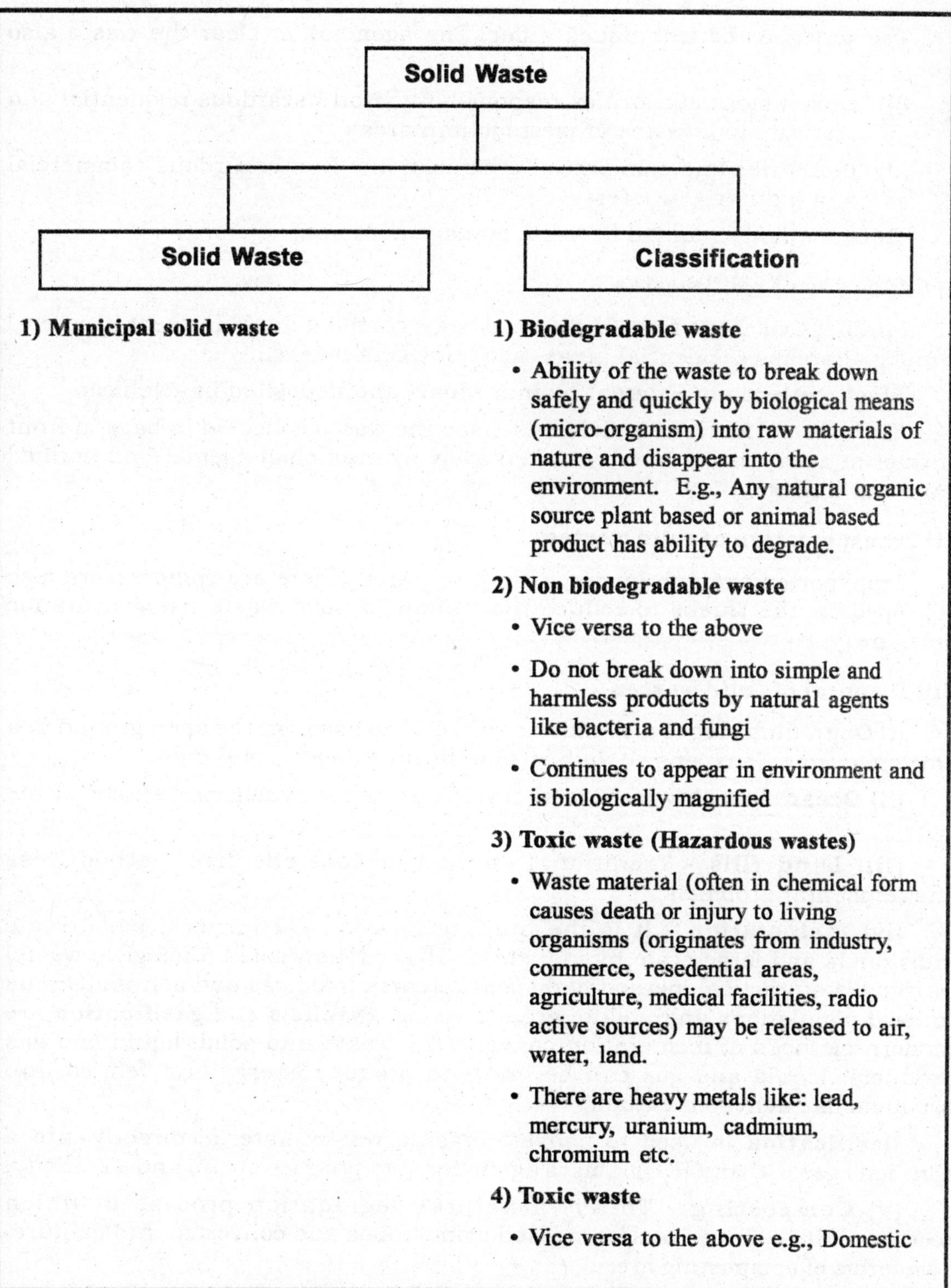

Fig. 3.63 Solid Waste Types

The practices or techniques differ. The agencies to clear the waste also differs.

(i) Government authorities responsibility: Non hazardous residential and institutional wastes in metropolitan areas.

(ii) Industries and commercial organisations: Non hazardous commercial and industrial wastes.

Three methods adopted in waste management are:

(i) Collection of solid wastes

May be in **Garbage bins**, in disposal bags, common dust bins kept in several municipal areas (Residential areas, shopping centers etc.).

Block collection: Brought by individuals and deposited in a vehicle.

Krebsite collection: Individuals place the waste collected in bags in front of their houses. This is later on taken away by municipal agencies on notified days and timings.

(ii) Transportation of solid wastes

Transported through lorries, trucks or carts. There are compressors also equipped on the trucks to reduce the volume of solid waste using hydraulic pressure.

(iii) Disposal of solid wastes

(i) Open dumping is a common method of disposal on the open ground in a particular area. Inexpensive, but certain disadvantages are there.

(ii) Ocean dumping in coastal cities; upsets the ecological balance of the sea.

(iii) Land fills - Traditional method, a cost effective method; less environmental problems.

(iv) Incineration - It is the burning in a special furnace; small-scale individuals and large scale by industries. Hazardous wastes (Biological waste) burning is a practical method of disposal creates toxic gas and ash-dangerous to local populations and pollute ground water. **Pyrolisis** and **gasification** are modern methods of incineration converts the waste into solid, liquid and gas products. Liquid and gas can be burnt to produce energy and refined into products like activated carbon.

Gasification is used to convert organic waste material directly into a synthetic gas (CO and H_2O). This is again burnt to produce steam and electricity.

(v) Composting - This is a natural degradation process in which biodegradable wastes are decomposed by microbes and converted into manure. Two forms of composting are:

(a) Aerobic composting: requires mixing and aeration to promote stable aerobic conditions; But expensive, creates bad odour; mixing and aeration is needed, uses additives, produces green house gases.

(b) Anaerobic composting: done in the absence of air; biodegradable component of wastes stabilizes the putrescible fraction of wastes into a soil conditioner. Does not produce bad odour; No attraction from insects or pests. To enhance soil quality, it can be applied to land. Quite useful in developing countries for disposal of wastes.

(vi) Volume Reduction - For easy handling in bulk due to less space methods are:

- Compacting (compressed; breaking up large or fragile items of waste)
- Shearing (sliced with heavy metal shears)
- Grinding (in a hammer mill).

(vii) Chemical processing - Costly, not affordable by poor countries only for some wastes, this method is advantageous because of recovery of certain usable materials and the prospect of energy production.

(viii) Recycling of waste - Burning of waste and utilize the heat to warm up residential buildings and generation of electricity, composting of organic waste for the preparation of manure and biogas, transformation of organic matter into sugar or protein. Use the refuse into building blocks, briquettes that can be used as a fill. Items recycled are: aluminum, beverage cans, steel and aerosol cans, plastic/glass bottles and jars, paper board, cartons, news papers, magazines, cardboard etc. Recycling needs less energy, water and other resources to produce new materials.

ROLE OF AN INDIVIDUAL IN THE PREVENTION OF POLLUTION

Pollution and Health effects

Air pollution claims one lakh lives in India and affects the health of 250 lakhs every year. Raw data is simply not enough. A lot of research on health impacts of pollution is needed. A simpler air quality index is necessary to increase awareness about pollution among people. Indoor air quality is also an important, but neglected area. We need an integrated approach as monitoring and data alone will do no good, unless we act to reduce pollution. Whether vehicles are meeting pollution control norms, is also to be examined.

Pollution aggravates asthma and wheezing lasts larger. Viral infections can only make a situation worse. Many parents take their young children out in traffic, while many children suffer due to adults smoking at home. Indoor air quality is equally important for good health. Particulate matter (PM) in air is a major health concern as it is small enough to penetrate deep into the lungs, cause inflammation and worsen preexisting heart and lung conditions. It leads to systematic inflammatory changes, their affect blood coagulability. They can also carry surface absorbed carcinogens into the lungs.

Ozone (O_3) is produced by a reaction between nitrogen oxide, hydrocarbons and sunlight. Ozone irritates the airways of the lungs. It produces alterations is breathing patterns. The principal source of NO_2 is road traffic. When asthmatics are exposed to nitrogen dioxide they experience brancho constriction. It lowers resistance and increases susceptibility to respiratory infections such as influenza. A major source of sulphur dioxide (SO_2) is fossil fuel combustion. It can cause brancho constriction, irritation in nose and throat.

Carbon monoxide (CO) is a toxic gas, which is entitled as a result of combustion. CO prevents the normal transport of oxygen in the blood and this leads to reduction in the supply of oxygen to the heart.

Lead exposure through batteries is linked to impairment of mental faculties and visual monitor performance. It also causes neurological damage in children.

The Central Pollution Control Board notified the first Ambient Air Quality standards on November 11, 1982 and revised it in 1994. The national ambient air quality is notified for six pollutants.

SO_2	SPM	Pb	NH_3
NO_2	RSPM	CO	

covering three types of areas - industrial, residential, rural and other areas; sensitive areas.

Disaster means:

- A great or sudden misfortune
- A complete failure
- A person or enterprise ending in failure.

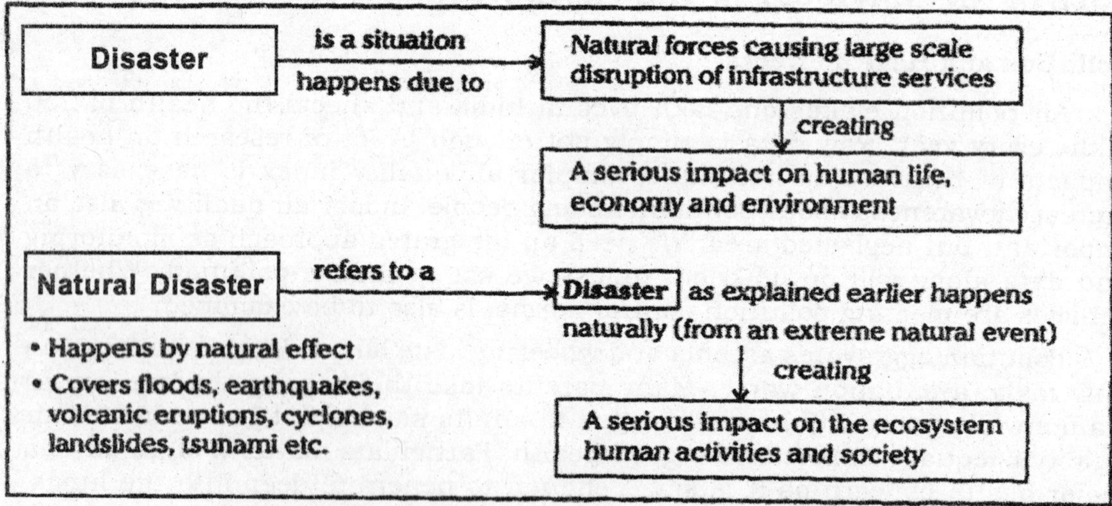

Fig. 3.64 Disaster and Natural Disaster

Natural disaster is only for natural extreme or geographical events but not for the following:

- Epidemics (diseases)
- Toxic spills

- Transportation accidents
- Industrial plants explosion
- Riots, terrorism (social disasters).

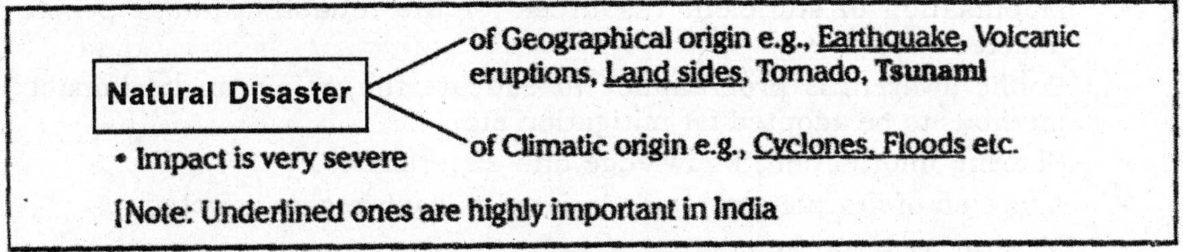

Fig. 3.65 Natural Disaster

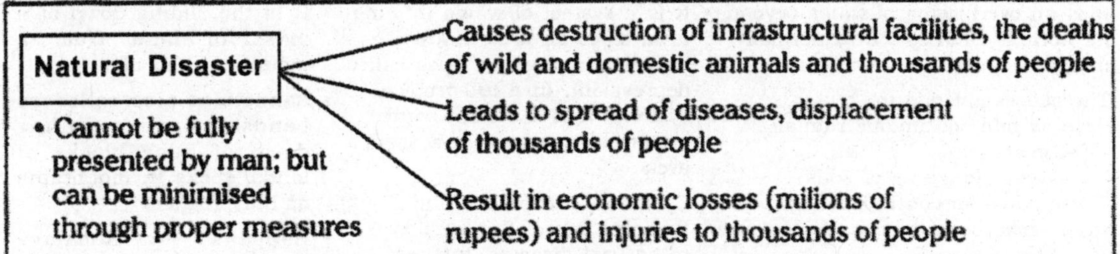

Fig. 3.66 Natural Disaster Impacts

Natural disaster impacts are shown in the above figure.

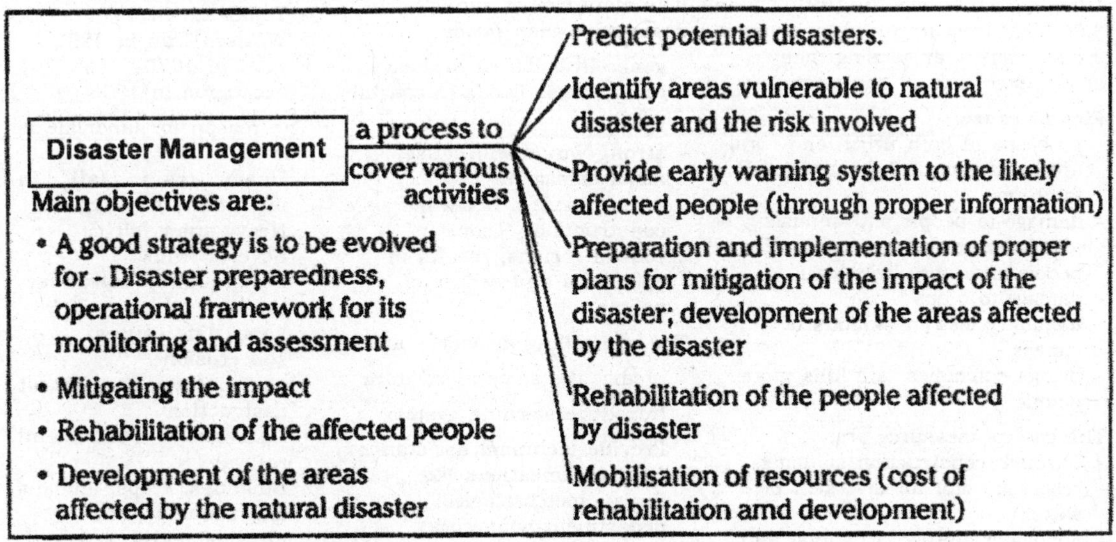

Fig. 3.67 Meaning of Disaster Management

Disasters can be reduced by certain essential requirements:

- Space Technology (Satellites) for early warning.
- Good strategy for preparedness and operational frame work.
- Mobilisation of sufficient resources for the rehabilitation of people affected.
- Public awareness programmes to educate the public on its impact, methods to be adopted for mitigation etc.
- Sharing information, knowledge and experiences.
- Adoption of flexible strategies tailored to each region affected.
- Monitoring hazards.

Floods	***Cyclones***	***Landslides***
• It is an overflowing of water beyond its normal confines (on to normally dry land) • The causes are due to - Heavy and continuous rainfall - Deforestation - Careless ploughing of soils These cause uncontrollable havocs which may be extensive or intensive • Floods are more in China, Bangladesh and India and cause more deaths than any other disasters. It may repeat. Eg. Bangladesh 3,00,000 lives lost in 1970, 1,30,000 lives in 1991, China 3,000,000 lives in 1931. In India, it occurs every year causing many deaths both human and animals • **Floods cause:** - problems in both urban and rural areas- damage to infrastructural facilities - damage to people and animals (displacement of thousands of people and more lives lost) - damage to crops - monetary loss in millions of rupees - brings epidemics and kills more people • The control measures are: - Through construction of dams, reservoirs etc. for diversion of water - For water storage, irrigation and power generation and for flood control (through flood ways also) - Through flood forecasting and warning system - Through re-forestation and good soil management methods cwc (central water commission in India is helping in major areas)	• It is a system of winds rotating inwards to an area of low barometric pressure (Also called depression). In a full tropical cyclone, it is a violent wind system of this kind in a small area • Cyclones, hurricanes and typhoons are of the same type of natural disaster. Intense storms in North atlantic ocean- **Hurricanes** Intense storms in the pacific ocean are called **Typhoons** • It is more violent and destructive than floods. - generally followed by heavy rains, cause floods in coastal areas - strong winds will cause major damage to infrastructure, houses, fragile constructions, crops in coastal regions, results in epidemics and deaths of people • The controlling measures are: - predict the same in advance - Introduce warning system - Provide technical assistance from organisations like Indian meteorological department who works through cyclone detection radars located in coasts • Proper sound structures may be built in cyclone prone areas; proper cropping strategy to be evolved for cyclone prone areas.	• It is the sliding down of a mass of land from a mountain, cliff etc. • Landslides also called as Landships where pulling down of huge blocks of lands, rocks in mountains or hilly regions • Happens in Himalaya mountains and Western Ghats in India • Occurred in - Mount St.Helens in Washington in 1980 - Tajikistan in 1971 - Western Iran in 1990 - Peru in 1970 - Nicaragua in 1998 • The reason for landslide is due to: - Heavy rain fall in mountain/hilly regions - Heavy snow fall - Severe winds - Earthquake, Volcanoes, etc. - Land slide causes: - soil erosion - up rooting and forest destruction - Damage to roads and railways - Buildings, crops, animals and people's lives - Flow of water affected; changes the direction of streams and rivers

How to Tackle Disasters?

- Existing Disaster management needs overhaul.
- On January 9, Government decided to set up a national disaster management authority and introduce a Bill in the budget session of Parliament to give it a statutory status. A high powered committee was set up.
- Shifting of disaster management from the agricultural ministry to the home ministry (with the exception of drought) suggested. With para military bodies handling relief, it makes little sense for the former to oversee operations. Home Ministry has skeleton staff to handle this.
- Civil Defence Organisation came into existence in 1962, after the China war, to manage was related disasters.
- A national emergency response force would be set up as a para military organisation like National Security Guard which handles hostage situations by terrorists. Such a force would have been of great utility in tsunami tragedy.
- We need to be active rather than reactive. A full fledged ministry of disaster management in place in many countries is needed. The central legislation for disaster management now announced by the government was long overdue. Civil defence, fire services also to be brought under one set up of disaster management.
- Our forecasting, warning and alert systems need to be updated.
- Our remote sensing and satellite capabilities need to be utilised fully.
- Issues of governance such as making embankments on rivers that have regular floods, shelters, depots with adequate stock of relief materials at important places; well equipped medical and healthcare. Use of Information Technology, capacity buildings, mapping, insurance, international and regional cooperation.
- Proper planning and funding at all levels with active procedures and systems help in preparedness and in disaster mitigation.
- Communities, NGOs and the media are emerging as roll players. In addition, Paramilitary organisations, ex-servicemen, NCC and similar institutions are to be involved.
- It is not only the coastlines and states having floods that need attention-big cities like Delhi in the seismic zone V are ticking bombs whereas our preparations are virtually zero.
- Gujarat, Orissa and AP have set up proper disaster management authorities after facing natural calamities. Delhi have yet to learn a lesson, perhaps waiting for a big tragedy to happen.
- Tsunami was not the first experience, but the biggest. Arunachal Pradesh, Assam and Bihar have had floods. There have been drought conditions in different states. There is a well laid procedure for disaster

management that requires officers at different levels to take steps to help people. The centre gives the affected states the funds. PMs relief fund is also there. All the main political leaders visited tsunami site.

- Sea coasts in Maharashtra and Kerala have walls along the sea casts to protect roads and houses.
- Now, the Union Home Ministry has taken up additional charge of disaster management after the nation was hit, literally by a bolt from the blue. The ministry is constantly fire fighting on different fronts. Shivaraj Patil the man at the helm expressed satisfaction at the way the crisis was handled regarding tsunami.

Disaster Management

In a country like ours, disasters are as given:

- Floods one day
- Droughts the other
- Earthquake in other part

If not natural, then man made-

- Gas leaks
- Bomb blasts
- Wars
- Train crashes
- Terrorist operations
- Fire breaks out, buildings crumbling

Note: **Famines** were more before independence. Now it is not there.

Major Earthquakes/Cyclones in India

We, as a country not prepared to respond to, or prevent disasters. Since the 90s alone, we have had major earthquakes and cyclones.

January 2001	Gujarat Earthquake	14,000 lives lost
September 1993	Latur quake	10,000 lives lost
October 1991	Uttar Kashi	2,000 lives lost
October 1999	Orissa Super Cyclone	10,000 lives lost
December 26, 2004 (Latest)	Tsunami in Tamil Nadu, Pondichery, Kerala, Andhra Pradesh	13,000 lives lost

Fig. 3.68 Major Earthquakes and Cyclones in India

Recent Earthquake in India and Pakistan on 8th October 2005

The recent earthquake happened on 8th October, 2005 at both Pakistan and India. 39,000 feared killed in Pakistan itself. In India, the figure may be around 2,000. New mega fractures developing across the Himalayan region were responsible for the earthquake that shook Pakistan and Northern India on 8th

October morning. Sesmicity was shifting from the north to the south and areas south of the ranges now more vulnerable. The foothills of the Himalayas and Indo Gangetic areas were developing into quake prone zones.

Earlier, when the Indian plate was colliding with the Tibetan plate, regions of north of Himalayas were more susceptible.

Mega fractures are energy release points and lead to displacement of earth's plates which causes an **earthquake**. There are several mega fractures in the Himalayas which release energy from the earths crust and cause earthquakes. New fractures are developing in the North West to South West direction.

The recent tsunami in India affected 20 districts, in four Indian States and one Union Territory. Mercifully only people along the beaches were affected, but they covered a 2500 km coastline on the mainland and 800 kms in the Andaman and Nicobar islands. Managing this task was not easy.

Major Earthquakes around the World

December 26, 2003	South Eastern Iran	6.5 (Richter)	41,000 killed
May 21, 2003	Northern Algeria	6.8	2,300 killed
March 25, 2002	Northern Afghanistan	5.8	1,000 killed
January 26, 2001	India	7.9	14,000 killed
September 21, 1999	Taiwan	7.6	2,400
August 17, 1999	Western Turkey	7.4	17,000
January 25, 1999	Western Columbia	6.0	1,171
May 30, 1998	Northern Afghanistan Tajikistan	6.9	5,000
January 17, 1995	Kobe, Japan	7.2	6,000
September 30, 1993	Latur, India	6.0	10,000
June 21, 1990	Northwest Iran	7.3-7.7	50,000
December 7, 1998	North West Armenia	6.9	25,000
September 19, 1985	Central Mexico	8.1	9,500
July 28, 1976	Tangshan, China	7.8-8.2	2,40,000
February 4, 1976	Guatemala	7.5	22,778
February 29, 1960	Morocco	5.7	12,000
December 26, 1939	Enzincan Province, Turkey	7.9	33,000
May 31, 1935	Quetta, India	7.5	50,000
September 1, 1923	Tokyo, Yokohama, Japan	8.3	1,40,000
December 26, 2004	South Asian Countries (including India)	9.0	2,40,000
October 8, 2005	Pakistan and India	7.6	50,000 (apprx) killed

Fig. 3.69 Major Earthquakes around the World

Types of Earthquakes

There are three types of earthquakes:

- Earthquakes (Normal)
- Earthquake that generated local tsunami
- Earthquake that generated pacific wide tsunami

What is a tsunami?

A **tsunami** (pronounced su-nah-me) is a **wave train**, or **series of waves**, generated in a body of water by an impulsive disturbance that vertically displaces the water column. Earthquakes, landslides, volcanic eruptions, explosions and even the impact of cosmic bodies, such as meteorites, can generate tsunami. These can savagely attack coastlines, causing devastating property damage and loss of life.

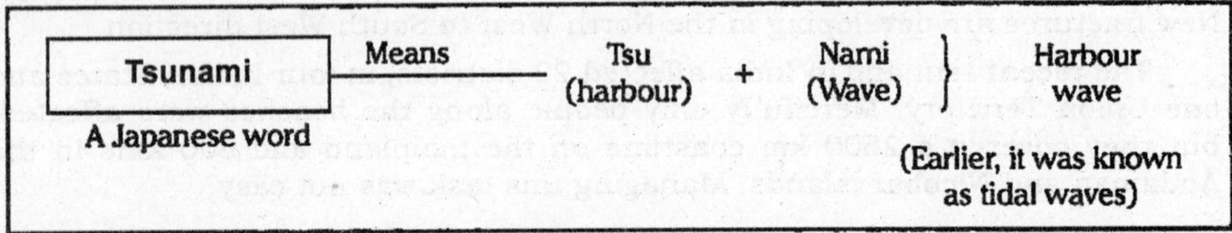

Fig. 3.70 Meaning of Tsunami

Tsunamis are unrelated to the tides, although a tsunami's impact upon a coastline is dependent upon the tidal level at the time a tsunami strikes. **Tides** result from the imbalanced, extra terrestrial, gravitational influences of the moon, sun, and planets. **Seismic** implies an earthquake related generation mechanism. But a tsunami can also be caused by a nonseismic event, such as a landslide or a meteorite impact.

Tsunami	*Wind generated waves*
Shallow water waves with long periods and wave length.	Water waves with shorter period and short wave length.
One hour and 100 km and more	10 seconds and 150m Rhythmically rolling in, one wave after another.
Shallow water waves (water depth to wavelength ratio is small).	
Moves at a speed of square root of the product of the acceleration of gravity and water depth.	
At 4000 m/depth-speed is 700 kms/hr.	
In 1960, Chilean tsunami travelled at 17,000 kms across to pacific to hit Japan.	
Earthquakes, landslides, volcanic eruption, cosmic collations generate tsunamis.	
When tsunami approaches the land, it begins to slow and grow in height.	
Maximum vertical height on shore (run up height).	
10, 20 and even 30 meters.	

Fig. 3.71 Difference between Tsunami and Wind Generated Waves

Magnitude of Tsunami

Tsunami waves of the recent one in South Asia packed:

- 350 Hiroshimas in it (350 times the Atomic Bomb dropped in Japan, Hiroshima)
- Most powerful releases of energy by the Mother Earth ever.
- Energy released 5 mega tonnes (Hiroshima Bomb was 15 kilo tons)
- This Earthquake at Sumatra had the power of 32,000 hydrogen bombs (one hydrogen bomb has the power to release one megaton of energy)
- Occurred at 10 kms below the seabed created the deadliest of all tsunamis which could travel right up to Somalia on the east cost of Africa which was 2,500 kms West of epicenter
- The release of energy in an earthquake always multiplies 32 times with every single point increase on the Richter e.g., If earthquake of 6 magnitude would release one megaton of energy then 7 magnitude would release 32 megatonnes of energy

Then 8 magnitude would release 1000 megatonnes of energy

Then 9 magnitude would release 32,000 megatonnes of energy

Fig. 3.72 Tsunami Wave of the Recent one in South Asia (26th December, 2004)

Dempo's Brazilian Striker Christiano Junior's death in the field who had heart attack may have left everyone numb, but it also started a public debate on whether we are equipped to handle emergencies on sports fields. Another incident, a fantasy park in Bangalore saw a joy ride crashing recently sending a huge scare amongst families. Six months ago (in 2004) dozens of kids were charred to death at Kumbakonam School which had been violating every rule in the notebook.

India is indeed a disaster prone country but we also seem to learn very little from experiences. Is India capable of handling disasters? Is that there is no room for disaster management of any kind in our dictionary? Just because we have so many people, have we become insensitive about losing lives?

How small small steps bring a resolution to avoid pollution?

Small steps which make a big difference:

(i) **Change the air filter:** Check car's air filter every month. It saves 360 kg of carbon dioxide and Rs.5,144 per year.

(ii) **Use recycled paper:** Make sure the printer paper is 100% post consumer recycled paper. It saves 2.2 kgs of CO_2 per realm of paper.

(iii) **Check the water heater:** Keeping the water heater thermostat not higher than and 49 degree Celsius. It saves 249.47 gms of CO_2 and Rs.1,187 per par.

(iv) **Take shorter showers:** Showers account two-thirds of all water heating costs. It saves 158.75 kg of CO_2 and 3917 per year.

(v) **Buy products locally:** Buying locally and saving on energy required to drive otherwise.

(vi) **Buy minimally packaged goods:** Less packaging could reduce garbage by about 10%. It saves 544.3 kg of CO_2 and Rs.39.575 per year.

(vii) **Buy fuel efficient car:** Getting a few KMs per litre makes a big difference.

(viii) **Don't leave the car idling:** It wastes money and fuel, and generates pollution and global warming causes emissions. Except when in traffic turn the engine off if the waiting period is more than 30 seconds.

(ix) **Plant a tree:** Trees suck up CO_2 and make clean air for us to breathe. Save 907 kg of CO_2 per year.

(x) **Replace old appliances:** Inefficient appliances waste energy.

(xi) **Air dry the clothes:** By avoiding using the dryer, 3175 kg of carbon dioxide is saved.

(xii) **Take cloth bags to the market:** Using cloth bags instead of plastic or paper bag reduces waste and requires no additional energy.

(xiii) **Turn off the computer:** By shutting off the computer when not in use saves, 90 kgs of CO_2. Energy conservation is possible by using the monitor sleep mode instead of a screen saver.

People all over the world are taking measures to reduce the greenhouse gases emitted as a result of the way we live.

Everybody can take action to combat climate change, and there is plenty of advice on how to do it. From carbon footprint calculators that allow us to evaluate our total carbon dioxide (CO_2) emissions, to specific actions we can take to reduce emissions, we can all become more conscious about our use of resources. In addition to the climate benefits, most of the recommended action result in long-term household financial savings, and many will lead to improved personal health and quality of life.

Together, the actions of millions of people could add up to considerable savings in greenhouse gases, but they will not, on their own, be sufficient to halt climate change. Individuals also need to put pressure on our government representatives and companies to take the larger - scale collective action necessary to achieve a reduction in emissions of 60 to 80 per cent.

Energy savings at home

Using less energy not only helps the planet, but also saves money on household bills.

An energy - efficient refrigerator could save nearly half a tonne of CO_2 a year, compared with an older model.

Locally produced, seasonal foods save the emissions resulting from transporting food long distances. or from heating greenhouses to grow out-of-season produce.

Compact fluorescent, spiral light bulbs are 75% more efficient than standard light bulbs.

Energy savings on the road....

Walking, cycling, using a car pool or taking public transport - all produce fewer emissions than those emitted by a single person in a car.

Keeping tires optimally inflated uses less fuel and cuts down emissions.

Choosing the most efficient car available and keeping any car well-maintained, will reduce emissions.

Driving at 5 kmph below the speed limit over a 10 km commute to work saves 250 kg of CO_2 per year.

Sharing a car, and avoiding short journeys by car, saves energy.

Pledge to see this film

Former U.S. Vice President and 2007 Nobel Peace Prize Winner, Al Gore, presents an eye - opening and compelling view of the future of our planet - and our civilization - in the MUST SEE documentary of the year. This is a wake-up call that cuts through myths and misconceptions to deliver that global warming is a real and present danger. An Inconvenient Truth brings home Core's persuasive argument that we must act now to save the earth. Each and every one of us can make changes in the way in which we live our lives and BECOME PART OF THE SOLUTION.

Ban the bulb!

- Replace all ordinary light bulbs with Compact Fluorescent Lamps (CFLs)!
- Reduce India's CO_2 emissions by 55 million tones!
- CFLs use only 20% of the energy used by an ordinary light bulb!
- CFLs are the most cost-effective and do not need to be changed too often!
- CFLs can replace Incandescents (ordinary bulbs), saving upto 75% of the initial lighting energy!

Cost comparison chart between CFLs and ordinary bulbs*

	15-Watt CFL	**75-Watt Ordinary Bulbs**
Cost of Lamps (Avg.retail price)	Rs.115	Rs.10
Lamp Life (6 hours/day use)	1000 days (2.7 years)	167 days
Annual Operating Cost	Rs.162	Rs.810
Lamps replaced in 2.7 years	0	6 nos.
Total Operating Cost	Rs.552.4	Rs.2187
Savings over Lamp Life	Rs.1634.6	0
Light Quality (color)	Cool day light	Yellowish
Environmental-friendliness	Most	Least

We can reduce the amount of carbon we release into the atmosphere with these eco-tips*

Carbon offsetting or "going carbon neutral 'or' green-tagging", is important. Each of our everyday action consume energy and produce CO_2 emissions, e.g., taking flights, driving our cars, cooling our homes, etc. Carbon Offsetting is a way of compensating for the emissions produced with an equivalent CO_2 saving.

Carbon offset your air travel

Every passenger km you fly emits 0.18 kg of CO_2. So if you fly about 5,600 kms on a round trip across the country, multiply that by 0.18 and you get approx, one tonne of CO_2 as your individual contribution to carbon emissions.

Flight kms per Year ..... x 0.18 = Year Total .....

Carbon offset your driving

Every litre of petrol you use emits about 2 kgs of carbon dioxide. To figure out your carbon emissions from driving: Car kms per Year x 2.0 = Year Total.

If the ice shelves keep melting at their current rate, coastal cities will become submerged. Droughts will occur inland, and food and water shortages will follow. Wildfires will increase, plants and animals will die. Diseases will increase as people are forced to live closer together, and there will be fewer natural resources to go around.

The planet will literally begin to die.

It sounds like the makings of a science fiction movie, but it isn't. It is the ultimate problem we are facing today.

The scientific community is increasingly veering to the consensus that **if we do not reduce carbon emission dramatically in the next ten years, it may be too late to do anything at all.**

These sites can help you calculate your personal impact in terms of.

Carbon offset your electricity

When you use electricity you'll emit an average 0.61 kg of CO_2 per kilowatt-hour: Electricity per Year ..... (kilowatt - hours) x 0.61 = Year Total .....

Carbon dioxide (CO_2) air pollution through air travel

Bangalore - Mumbai:	89 kg per person.
Bangalore - Delhi:	190 kg per person.
Bangalore - Chennai:	41 kg per person.
Bangalore - Calicut:	49 kg per person.
Bangalore - Hyderabad:	61 kg per person.
Bangalore - Kolkata:	199 kg per person.

Jet engine's exhaust pollutes the earth at 2 to 4 times the rate of ground level CO_2. And it'll stay in the air for at least 5 years.

A fantastic site which calculates your CO_2 emissions for any flight you take between two airports in India. WWW.Cheap-parking.net/flight-carbon-emissions.phpz

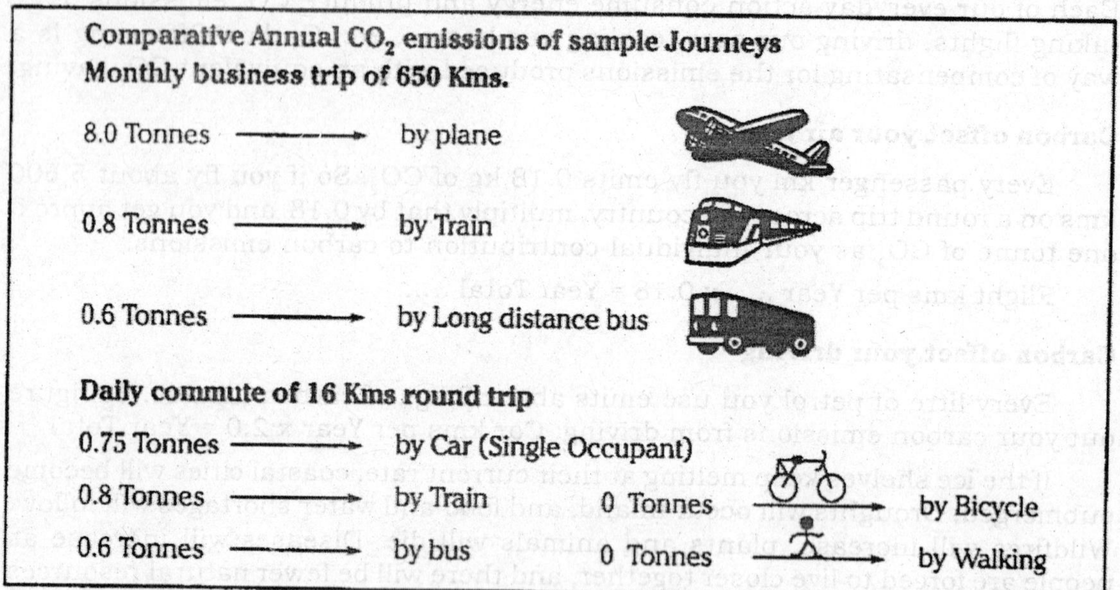

Comparative Annual CO_2 emissions of sample Journeys

Monthly business trip of 650 Kms.

8.0 Tonnes → by plane

0.8 Tonnes → by Train

0.6 Tonnes → by Long distance bus

Daily commute of 16 Kms round trip

0.75 Tonnes → by Car (Single Occupant)

0.8 Tonnes → by Train

0.6 Tonnes → by bus

0 Tonnes → by Bicycle

0 Tonnes → by Walking

Fig. 3.73

India and other developing countries stand firm against scrapping Kyoto pact

Nitin Sethi | TNN

New Delhi: Talks in Bali hit a dead-lock on the first day of the high-level ministerial meeting of the UN climate change conference with Indian and other developing countries taking a dissenting position against US and most other developed countries which are demanding that the existing Kyoto Protocol be scrapped.

"There is a logjam on the future of the global treaty on climate change", science and technology minister Kapil Sibal, leading the Indian delegation told from Bali. "India has made its position emphatically clear to the gathered countries and we will continue to insist on it. We hope an understanding emerges over the next two days", he added.

India wants a two-track process on the UN treaty's future. It wants the Kyoto Protocol, which puts mandatory and quantified commitments to cut emissions on rich countries, to be reviewed separately while the long-term review of the entire UN treaty continues alongside.

The first phase of the protocol will expire in 2012 and the kind of cuts rich countries would have to taken in the second phase is open to discussion. A

• CO_2 – carbon dioxide – emissions from burning fossil fuels are the major contributor to greenhouse gases, which cause global warming

What's your CARBON footprint?

What difference does it make if we drive everywhere or use public transport, a bike or our own feet? Live in a big house or a small one? Eat imported foods or locally grown? The answer is tonnes of CO_2.

First steps toward a solution

Calculate your carbon footprint, an estimate of the amount of carbon dioxide you produce, so you can see the effect you have on climate and lessen it

SAMPLE CARBON CALCULATOR

Many environmental organisations have carbon calculators on their websites. Here's some of the questions they ask:

- How fuel efficient is your car?
- How many miles do you drive?
- How many plane trips do you take?
- How far do you fly?
- Do you live in a large house? A small one? An apartment?
- How do you heat your home?
- Do you eat beef frequently?
- Do you recycle? If yes, how often and how much?

Biggest feet

Top countries for carbon dioxide emissions, in millions of metric tonnes of CO_2, 2004

United Kingdom 580

Germany 862

Italy 485

Japan 1,262

South Korea 497

India 1,112

© 2007 MCT
Source: Carbonfund.org, U.S. Environmental Protection Agency, Wired magazine, Jamais Cascio of Open the Future
Graphic: Pat Carr, Lee Hulteng

How Americans contribute

The average American adds 23 tonnes (more than 50,000 lb/22,700 kg) of CO_2 to the atmosphere yearly

DIRTY DRIVE	PLANE TRUTH	HOUSE THAT	FOOD FOR THOUGHT
Average CO_2 emissions from cars yearly (lb/kg), by fuel efficiency	Average CO_2 emissions from planes (lb/kg), by distance flown	Average CO_2 emissions (lb/kg) from home air conditioning, by area	One researcher's estimate of the maximum yearly carbon footprint of that US institution: the cheeseburger*
41+ mpg (66 kpg)	6,000 mi (9,660 km)	<1,000 sq ft (92 sq m)	
6,000/2,700	2,500/1,130	11,000/5,000	
29-40 mpg (47-65 kpg)	20,000 mi (32,200 km)	1,001-1,499 (93-138)	Per burger
8,000/3,600	8,350/3,800	16,500/7,500	6.3-6.8 lbs (2.9-3.1 kg)
19-28 mpg (31-46 kpg)	40,000 mi (64,400 km)	1,500-2,499 (139-232)	
12,000/5,400	16,700/7,600	27,500/12,500	Per person
10-18 mpg (16-30 kpg)	100,000 mi (160,900 km)	2,500-4,000 (233-372)	941-1,023 lbs.
20,000/9,000	[illegible]1,750/18,900	[illegible],000/20,000	(428-465 kg)

* Assumes the average American eats 150 burgers a year; includes production, storage, transportation of beef and cheese, as well as cooking the burgers

Fig. 3.74

parallel debate on at Bali is to review the principle governing climate change at UN which in the long-run could also mean greenhouse gas cuts for India.

India is keen that while the long-term treaty overhaul process is negotiated (and this can take years), rich countries are not left off the hook on their existing commitments. "The global community knows that despite the existing Kyoto protocol demanding emission reduction from these industrialized countries by 2012, the greenhouse gas emissions have increased over the past five years for most. They have to prove their credibility by achieving these goals before India and other developing countries think of committing to any long-term framework", another Indian official at Bali explained.

The rich countries want the two processes to merge. US, EU and all other rich countries want one complete overhaul of the existing framework. "But that would allow the industrialized countries to paper over their existing failures which we don't want to happen", the official said.

"There can be no deviation from the Kyoto Protocol. Bali should carve out the roadmap for implementation of the existing deal and look at enhancing implementation, not throwing it out", Sibal said. With two days remaining for the 190 countries to come to an understanding, pressure was building on the delegates. The Bali meeting, is expected to see the general principles of future negotiations emerge. This emerging framework is considered critical as it could impact Indian economy severely for decades to come, for good or for bad.

CASE STUDY

BATTLE OF BHOPAL (BHOPAL GAS TRAGEDY)

SC Judgement is not the end of the affair.

The Supreme Court's decision, to finally disburse the Rs.1,500 crore compensation from Union Carbide to victims or kin of the 1984 Bhopal gas tragedy, is a significant milestone, but one sans the attributes of a climax. The good news is soured with the knowledge that the BJP government of Madhya Pradesh wishes to use part of the amount for the city of Bhopal. The SC must ensure that the money goes to the victims and not into the grubby paws of local corporators. This sorry case begs an examination of a larger attitudinal issue: The disposition of the powers that be to such victims. From Bhopal to Kumbakonam, we have been repeatedly assaulted by images of abject grief, of victims of largely avoidable man-made disasters. In almost all these cases, the victims fate is made more tragic by the culpability of the state in not ensuring that proper procedures were being followed. Speedy relief and some clear demonstration of the caring hand of the state are immediate actions necessary to ameliorate grief, but these are rarely found together. It's high time the government pulled up its baggy socks on disaster management policies, strategies and procedures.

In this case, the administration has appeared lackadaisical from the start Bhopal was the single largest industrial accident in the world that ultimately affected over five lakh people, and the government only got 8470 million as compensation! This is a paltry amount, especially when measured against the billion dollar payouts to American victims of similar accidents. Quite clearly, it isn't over yet. The government must actively push cases against both Warren Anderson and Dow Chemicals, the present owners of Union Carbide, and at least get the firm to thoroughly clean up the abandoned Bhopal complex that is still leaking toxins into the environment. That much is owed to the people of the city. Ultimately, no one doubts the immense value of the compensation that will be paid to the Bhopal survivors. But we must understand that this particular decision is more about the delivery, however delayed, of some justice to a struggling few than any compensatory largess being doled out to them.

KYOTO PROTOCOL FOR CUTTING EMISSIONS

The 1997 **Kyoto Protocol** now came into effect after 7 years wait requires participating countries to cut back emissions by **2012 to 5.2%** of the 1990 levels. The activation of the protocol has indicated the efforts by complying countries, particularly EU members, who have been consciously reducing industrial emissions by promoting green practices (limits on emissions of carbondioxide and other gases) for raising world temperatures, melting glaciers and rising oceans. Kyoto protocol took effect the **support of 1'41 nations** but a boycott by the **biggest polluter US.**

Kyoto protocol brings with it credibility, specific instruments, the possibility of going beyond. It also gives developing countries the leverage required to catch up on the economic front, as they are exempt from the quota deadline that is mandatory for industrialized countries. Scientists have warned us that the one degree Fahrenheit increase in global temperatures on the 20th century was due to excessive fossil fuel-burning. Yet **the US and Australia have refused to ratify the protocol, as the cat back clause did not apply to India and China.** Infact from the 'Asian' brown haze over the Indian ocean to the dark clouds over Bihar, US supported **climate studies** have been building up **'evidence' against developing countries,** particularly in the South Asian ones. It is facile to lay the blame for global climate change entirely on smoke emitting choolas and methane expelling animal waste fuels in the Indo-Gangetic plain, which are at any rate more environment friendly than energy-guzzling electric appliances and heavy industry.

US releases	**25% of the world's greenhouse gases**
China and India put together	<12.5% of the world's greenhouse gases.

America is unwilling to subsidies any economic slowdown at home if it were to reduce industrial emissions. US keeps harping on how it is focusing instead of developing clean technology while **planting trees** and **preserving forests as carbon sinks.** These measures, however, are not enough to offset the warming process that requires a far more aggressive emissions control policy. The **global warming issue** have been politicized by bigger polluter consumer countries like the US and Australia, who have declined to be part of any international accord on the environment. The Kyoto protocol has come into effect only because Russia made the decision to ratify it, thereby fulfilling the protocol's requirement that **atleast 55% of greenhouse gas emitters** must concur. The ratification should be seen as the first step towards shifting focus from **hunting for scape goats** to promoting cleaner technology and energy conservation and other green practices that are part of its tradition.

Kyoto protocol is quite a challenge if we see where countries are in terms of realizing (emission reduction) commitments. If we reduce emissions by 5.2% (over 1990 levels) between 2008 and 2012 and if countries such as Britain and Germany, which are in a leadership position in Europe do it, it would be a huge step. Political momentum is expected to come from G8 group this year. Britain has the presidency. **2005 is an important year for the agenda of sustainable development.** US remains out of the protocol. US is the largest emitter of greenhouse gas emissions and is blamed for accelerating global warming.

The reports indicate that climate is changing across the world, the protocol targets will not be enough. Climate change is a very important factor. The UN reform paper has linked it with a new strategy for peace. It is underlining the link between environment and security. We can only underline that **sustainable development** and the **fight against climate change** is very important. It will contribute to peace policy in the future to disarmament. There has been talk on water stimulating tensions, causing wars. The realization of millennium development goals is altogether dependent on **environment capital.**

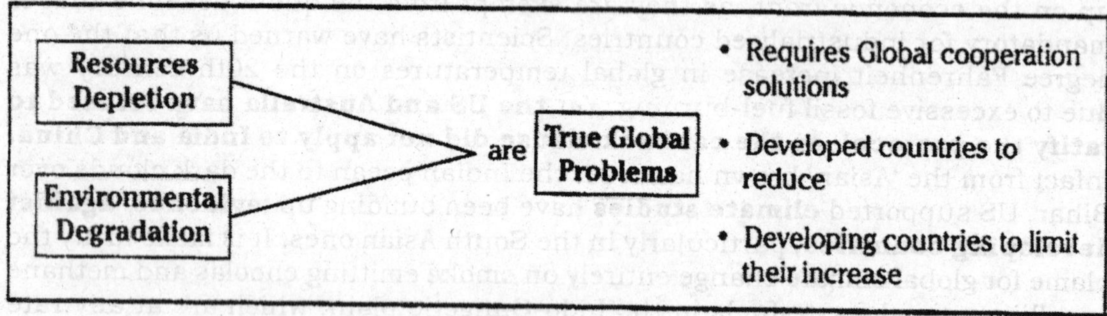

Fig. 3.75 The Global Problems

The broader range on partnerships is not a burden, it is a chance. It should stimulate the development agenda.

Japan says that it is regrettable, since US has not joined the Kyoto pact. The agreement, negotiated in Japan's ancient capital of Kyoto in 1997, with the support of 141 nations.

More than 300 environmental activists marched through Kyoto under persistent rain to celebrate the start of the pact, despite years of doubt, with some dressed as monkeys or penguins or weaving mock tiger ears to highlight **global warmings impact on animals.**

3.3 The Ethics of Conserving Depletable Resource

SOCIAL ISSUES AND THE ENVIRONMENT

A number of social issues are connected with the environment. Some of these are discussed in figure 3.76.

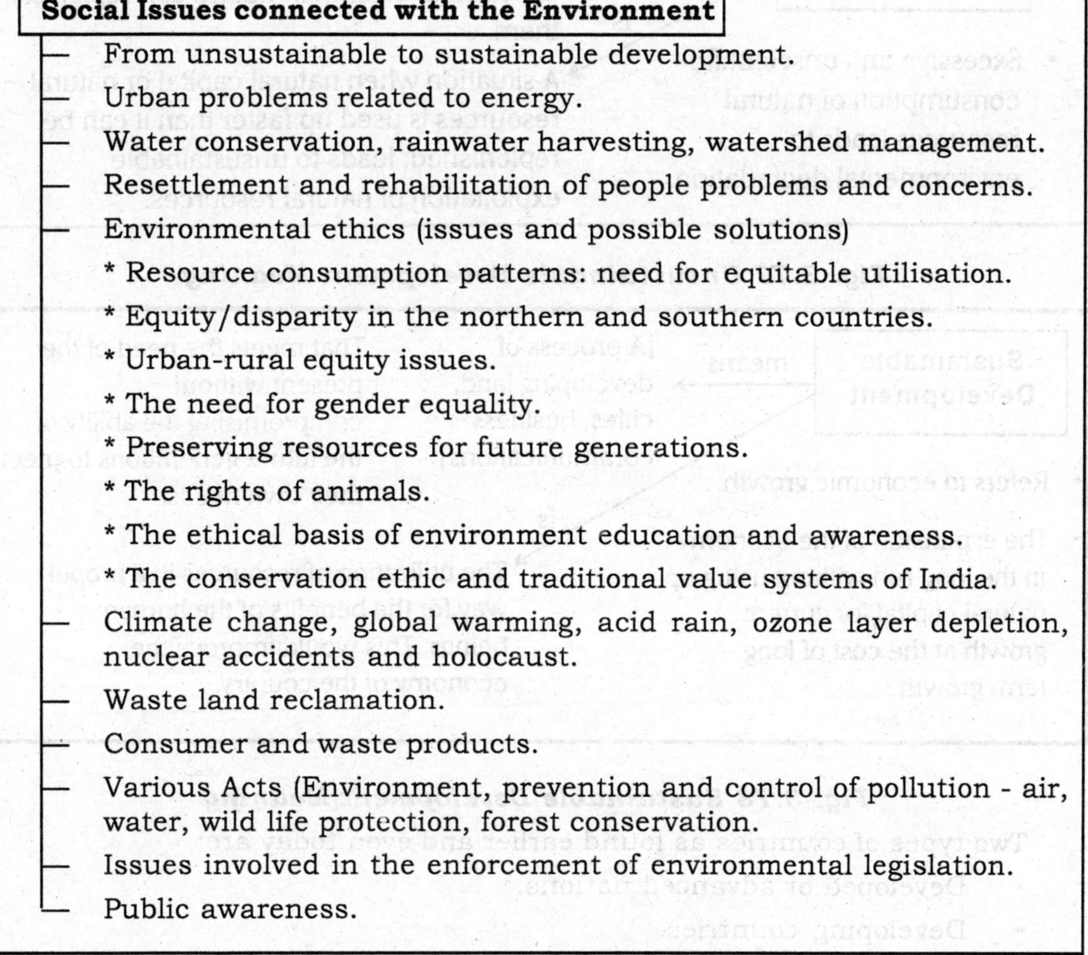

Social Issues connected with the Environment

- From unsustainable to sustainable development.
- Urban problems related to energy.
- Water conservation, rainwater harvesting, watershed management.
- Resettlement and rehabilitation of people problems and concerns.
- Environmental ethics (issues and possible solutions)
  * Resource consumption patterns: need for equitable utilisation.
  * Equity/disparity in the northern and southern countries.
  * Urban-rural equity issues.
  * The need for gender equality.
  * Preserving resources for future generations.
  * The rights of animals.
  * The ethical basis of environment education and awareness.
  * The conservation ethic and traditional value systems of India.
- Climate change, global warming, acid rain, ozone layer depletion, nuclear accidents and holocaust.
- Waste land reclamation.
- Consumer and waste products.
- Various Acts (Environment, prevention and control of pollution - air, water, wild life protection, forest conservation.
- Issues involved in the enforcement of environmental legislation.
- Public awareness.

Fig. 3.76 Social Issues

From Unsustainable to Sustainable Development

Let us understand the terms 'unsustainable development' and 'sustainable development'.

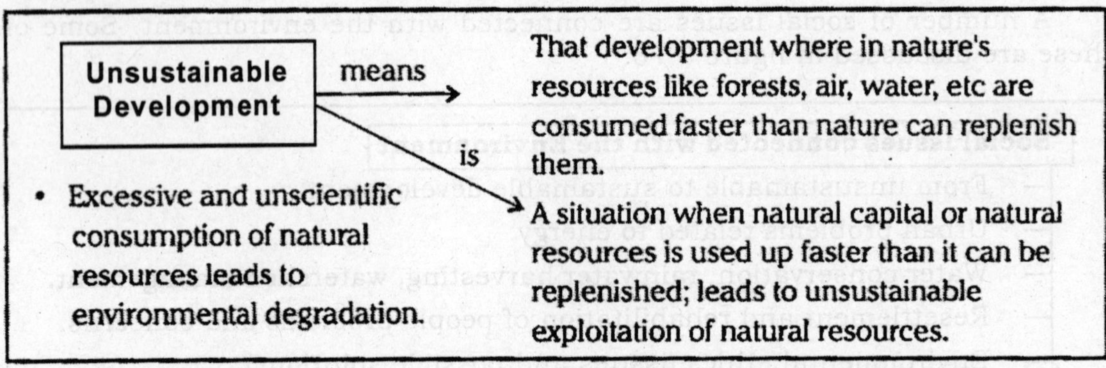

Fig. 3.77 Unsustainable Development Meaning

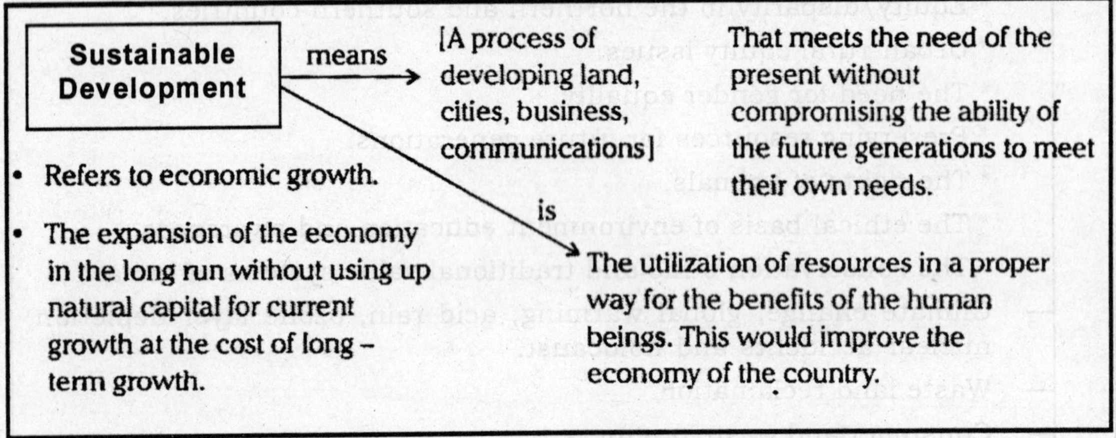

Fig. 3.78 Sustainable Development Meaning

Two types of countries as found earlier and even today are:

- Developed or advanced nations.
- Developing countries.

The under-developed countries also exist. In the European and American countries most of them are called as **advanced countries** as they became industrialized at an early stage. The world look at only economic status as a measure of human development. Now a days (after 1970s), these have changed. The specialists started looking rest, not only the economic growth but also the improvement of environmental conditions. If only economic status is looked into those countries might suffer from serious environmental problems like:

- Air and water pollution.
- Waste management.
- Deforestation.
- Other ill effects are in plenty that seriously affected peoples well-being and health.

Added to this, serious equity issues like 'haves' and 'have nots' in society, at the national and global levels are found. Unsustainable development strategies will further worsen the disparity in the life styles between the rich and the poor.

Concept of Sustainable Development and its Significance

As per this, it signifies that the natural resources are exhaustible. The development process should be aimed at both the needs of the present generation and without compromising the ability of the future generation to meet their needs.

Sustainable development must overcome environmental degradation. It must preserve environment without ignoring the needs of economic development as well as social equity and justice.

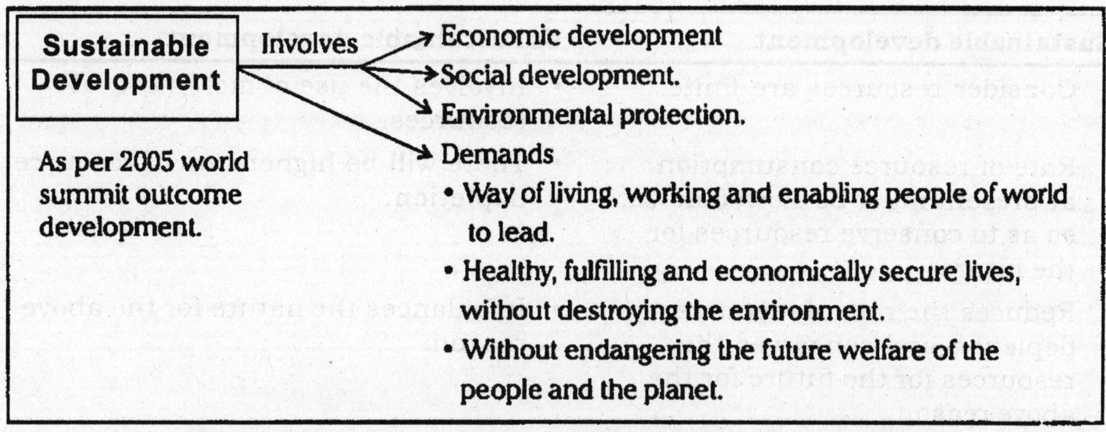

Fig. 3.79 Involvement of Sustainable Development

The current strategies of economic development are using up resources of the world rapidly. Our future generations will have serious environmental problems, much worse than what we are having at present. Current development strategies have come to be considered unsustainable for the world's long term development. The newer concept of development is known as **sustainable development: Rio de Janeiro declaration on environment and development 1987** has become an accepted goal of environmental policy for sustainable development. There has been a shift in emphasis from unsustainable development to sustainable development. The **UN's Brandland Report** "Our common future" also highlighted the concept of sustainable development. Sustainable development considers the equity between countries and continents, races and classes, genders and ages. It includes, social development and economic opportunity on the one hand, and the requirements of the environment on the other.

Certain documents created for the United Nations Conference on Environment and Development (UNCED) brought out the fact that environment and development are closely linked. There is a need to 'care for the earth'.

How to achieve sustainable development? - Guidelines

- Change in people's attitudes and value system.
- Involvement of everyone; Industries to produce efficient and innovative goods using few resources which offer better values.
- Government to set higher environmental standards (energy consumption and conservation policies).
- Substantial reduction in population growth rates.
- Provision for basic needs like house, clothing, shelter, health care, etc. to all.
- Education and empowerment of women - much more in rural areas.
- Change in methods of production and consumption in line with the sustainability of the environment.

Sustainable development	Unsustainable development
• Consider resources are finite.	• Involves the use of more natural resources.
• Rate of resource consumption at present must be slowed down, so as to conserve resources for the future.	• There will be higher rate of resource depletion.
• Reduces the rate of resource depletion and conserves the resources for the future for the above reason.	• Imbalances the nature for the above reason.
• Emphasises reuse or recycling of waste matter scientifically.	• Results in disposing of the waste matter unscientifically.
• Substitutes renewable resources for non-renewable resources.	• It is the other way.
• In the long run, it is ideal.	• No future thinking; look for to-day's comfort.

Fig. 3.80 Sustainable Development vs. Unsustainable Development

- Afforestation in a large scale.
- Non-conventional energy resources by industries.
- Proper treatment of urban water and industrial effluents.
- People's education, participation in conservation and improvement of environmental quality.
- Efficient use of resources without much wastage and high utilization.

Urban Problems Related to Energy

More and more people are moving to cities in these days in both developed and developing countries. The migration of human population to cities is because of employment opportunities and to enjoy city's luxury life. Out of a total of 6 billion people at present in the world, more than 2 billion people will be living in urban areas. This is more in the developing countries.

Urban areas are enormous quantities of energy. Earlier urban housing needed only smaller amounts of energy than we use at present. The materials used in housing are woods and bricks, which handled temperature changes well. But the materials used now are concrete, glass and steel of ultra modern building, which requires more energy for temperature adjustments needed by human.

Consumption of energy in urban areas

There is a sudden spurt in the consumption of energy in urban areas. The important reasons are as under:

- Increase in population in urban areas.
- Higher standard of living; Better life styles.
- High per capita consumption of energy (sophisticated gadgets and better lighting).
- Industrial growth and development (very large number of industries both big and small).
- Transportation development in large scale (roads, railways and airways).
- Energy intensive materials are used in urban housing and in industries, now a days for better aesthetic appearance.
- Energy consumption has become a measure of quality of life of an individual, society, better standard of living.

Embodies energy

Materials used in the recent days in urban housing are more of iron, glass, aluminum, steel, cement, marble, burnt bricks etc., need high energy - energy intensive. The process of extraction, refinement, fabrication and delivery are all energy consuming and add to the pollution of the earth, air and water. The energy consumed in the process is known as **'embodied energy'**.

Urban problems pertaining to energy

- Shortage in the supply of energy because of more consumption of energy by people.
- Excessive and reckless consumption of energy by people, causes environmental pollution.

  [**Note:** Switching the lights, fans, geysers, TVs, radio etc., even when not in use]

- Large scale use of energy for household appliances (Refrigerators, Washing machines, Vacuum cleaners etc.).
- Inadequate use of non-conventional energy sources like solar energy. Mainly depends on conventional (Hydro-electricity, petroleum etc.).
- Large-scale usage of fossil fuels by industries cause air/water pollution.
- Noise pollution by using a number of household appliances.
- Enormous wastages in the case of energy, petrol, diesel, hydro-electricity. Poor maintenance of roads, vehicles, transmission lights etc.

Each of us, as an environmentally conscious individual, must reduce our use of energy. If we learned to save electricity, we would begin to have a more sustainable life style.

Measures to solve the energy crisis in urban areas

These are to:

- Increase the supply of energy like petroleum and hydroelectricity.
- Check waste in the use of all sources of energy.
- Control the energy transmission losses.
- Control the excessive and reckless consumption of energy by road vehicles and in houses.
- Shift in the source of energy from conventional to non-conventional (like solar).
- Control environmental pollutions (air, water etc.) created by industries vehicles etc., using fossil fuels.
- Create public awareness more than anything among the urban people regarding excessive use and wastage.

Water Conservation, Rainwater Harvesting and Watershed Management

(1) Water conservation

- Conserving water is a primary environmental concern. Clean water is scarce all over the globe. When deforestation takes place, surface-runoff increases; sub-soil water table drops since water has no time to seep slowly into the ground, once the vegetation is cleared.
- Wells are dug deeper and deeper, as this is a main source of water in many areas. This adds to the cost and further depletes underground stores of water.
- Because of deforestation and desertification gives rise to extensive changes in land use. The perennial rivers are turning into seasonal rivers.

- Water is being used by us in several ways and we do not bother that it, affects the lives of all of us in different ways. Its overuse and misuse due to various activities that waste water or cause pollution has led to a serious shortage of potable drinking water.

Several methods for conservation of water exists. These methods are described below:

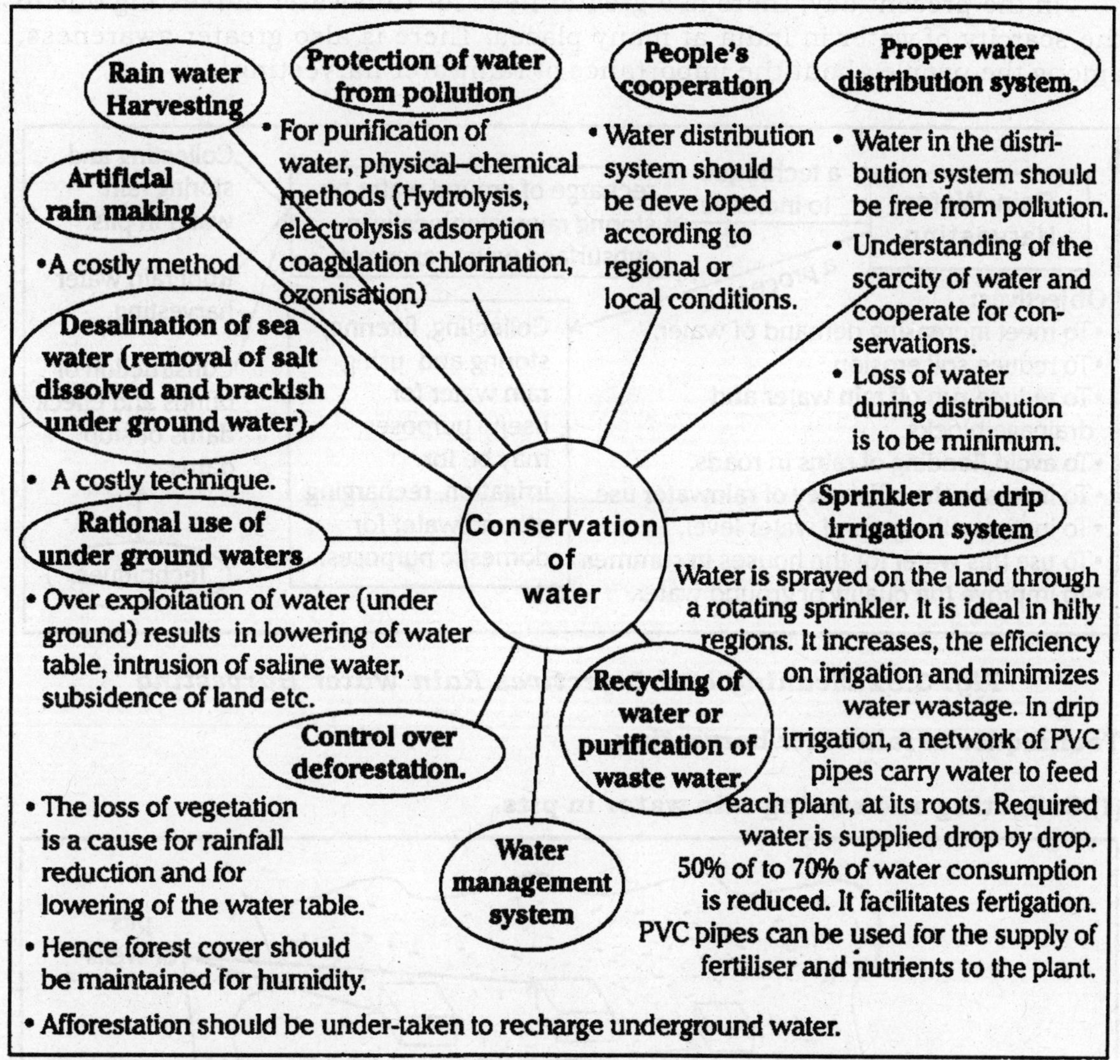

Fig. 3.81 Various Methods of Conservation of Water

Rainwater Harvesting

To save the water shortage threat, every drop of water if used efficiently will have great value. One of the methods is to manage rain water in such a way that it is used at the source. It has already been followed in India. There were other advanced rain harvesting system like tanks, wells, canals etc., in the ancient times in India. In Hilly and mountainous regions, rainwater harvesting from roof tops was practiced. The stored water has to be kept pollution free and clean so s to use it for drinking purposes. Stored water can grow algae and zoo plankton (microscopic animals) which is pathogenic and cause infections. Hence keeping the water uncontaminated is important.

In the present day, there is a greater need for rain water harvesting due to the scarcity of water in India at many places. There is also greater awareness, among the people about the importance of rainwater harvesting.

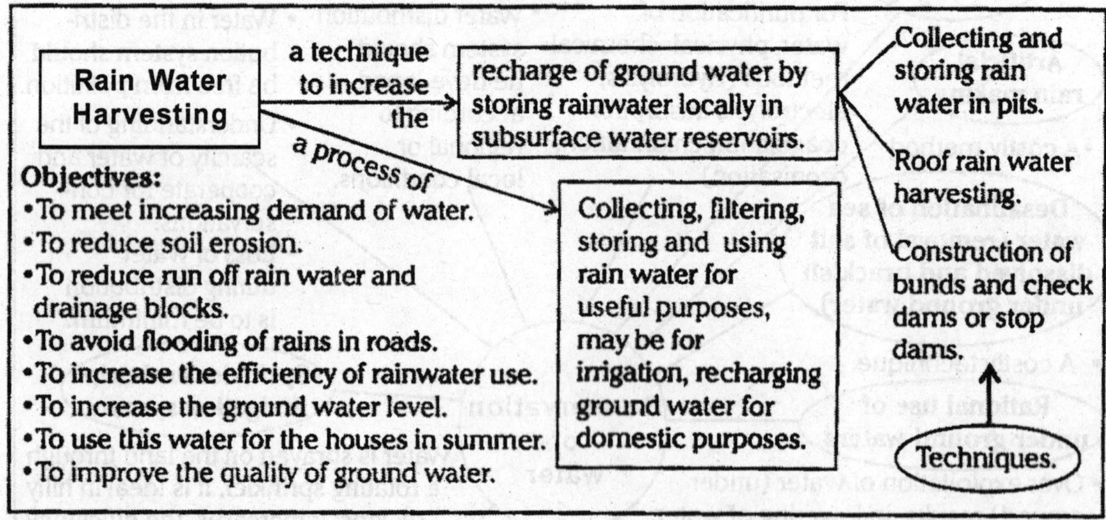

Fig. 3.82 Meaning and Objectives Rain Water Harvesting

Techniques of rainwater harvesting

(I) Collecting and storing rain water in pits

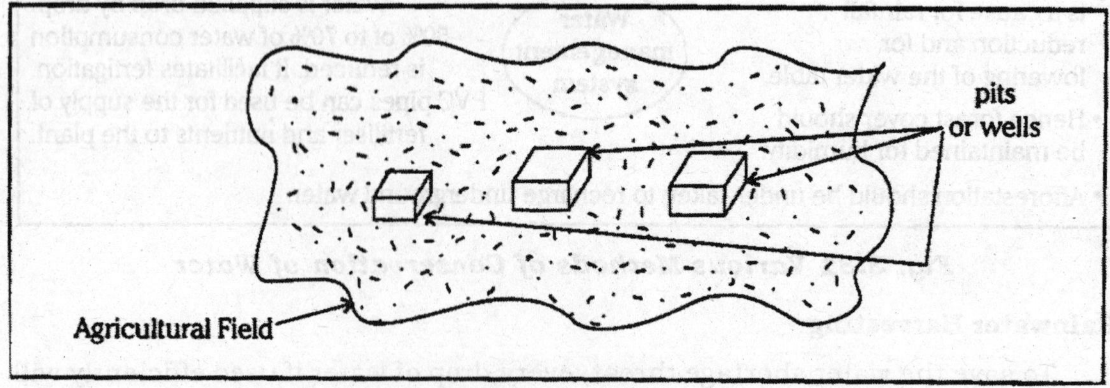

Fig. 3.83 Storing Rain-water in Pits or Wells

- Rain water is collected and stored in pits in fields used for irrigation.
- To increase the ground water level in the fields.
- Even in residential areas, rain water can be stored in pits and used for domestic purposes.
- Rain water falling from roof tops of residential buildings commercial buildings can be collected in pits/tanks/drums.
- These can be used for domestic purposes, washing, cleaning etc.

(II) Roof rainwater harvesting

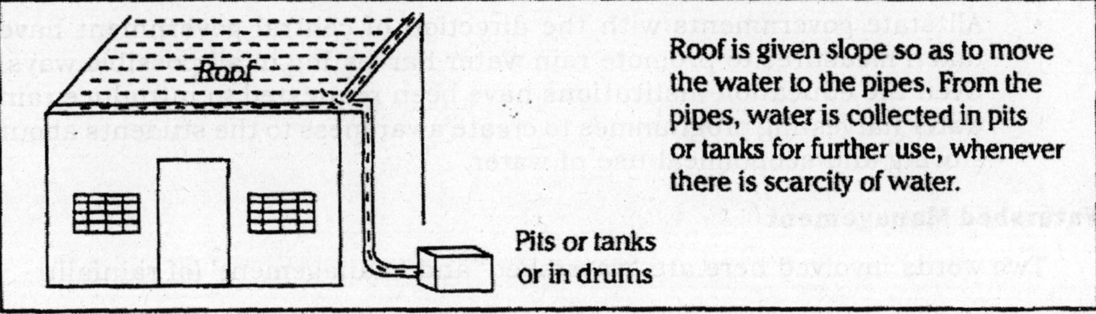

Fig. 3.84 Roof Rainwater Harvesting

(III) Bunds construction and check dams

Merits and Demerits of Rainwater harvesting

Merits of rainwater harvesting	*Demerits of rainwater harvesting*
• Improvement in irrigation facilities to agricultural lands; drinking water for the houses or even at least water, for other domestic purposes can be got through roof rain water harvesting.	• But this is a limited quantity as the storage is less.
• The ground water level of open wells and bore wells can be increased.	• Rainwater harvesting is only in rainy seasons.
• The requirement of water for domestic purposes can be met to a certain extent through roof rainwater harvesting.	• Wastage of rainwater through pipes and on the roads are enormous. Similarly through canals and pipes carrying water from dams to the consumer forms a higher percentage of loss during transfer.

Fig. 3.85 Merits and Demerits of Rainwater Harvesting

- State Governments are now insisting that rainwater collection and usage in new houses is a must for issuing license for new house constructions. In spite of this, concerned people are not serious and education is a must for such people.

- No doubt seminars have been organized regarding the importance of rain water harvesting to minimise the problem of scarcity of water both in rural and urban areas.
- People have been asked to associate and take interest in the programmes. Non governmental organisations, business houses, local bodies have been asked to participate in the programmes.
- Rain water harvesting programmes are being promoted through watershed management programmes, artificial recharge of ground water etc. Rain water harvesting could help to recharge about 210 cubic meters of run-off water for ground water tables.
- All state governments with the direction of central government have taken measures to promote rain water harvesting in all possible ways. Even the education institutions have been requested to introduce rain water harvesting programmes to create awareness to the students about storing and economical use of water.

Watershed Management

Two words involved here are 'watershed' and 'management' (of rainfall).

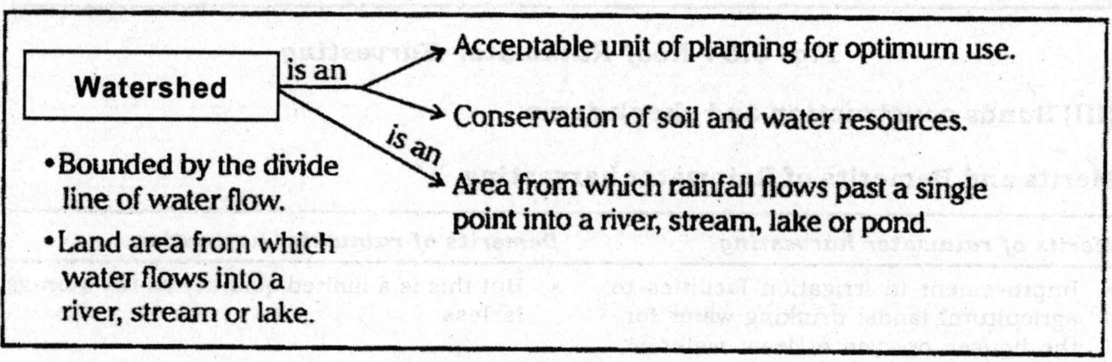

Fig. 3.86 Watershed

Management in this context is the management of rainfall and the resultant run-off to a destination is very important and is based on watershed. Each watershed is an independent unit.

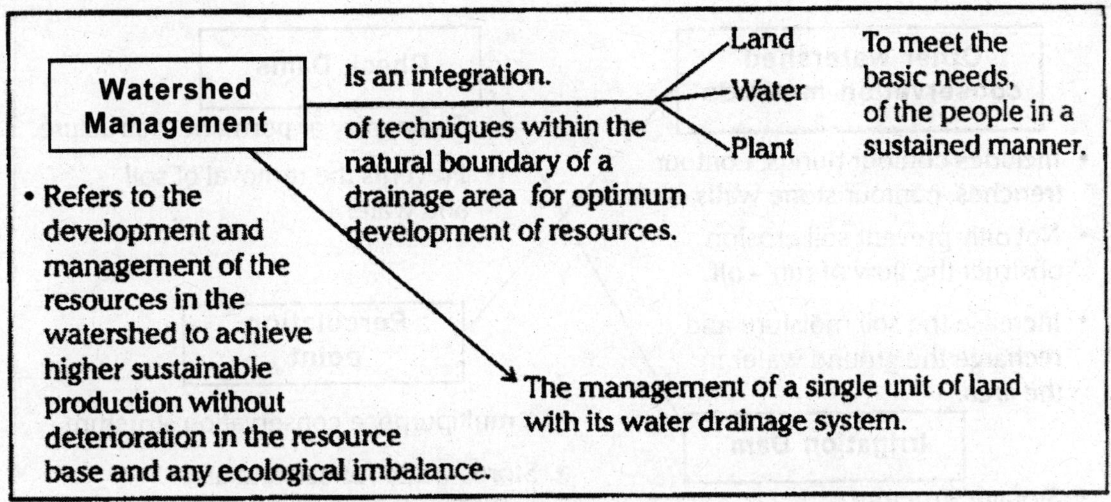

Fig. 3.87 Meaning of Watershed Management

Watershed management is a technique that has several components:

- Soil and Water management.
- Developing vegetative cover.

If managed properly, the natural drainage pattern can bring about local prosperity. It provides a year round supply of water, improves the quality of life in the area, improves health in the community with clean water, enhances the growth of agricultural crops and can grow more than one crop a year in dry areas.

Benefits of watershed management

- Provides for optimum use of resources in the watershed without adversely affecting the soil and water base.
- Eliminates unscientific land use, inappropriate cropping pattern, and soil erosion, improves and sustains the productivity of resources contributes to higher income and better living standards of the people.

Watershed management principles

- A land management programme looking at a region from the perspective of all its water related issues. It can also be used to manage a river from its source to termination; It can also consider the management of a single valley as a unit, based on its small streams. Saving water from its local source and allowing it to percolate into the ground and construct dams instead of allowing it to run off rapidly along the surface during the monsoon is a major aspect. Underground aquifers will fill when once the ground water is recharged. Deforestation is the major cause for water supply. Afforesting such degraded areas is an important aspect of watershed management.

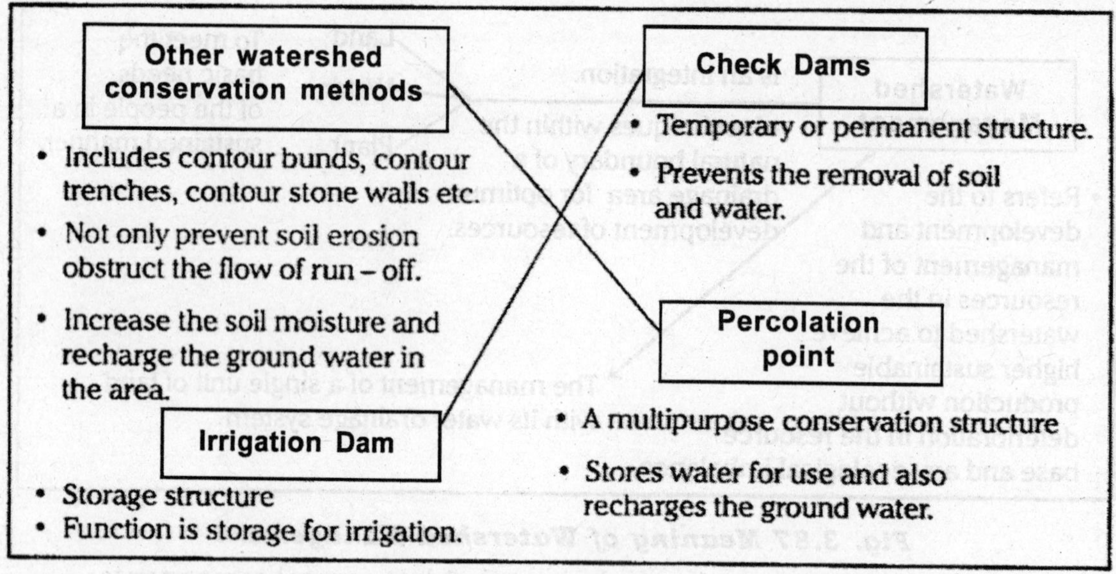

Fig. 3.88 Watershed Conservation Practices

Resettlement and Rehabilitation of People: Its Problems and Concerns

The lives of the people are disrupted when major projects like dams, mines, express ways or national parks take place. The people who live in that are to be relocated to alternative sites. Making people to shift to other places is a serious issue, when once they are settled at some place having their homes. For tribal people, it is more difficult to adapt to a new way of life in a new place as they have already adjusted to the natural resources. In India, Lakhs of people have been displaced by the thousands of dams built after independence during the green revolution period.

Resettlement requires alternate land. Ours is a over populated country and we do not have quality land. Such people who needs resettlement are not given the right type of land. But they are given unusable waste land.

Features associated with displacement and resettlement of people

- Depends on the number of people affected, numbers affected directly and indirectly are underestimated.
- Involuntary and forced in most cases.
- Seen as a project that enforces certain technical and economic choices. These choices involve least social and environmental costs.
- Very little meaningful participation of the affected people in the planning and the implementation of the project; Last to receive meaningful information on the project.
- Delayed relocation of displaced people.

- Denial of development opportunities to those relocated for years due to long and uncoordinated displacement and resettlement process.
- There is inadequate understanding of the exact nature and extent of the negative effects.

Risks associated with Resettlement and Rehabilitation of affected people

- Programmes are focussed on the process of physical relocation but not on the economic and social development of the displaced people.
- The displaced people are inconvenienced due to:

— Loss of livelihood

— Income sources

— Common property sources like forests, grazing lands, surface water, fisheries etc.

— Changed access

— Control of productive resources

— Loss of economic power due to the breakdown of the livelihood system (affects household food security and undernourishment)

— Decline in the living standards

— High incidence of diseases (giving raise to mortality of displaced persons).

However, there are arguments also in favour of displacement and resettlement. They are:

(i) National Interest (An opportunity to work in large developmental projects).

(ii) Long term benefits.

Main Problems associated with Resettlement and Rehabilitation

(i) Cost of resettlement programme is underestimated; adequate budget not made for resettlement. Any financial problems in the project, the budget of resettlement/rehabilitation is reduced.

(ii) Resettlement sites selected without reference to livelihood opportunities and the preference of the displaced people.

(iii) Most resettlement programmes have failed to encourage successful self-employment strategies, skills and capacity building etc., for the displaced.

(iv) Effective resettlement/rehabilitation happened by problems like:

- Institutional weakness
- Lack of coordination between various departments etc.

(v) Good projects (with well structured institutions and trained staff) have failed because of lack of policy and effective mechanism to monitor compliance.

(vi) Participation of displaced people not considered important by those responsible for the execution of the project.

(vii) The house sites allotted to the displaced persons are often temporary structures.

(viii) Large families and communities are broken up and resettled over a wide area.

(ix) Forced relocation, implicit in resettlement, usually results in shifting of people from a social ecology hampers the development of the displaced.

(x) Most of these are long drawn programmes; completion takes a long time. Long interval between the date of notification of displacement and the actual resettlement; Intervening period is full of uncertainties and anxieties.

(xi) Resettlement sites are selected often without reference to availability of livelihood opportunities and the preference of the displaced people.

(xii) The Resettlement sites are underdeveloped in terms of essential infrastructure facilities and amenities for decent living.

Successful Resettlement and Rehabilitation programmes need following requirements:

- It is not a mere physical relocation or mere restoration of incomes. It should be a planned, integrated and a comprehensive development project.
- It ensures that resettlement results in:

  - Enhancement of people's capabilities.

  - Expansion of social opportunity.
- It is nothing but a participative development - not a forced relocation.
- For success of the programme, it is not just the participation of affected community but its ownership and control of the project.
- It is to be governed by law, not to be left to the discretion of the executives consumed with the administration of the programme.

Environmental Ethics: Issues and Possible Solutions

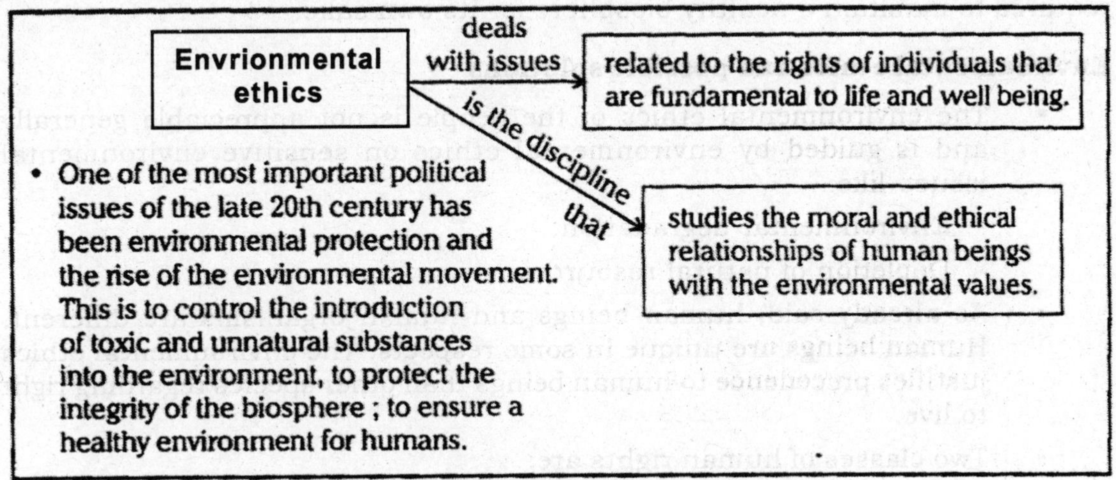

Fig. 3.89 Environmental Ethics

Environmental ethics deal with issues like:

- The needs of each person today.
- The needs of the people who live after us.
- The rights to other living creatures that inhibit the earth.

The environmental movement has led to an increased awareness among people that they have a responsibility to use their knowledge and issues to help protect the environment. As concern about the environment has grown, ethicists have turned their attention to the ethical dimensions of environmentalism.

In the late 1960s, an area of study called **environmental ethics** was formulated, seeking to explore the ethical roots of the environmental movement and to understand what ethics tells us about our responsibility to the environment.

Western ethical tradition is **anthropocentric** (human beings only have moral standing). Animals and plants are important only in respect to their usefulness to humans. This type of thinking is often evident within the environmental movement in which a case is sometimes made for the protection of rare plants based on their potential for providing new medicines. If animals, trees and other components of the environment have no moral standing, then we have no ethical obligations towards them beyond maintaining their usefulness to humans. There are other ways also to view the moral standing of the environment.

Do we belong to nature or does nature belong to us? If animals can suffer and feel pain like humans, should they have formal standing? If animals have moral standing, how far does this extend to other life forms such as trees? These questions are not easily answered. Many people believe that the environment, and specially animals and plants do have standing beyond their usefulness to humans. Humans are just one component of the environment and that all components have equal standing. It is the utmost duty of everyone to do what is required to maintain a healthy biosphere for its own sake.

Environmental ethics and possible solutions

- The environmental ethics of the people is not appreciable generally and is guided by environmental ethics on sensitive environmental issues like:
  - Environmental degradation.
  - Depletion of natural resources.
- As already said, human beings and human organisms are different. Human beings are unique in some respects. The environmental ethics justifies precedence to human beings than other species regarding right to live.
- Two classes of human rights are:
  - Strong (Right to life and security)
  - Weak (Right to property) this can be overridden by consideration like the good of the whole community i.e., the welfare of the whole community.
- Human beings can enjoy the benefits of environment. It is wrong if they bring harm on environment for the reason of greedy realization of their personal needs.
- Human beings harm the environment by performing certain activities e.g., Certain disease eradication programme. Human life can be safeguarded even at the cost of environmental degradation in such cases as per environmental ethics.
- Regarding the present generation and the due share of the rights of the future generation, environmental ethics suggests.
  - Such situations are to be tackled by reconciling the needs of both the generations.
  - Moral obligations exist on the present generation to pass on those to the future generation what it has inherited from the past generation.

Important Parameters of Environmental Ethics

Environmental Ethics (Deals with)	
Green house gases CO_2, Nitrogen Oxides, CFCs, HFCs, Halogens Convert Hydrocarbons to Cl_2, Fl_2, Br_2 and I_2 and replace H_2	**Ozone** It is an atmosphere and protects life against harmful ultra violet radiation. But at groundlevel it is harmful to life and breathing disorders. Its depletions causing holes at poles where the UV radiations is leaking; In strategy. (i) Reactive stragey, (ii) Defensive stragey, (iii) Strategy of accommodation.
	Whistle Blowing An attempt by an employee to disclose what is proclaimed to be wrong doing by an organisation, reporting misdemeanor to someone
	Environmental threats Greenhouse gases, depletion of ozone layer, acidificationof water/soil urban pollution, Noise, Metals effects, organic pollutants-effects, land and water in-appropriate use, land, water exploitation, Housing/Industrial /Infrastructure, Pressure on conservation, Non-cyclic Material flows and hazardous residues.
	Greenhouse effect Ideal global temperature is average 15°C, or else the world will freeze, the emissions of CO2, cause alarming temperature increase and polar ice caps melt and increased water levels which may submerge many parts of low lying areas, causing hardships for human residents.

Fig. 3.90 Environmental Ethics

Reactive strategy: Resistance of public or government pressures by legal means.

Defensive strategy: A firm depends its position by less aggressive means. The firm does the minimum requirements and not more, unless compelled to do so.

Strategy of accommodation: More progressive of the strategies, include acceptable of ideas for social changes, firm's resistance is to the extent of what is not in its best interests. Most companies adopt this strategy.

Climate Change: Global Warming, Acid Rain and Ozone Layer Depletion

Note: The following changes taking place on the climate:

- The temperature (average) in many regions has been increasing.
- The global surface temperature has increased by 0.6°C - 0.2°C over the last century.
- 1998 - warmest year.
- 1990s - warmest decade.
- Rainfall has increased in many countries.
- Intensity of droughts increased in certain parts of Asia and Africa.
- Storms have been more frequent, intense, persistent in the recent days.
- It is expected in the near future, global mean surface temperature will rise by 1.4° to 5.8°C; warming will be greatest over land areas and at high latitudes.
- Rate of warming is higher than that occurred in the last 10,000 years.
- Frequency of weather extremes is likely to increase, leading to floods or drought. There will be fewer cold spells but more heat waves.
- More than 50% of the world's population lives within 60 KM of the sea.

Fig. 3.91 Climatic Charges Taking Place

Like these several points could be seen regarding the climate change, on the whole. HUman societies will be seriously affected by extremes of climate such as droughts and floods. Changing climate is also a fundamental concern for human health. Public health depends on:

- Safe drinking water (water may be contaminated and sewage systems may be damaged).
- Sufficient food.
- Secure shelter.
- Good social conditions.

The risk of spread of infectious diseases such as diarrhea disease will increase. Food production will come down in vulnerable regions through an increase in pests and plant or animal diseases, leading to starvation and malnutrition with long term health consequences for children.

Changes in climate may affect the distribution of **vector species** (mosquitoes as an example) will increase the spread of diseases.

Global warming

It is one of the most significant threats facing human kind which shows how climate change in the past led to famine, wars and population decline. The world's growing population may be unable to adequately adapt to ecological changes brought about by the expected rise in global temperatures. The warmer temperatures are probably good for a while, but beyond some levels, plants will be stressed. With more droughts and a rapidly growing population, it is going to get harder and harder to provide food for everyone and that we should not be surprised to see more saturation and probably more cases of hungry people clashing over scarce food and water. Trawling through history and working out correlative patterns, it is found that temperature declines were followed by wars, famines and population reductions (the time period between 1400 and 1900) or the little Ice age, which recorded the lowest average global temperatures around 1450, 1650 and 1820, each separated by slight warming intervals. When such ecological situations occur, people tend to move to another place. Such mass movements lead to war. In the 13th century, the Mongolians suffered a drought and they invaded China.

Climatic change will put half the world's countries at risk of conflict or serious political instability. A London-based conflict resolution group identified 46 countries - home to 2.76 billion people where it said the effects of climate change would create a high risk of violent conflict. Another 56 states there was a risk of political instability. Certain experts analysts expect some pretty serious conflicts that are clearly linked to climate change on the international scene by 2020.

World's Weirdest creatures are headed for extinction

Experts say that 85% of the world's top 100 strongest species will disappear soon. For example, pigmy hippopotamus, the bumblebee bat, rare slender loris. These are receiving very little, conservation attention and will disappear if no action is taken. The fund raising initiative for amphibian conservation known as EDGE aims to save animals has been launched. Tragically amphibians tend to be the overlooked members of the animal kingdom. One in three amphibian species is currently threatened with extinction, the proportion is more than that of the bird or mammal species. These species are highly sensitive such as climate change and pollution. If we lose them, other species will inevitably follow. The EDGE programme strives to protect the world's forgotten species and ensure that the weirdest species survive the current extinction crisis and astound future generations with their extraordinary uniqueness. Zoological Society of London (ZSL) has identified 10 species to protect them which includes EDGE amphibian species. These include:

- Chinese giant salamander
- Ghost frogs of South Africa
- Purple Frog
- Sagalla caecilian
- Lungless salamanders of Mexico, Ohm etc.

These animals may not be cute and cuddly but hopefully their weird looks and bizarre behaviours will inspire people to support their conservation.

This was caused at least in part by the reckless use of fossil fuels. Now it has begun to than the frozen Arctic. The melting ice is exposing potentially huge deposits of hitherto unreachable natural resources including hydrocarbon reserves in the seabed below. Due to this, nations are suddenly scrambling to claim these subterranean land as their own in order to exploit the economic wealth of the ocean. As per US, Geological survey, an estimation upto 25% of the world's uncovered oil and gas remain locked up beneath these frigid waters. A Russian submersible recently planted that country's flag under the North pole. The idea behind the expedition was to prove that Lomonsov Ridge, an arctic under water mountain range is an extension of Siberia and therefore belong to Russia. Denmark claims the ridge as an extension of Greenland and should belong to it. Canada says it is part of its own continental shelf and thus, logically belongs to it. The US asserts the shelf actually extends northwards form Alaska. In the fray are also Finland, Iceland and Norway.

The up folding conflicts of interest could easily spin out of control if proper steps are not taken now. The 1982 UN conventional law exists for challenging claims. In any cases with oil prices teetering over $70 mark, who is willing to listen in a hurry. The Arctic could create overt economic hostility or even political fisticuffs. A treaty can be set aside as a common scientific preserve and ban all military activity. What do they have lose besides some more oil? It's degraded the Arctic anyway.

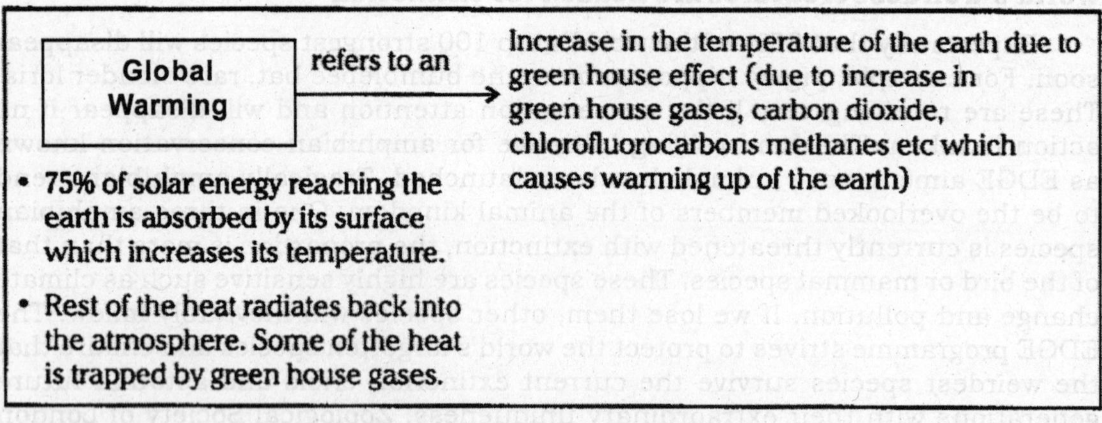

Fig. 3.92 Global Warming

The average surface temperature of the earth is about 15°C. This is about 33°C higher than what it would have been without the greenhouse effect (i.e., it would have been at - 18°C, without such gases i.e., mean air temperature of - 18°C).

In the recent days, human activities have increased because of industrialization and population growth. This has polluted the atmosphere in such a way to seriously affect the climate. The carbon dioxide in the atmosphere has increased by 31% causing more heat to be trapped in the lower atmosphere. The carbon dioxide level is further increasing as per the scientists. Many countries have signed a convention to reduce green house gases (GHGs) under the UN frame work convention on climate change (UNFCC).

Global warming is alarmingly increasing than what was calculated by climatologists few years back. The prediction in 1995 was that global warming would raise temperatures by 3.5°C to 10°C during the 21st century, if the present trend continues. The amount of rainfall would increase. India may see a great annual fluctuations in rainfall leading to floods and droughts.

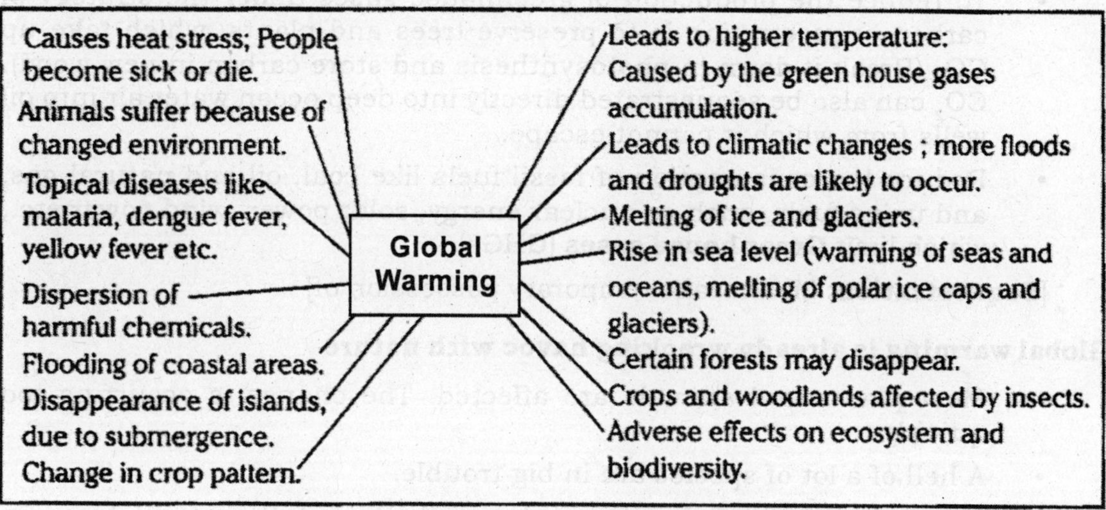

Fig. 3.93 Effects of Global Warming

For millions of years, gases in the earth's atmosphere have trapped sufficient heat from solar radiation to sustain life. However, an increase in human activity may now be rising levels of greenhouse gases such as CO_2, so that excess heat is trapped into the atmosphere.

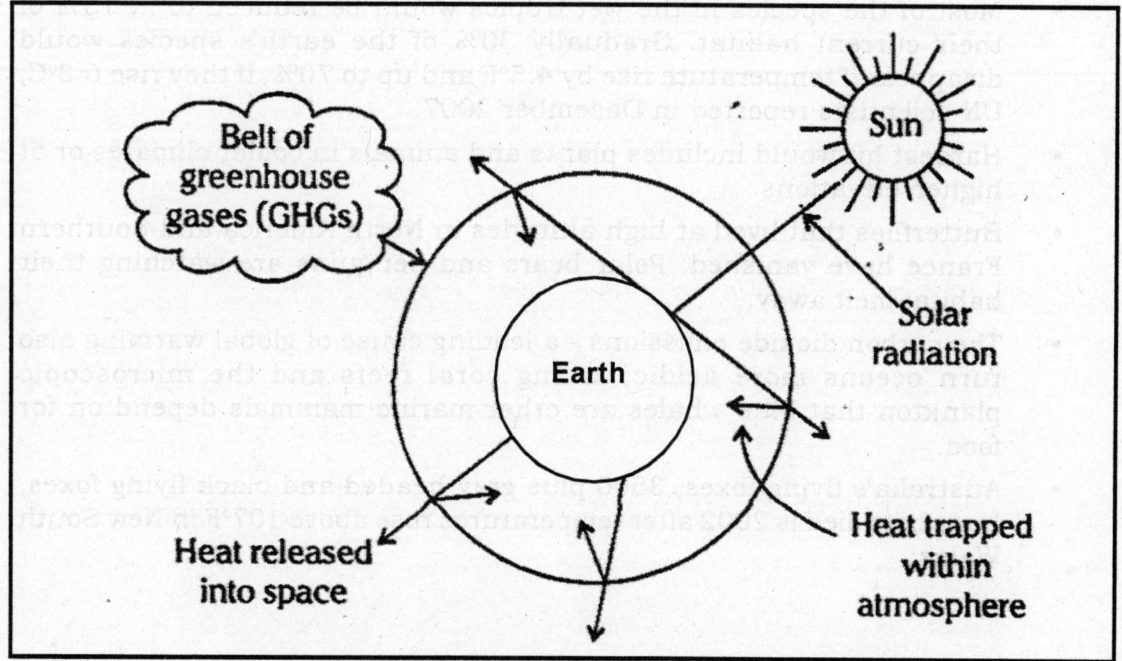

Fig. 3.94 Demonstration of Global Warming

Measures for controlling global warming

Three ways are there:

- Keep the carbon dioxide out of the atmosphere by storing the gas or its carbon component somewhere else - known as **carbon sequestration**.
- To reduce the production of greenhouse gases under the strategy of carbon sequestration is to preserve trees and plants, which take up CO_2 (Break it down in photosynthesis and store carbon in new wood). CO_2 can also be sequestrated directly into deep ocean water air into oil wells from which it cannot escape.
- Reduce the consumption of fossil fuels like coal, oil and natural gas, and using fuels, such as nuclear energy, solar power, wind power etc., which limit **Greenhouse gases** (GHGs).

[**Sequestration:** Means take temporary possession of]

Global warming is already wrecking havoc with nature

- Most plants and animals are affected. The change is occurring too quickly.
- A hell of a lot of species are in big trouble.
- More than 3000 flying foxes dropped dead, falling from trees in Australia.
- Giant squid migrated north to commercial fishing grounds off California, gobbling anchovy and hake.
- Butterflies have gone extinct in the alps.
- Most of the species in the wet tropics would be reduced to ... 15% of their current habitat. Gradually 30% of the earth's species would disappear if temperature rise by 4.5°F and up to 70%, if they rise 6.3°C, UN scientists reported in December 2007.
- Hardest hit would includes plants and animals in colder climates or at higher elevations.
- Butterflies that lived at high altitudes in North America and Southern France have vanished. Polar bears and penguins are watching their habitat melt away.
- The carbon dioxide emissions - a leading cause of global warming also turn oceans more acidic, killing coral reefs and the microscopic plankton that blue whales are other marine mammals depend on for food.
- Australia's flying foxes, 3500 plus gray headed and black flying foxes, huge bats died is 2002 after temperatures rose above 107°F in New South Wales.

Impact of global warming
• Heat waves and periods of unusually warm weather. • Ocean warming, rise in sea level and constant flooding. • Glaciers melting. • Aretic and Antarctica warming. • Spreading disease. • Spring arrives earlier. • Plant and animal range shifts and population changes. • Coral reef bleaching. • Downpour, heavy snowfall and flooding. • Drought and fire.

The inconclusive Bali summit 2007 may not have set any target for developing countries like India. To review climate change issues:

- Priorities the causative factors confronting the state.
- Recommend strategies, ways and means to improve the standards and adopt cleaner technologies.
- Create awareness and capacity building to mitigate and manage climate change variability and to achieve sustainable development.
- The world leaders and environmentalists are still grappling to find a solution even as developed and developing countries try to shift the responsibility to each other.

What reduces global warming?

- Scientific irrigation
- Use of bio-fertilisers and pesticides
- Organic cultivation
- Preservation of crop diversity
- Energy efficiency
- Cleaner and greener technologies
- Scientific management of waste
- Fuel substitution with renewables or gas
- Cleaner fuels
- Mass transport
- Improved road network
- Promotion of renewable energy

- Rain water harvesting
- Afforestation
- Social forestry.

How we can help?

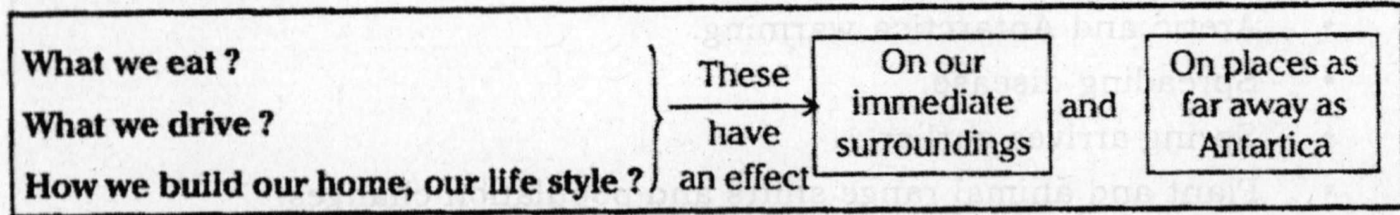

As we all contribute is global warming, we all need to be part of the solution. Simple actions in our daily life like using. "Sleep mode" instead of a screen saver in a computer monitor, taking shorter showers, using recycled paper and changing air filters will help in freezing and reducing carbon dioxide emissions and saving the planet.

Acid Rain

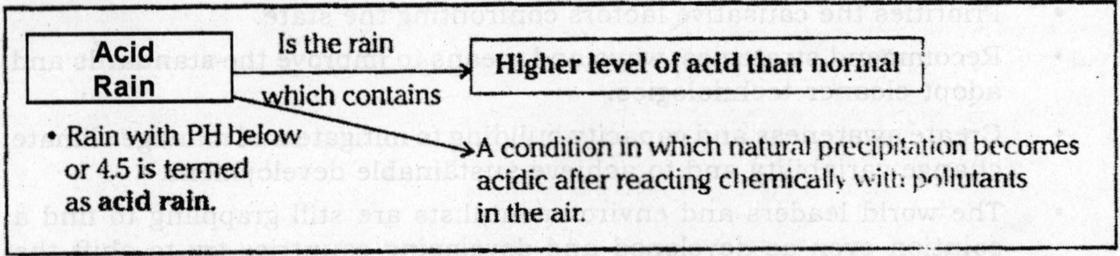

Fig. 3.95 Meaning of Acid Rain

The clouds that produce acid rain are formed, when polluting gases, such as sulphurdioxide and nitrogen oxide combine with oxygen and moisture in the air. The resultant precipitation is **acid rain**.

Acid rain causes forestry damage as well as hastening the erosion of many ancient buildings and sculptures.

The oxides formed are swept into the atmosphere travels a long distance. The longer they stay in the atmosphere, the more likely they are oxidized into acids like sulphuric acid and nitric acid. When they dissolve in the water in the atmosphere, they may fall to the ground as **acid rain** or may remain in the atmosphere in clouds and fogs. Volcanoes, fires etc., are the natural causes for acid rains. Decomposing matter emitting pollutants is also a cause for acid rain.

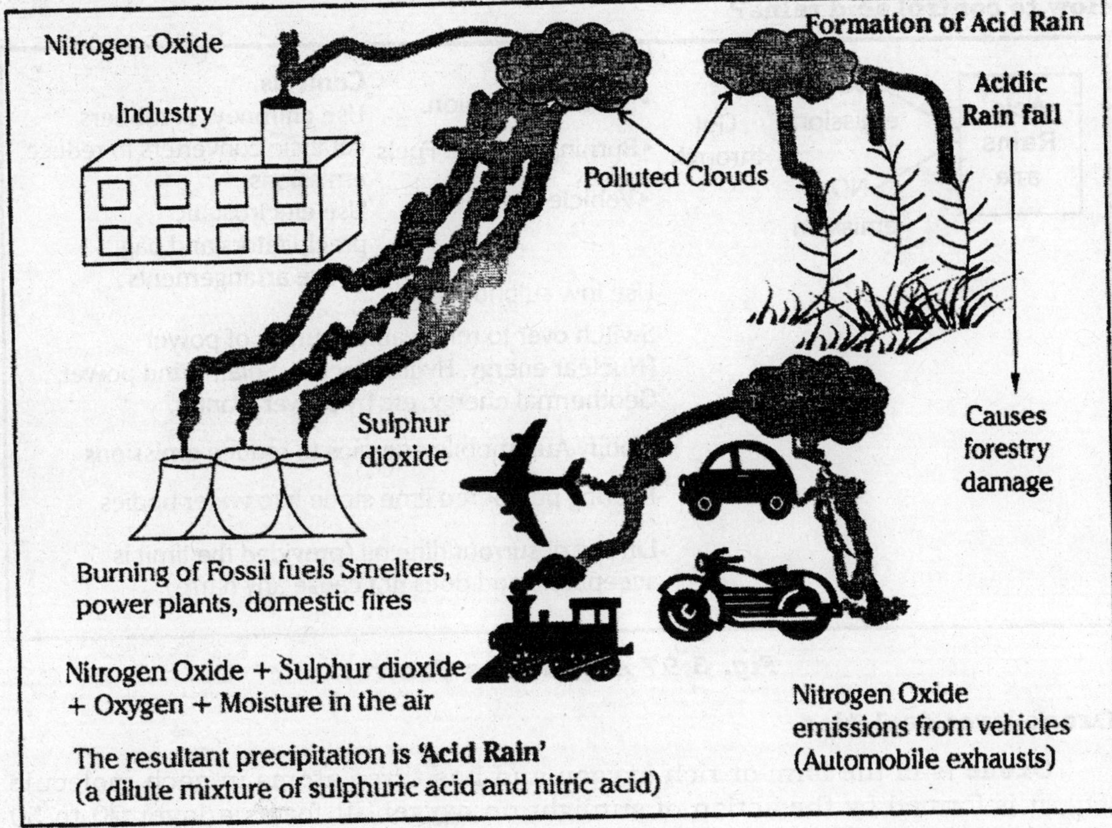

Fig. 3.96 Acid Rain

Ill Effects of Acid Rains

Rain water is slightly acidic because CO_2 is dissolved is it, reacts to form a weak acid, which is not harmful.

These Acid rains will have several environmental implications.

- Ill effect on vegetation (dropping of leaves and discolouring of leaves and flowers) - resulting in the loss of trees.
- Acidification of lakes and streams (affect aquatic life).
- Ill effect on soils (soil gets acidified - lead to loss of productivity and damage to plant roots).
- Affects crop productivity.
- It has ill-effect on monuments, statues and buildings.
- It has ill-effect on man. Human health is affected by increased respiratory and skin problems; causes irritation to skin.
- Accelerate the decay of building materials and paints.

How to control acid rains?

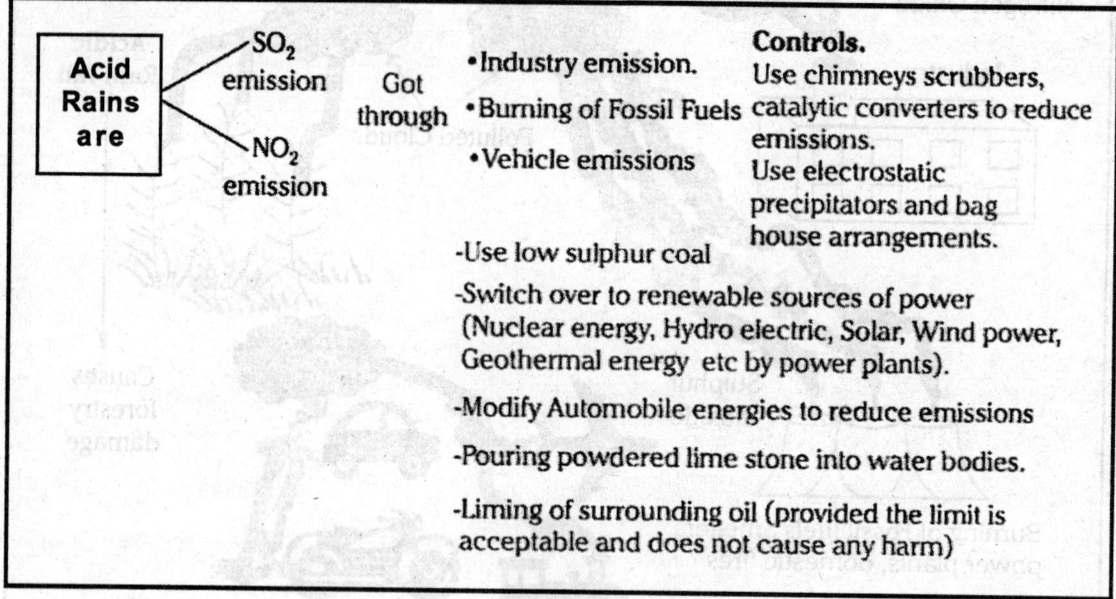

Fig. 3.97 Acid Rains Control

Ozone layer depletion

Ozone is in the form or rich oxygen and has three atoms in each molecule (O_3), it is formed by the action of sunlight on oxygen. It forms a layer 20 to 50 kms above the surface of the earth.

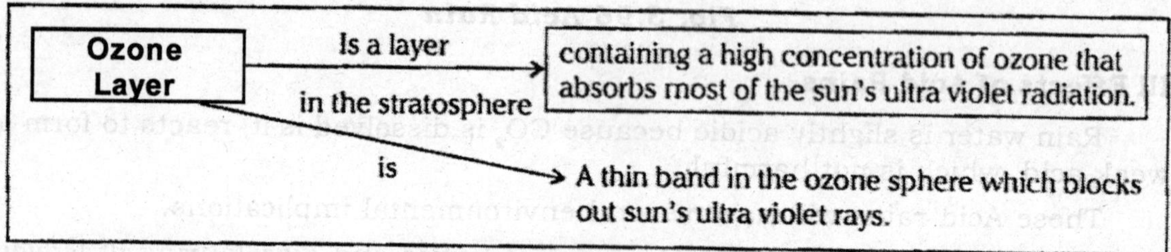

Fig. 3.98 Ozone Layer

Ozone is a slightly poisonous gas with a strong odour. It is considered a pollutant at ground level and constitutes a health hazard by causing respiratory ailments like asthma and bronchitis. It causes harm to vegetation and leads to deterioration of certain materials like plastic and rubber. Ozone is an important constituent in the upper atmosphere and is vital to all forms of life. It protects the earth from the sun's harmful ultra-violet radiation. The ozone in the upper atmosphere absorbs the sun's ultraviolet radiation, preventing it from reaching the earth's surface. However the chemicals discovered in 1970 known as chloroflourocarbons (CFCS) used as refrigerants and aerosol spray propellants fire a threat to the ozone larger. The CFC molecules are undestructible. However, if these reach the stratosphere, the UP breaks them down to release chlorine atoms, in turn these react with ozone molecules to form oxygen molecules which do not absorb ultraviolet radiation. Scientists in 1980 detected a thinning of the ozone layer in the atmosphere above Antarctica and now a days being deducted in several places including Australia. Another danger with the ozone large is that the destruction of the ozone layer causes an increased incidence of skin cancer and cataracts. It also causes damage to certain crops and plankton, thus affecting natural food chains and food webs. In turn, the decrease in vegetation leads to an increase in carbon dioxide.

In 1987, signing of the Montreal protocol took place, a treaty for the protection of ozone layer.

In 2000, the use of CFCs was to be banned, expecting ozone layer would be recovered slowly in a period of about 50 years.

Presently, although CFCs have been banned and reduced in many countries, the chemicals and industrial compounds like bromine, halocarbons, nitrous oxides from fertilizers are still attacking the ozone layer.

Holocaust (Nuclear accidents)

Holocaust is a case of large scale destruction especially by fire or nuclear war.

Holocaust also gives a meaning of the mass murder of the Jews by the Nazis (1941-45) based on Greek Kaustos meaning "brunt". It refers to wholesale destruction caused by fully burnt nuclear weapons or bombs.

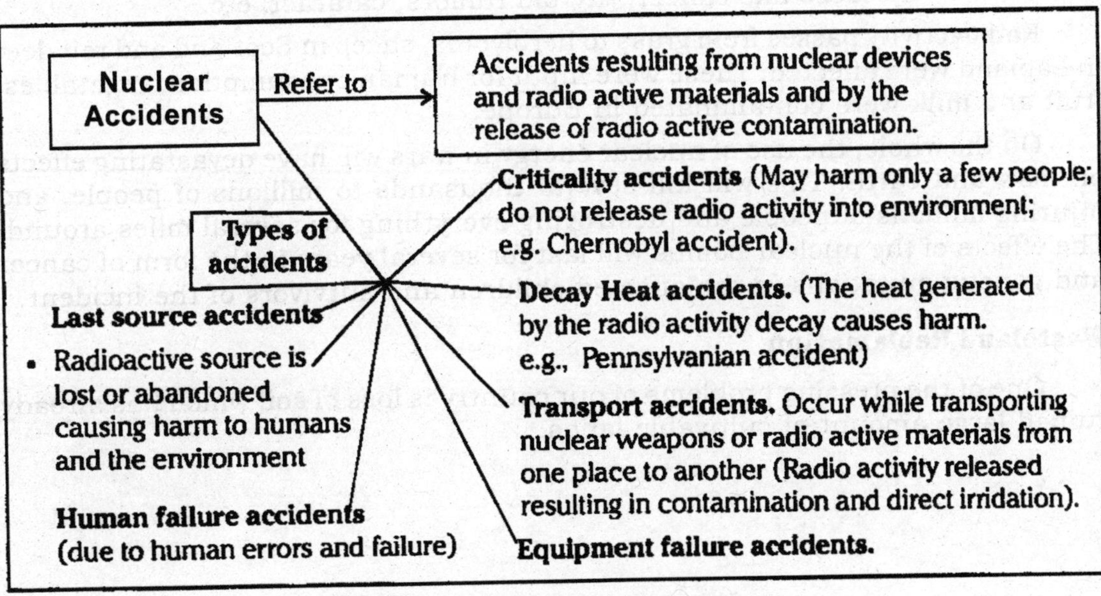

Fig. 3.99 Nuclear Accidents

The examples of nuclear holocausts are:

(a) Dropping of atom bombs on Hiroshima and Nagasaki Cities in Japan by the American Army Air Force

Day: 6th August 1945

Period: Second world war

Damage: Gravity bomb with 60 kgs (130 lbs) of uranium - 235 was dropped on the city of Hiroshima (1,40,000 people died); Another bomb, three days later of 6.4 kg (14.1 lbs of plutonium-239, was dropped over Nagasaki in Japan (74,000 people died; Not by bomb alone and due to its side effects).

(b) Nuclear power station at Chernobyl (in the earlier USSR)

The power station developed a problem leading to a big fire and a number of explosions in its nuclear reactor.

Year: 1986

Damage: The radio active dust spread over many kilometers, covered Europe and North America; 3 people died in the explosion and 28 later on, due to radiation exposure, 259 sick people admitted to hospitals. The area was evacuated immediately, 1,35,000 people moved from there immediately. In 1991, another 1.5 lakhs moved. Because of the radio active fallout continuation, more people moved 6.5 lakhs people in total were seriously affected. They may get various deadly diseases like cancer, thyroid tumors, cataract, etc.

Radioactivity passes from grass to herbivores, sheep in Scotland and reindeer in Lapland were affected. These were input for human consumption; vegetables, fruit and milk were contaminated in Europe.

On the whole, the use of nuclear energy in wars will have devastating effects on man and earth. This will kill several thousands to millions of people, and injuring millions of people and destroying everything for several miles around. The effects of the nuclear bombs will last for several years in the form of cancer and genetic mutations in the affected children and survivors of the incident.

Wasteland Reclamation

One of the pressing problems of our country is loss of soil which has already ruined large amount of cultivable lands.

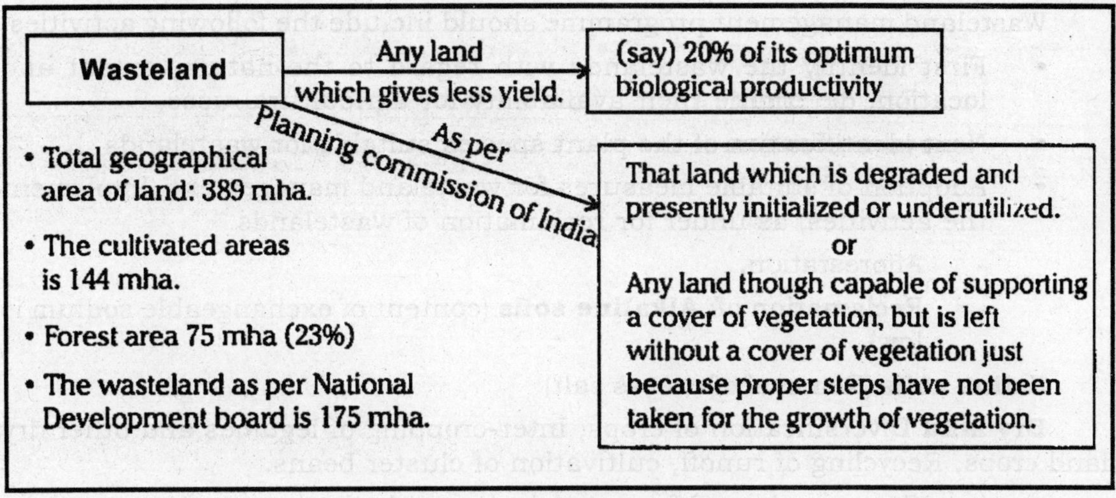

Fig. 3.100 Wasteland

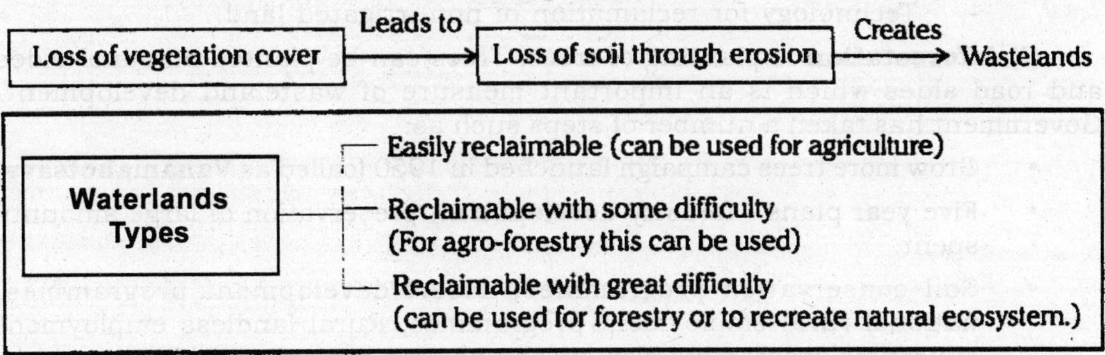

Fig. 3.101 Types of Wastelands

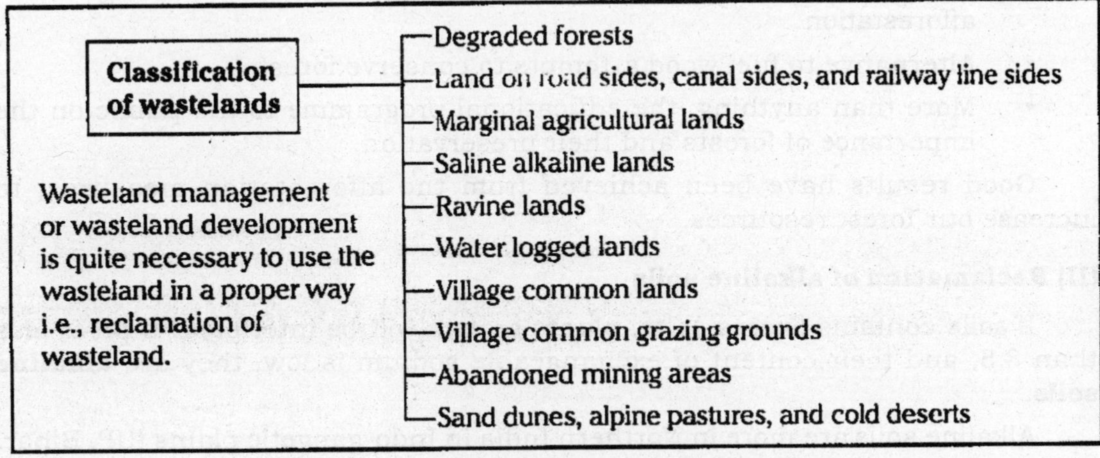

Fig. 3.102 Wastelands classification

Wasteland management programme should include the following activities:

- First identify the wastelands with regard to the nature, extent and location, determine their availability for agricultural uses.
- Next identification of the plant species suitable for wastelands.
- Adoption of suitable measures for wasteland management (Implement the activities) as under for reclamation of wastelands.
  - Afforestation.
  - Reclamation of: **Alkaline soils** (content of exchangeable sodium is low)

Saline soils (Removal of excess salt)

Dry land Diversification of crops; Inter-cropping of legumes and other dry land crops, Recycling of runoff, cultivation of cluster beans.

- Conservation of farm ponds (watershed management practices brings down dam sedimentation).
- Technology for reclamation of non-irrigated land.

(I) Afforestation is planting of trees. Trees can be planted on canal sides and road sides which is an important measure of wasteland development. Government has taken a number of steps such as:

- Grow more trees campaign launched in 1950 (called as **Vanamahotsava**)
- Five year plans - forestry development, preservation of large amounts spent.
- Soil conservation programmes, desert development programmes, national rural employment programmes, Rural landless employment guarantee programme, drought prone area programme with the object of expanding forest cover.
- International aid was sought and the funds used for large scale afforestation.
- Alternative to fuel wood attempts to conserve forests.
- More than anything, the educational programme to the public on the importance of forests and their preservation.

Good results have been achieved from the afforestation measures, to increase our forest resources.

(II) Reclamation of alkaline soils

If soils contains excess salts, plants growth will be interfered. If pH is less than 8.5, and their content of exchangeable sodium is low, they are **alkaline soils**.

Alkaline soils are more in Northern India in Indo-gangetic plains (UP, Bihar, WB, Punjab etc.).

As canal irrigation facilities have improved, alkalinity/salinity problems are serious in India, amounting to 7 million hectares of land, lying uncultivated.

Reclamation of saline soils

Saline soils are found mostly in the coastal areas, arid and semi arid regions of the country.

Reclamation involves removal of excess salt through leaching and flushing. In the coastal areas, salt (sodium chloride) is high and is the cause of salinity. The aim of leaching is to lower the salt content levels tolerated by crops. Gypsum can be used. Proper drainage to carry away excess salt is needed. The green manure cultivation helps in checking the rise of salt during summer.

The rural population is a large percentage of population in India depends on local natural resources for their survival. The development of agro-forestry based agriculture and forestry has become the prime pre-requisite for an overall development of the economy in the country. The only hope of increasing productivity lies in bringing appropriate improvement in the categories of waste land spread over the country.

Consumerism and Waste Products

People in the industrialized countries make up 20% of the world population consume 80% of the world's resources and produce 80% of wastes. It looks like a Pareto's Law. This is due to a pattern of development ensures that people go on consuming even more than what they actually need. India is now moving rapidly into this type of unsustainable pattern of economic growth and development.

Consumerism has become one of the social issues connected with environment. It causes

- Pollution
- Degradation

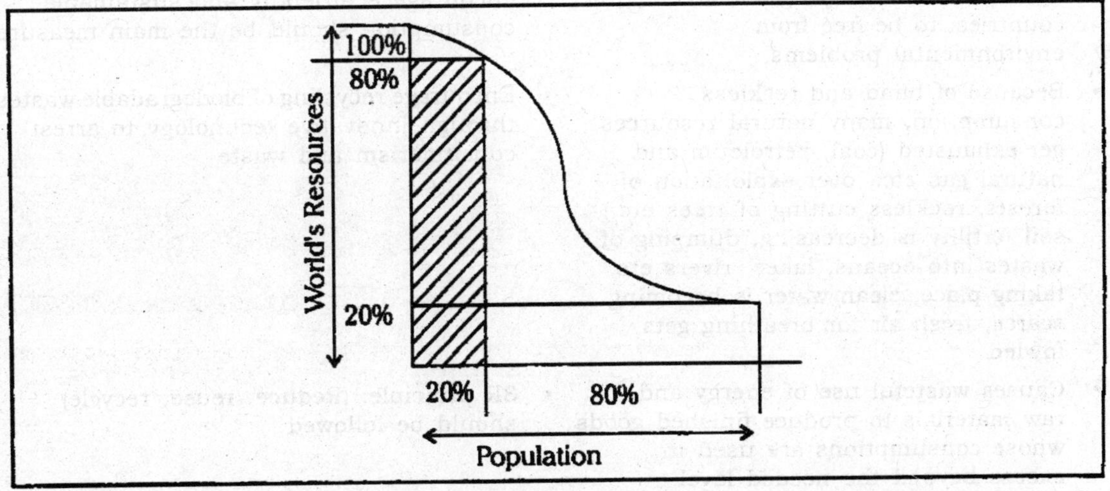

Fig. 3.103 Consumption Pattern of People (Follows Pareto's Law)

It is more in developed countries and is present even in developing countries.

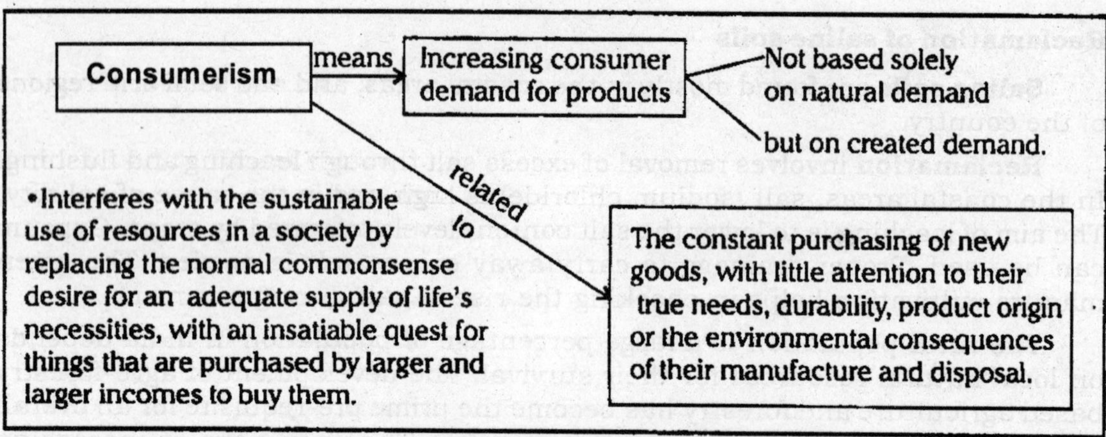

Fig. 3.104 Meaning of Consumerism

The inordinate amount of waste that is generated by consumer oriented-societies around the world is now a serious environmental issue.

Consumerism

Consequences	*How to get rid off?*
• Results in excessive wastes (200 billion tons can, bottles, containers, paper cups-all plastic items thrown away every year in developed countries)	• Buying quality products free from defects and failure with longer life arrests consumerism and wastes
• Leads to environmental pollution (reckless throwing away of wastes)	• Wise use of resources and products
• Developed countries may dump toxic waste in the developing and free countries, to be free from environmental problems	• Remove the practice of blind consumption, encourage ecofriendly and sustainable consumption should be the main measure
• Because of blind and reckless consumption, many natural resources get exhausted (coal, petroleum and natural gas etc., over exploitation of forests, reckless cutting of trees etc.) soil fertility is decreasing, dumping of wastes into oceans, lakes, rivers etc. taking place, clean water is becoming scarce, fresh air for breathing gets fowled	• Encourage recycling of biodegradable wastes through innovative technology to arrest consumerism and waste
• Causes wasteful use of energy and raw materials to produce finished goods whose consumptions are used in excess beyond the needed level	• 3R principle: (Reduce, reuse, recycle) should be followed
• Consumerism is harmful and it is to be checked.	

Different Acts to Protect Our Environment and Resources

The different acts are as under:

— The Environment (Protection) Act 1986.

— The Air (Prevention and Control of Pollution) Act 1981.

— The Water (Prevention and Control of Pollution0 Act 1974.

— The Wildlife protection Act 1972.

— Forest Conservation Act 1980.

— Forest Rights Act 2008.

The Acts are explained in the following table:

The environment (protection) Act (EPA)	***The air (prevention and control of pollution) Act***	***Act the water (prevention and control of pollution) Act***
Came into force in India on 19th November 1986: Spirit of the proclamation adopted by UN Conference on Environment (stock holm) in June 1972. • **Objective** is for the protection and improvement of environment and the matters connected with. • **Certain terms were defined in section 2 of the Act like:** - Environment - Environmental pollution - Environmental pollutant • There was a need for an authority of study, plan and implement the long term requirements of environmental safety, and direct and coordinate a system of appropriate response to emergencies threatening the environment. Hence this act was introduced as there was a growing concern over the deteriorating state of the environment. • Public concern and support is crucial for implementing the EPA. • In section 3 of the Act, it covers the powers of the central Government for the purpose of protecting and	**Came into force in India on 29th March 1981:** It is to clean up our air by controlling pollution; Industry, vehicles, power plants etc. are not permitted to release particulate matter Lead, CO, SO_2, Nitrogen oxide etc. or other toxic substances beyond a prescribed level. **The main objectives:** To provide for the prevention, control and abatement of air pollution, establishment of central and state boards to implement the Act. To confer on the boards, the powers to implement and assign functions relating to pollution. **Important Features:** - Empowers central and state pollution control boards to declare pollution control areas, restriction on certain industrial units, authority of the boards to limit emission of air pollutants, power of entry, inspection, taking samples, analysis, penalties, offences by companies etc. - Empowers State Government to designate air pollution areas and to prescribe the types of fuel to be used in the areas, operation of the industries	**Came into force in India on 23rd March 1974:** Amended on 1988. It is to prevent the pollution of water by industrial agricultural and house hold waste water that can contaminate our water sources. Waste waters with high levels of pollutants that enter waste lands, rivers, lakes, wells, sea, are serious health hazards. **The main objectives:** To provide for prevention, control and abatement of water pollution and the maintenance or restoration of the whole-someness of water. It is designed to assess pollution levels and punish polluters. The central/state governments have setup Pollution Control Boards (PCBs) to monitor water pollution. **Important features of this Act** - Establishment of central and state pollution control boards. - The boards are given powers to prevent water pollution, take samples of water and analyse, discharge of sewage, trade effluents etc. - There should be no discharge of trade effluent

improving the quality of the environment. Preventing and controlling and abating environmental pollution.

The central government can take measures on:

- Coordination of actions by the state governments, its officials.
- Planning and execution of a nationwide programme.
- Laying down quality standards, of environment, procedures and safe guards for the prevention of accidents causing and environmental pollution as well as handling of hazardous substances; standards for emission or discharge of environmental pollutants from different sources.
- Restriction of areas for industries and their operations, processes etc. for safe guard.
- Examination of manufacturing processes, materials, substances, responsible for pollution.
- Collection and dissemination of information on pollution etc.

without the consent of the state board to be examined.

- Central board to advise the central government, coordinate the activities of the state boards, lay down quality standards, trained human resources to monitor pollution.
- State boards are empowered to establish laboratories for analysing sample of air or emissions for purposes of implementing this Act.
- The state governments are empowered to declare any area within the state as air pollution control area after consulting state board.
- It can prohibit the use of certain fuels, materials or appliances which may cause air pollution.

or sewage without the permission of state board. Industry would be closed it it violates.

- The state board can demand any information from any person in order to ensure compliance with the provisions of this Act.

• The central and state can advise the respective governments on any matters concerning the prevention and control of water pollution.

• Penalties are charged for acts that have caused pollution.

The Wild Life (Protection) Act	***Forest Conservation Act***
Came into force in India in the year 1972. Amendment came in 1983, 1986, 1991, 2002. It deals with the declaration of National parks and wild life sanctuaries and their notification. **The objective is to provide for the protection of wild animals, birds and plants; to ensure ecological and environmental security of the country. The new act in 2002** is more stringent and prevents the commercial use of resources, by local people. New concepts introduced such as the creation of community reserves. Several definitions were altered. Under animals, fish was included. Forest produce redefined. The new act has serious issues concerned with its implementation. **Important features of this Act** • Establishment of wild life advisory board in each state.	**Came into force** in India in the year 1980 amended in 1988 (First Forest policy was enunciated in 1952). It was realized in 1980 that protecting forests for timber production alone was not acceptable. Protecting the services that forests provide and its valuable assets such as **The new** biodiversity overshadowed the importance of revenue earnings from timber. A new act came in 1988. The **objective** is conservation of forests as a natural heritage to find a place in the new policy for preservation of forests of its biological diversity and genetic resources. It also values meeting the needs of local people for food, fuelwood, fodder and NTFPs. **Important features of this Act** • Covers all types of forests (including reserved).

- Regulation of hunting of wild animals and birds.
- Provide penalties for the contravention of the act.
- Provide for captive breeding programme for endangered species.
- Lay down the procedure for declaring areas as sanctuaries, national parks etc.
- Regulate possession, acquisition or transfer or trade in wild animals, animal articles etc.

Forest Rights Act

The central government on 1st January 2008, issued a notification for implementing the provisions of the scheduled tribes (ST). Forest Rights Act which gives the forest dwellers exclusive rights over its resources. The Act essentially aims to provide a framework to recognise these rights.

The Act will be beneficial to STs and other forest dwellers living in and depending on forests for their livelihood for three generations (or 75 years) prior to December 13, 2005.

- The central government has full powers and nits permission is needed regarding leasing of forest land to persons or any authority/ corporation etc. clearing of trees which have grown naturally in any forest land (re-afforestation).
- A punitive provision is provided in the act for the enforcement machinery.
- The 1992 amendment act allows certain non-forest activities in forests for limited cutting, setting up of transmissions lines, drilling and hydro-electric projects, sesmic surveys, exploration etc.
- Exception for wild life sanctuaries, national parks etc. are totally prohibited for any exploration or survey (even for tree felling) without central governments prior approval.

Cultivation of coffee, species, rubber (cash crops) included in non-forestry activity is not allowed in reserve forests.

- Cultivation of fruit bearing trees, oil yielding plants or plants of medicinal values in forest areas has to be first approved by Central Government.
- Mining is a non-forestry activity; mining in a forest area needs central government approval. It is mandatory.

Issues Involved in Enforcement of Environmental Legislation

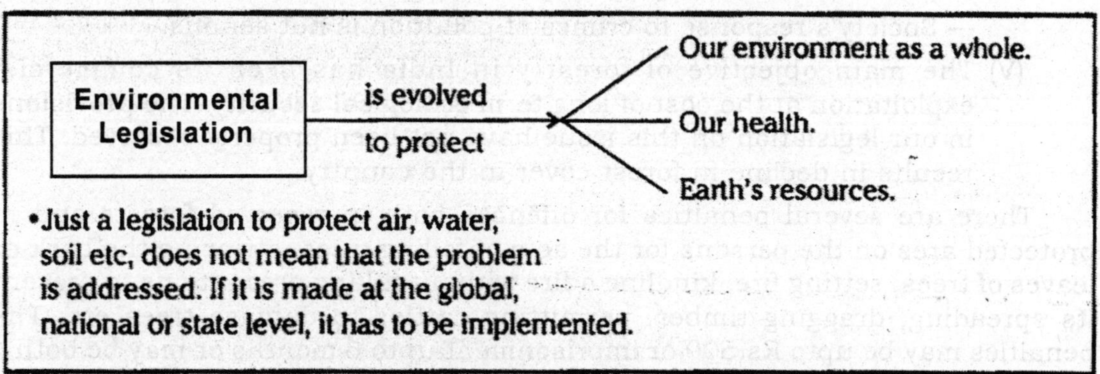

Fig. 3.105 Environmental Legislation

To protect our environment, there are number of legislations in India:

- Constitutional provisions (Articles 48A, 51A)
- About 200 central and state legislations.

A wide gap exists between what appears in the legislation and what is actually practiced in regard to environmental protection. Some issues or problems are found in the enforcement of environmental legislation.

(I) Despite the Wild Life Act provided, poaching of wild animals is going on. Several species of wild life are wiped out. Poaching is not effectively checked, as there are no stringent provisions in the act to punish the poachers. Further, many are not perturbed by large scale poaching of wild life.

(II) In the Environment Protection Act, the state governments do not have sufficient powers to enforce the provisions of the act as all the powers are vested in the hands of the central government. This centralization of power is a major hurdle for the efficient enforcement of the provisions of this Act.

One of the clauses provides that if an offence is punishable under this Act and under any other Act, the offenders should be punished under the other acts and not under this Act. The penal provisions of the other Acts are less stringent than the penal provisions of this Act. This has reduced the effectiveness of penal provisions. Offenders are escaping from severe punishments. Only minor punishments are given.

(III) As already said, there are enough legislations in India for the protection of environment. But the authorities responsible for the enforcement of the environmental decisions are different which may not be so effective on account of this. Ineffective enforcement of the safety provisions of some of the environmental legislations (Pollution Control Act, Factory Act etc.) is a major issue.

(IV) In order to effectively implement environmental legislations, following will act as hurdles:

— Lack of knowledge of the pollution control laws by the individuals and the business community.

— Indifference of intellectuals to the environmental degradation.

— Society's response to crimes of pollution is not serious.

(V) The main objective of forestry in India has been its commercial exploitation at the cost of long term ecological security. The provisions in our legislation on this issue have not been properly observed. This results in decline in forest cover in the country.

There are several penalties for offences both in reserved forests and in protected ares on the persons for the acts of felling trees, stripping the bark or leaves of trees, setting fire, kindling a fire without taking precautions to prevent its spreading, dragging timber, permitting cattles to damage trees etc. The penalties may be upto Rs.500 or imprisonment upto 6 months or may be both.

Environment Impact Assessment (EIA)

For development of any project government or private, the ministry of environment and forests (MOEF) requires an impact assessment done by a competent organisation. EIA must look into physical, biological and social parameters, before clearing the project on environmental grounds. If the anticipated impacts are likely to be severe, the project is to be dropped.

Citizens Actions and Action Groups

Citizens can act as watchdogs to protect their own surroundings/ environment from the consequences of unsustainable projects around them.

Well-informed citizens not only have rights but also have a duty to perform. They can join together and form groups to strengthen the environmental movements. They are the action groups to represent the citizen's actions for the country, state, city, town or village.

Public Awareness

In our country, environmental sensitivity can only grow through a major public awareness programme. The various tools are:

- News papers and magazines.
- TV channels.
- Other electronic media.
- School and college education.
- Adult education etc.

Each one of the above complements other.

Environmental problems in the recent days are at the peak owing to:

- Population growth
- Industrialization
- Urbanization.

These brings out lot of stress on environmental problems in the Government's policies of economic development. Unless the public supports and participate, the implementation of the policies of the Government will not be possible and even by force if it is done, it would be ineffective. Hence public awareness and understanding of all the important environmental problems by them is absolutely necessary.

Several days of the year have been marked for various activities which creates public awareness pertaining to the environment all over the world.

(i)	**February 2**	World Wetland Day - about wetlands and their value to mankind.
(ii)	**March 21**	World Forestry Day - about rapid disappearance of our forests
(iii)	**April 7**	World Health Day (by WHO) - about issues of public/occupational health etc.
(iv)	**April 18**	World Heritage Day - about our heritage like forts, museums, monuments, visits to students are arranged.
(v)	**April 22**	Earth Day - to know about increasing environmental problems caused by humans on earth.
(vi)	**June 5**	World Environment Day - to share their concern over human progress at the expense of the environment.
(vii)	**June 11**	World Population Day - to discuss on the vital link between population and environment.

(viii)	**August 6**	Hiroshima Day - (In India) to discuss on Bhopal gas tragedy and the Chernobyl Disaster.
(ix)	**September 16**	World Ozone Day - for the preservation of ozone layer.
(x)	**September 28**	Green Consumer Day - to create awareness among consumers about various products.
(xi)	**October 7**	Wild Life Week - conserving our species and threatened ecosystems.

Climate change is damaging our world

- Climate change is a serious and long term challenge that has the potential to affect each and every one of us. It is one of the biggest issues facing the world today - a global threat, no nation can resolve alone.
- Today many organizations across the world are joining hands to raise awareness among climate change and taking remedial action to reduce the impact of human induced climate change.
- We believe a combined and sustained effort by corporate and the media can make a major contribution towards making climate change a national priority.
- There is an increasing need to provide credible and technically sound leadership to identify and foster actions across several sectors with special reference to mitigation and adaptation imperatives related to climate change and global warming.
- In India, the centre for environment education (CEE) was established in 1984 having its head office in Ahmedabad and branches at other places in India (Bangalore also) mis working in this area. It is also technically supported by the Energy and Resources, Institute (TERI). There is also an award created called as "The Earth Care Award"-a pioneering step taken by JS Wand and The Times of India, jointly. This is an award for excellence on climate change mitigation and adaptation.
- The different ways of creating public awareness as already said is through:
  - — NGOs (Non-Governmental Organizations) are to be enlisted for creating public awareness and public support for environmental problems.
  - — Through environmental education at the schools and colleges, training of teachers on environmental issues, development of research centers etc.
  - — Through News papers, Technical magazines, Pamphlets issuing etc.
  - — Sharing of information, knowledge, experience on environmental issues and their solutions should be strengthened.
  - — Behavioural and attitude changes by the individuals and society towards environmental issues should be motivated through media (print media, radio, television etc.).

— Create public awareness on the adoption of flexible strategies pertaining to each region.

— By having local, national and international sewminars and workshops on environment issues.

Climate change affects peace and stability in the world

This is as observed by R.K.Pauchauri, the Nobel prize winner. Inter governmental panel on climate change (IPCC), the Nobel prize committee has signalled the importance of stabilising the earth's climate for ensuring peace and stability in the world.

(I) There are major equality issues associated with climate change, essentilaly arising out of the fact that the high concentration of greenhouse gases in the atmosphere - that are causing climate change has been created cumulatively, by the developed countries.

Some of the worst suffers from the impacts of climate change are the poorest societies largely in Africa and parts of Asia.

- In some African countries, yields, could be reduced upto 50% by 2020.
- Crop net revenues could fall as much as 90% by 2100.
- In central and south Asia,, yields could decrease upto 50% by 2050.
- The poorest countries in the world to import adequate quantities of foodgrains for their population at higher prices.
- The most significant impact of climate change is expected in respect to availability of water. There are several regions that are afflicted by water stress due to changes in precipitation patterns, increasing salinity of ground water, due to increase in sea level and melting of glaciers which would result in decreased river flow.
- IPCC estimates that in south Asia alone perhaps 500 mjllion people would be affected by reduced river flows in the northern part of the subcontinent and about 250 million in China.
- Water scarce is already a source of tension between several states of India and certainly between India and Bangladesh.

By 2020, people exposed to increased water stress would include

- 120 mln to 1.2 bln in Asia
- 75 to 250 mln in Africa- 12 to 81 mln in Latin America.

- A major impact, of climate change resulting from sea level rise would be the threat of coastal flooding (serious in cities like Dhaka, Kolkata and Shangai where the density of population is extremely high and the threat of coastal flooding is serious).
- Droughts and floods are increasing in several parts of the world in frequency and intensity could displace large numbers of people with consequences for the stability of society.

- Social scientists have not devoted adequate attention to the consequences of climate change, but projections of the future clearly indicate that the severity of the problem justifies considerable research and investigation into associated prospects for peace and security.

3.4 Consumers Markets and Consumer Protection

Introduction to Marketing

The question in marketing is: Why should marketers worry about ethics? What role do moral values play in an economic system? Do competitive pressures conflict with ethical considerations in marketing? Does the legal system provides too many or too few ethical constraints on the marketer? While most marketers have always been conscious of ethical considerations, today's climate of consumerism renders many traditional attitudes obsolete. Marketers must adopt a broadly based view of ethics if they really want to understand and meet the needs of today's customers.

Is marketing completely unethical? More extreme critics appear to think so. Others find it hard to see anything unethical about attempting to meet customer's needs with appropriate goods and services. These contrasting view points span a variety of differing opinions on what constitute ethical practice in marketing. In this chapter, we provide to explore the issue raised by these opinions and to provide some guidance to the marketer, who is increasingly be leagued by ethical criticism.

Marketing consists of the performance of business activities that direct the flow of goods and services from producer or manufacturer to consumer or user. A number of distinct functions is coming under this broad characterisation which includes:

- Product Development
- Distribution
- Pricing
- Promotion
- Sales

Virtually all aspects of marketing-from the development of new products to pricing, promotion and sales-raise ethical questions that do not always have an easy answer. Advertisement, similar to safety in the development of new products raises numerous ethical concerns.

Direct Marketing

Mass Marketers have typically tried to reach millions of buyers with a single product and a standard message communicated via the mass media. Consequently, most mass marketing communications were the one way communications directed to consumers rather than the two way communications with consumers. Today, many companies are connected to **direct marketing** in an effort to reach carefully targeted customers more efficiently to build storage, more personal, one to one relationships with them.

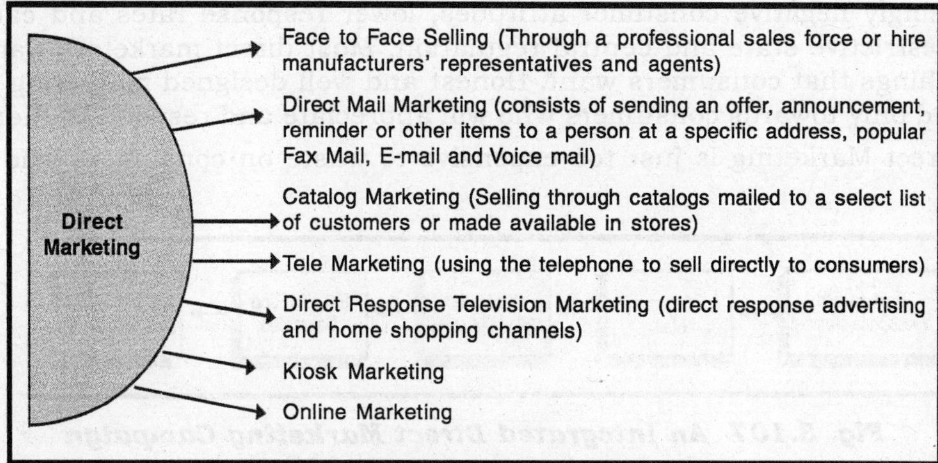

Fig. 3.106 Direct Marketing

The main forms of direct marketing are:

Direct Marketers and their customers enjoy mutually rewarding relationships. However, a darker side also emerges. The aggressive and sometimes shady tactics of a few direct marketers can bother or harm consumers, giving the entire industry a blackeye. Abuses range from simple excesses that irritate consumers to instances of unfair practices or even outright deception and fraud. It has also faced recently growing concern about invasion of privacy issues. Direct Marketing excesses sometimes annoy or offend consumers. Sometime television commercials are felt as too loud, too long and too inconsistent. Television shopping shows and programme long "Informercials" seem to be the worst culprits. They feature smooth talking hosts, elaborate stage demonstrations, claims of drastic price reductions, unequalled ease of purchase to inflame buyers who have low sales resistance.

Fraudulent schemes such as investment scams or phony collection for charity have also multiplied in recent years. Other direct marketers pretend to be conducting research survey when they are actually leading questions to screen or persuade consumers. Crooked direct marketers can be hard to catch: Direct marketing customers often respond quickly, do not interact personally with the seller and usually expect to wait for delivery. By the time buyers realise that they have been bilked, the thieves are usually somewhere else plotting new schemes. Some will give wrong telephone numbers, addresses, unheard references etc. to make the customer to check but in vain. Thus Irritation, Unfairness, Deception and Fraud are very common in Direct Marketing.

Invasion of privacy is perhaps the toughest public policy issue now confronting the direct marketing industry. It seems that almost every time consumers order products by mail or telephone, enter a sweepstakes, apply for a credit card or takeout a magazine subscription, their names are entered into some company's already bulging database. Using sophisticated computer technologies, direct marketers can use these databases to 'microtarget' their selling efforts.

The Direct marketing industry is addressing issues of ethics and public policy. Direct marketers know that, left unattended, such problems will lead to increasingly negative consumer attitudes, lower response rates and calls for more restrictive state and central regulation. Most direct marketers want the same things that consumers want. Honest and well designed marketing offers targeted only towards consumers who will appreciate and respond to them.

Direct Marketing is just too expensive to waste on consumers who don't want it.

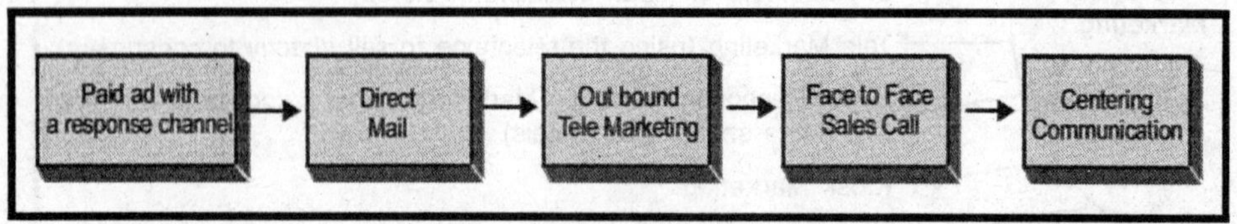

Fig. 3.107 An Integrated Direct Marketing Campaign

Marketing Ethics and Consumer Rights

The laws and regulations are generally designed to protect the consumer from unethical practices by businesses. These laws recognise that consumers have certain basic rights in the market place. However, some unethical practices are just one step short of being unlawful and are therefore overlooked by the regulatory agencies. Ultimately each marketer must rely on his/her own value system to determine what is and is not ethical. That value system should recognise consumer rights to safety, to full information, and to value for the price paid.

American Marketing Association (AMA) has established a codes of ethics to provide guidelines for ethical conduct. It says, in part, that, "Marketers shall uphold and advance the integrity, honour and dignity of the marketing profession, by being honest in serving consumers, clients, employees, suppliers, distributors, and the public."

The code then outline responsibilities for each component of the marketing mix:

Marketing Mix

As further insurance of consumer rights, AMA code states that marketers should provide the means to hear customer complaints and to adjust them equitably.

Many of the actions cited by the AMA code as unethical, are also illegal. Some are not unethical. For example, ignoring a consumer's complaint, even the AMA code is not sufficient to provide guidelines for ethical action. For example,

- An individual to work for a cigarette company, if he believes that cigarettes cause cancer
- An international marketer subscribe to the practice of offering bribes, if all the competitors are doing it

Marketing Mix	As per AMA Code			
	Products & Services	*Advertising*	*Distribution*	*Pricing*
	Marketers have the responsibility to ensure product safety to disclose all product risks, and to identify any factor that might change product performance. E.g. General Motors failed to fulfil the responsibilities by providing faulty brakes for 1.1 million X-body cars.	Marketers must avoid deceptive and misleading communications must repeat high pressure sales tactics, and must avoid manipulating consumers to buy. E.g. Warner Lambert failed to fulfil the responsibilities when advertised listerine as preventing colds.	Suppliers should not coerce their intermediaries into taking unwanted products they should not create false shortages to drive up prices of their products. E.g. Chrysler did not fulfil these responsibilities in early 1960s when it forced dealers to take unwanted cars during an economic downturn.	Marketers must not engage in price fixing or predatory pricing and must disclose all prices associated with the purchase including service, installation and delivery. E.g. GE did not fulfil these responsibilities in the 1960s when several of its executives were indicated for price fixing?

Fig. 3.108 Marketing Mix

- A manager to approve of buying a competitor's product, analysing it and then duplicating it.

And many more like the above.

These areas are not covered by the law or the AMA Code. In every such issue, the question of marketing ethics must bear directly on the level of integrity of the individual marketer.

Ethics Concept and Consequents

Ethics definition mentioned in chapter 1 necessarily implies some set of criteria by which to judge the merits of a given act. These criteria are moral value, or the rules of conduct deemed acceptable by society at a given time.

For the marketer, whose promotional activities render him a very visible agent in society, two acute problems emerge from the definition of ethics.

- Society is by no means homogeneous in its ethical values.
- Ethical values though defined 'at a given time', are not fixed and unalterable. They change over time.

The focus of ethics is normative, 'what should be', rather than 'what is', notions of the ideal vary from group to group and from time to time. Marketers who wish to avoid criticism of their ethics are faced, therefore with the unenviable task of attempting to make decisions which do not necessarily conflict with variety of changing ethical ideals. This type of balancing act should not, however, be strange to the marketer.

Example: **Segmentation strategies** reflect social heterogeneity. Yet marketing seems able to adopt to this complexity reasonably well. It would be a very unperceptive and probably unsuccessful marketing manager who did not recognise the fact that markets of the nineties will differ from those of the seventies or eighties. Change and adaptation are not new to him.

However, the ethical problems of the marketer can be painful. Swept by the rising tide of consumerism, business leaders who perceive themselves as acting with commendable moral diligence are pilloried by consumerists whose moral percepts are quite different. For example, the controversy over television advertising to children. Until nineteen sixty, there were virtually no guide lines or disapprobation. Some questionable marketing practices were not unknown. Over the years these have changed to depict product features and benefits more accurately. Some interest groups and individuals remain adamantly against any children's advertising on principle. Such fundamental differences are clearly difficult, to resolve on logical or empirical grounds.

Many managers regard adherence to legal standards as sufficient guarantee of ethical acceptability. But in most cases, the law represents the only available written embodiment of ethical standards. However, at least in part, because of the nature of political and legislative processes, adherence to legal standards provides no guarantee of freedom from ethical criticism. The concern of consumerists focuses on the inadequacy of existing law.

Criticisms of Ethics in Marketing

From a variety of sources, criticism emanates. These are:

- Opposed to the whole marketing system, attacking the goals, methods and results of the marketing activity.
- Specific practices in marketing, without questioning the ethics of the system as a whole.

(i) Criticism of the former

Promotion of morally 'bad' values, such as the excessive consumption of private rather than public goods and services comes under this. Galbraith's opposition to materialism is widely shared among social critics and recent public concern over ecological issues has increased the saliency of their views. They generally relate much less directly to the marketers' decisions than do criticisms of specific marketing practices. These criticisms reflect a set of ethical values widely divergent from those of most managers, managers should be familiar with them.

(ii) Criticism of Specific practices

These are frequently based on assumptions drawn from system level critiques. Similar values are held by many young persons who are prospective employees as well as consumers.

The criticisms are:

- **Visible institutions and practices:** These cannot help but the subject of public debate and controversy at some time. Marketing is no such exception. Criticism has provided the stimulus for much needed legal reform. Today, many of the issues seems less clear-cut, a factor may be responsible for the difficulty of reaching agreement on just what constitutes ethical marketing conduct.
- **Advertising** has been the target for some of the most vehement criticism. It has been accused of failing to provide useful information, deceiving the consumer, exhibiting poor taste, penetrating the wrong values (hedonism, excessive consumption or male chauvinism), adding to the cost of products, and influencing particular audiences (children or the poor) unduly.
- **Personal selling** though less, is another area of criticism because of its lesser importance in consumer marketing. The ethics of the relationship of sales people to customer are the subject of continuing scrutiny by buyer and seller organisations.
- **Public relations**, a definite part of the firms promotional program is not free from criticism. Lobbying activities are the focus of criticism, and the founding of such organisations as common cause may be attributed to concern over the 'privileged' position of business lobbyists.
- **Packaging and labelling practices** are the critics distaste.
  - Irregularities of package size and shape.
  - Provision of intelligible labelling information.
  - Ecological issues are also in the forefront (Recycling centres established by aluminum companies).
  - Pricing practices (criticism concerning ethics during implementation periods).

Here price differentials between national and private brands and the effects of promotional expenditures on price are the focus of criticism.

Reasons for Unethical Practices

The major reason is undoubtedly the pressure of **competition**. Unless a firm can turn ethical restraint to competitive advantage, it has little economic motivation to maintain higher ethical standards. With more widespread activism and concern on the part of the consumers, the chances that economic benefits will accrue to the more ethical market are definitely enhanced.

Although ethics and profits are not necessarily mutually inconsistent, there is quite often little likelihood or immediate economic benefit to the more ethical competitor. Legal standards represent the only set of rules which the competition may be expected to obey, the astute manager will also adopt them. If a given firm or manager wished to employ more stringent standards, it could not without risking possible loss or profits!

Another factor bearing on ethical conduct is the prevailing practice in a department, firm or industry. The influence of such practices may cause a manager to act in a way that he would otherwise consider unethical. Prevailing practice becomes the dominant influence.

- The time span within which decisions are made also favours the expedient over the conscientious decision. Even though the marketer may believe that ethical conduct will produce more profit in the long-run, emphasis on immediate profits and the short-run focus of managerial objectives and evaluation systems often tend to prohibit a long-run view.
- Mitigating against the various pressures towards unethical behaviour are opposing forces including in many cases, the values of the manager. Consumer and religious groups and the publicity they generate also have an inhibitory effect, as do investigative report by the media.
- Government agencies, by no means insulated from the pressures of public opinion are frequently in a position to exert direct influence on marketers to change their behaviour.
- The attempts by various business leaders, companies, associations, and professional bodies to establish and maintain ethical standards of behaviour undoubtedly counterveil some of the tendencies to unethical behaviour.

Establishing Ethical Standards

The considerable concern over ethics is reflected in the large number of organisations that have attempted to codify ethical standards. Such codes are usually based upon legal standards, industry practice, religious ethical ideals, and the values professed by their developers etc. Standards must be communicated before they can be effective. It can certainly be argued that there are merits to an explicit statement of ethical ideals. The exercise seems futile, however, unless employees or members comply with those standards. Ensuring compliance is a weakness of most codes. For the manager who wishes to secure subordinate's adherence to a set of ethical standards, there is no practicable alternative to making those standards part of the system of performance evaluation and control.

For maintaining ethical standards in marketing, the firm itself must provide the standards and the control system, should it not be satisfied with existing performance.

Implications

These are:

- **Ethical attacks** on marketing will continue, as long as there is heterogeneity of opinion over what are the 'right' moral values, there will be conflict. There is also an inherent danger of the competitive system inducing downward spiralling of ethical standards, to a lower bound set by legal standards.
- A good case can be made that it is unfair to expect firms in competitive industries to do other than stay within the law. Critics must look to the law, rather than spontaneous action of companies for setting new ethical standards for marketing practice. Only then consistent standards may be obtained.
- Many marketing managers do not view the regulatory incursions of government dispassionately. The onus on those who feel the way is to provide a non-governmental remedy, through establishing and maintaining by management control, effective ethical standards for company decisions. A first step toward such a system is to open up lines of communication to those who criticise marketing ethics.

Ethics in Personal Selling

The salesperson will sell a company's products or services in an ethical manner - making a good faith effort to determine what the customer wants, conveying truthful and accurate information about the company's products, trying to provide customers with full information and addressing any subsequent customer complaints. Unfortunately such is not always the case. We have all, at one time or another experienced undesirable high pressure sales tactics. Most sales people, however, conduct themselves in a responsible manner, especially with today's emphasis on a **problem solving approach**. The greatest problem is with order getters, since their **canned approach** of one-way communication from seller to buyer does not encourage an attempt to understand and satisfy customer needs. In trying to close a sale, order getters have occasionally forgotten their obligation to be truthful and to keep the customers best interests in mind. There is nothing inherently unethical about order getting. Many order getters are truthful, responsible and responsive to customer needs.

Government can do little to legislate fair sales practices. If outright fraud has occurred, consumers have recourse in the courts. Otherwise consumers rely on the self-regulation imposed by companies. Companies have become sensitive to the need to maintain high standards in selling.

Strategies for Pricing New Products

Developing a price for new product is difficult, since managers have little basis for assessing consumer demand. The more innovative the product, the more difficult it is to assess consumer reactions to price prior to market introduction. **Pricing strategies** for existing products focus on establishing the appropriate price level and on deciding whether to change prices from current levels or maintain price stability.

Pricing Strategies for New Products

These include two types of pricing:

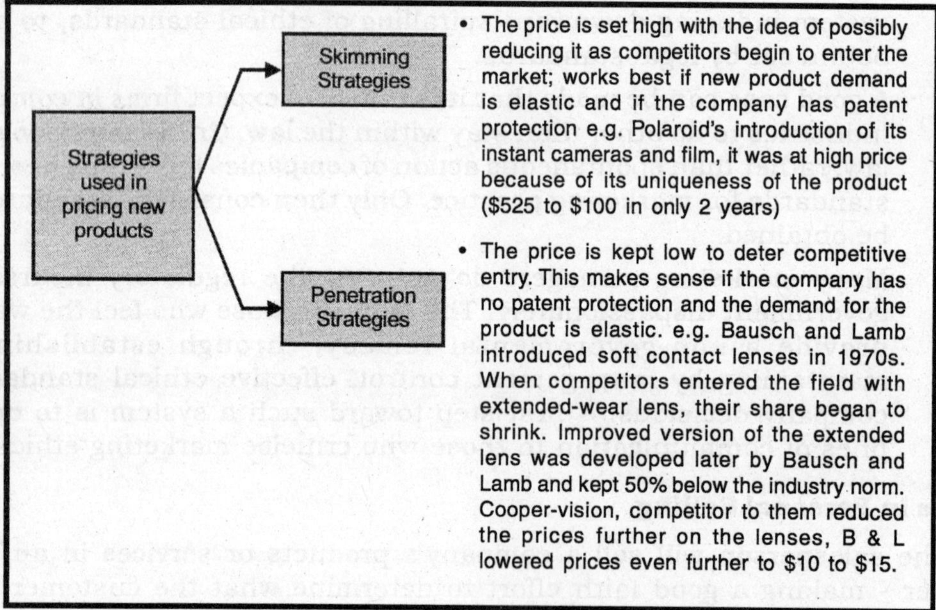

Fig. 3.109 Strategies used in Pricing New Products

In **penetration strategy**, it is to set prices for foreign goods based on total costs. If the firm exports its products, this approach is likely to lead to prices higher than those in the firm's home markets because of higher costs of distribution. Hence, firms pricing on a total cost basis might find themselves at a disadvantage compared to local competitors. Companies following this strategy do not distinguish between products stated for domestic or foreign markets. Foreign operations are viewed as profit centers that must cover total costs.

Strategies for Pricing Product Lines

A firm can create more profits by offering products to different price segments of the market. Establishing a product line targeted to different segments at specific price points is called **price lining**. In following such a strategy, the company is covering the demand curve by marketing products to appeal to:

- Economy minded customers
- Customers at the mid-price level
- Customers interested in prestige products

Each product is aimed at a segment with a different price elasticity. Pricing line is an important strategic tool. A company following a strategy of price lining must determine the optimal pricing level for each product in its line.

Ethics and Regulations in Pricing

Pricing practices are regulated by the government more forcefully than other areas of the marketing mix (such as personal selling, distribution, advertisement) in that pricing illegalities are made explicit in acts such as:

- FTC Act (Federal Trade Commission Act)
- Robinson-Patman Act

Four areas of pricing are considered unethical and illegal. (See figure on the next page).

(i) Deceptive Pricing: Bait and Switch Pricing is one type of deceptive price-a low price offer intended to lure customers into a store, where a sales person tries to influence intended to lure customers into a store. Thereafter, a sales person tries to influence them to buy a higher-priced item.

e.g. Audi in USA was accused of Bait and Switch tactics in 1998. It offered rebates on a product, which was phased out and was often unavailable, leaving customers to consider other products without rebates.

Another deceptive practice is to offer a discount off an inflated price. e.g. In India buy one saree take two sarees free; the price would have been jacked up on the first saree covering the prices of other two sarees.

(ii) Unfair Pricing: When competitors are driven out by low prices (less than cost) the company raises price back to their former level. This happened even for a reputed public sector company like HMT in 1990s in the dairy machinery area from their competitors to suffer losses. The survival for existence was a problem.

(iii) Price Discrimination: Though theoretically, price discrimination maximises profits by enabling sellers to charge price-inelastic customers high prices than elastic customers are charged. It can be unethical if similar buyers are charged different prices for the same goods based on their ability to pay.

The **Robinson-Patman Act** (1936) states that price discrimination is illegal as it makes a number of important exemptions. Applies only to sales to organisational buyers, not to final consumers. Maruti Motors cannot sell the same cars at different prices to its dealers. The dealers can charge customers different prices for the same car. Price differences to similar buyers are legal if such differences have some cost justification. The Gas prices are different in USA at different places. So also in India for petrol and diesel (price of petrol and diesel are cheaper at Delhi than at Bangalore).

As with other areas of marketing mix, most firms have acted ethically in setting prices. They do not attempt to deceive customers or to use pricing actions to restrain competition. A firm willfully deceiving consumer through pricing actions will eventually lose out to more responsible competitors as consumers learn that they are being duped. Though Government regulation is important in pricing, competitive forces are the best regulators in insuring ethical pricing.

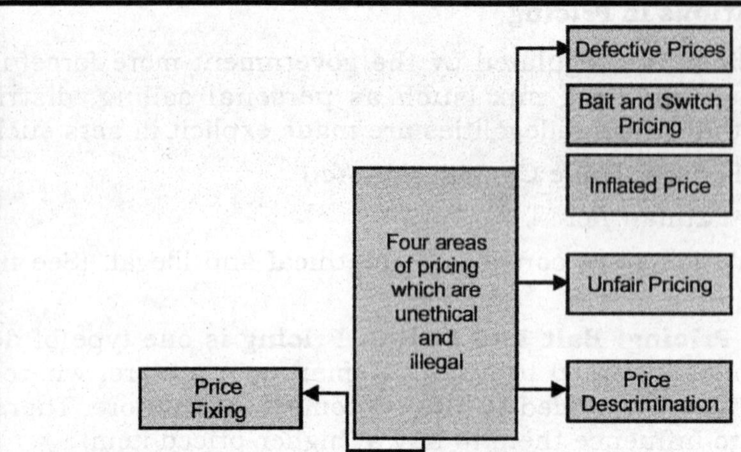

1. **Deceptive Prices** - Meant to deceive customers and to take advantage of them; Illegal under the FTC Act
   (i) **Bait and Switch Pricing.**
   - One type of deceptive price-a low price offer intended to lure customers into a store, where a sales person try to influence them to buy a high priced item. e.g. Audi in 1988 adopted this tactics (offered rebates on its 5000 line, which was phased out and was often unavailable, leaving customers to consider other lines)

   (ii) **Inflated Price**
   - To offer a discount off an inflated discount. The consumer is not actually getting a discount.
2. **Unfair Pricing** - Uses pricing practices to drive competitors out of business.
   (i) **Predatory Pricing**
   - Decreasing in prices, even below cost when competition are driven out, the company then raises prices back to their former level (Sherman Act prohibits such practices) FTC brought action against General Foods for predatory pricing in 1976.
3. **Price Discrimination**
   - Involves selling the same product to buyers at different prices without any cost justification. Theoretically, this maximises profit by enabling sellers to change price-inelastic customers higher prices than elastic customers are charged. It can be unethical if it leads to charging similar buyers different prices for the same goods based on their ability to pay. **Robinson-Patman Act of 1936** states that price discrimination is illegal, makes also certain important exemptions. Though Maruti cannot sell the same cars at different prices, dealers can do.
4. **Price Fixing**
   - It is an agreement among firms in an industry to set prices at certain levels. The **Sherman Act** prohibits it because such actions restrict price competition. Two types of price fixing are:

     Horizontal Price Fixing: Agreements among competitors to fix prices at artificially high levels.

     Vertical Price Fixing: Price fixing agreements between manufacturers and retailers or between manufacturers and distributors. This involves an agreement that the product will be sold at the manufacturer's suggested price and will not be discounted by the retailer or wholesaler.

     Panasonic was accused of vertical price fixing by forcing its retailers to raise prices by 5-10%; Retailers not cooperative were threatened.

Fig. 3.110 Four Areas of Pricing which are Unethical and Illegal.

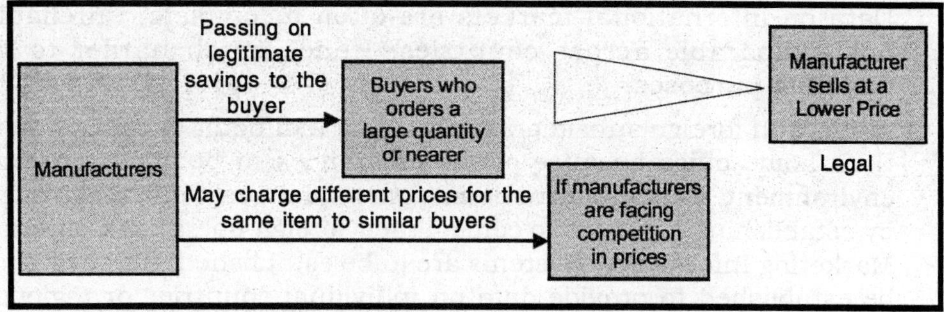

Fig. 3.111 Price Differences to Similar Buyers

Product Packaging and Labelling

Consumers need a certain amount of information to make rational choices. This information is not easily obtained. For example, A consumer examining a frozen apple pie in a sealed, opaque cardboard box. Without information on the label, consumers have no practical means for determining the size of the frozen pie, the ingredients used, the nutritional content, or the length of time the product was frozen etc. Health conscious consumer are disadvantaged by the welter of claims about low fat and salt content and the unregulated use of words such as light and healthy. The more information is provided, consumers can better protect themselves in the market place. There are acts like:

- **Fair packing and labeling Act** of 1966 to enable consumers to make meaningful value comparisons
- **Nutrition Labeling and Education Act** of 1990 (NLEA) states that the labels on packaged food products contain information about certain ingredients expressed by weight and as a percentage of the recommended daily diet in a standard serving size.

Manufacturers offer a number of reasons for not providing more information. These are often misunderstood by consumers who reject older products that are still good and packaging has to be designed with many considerations in mind. The objectives of the above mentioned acts, manufacturers argue, need to be balanced against a number of practical constraints.

Ethics in International Marketing

The nature of international operations has created several ethical issues that have prompted debate in the business community. The process of international marketing planning, evaluating and controlling the marketing effort, is more difficult than in domestic marketing for reasons indicated below:

- International marketers have less control over price because of tariffs and trade regulations. The international firm must price its products higher than anticipated

- Data on international markets are often incomplete, unreliable, and not comparable across countries; Hence much harder to use for planning purposes
- Firms with foreign subsidiaries often find it difficult to control them from their home office because of the differences in business customs and environment. Hence International firms must overcome these difficulties by establishing a system to control their foreign operations. International Marketing Information Systems are to be established. Sub-systems must be established to provide data on individual countries or regions. Data used to develop estimates of market potential and opportunity must be comparable across countries and regions. International Information Systems have more emphasis on environmental scanning than domestic systems due to the importance of monitoring variations in political, economic and cultural factors across countries.

The three ethical issues involved are:

- **Should an international marketer offer payoffs to buyers abroad if such payoffs are accepted mode of doing business?**

(Such pay offs are little more than bribes for doing business. The fact that competitors offer them does not make the practice ethical. A firm could very well take that it sells its products based on quality and payoffs will not be considered. Such a policy will be most effective if the largest sellers were to publicise it and discourage others from offering payoffs)

- **Doing business in countries regarded as having unethical political policies, such as the policy of apartheid in South Africa**

(Most US companies have withdrawn from South Africa at the urging of the US Government. However, Mobil remains in South Africa arguing it is better to continue and support blacks economically through higher wages)

- **Some companies from industrialised nations sell products to underdeveloped third world countries that have harmful effect on consumers or take unfair economic advantage of them.**

Example: In 1970s-serious health problems among babies in underdeveloped countries being fed Nestle's infant formula products.

Ethics and Marketing

Ethics are standards of moral conduct. To act in an ethical fashion is to conform to an accepted standard of moral behaviour. Undoubtedly, virtually all people prefer to act ethically. It is easy to be ethical when no hardship is involved i.e., when a person is winning and life is going well. The problem comes when it is the other way-Pressures build. These pressures arise in all walks of life; marketing is no exception. Marketing executives face the challenge of balancing their own interests in the form of recognition, pay, and promotion, with the best interests of consumers, their organisations and society into a workable guide for their daily activities. In any situation, they must be able to distinguish what is ethical with unethical and act accordingly, regardless of the possible consequences. Many organisations have formal codes of ethics that identify specific acts (bribery, accepting gifts etc.) as unethical and describe the standards employees are expected to live upto. These guidelines lessen the chance that an employee will knowingly or unknowingly violate a company's standards. Codes of ethics strengthen a company's hand in dealing with customers or prospects that encourage unethical behaviour. For young or inexperienced executives, these codes can be valuable guides, helping them to resist pressure to compromise personal ethics in order to move up in the firm.

Every decision cannot be taken out of the hands of the manager. Determining what is right and what is wrong can be extremely difficult. It is not possible to construct in an organisation to construct a two column list of all possible practices under the headings 'ethical' and 'unethical.' A marketer also finds it difficult to evaluate a situation and formulate a response.

Arthur Anderson and company has developed an ethical reasoning model that can be taught to current and future managers. The procedure consists of:

Step 1: Identifying the decision options and the likely consequences of each.

Step 2: Identifying all individuals and organisations that will be positively or negatively affected by the consequences of each option.

Step 3: Estimating the negative impact (costs) and positive impact (benefits) of each option from the point of view of each affected party, taking into consideration their particular interests and needs.

Step 4: Ranking the costs and the benefits of each option and making a decision.

This approach is an attempt to be systematic and logical in ethical decisions. It works only if the decision maker can be objective and impartial. Ethical situations are freely charged with emotion. An alternative approach that attempts to personalise the situation may be more effective. Faced with an ethical problem, one should be honest in answering the following questions which indicates the route to follow:

- Would I do this to a friend?
- Would I be willing to have this done to myself?
- Would I be embarrassed if this action were publicised nationally?

Pragmatic Reasons for Behaving Ethically

Ethical behaviour should be practiced by marketing executives because it is morally correct, simple and beautiful in concept. There is not sufficient motivation for everyone.

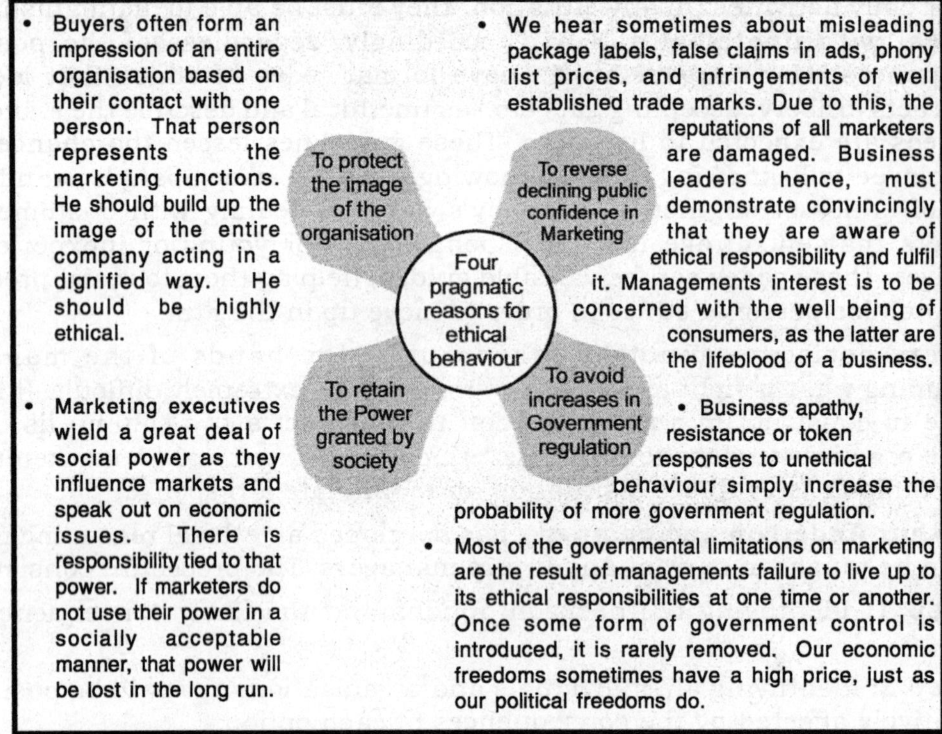

Fig. 3.112 Four Pragmatic Reasons for Ethical Behaviour

Unethical Marketing Behaviour	
A. Product	
• Safety	Manufacture of flammable stuffed animals
• Shoddy goods	Products that cannot withstand ordinary wear and tear
• Inadequate warranties	Warranties with insufficient time or parts coverage
• Environmental pollution	Manufacture of Non-biodegradable plastic products
• Mislabeled products	Flavoured sugar water sold as apple juice for babies
• Development	Bribery of FDA officials to secure agency approval of generic pharmaceuticals
• Manufacturing	Unauthorised substitutions in generic drugs after FDA approval
• Brand 'Knock-offs'	Counterfeit branded goods sold as originals
B. Price	
• Excessive Markups	High prices used by retailers to connote quality
• Price differentiation	Yield management pricing of airline tickets, resulting in day to day differential pricing of adjacent seats
• Price discrimination	Favoured pricing to preferred ethnic groups
C. Promotion	
• Exaggerated Claims	One blade company claims its razor as 'the smoothest, most comfortable shave known to man.' Another company challenges.
• Tasteless advertising	Sexual innuendoes and gender disparagement

• Inappropriate Targeting	
• Deceptive advertising	
• Persuasive role models for inappropriate products	Celebrity spokes persons in beer, liquor, cigarette ads targeted to youths
• Naive audiences	Bill boards for cigarette and alcohol in poor urban neighbourhoods where many people are dying from related causes.
• Telemarketing	Offers of fabulous prizes in return for credit card purchases of touted goods
• Captive audiences	Mandatory viewing of TV commercials by students in schools
D. Distribution	
• Fraudulent Sales	Phony markdowns based on 'Kited' retail prices
• Bait and Switch tactics	Living consumers with ads for low priced merchandise for the purpose of switching them to high priced models
• Direct Marketing	Deceptive, misleading product size and performance claims
E. Packing	
• Deceptive Quantities	Some marketers use 'packaging-to-price' tactics that mask a decrease in product quantity while maintaining the same price and traditional package size.

Fig. 3.113 Unethical Marketing Behaviour

Unethical Consumer Practices

- Shop lifting
- Switching price tags
- Returning clothing that has been worn
- Abusing products and returning them as damaged goods
- Redeeming coupons that have expired
- Redeeming coupons without the requisite purchase
- Returning cloth bought at full-price and demanding a refund for the sales price differential
- Returning products bought at sale and demanding the full price refund
- Stealing belts from store clothing
- Cutting buttons off of store merchandise
- Returning partially used products for full store credit
- Abusing warranty or unconditional guarantee privileges
- Damaging merchandise in a store and then demanding a sales discount
- Copying copy righted materials (books, videotapes, computer software without permission)

Fig. 3.114 Unethical Consumer Practices

Portrayal of Women and Minorities

Another area in which advertising is sometimes socially irresponsible is in its portrayal of **women and minorities**. Advertising review board found that until 1970s women were shown as 'Stupid-too dumb to cope with familiar everyday chores unless instructed by children or a man.' In 1980s, alternatively women were portrayed as super woman-working woman as well as a housewife taking care of kids, stimulating conversation with her husband.

Today, advertisers are portraying women in more realistic roles. Offensive role portrayals of women still linger.

Advertising's portrayal of blacks has also improved over time. Earlier, blacks have been portrayed in subservient roles such as:

- Waiters and Porters
- Inept or motivated

Ten years ago, most portrayals of the black male were of the 'can't-do-anything-but-have-a-good-time' type.

Today, the black male is characterised as 'more ambitious' type and is portrayed in more realistic roles.

Ethical Consumerism

Ethical consumerism should be about using our purchasing power to make the world a better place - Feeling pure will not help the worlds pure. It is characterised by three almost religious convictions:

- Multinationals are inherently bad
- The natural and organic are inherently superior
- Science and technology are not to be trusted

Irrational prejudice against multinationals is connected to incoherent opposition to globalisation. Antiglobalisation compaingners seem blind to the irony that it was precisely the increased interconnectedness of peoples and trade characteristic of globalisation that allowed their worldwide opposition movement to flourish. The growth of multinationals is just one aspect of globalisation and the homogeneity it brings is regrettable. If you care about morality, the multinationals can be a force for good. For instance, say you fancy a coffee in Italy. Go to a local cafe and the chances are the beans they grind have been bought to market prices from farmers who receive so little that they can barely make a living. Starback is a huge purchaser of coffee worldwide and should be lauded and encouraged to go further by ethical consumers. Instead it is only one of the first targets for antiglobalisation protesters bricks.

There is nothing wrong with most non-organic foods; The feeling that we defile the inner sanctums of our bodies by eating food treated by pesticides is rooted in an almost religious, supersitious worship of 'the natural'. Dressing this up as an 'ethical' choice is self serving self deception. Further, the deep mistrust of science, which goes beyond reasonable suspicion. It is not just that we do not trust scientists or technology. We seem to feel that for any scientific fix there must be a price. Natural justice demands that cheaper, longer lasting tomatoes come at a cost. Even the poor are not allowed to get richer, if it means using more technology.

Ethical consumerism requires a harderheaded look it what is in the interests of the world's poor. If that means ripping up the standard ethical consumer's checklist and starting again, so be it.

Rights and Duties of Parties in the Marketing Exchange Process

Participants in the marketing exchange process should be able to expect that:

1. Products' and services offered are safe and fit for their intended uses;
2. Communication about offered products and services are not deceptive;
3. All parties intend to discharge their obligations, financial and otherwise, in good faith; and
4. Appropriate internal methods exist for equitable adjustment and/or redress of grievances concerning purchases.

It is understood that the above would include, but is not limited to the following responsibilities of the marketer:

In the area of product development and management,

- disclosure of all substantial risks associated with product or service usage;
- identification of any product component substitution that might materially change the product or impact on the buyer's purchase decision;
- identification of extra cost-added features.

In the area of promotions,

- avoidance of false and misleading advertising;
- Rejection of high pressure manipulations, or misleading sales tactics;
- avoidance of sales promotions that use deception or manipulation.

In the area of distribution,

- not manipulating the availability of a product for purpose of exploitation;
- not using coercion in the marketing channel;
- not exerting undue influence over the resellers' choice to handle a product.

In the area of pricing,

- not engaging in price fixing;
- not practicing productory pricing;
- disclosing the full price associated with any purchase.

In the area of marketing research,

- prohibiting selling or fund raising under the guise of conducting research;
- maintaining research integrity by avoiding misrepresentation and omission of pertinent research data;
- treating outside clients and suppliers fairly.

Organisational Relationships

Marketers should be aware of how their behaviour may influence or impact on the behaviour of others in organisational relationships. They should not demand, encourage or apply coercion to obtain unethical behaviour in their relationships with others, such as employees, suppliers, or customers.

1. Apply confidentiality and anonymity in professional relationships with regard to privileged information;
2. Meet their obligations and responsibilities in contracts and mutual agreements in a timely manner;
3. Avoid taking the work of others, in whole, or in part, and represent this work as their own or directly benefit from it without compensation or consent of the originator or owner;
4. Avoid manipulation to take advantage of situation to maximise personal welfare in a way that unfairly deprives or damages the organisation of others.

Any AMA member found to be in violation of any provision of this Code of Ethics may have his or her Association membership suspended or revoked.

3.5 The Due Care Theory

Product Liability

The right of consumers to be protected from harmful products raises a number of problems for manufactures as products can injure, and even kill people (if products are used improperly).

Every dangerous product can be made safer at some cost. Is there any limit to the safety improvements that a manufacturer ought to provide? Do manufacturers have a responsibility to ensure that the product is safe before it is put in the market?

There exists three theories which are in common use to determine when a product is defective and what is owed to the victims of accidents caused by defective products.

Which theory of liability is applied by the courts is of immense importance to manufacturers and consumers. This is a matter to be decided in part by legal and political considerations. There are important ethical issues in the debate. The theories rest on different ethical foundations.

The Due Care standard

The standard of due care for manufacturers or other persons involved in the sale of a product to a consumer including wholesalers and retailers, covers a wide range of activities. Among them are:

- **Design** - Designed in accordance with government and industry standards to be safe.
- **Materials** - Materials specified in the design; should meet government and industry standards.
- **Production** - Due care should be taken in fabricating parts to specifications and assembling them correctly.,
- **Quality control** - A systematic programme to inspect products between operations at the end to ensure that they are of sufficient quality.
- **Packaging, labeling and warnings** - Product should be packaged so as to avoid any damage in transit.

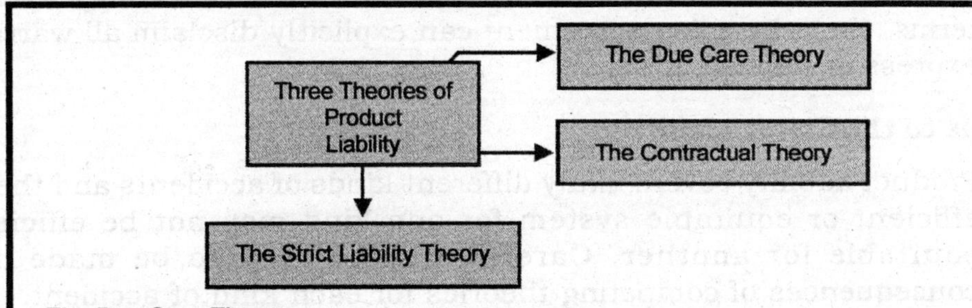

The Due Care Theory

- Manufacturers ought to exercise due care. Their obligation is to take all reasonable precautions to ensure that products they put on the market are free of defects likely to cause harm. It is based on the Aristotelian principle of compensatory justice, the contractual theory, on freedom of contract and strict liability, largely on utilitarian considerations. The disadvantage of this theory is the difficulty of deciding what constitutes due care and whether it was exercised.

The Contractual Theory

- The responsibility of manufacturers for harm resulting from defective products is that specified in a sales contract. The seller and buyer relation is viewed here as a contractual relation, which is subject to the terms of a contract. Even in the absence of an explicit, written contract, there may be an implicit, understood contract between the two parties that is established by their behaviour. It is the least satisfactory because of the power of manufacturers to write warranties and other agreements to their own advantage and to offer them to consumers on a 'take it or leave it' basis.

The Strict Liability Theory

- Manufacturers are responsible for all harm resulting from a dangerously defective product even when due care has been exercised and all contracts observed; Now gaining wider acceptance in the courts. Here, Law is strict liability, a manufacture need not be negligent nor be bounded by any implied or express warranty to have responsibility. Despite the absence of fault, is arguably the best theory. It provides a powerful incentive for manufacturers to take extreme precautions and creates a workable legal framework for compensating consumers who are injured by defective products. To be just, the costs have to be properly distributed so that they are fair to all parties.

Fig. 3.115 Three Theories of Product Liability

- **Notification** - The manufacturers of some products should have a system of notifying consumers of hazards that only become apparent later.

One question arises that in due care theory is whether manufacturers have an obligation to ensure that a product is safe to use as intended or to anticipate all the conditions under which injury could occur.

The Problem of Misuse: This duty also extends to foreseeable misuse by the consumer.

The Concept of Negligence: The major difficulty with the due care theory is establishing what constitutes due care.

Objections to the Contractual Theory: The objections are:

- The understandings in a sales agreement, which are the basis for implied and express warranties, are not very precise.
- A sales agreement may consist of a written contract with language that sharply limits the right of an injured consumer to be compensated. If buyers and sellers are both free to contract on mutually agreeable terms, then the sales agreement can explicitly disclaim all warranties express or implied.

Objections to the Strict Liability

- Product liability covers many different kinds of accidents and the most efficient or equitable system for one kind may not be efficient or equitable for another. Careful studies need to be made of the consequences of competing theories for each kind of accident.
- The view that corporations are able to distribute the burden of strict liability to consumers effortlessly is not always true.

The Ethical arguments for Strict Liability

This rests on two distinct grounds of:

- Efficiency
- Equality

One argument is purely utilitarian and justifies strict liability for securing the greatest amount of protection for consumers at the lowest cost. The second argument is that strict liability is the farthest way of distributing the costs involved in the manufacture and use of products. Both of these arguments recognise that there is a certain cost in attempting to prevent accidents and in dealing with the consequences of accidents that do on product safety. Preventing accidents requires that manufacturers expend greater resources on product safety. The efficient argument hold by one advocate that responsibility be fixed wherever it will most effectively reduce the hazards to life and health inherent in defective parts that reach the market.

The equity argument principle holds as expressed by Richard A.Epstein as follows:

'The defendant who captures the entire benefit of his own activities should....also bear its entire costs.' In so far as manufacturers are the beneficiaries of their profit making activity, it is only fair, according to this principle, that they be forced to bear the cost, which includes the cost of the injuries to consumers as a result of defective products. Much of the benefit of a manufacturer's activity is shared by consumers, however. But they also share the cost of compensating the victims of accidents through higher prices. It is also just that they do so insofar as they reap some benefit.

3.6 The Social Costs Views

The term corporate citizenship is often used to communicate the extent to which business strategically meet the economic, legal, ethical and philanthripic responsibilities placed a term by various stakeholders. The economic is affected by the way companies relate to shareholders and other investors, employees, customers, competitiors, the community and even the natural environment. When people talk about the 'economy' they generally mean cyclical conditions such as inflation, recession and employment rates or economic concept such as supply and demand. The economic aspects of social responsibility relate to new business use resources and respon to changes in business cycles. An organisations sense of economic responsibility is especially significant for employees because it raises such issues as equal job opportunities, work place durerniz, rod safety, health and emplyee privacy.

3.7 Advertising Ethics

Some of the advertising topics have already been covered in para 3.4.

Socially Responsible Advertising

Most advertising is socially responsible. Unfortunately, some advertising has willfully deceived or misinformed the public, has taken advantage of the naivete of younger children or has alienated key consumer groups such as women or minorities with insulting or distasteful representations of their roles.

Deceptive Advertising

Advertising that gives false information or that willfully misleads consumers about the benefits of the brand is **deceptive advertising**. It is unethical, and is controlled both through the self-regulation of responsible advertisers or through government action.

Corrective Advertising

The company must publicly correct a false impression created by past advertising. So, a second remedy is sometimes applied known as **corrective advertising**.

Advertising to the Children

Advertisers have a responsibility to avoid manipulating younger children, who tend to be more gullible than the rest of the population. One study found that a child requested a product because it was seen on TV, the parent was more likely to buy it. Yet younger children cannot adequately process information to evaluate advertising claims. The potential for taking advantage of children has led to propose a ban on advertising sugar coated foods on children's programs. Others have suggested prohibiting all advertising on programs watched by a significant proportion of children under the age of eight, which is rather difficult to implement.

Ethical and Social Issues in Advertising

Advertising plays in the recent times a unique role in information dissemination on various products and services marketed by different firms. It aids the consumers in:

- Understanding process
- Increasing their ability to make a better choice

Marketers use this for:

- Creating awareness
- Developing consumers interest
- Stimulating demand for various products and services

It is unfortunate that the consumers nor the competitors are getting full benefit out of it due to the misuse of this by various ways. A few issues of advertising has emerged as sensitive as ethical standards and practices. The result is the misallocation of resources, disappointed or even injured consumers and damaged competitors - known as **'perennially beleaguered business'**; a subject of debate for the social scientists, consumer bodies.

The question is:

- What is the consumer perception of about the use of some unethical practices followed by advertisers in their advertisements?
- Which category of advertisements contain these practices more?
- What are the most important deceptive practices to be controlled?
- What type of institutional arrangement is most suitable to control it?

When we speak about ethics as related to advertising activities, we are dealing with the judgement that certain types of advertisements are inappropriate. We do not have infact, a list of ethical or unethical practices that would cover all situations. One would encounter in advertising, the several uses of which are controversial. Opinion associate with certain practices which are heavily interwoven, with fundamental values and beliefs about how a society does and should operate. Much depends on the perspective of a particular situation and therefore, any debate is highly subjective.

Common Deceptive Practices

Unanimity is not found among advertising professionals and marketing clients regarding such questionable practices. In one aspect they are agreeable, while considering the question of unethical practices the focus must be to safeguard the interest of buyers at the micro-level and the society at the macro-level, since their satisfaction is the key for success.

A survey has been conducted at USA among eight randomly selected consumers. Half of the respondents are serious readers of advertisements, while others are casual readers.

The survey depicted that more than three fourth of the respondents, feel that most of the advertisement appearing in any media contain one or more of the above mentioned deceptive practices, especially in product advertisements than in service advertisements.

Common deceptive practices all over the world are:

- False and misleading presentation of facts
- Deliberate omitting of required information
- Implying a benefit that hardly exists
- Trade puffing and exaggerations
- Using unnecessary, unwanted technical jargons
- Creating cultural degeneration
- Creating ambiguities in the minds of consumers
- Creating fear in consumers
- Plagiarism (Take another writings as his own)
- Open criticism of competitors

Fig. 3.116 Common Deceptive Practices

Sl. No.	Unethical Practices	Opinion (% of respondents)		
		More in Product ads	More in Service ads	Equal in both
1	False and misleading presentation of facts	68.5	12.5	20.0
2	Deliberate omitting of required information	37.5	57.5	5.0
3	Implying a benefit that hardly exists	55.0	35.0	10.0
4	Trade puffing and exaggerations	31.0	30.0	39.0
5	Using unnecessary, unwanted technical jargons	64.0	20.0	16.0
6	Creating cultural degeneration	75.0	12.0	13.0
7	Creating ambiguities in the minds of consumers	30.0	60.0	10.0
8	Creating fear in consumers	22.5	20.0	59.5
9	Plagiarism (Take another writings as his own)	28.0	21.0	51.0
10	Open criticism of competitors	70.5	12.5	17.0

Fig. 3.117 More Deceptive Practices in Product Advertisements, than in Service Advertisements

Most Common Types of Advertising

The most common types of advertising are as under:

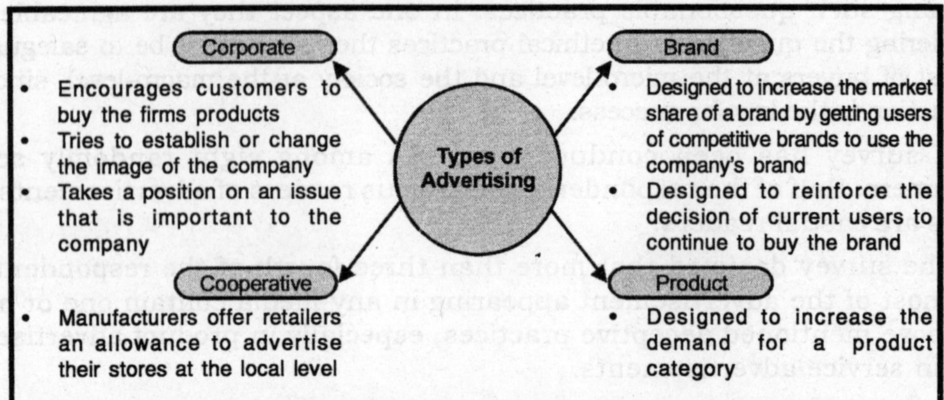

Fig. 3.118 Most Common Types of Advertising

Advertising Critics

Advertising critics has several adverse effects on society: It degrades people's tastes, it wastes valuable resources, and it creates monopoly power. The criticisms are:

Psychological Effects in Advertising

(i) It debases the tastes of the public by presenting irritating and aesthetically unpleasant displays. Advertisements to be effective, it must often be intrusive strident and repetitive to be understood by the most simple minded person. Advertisements are often boring, insiped and insult the intelligence of viewers. For example, while illustrating the use of toothpaste, mouth washes, deodrants and undergarments for example, advertisements sometimes employ images that many people find vulgar, offensive, disgusting and tasteless. However, they do not seem to raise important ethical issues. Advertisements do not measure up to our aesthetic norms. But this does not imply that they also violate our ethical norms.

(ii) Advertising debases the tastes of consumers by gradually and subtly inculcating materialistic values and ideas about how happiness is achieved. Personal efforts are divested from 'nonmaterialistic' aims and objectives, which are more likely to increase the happiness of the people and are instead channeled into expanded material consumption.

A person's beliefs and attitudes are notoriously difficult to change without there being a willingness to accept the message being offered. The success of advertising may depend more on its appeal to the values consumers already posess than on its ability to instill new values.

Advertising is Wasteful

It is another major criticism. Economics distinguish between production costs and selling costs.

- Production costs are the costs of the resources consumed in producing or improving a product.
- Selling costs are the additional costs of resources that do not go into changing the product, but are invested instead in persuading people to buy the product. E.g., advertising, critics claim etc. These are not used to improve the product, but to merely persuade people to buy it (advertisements do not add anything to the utility of the product). Such resources, critics conclude are wasted because they are expended without adding to consumer utility in any way.

Advertising adds to the consumer utility by serving as an incentive to greater consumption and thereby indirectly motivating a greater productivity, efficiency and a lower price structure. It is felt that many advertising serves to produce a beneficial rise in demand for all products. There is also a substantial uncertainty surround the question of whether advertising is responsible for a rise in the total consumption of goods. It fails to stimulate consumption of a product, and consumption in many industries has increased despite minimal advertising expenditures. It shifts consumption away from one product to another. If this is true, beyond the level needed to impart information, advertising becomes a waste of resources since it does nothing more than shifting the demand from one firm to another.

Even if advertising were an effective spur to consumption, many argues that this is not necessarily a blessing. Several economists like E.F.Schumacher and Herman E.Daly have claimed that the most pressing social need at present is finding ways of decreasing consumption to lessen the rapid industrial expansion that has polluted much of the natural environment and has rapidly depleted our nonrenewable resources. Unless we limit consumption, we will soon outturn the finite natural resources of our planet with disastrous consequences.

Advertising and Market Power

Advertising is supposed to reduce competition and raise barriers to entry into markets. For a long period, massive advertising campaign of modern manufacturers enable them to achieve and maintain a monopoly (or oligopoly) power over other markets. These campaigns create in consumers a loyalty to the brand name of the manufacturer, giving the manufacturer control of a major portion of the market. Small firms are unable to break into the market because of lack of finance for the expensive advertising campaigns needed to make consumers to switch their brand loyalties. A few large oligopoly firms emerge in control of the consumer markets from which small firms are effectly barred.

Is there any connection between advertising and the market power? If advertising does raise costs for consumers by encouraging monopoly markets, there should be a statistical connection between the amount of advertising amount spent by an industry and the degree of market concentration in that industry. More concentrated and less competitive industries should exhibit high levels of advertising. Vice versa similarly, whether advertising harms consumers by diminishing competition? The criticisms of advertising based on its social effects are inconclusive for the simple reason that it is unknown whether it has the capacity to produce the effects that the criticisms assume it has.

Creation of Consumer Desires

John K.Galbraith and other eminents in the advertising line have argued that advertising is manipulative. It is the creation of desires in consumers for the sole purpose of absorbing industrial output. He distinguished two kinds of desires:

- Those that have a 'physical' basis - Desires for good and shelter
- Those that are 'psychological in origin' - Individual's desires for goods that give him a sense of personal achievement (accord him a feeling of equality with his neighbors, direct his mind from thought, serve sexual aspiration, promise social acceptability, enhance his subjective feeling of health, contribute by conventional canons to personal beauty or otherwise psychologically rewarding).

(i) The physically based desires onginate in the buyer and are relatively immune to being changed by persuation. The psychic desires, however, are capable of being managed, controlled and expanded by advertising. Because the demand created by physical needs is finite, producers soon produce enough to meet these needs. If production is to expand, the producers must create new demand by manipulating the pliable psychic desires through advertising. Advertising is used to create psychic desires for the sole purpose of 'ensuring that people buy what is produced' (to absorb the output of an expanding industrial system). The effect of this management of demand through advertising is to shift the focus of decision in the purchase of goods from the consumer where it is beyond control to the firm were it is subject to control. Production is not moulded to serve human desires. But vice versa. If Galbraith's view is correct in the above, then advertising violates the individuals right to choose himself. Advertising manipulates the consumer. The consumer is merely used as a means for advancing the ends and purposes of producers and this deminishes the consumers' capacity to freely choose for himself.

(ii) The psychological effects of advertising are still not clear. Consequently, it is unclear whether psychic desires can be manipulated by advertising in the wholesale way that Galbraith's argument assumes. Few others like Von Hoyek have pointed out, the 'creation' of psychic wants did not originate with modern advantings. New wants have always been 'created' by the invention of novel and attractive products (like first painting, the first perfume etc.) and such a creation of wants seems harmless enough.

Some particular advertisements are at least intended to manipulate with a psychological desire for the product by the consumer without his knowledge and without knowing whether the product is in his own best interests.

3.8 Consumer Privacy

An ethical issue is a problem, situation, or opportunity that requires an individual or organisation to chook among several actions that must be evaluated as right or wrong, ethical or unethical.

Ethical issues typically arise because of conflict between individuals' personal moral philosophe's and values and the values and attitudes of the organisations in which they work and the society they live. There are five categories of ethical issues. Honesty and fairness, conflict of enterent, fraud, discrimination and technology ethical issues related to technology are on the rise with advences in technology. Among the most challenging are employee privacy, consumer privacy and the protection of Intellectual property.

The first category of ethical issues relates to technology and the numerous advances made in Internet and other forms of electronic communication in the last few years. The second ethical issue created by advances in technology relates to consumer privacy. There are two dimensions to this issue: Consumer awareness of information collection and a growing lack of consumer control over how companies use the personal information they collect. Online purchases, random web surfing etc can be tracked with consumer's knowledge. A third ethical issue related to the technology involves the legal protection of intellectual properties (music, books and movies). Various acts (Copyright etc) are designed to protect the creation of Intellectual propesty.

Advances in computer processing power, data base software and communication technologies have given us the power to collect, manipulate and disseminate personal information about consumers on a scale unprecedented in the history of the human race. This new power over the collection, manipulation, discremination of personal information has enable mass invarious of the privacy of consumers and has created the potentical for sifnificant harms arising from mistakes or false information. **The right to privacy** is the right of persons to determine what, to whom, and how much information about themselves will be disclosed to other parties. There are two types of privacy. Psychological and physical. Psychological privacy in with respect to a person's inner life; **Physical Privacy** is with respect to a person's physical activities.

Importance of privacy is to:

- Protect individuals from shame, interference, hunting loved ones, self-incrimination
- Enables the development of personal relationships, professional relatinships, distinet social roles, and self determination.

Legetimate business needs with the right to privacy include:

— relevance
— informing
— consent
— accuracy
— purpose
— recipients and security

Questions

1. Which are the distinct functions coming under the broad characteristics of marketing raise ethical questions that do not have an easy answer?
2. Explain the main forms of Direct Marketing. Explain the shady tactics of a few direct marketers can harm or bother consumers giving the entire industry a black eye.
3. 'Irritation, Unfairness, Deception and Fraud are very common in Direct Marketing' as per some critics. Comment.
4. 'Invasion of privacy is perhaps the toughest public policy issue now confronting the direct marketing industry'. Explain your views.
5. Explain an integrated direct marketing campaign.
6. What are the laws and regulations generally designed to protect the consumer from unethical practices by business?
7. What is the purpose of establishing a code of ethics by American Marketing Association (AMA). How does the AMA code outlines the responsibilities for each component of the marketing mixed.
8. 'Many of the actions cited by the AMA code as unethical, are also illegal.' What are your views?
9. Why should marketers worry about ethics?
10. What role do moral values play in an economic system?
11. Do competitive pressures conflict with ethical considerations in marketing?
12. Does the legal system provides too many or too few ethical constraints on the marketers?
13. List out the criticisms of ethics in marketing?
14. What are the implications found for maintaining ethical standards in marketing?
15. Explain the reasons for unethical practices.
16. What is socially responsible advertising?
17. Explain ethical and social issues in advertising.
18. Which are the common deceptive practices found in advertising all over the world?

19. What is deceptive advertising? What aspects to be considered while advertising to the children?
20. Do you feel a regulatory body to control the unethical practices is required? What are your views?
21. What do you mean by tunnel vision?
22. What are hot button issues?
24. Explain the strategies used in pricing new products. What ethical issues are found in these strategies?
25. Which are the four areas of pricing considered as unethical and illegal?
26. Explain the FTC Act and Robinson-Patman Act and Sherman Acts introduced at USA to prevent unethical and illegal activities of marketing.
27. What are the ethical issues found in product packaging and labeling? Mention any two acts which are applicable in this area.
28. Mention some of the ethical issues observed in the international marketing operations.
29. Explain the steps involved in the marketing model developed by Arther Anderson and Company which can be taught to the current and future managers of any company.
30. Explain the four pragmatic reasons in marketing for behaving ethically.
31. List down unethical marketing behaviours found in various marketing areas. Explain them briefly.
32. List down atleast ten unethical consumer practices generally found in marketing.
33. Explain the three theories of product liability, which are of common use in marketing.
34. Which are the theories which determines when a product is defective and what is owed to the victims of accidents caused by defective products. Explain them.
35. Which theory of product liability is applied by the courts is of immense importance to manufacturers and consumers? Explain.
36. Explain the two distinct grounds on the ethical arguments for strict liability.
37. What are the most common types of advertising? Explain the ethical issues involved in it.
38. What creates opportunities and threats in the marketing environment?
39. Why does marketing opportunity always have some threat? How can an environmental threat frequently be turned into an opportunity?
40. What is Environment?
41. Why should we study the state of the Environment?
42. Explain the modern environmental concepts and the need for information for the same.
43. Define Environmental Study.

44. What are the components of Environmental Study?
45. What is the scope of Environmental Study?
46. How does the technology affects the Environment?
47. Explain a Clock Face Metaphor. What have we observed?
48. How do you say that human beings have to depend on nature so much and any lack of protecting Environmental Resources available on the Earth, human would suffer and cannot continue to live.
49. Explain the different types of Natural Resources available on the Earth. Classify the resources.
50. Everyone of us should be concerned about our environmental assets and change our ways of wastage if any? Discuss on this issue.
51. What is the importance of Environmental Study?
52. Discuss on the life support systems of human beings.
53. How are the misuse of resources taking place? Explain each one of them. What are the harms created by Waste?
54. To preserve the Environment, who has to act on it? Is it Government or the individual or both? If it is individual, how he can help?
55. Explain the multidisciplinary nature of Environmental Studies?
56. What do you mean by exceptional recreation values?
57. What do you mean by the value of nature? What are its types? Explain each one of them.
58. What is Environmental Degradation?
59. What is the need for public awareness in the prevention of environmental degradation?
60. Which are the various institutions involved in the study? Environment in both, Private or Government of India?
61. Explain the terms:

    Atmosphere   Biosphere   Troposphere

    Lithosphere   Stratosphere   Hydrosphere
62. Explain briefly the terms:

    Ozone layer   Greenhouse effect

    Global warming   Green house gas

    Green house
63. Explain the 'green house effect' in the atmosphere and how does this lead to 'global warming'
64. What are the characteristics of Biogeographical assets?
65. Explain an hydrological cycle with a sketch. What is the purpose of this cycle?

66. What are Natural resources? What does these include?
67. Explain the terms 'Biotic' and 'Abiotic'.
68. Explain with a sketch an understanding of Natural resources and Ecosystems.
69. Distinguish between renewable and non-renewable resources.
70. Which are the resources renewable only within certain limits?
71. How do you increase forest cover in addition to protecting our forests?
72. What are the India's serious environmental problems connected with forest resources?
73. Discuss on the biggest challenge involved in this century in the world, a need to retting about the overall management of world resources, specially involved in water resources.
74. There is a large thinking that there might be wars between countries due to shortage of fresh water. Discuss.
75. What is a mineral? What are the characteristics? Which are the mineral resources found in the earth crust?
76. What is .mining and mining technology? Which are the different types of mines?
77. Which are the major environmental concerns found in mining and processing of minerals? What type of global public awareness created by the government to prevent the damage to the natural environment?
78. Discuss on Food resources in India? Do you agree that the modern method of agriculture pollute our environment as they use excessive fertilizers and pesticides? What are your comments?
79. Explain the usage of :

    Organic Fertilisers

    Inorganic Fertilisers and pesticides.

    Integrated crop Management.
80. Forests, grass lands, wetland are being converted for agricultural use. Will there be any serious ecological questions arising from this? Comment.
81. What is land? Explain the use of land resource.
82. How do you say that Land is overused or misused?
83. What are the main reasons for land utilization?
84. What do you mean by land degradation? Mention the factors for land degradation.
85. Discussion the land use pattern in India.
86. Which are the main sources of energy in India?
87. Distinguish between commercial and noncommercial energy resources.

88. Distinguish between conventional and non-conventional energy resources.
89. What is the necessity for non-conventional source of energy?
90. Discuss briefly on the following energy resources:

    Solar energy

    Wind power

    Tidal power

    Biogas

    Geothermal power
91. How do you conserve energy resources?
92. Define soil. What do you mean by soil erosion?
93. What are the causes for soil erosion?
94. Discuss on the effects of soil erosion.
95. How do you conserve soil?
96. What are the techniques of soil conservation?
97. Explain the following terms in two to three sentences.

    Afforestation

    Strip cropping

    Terracing

    Shelter belts

    Mulching

    Crop rotation

    Contour farming

    Gully plugging.
98. Give the meaning of desertification.
99. What are the causes of desertification?
100. Explain the consequences of desertification.
101. Explain the measures of desertification.
102. What do you mean by sustainable development?
103. Which are the points to be covered while taking care for sustainable development?
104. How sustainable development can be attained ecologically and what measures are to be adopted?
105. Explain equitable use of resources for sustainable style.
106. Give the meaning of conservation of natural resources.
107. What is the role of an individual in conservation and protection of natural resources?

108. Give the meaning of Pollution.
109. How do you classify pollutants? Explain each one of them.
110. How does pollution create harmful effects on plants, animals and human beings?
111. What are the different types of pollution? Name them and explain each one of them briefly.
112. What do you mean by air pollution? How is the air polluted?
113. Give the meaning of primary pollutants and secondary pollutants. Compare and contrast primary and secondary pollutants.
114. What is a particulate? List down the type of particulates. Explain each one of them.
115. Which are the five primary pollutants? Explain each one of them.
116. What do you mean by indoor and outdoor pollutants?
117. How do the pollutants entered into the troposphere of the atmosphere behave at different timings of the day?
118. How do the secondary pollutants come down on earth's surface behave?
119. What do you mean by acid rain or acid deposition? When is this harmful?
120. In what way the acid rain affects the humans and plants?
121. What are the effects of air pollution on living organisms?
122. What are the effects of air pollution on plants and on materials?
123. What do you mean by ozone layer? Explain.
124. Explain the terms: - Ozone layer - Chloroflouro carbons - Ozone depletion.
125. What are the effects of Ozone layer on human health, food production, plants and animals, materials and climate.
126. What do you mean by Greenhouse effect? Explain.
127. What is Green House? Why it is called so?
128. Define Global warming. What are the reasons for global warming? What are the adverse effects of global warming?
129. How do you control air pollution. Explain the techniques of air control.
130. What do you mean by atmospheric radiation? From where it originates?
131. Write a note on air pollution in India.
132. How do you say water is a very precious resource?
133. How do you conserve water?
134. 'People say that the countries may fight in the future for fresh water and there may be wars'. Put forth your argument in favour of this.
135. Fill in the blanks:
    (i) % of the earths surface is covered by water and .... % forms the land surface.

(ii) .... % of the total water available is found in the form of oceans, out of which .... % is available to as fresh water.

(iii) .... % out of the total fresh water .... % is locked up in ice caps or glaciers.

(iv) Out of .... % available as fresh water, only .... % of the earth's total volume of water is available to us as soil moisture, ground water, water vapour and water in rivers, lakes, streams and wet lands.

136. Fresh water availability is in three forms. Explain each one of them.
137. Write a note on water pollution.
138. What do you mean by water pollution?
139. What are the sources of water pollution? Explain each one.
140. What are the signs of water pollution?
141. Write a note on water pollutants.
142. Explain the different classes of water pollutants. Explain the harms created by water pollutants on humans.
143. What is anaerobic bacteria?
144. Explain the terms: (i) Eutrophication (ii) Bioaccumulation (iii) Biomagnifications.
145. Explain water pollution prevention through control measures.
146. Explain the terms 'soil' and 'soil pollution'.
147. What are the constituents of the soil?
148. What do you mean by 'Soil Horizon'?
149. How are the soil horizons classified?
150. What is loam?
151. Explain why soil degrades?
152. What is soil erosion? How the soil erosion is accelerated by human activities?
153. What are the soil conservation measures?
154. Explain the treatments used in soil conservation.
155. What do you mean by pesticides?
156. List down the problems of using pesticides.
157. Define Integrated Pest Management (IPM)?
158. Explain the terms 'salination' and 'water logging'.
159. Explain the terms 'Marine pollution'.
160. What are the causes that pollute marine waters?
161. Explain how sewage water and organic wastes are the major causes of marine pollution. Give your own example citing an industry.

162. What are the control measures to reduce the pollution load on marine waters?
163. Explain the different types of treatment done to prevent Marine pollution?
164. Explain the importance of oil pollution of the sea and which are the sources through which the soil can reach the sea.
165. Which are the affect and control measures for oil pollution?
166. Give the meaning of the terms 'Noise' and 'Noise pollution' from where the noise emanates?
167. What are the harmful effects of noise?
168. What do you mean by thermal pollution?
169. Explain the effects, prevention and control of thermal pollution.
170. Reduction of Emission's will cost India a high price. Discuss.
171. What do you mean by nuclear hazards?
172. Explain the sources, effects and control of radioactive pollution.
173. Give the meaning of solid~waste and explain its effects.
174. What do you mean by solid waste management? How it is useful?
175. Explain the sources and classification of solid waste.
176. What is the methodology involved in solid waste management? Explain each one of the methods adopted.
177. Discuss on the role of an individual in the prevention of pollution.
178. What do you mean by disaster and natural disaster?
179. Explain natural disaster impacts.
180. Give the meaning of disaster management.
181. Explain floods, cyclones, landslides and how it is caused?
182. How do you tackle disasters?
183. Write a note on various disasters occurred in India and neighbouring countries.
184. Explain earthquake on Tsunami faced by India.
185. Suggest small steps which make a big revolution to avoid pollution.
186. America blames India and China are the main polluters ignoring themselves. Is it true? What is the reason behind it?
187. What are the social issues connected with the environment?
188. What do you mean by 'sustainable development' and 'unsustainable development'?
189. What is the concept of sustainable development? Explain its significance.
190. Explain the involvement of sustainable development.
191. How do you say that our future generations have serious environmental problems?

192. Compare and contrast sustainable development and unsustainable development.
193. How to achieve sustainable development? Give the guidelines.
194. What are the urban problems related to energy?
195. Explain the consumption of energy in urban areas.
196. What is the meaning of embodied energy?
197. Explain the measures to solve the energy crisis in urban areas.
198. What do you mean by water conservation? Explain the various methods involved.
199. Explain rainwater harvesting.
200. Define rainwater harvesting and what are the objectives of rainwater harvesting?
201. Explain the techniques of rainwater harvesting.
202. Explain roof rainwater harvesting with a sketch. What are the merits and demerits of rainwater harvesting?
203. Give the meaning of 'watershed' and 'watershed management'.
204. What are the principles and benefits of watershed management?
205. Explain the techniques of watershed management.
206. List down the watershed conservation practices. Explain each one of them.
207. Discuss the problems and concerns of resettlement and rehabilitation of people.
208. What are the risks associated with resettlement and rehabilitation of affected people?
209. Explain the requirements needed for successful resettlement and rehabilitation programmes.
210. Define environmental ethics. What are the issues involved and possible solutions.
211. Explain the important parameters of environmental ethics.
212. Explain the following environmental threats.

     Ozone layer depletion

     Green house gases

     Green house effect
213. Define reactive strategy and defensive strategy.
214. What are reasons for climate change? Give suitable examples.
215. Explain the following terms.

     Global warming

     Acid rain

216. Define global warming. What are the effects of global warming?
217. 'It is felt that global warming is alarmingly increasing than what was calculated by climatologists few years back'. Comment.
218. Demonstrate with a sketch how global warming takes place?
219. What are measures for controlling global warming?
220. Give the meaning of sequestration.
221. Give the meaning of acid rain. Show with a sketch. How an acid rain takes place?
222. How do you control acid rain?
223. Give the meaning of Ozone layer. Explain the functions of Ozone. What do you mean by Ozone layer depletion?
224. Explain the terms
    (i) Chloro fluoro carbons (CFC_s)
    (ii) Holocaust
225. Give the meaning of holocaust. Explain the same with a few examples.
226. What do you mean by wasteland reclamation?
227. Define wasteland. What are the types of wasteland? What are its classifications?
228. Explain wasteland management programme. What activities does it include? Explain each one of the activities.
229. Explain the terms.
    (i) Afforestation
    (ii) Desertation
    (iii) Reclamation of Alkaline and Saline soils
230. Define consumerism. Explain consumption pattern of people on the recent days.
231. What are the consequences of consumerism and how to get rid off?
232. What are the environment protection act 1986 indicating the main objectives and features?
233. Explain the environment protection act 1986 indicating the main objectives and features.
234. Explain the air prevention and control of pollution act 1981 indicating the main objectives and features.
235. Explain the water prevention and control of pollution act 1974 indicating the main objectives and features.
236. Explain the wild life protection act 1972 indicating the main objectives and features.
237. Explain the forest conservation act 1988 indicating the main objectives and features.

238. Explain the forest rights act 2008 indicating the main objectives and features.
239. Define environmental legislation. What are the issues involved in enforcement of environmental legislation?
240. What is environmental impact assessment?
241. Discuss on citizens actions and action groups and the tools of public awareness need for environmental sensitivity growth.
242. What is climate change? What are our observations on the climate change in the recent days? How is it damaging our world?
243. 'The peace and stability in the world is affected by climate change' as per Indian' noble prize winner R.K. Pauchauri comment.
244. 'Global warming is already wrecking with nature'. Discuss.
245. 'India has to spend lot of money to reduce emissions'. Comment.
246. What IS the impact of global warming? What reduces global warming? How we can help?
247. Discuss on Kyoto protocol for cutting emissions.
248. What are the true global problems pertaining to global change and sustainable development.

MODULE 4

Internal Context - Employee

JOB DISCRIMINATION

4.1 Its Nature and Extent

Job discrimination, in particular, has been a 'vicious cycle'. Many minority-group members have had little incentive to seek an education as they could not hope for better jobs. Whatever is available to them, the educated minorities will seek them. Discrimination runs counter to American ideal of equal opportunity for all citizens of USA. When blacks, women, Hispanics and other minorities have present demands for fair treatment, many members of the business community have responded.

Discrimination describes a large number of wrongful acts in employment, housing, education, medical care and other important areas of public life. This takes different forms in the above areas. What is common is that a person due to the above is deprived of some benefit, opportunity because of membership in some group toward which there is substantial prejudice.

It is a form of unequal treatment but not all unequal treatment is discrimination. An employer shows favouritism in deciding promotions.

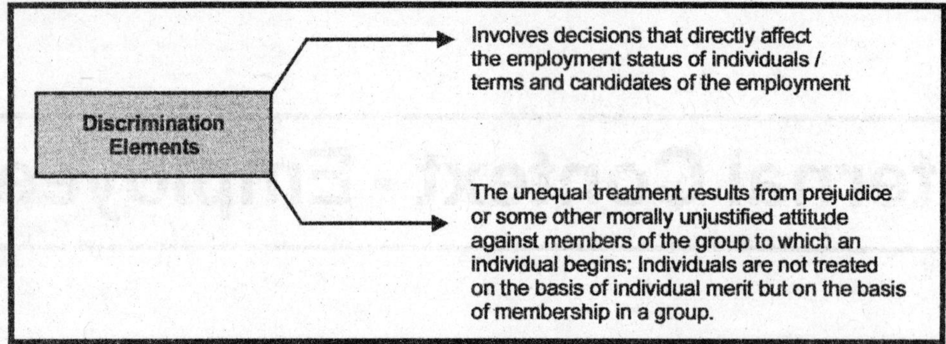

Fig. 4.1 Discrimination Elements

Employment policies that do not explicitly involve classifying employees by race, sex, religion or other impermissible characteristics can still serve to exclude members of these groups in disproportionate numbers.

Although a person's racial and sexual prejudica are on individual ethical concern, racial and sexual discrimination in the work place creates ethical issues in the business world. Ethical issues related to technology have increased with advances in technology. Among the most challenging are employee privacy. Consumer privacy and the protection of intellectual poverty.

Discrimination is not solely a matter of intention but also of consequences. **'Disparate treatment'** is the discrimination of the first kind while the latter is 'disparate impact'. The various forms of discrimination are shown below:

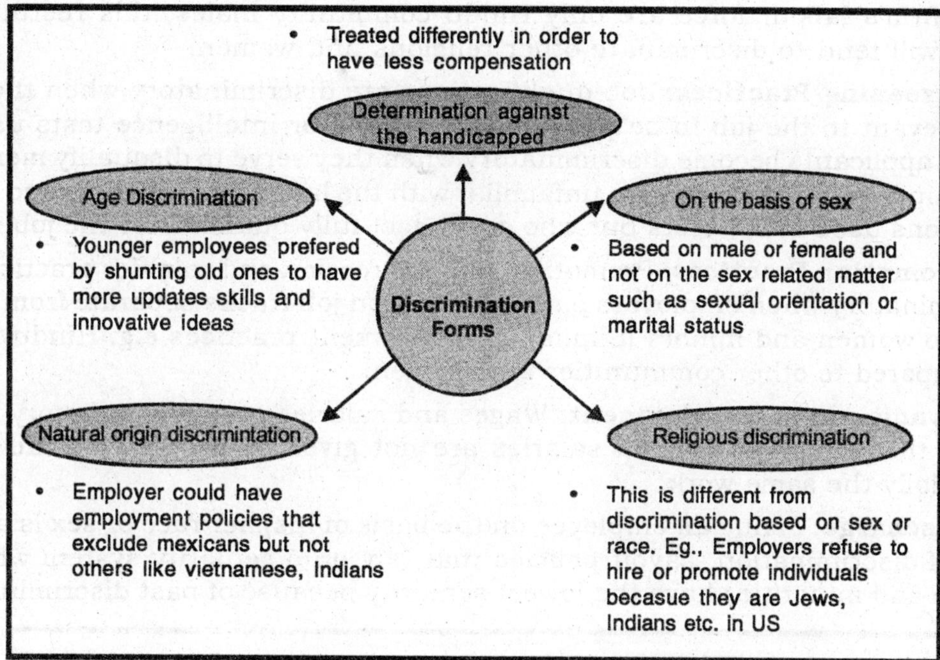

Fig. 4.2 Discrimination Forms

The discriminatory practices now widely recognised are as under:

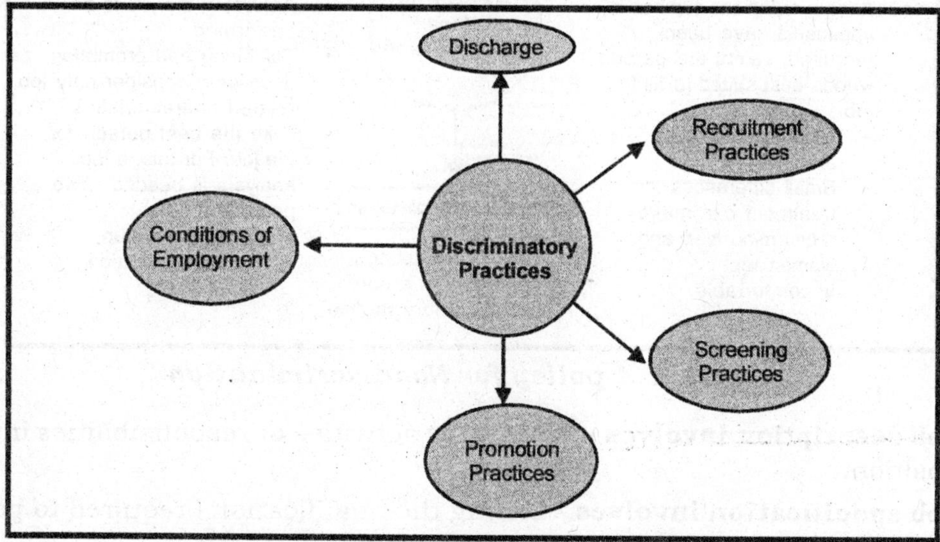

Fig. 4.3 Discriminatory practices

Recruitment Practices: Firms that rely solely on the word-of-mouth referrals of present employees to recruit new workers tend to recruit only from those racial and sexual groups that are represented in their labour force. For example:

If the firm's labour force are only Hindu community males, this recruitment policy will tend to discriminate other religions and women.

Screening Practices: Job qualifications are discriminatory when they are not relevant to the job to be performed. Aptitude or intelligence tests used to screen applicants become discriminatory when they serve to disqualify members from minority cultures who are unfamiliar with the language, concepts and social situations used in the tests but who are in fact fully qualified for the job.

Promotion Practices: Promotion, job progression and transfer practices are discriminatory when employers place majority on job tracks separate from those open to women and minors (Similar to recruitment practices e.g. Hindu males as compared to other communities and women).

Conditions of Employment: Wages and salaries are discriminatory to the extent that equal wages and salaries are not given to people who are doing essentially the same work.

Discharge: Fixing an employee on the basis of his/her race or sex is a clear form of discrimination. Layoff policies that rely on a seniority system wherein women and minorities have the lowest seniority because of past discrimination.

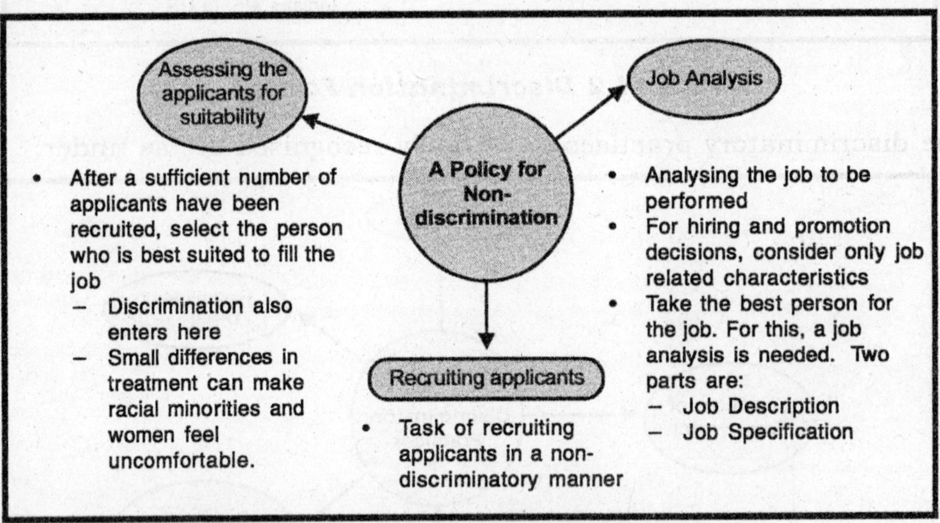

Fig. 4.4 A policy for Nondiscrimination

Job description involves - Details the activities or responsibilities involved in a position.

Job specification involves - Listing the qualifications required to perform the job as required.

During the hiring and the promotion process, two other important sources of discrimination are objective tests and subjective evaluations (on the basis of personal interviews and recommendations of supervisors).

Objective tests are of three types:

Tests that

- measure specific knowledge and skills (eg. Book Keeping, Typist, Computer Operator)
- measure intelligent and general aptitude for measuring certain kinds of work.
- attempt to gauge an applicant's suitability for employment; extent to which an applicant will fit into a specific work environment.

These are ethically and legally permissible, as long as they do not have disparate impact and are validated.

Personal interviewers and supervisors evaluations are apt to be influenced by irrelevant factors (A person's appearance, manner and by conscious/ unconscious prejudice, if evaluators are not well trained for the task).

Ethical arguments against discrimination

The three arguments that shows discrimination is wrong, each in its own way are explained below:

Utilitarian	*Kantian*	*Based on Justice*
• Straight forward arguments how discrimination harms individuals, business firms, society as a whole. • Discrimination creates an economically inefficient matching of people to jobs. • It is economically disadvantageous for employees to discriminate by refusing to work with blacks or women and for customers to discriminate by refusing to patronise minority owned businesses. • Harm that discrimination does to the welfare of society as a whole by perpetuating the effects of racism and sexism they impose an external cost on society. • In a free market, employers with a taste for discrimination are liable to be driven out of business and discrimination to be reduced over time. • An externality is imposed when employers attempt to cut costs by refusing to hire the handicapped; the savings to employers may be more than offset by the cost to the handicapped themselves and to the society that is forced to take for them.	• Appeals to the Kantian notions of human dignity and respect for persons. • Discrimination based on contempt or enmity for racial minorities or women involves a racist or sexist attitude that denies individuals in these groups the status of fully developed human beings who deserve to be treated as the equal of others. • The victims of racial and sexual discrimination are force to have undesired jobs with low pay and also deprived of a fundamental moral right to be treated with dignity and respect. • The moral right is also denied when individuals are treated on the basis of group characteristics rather than individual merit; stereo types, which are a part of racism and sexism clearly result in a denial of dignity and respect.	• Based on various principles of justice. • Fundamental to many principles of justice is the requirement that we will be able to justify our treatment of another people giving good reasons, but to discriminate is to treat people differently when there is no good reason for doing so. • Aristotle's principle of justice as proportional equality like cases should be treated alike. Unlike cases should be treated differently in proportion to the relevant differences. • Characteristics such as race and sex are generally irrelevant to the performance of a job. • John Rawls says 'Social and economic inequalities are to be arranged so that they are...attached to offices and positions open to all under conditions of fair equality of opportunity.

Fig. 4.5 Utilitarian Vs Kantianism Vs Based on Justice (Ethical arguments against Discrimination)

Avoiding Discrimination

- To become a truly nondiscriminatory employer is not an easy task
- They should have good-faith compliance with the law
- Employers must be aware of some subtle and surprising sources of discrimination.

4.2 Job Discrimination - Utility, Rights and Justice

This portion of the matter has been discussed in para 2.2 under Teleology.

A set of guidelines has to be used by business as a need for thinking about ethics. These guide lines would help corporate managers and employees in:

- Identifying the nature of the ethical problem
- Deciding the course of action likely to produce the best ethical result.

Three methods involved in ethical reasoning used for analytical purposes are as under:

(a) Utilitarian: The utilitarian is explained in the further chapters. Definition of utilitarianism is already given in chapter 2 and also in figure 4.6.

Example: In the month of May 1995, a leading battery factory in the gulf at Muscat got fire during the night. The fire destroyed 30% of the factory. As a result of that, the entire factory's production got affected. Though the company recovered the money from their insurance company, the morale of the company came down and the employees productivity affected in other areas also. However, the company took the opportunity and tried to relay the factory with a new plan (Business process reengineering) by redesigning the processes, trying to cover all the defects they had encountered in their earlier layout. The management had different options such as worked out by their in-house team as under:

(i) Rebuild the destroyed area only, with new building, installing new plant and machinery at that place and by redesigning the critical processes.

(ii) Taking the opportunity, relay the entire factory rectifying all the defects in the layout faced earlier including point No.(i) within a short period.

(iii) Destroy the entire setup and adopt 'business process re-engineering technique' (construct the entire factory as though it is a new one to increase productivity, after demolishing the entire buildings and adopting new planning design, improving the processes and technology). This is known as BPR, Covers: (a) Fundamental rethinking of business processes, (b) Adopt redesigning of business proceses, (c) Dramatic improvements in performance in critical, contemporary measures of performance such as cost, quality, service and speed.

After analysing the various utilitarian methods, company found that it is advantageous to adopt to point No. (ii) as it is not much time consuming and the orders on hand could be executed to their customers without much delay.

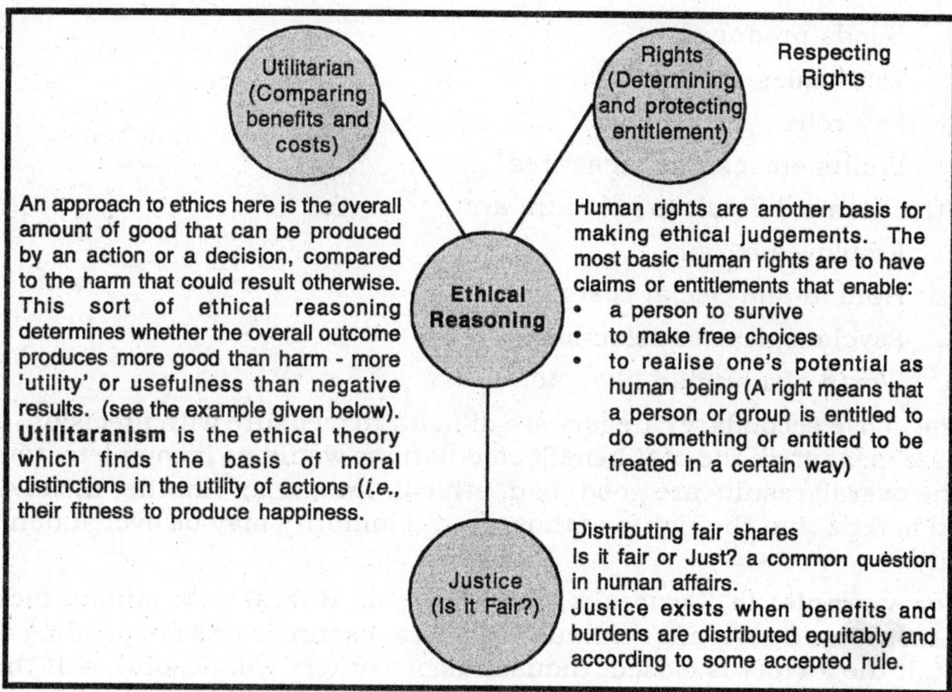

Fig. 4.6 Ethical Reasoning

Methods as per point No. (i) is not of much advantage as the existing problems in other areas would continue. Similarly method as per point No. (iii) would involve lot of planning, designing and construction of work in addition to other activities which would have taken more time involving heavy cost and labour dissatisfaction, temporary termination involved. Further, there were chances of losing the customer orders to their competitors in view of the delay anticipated.

Considering many of the aspects including benefits and costs, the 2nd proposal was taken up. This kind of ethical approach is called utilitarian reasoning since it avoided plant closing more good than harm resulted. Otherwise, workers would have been jobless for some time resulting in, both employee and customer dissatisfaction.

According to the concept of utilitarianism, the right decision is the one that produces the **greatest good for the greatest number of people.** It is the philosophy used in making ethical decision that aims to achieve the greatest good for the greatest number. If you were a manager using this approach, you would try to figure out the impact of all the alternative actions on everyone concerned, then choose the alternative that created the most satisfaction for the majority of the people and reject alternatives that catered to narrow interests or that failed to satisfy the needs of the majority skill. The value of this approach would depend on your ability in estimating the effect of your decisions. The challenge would lie in coming up with a decision that would benefit the majority of the people.

The main drawback in Utilitarian reasoning is difficulty in accurately measuring both costs and benefits. Certain things like:

- Goods produced
- Total sales
- Pay rolls
- Profits etc. can be measured

Other items difficult to measure are:

- Employee morale
- Human and Social costs
- Psychological satisfaction
- Worth of a human like, etc.

The above secondary category are difficult to measure with precision. Unless these are measured, the cost benefit calculations would be incomplete, to ensure that the overall results are good, bad, ethical, unethical. Another disadvantage we find here is that the rights of those in the minority may be overridden by the majority.

For example: In Karnataka, the known as Bharat gold mining factory at Kolar known as 'BGML' after exhausting all its resources was not yielding desired output. If the factory is closed, thousands of workers will be jobless. If the work is continued, it is a heavy burden to the company as well as to the Government every year. The people were not interested to move out to other places even if alternate jobs were given to them due to their long settlements in that area. Closing an outmoded plant may produce "the greatest good for the greatest number".

But this good outcome will not help the workers left behind jobless. The problem gets more aggravated for the old workers or those not well educated from minority groups. A utilitarian solution may leave them in the lurch. Here this method will not produce an ethical outcome. In spite of the limitations as explained above, the cost benefit analysis is still a widely used method in business. Business judge their own success or failures on this basis. If its costs are continuously higher than its revenues, financial failure is just around the corner. Business managers generally are tempted to rely on it to decide important ethical questions without fully aware of its limitations or the availability of still other methods to improve the ethical quality of their decisions.

(b) Human Rights

> **Example:** "A well experienced person in a company who was ideally fit for a profit implementation job abroad was denied that opportunity and a junior employee selected with that opportunity without much experience and knowledge was sent in his place"

Such things, we find common in many of the Indian organisations sometimes even in foreign countries whether it is private or public sector.

Denying those rights or failing to protect them for other persons and groups is normally considered to be unethical. The company interests would be lost and it has to pay a very heavy penalty respecting others, even those with whom we disagree or whom we dislike, is the essence of human rights provided that the others do the same for us. This approach to ethical reasoning holds that individuals are to be treated as valuable ends in themselves just because they are human beings. For your purposes if you use others, it is unethical, at the same time, you deny them their goals and purposes. For example, dumping your unwanted materials on the back of other industries compound may be guilty of ignoring the rights of others.

One of the major limitations, we find here is the difficulty of balancing conflicting rights. For example: an employees right to privacy may be disturbed with an employer's right to protect the firms cash by testing the employees honesty with secret watch and ward.

Individual rights is a philosophy used in making ethical decisions that aims to protect human dignity (guided by a belief). Because a belief in another persons rights implies that you have a duty to protect those rights. You would reject any decision that violated these rights.

Example: You would not deceive people nor trick them into acting against their own interests.

You would respect their privacy and right to express their opinion openly; You would not force people to act in a way that was against their religion or moral beliefs; You would not punish a person without a fair and impartial hearing; Though you might be guided by a desire to achieve the greatest good for the greatest number of people, you would reject any choice that violated the rights of even one person. In an era when individual workers expect and demand their rights, this philosophy is becoming a practical necessity.

The protection and promotion of human rights is an important ethical benchmark for judging the behaviour of individuals and organisations. Majority would certainly agree that the denial of a person's fundamental rights to:

• Life • freedom • privacy • growth • human dignity

Human dignity is generally unethical. By defining properly the human constitution and pointing the way to realisation of human potentialities, such rights become a kind of common denominator of ethical reasoning, leading to the essential conditions for ethical actions and decisions.

(c) Justice

Justice is the philosophy used in making ethical decisions to ensure the equal distribution of burdens and benefits. These principles include a belief that people should be treated equally, that rules should be applied consistently and that people who harm others should be held responsible and make restitution.

A justice decision is one that is fair, impartial, reasonable in the light of the rules that apply to the situation.

> **Examples:** Many people will be eager to know when budget is presented on 29th March every year in India, as they would like to know what would be the burden and who will escape paying their fair share? A fair distribution does not mean equal distribution. For society as a whole,

social justice means that a society's income and wealth are distributed among the people in fair proportions. In the case of fair distribution, the shares received by the population depend upon the society's approved rules for getting and keeping income and wealth. Rules vary from society to society. Most societies try to consider people's needs, abilities, efforts, and the contributions they make to societies welfare. Since these are not equal, fair shares vary from person to person and as well as group to group.

4.3 Job Discrimination

Affirmative Action

In 1964, Civil Rights Act was passed in USA. After this employers scrutinised their hiring and promotion practices to eliminate sources of discrimination. As a result of past discrimination, women and minorities do not have the same skills as their counterparts ie., white male. The former are now under represented in the most prestigious and desirable job positions. Even with the best efforts of the components, they could not succeed in increasing the advancement opportunities for women and racial minorities in USA.

To rectify the effects of past discrimination, many employers have instituted **'Affirmative Action Programs'** designed to achieve a more representative distribution of minorities and women within the firm by giving preference to women and minorities. It is now legally required of all firms that hold a government contract.

In view of the future demographic trends, that enlightened self interest should also prompt business to give women and minorities a special hand. If businesses do not accommodate themselves to these new workers, American businesses will not be able to find the workers they need and they will suffer recurrent and crippling shortages over the next decade. Businesses will not be able to rely on the small pool of traditional white male workers to fill all their requirements for skilled and managerial positions. Lots of Asians and out of which a majority of Indians have taken responsible positions in the jobs given to them in USA.

Affirmative action has some significant undesirable consequences that must be balanced against the undesirable utilitarian benefits of preferential treatment programs. These arguments are putforth by opponents of affirmative action as shown in figure 4.7.

Affirmative action as a form of compensation are based on the concept of 'compensatory justice'. **Compensatory justice** implies that people have an obligation to compensate those, whom they have intentionally and unjustly wronged. The principle requires that compensation should come only from those specific individuals who inflicted a wrong, and it requires them to compensate only those specific individuals whom they wronged. Arguments and counter arguments exist on these issues by various authors.

A second set of justifications advanced in support of affirmative action programs mention that the programs are morally legitimate instruments for achieving morally legitimate ends.

Example: Utilitarians have claimed that affirmative action programs are justified because they promote the public welfare. They have also argued that past discrimination has produced a high degree of correlation between race and poverty. They also question whether the social costs of affirmative action programs weighs their obvious benefits? Defenders reply that the benefits far outweigh their costs. Utilitarians argue that all minorities and women have been impoverished and psychologically harmed by past descrimination. As a result, race and sex provide accurate indicators of need.

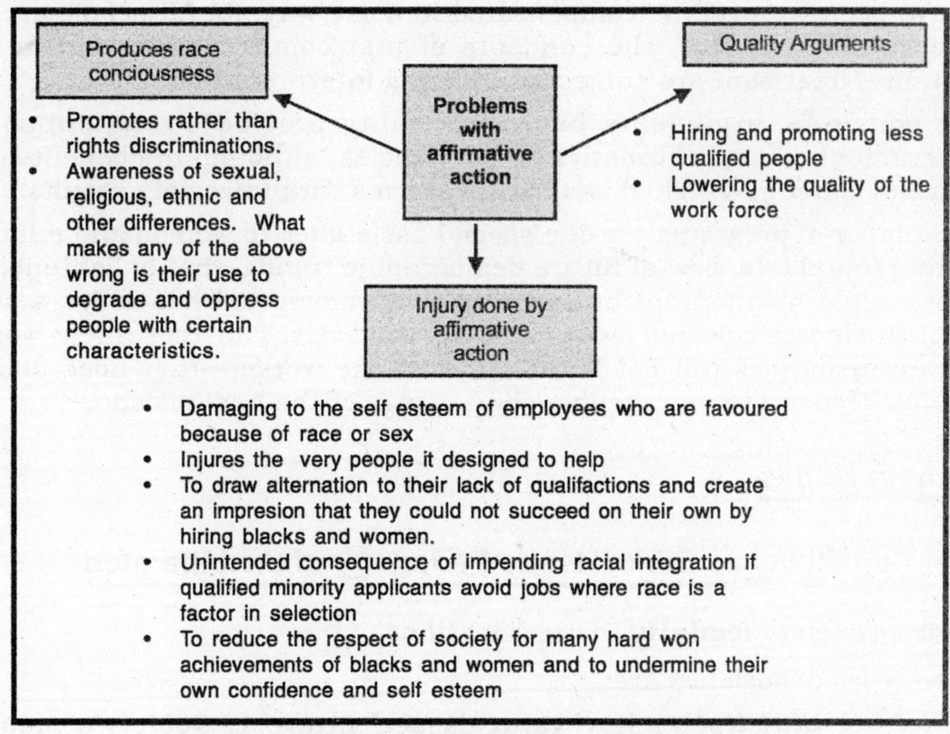

Fig. 4.7 Problems with Affirmative Action

Utilitarians in support of affirmative action programs have proceeded in two steps:

(a) They argue that the end envisioned by affirmative action programs is equal justice.

(b) Secondly they argue that affirmative actions are morally legitimate means for achieving this end.

A third end of affirmative action is to neutralise these competitive advantages with which women and minorities are currently burdened, when they compete with white males and thereby bringing women and minorities to the same starting point in their competitive race with others. This would ensure an equal ability to the latter to compete with white males. The basic end that affirmative action seeks is a more just society-a society in which an individual opportunities are not limited by his or her race or sex. This goal is morally legitimate in so far as it is morally legitimate to strive for a society with greater equality of opportunity.

The ethical issues surrounding discrimination and affirmative action creates problems. In these issues, **Rights** prominently figure as under:

- Rights of people who have been victimised by discrimination
- Rights of people who now bear the burden of correcting past wrongs.

Consideration of justice also have a role (a) Justice requires that people who have been wronged be compensated in some way. (b) All people are to be treated equally. (c) But, the concepts of just compensation and of equal opportunity/treatment are subject to differing interpretations.

To conclude, arguments based on utility provide strong support for antidiscrimination and affirmative action policies, although the benefits of any given policy must be weighed against the harms with uncertain results.

A number of programs provide special assistance to women and minorities on moral grounds. In view of future demographic trends, that enlightened self-interest should also prompt business to give women and minorities a special hand. If businesses do not accommodate themselves to these new workers, American businesses will not be able to find the workers they need and they may suffer recurrent and crippling shortages over the next decade.

4.4 Gender Issues

Gender Sensitivity as Ethical Issue-Pedagogy of the Liberated

Towards a touch of feminity in organisations

Two types of societies are:

(i) ***Individualistic:*** Key value is self interest. Society's modes of functioning are self interest (Swartha); "ego"/Swartha driven demonic; mind set as per Gita.

(ii) ***Collectivistic:*** Emphasis is on the centrality of collectivity (Paramartha) "eco" signifies concern for the ecosystem (concern for others). Societies tend to pass these values to the new generations through number of metaphors. A shift could occur if certain types of metaphors of values are emphasised over other metaphors; divine mind set as per Gita.

Societies are also classified as:

(i) ***Masculanity:*** Implies the aggressive instinct. **Yang** represent, aggression and masculanity; over intellectual, excessively rational, particularistic, extrovert. Human actions are largely governed by the grabbing orientation.

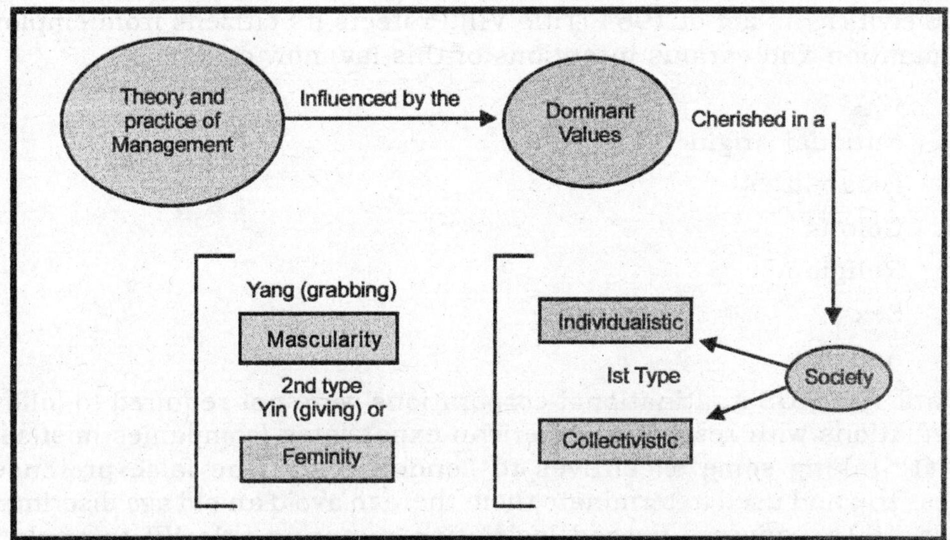

Fig. 4.8 Towards a Touch of Feminity in Organisations

(ii) ***Feminity:*** Indicates the empowering instinct. **Yin** is creative and feminine. It is instinctive and intuitive. It cares for feeling and is emotional. Its passivity is more enduring. Holistic; Introvert. Cooperation and sharing are the basic ethics and human actions are largely governed by the **giving** orientation.

Individualistic and collectivistic nations differ most significantly in that of gender equality.

United Nations 1948 declaration of human rights promotes the concept:

- All human beings are born free and equal in dignity and rights.

Mayer and Cava in 1993, p.701 mentions that 'unequal ethical terrain' exists internationally in the areas of gender and racial equality. We find countries like Sweden, USA and Denmark have made significant advances in the Gender equally, whereas we find Japan and Saudi Arabia are nations that seem to emphasize gender inequality favouring men over women, in all the important positions or leadership roles in business organisations. India is not an exception and it falls in line with these countries. Only fortunate thing in India was, we had a prime minister Indira Gandhi who lead the nation. We had also several central women ministers occupied several portfolios though not key positions. A lady was also a speaker Nazma Heptulla in the Rajya Sabha. What is considered to be acceptable and ethical treatment of women in some nations is viewed as reprehensible in others. In Japan, in the late 1980s, the dean said in an university college that it is a waste of time for females to take up law-this statement made the students to agitate and one of the girls held a sign with, "For women, Sweden is heaven and Japan is hell".

Source: Adapted from Subash Sharma, *Management in New Age: Western Windows Eastern Doors*, Published from New Age International Publishers, New Delhi, with his kind permission.

US civil rights act of 1964 (Title VII) Protects its citizens from employment discrimination and various intentions of this law now cover:

- Race
- National origin
- Disabilities
- Colour
- Religion
- Sex
- Age

Until 1991, US multinational corporations were not required to follow title VII regulations with respect to American expatriates (companies misused this and were taking some executives to London under the false pretense of a business trip and used to terminate them there to avoid an old age discrimination suit). In 1991, congress passed legislation requiring title VII to apply 'extra territorially'.

Discrimination against women were handled by US by having suitable laws to protect them and these are there for decades. However, USA does limit women from working in a few selected areas. Most US women have combat zone restrictions during the war. Over the past 25 to 30 years, there has been a constant tension in the government between those who want to create special programs to help women and minorities move up the economic ladder and those who prefer to minimise to government intervention.

Affirmative action has benefited the minorities section. Women seemed to have fared better than others in USA. Women have filled two thirds of the new jobs created and out number white men in the labour force. The most hazardous jobs tend to be in the manufacturing sector. As the economy shift toward services, the number of work related illness and accidents is expected to decline. Women are not supposed to work in riskiest industries.

4.5 Job Discrimination - Employees Obligation to Firm

Employees main moral duty is to work:

- Towards the goal of the firm.
- To avoid any activities which might cause harm to those goals.
- To obey organisational superiors.

To be unethical, basically is to deviate from the above in order to serve one's own interests in ways that, if illegal, are counted as a form of **'white collar crime'**.

Conflicts of Interest

Conflicts of interest in business arise when an employee or officer of a company is engaged in carrying out a task on behalf of the company and the employee has private interest in the outcome of the task.

- Possibly antagonistic to the best interests of the company.
- Substantial enough that it does or reasonably might affect.
- The independent judgement the company expects the employee to exercise on its behalf.

Conflicts of interest need not be financial. It can also arise when officers or employees of company hold another job or consulting position in an outside firm with which their own company deals or competes with. It may be actual or potential. Conflicts of interest can be created by a variety of different kinds of situations and activities. Two kinds of situations and activities demand further attention:

- Bribes
- Gifts

A **commercial bribe** is a consideration given or offered to an employee by a person outside the firm with the understanding that when the employee transacts business for his own firm, the employee will deal favourably with that person or with that person's firm. The consideration may consist of money, tangible goods, the 'kickback' as part of an official payment, preferential payment, or any other kind of benefit. Accepting gifts may or may not be ethical. The purchasing agent for example, who accepts gifts from the sales person with whom he or she deals without asking for the gifts and without making said gifts a condition of doing business with them, may be doing nothing unethical. The employee of a firm has a contractual agreement to accept only certain specified benefits in exchange for his labour and to use the resources and goods of the firm in pursuit only of the legitimate aims of the firm.

Employee theft is often petty involving the theft of small tools, office supplies or clothing. It occurs at the managerial level through:

- Padding of expense accounts
- White collar crime (embezzlement, larceny, fraud in the handling of trusts, or receiverships, and forgery)

Enbezzlement is the fradulent approapriation of anothers properity by the person to whom it was entrusted.

Larceny is the legal term in England and Ireland for stealing; theft.

The ethics of these forms of theft are not clear. Modern kinds of theft are thefts of various forms of information.

The ethics of using a computer to gain entry into a company's data bank for copying company's computer programs.

Trade secrets: 'Proprietary information' or 'trade secrets' consist of nonpublic information concerning:

- Company's own activities, technologies, future plans, policies or records, if known by competitors affect the company's ability to compete.

- Owned by the company might not be patented or copyrighted since it was developed by the company for its private use from resources it owns or purchased for its private use with its own funds.
- The company indicates through explicit directives through security measures or through contractual agreements with employees that it does not want anyone outside the company to have that information.

4.6 Job Discrimination - Firms Duties to the Employees

The basic moral obligation of the employer to the employees according to the rational view of the firm is to:

- Provide them with the compensation they have freely and knowingly agreed to receive in exchange for their services.

Two main issues related to this obligation are:

- The fairness of wages
- The fairness of employee working conditions.

Working conditions inadequacy, inadequate wages will make the work contract unfair.

Under working conditions, two major things are:

- Job satisfaction (job specialisation is essential at all levels. Jobs must be expended in five dimensions: Skill variety, Task identity, Task significance, Autonomy, Feedback)
- Health and safety (Job accidents are due to work place hazards and hazardous occupations, safety programs are to be implemented).

4.7 Job Discrimination - The Employee Rights

Employers are generally regarded as having the right to make decisions about:

- Hiring
- Promotion
- Discharge as well as wages
- Job assignments and
- Other conditions of work.

Employees have a corresponding right to accept or refuse work on the terms offered and to negotiate for more favourable terms. In the absence of a contract that spells out the conditions under which employment can be terminated, employees can be legally dismissed for any reason or for no reason at all.

Employment at Will

'Employment at will' is a doctrine connected with the moral and legal basis for this particular assignment of rights for employers and employees. **Employment**, according to this doctrine, is an 'at will' relation that comes into existence when two parties willingly enter into an agreement, and the relation continues to exert only as long as both parties will that it do so. Employers and employees both have the right to enter into any mutually agreeable arrangement without outside interference. The task is to examine the justification with regard to the rights that employees have against unjust dismissed and other adverse treatment at the hands of employers.

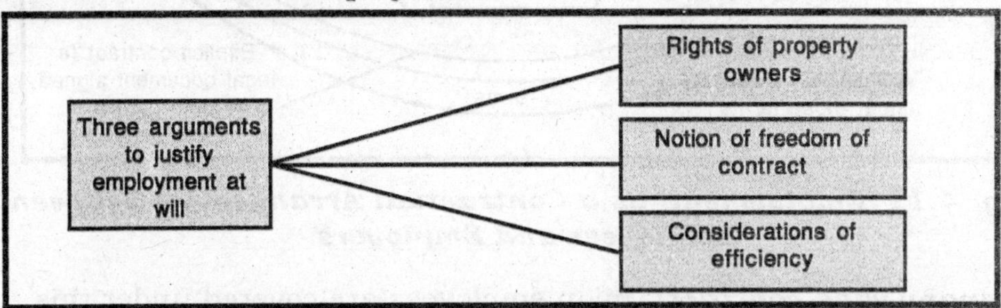

Fig. 4.9 Three Arguments to Justify Employment at Will

The above arguments upholds certain rights of employers. These can also be used to make a strong case for the rights of employees and to provide greater protection from unjust dismissal than the prevailing legal interpretation of employment at will.

(a) Property Rights Argument

Here the assumption is that both employers and employees have property of some kind.

(i) The owner of a factory owns the machinery, raw materials (for the manufacture of the product), some money (for wages); But he lacks labour for operating the machinery and turning the raw material into a finished product.

(ii) Labour (productivity labour) has an economic value, can be said to be a kind of property 'owned' by the worker.

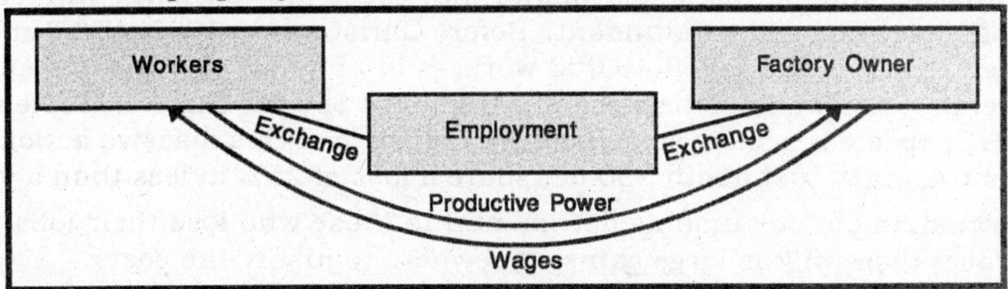

Fig. 4.10 'Employment' as an Exchange of a Worker's Productive Power for the Wages given out in Return by the Factory Owner.

In this exchange, both parties are free to exercise the rights of property ownership.

(b) Freedom of Contract Argument

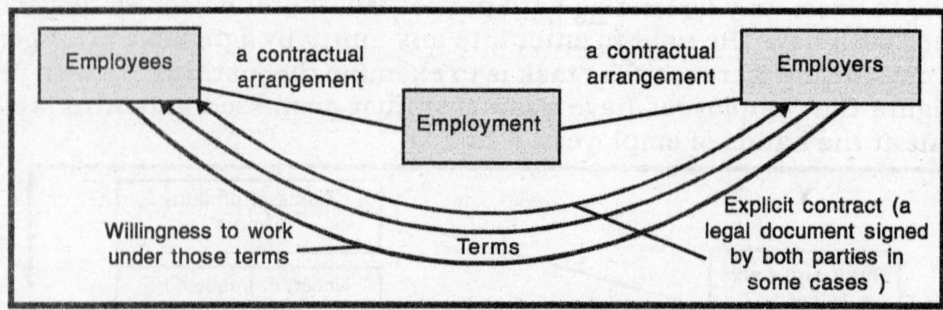

Fig. 4.11 'Employment' as a Contractual Arrangement between Employees and Employers.

Company wide contract: Union employees are covered under this.

Implicit contract: Conditions of employment are understood and tacitly accepted by both parties.

Freedom of contract, like the right to property, is not absolute. Outside the employer-employee relation, there are a number of moral and legal limits on the right of individuals to enter into contractual relations. Children and people who are mentally incompetent cannot be parties to a contract. Children, retarded and insane do not have the mental or emotional capacity to understand the terms of a contract. They are not able to give their consent in a meaningful way.

(c) An Autonomy Agreement

Autonomy can be used to support freedom of contract and with it the doctrine of employment at will - the same concept can also serve as the basis for an argument against employment at will.

Layoffs

Layoffs meaning a dictionary shows that these are discharge (unneeded workers) temporarily; make redundant. Before Christmas in 1995, AT&T in USA announced that it would layoff 40,000 workers in an effort to cut costs and to boost revenues. At that time, the stock was trading at $65 per share. In September 1996 AT&T expected to show some positive response of this massive action, its stock was trading at just about $50 per share a loss of 25% in less than a year.

If **downsizing** is presumably detrimental to those who lose their jobs, one would expect there will be large gains somewhere to justify the costs.

Question is whether downsizing ever ethical? Organisations in every segment of business, industry, government and education are downsizing. Forcing people to leave their employment in rife with ethics related questions. Is downsizing ever ethical? **Downsizing** is not necessarily a desperate move on the part of failing organisations. It can be/probably should be a strategic choice designed to serve the best interests of the organisation. A healthy profit picture and downsizing are not mutually exclusive. It is only a partial answer to the question. Organisation downsizing is not intrinsically unethical.

Wages Empowerment of the Weakest and Uniquest

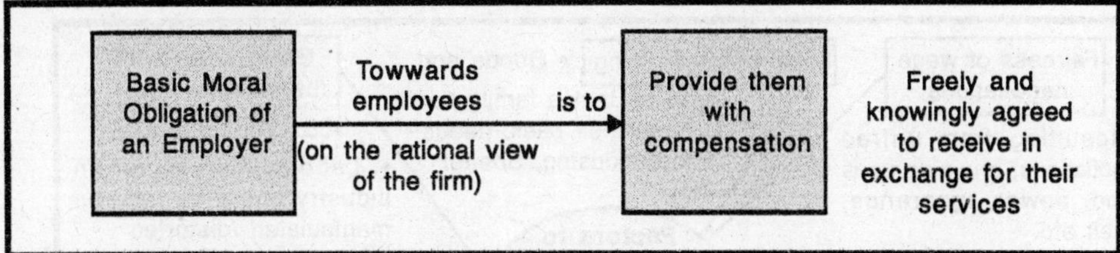

Fig. 4.12 Basic Moral Obligation of an Employer

Two main issues for this obligation are:

- Fairness of wages
- Fairness of employee working conditions.

Both the above are aspects of the compensation employees receive from their services and are related to the question of whether the employee is contracted to take a job freely and knowingly. If the employee is forced to accept a job with inadequate wages or inadequate/improper working conditions, the work contract would be unfair.

Wages

Wages are the principal means (and perhaps the only means) for satisfying the basic economic needs of the worker and the worker's family. Wages are a cost of production and hence to be lowered otherwise, the product will be priced out of the market. Hence every employer is faced with a dilemma of setting fare wages. Two things to be balanced are:

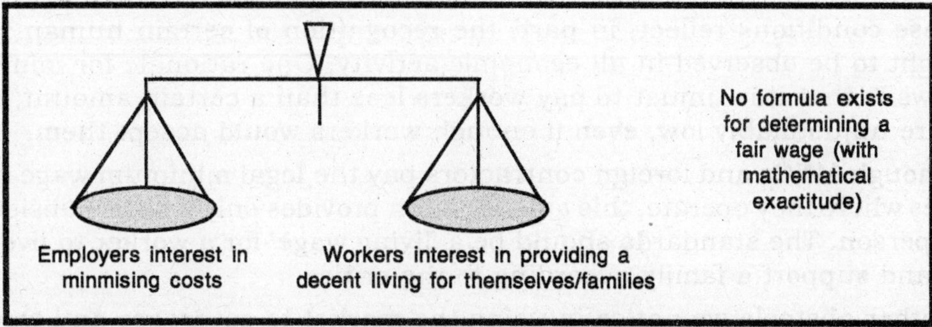

Fig. 4.13 Employers and Workers Interest are to be Balanced

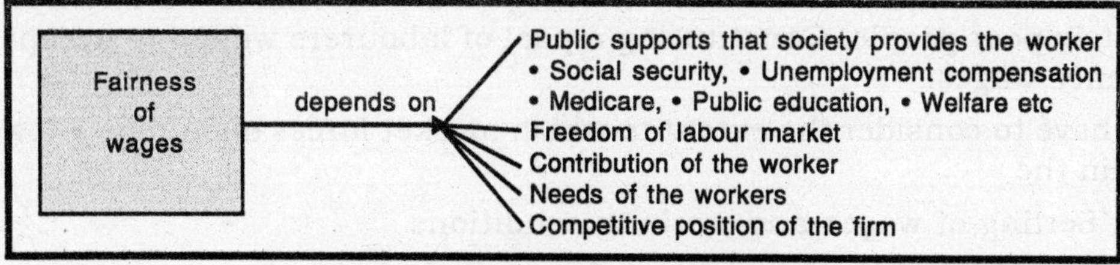

Fig. 4.14 Fairness of Wages

However, following factors to be considered while determining wages and salaries.

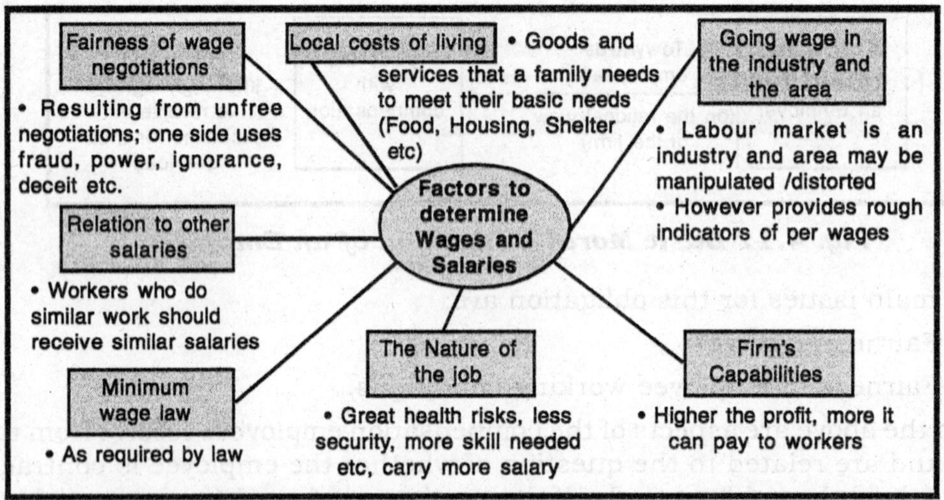

Fig. 4.15 Factors to determine Wages and Salaries

In developed countries, the determination of wages and working conditions results primarily from:

- the competition among employers for desirable workers which compels them to offer high wages and good working conditions
- certain minimum conditions set by law, such as minimum wage laws, fair labour standards and health and safety regulations but not rely solely on the market.

These conditions reflect, in part, the recognition of certain human rights that ought to be observed in all economic activity. One rationale for minimum wage laws is that it is unjust to pay workers less than a certain amount, some wages are unjustifiably low, even if enough workers would accept them.

Although MNCs and foreign contractors pay the legal minimum wage in the countries where they operate, this amount often provides only a basic subsistence for one person. The standards should be a 'living wage' for a worker to live with dignity and support a family according to the critics.

Another obstacle we notice in using the market to set wages and working conditions is the possibility that the conditions for a free market are lacking.

In less developed countries, there will be the mass of unemployed, desperately poor people. Constituting a pool of labourers willing to accept bare subsistence wages.

We have to consider the extent to which market forces should be allowed to operate in the

- Setting of wages and working conditions
- Principles of human rights to be applied

The Working Condition

This can be discussed under two headings:

- **Health and Safety**
- **Job satisfaction**

Health and Safety are discussed in the following para.

Health and Safety

Work place hazards include many hazards like:

- mechanical injury
- extreme heat and cold
- textile fibre dust
- electrocution
- noisy machinery
- chemical fumes
- burns
- rock dust
- skin irritants
- radiation
- mercury, lead, beryllium, arsenic, corrosives, poisons

Although more attention is now being paid to worker safety, occupational accident rates have not declined.

Risk is another unavoidable past of many occupations. Example, a race car driver, a circus performer, a cinema stunt man all accept certain hazards in part of their jobs. If they are fully compensated for taking these risks and freely and knowingly choose to accept the risk in exchange for the added salary, then we may assume that their employer is ethically acted.

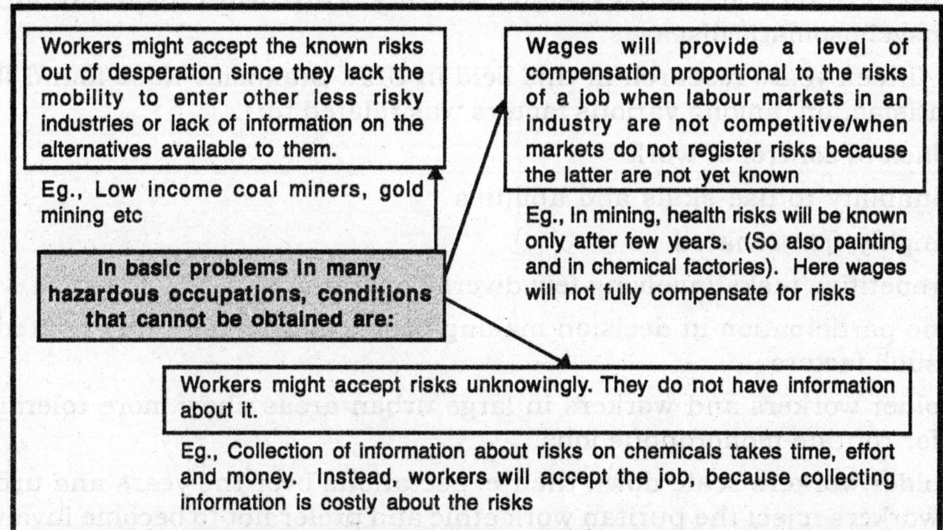

Fig. 4.16 Basic Problems in Many Hazardous Occupations

Employer has a duty in such cases to take steps to ensure that the worker is:

- not being unfairly manipulated into accepting a risk unknowingly, unwillingly (all information about hazards to the jobs are made known to workers)
- Without due compensation; (should offer wages that reflect the risk premium prevalent in other similar competitive labour markets)
- ensured against unknown hazards (with suitable health insurance programmes).

Job Satisfaction

Jobs can be specialised in two dimensions:

- **Horizontal** - Restricting the range of different tasks contained in the job and increasing the repetition of the narrow range of tasks. E.g. painters job.
- **Vertical** - Restricting the range of control and decision making over the activity that the job involves. E.g. plant manager's job.

Job specialisation is most obvious at the operating levels of the organisation. The debilitating effects of this on workers were noted 200 years back by Adam Smith.

- Assembly line work - closely supervised, repetitive type, simple tasks
- Low level clerical jobs - closely monitored, repetitive, dull, fragmented some studies found that workers suffered from mental health problems, ulcers, lack of self-esteem, anxiety and other psychological, psychosomatic diseases.

After fifteen years research in this field in USA, Stamislav Kase found that low job satisfaction, among various factors was related to:

- lack of control of work
- inability to use skills and abilities
- highly fractionated
- repetitive tasks involving few diverse operations
- no participation in decision making poor mental health was related to such factors
- older workers and workers in large urban areas show more tolerance for routine monotonous jobs
- older workers scale down their expectations over the years and urban workers reject the puritan work ethic and prefer not to become involved in their work

How should these problems of job dissatisfaction and mental injury be dealt with is the question?

Oldham, Jansen and Purdy have suggested that there are three determinants of job satisfaction and job must be expanded to influence these three determinants in five dimensions as under:

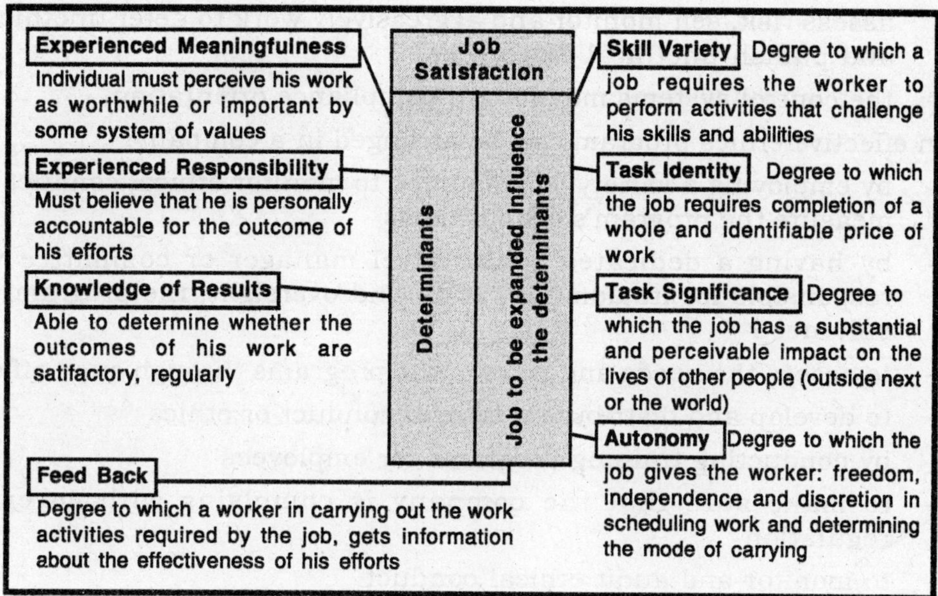

Fig. 4.17 Job Satisfaction Determinants and Jobs to be Expanded to Influence the Determinants

The solution to dissatisfaction is perceivable enlargement of the narrow specialised jobs that give rise to dissatisfaction.

4.8 The Need for Organisaitonal Ethics Program

Organisations develop ethics programs by:

— establishing

— communicating

— monitoring ethical values, and

— monitoring the legal requirements.

The above characterise the organisation's history, culture, industry and operating environment.

Ethics program helps to:

— scrutinise employees to potential legal and ethical issues within their work environments.

— ensure employees understand companies values.

— comply with companies policies and conduct

— make employees to determine what behaviours a company deems acceptable

— work as organisational control systems to create predictability in employee behaviour. Organisations are to encourage companies to assess risk, self monitor and aggressively work to deter unethical acts and punish unethical employees

— the control systems may have a compliance orientation.

An effective ethics program can be arranged in a company:

— by employing a variety or resources to monitor ethical conduct and to measure the program's effectiveness

— by having a dedicated senior level manager or committee who is responsible for its administration and oversight, the program can be enhanced

— to assess the needs and risks of the programs through such officers

— to develop and distribute a code of conduct or ethics

— by conducting training programs for employees

— to make sure that the company is complying with government regulation

— to monitor and audit ethical conduct

— to take action on possible violations of the company's code

— to review and update the code

— to establish and maintain a confidential service to answer questions about ethical issues

— to reduce the possibility of penalties and negative public reactions to misconduct

— as good corporate citizen and to recognise the importance of ethics to successful business activities of the company.

Ethical compliance can be ensured:

— by designing activities to achieve organisational objectives using available resources and given existing constraints

— with proper codes of ethics so that the company complies with values, rules and policies that support an ethical climate

— with uniform policies and standards, employees will have no difficulty in determining what is acceptable behaviour in the company.

Both ethics and compliance programs are implemented in many firms which are used:

— to avoid common mistakes generally made

— failure to answer fundamental questions about the goals of such programs

— to avoid in not setting realistic and measurable program objectives

— failing to have its senior management taking the lead of the ethics program

— developing program materials to cover the needs of the average employee etc.

To develop an ethics program, follow these steps:
• Firms values are to be assessed (self assessment) and the ethics and compliance programs as on date followed • Top managers to commit for their involvement • Publish, post, make codes of ethics available • Communicate ethical standards and understandable to all the concerned • Provide timely training to provide enough knowledge to the concerned • Provide resources; employees can seek advice and report their problems from such resources • Ensure consistent and thorough implementation • Enforce consistently, fairly and promptly • Use appropriate methods to monitor and assess • Ensure continuous improvement

4.9 Codes of Conduct

Codes may refer to general areas of business conduct or may apply to a specific area of the firm's business.

E.g. Reebok has human rights production standards in ensuring that the factories it uses have humane working conditions. Other strategies exist like (i) to communicate corporate values (ii) to continually update corporate programmes to work effectively. Some firms have used corporate ombud persons. An **ombudperson** is someone who is neither an advocate for the firm nor for an employee; Instead he administers a general reporting structure that holds fairness to all as an important goal.

Company Codes

Codes of practice and codes of conduct tend to be the most prescriptive in time. The differences between the two are less significant than the fact that they exist at all. Some might argue that good people will not need the guidance of such a code, where as the malicious, selfish or even stupid will ignore it. In both the cases, the existence of a code makes no difference. From this, we understand that good people always know what to do, and that those who do the wrong thing always do so for reprehensible reasons. It depends on the assumption that we can divide the people neatly into the good and the bad, though this is more transparently false.

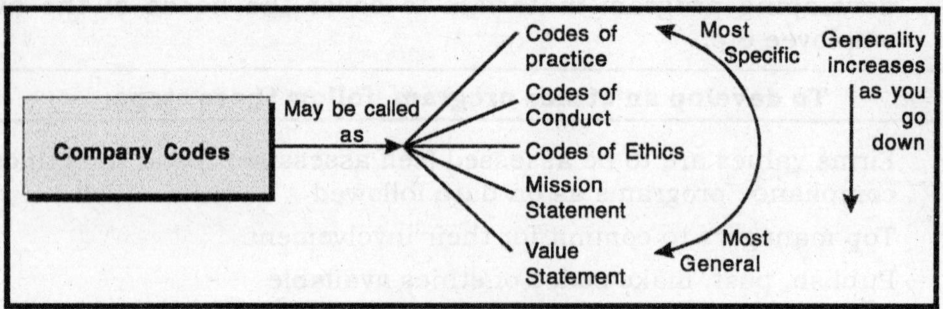

Fig. 4.18 Company Codes

We all need to know, or try to work out, how general principles are to be made to apply to concrete particular cases. Different people may, in good faith and quite justifiably, come to different conclusions about the rightness of a particular act in particular circumstances, and in private life this may not matter.

For example: A judgement to promote a particular person may be totally defensible, but it has to be seen in the light of a company's record on promoting, say, women or members of the minorities. The persons promoted, or not promoted, have a right to be treated not yet reasonably but equitably. Those who operate the procedures, must not be seen as personally responsible for the outcome.

One way of seeing codes is by analogy with the law. Just as case law and rules of process are needed in order to make it possible for statute and common law to be implemented, a code of practice mediates between general.

Surveys conducted *in UK & USA*	Year	No.of *companies surveyed*	Usable *responses*	Company codes *found in companies*
Wesley's Survey	1988	300	100	55
in UK	1992	400	159	113
Langlois and Schlegel milch	1990	1481	370	186@
Weaver's Survey	1992	NA	NA	83% of the
	1992	Fortune 1000	1000	companies surveyed 930

@ 22.8% had policy statement on ethics

42.6% had guidelines for the proper conduct of business.

From the above, it may be noted that in the USA, the members and percentages of companies having codes of ethics is higher than that is found in the UK.

The summary found by Weaver in 1993 is as under:

Survey at:	**Codes found in companies**
USA companies	83% (Second survey showed 93%)
European companies	50%

Nash in 1992 made a comparative survey of USA and European companies and observed as indicated below:

USA Companies	Ethics activity is more widespread, more sophisticated, moving deeper into the organisation.
European Companies	Ethics activity is still not attracted to formalise ethics statements and codes. Codes and Ethics programmes appeared to be less frequent. These are new and more found in large companies but more widely disseminated than in the USA.

Reasons for adopting a Code of Conduct

(a) One of the reasons for adopting a code of conduct may be to see themselves as self-regulatory in order to avoid regulation by government.

E.g. Strategy adopted by press, customs, stock market, industries like tobacco, liquor sellers in regard to advertising.

(b) This may be a wish by a profession or a company to improve its image with the general public, or with its peers in the industry. Reasons might be prudential, since they are aimed at benefiting (or avoiding harm to) the company or profession in question.

(c) In some cases, drawing up codes of behaviour are clearly moral in character. Companies where they feel that they have to face special problems or particular temptations and cannot cope up with ordinary moral judgement.

A successful code is the result of following three conditions:

Three major concerns.

- How business may make effective use of company codes?
- The impact of company codes on business practice from a variety of perspectives?
- To analyse company codes using theories of ethics?

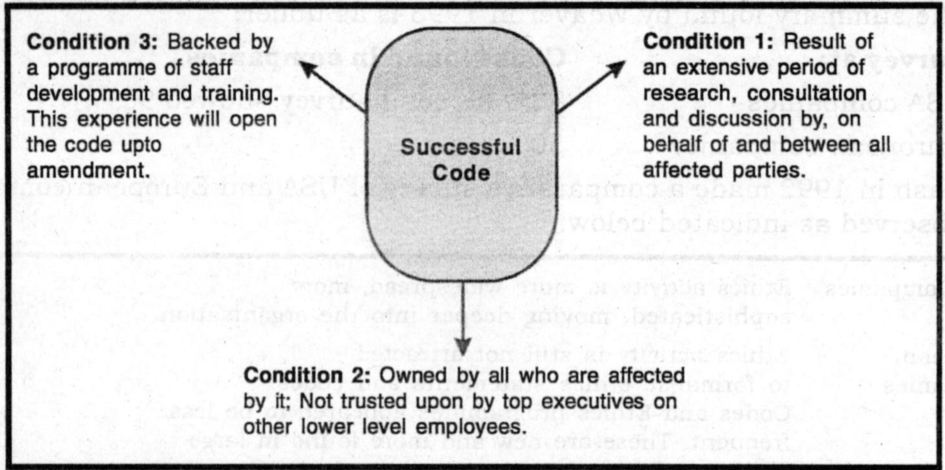

Fig. 4.19 Successful Code and Conditions

Individual codes draw upon:

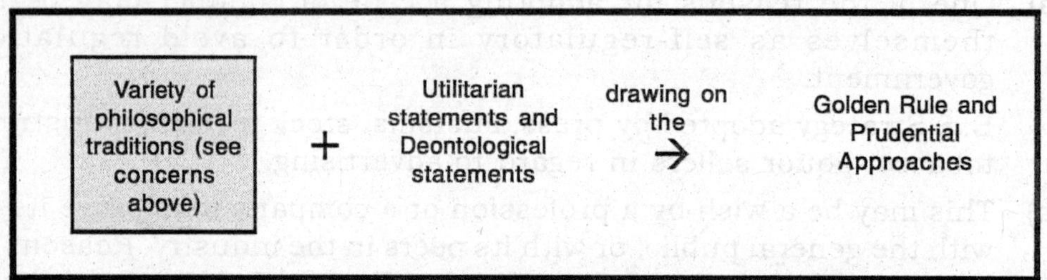

Fig. 4.20 Golden Rule and Prudential Approaches

The contents of the codes lack many a times philosophical consistency (may be due to the product of the circumstances in which the code is drafted and the positions of those responsible for drafting it).

Most of the codes which are developed are found to be mostly by senior managers of the company from a defensive posture. They would have developed a prudential tone with some basis in utilitarian theory. They would have developed a code for their employees which lays down clear and enforceable rules concerning relations with the outside related agencies at all levels (like government). However the code might ignore many other aspects of employee behaviour which have ethical implications. The code has been fashioned to suit particular circumstances for particular reasons. Special guidance/advice may be needed in order to protect their members or employees from moral risk. Finally, they may feel the need for disciplinary sanctions against a minority for the sake of either general public or their own members or employees. A code may also be used to play a training role in inculcating and promoting the particular values and standards which characterise a profession or a company and which members or employees needed to be internalised in order to play a dominant role.

Differences exist between professional and company codes in some respects.

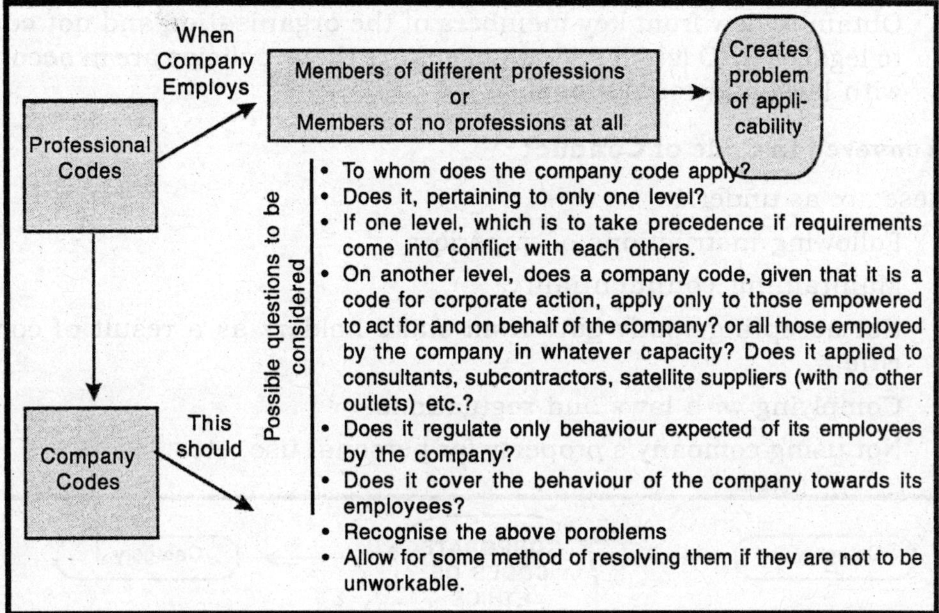

Fig. 4.21 Differences between Professional and Company codes

How to Develop Codes of Ethics

- There is an universal feeling or may even be considered as a real risk that codes exist only on paper and not in practice. Cynic's always claim that codes are for impressing outsiders. They are not for affecting the behaviour of the company or its employees codes are always to be:
- Explicit
- Sufficiently detailed
- Internalised by those to whom and by whom they will be applied
- Worthy of name must be embodied in the behaviour and the practices of the relevant group of people.

Two major activities found are

- Actually producing the written part of the code
- Implementation (cannot be done only once. It is a continuous process)

How to develop a Code of Conduct?

Carter McNamara suggests the following three guide lines:

1. Identify key behaviours (needed to adhere to the ethical values proclaimed in your code of ethics).
2. Include wording (that indicates all employees are expected to conform to behaviours specified in the code of conduct).

3. Obtain review from key members of the organisation and not confined to legal or HRD (such reviews to ensure these policies are in accordance with laws and regulations).

Topics covered in Code of Conduct

These are as under:

- Following instructions of superiors
- Maintaining confidentiality
- Not accepting costly gifts from stake holders as a result of company rule
- Complying with laws and regulations
- Not using company's property for personal use, etc.

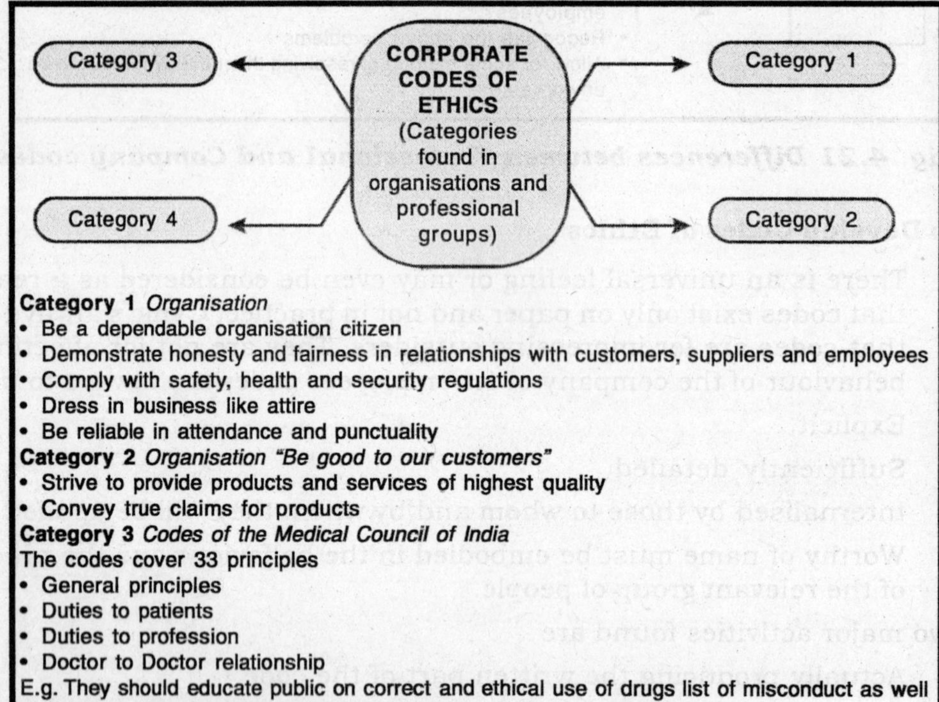

Category 1 *Organisation*
- Be a dependable organisation citizen
- Demonstrate honesty and fairness in relationships with customers, suppliers and employees
- Comply with safety, health and security regulations
- Dress in business like attire
- Be reliable in attendance and punctuality

Category 2 *Organisation "Be good to our customers"*
- Strive to provide products and services of highest quality
- Convey true claims for products

Category 3 *Codes of the Medical Council of India*

The codes cover 33 principles
- General principles
- Duties to patients
- Duties to profession
- Doctor to Doctor relationship

E.g. They should educate public on correct and ethical use of drugs list of misconduct as well given eg. refusing to perform a sterilisation operation on religious grounds

Category 4 *All India Management Association (AIMA)*

A member of a management association affiliated to AIMA shall:
- Try his best to organise the resources available to him with a view to optimise their use in attaining the objectives of the organisation
- Consider the guide to good management practices conveyed by AIMA from time to time in carrying out his tasks
- Comply with the Indian laws relating to the management of his organisation and do his best to operate within the spirit of these laws
- So order his conduct as to uphgold and further the reputation of professional management and management movement

Fig. 4.22 Corporate Codes of Ethics (As examples)

Gary Edwards, Director of the Ethics Resource Centre says over 90% of United States Corporations had ethics codes in 1985.

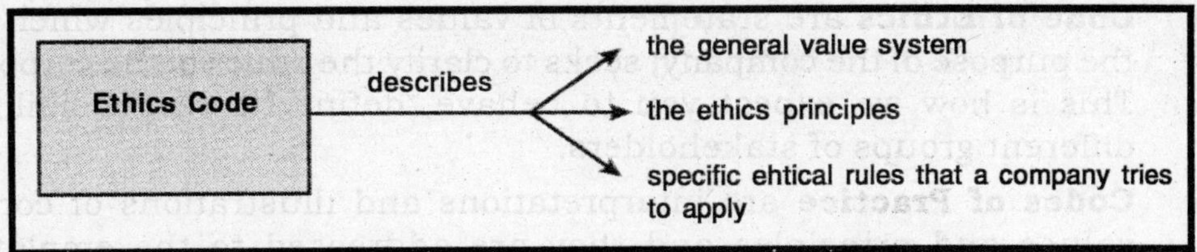

Fig. 4.23 What Does Ethics Code Describes?

Ethical codes help employees know what is expected in ethical terms when they face an uncertain situation. Codes vary considerably among companies.

A codes impact on employee behaviour is weakened if its purpose is primarily to make the company look good or if it is intended to give the company's top executives a legal defense when illegal or unethical acts are committed by lower ranking employees. The most effective codes are those drawn up with the corporation and participation of employees and those having rewards and penalties that are spelled out and enforced. Majority of managers are under the impression that a self developed code will help improve ethical behaviour in their industries.

Corporate Codes

A firm must first articulate its values, its priorities. The most important form of values articulation and communication is:

- A corporate mission
- Code of conduct or code of ethics

After defining the firms individual value structure, individual decision makers within the firm have guidance in connection with difficult dilemmas. Codes refer to:

- General areas of business conduct

or

- Specific area of the firm's business.

Some firms use corporate ombudspersons to communicate corporate values as well as to continually update corporate programmes and make them more effective. An **ombudsperson** is a person officially appointed to investigate complaints against public authorities. He is neither an advocate for the firm nor the employee but he or she often administers a general reporting structure that hold fairness to all parties.

Michael Deck explains research conducted to gather and to analyse 200 codes of conduct. Many firms have codes. But they are not communicated to stakeholders and also not adhered to. 'Codes of Ethics,' 'Codes of Conduct' and

'Code of Practice' are used interchangeably. However each basic code type has a different intent and purpose.

- **Code of Ethics** are statements of values and principles which define the purpose of the company; seeks to clarify the ethics of the corporation. This is how we expect you to behave, define its responsibilities to different groups of stakeholders.
- **Codes of Practice** are interpretations and illustrations of corporate values and principles and they are addressed to the employee as individual decision maker.
- **Codes of conduct** are statements of rules (comprised of a list of rules). It says 'This is what you must not do or you must do.'

4.10 Ethics Training Programmes and Communication

Elements of Programmes for Building Commitment to Ethics

The following six elements of programmes for building commitment to ethics are needed. Out of which ethics training is one among them.

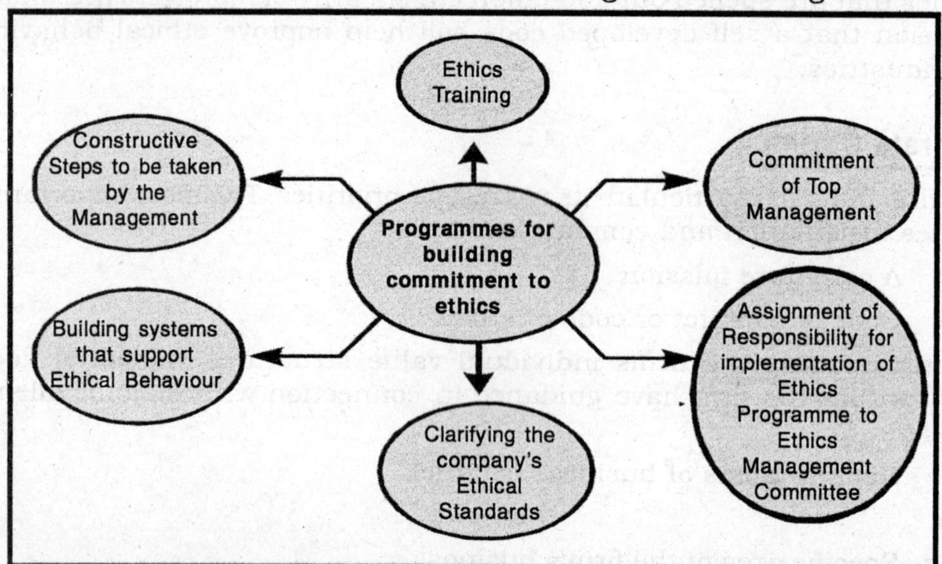

Fig. 4.24 Programmes for Building Commitment to Ethics

(i) Commitment of Top Management

- Top management to ensure the following:
  - adequate resources are invested
  - ethical behaviour is truly supported
  - to provide leadership through example

- ethics is folded into every aspect of corporate life-including strategic planning process e.g. (i) Strategic management, (ii) HRM, (iii) Participative management, (iv) Quality management, (v) Ethical decision making
- involving the chairman of the company to fully support ethics programme and also announce it and ensure its implementation
- formation of an ethics committee at board of director's level. After establishing it has to oversee development and operation of ethics programme

(ii) Assignment of responsibility for implementation of Ethics Programme to Ethics Management Committee

Some senior level manager is to be made responsible for development, coordination of ethics programme. He is to be assisted by full time manager to implement the ethics programme. The full time manager is well versed in business aspects and as well as act as a business ethics specialist and function as ombuds person. He can also have ethics management committee of senior officers for administrating policies and procedures. The most important aspect is the process of reflection and dialogue while preparing codes, policies and procedures etc. The ethics management committee takes decisions in groups, which should be cross functional teams. These code of ethics can avoid the occurrence of ethical dilemmas.

(iii) Clarifying the Company's Ethical Standards

In written statements or ethical code or credos, "codes of ethics," this includes:

- Company's mission, purpose or beliefs.
- Main stockholders, employees, suppliers, consumers, community etc. are stakeholders to whom company is obliged. Specific obligations to above groups or behaviours required or permitted are to be laid.
- Penalties for violation of obligations of the management.
- An organisational code of ethics is to be firmly supported by top management and equitably enforced through the reward and punishment system (Robert Kreitner has said that selective or uneven enforcement is the quickest way to kill the effectiveness of an ethical code).

(iv) Building Systems that support Ethical Behaviour and Communications

The two aspects are:

- Ensuring that systems are established e.g. audit is done to monitor and enforce the ethical behaviour

- New employees are being informed of ethical standards
- Annual performance appraisal includes observance of standards and deviations noted in files (corrective actions, managers have taken or not?
- Ethical guidelines also indicates that personal integrity and moral fibre are as important to advancement as technical competence (as per GTE Corporation, USA)

- Communicating the company's values to all employees is vital
  - Employees should alert the company about any unethical behaviour that is "Internal whistle-blowing" made higher management aware of violations in time.
- Communicate the company's values and standards of ethical business conduct to employees.
- Inform employees of company's policies and procedures regarding ethical business conduct.
- Establish processes to help employees obtain guidance and resolve questions regarding compliance with the company's standard of conduct and value.
- Establish criteria for ethics education and awareness projects and for coordinations compliance overnight activities.

(v) Constructive steps taken by the Management

The challenge for today's management is to create a suitable organisational climate wherein the "**whistle blowing**" need is reduced. The various steps are:

- Encourage the free expression of controversial and dissenting view points
- Streamline the organisation's grievance procedure so that problems receive a prompt and fair hearing
- Find out what employees think about the organisation's social responsibility policies and make appropriate changes
- Make the employees aware that management respects them and is sensitive to their individual consciences
- Recognise the harsh treatment of a whistle blower will probably lead to adverse public opinion
- Company to provide advisory service in case doubts/clarification.

(vi) Ethics Training

In all disciplines and areas, business firms train their employees like:

- accounting methods
- sales and marketing techniques
- purchasing procedures

- safety procedures
- technical systems etc.

The question arises why not training in ethics also? More corporations are providing training in ethics also. Managers are given training in some companies like General Dynamics, McDonnell Douglas in USA. Even the supervisors as well as others who are likely to encounter an ethical question at work are provided with training. The training programmes acquaint employees with:

- Official company policy on ethical issues; How such policies can be translated into the specifics of every day decision making.
- Simulated case studies based on actual events in the company used to illustrate how to apply ethical principles on the job problems of everyday.

Arrange Workshops for employees frequently and to make aware of company commitment to ethics. These workshop may be for half days and are arranged by line managers. Thus concerted and systematic attention to ethics will reduce and eliminate such risks. Carefully designed and administered ethics training programems can bring positive contributions to the company.

Rober Kreitner has specified key features of effective training programmes.

- Top management support
- Open discussion on resolving of realistic cases/dilemmas
- A clear focus identification on ethical themes in all training
- A mechanism for anonymously reporting ethical violations
- An organisation climate that rewards ethical conduct
- Provide all staff with a copy of code of ethics and also code of conduct. Also explain all employees the working of the same with their role.

Can Ethics be taught?

It would be interesting to know just why some college and university programmes require their students to take a course on ethics. Does this requirement rely on a belief that ethics or moral philosophy is designed to make people good and is capable of doing that.

Similarly, Question of 'whether ethics can be taught? the students will give different answers:

"If it can't be taught, why are we taking this class?"

"Look at public immorality"

"These people haven't been taught properly"

"Although certain ideas or types of knowledge can be taught, ethical matter cannot, because it is a matter of individual choice"

"Ethics could be taught, but some people do not learn the lessons well"

The general conclusion can be drawn from the above, we tend to think of ethics as the set of values or principles held by individuals and groups.

Each individual has his own ethics and groups also have sets of values with which they tend to identify. We can think of ethics as a study of the various sets of values that people do have. This could be done historically and comparatively, for example, or with a psychological interest is determining how people form their values and when they tend to action them. Ethics also can be thought as a critical enterprise. We would then ask whether any particular set of values or beliefs is better than any other? Are there good reasons for preferring them?

We will examine various ethical values and types of reasoning from a critical or evaluative stand point. This examination will also help us come to a better understanding of our own and various societies' values.

Ethics is a branch of philosophy. 'Ethics' or 'moral philosophy' asks basic questions about the good life, about what is better and worse, about whether there is any objective right or wrong, and how we know if there is. Although not everyone agrees on what philosophy is, let us think of it as a discipline or study in which we ask and attempt to answer-basic questions about key areas or subject matters of human life and about pervasive and significant aspects of experience.

Ethics Hot Lines

Ethics Hot Lines are direct channel of communication between the affected employee on ethica

l issues and a member of ethics committee, who on receiving the confidential call, quickly investigates the problem.

Steps are taken the identity of the caller as secret, in order to encourage more and more employees to report any deviant behaviour.

To overcome problems, an ethical organisation should adopt the following system known as **Ethics Hotline**.

- The organisation should install a toll-free telephone number that any employee can call to report suspected legal or ethical violations to an 'ethics officer' whose full-time responsibility is responding to any calls that come in. If the employee wishes to remain anonymous he or she is assigned a number that can be used for identification in any future communications.
- The ethics officer should be empowered to conduct a full investigation of the allegations and to take the results of the allegations to the higher management or corporate management.
- Such a toll-free telephone is called the **'Ethics Hotline'**. The organisation must ensure that all employees are aware of the hotlines and are encouraged to use it.

4.11 Systems to Monitor and Enforce Ethical Standards

Building systems that support ethical behaviour and communications/ standards etc has already been in para 4.10.

Establishing Ethical Standards

The ethics programme and compliance programs and the systems and regarding ethical standards are mentioned in para 4.8.

The considerable concern over ethics is reflected in the large number of organisations that have attempted to codify ethical standards. Such codes are usually based upon legal standards, industry practice, religious ethical ideals, and the values professed by their developers etc. Standards must be communicated before they can be effective. It can certainly be argued that there are merits to an explicit statement of ethical ideals. The exercise seems futile, however, unless employees or members comply with those standards. Ensuring compliance is a weakness of most codes. For the manager who wishes to secure subordinate's adherence to a set of ethical standards, there is no practicable alternative to making those standards part of the system of performance evaluation and control.

For maintaining ethical standards in marketing, the firm itself must provide the standards and the control system, should it not be satisfied with existing performance.

Implications

These are:

- **Ethical attacks** on marketing will continue, as long as there is heterogeneity of opinion over what are the 'right' moral values, there will be conflict. There is also an inherent danger of the competitive system inducing downward spiralling of ethical standards, to a lower bound set by legal standards.
- A good case can be made that it is unfair to expect firms in competitive industries to do other than stay within the law. Critics must look to the law, rather than spontaneous action of companies for setting new ethical standards for marketing practice. Only then consistent standards may be obtained.
- Many marketing managers do not view the regulatory incursions of government dispassionately. The onus on those who feel the way is to provide a non-governmental remedy, through establishing and maintaining by management control, effective ethical standards for company decisions. A first step toward such a system is to open up lines of communication to those who criticise marketing ethics.
- Building systsm to monitor and enforce ethical standards is essential in the organisations who are concerned with ethics.

4.12 Ethical Audit

Ethical audit is unique to each company based on:

— Size of the company

— Industry

— Corporate culture

— The risks involved

— The regulatory environment in which it operated

The framework for conducting ethics involves following steps:

— Securing the commitment of the firm's top management and its board of directors. Top management support is needed for the success of audit.

— Establishing a committee or team to oversee the audit process. Auditing ethics is conducted by either the board of director's financial audit committee or by its managers or ethics officers. An inside official from the firm or an outside consultant may be recruited to coordinate the audit and report the results.

— Establish the scope of the audit; considering the risk of the firm available opportunities to manage ethics; define the key subject matter, risk areas important to the ethics audit.

— Review of firm's mission, goals, values and policies examine both formal documents that make explicit commitments with regard to ethical, legal or social responsibility with less formal documents (market materials, work place policies, ethics policies and standards for suppliers or vendors).

— Identify tools or methods that can be employed to measure the firm's progress and then collect and analyse the relevant information.

— Verification of the results of the data analysis by an independent party such as a social/ethics audit consultant or a financial accounting firm that offers social auditing services or a non-profit special interest group with auditing experience.

— Report the audit findings to the board of directors and top executives and if approved, to external stockholders. The report informs the purpose, scope, the methods used in the audit, the role of the auditor, auditing guidelines followed, reporting guidelines followed by the company.

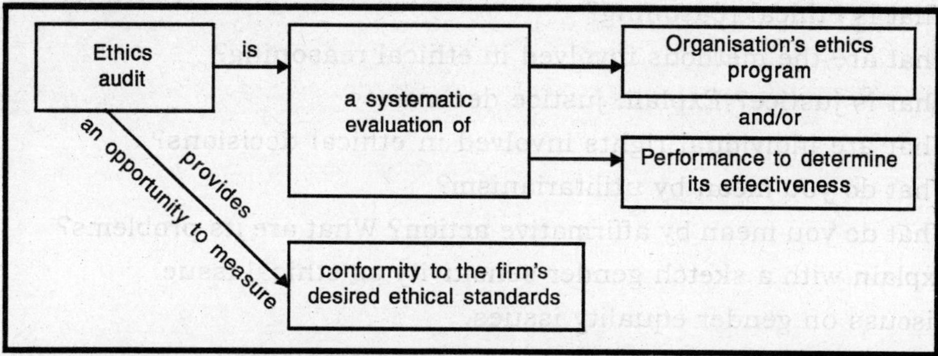

Fig. 4.25 Definition of Ethics Audit and Purpose

Ethics Audit may be conducted as a component of social audit (social audit is the process of assessing and reporting a business's performance in fulfilling the economic, legal, ethical and philanthric social responsibilities needed by its stakeholders)

Ethics auditing helps:

— as a tool to be employed by the company to identify and measure its ethical commitment to stakeholders.

— to demonstrate its commitment to improve strategic planning including their compliance with legal, ethical, and social responsibility standards.

— highlights trends, improve organisational learning, facilitates communication and working relationships

— improved relationship with stakeholders in businesses

— presents the public relation arises associated with ethical or legal misconduct

— potential to create risks is a drawback.

Questions

1. Explain what is job discrimination? Discuss on its nature and extent.
2. Which are the discrimination elements. Explain discrimination its elements, forms, practices.
3. Define disparate treatment.
4. Which are the diffent job dicrimination forms? Explain each one of them.
5. Explain the different discriminatory practices widely recognised?
6. Explain a policy for non-discrimination.
7. What do you mean by Job analysis, Job description, Job specification.
8. Discuss on the ethical arguments against discrimination.
9. How do you avoid discrimination?

10. What is ethical reasoning?
11. What are the methods involved in ethical reasoning?
12. What is justice? Explain justice decision.
13. What are individual rights involved in ethical decisions?
14. What do you mean by utilitarianism?
15. What do you mean by affirmative action? What are its problems?
16. Explain with a sketch gender sensitivity as ethical issue.
17. Discuss on gender equality issues.
18. What are the employer's obligations to an employee?
19. What are the employer rights and organisational policies in an organisation?
20. Explain all aspects about employee's duties to the firm.
21. What do you mean by layoffs? Explain.
22. Explain the following:
    (a) Balance of employers and workers' interest
    (b) Fairness of wages
    (c) Factors to determine wages and salaries
23. What are the basic moral obligation of an employer?
24. Explain the fairness of wages and what are the factors to determine wages and salaries?
25. Explain the need for organisational ethics program?
26. Define code, explain company code. Explain how codes of practice and codes of conduct are helpful in the organisation? How do you develop them?
27. What are the reasons for adopting codes of conduct?
28. What does ethics code describes? Explain the function of corporate codes.
29. Discuss on ethics training program and the way of communicating company's values to employees.
30. Can ethics be taught?
31. Explain the need for systems to monitor and enforce ethical standards?
32. Write notes on:
    (a) Ethics hot line
    (b) Ethical audit and its purpose.

MODULE 5

Business Ethics in a Global Economy

5.1 Ethical Perceptions and International Business

Globalisation is the process by which the economic and social systems of nations are connected together so that goods services, capital, and knowledge move freely between nations.

Economic System: is the system a society uses to provide the goods and services it needs to survive and flowrish. The two main economic tasks are : Commands and markets.

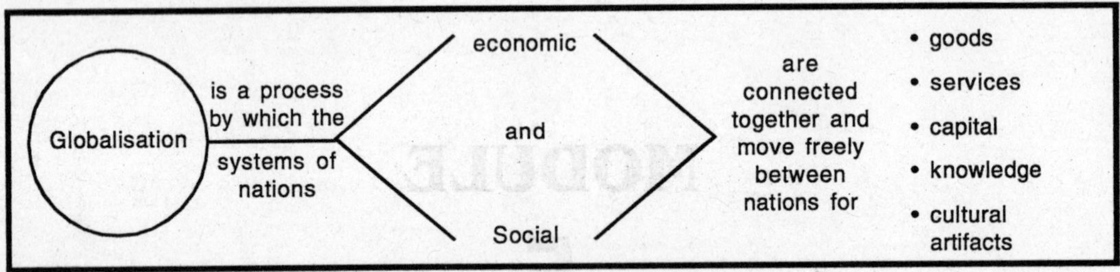

Fig. 5.1 Globalisation

A **multinational Corporate** is a company that maintains in many host countries the following operations:

— Manufacturing
— Marketing
— Service
— Administration

Globalisation process has several components:

— Lowering of trade barriers
— Raise of world wide open markets
— The creation of global communication
— Transportation systems such as the Internet and Global Shipping.
— The development of international trade organistions such as world trade organisation, the establishment of international financial institutions such as the World bank and the International Monetary fund (that have facilitated the international flow of capital and the spread of multinational corporations).

It has brought the world significant economic benefits and multinationals have established several factories in different countries with low labour cost; bring jobs, skills, income, technology to all regions of the world including the underdeveloped, raising the standard of living, providing consumers everywhere with lower priced goods. It has reduced the poverty of over 3 billions people in developing nations, opened their borders to global trade in India, China, Bangladesh, Brazil etc.

Global Business

Business is being conducted across national boundaries. We have seen many large multinational corporations (MNCs) that have long operated in other countries are being joined by many smaller domestic firms going abroad for the first time. Intense competition is forcing companies worldwide to enter the global market place whether they are ready or not. Especially in India, software companies in IT has grown tremendously and are entering globally. Such development presents a host of ethical problems that managers are unprepared to address. Many of these problems arise from the diversity of business standards around the world and especially from the lower standards prevailing in less developed countries (LDCs). Some of the companies experience difficulty and hence adopt:

- Paying low wages (exploitive wages)
- Imposing stringent or unsafe working conditions (standards are kept low compared to US, but high compared to local standards)

Countries with pervasive corruption

- Violation of human rights.
- May even try to avoid fair share of taxes.

MNCs exploit the cheap labour and natural resources of LDCs without making investments that would advance economic development. The above working though it benefit to some extent to LDCs, it still have disadvantage in the distribution of the gains which is usually unequal.

The other question arises about the companies operating in foreign countries is the proper role of corporations in political affairs. They consider themselves as guests in the host countries and refrain from influencing local governments. Further bribery is universally recognised as wrong. It is a practice that is viewed differently around the world. A thorough examination of the difference in the ethical outlook of business people in different parts of the world (specially in Asia) and the development of ethics of codes that attempt to guide responsible business conduct worldwide is needed.

Major Questions about Companies who go Globally

The main charge against global corporations who move to different parts of the world is that they adopt different standards, doing in less developed as wrong. However, many criticised practices are said to be legal in the countries in question and are not considered to be unethical by local standards.

(i) Should global companies are bound by the prevailing morality of the home country?

(ii) Should they follow the practices of the host country and adopt the adage (Be a Roman, while you are in Rome).

(iii) Are there special ethical standards that apply when business is conducted across national boundaries?

(iv) What are the appropriate standards for global business?

No easy answers are available for these questions.

For question (ii), there are two extremes to answer:

- **Absolutism** (when in Rome or anywhere else, do as you would at home)
- **Relativism** (when in Rome, do as the Romans do)

In absolutism, business ought to be conducted in the same way the world over with no double standards; to observe a single code of conduct in their dealings everywhere.

In Relativism, the only guide for business conduct abroad is what is legally and morally accepted in any given country where it operates. There seems to be no fault in adopting this, and at the same time it is not wholly justified either.

The debate over Absolutism and Relativism is shown under four points:

Ethical Convergence

Having studied the diversity of ethical outlooks in the world, is it possible to agree on ethical convergence or a set of standards for business worldwide. Such a goal is possible if globalisation is to succeed. The very phenomenon of globalisation makes it clear that there must be a globalisation of ethics as per Hans Küng Full agreement is not needed or even desirable. But globalisation requires a commitment to some core standards or atleast a willingness to abide by them.

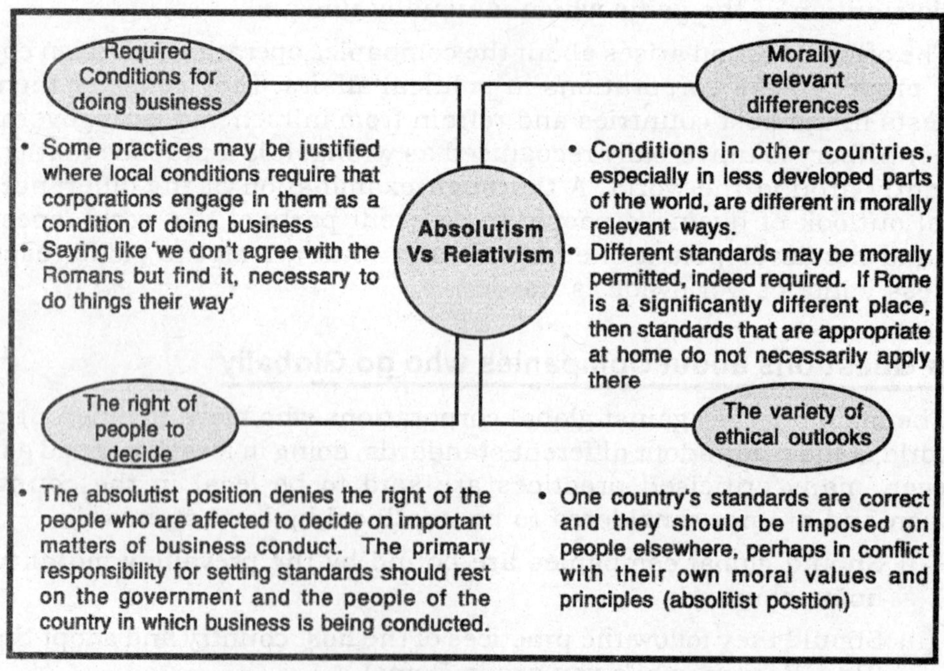

Fig. 5.2 Absolutism Vs Relativism

The Ethical Relativism is again explained at the end of this moduel in Page No.

Substantial agreement is being achieved through a number of codes that have been developed by international organisations involving:

- governments
- religious bodies
- private individuals

Foundational document for human rights

- United Nations Universal Declaration on Human Rights - 1948
- UN adopted two agreements (subsequently ratified by the major countries of the world; International covenant on Social, Economic, and Cultural Rights and the International Covenant on Civil and Political Rights) - 1966
- UN has been developing a code of conduct for multinational corporations (yet to be completed or adopted) - Since 1972
- UN Secretary General Kofi Annan challenged world business leaders to "embrace and enact" the Global Compact (consists of 9 principles covering human rights, labour and the environment) - 1999
- ILO which dates from 1919 and is now a specialised agency of UN, sets many international standards, including those of the Tripartite Declaration of Principles concerning Multinational Enterprises and Social Policy - 1977
- Recently, OECD (members are the more developed countries of the world) has adopted the OECD guidelines for multinational enterprises. Several interfaith religious bodies have developed codes:
  - The principles for Global Corporate Responsibility adopted by the US based Interfaith Centre on Corporate Responsibility and similar organisations in Great Britain, Ireland and Canada adopted by Interfaith Declaration on International Business Ethics which resulted from a dialogue among Christians, Jews and Muslims.
  - A group of world business leaders, meeting in Caux, Switzerland, developed the Caux Roundtable Principles for Business.

These codes have many guidelines in common and cover the areas of employment practices, consumer protection, environmental preservation, involvement in politics, including bribery, and basic human rights.

Operating outside the home country, specially in LDCs, create dilemmas that lead to charges of serious ethical failings. MNCs generally recognise a social responsibility and attempt to fulfill their responsibilities everywhere they are located. The major cause of occasional failures to act responsibly is not because of lack of effort but the diversity of political and legal systems around the world and differences in economic development.

Foreign operations create challenges as well as opportunities for misconduct that simply do not exist for purely domestic enterprises. The question for MNCs is deciding which standards to follow. Neither of the two extreme positions is satisfactory. Ultimately, the solution to many of the ethical problems of international business lies in the development of international agreements and codes of ethics.

Ethics in Global Business

It is said that one's actions will be judged according to the norms of the environment in which it takes place, which may not be true always in all the cases. In many circumstances, we believe that in whatever way we proceed, we pressure that as the right way and the other alternatives are not acceptable to us.

Consider what you would think or do if the only way to obtain a certain permit or contract is to offer a bribe and that all others also do it. A firm may contend that if it does not act similar to firms local to that country, it may lose business and it has to bundle up and leave the country. Does that make it acceptable? Everyone knows that bribery is wrong or unethical because it allows certain parties to obtain a privilege not afforded to others. Many competing firms do not believe it is wrong or unethical to eat meat; Individuals in other countries may consider eating meat is wrong and unethical. In India and even in USA, men are generally restricted to one wife. Whereas in other countries that is considered as unthinkable and humiliating. Who is right? Who should answer that question? Are there any objective rights and wrongs? Both western and non-western values may have a great deal in common. e.g., Donaldson links the western values of individual liberty and human rights to the values of other regions.

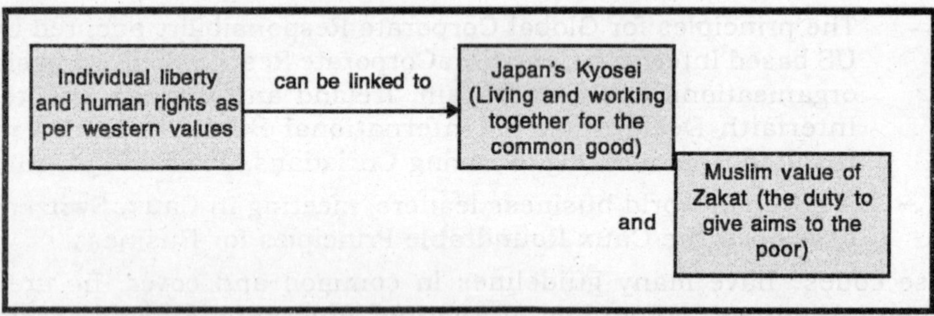

Fig. 5.3 Individual Liberty and Human Rights

The integrative **social contracts theory** as per Donaldson and Thomas Dunfie suggests that one can differentiate between those values which are fundamental across culture and theory (hypernorms) and those values which are determined with moral 'free space' and not hypernorms. One has to look to the convergence of religious, cultural and physiological beliefs around certain core principles as a clue to the identification of **hypernorms**. Example of hyper norms are freedom of speech, the right to personal freedom, the right to physical movement and informed consent. When you consider these far reaching rights, do you believe that all reasonable thinkers would agree to their predominance and worthiness of a protection.

Donaldson's and Dunfee's effort is to propose a means by which to apply ethical standards across borders. The proposed codes of conduct include:

- US Model Business Principles
- Caux Round Table Principles

One has to judge the similarities and differences between the proposed models of business behaviour.

If differences found, do these difference in themselves evidence the fact that there is no general agreement regarding business conduct.

By creating a model code of conduct for a global firm, would it resemble any of these codes?

Firms complain that adhering to these codes of conduct is costly imposing higher costs on them than those imposed on firms in other countries. Adherence to the codes tends them to be at a competitive disadvantage in comparison to firms in a less regulated countries.

In addition to compliance to a central code of business behaviour, firms must be sensitive to cultural differences in those countries in which they do business. The flavours, the type of products preferred by the community, the packaging concept, the mode of advertisements etc. all have a bearing related to culture suited to that country. Challenges to this cultural sensitivity are strong. If one culture's standards seriously violate a norm that is generally accepted by many other cultures, can you take the majority as right?

How can one determine right from wrong in the global arena? Is the most significant question. Right and wrong depends on the standards by which you are judging the act or decision. As the national boundaries within our world market become increasingly blurred, so too do the cultural differences.

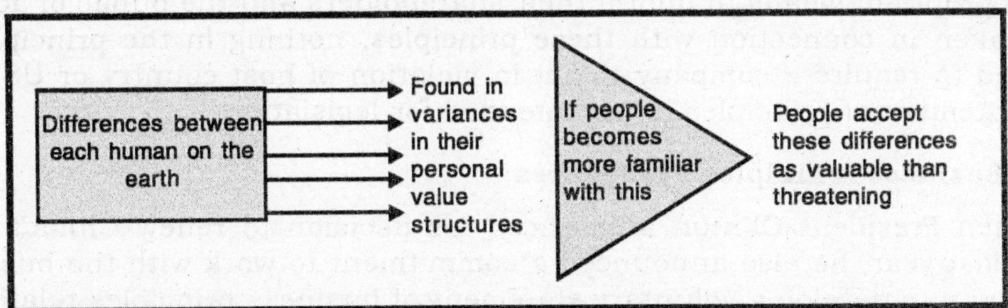

Fig. 5.4 Differences between Each Human on the Earth

Model Business Principles of USA

The US Department of Commerce (DOC) to codify the expectations of the US Market issued its **Model Business Principles** in 1995 as guidelines for business conduct in the US and abroad. The principle comprise a voluntary code of conduct. DOC hopes that they will encourage appropriate behaviour.

The US administration encourages all businesses to adopt and implement voluntary codes of conduct for doing business around the world in upholding and promoting adherence to universal standards of human rights worked out the minimum following areas:

- Provision of a safe and healthy work place
- Fair employment practices (Avoidance of child and forced labour avoidance of discrimination based on race, gender, national origin or religious beliefs; respect for the right of association and the right to organise and bargain collectively)
- Responsible environmental protection and environmental practices
- Compliance with US and local laws promoting good business practices (including laws prohibiting illicit payments and ensuring fair competition)
- Maintenance, through leadership at all levels (A corporate culture that respects free expression consistent with legitimate business concerns, and does not condome political coercion in the work place; that encourages good corporate citizenship and makes a positive contribution to the communities in which the company operates; and where ethical conduct is recognised, valued and exemplified by all employees)

Fig. 5.5 Areas Adhered to Universal Standards of Human Rights

In adopting voluntary codes of conduct that reflect these principles, US Companies should serve as models, encouraging similar behaviour by their partners, suppliers and subcontractors. Adoption of codes of conduct reflecting these principles is voluntary companies are encouraged to develop their own codes of conduct appropriate to their particular circumstances. Companies should final appropriate means to inform their shareholders and the public of actions undertaken in connection with these principles, nothing in the principles is intended to require a company to act in violation of host country or US Law. This statement of principles is not intended for legislation.

Model Business Principles:Procedures

When President Clinton announced his decision to renew China's MFN status last year, he also announced a commitment to work with the business community to develop a voluntary statement of business principles relating to corporate conduct abroad. The President made clear that U.S. business can and does play a positive and important role promoting the openness of societies, respect for individual rights, the promotion of free markets and prosperity, environmental protection and the setting of high standards for business practices generally.

The Administration today is offering an update on our efforts to follow-through on the President's commitment to promote the Model Business Principles and best practices among U.S. companies. The Principles already have gained the support of some U.S. companies. A process is ongoing to elicit additional support for these Principles and to continue to examine issues related to them.

The elements of this process are:

(i) Voluntary Statement of Business Principles.

(ii) Efforts by US Business

- Conferences on Best Practices Issues
- Best Practices Information Clearing house and Support Services

(iii) Efforts by the US Government

- Promote Multilateral adoption of Best Practices
- Presidential Business Discussions.

1. **Voluntary Statement of Business Principles**. The Administration, in extensive consultations with business and labour leaders and members of the Non-Governmental Organisation (NGO) community, developed these model principles, which were reported widely in the press earlier this spring. This model statement is to be used by companies as a reference point in framing their own codes of conduct. It is based on a wide variety of similar sets of principles U.S. companies and business organisations already have put into global practice. The Administration encourages all businesses every where to support the model principles (Copies of the model statement are available by calling the U.S.Department of Commerce Trade Information Center, 1-800-USA-TRADE).

2. **Efforts by US Business**. As part of the ongoing effort, U.S.businesses will engage in the following activities:

(a) **Conferences on Best Practices Issues**. In conjunction with Business for Social able corporate practices, and/or other appropriate organisations, the Administration will work to encourage conferences concerning issues relating to the practices contained in the Model Business Principles. Such conferences can provide a forum for information-sharing on new approaches for the evolving global context in which best practices are implemented (For further information on Business for Social Responsibility, contact Bob Dunn, President, (415) 865-2500).

(b) **Best Practices Information** Clearing house and Support Services. One or more non-profits will work with the U.S. business community to develop a clearinghouse of information regarding business practices globally. The clearinghouse will establish a library of codes of conduct adopted by U.S. and international companies and organisations, to be cataloged and made available to companies seeking to develop their own codes. The clearinghouse would be available to provide advice to companies seeking to develop or improve their codes, advice based on the accumulated experience of other companies. Business for Social Responsibility (described above) is highly respected and is one resource that businesses and NGOs alike can turn to for information on best business practices.

3. **Efforts by the U.S. government**. The U.S. Government also will undertake a number of activities to generate support for the Model Business Principles:

(a) **Promote Multilateral Adoption of Best Practices**. The Administration has begun and will continue its effort to seek multilateral support for the Model Business Principles. Senior U.S. Government officials already have met with U.S.company officials and U.S. organisations operating abroad as well as with foreign corporate officials to seek support for the Principles. For example, the American Chambers of Commerce in the Asia Pacific recently adopted a resolution by which their members agreed to work with their local counterparts in the countries in which they operate to seek development of similar best practices among their members. The United States also will present the Model Business Principles at the Organisation for Economic Cooperation and Development (OECD) and the International Labour Organisation (ILO) as part of these organisations' ongoing behaviour. Therefore, on an annual basis, the Administration will offer a series of awards to companies for specific activities that reflect best practices in the areas covered by the Model Business Principles. The awards will be granted pursuant to applications by interested companies. NGOs ad private citizens will be encouraged to call attention to activities they believe are worthy of consideration (For further information on the Best Practices Awards Programme, contact Melinda Yee, U.S. Department of Commerce, (202) 482-1051).

(b) **Presidential-Business Discussions**. The President's Export Council (PEC), a high-level advisory group of Chief Executive Officers, provides a forum for the President to meet regularly with U.S. business leaders to discuss issues relating to U.S. industries' exports and operations abroad.

5.2 Global Values

The corporate code have already been dealt in para 4.9. These include:

- Code of ethics
- Code of practive
- Codes of conduct

The basic ethical ideals are explained in the Caux principles.

The Caux Principles

Two basic ethical ideals found in the Caux Principles are:

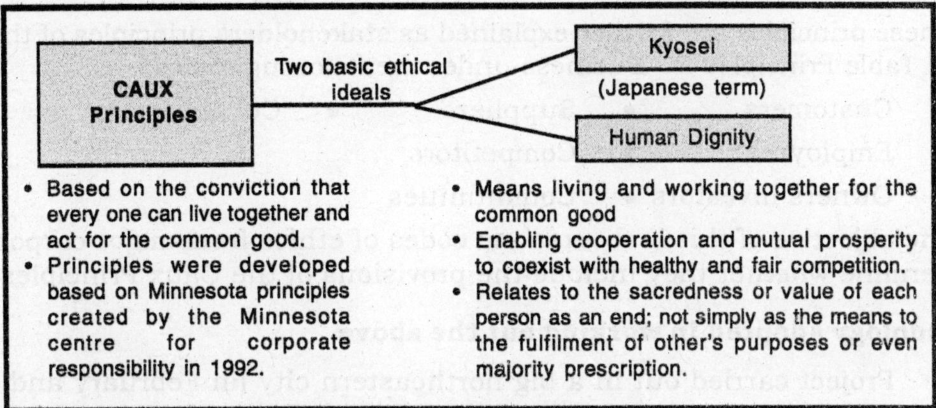

Fig. 5.6 CAUX Principles

The Caux Round Table: This works with a group of international executives based in Caux, Switzerland. The group shared a belief that business organisations can be a powerful group for positive change in the quality of life of the world (Business leaders represented the US, Europe and Japan).

International ethics standards for business are:

- NAFTA
- Caux Principles
- US Corporate Code of Ethics

NAFTA: The implementation of the multilateral international trade agreement which addresses the mean issues of multinational trade, environment protection, intellectual property and employment, among others is known as **NAFTA** executed on 1st January 1974 among the US, Canada and Mexico to promote free trade by eliminating tariff and non-tariff barriers was the creation of the Caux Principles (considered to be the first international code of ethics for business). The Caux Principles promote action to strengthen the two main concepts of fairness and respect for others. This can be ensured by:

- promoting free trade
- environmental and cultural integrity
- prevention of actions that fall in the category of foreign corrupt practices as defined by US law like bribery, money laundering etc.

Among the principles that expand on the two main concepts are the following general principles:

- The economic and social impact of business
- Respect for the rules

- Support for multilateral trade
- Respect for the environment
- Avoidance of illicit operations

These principles are further explained as stakeholders principles of the Caux Round Table Principles for Business under the following topics:

- Customers
- Suppliers
- Collaborators
- Employees
- Competitors
- Owners Investors
- Communities

The objective of this is to examine codes of ethics from major corporations to determine whether they include the provisions of the Caux Principles.

Methodology adopted in working out the above

- Project carried out in a big northeastern city (in February and March 1994)
- Codes of ethics solicited from businesses represented in the area (Yellow pages)
- Businesses chosen on criteria: size and industry
- Larger businesses were considered because they are likely to have formal code of ethics; sample was limited to businesses with national prominence
- Industries selected were retail (fast food, grocery stores, departmental services), financial services, utilities and health services
- Each business was contacted to determine the name of the person to be contacted through letters. A letter soliciting the company code of ethics was sent by the researchers. A following phone call to the businesses who have not given reply within a 2 month time period resulted in a response rate of 84%, 37 letters sent and 31 codes received
- Each corporate code of ethics was read by one of the researchers and references to important concepts were noted. The researchers each read a subset of the other researchers codes so that the coding would be uniform
- Salient concepts were decided upon before the coding process by combining principles mentioned in NAFTA with those from the CAUX Principles

The subject of Caux Principles can be grouped under 3 sections:

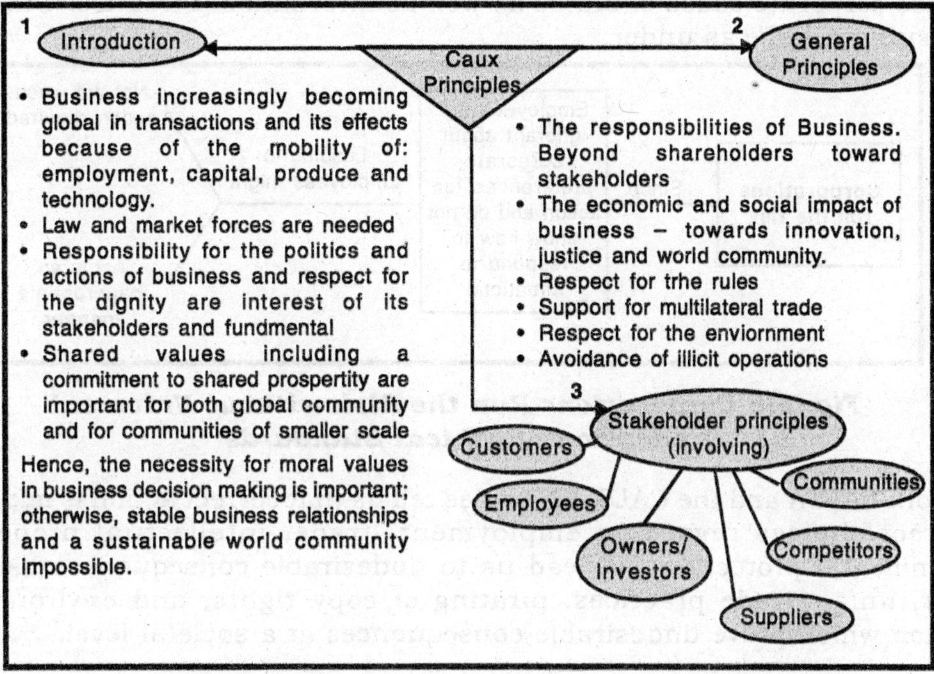

Fig. 5.7 Grouping of the Subject of CAUX Principles

The Caux Principles contain a broad statement of ethical principles encompassing and enlarging upon the NAFTA provisions. The final coding scheme consists of five all-encompassing concepts shown in the above figure marked as (→) under General Principles. These would mean as under in corporate code of ethics.

- The economic and social impact of business is Importance of ethnicity employee culture, equal opportunity, equal conditions (Data set: 11 No. of codes of ethics)
- Respect for the rules like Intellectual property, copy right, trade marks (8 Nos.)
- Support for multinational trade in Trade, relationship with suppliers, free trade (11 Nos.)
- Respect for the environment is to improve or promote sustainable development, present waste, environmental protection (4 Nos.)
- Avoidance of illicit operations like corrupt practices, bribes, arms, other corrupt practices (31 Nos.).

Universal adoption of ethical standards such as the Caux Principles will enhance corporate codes of ethics as well as international treaties. Otherwise, the result would be as under:

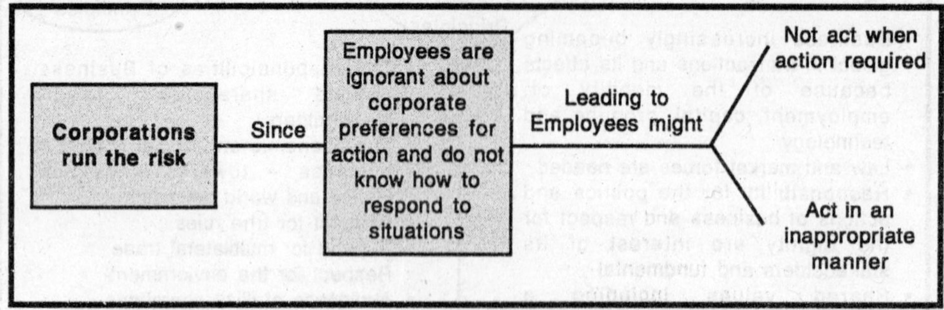

Fig. 5.8 Corporations Run the Risk without Universal Adoption of Ethical Standards

Both NAFTA and the CAUX Principles tell us that correct action is important; Incorrect choices regarding employment, trade, intellectual property or environmental protection will lead us to undesirable consequences like child labour, unfair trade practices, pirating of copy rights, and environmental pollution which prove undesirable consequences at a societal level.

Guidelines for Global Companies

If neither home country nor host country standards provide complete guidance, what principles or sales should global corporations adopt? Three kinds of guidelines have been offered are as under:

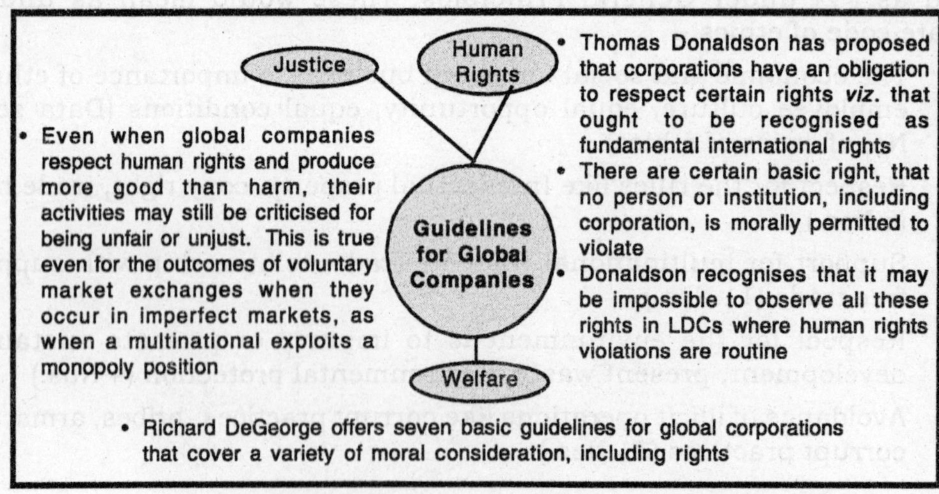

Fig. 5.9 Guidelines for Global Companies

Human Rights

Donald's suggestion for the fundamental rights as a moral minimum:

The right to:

- Freedom of physical movement
- Ownership of property
- Freedom from torture
- A Fair trial
- Nondiscriminatory treatment
- Physical security
- Freedom of speech and association
- Minimal education
- Political participation
- Subsistence

Fig. 5.10 Donald's Suggestion for the Fundamental Rights

Sample applications to this are:

- Failing to provide safety equipment to protect employees from serious hazards (the right to physical security)
- Bribing government officials to violate their duty or seeking to overthrow democratically elected governments (the right to political participation)
- Employing child labour as found mostly in India (the right to minimal education)

On the whole, Guidelines based on human rights provide a bedrock moral minimum. However, the application of rights based guidelines are uncertain in more controversial situations where we are most in need of guidance, and they are inapplicable to many other pressing matters.

Welfare

The guidelines offered by Richard DeGeorge are:

Global Companies should:

- Do no intentional direct harm
- More good than harm for the host country
- Contribute by their activity to host country's development
- Respect the human rights of their employees
- To the extent that local culture does not violate ethical norms, respect the local culture and work with and not against it
- Pay their fair share of taxes
- Cooperate with the local government in developing and enforcing just background institutions

Fig. 5.11 Guidelines Offered by Richard Degeorge

The first three express in different ways a duty to consider the welfare of the people in a host country.

Global companies are criticised primarily in cases where they take more than a fair share by exploiting their superior position in an imperfect market.

Manuel G.Velasquez observes DeGeorze's approach fails to take seriously the importance of justice in evaluating the activities of multinationals.

Justice

One kind of unfairness cited by critics is the often one-sided division of the benefits from foreign investment. The gap between the rich and poor countries is an urgent moral concern and MNCs have much to offer. DeGeorges guidelines to should contribute by their activity to the host country's development. The main questions are: who should act? What should be done? Since National governments and world organisations are the primary actors.

Another kind of unfairness in violating the rules of the market place, which is to say engaging in unfair competition and otherwise taking unfair advantage.

Tax avoidance through transfer pricing is a critical problem for both developed and developing countries (Transfer pricing are the values assigned to raw materials and unfinished products that one subsidiary of a company sells to another).

Wages and Working Conditions

All major American shoe and clothing companies as well as software companies have outsourced the actual assembling of their products as well as business processes to contractors in South East Asia, Central America and India. This development benefits consumers everywhere by lowering the cost of goods and for job creations in the above mentioned countries that desperately need them. The manufacture of goods in countries with low labour costs is advantageous to developed and developing countries alike. However, the benefits must be weighed against a long list of wrongs that include very low wages, substandard working conditions, the use of child labour and association with repressive regimes. Some of the factories operated by MNCs and their foreign contractors are alleged to be 'sweat shops' of the kind that operated in developed countries until the passage of protective legislation in the 20th century. Instead of improving the lives of people, they charge, the contracting system leads to greater misery for the bulk of the population and to a wider gap between the rich and the poor. Although the jobs that are exported overseas are a boon to workers in LDCs, they reduce job opportunities in the developed world.

Whatever may be the controversies on the above, 'how should the standards for wages and working conditions be determined?' is a question, for which many say that these standards are set by the market. In developed countries, the determination of wages and working conditions results primarily from the competition among employers for desirable workers, which compels them to offer higher wages and good working conditions. On this view, there is nothing unjust about jobs with lower pay and poor conditions so long as the workers are ready to accept the jobs on the terms offered. Any arrangement is justified. However, using the market to determine the standards and working conditions in developing countries encounters two obstacles:

- Developed countries do not rely solely on the market but certain minimum conditions by law, such as minimum wages laws, fair labour standards, and health and safety regulations. These reflect certain human rights that ought to be observed in all economic activity.
- Using the market to set wages and working conditions is the possibility that the conditions for a free market are lacking. The mass of unemployed, desperately poor people in LDCs constitute a pool of labourers willing accept bare subsistence wages. The market for labour in any given country may also be artificially low because of political repression that prevents workers from organising.

We need to consider the extent to which market forces should be allowed to operate in the setting of wages and working conditions and the extent to which principles of human rights to be applied.

Justified wage means what?

Wages paid by the global companies are usually above the minimum wage and the prevailing market rate. As a result the jobs in these factories generally pay better than work in local enterprises and regular employment in the formal economy is vastly superior to work in the informal sector (includes agriculture, domestic service and small, unregulated manufacture). Well intentioned efforts to better the condition of factory workers will ultimately reduce the number of jobs and the level of foreign investment. Low labour costs constitute a competitive advantage for a poor country and attracts investment on the basis provides jobs that can lead to greater development (Earlier low wage countries are Korea, Taiwan, Malaysia, India, China) have successfully employed this strategy for creating higher paying jobs. Countries like Vietnam and Indonesia not taking the advantage of low cost labour, they are not utilising the opportunity to use their main competitive edge, namely unemployed workers, to begin the process of development. Wages also applies to working conditions in as much as both are matters of cost.

World bank's report says 'Reducing hazards in the workplace is costly and the greater the reduction the more it costs.' As a result, setting standards too high can actually lower workers welfare. Investment to improve working conditions may come at the expense of wages.

The dispute between those who advocate paying the market rate for labour and those favouring a living wage is not over the ultimate end which is to improve the welfare of people in developing countries. However, there is general agreement on standards for working conditions.

Child labour presents a thorny issue. An estimation shows more than 150 million children below 14 years work worldwide. 5% of these make goods for exports. Some are employed even in most dangerous jobs. Virtually every country bans child labour but enforcement is ineffective.

ILO (International Labour Organisation) has worked with governments and businesses to establish special schools for 10,000 children approximately who worked in garment factories and to pay their parents for the lost wages. The solution to the problem of child labour is not merely to prohibit the employment of underage workers but also to provide schooling for children and jobs for parents so that child labour is no longer an economic necessity.

5.3 Various Ethical Issues Around the Globe

Many of the global ethical issues have been explained in para 5.1.

Some of the major ethical issues are:

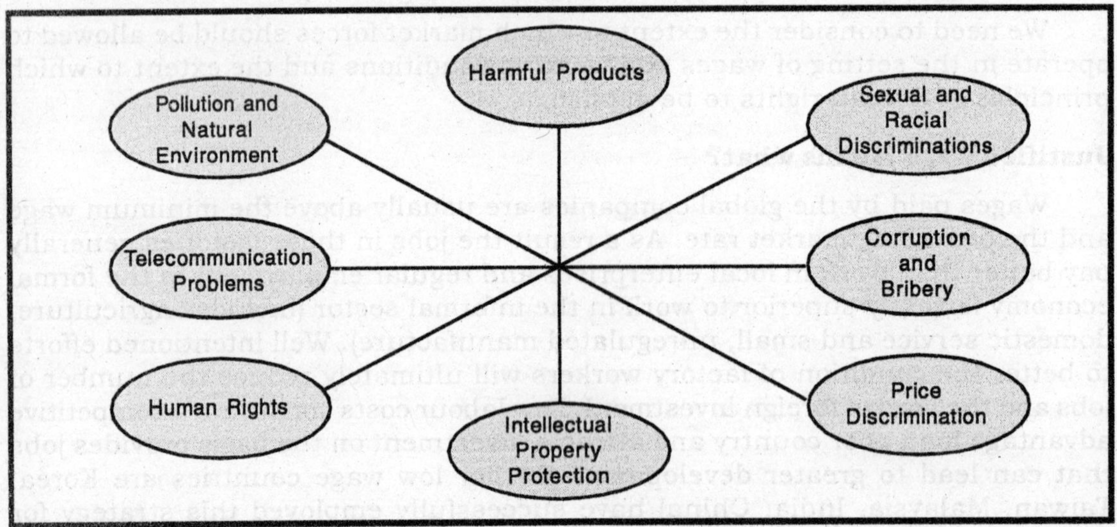

Fig. 5.12 Major Ethical Issues

Countries have joined together to establish various organisations to provide guidance on such international business issues:

(i) Sexual and racial discrimination

Refer para 4.2

The problem of discrimination on the basis of sex, race and religion exist in many countries. Though the respective governments both in Europe and USA have made suitable laws to prohibit business from discriminating on the basis of above, it still remains. Everywhere we find people from other nations would have entered seeking employment or the natives may be available for jobs. These people are paid less compared to the other citizens. For example, In USA, the Mexicans and in UK, the east Indians have been relegated to the lowest paying, least desired and harmful jobs. So also in Germany the government will not grant citizenship to Turkish workers. This happens everywhere in every country including Jafna, Australia. Business women are not found in numbers in the middle eastern nations. Even the education is denied for women in several countries. Women do not want to go to certain fields, as these restricts them to find jobs. Women sales representatives are not many in most of the countries as they find that they will be unsuccessful and not liked by the society if they work in those areas and the cultural norms in those societies do not encourage.

(ii) Corruption and Bribery

Indian society has to face the biggest challenge of tackling and ending **corruption**. Though governmental regulation and social awareness are there, this menace is still continuing without any instant cure. Our social problems are very much like that of other civilized countries in the world. But the problems are peculiar in nature only to this country because of diversity in culture, social setup, religion, certain other historical and political reasons. The problems which we are facing are of many types.

- Juvenile delinquency
- Gambling
- Drinking
- Prostitution
- Beggary
- Ecological
- Minorities
- Sex
- War with neighbouring country etc.

These affect mostly our rapid industrialisation and urbanisation on one side and disallocation of old institutions like joint family, panchayat etc., on the other side.

Corruption and Moral degeneration problems are the result of the way we have been living in the last several decades. The social, religious, and cultural aspects, of our lives many a times dictates our vulnerability to corruption. The corruption we find generally in India are from:

- Politicians.
- Officials from government or even public sector companies.
- Lower staff in the government and public sector companies.
- Policemen.
- Businessmen.
- Educational institutions.
- Individuals.
- White collar criminals.

Corruption takes place both in public and private sector enterprises. The private entrepreneurs aim at:

- To earn maximum profit by way of evading tax
- Illegal procurement of raw materials
- Hoarding the goods
- Black marketing, etc.

Likewise in the public undertakings also, business executives play an important role by encouraging corruption due to the influence of politicians. Most of the business organisations are under the mercy of political leaders to help them during election time and at the other critical junctures in order to obtain their favour when they are in power. While obtaining the license and at the starting of the business, the private enterprise owners have to approach politicians for the latter's favour. Corruption is found in various stages during:

- Construction of building
- Erection of plant and machinery
- Recruitment of people, etc.

How Does Corruption Take Place?

The vicious circle of petty corruption is as given under:

The Government due to its shortage of funds cannot meet the salary bill of the employees on time and also they do not pay the employees adequately. Low/ Late payments are the result (Fig. 5.13). Hence the employees (both clerks and officials) are thirsty for additional money which can be called as 'extras'. Naturally, they will try to seek alternate income. Some of the employees work outside the companies in their leisure time and earn extra money, though sometimes not permitted by the government, since it affects the performance of the work and as well as affect the health of the employees. Some others engage themselves in corrupt practices. Thus they will try to get alternate incomes, as the main income is not sufficient to lead a good life. This will show the hidden economy. In the private companies, officials also try to avoid tax by all possible means (also keeping two accounts, one for the company, another for the tax department - Rama's account, Krishna's account).

The government, as a result of the above, collects low revenues and hence they are unable to pay sufficiently to their employees. This is a vicious circle. As a result, the corruption, is found with the employees, as well as other criminal causes will result. From the government side, poor services and poor results due to lack of honesty and efficiency are found. The services will be poor to the public and the public gets annoyed. Again the public wants better services somehow if not by the government, through some other ways. For this they have to pay money. In order to meet this additional burden, one may also resort to corruption to meet their ends.

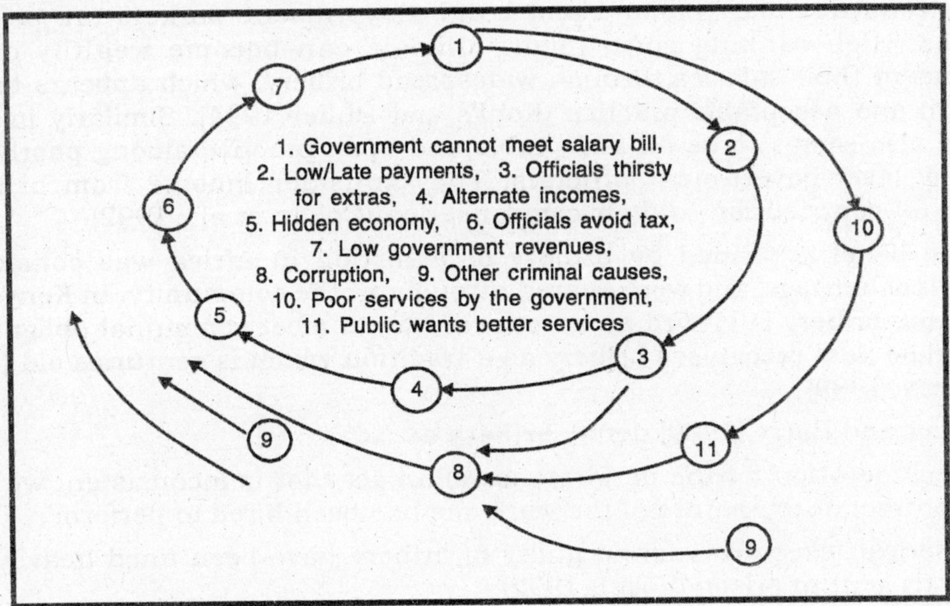

Fig. 5.13. The vicious circle of petty corruption

Two levels of corruption are to be understood:

- **Petty corruption**
- **Grand corruption**

Petty corruption is a sort of endemic in many countries which is a different thing and is totally different from the 'grand corruption' which is so common in 'International aid programmes' and in the 'Armaments Industry'.

Bribes

Bribes are personal payments, gifts, or special favours granted improperly to influence the outcome of decision.

Bribery affects citizens, because:

- It raises the costs of goods sold.
- Leads to perceptions of unfair treatment of some companies and groups at the expense of others.
- Decreases the level of trust across groups.
- Different forms of bribery also lead to differential perceptions that can further decrease trust.
- Some Americans decry outright pay-offs to obtain business contracts.
- Some foreigners see large financial contributions by interest groups to American political campaigns. This is much more damaging than a modest financial payment that is straight forwardly offered and accepted.

In countries like Thailand and India, Government workers are paid low salaries. High ranking government officials can become wealthy or can supplement their salaries through widespread bribery, which appears to be a common and acceptable practice (Kohl's and Buller 1994). Similarly in Peru, bribery also seems to be an acceptable and open practice among poorly paid and low level government officials. They consider income from bribes a significant contribution to their compensation (Cohen et al., 1992).

The benefits reaped by bribery or extortion in Africa was considered 'communal heritage' and were shared throughout the community. In Kenya and Indonesia, bribery is viewed as an ethical way to meet communal obligations. The Middle East recognises bribery as a tradition which is centuries old (Shaw and Barry, 1989).

Shaw and Barry (1989) define **bribery** as:

'Remuneration for the performance of an act that is inconsistent with the work contract or the nature of the work one has been hired to perform'.

American executives found guilty of bribery have been fined heavily and frequently sent to prison (Vogel, 1992).

In Malaysia, influenced by the Moslem Prescriptions against bribery, execution of executives is legal. So also in Saudi Arabia.

Bribery is said to be more extensive in developing nations and those stressing a high degree of collectivism. Though American regulations are against bribery, many parts of the business would consider it as an acceptable or normal practice, regardless of whether it is considered legal. **Bribes** are personal payments, gifts or special favours granted improperly to influence the outcome of a decision. A conflict of interest exists when an individual is in the position of having to decide whether to advance the interests of the business or to operate in his or her own personal interests. In an ethical environment, employees scrupulously separate their private financial interests from their business dealings. Asian, African and Middle East countries seem to consider bribery an acceptable or normal practice, regardless of its legality. In some of the African nations, bribery is a strong and common norm and the benefits reaped by bribery is shared throughout the community. Similarly in Kenya and Indonesia (collectivistic countries), bribery is viewed as a way to meet communal obligations by distributing the wealth to members of the communities inner circle. Middle East recognises bribery as a tradition which is centuries old.

In India and Thailand, government workers have low salaries. High ranking government officials can become wealthy only through widespread bribery to supplement their salaries, which appears to be a common and acceptable practice (Kohl's and Buller, 1994). In Peru also, bribery seems to be an acceptable and open practice among poorly paid government officials, who consider this income a significant contribution to their compensation (Cohen et al., 1992).

Some nation's tolerance of bribery in conducting business is higher than others. Japan for instance although having a partial code against bribery, seems to maintain a high tolerance level for this practice (Dr.George, 1986). Bribery in Japan is an "open kind of activity which is culturally accepted". American managers consider bribery as an unethical act than German and French managers (Becker and Fritzsche, 1987).

Universally, bribery is not accepted as an immoral, illegal, or unethical business practice, despite the American desire to level the playing field and ascertain a utilitarian ethical approach to replace all forms of bribery internationally with competition based solely on the merit of the products and services offered by nations (De George 1986) - Between intended meaning of the law and the execution, there is a gap. E.g. Venezuela, payments and commissions to public entities and unlawful gifts and payments to civil servants are condemnable type of behaviour. However, like Japan, this type of corruption is quite common in Venezuela. It is also to be noted that bribery is a standard way of doing business in many countries, the US made provisions for corporations to either use or succumb to small bribes, which are required to travel or work in less or developed countries. **Cumshaw, baksheesh, grease payment** are different terms. Foreign Corrupt Practices Act stipulates that American employees and managers can legally be reimbursed for such payments.

Bribery is a way of life for many foreign business professionals and government officials. It is frequently accepted that government officers will not accept bribes but they are motivated to actively solicit them because of their low salary. Many countries have legislation prohibiting bribery, few actually seem to enforce violations or confront individuals involved in bribery.

A conflict of interest exists when an individual is in the position of having to decide whether to advance the interests of the business or to operate in his or her own personal interests. In an ethical environment, employees scrupulously separate their private financial interests from their business dealings. They do not accept bribes.

Commercial Bribes and Extortion

As already said in page 209 a **commercial bribe** is a consideration given or offered to an employee by a person outside the firm with the understanding that when the employee transacts for his own firm. The employee will deal favourably with that person or that person's firm (in the form of money, tangible goods, the kickbacks of part of an official payment, preferential treatment, or any other kind of benefit) e.g. a purchasing agent accepts a bribe in the form of money or a present from a supplier (to receive a favoured treatment in the agents purchasing decisions).

Extort is to gain or draw from by compulsion or violence.

Extortion is illegal or oppressive exaction; that which is extorted.

Extortion on the contrary to bribe, an employee is engaged in a commercial extortion if the employee demands a consideration from persons outside the firm as a condition for dealing favourably with those persons when the employee transacts for his firm e.g. purchasing agents buy only from those sales people who give them certain goods or services.

Extortion and the acceptance of bribes obviously create a conflict of interest that violates the moral duty that the employee's work contract establishes.

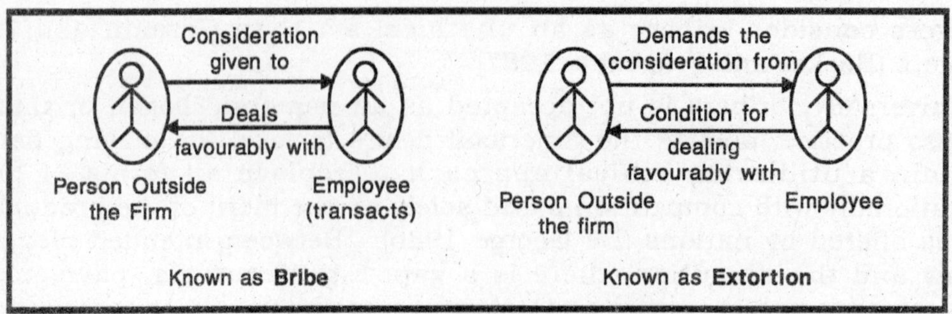

Fig. 5.14 Bribe Vs Extortion

Foreign Bribery

Bribery is one of the most common and controversial issues that global companies face. It is universally condemned and no government in the world legally permits bribery of its own officials. The major cases we have seen are Lockheed in Japan, Bofors in India. However corruption exists to some extent in every country and is epidemic to more than a few. The main ethical question is whether companies are justified in making payments when they are necessary for doing business in a corrupt environment. Although the demand for a bribe may be unethical, is it unethical to give in to a demand?

Foreign Corrupt Practices Act (FCPA) in US was introduced in 1977 forbids American Corporations to offer or make any payment to a foreign official for the purpose of "influencing any act or decision of such foreign official in his official capacity or of inducing such foreign official to do or omit to do any act in violation of the lawful duty of such official" in order to obtain or retain business (includes payment to political parties and candidates for offices in foreign countries).

Bribe is a payment made with an intention to corrupt. The payment is made with the intention of causing a person to be dishonest or disloyal or to betray a trust in the performance of official duties.

Certain kinds of payments are legally permitted and do not constitute bribes. These include 'facilitating payments' which are made to expedite the performance of "routine governmental action." Also called "**Grease payments**." These are small sums paid at lower level officials to lubricate the rusty machinery that provides government services. Facilitating payments do not include anyone to violate a duty or trust. Also excluded from the category of bribes are reasonable expenditures for legitimate expenses, such as entertaining a foreign official in the case of doing business. Any payments that are permitted or required by the written laws of the country in question are legal under the FPCA. FPCA was enacted by Congress in past to protect American interests.

The immorality of demanding or accepting bribes is implicit in the definition of bribery. A government official violating a duty or a trust. Inducing such a violation by offering a bribe is commonly recognised as wrong. Corrupting others is as wrong as being corrupt oneself. The principal ethical objection to foreign bribery is that systematic and widespread corruption inhibits the development of fair and efficient markets. Although corrupt government officials bear chief responsibility for the economic consequences of bribery, major foreign corporation s contribute to the problem when they actively participate in corruption and take no steps to combat it. Corruption in Russia for example does not affect the Russian people alone. It also makes Russia a less attractive environment for investment by corporations from US, Europe and other developed countries.

The justification for prohibiting foreign bribery is rather straight forward. A double standard is employed if a country permits its companies to do abroad what they are forbidden to do at home. Bribery impose, harms and violates basic rights. Some have argued that FCPA is a form of **"ethical imperialism"** that imposes our values on other countries.

World attitudes are now changing. The proposed code of conduct developed by the United Nations Commission on Multinationals has contained a prohibition on bribery, although the code has yet to be adopted by the organisations membership. The US has fought, largely without success, to gain agreement for a ban on bribery through the world trade organisation. However, in 1990s, leading financial institutions, including IMF and the World Bank have stressed the economic consequences of foreign bribery and placed restrictions on aid recipients to limit the practice.

The most significant development is the adoption of a legally binding treaty by the 29 number organisation of Economic Cooperation and Development (OECD) in April 1996 which commits each member country to change its laws to accord roughly with the FCPA. OECD includes the world's richest nations have agreed to:

- prohibit bribery of foreign officials
- impose criminal penalties on those found guilty
- allow for the seizure of profits gained by bribery.

This initiative concentrates on the 'supply' side by changing the conduct of corporations that have been paying bribes. Many opine that OECD treaty will significantly reduce the incidence of foreign bribery and produce a more level playing field for all multinational corporations.

(iii) Price Discrimination

Ethics and Regulations in Pricing

Pricing practices are regulated by the government more forcefully than other areas of the marketing mix (such as personal selling, distribution, advertisement) in that pricing illegalities are made explicit in acts such as:

- FTC Act (Federal Trade Commission Act)
- Robinson-Patman Act

Four areas of pricing are considered unethical and illegal. (See figure on the next page).

(i) Deceptive Pricing: Bait and Switch Pricing is one type of deceptive price-a low price offer intended to lure customers into a store, where a sales person tries to influence intended to lure customers into a store. Thereafter, a sales person tries to influence them to buy a higher-priced item.

e.g. Audi in USA was accused of Bait and Switch tactics in 1998. It offered rebates on a product, which was phased out and was often unavailable, leaving customers to consider other products without rebates.

Another deceptive practice is to offer a discount off an inflated price. e.g. In India buy one saree take two sarees free; the price would have been jacked up on the first saree covering the prices of other two sarees.

(ii) Unfair Pricing: When competitors are driven out by low prices (less than cost) the company raises price back to their former level. This happened even for a reputed public sector company like HMT in 1990s in the dairy machinery area from their competitors to suffer losses. The survival for existence was a problem.

(iii) Price Discrimination: Though theoretically, price discrimination maximises profits by enabling sellers to charge price-inelastic customers high prices than elastic customers are charged. It can be unethical if similar buyers are charged different prices for the same goods based on their ability to pay.

The **Robinson-Patman Act** (1936) states that price discrimination is illegal as it makes a number of important exemptions. Applies only to sales to organisational buyers, not to final consumers. Maruti Motors cannot sell the same cars at different prices to its dealers. The dealers can charge customers different prices for the same car. Price differences to similar buyers are legal if such differences have some cost justification. The Gas prices are different in USA at different places. So also in India for petrol and diesel (price of petrol and diesel are cheaper at Delhi than at Bangalore).

As with other areas of marketing mix, most firms have acted ethically in setting prices. They do not attempt to deceive customers or to use pricing actions to restrain competition. A firm willfully deceiving consumer through pricing actions will eventually lose out to more responsible competitors as consumers learn that they are being duped. Though Government regulation is important in pricing, competitive forces are the best regulators in insuring ethical pricing.

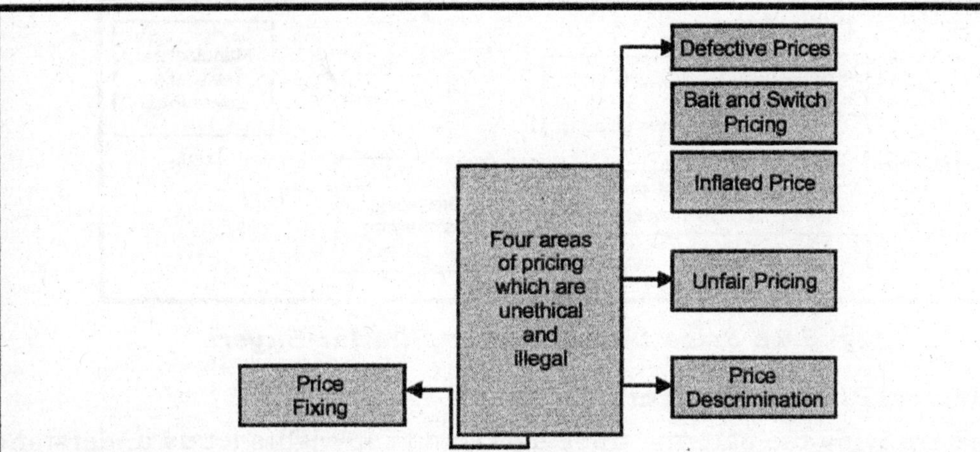

1. **Deceptive Prices** - Meant to deceive customers and to take advantage of them; Illegal under the FTC Act
   (i) **Bait and Switch Pricing.**
   - One type of deceptive price-a low price offer intended to lure customers into a store, where a sales person try to influence them to buy a high priced item. e.g. Audi in 1988 adopted this tactics (offered rebates on its 5000 line, which was phased out and was often unavailable, leaving customers to consider other lines)

   (ii) **Inflated Price**
   - To offer a discount off an inflated discount. The consumer is not actually getting a discount.
2. **Unfair Pricing** - Uses pricing practices to drive competitors out of business.
   (i) **Predatory Pricing**
   - Decreasing in prices, even below cost when competition are driven out, the company then raises prices back to their former level (Sherman Act prohibits such practices) FTC brought action against General Foods for predatory pricing in 1976.
3. **Price Discrimination**
   - Involves selling the same product to buyers at different prices without any cost justification. Theoretically, this maximises profit by enabling sellers to change price inelastic customers higher prices than elastic customers are charged. It can be unethical if it leads to charging similar buyers different prices for the same goods based on their ability to pay. **Robinson-Patman Act of 1936** states that price discrimination is illegal, makes also certain important exemptions. Though Maruti cannot sell the same cars at different prices, dealers can do.
4. **Price Fixing**
   - It is an agreement among firms in an industry to set prices at certain levels. The **Sherman Act** prohibits it because such actions restrict price competition. Two types of price fixing are:
     Horizontal Price Fixing: Agreements among competitors to fix prices at artificially high levels.
     Vertical Price Fixing: Price fixing agreements between manufacturers and retailers or between manufacturers and distributors. This involves an agreement that the product will be sold at the manufacturer's suggested price and will not be discounted by the retailer or wholesaler.
     Panasonic was accused of vertical price fixing by forcing its retailers to raise prices by5-10%; Retailers not cooperative were threatened.

Fig. 5.15 Four Areas of Pricing which are Unethical and Illegal.

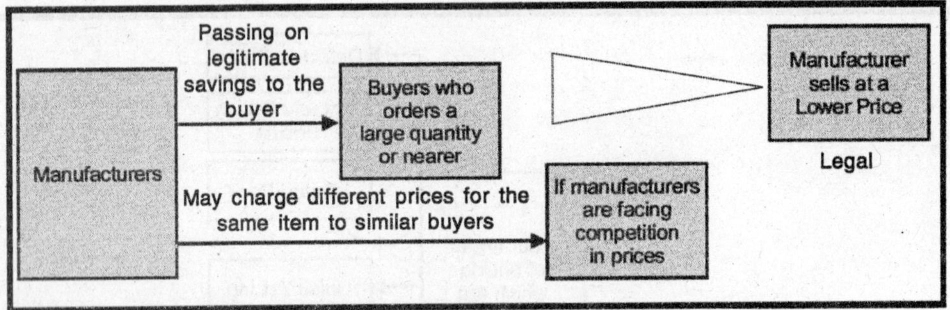

Fig. 5.16 Price Differences to Similar Buyers

(iv) Intellectual Property Protection

Before studying the patents, trademarks and copyrights let us understand the design first.

Design

A **design** means only the features of shape, configuration, pattern or ornament applied to any article by any industrial process, or means, whether manual, or chemical, separate or combined, which in the finished article appeal to and are judged solely by the eye; but does not include mode or principle of construction or anything which is in substance a mere mechanical device, and does not include any trademark.

In simple terms, the dictionary meaning of **design** is art of producing; sketch or plan for product; lines of shapes as decoration; layout; established form of product; mental plan; purpose etc.

A design is registered only if it is new or original. The Controller General of Patents and Designs will not register a design if the same is already registered or published in India in respect of the same or any other article prior to the application of registration. The registration of a design confers on its proprietor valuable rights to use the registered design exclusively by him. Article with registered design shall be marked 'Registered' along with the Registration number.

Trademarks, Patents and Copyrights

Trademarks, patents and copyrights affect the growth and prosperity of every industry and more so with the following industries:

- Chemicals and pharmaceutical industries, boilers, valves, regulators etc.
- Printing, publishing, entertainment industries like the files and recording industries.
- Computer software industry.

It is essential to be familiar with the law relating to the above subjects as these are fundamental to business strategy. It is significant to know the rights and options as well as the legal formalities and requirements necessary for protecting the products and ideas in the present day's competitive markets.

The above are governed by separate laws and they have to be studied separately.

A comparison of the above is as given in the table on page no. 201:

Copyright protection is explicit and clear cut. It protects against copying of entire programs or their part. Damages and relief are readily obtained for infringement.

The central ethical issue posed to individual concerned are:

- Should you copy for your own use a product protected by trade secret, copyright and/or patent law? If every one copies product, very little new products would be produced because creators could not benefit from the results or their work.

Does Your Work Involve Intellectual Property Rights?

Intellectual Property (IP), a creation of the mind, is an asset, and as such it can be bought, sold, licensed, exchanged, or gratuitously given away like any other form of property. Further, the IP owner has the right to prevent the unauthorised use or sale of the property. The most noticeable difference between IP and other forms of property, however, is that IP is intangible, that is, it cannot be defined or identified by its own physical parameters.

Educational institutes deal mainly with copyrights, though some of them do sometimes deal with other IP including trademarks and patents. **Copyright** is an exclusive right to reproduce an original work of authorship fixed in any tangible medium of expression, to prepare derivative works based upon the original work, and to perform or display the work in the case of musical, dramatic, choreographic, and sculptural works. Copyrights are protected in India, by the Copyright Act of 1957 along with the Copyright Rules, 1958, several subsequent amending Acts, and the latest Copyright (Amendment) Act of 1999.

Copyrightable Work

Works of authorship that fall within the definition of copyrightable work include:

- Literary works (books and other writings, musical compositions, paintings, sculpture, computer programmes and films);
- Musical works and accompanying lyrics;
- Dramatic works;
- Pictorial, graphic, and sculptural works;
- Sound recordings; and
- Cinematograph films.

Copyright protection comes into existence from the moment the work is fixed in a tangible expression. Copyright registration is not mandatory. However, it is advisable to register because in India copyright registration constitutes prima facie evidence of the validity and ownership of the copyright.

The **Trade Related Intellectual Property Rights (TRIPS)** Agreement, under the World Trade Organisation (WTO), provides a minimum standard for duration of copyright protection. In the case of a person, the term is the life of the author plus 50 years. In the case of a corporate entity, it is 50 years from the end of the calendar year of authorised publication or, in the absence of publication, from the end of the calendar year of making. The term of protection for live performances that are recorded is 50 years for the performer and producer, and 20 years for the broadcaster of the work from date of publication. India is a signatory to the Berne Convention and Indian Copyright laws conform to all the WTO requirements.

In the past, educational institutes flourished in homegrown, local environments. Resources that were developed in-house were used only for the benefit of the students and faculty of the institute. Several times, teaching staff wrote textbooks and reaped the rewards of admiration from within the local community as well as limited commercial benefits.

In view of globalisation and the eminent enforcement of TRIPS, India and other smaller/less developed nations and institutions that fail to claim or register their IP rights stand the risk of losing their rights to international institutes.

The faculty and research staff of Indian educational institutes are capable of creating IP but are not adequately aware of how they can protect these rights. In fact, many times, they are not even aware that the IP they create is eligible for protection. For instance, teachers prepare test papers and examination papers, which are copyrightable. These papers are freely copied by students, shared with friends; often given to opportunists, commercial copying centers that sell them to students of other institutes for monetary value. It is necessary to raise the awareness of those involved in the creation of IP, so that they can realise the potential of creating and avail of the benefits of IP rights. It is also necessary to develop in-house systems to help these individuals protect their rights. Educational Institutes in certain developed countries do not permit students to take copies of the test papers with them at the end of a test.

In fact, educational institutes in several developed countries actively protect their IP and exploit it for monetary gains. Most universities that are involved in research and technology development have dedicated departments within the university with qualified scientists and lawyers. They continually work to protect IP created by the different in-house departments and actively court businesses to license use of their IP.

Fair Dealing

The exclusive rights granted to the copyright owner do not include the right to prevent others from 'fair dealing' with, or making 'fair use' of, the owner's work. Such 'fair use' may include use of the work for purposes of criticism, comment, news reporting, teaching or education, and scholarship or research. The nature of the work, the extent of the work copied, and the impact of copying on the work's commercial value are all considered in determining whether an unauthorised use is a 'fair use'. This enables educationists to use parts of a copyrighted work for the enhancement of education. For example, a professor, the owner of a text book, makes 30 photocopies of one page or one chapter of the book. This may be covered by 'fair use'.

Plagiarism

When students prepare reports, write articles or critiques they liberally borrow from material that is 'freely' available, it is considered **plagiarism**. Using existing material in subsequent works, without prior permission from the copyright owner, is **plagiarism**. For instance, it is simple to access and copy material available on the internet but it is not 'free' just by virtue of ready availability.

Plagiarism, the illegal copying of material is a **violation of IP rights**. Students, for the most part, are not even aware that they are violating laws by copying from existing matter. To avoid plagiarism, an individual who uses prior existing material, should give credit to the source and author of the matter used. Even if students quote or cite from other material they should provide information regarding the source and author. Obtaining prior permission from the copyright owner to use the material also protects students and institutes.

IP violations are myriad even though they are punishable by law. It should be noted that educational institutes could be held liable for plagiarism and copyright violations of their students, staff members, faculty etc. Among several factors, the lax enforcement of laws and the delay in the judicial disposal of matters in India, contribute to the rampant illegal use of protected IP. As the courts in India move slowly, the legal repercussions of IP violations may not be immediate.

However, reports of IP violations in the press harm the reputation of the institute. In addition to having an effective judicial system in certain developed countries, educational institutes have stringent codes of ethics that emphasise the illegality of plagiarism and the unauthorised use of other types of IP. For instance, in certain extreme cases, students guilty of plagiarism are rusticated or allowed to withdraw from the institute. Indian institutes can develop similar systems.

(Poorvi Chothani is a U.S. attorney at law and an advocate,
The Times of India, 12th July 2004)

The abuse of intellectual property (IP) rights in general is well documented, and applies equally in the world of technical standards. Based on some work done in the US, and supported anecdotal evidence in Europe, for every dollar we earn from the sale of standards, we lose a further dollar to illegal copying, transmission or unlicensed use. And that's probably a conservative estimate.

Some years ago, before the digital revolution. British Standards Institution in the UK did research suggesting that every printed standard they sold was illegally photocopied an average of five times.

Theft Costs the Community

Creating, maintaining and distributing a contemporary, technically valid collection of standards is an expensive exercise, sustained by the dedication and altruism of the many thousands of experts who freely contribute their time and expertise. So every time an illegal copy is made, or a single-user electronic document is passed on or networked, it increases the cost to legitimate purchasers, and the volunteer experts have their contribution devalued.

Scale of Copyright Abuse

The scale of copyright abuse is enormous. Based on some recent industry estimates, the US dollar losses from illegal use of material are:

Music Industry - USD 5 billion

Software Industry - USD 13 billion

Movie Industry - USD 4 billion

Standards Industry - USD 1 billion

Digital Rights Management-The Emerging Solution

A powerful long-term solution to this widespread devaluation of intellectual property, now being explored within the international standards community, is the coordinated use of a **Digital Rights Management (DRM) strategy.**

What is DRM? A definition offered by the American National Institute of Standards and Technology is that "**DRM** is a system of IT components and services, along with corresponding law, policies and business models, which strive to distribute and control intellectual property and its rights. Product authenticity, user charges, terms-of-use and expiration of rights are typical concerns of DRM."

In practice, it is a way of indelibly encrypting digital 'content' so that its future use can be inextricably tied to a particular piece of hardware, a specific user, a defined set of licensing conditions, or a pay-per-use financial arrangement.

Why is DRM so important to standardizers? Because standards organisations have been world leaders in moving away from paper and making their intellectual property available via advanced technologies. Virtually all major national and international collections are now available for instant access via the web-standards which less than five years ago would have required days of waiting by post, or the inconvenience of a visit to a specialist bookshop are now on line.

- In a booming global economy, where standards are being used to an ever-increasing extent, commercial revenue from the sale of standards worldwide has been flat or falling.

- A lack of understanding - a lack of education - amongst users on the nature and economic importance of copyright in general, and in particular where electronic documents are concerned.
- Confusion and differences amongst copyright owners as to how to educate and enforce copyright (a lack of standardization!).

These are challenges that will not go away, and in the longer term they represent a danger to the health, even the very existence of standardizing organisations and the current commercial model. If nothing is done to protect against the current devaluation of copyright, then the existing 'from the few to the many' model could wither, at very high cost to the general community.

By deploying Digital Rights Management systems, the industry may help both itself and its customers in ensuring an equitable long-term outcome for both.

DRM is not a single technology, but an aggregation of several intermeshed technologies.

DRM does not replace or substitute for copyright and legal constraints.

Perhaps the best comparison is to speed cameras. Like it or not, they help motorists comply with their driving license conditions. DRM is a tool that will help users avoid contravening their copyright licence obligations.

DRM has two aspects. Firstly, there is the Management of digital rights - how a digital product (book, film, music, software), with rights attached, can be managed. Effectively, this is the definition and licensing of rights.

A Brief History of Copyright

Intellectual property is fully recognised in law, and afforded extensive protection. It wasn't always so. Scholars in ancient Greece were the first to be concerned about being recognised as the authors of their works, but they had no economic rights. It was only with the invention of printing in the late 15th century that any form of copyright was devised. Before that, there was little need! Copying of manuscripts was a painstakingly slow process. And with a largely illiterate population, demand was small. In English law the first copyright act was only enacted in 1710.

Copying and distribution outside of the provisions of the current copyright legislation is illegal. It is theft. But people who would never dream of breaking into a home and stealing the family silver often don't think twice about misappropriating the intellectual family silver though illegal copying, transmission and use. It deprives the intellectual property owner in no less a tangible way.

Secondly, there is the Digital Management of Rights. This focuses on protection; how the rights attached to the object can be enforced by processes such as encryption, watermarking and other types of access and usage control.

The other major characteristic of an effective DRM system is that it must be a unique and indelible part of the intellectual property it protects. Effectively it is a digital fingerprint, so that whenever that document is accessed, its DRM system ensures that only licensed use is permitted.

The Danger-Throwing out the Baby, not the Bathwater

Electronic sale and distribution of standards has been the greatest single advance in the popularisation and use of standards. It provides 24/7 access, and more importantly, legal networking. And although not yet apparent, it has significant potential for reducing end user cost. These benefits must not be compromised. But there are downsides from the IP owner's viewpoint. While it is easy to control initial access to a document, it is difficult to control what people do with it afterwards. Users poorly understand that they are in serious breach of copyright when sharing files. Perfect copies can be made at the click of a mouse, and networking allows infinite, instantaneous sharing of digital content at virtually zero marginal cost.

The Need for User Education

But a heavy-handed approach to these issues could turn back the clock and even sacrifice revenue. The progressive introduction of DRM systems will be both a learning process for intellectual property owners, and require extensive education programmes for users. IP owners, especially in the standards world, have been culpable in failing to regularly and systematically educate their users in the value and community benefit of copyright, and the illegality and economic losses where breaches occur. ISO and its members are committed to rectifying this omission, and to provide much clearer education and guidance as DRM systems begin to move into the mainstream of our distribution systems.

All Saints and Sinners

Copyright abuse is an area in which we are all saints and sinners. Few of us have not copied something that clearly has the (C) mark on it. Or taped a piece of music for a friend. No harm in that. Except that the recorded music industry estimates its annual losses in billions of dollars to illegal copying, exacerbated by the advent of digital systems where the definition of what is original and what is a copy is practically, if not legally, blurred.

Microsoft to appeal $520-mn patent ruling

Microsoft Corp. says it will appeal a jury's ruling that it pay more than $520 million in damages to a university and a software company because its popular Web browser infringed on a patent.

The jury could have awarded as much as $1.2 billion to University of California and Eolas Technologies Inc., based in Chicago. "We are very satisfied," Eolas attorney Martin R.Lueck said Monday. "It shows the jury system works. Patents need to be respected regardless of the size and the market power of the company involved."

Microsoft attorney Andy Culbert said Monday's finding would be appealed.

Details	*Patents*	*Trademarks*	*Copyrights*
1. Definition	It is a monopoly right granted to a person who has invented a new and useful article, or new process of making an article. It consists of an exclusive right to manufacture the new article invented or manufacture an article according to the invented process for a limited period. After the expiry of the duration of patent, anybody can make use of the invention.	It is a visual symbol in the form of a word, device, name, letter, numerical, brand, heading, signature or label or any combination of these, applied or used in relation to goods so as to indicate a connection, in the course of trade between the goods and some person who is the proprietor or registered user of that trademark. The identity of that person may or may not be disclosed.	It is a negative right which prevents the appropriation of the fruits of man's work, labour or skill by another person. This protection is given by making any infringement of copyright as unlawful; copyright prohibits any person from reproducing or copying any "literary, dramatic, musical or artistic work" without the consent of the owner of the copyright in that work.
2. Dictionary meaning (Little Oxford dictionary)	Document conferring right, title etc., to sell some invention or process so protected.	Device or name legally registered to represent a company or a product, distinctive characteristic.	Exclusive right to print, publish, perform etc., material.
3. Benefits	They encourage inventions on a commercial scale and ensure that ultimately the patented article or process is utilised for the general good of the people at large.	It distinguishes the goods as regards their manufacture or quality, dealt by a particular person, company or firm, from similar goods manufactured or dealt by other persons, companies or firms.	It ensures that any intellectual or artistic work, which often is immeasurable in terms of money, belongs to its rightful owner or author, and none else is able to derive any benefits by annexation of its fruits.

Details	*Patents*	*Trademarks*	*Copyrights*
4. Governing Act	**The Indian Patents Act, 1970,** contains the law governing patents. This Act extends to the whole of India.	**The trade and Merchandise Marks Act 1958**, provides for the registration and better protection of trademarks and for the prevention of the use of fraudulent marks on merchandise. It extends to the whole of India and came into force on 25th Nov. 1959.	**The Copy Right Act 1957**, contains the law relating to copyright. It extends to the whole of India and came into force from 21st Jan.1958. It set up a copyright office under the control of the registered officer for the registration of copyrights. Important amendments were made in the Acts in 1984 and 1992. The copyright 1992 which is pending before parliament, seeks to extend more than effective protection to owners of copyright in the context of technological developments, affecting the reproduction of musical compositions, videotapes of films and various computer programs and computer generated works.
5. Registration	Section 134 provides that where any country does not accord to citizens of India the same rights in respect of the grant of patents and its protection as it accords to its own nationals, then no national of such country shall be entitled to apply for the grant of patent or be registered as assignee of the proprietor or other privileges granted by the Act. Subject to the above provision, an application for a patent for an invention may be made by:	A register of trademarks is kept at the head office of the trademarks registry in which all trademark, registered are entered with the relevant particulars. This register is divided into two parts. Part A and B. The qualification for registration in Part B is less stringent than Part A registration. The validity of Part A cannot normally be challenged after the expiry of 7 years from the date of registration. Contents:	A register of copyright will be in the copyright office in which the names or titles of the works, the names and addresses of authors, publishers and owners of copyright and certain other particulars are entered on making an application to the registrar. Such registration is however, optional and is not a condition for acquiring copyright. The advantage of registration is a certified copy of an entry in the registrar of copyrights as a

Details	*Patents*	*Trademarks*	*Copyrights*
	Any person claiming to be the true and first inventor of the invention by any person being the assignee of the person mentioned above. By the legal representative of any deceased person who immediately before his death was entitled to make such an application.	1. The name of a company individual or firm represented in a special or particular manner. 2. The signature of the applicant for registration or some predecessor in his business. 3. One or more invented words. 4. One or more words having no direct reference to the character or quality of the goods, not being a geographical name or a surname or a personal name or the name of a sect, caste or tribe in India. 5. Any other distinctive mark.	primafacie evidence of the particulars entered there in all courts without further proof of production of the original. The registrar publishes in the official gazette all entries made in the register of copyrights. The author of a work has the right to claim authorship of the work as well as the right to restrain or claim damages in respect of (a) any distortion, mutilation or other modification of his work, or (b) any other action in relation to his work which would be prejudicial to his honour or reputation.
6. Terms	Every patent granted under this Act shall be in respect of the process of manufacture of food or a medicine or drug, 5 years from the date of sealing of the patent, whichever is shorter. In respect of any other invention, 14 years from the date of the patent. A patent shall cease to have effect on the expiration of the aforesaid period, unless it is renewed.	On registration of a trademark, the registrar will issue a certificate of registration in the prescribed form, with the seal of trademarks registry. The registration will be for a period of 7 years but may be renewed from time to time on payment of the prescribed renewal fee. A trademark removed from the register for failure to pay the renewal fee can be restored on application.	In published literary, dramatic, musical and artistic work (other than a photograph). Sixty years from the beginning of the calendar year next following the year in which the author dies. In case of work of a joint authorship, the reference to the author shall be construed as to that author who dies last. In case of a photograph the copyright shall subsist for 50 years from the beginning of the calendar year following the year of publication. In case of cinematograph films and records, this shall subsist until 50 years from the beginning of the calendar year next following the year in which the film or the record, as the case may be, is published.

(v) Human Rights

'Human Rights', constitutes two words: 'Human' and 'Rights'. 'Human' means 'belonging or pertaining to man' or 'having the qualities of man'. From these, we can clearly understand the word 'human' refers to persons who possess the characteristics of a man. He should not behave like animals or in a mechanical way. This has been very well depicted by OSHA'S model by Subash Sharma in his book on ethics and Human Values in Management.

- Progress of the humanity can be seen in terms of material abundance; Material satisfaction is found outwardly; But there is no mental satisfaction for the human.
- Earlier in the pre-industrial agricultural society, the man was in relatively greater harmony with nature. In the recent times, as the civilisation progressed, man has lost his mental happiness because of the emergence of a mechanical society and man is almost working like a machine. The machine simile became a dominant simile in organisational and social life.
- The fall of man is felt inevitable with the advent of the information revolution in this robotic age. How to prevent the fall of man and to restore his harmonic nature is the question. Can 'OSHA' model help to know this and to understand the same? The answer is 'yes' and the model has relevance for preventing the fall of man.

OSHA model depicts human behaviour and the actions.

Level 0: Highest and the **Best** human behaviour and the action is First alphabet of 'OSHA' O. **'O'** is termed as **'Oneness** with nature' and the man who achieves this can be equated with the giver of "devine-energy". This level is very difficult to be reached by a normal human being. If once achieved, he is considered a superhuman. This is the stage of **'Nirvana**,' liberation from all bondages of the attributes. The transcendence of all attributes shown under level 1 to 3 below is depicted by 'O'.

Level 1: Next alphabet of 'OSHA' is 'S'. **S** is a higher category of attribute - a **spiritual** attribute. If an individuals behaviour is dominated by this spiritual attribute, he is nearing oneness with nature and help. On the verge of reaching Level 0. This level is also extremely difficult to achieve and the percentage of the people who are endowed with this behaviour is too small. But every person has the ability to achieve it but with full determination and effort.

Level 2: The alphabet following S in OSHA is **'H'**, a lower category of attribute - a **human** attribute (attributer's is also termed as guna). We find in this category (people of H attribute) considerable in number.

Level 3: Last alphabet of 'OSHA' is **'A'** which represents **animal** attribute, the lowest category of attribute with **majority of people falling under this category**.

The 'OSHA' model conceptualises the three modes of behavioural tendencies in terms of:

- **Spiritual**
- **Human**
- **Animal**

These three tendencies are again the reflections of the **Indian Psycho-Philosophy** which are referred to the three gunas as:

- **Sattva** (essence attributes)-Refers to purity and illumination. Binds the individual to **bliss**.
- **Rajas** (Energy attributes)-Refers to craving and attachment; Binds the individual to **action**.
- **Tamas** (Inertia attributes)-Means darkness; Arises out of ignorance and dilution i.e., (agnana and mosa).

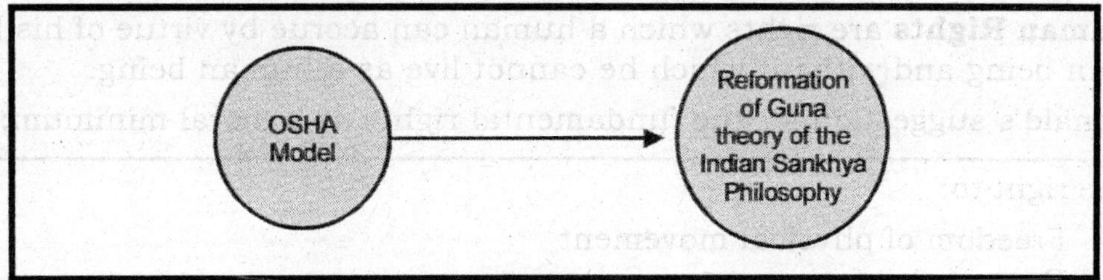

Fig. 5.17 "OSHA" Model Meaning

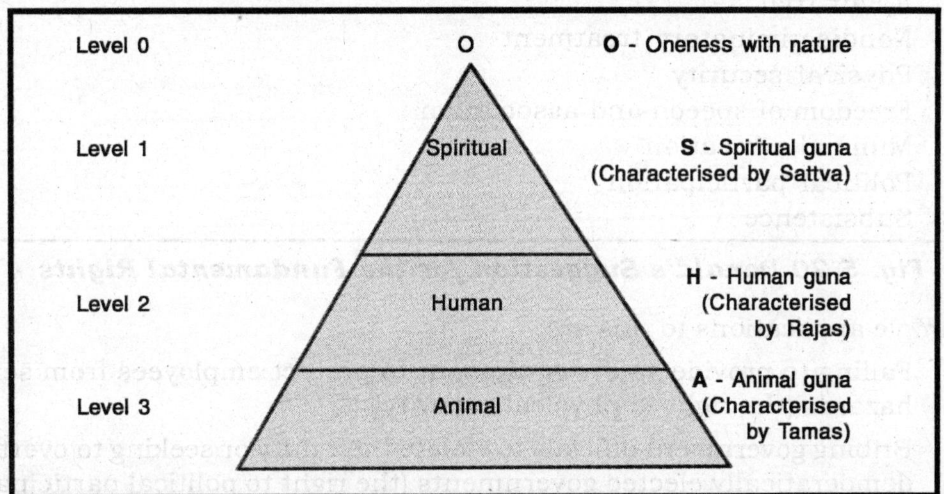

Fig. 5.18 OSHA Model

***[Ref:* Book Ethics and Human values in Managemement' by Subash Sharma]**

Human Rights represent an attempt to protect individuals from oppressing exploit and injustices. Human rights is the core of civil liberties of a man.

Human Rights are the natural rights, inalienable inherent in all human benings by virtue of their being human beings alone. Irrespective of civilization, religion and philosophy, there exists certain rights for the human called **'Human Rights'**.

Definition

Human rights have been defined by different authors in different ways. The dictionary meaning is.

Fig. 5.19 Human Rights

World conference on human rights says. "All human rights derive from the dignity and worth inherent in the human person, and that the human person is the central subject of human rights and fundamental freedoms".

Human Rights are rights which a human can accrue by virtue of his being a human being and without which he cannot live as a human being.

Donald's suggestion for the fundamental rights as a moral minimum:

The right to:

- Freedom of physical movement
- Ownership of property
- Freedom from torture
- A Fair trial
- Nondiscriminatory treatment
- Physical security
- Freedom of speech and association
- Minimal education
- Political participation
- Subsistence

Fig. 5.20 Donald's Suggestion for the Fundamental Rights

Sample applications to this are:

- Failing to provide safety equipment to protect employees from serious hazards (the right to physical security)
- Bribing government officials to violate their duty or seeking to overthrow democratically elected governments (the right to political participation)
- Employing child labour as found mostly in India (the right to minimal education)

On the whole, Guidelines based on human rights provide a bedrock moral minimum. However, the application of rights based guidelines are uncertain in more controversial situations where we are most in need of guidance, and they are inapplicable to many other pressing matters.

Example: "A well experienced person in a company who was ideally fit for a profit implementation job abroad was denied that opportunity and a junior employee selected with that opportunity without much experience and knowledge was sent in his place"

Such things, we find common in many of the Indian organisations sometimes even in foreign countries whether it is private or public sector.

Denying those rights or failing to protect them for other persons and groups is normally considered to be unethical. The company interests would be lost and it has to pay a very heavy penalty respecting others, even those with whom we disagree or whom we dislike, is the essence of human rights provided that the others do the same for us. This approach to ethical reasoning holds that individuals are to be treated as valuable ends in themselves just because they are human beings. For your purposes if you use others, it is unethical, at the same time, you deny them their goals and purposes. For example, dumping your unwanted materials on the back of other industries compound may be guilty of ignoring the rights of others.

One of the major limitations, we find here is the difficulty of balancing conflicting rights. For example: an employees right to privacy may be disturbed with an employer's right to protect the firms cash by testing the employees honesty with secret watch and ward.

Individual rights is a philosophy used in making ethical decisions that aims to protect human dignity (guided by a belief). Because a belief in another persons rights implies that you have a duty to protect those rights. You would reject any decision that violated these rights.

Example: You would not deceive people nor trick them into acting against their own interests.

You would respect their privacy and right to express their opinion openly; You would not force people to act in a way that was against their religion or moral beliefs; You would not punish a person without a fair and impartial hearing; Though you might be guided by a desire to achieve the greatest good for the greatest number of people, you would reject any choice that violated the rights of even one person. In an era when individual workers expect and demand their rights, this philosophy is becoming a practical necessity.

The protection and promotion of human rights is an important ethical benchmark for judging the behaviour of individuals and organisations. Majority would certainly agree that the denial of a person's fundamental rights to:

- Life
- Freedom
- Privacy
- Growth
- Human dignity

Human dignity is generally unethical. By defining properly the human constitution and pointing the way to realisation of human potentialities, such rights become a kind of common denominator of ethical reasoning, leading to the essential conditions for ethical actions and decisions.

Foundational document for human rights

- United Nations Universal Declaration on Human Rights - 1948
- UN adopted two agreements (subsequently ratified by the major countries of the world; International covenant on Social, Economic, and Cultural Rights and the International Covenant on Civil and Political Rights) - 1966
- UN has been developing a code of conduct for multinational corporations (yet to be completed or adopted) - Since 1972
- UN Secretary General Kofi Annan challenged world business leaders to "embrace and enact" the Global Compact (consists of 9 principles covering human rights, labour and the environment) - 1999
- ILO which dates from 1919 and is now a specialised agency of UN, sets many international standards, including those of the Tripartite Declaration of Principles concerning Multinational Enterprises and Social Policy - 1977
- Recently, OECD (members are the more developed countries of the world) has adopted the OECD guidelines for multinational enterprises. Several interfaith religious bodies have developed codes:
  - The principles for Global Corporate Responsibility adopted by the US based Interfaith Centre on Corporate Responsibility and similar organisations in Great Britain, Ireland and Canada adopted by Interfaith Declaration on International Business Ethics which resulted from a dialogue among Christians, Jews and Muslims.
  - A group of world business leaders, meeting in Caux, Switzerland, developed the Caux Roundtable Principles for Business.

These codes have many guidelines in common and cover the areas of employment practices, consumer protection, environmental preservation, involvement in politics, including bribery, and basic human rights.

Operating outside the home country, specially in LDCs, create dilemmas that lead to charges of serious ethical failings. MNCs generally recognise a social responsibility and attempt to fulfill their responsibilities everywhere they are located. The major cause of occasional failures to act responsibly is not because of lack of effort but the diversity of political and legal systems around the world and differences in economic development.

Foreign operations create challenges as well as opportunities for misconduct that simply do not exist for purely domestic enterprises. The question for MNCs is deciding which standards to follow. Neither of the two extreme positions is satisfactory. Ultimately, the solution to many of the ethical problems of international business lies in the development of international agreements and codes of ethics.

(vi) Pollution and Natural Environment

This matter has already been covered in para 3.1 of Module 3.

Ecological Concerns

The difficulty of balancing business and environment is very important. One of the companies in USA manufacturing paint pigments was dumping its waste from the manufacturing process in its own dump site on 68 wooded acres behind the plant. Recently the government ordered the firm to clear up the site with a US $60 million price tag. With annual sale of only US $30 million, it opted to close its doors. Now the company is out of business, its customers are scrambling to line up new sources of pigment, the employees are out of work, and the toxic waste remains.

In a situation like this, there are no winners.

Toxic wastes are not the only form of pollution threatening our environment. Our air, our water, and our land are all subject to abuse as a consequence of industrial activity. Pollution are threats to the physical environment caused by human activities in an industrial society.

Air Pollution

The air we breathe is threatened by two forms of pollution.

- Gaseous discharges
- Dust particles

More than 200 million tons of pollutants spill into the air each year, and each type of pollutant has a different effect. For example, hydrocarbons (gases released when fossil fuels are burned) combine with sunlight and under certain atmospheric conditions produce smog, which burns the eyes, sears the throat, and distresses those who suffer from asthma, bronchitis, and emphysema. Such far reaching heath consequences have made fighting smog in several areas.

One more sort of air pollutant is rain with a high acid content which is created when nitrous oxides and gaseous sulphur dioxide react with air. This 'acid rain' has been blamed for damaging lakes and forests in south-eastern Canada and the north-eastern United States. Most of the harmful emissions come from coal burning factories and electric utility plants. Coal admissions also have another disadvantage contributing to a 'green house effect' where the heated gases form a layer of unusually warm air around the earth, which trap the suns heat and prevent the earths surface from colling. Some scientists believe that the greenhouse effect will eventually cause dramatic changes in the earth's climate, including a general increase in temperature, changes in rainfall, and a rise in the level of oceans. But threat serves as a warning under these uncertainty about setting air pollution continue unchecked.

An air pollution problem with more immediate implications is posed by the airborne carcinogens (cancer-causing agents) that are emitted into the atmosphere during some manufacturing process. These toxins, according to environmentalists, are responsible for more than 20,000 cancer deaths each year.

Water Pollution

Our air is not the only part of our environment to suffer. Approximately, 11% of our river water and 30% of our lake water is polluted. The harbours and coastal waters are in trouble as well. This pollution comes from a variety of sources:

- Municipal industrial facilities.
- Oil Spills (In the largest spill in US history, the Exxon Valdez discharged 10 million gallons of oil into the ocean off the coast of Alaska, destroyed wild life and scenic beauty along 800 miles of shoreline).
- Run off from farm lands and construction sites and urban areas.
- In areas that are heavily industrialised, water, pollution levels are very high. Boston harbour is a 50 square mile soup of arsenic chromium, lead and PCBs dumped there by some 6000 factories. Hence fishing in the harbour is not outlawed. The flounder pulled out from the water have tumours and cancerous sores.

Even if all waste water were purified before being discharged the ground water would still be endangered by leakage from the millions of tons of hazardous substances that have been buried in the ground or dumped in inadequate storage sites. Several hundred cases of ground pollution reports exist.

In India, water pollution is very heavy especially from the discharge of industrial surplus. Waste and effluents disposal system are not properly enforced.

Industrial surplus is defined as those materials which are in excess of reasonable operational requirements of the concern. Surplus is the state of an item when stock is likely to last larger than a reasonable period or when it is no longer required for use. Industrial wastage is a residue or piece, cut of raw materials during the manufacturing process. There may be other type of waste. Waste is produced by industrial establishment and plant personnel.

Waste can be classified as under, in terms of its disposal.

- Salvageable waste
- Non salvageable waste

Non salvageable waste, have no salvage value, but need further processing and treatment for disposal. These are dangerous to the surrounding population and animal life, as it contains chemical toxins and disease producing organisms. There is bound to be pressure on the existing sanitation services if proper planning is not undertaken before locating industries. Ethical issue arises if lack of facilities for the disposal of non-salvageable industrial waste and sewage leads to pollution of water supply, contamination of soil with parasites and their ova.

Land Pollution

The disposal of industrial wastes directly into the ground probably the single greatest threat facing the environment today. Two thirds of the hazardous waste produced in the USA is disposed of in or on the land. And a large portion of this waste, - some estimates reach as high as 90 per cent - is disposed off unsafely. The USA government has identified some 20,000 dump sites around the country that are seriously contaminated. Almost half of the population lives in countries that contain one of these sites.

Ecology

It is the relationship among the living things in the water, air and the soil and the nutrients that support them. Pollution problems became the subject of widespread public concern in the 1960s, when ecology or the balance of nature, became a popular case. In 1963, Federal, State, and local governments in USA began to act laws and regulations aimed at reducing pollution. National environmental act of 1969 to control pollution established a structure for coordinating all federal environmental programs. This act was followed by a presidential order in December 1970, established the Environmental Protection Agency (EPA) to regulate air and water pollution by manufacturers and utilities, supervise auto pollution control, license pesticides, control toxic substances and safeguard the purity of drinking water.

After some initial conflict, the EPA and the industry established a relatively smooth working relationship, their willingness to work together brought advances in pollution control during the past decade, the influence of the EPA has diminished. The political climate has favoured deregulation and a relatively relaxed approach to the enforcement of environmental regulations. Much of the burden of environmental protection has shifted to state and local governments and to industry itself.

The current approach to pollution control recognises that the health threat posed by a given industrial pollutant must be weighed against the economic cost of limiting or eliminating its use.

Earth's Warming Due To Human Activity

Who has 'done the climate in'? Man or nature? As scientists desperately seek an answer, William K Stevens of The New York Times breezes through recent theories on climate change...

As evidence that the earth's atmosphere is warming continues to accumulate, scientists are making slow progress towards an answer to the big question:

How much of the warming is due to human activity and how much due to natural causes?

The United Nations' Inter-governmental Panel of Climate Change, the group of scientists widely considered the most authoritative voice of the subject, has already concluded that there is a "discernible human influence" on the global climate. While the group's conclusions are unformed, some experts on the problem say the human imprint on climate is becoming clearer, and may even have been the dominant factor in the global warming of recent decades. Not everyone agrees - there is a range of judgements and virtually all experts say that in any case, a reliable estimate of the human imprint's magnitude still remains some distance off.

A number of influences, both natural and man-made, cause the planet's temperature to vary. The natural ones include changes in solar radiation, and sulphate droplets called aerosols cast aloft by crupting volcanoes, which cool the atmosphere by reflecting sunlight. The human influence stems mostly from emissions of waste industrial gases like carbon dioxide, which trap heat in the atmosphere, and sulphate aerosols from industrial smoke stacks. The combined impact of industrial 'aerosols' and greenhouse gases creates complex and distinctive temperature patterns. It was mostly an analysis of those patterns that led the inter-governmental panel in 1995 to abandon its previous position that global warming observed over the past century might as easily be natural as human-induced. Human factors appeared to be playing a part, the panel said then, but it offered no judgement on whether that part was big, small or in between.

One recent piece of evidence suggesting a strong human influence, which seems likely to carry some weight with the inter-governmental panel, appeared recently in the journal 'Nature'. Scientists at the Henley Centre for Climate Prediction and Research, a British Government organisation, analysed the global climate record of the last century in an effort to isolate and quantify the major factors producing the century's rise of about 1 deg.F. in the earth's average surface temperature.

The research team led by Dr.Simon FB Tett found that in the earlier part of the century, the rise could be explained either by an increase in solar radiation or a combination of stronger solar radiation and heat-trapping greenhouse gases emitted by industrial economies. But they found that after the mid-1970s, when about half the century's warming took place, the warming resulted largely from the greenhouse gases.

This and other analysis have found that the warmest years of all occurred in the 1990s, with 1998 the warmest on record. EL Nino, the great pool of warm water in the tropical Pacific Ocean that from time to time heats the atmosphere and disrupts weather patterns, was responsible for some of the 1998 heating. A preliminary analysis by Dr.Wigley, however, has shown that when EI Nino's effects are filtered out of the global temperature record statistically, 1998 still ranks as the warmest year (Year 1999 is also shaping up as unusually warm, but not as warm as 1998).

Experts have difficulty in getting a handle on the constantly shifting amounts and patterns of industrial aerosols, and they have a similarly hard time establishing the varying strength of solar radiation.

Some mainstream scientists say that because the earth's average surface temperature has not varied by more than a degree or two since the last ice age, variations in the strength of the sun's radiation must be relatively small.

This is a measure of the climate system's sensitivity to "forcing", as experts call it, by external heating and cooling influences, and many mainstream scientists agree.

Now attention is shifting to the relative strength of the external forcing. This is the crux of the problem of figuring out the magnitude of human influence on the climate. There are basically three main forcing: greenhouse gases and solar radiation, which warm the atmosphere, and sulphate droplets, or aerosols, from both volcanoes and industrial sources, which cool it.

The amount of carbon dioxide and other greenhouse gases in the atmosphere has been firmly established, and continuously monitored, though it is difficult if not impossible to predict how much there will be in the future.

Sulphate aerosols from volcanoes sometimes spread to the stratosphere, where they, too, diffuse globally and cool the earth. But they dissipate in two or three years. Sulphate aerosols from industry generally rise only into the lower part of the atmosphere and fall out, as acid rain, within a few days. Moreover, their extent and impact is mostly regional rather than global. Until recently, they affected primarily the industrial countries of Europe and North America, but scientists now believe that they are diminishing in that part of the world because of controls on pollution. They are growing fast, however, in India, China and Southeast Asia.

The ethical issues now stands on the human factors of the emission of industrial aerosols and greenhouse gases which are prevalent in India affecting the climate as well as the health of the people and other creatures.

Cruelty To Animals

Have you at any moment remained a silent spectator to various forms of cruelty being perpetrated on animals all around? This is in short an "abetment" to the crime. It is time that each one raise their voice against the inhumanities heaped on these dumb creatures and joins animal lovers towards fighting for their rights.

The few common forms of "cruelty" are also the prescribed forms of cruelty as per the Prevention of Cruelty to Animals Act (PCA), 1960. Beating, kicking overriding, overloading, torturing, causing unnecessary pain to an animal, employing in any work a wounded or sick animal, carrying an animal in a vehicle in a manner or position that causes unnecessary pain or suffering, keeping or carrying an animal in a care that does not permit the animal to move freely,... the list is endless.

It is common slighter to witness the above forms of cruelty on our roads. The bullock cart heavily laden with cement, stones or iron rods, the poor animals trudging wearily, the cartman incessantly lashing with his whip at the already wounded and emaciated bodies. On closer observation most of them have grey mottled skin and congested lungs due to the traffic pollution that they are constantly exposed to. Their eyes speak a saga of suffering and deprivation. Have you seen the man racing on the bicycle or autorickshaw laden with hens from side to side. Many of the birds die of asphyxia even before they reach their destination.

You really do not have to look very far for the various forms of cruelty. Does your neighbour's dog bark continuously because it is kept tied throughout or is chained with a rope, which does not allow it to lie down properly?

These are also punishable forms of cruelty as per the PCA Act.

Unfortunately, the Act is ill equipped to deal with the offenders of the provisions of the Act. The punishments meted out to the offenders are silly. For any of the above-mentioned offences, the minimum fine is Rs.10 and a maximum of Rs.50. For subsequent offences committed within three years of the previous offence, the minimum fine is Rs.25 and carries a maximum of Rs.100 rupees or with imprisonment for a term which may extend to three months or both.

The fact that there is a special chapter in the PCA Act on "performing animals" namely chapter V is an indicator of how backward our animal laws are. The very thought of a performing animal would make any animal love blanch but our laws actually to us what kind of animals can be used to "perform" and how to go about it!

The rules under the PCA Act prescribe certain maximum load for draught animals.

Some of the examples are:

Up in rows slaughter while one animal is dragged by Small bullock drawing a two small bullock drawing a two-wheeled vehicle fitted with pneumatic tyres - 750 kgs.

Small bullock drawing a two wheeled vehicle not fitted with pneumatic tyres - 500 kgs.

Large bullock drawing a two wheeled vehicle not fitted with pneumatic tyres - 900 kgs.

Horse or mule drawing a two wheeled vehicle not fitted with pneumatic tyres - 500 kgs.

Large bullock is described as one whose weight exceeds 350 kgs while a small bullock is one whose weight does not exceed 250 kgs.

Rule 6 is the most flouted one which states that the draught animals should not carry a load for a period of more than nine hours a day; they should not be made to work for more than five hours continuously without a break and should also not be made to world from 12 noon to 3.00 p.m.

But while the human-animal conflict in the countryside and hunting's abetted by religious dogmas have encouraged man's brutality towards animals, no such excuse can be given for wanton cruelties perpetuated on the domesticated animals including cattle. At every step, the provisions of the Prevention of Cruelty to Animals Act are ignored and the animals flayed while they forth at the mouth. A scenario common in all the six major slaughter houses in the City.

According to Mr.P.Sanjay, Animal Welfare Officer of CUPA, the slaughter of animals defies all laws and is an assault of human sensibilities. "The animals are tied its tail and its throat slit and flung one hook and hanged, the other animals witness the proceedings. They defecate and urinate in horror since, by then, the mute creatures know what is in store for them. The flailing of the animals, which bleed to die a slow and agonizing death, is also done in full view of other animals. The bleating and shricks are silenced only when the slaughter for the day is completed, Mr.Sanjay, "who has visited some of the slaughter houses?"

The laws is clear that no animal should be slaughtered in the presence of other animals and that the killing should be done in a humane manner. A veterinarian should be present to oversee that the slaughter is done according to the provisions of the law. However, the law is given a quiet burial and the authorities seldom bother to implement them since these animals are doomed to die anyway.

"The suffering at the slaughter house are nothing compared with the agony of these animals during their march from distant places," says Mr.Sanjay. "The cattle are bundled into a truck in a group of 40 to 50 animals. No water, no food is provided for days and the reasoning is that 'there is a little urine and faces passed by the hapless creature at the time of slaughter', If they fall exhausted, then they are beaten black and blue till they are forced to stand and walk. If all else fails, chilli powder is smeared into the eyes of the cattle so that they jump to their feet out of excruciating pain".

Organisations such as CUPA have taken up cudgels on behalf of the mute creatures. It has been dealing with overloading of bullock carts for the past 18 months and sensitizing owners of bullock carts to the suffering silently endured by the animals. The organisation has organized awareness programmes to sensitize people and also the police to the need to effectively implement the law. "Many a time we find that the constables are not aware of the existing laws," says an officer-bearer of CUPA.

Another mission of CUPA is to focus on schools and colleges to sensitize children and youth to the cruelties inflicted on animals. The response, though encouraging, may not yet mitigate the sufferings of the animals until participation in the cause of the animal assumes the proportion of a mass movement. Where do ethics stand on this brutal act of human being?

(**Source**: R.Krishna Kumar in 'The Hindu' Feb.8, 1999 Sudha S.Naraynan, 16 Nov.1997).

Battle of Bhopal (Bhopal Gas Tragedy)

SC Judgement is not the end of the affair

The Supreme Court's decision, to finally disburse the Rs.1,500 crore compensation from Union Carbide to victims or kin of the 1984 Bhopal gas tragedy, is a significant milestone, but one sans the attributes of a climax. The good news is soured with the knowledge that the BJP government of Madhya Pradesh wishes to use part of the amount for the city of Bhopal. The SC must ensure that the money goes to the victims and not into the grubby paws of local corporators. This sorry case begs an examination of a larger attitudinal issue: The disposition of the powers that be to such victims. From Bhopal to Kumbakonam, we have been repeatedly assaulted by images of abject grief, of victims of largely avoidable man-made disasters. In almost all these cases, the victims' fate is made more tragic by the culpability of the state in not ensuring that proper procedures were being followed. Speedy relief and some clear demonstration of the caring hand of the state are immediate actions necessary to ameliorate grief, but these are rarely found together. It's high time the government pulled up its baggy socks on disaster management policies, strategies and procedures.

In this case, the administration has appeared lackadaisical from the start. Bhopal was the single largest industrial accident in the world that ultimately affected over five lakh people, and the government only got $470 million as compensation! This is a paltry amount, especially when measured against the billion dollar payouts to American victims of similar accidents. Quite clearly, it isn't over yet. The government must actively push cases against both Warren Anderson and Dow Chemicals, the present owners of Union Carbide, and at least get the firm to thoroughly clean up the abandoned Bhopal complex that is still leaking toxins into the environment. That much is owed to the people of the city. Ultimately, no one doubts the immense value of the compensation that will be paid to the Bhopal survivors. But we must understand that this particular decision is more about the delivery, however delayed, of some justice to a struggling few than any compensatory largess being doled out to them.

(vii) Harmful Products

Hearing Damages

In daily life, acoustics is usually associated with positive sounds like music and speech communication. Unfortunately, however, acoustics also has a grave negative side which becomes obvious when sound turns into noise.

It is said that some 20% of the total population in Europe is exposed to noise levels in their living environment that exceed the acceptable limits set by the scientific and medical community, leading to manifold physical and psychological irritations for the people concerned. Such effects are, however, difficult to quantify. More solid data exist for noise-induced hearing damages at workplaces, however. In Germany, for instance, hearing impairment has been at the top of all occupational impairments for many years, and the resulting annual social and economic costs are of the order of magnitude of 120 million USD. Other industrilized countries are faced with similar problems.

Hazards are Everywhere

Our workplaces are full of hazards (potential sources of harm). To name but a few: a guillotine on a paper-cutting machine could slice off a worker's hand, a crane that is too overloaded will fail mechanically, exothernic reactions in a chemical plant could reach a runaway condition, hydrocarbons on an oil refinery could leak and iugnite, and the dynamic positioning system of a ship must continuously adjust the thrusters correctly to avoid collision with a nearby installation.

Our first aim is always to eliminate the hazards at source. This can be achieved by the application of inherent safety principles and good engineering pracvtice. However, in many industrial scenarios it is not practicable to eliminate every hazard. For example, guillotines need a sharp blade to cut paper, an exothermic reaction may be the only way to produce a particular chemical, and oil refineries always contain hydrocarbons.

Fortunately, these hazards very rarely materialize because we design control or protection systems to ensure safety. These safety related systems defend against the remaining hazards by monitoring the state of the process under control and taking specific action to prevent an unsafe state occurring. In many cases the specific action is to shut down part or all of the process being monitored. If there is no simple safe state, such as with a ship's dynamic positioning system, the safety-related system will have to continuously control the process.

Safety that depends on a control or protection system operating correctly in response to its inputs is called **functional safety**.

Vibration and Shock Affect Peoples' Lives

When assessing the effects on vibration and shock on workplace safety, the first consideration is the nature of dynamic forces at work. They vary widely from steady state vibration to low range impulsive forces to high level shock, and each requires different methodology, monitoring cycles and assessment tools. Humans, machines, vehicles and structures, all factors in workplace safety. More specifically, its scope includes the general areas of mechanical vibration and shock pertaining to: terminology and nomenclature; actuators, sensors and associated signal analysis instrumentation; vibration and shock reduction and control methods; and, finally, the measurement and evaluation of the exposure of humans, stationary structures, vehicles and machines. In addition, standard methods of data processing, data acquisition, diagnostic measurement methods, transducer calibration and condition monitoring of machines and structures are actively being developed. All these subjects are related to workplace safety either directly through assessment of human exposure, potential workplace hazards and application of hazard control or indirectly by diagnosing and predicting future workplace hazards.

"Human exposure to whole-body vibration is a widespread occupational factor that may cause adverse effects on safety and health"

Major category of workplace hazards is the catastrophic failure of machines or structures leading to injury.

Cross-cultural contradictions

Ethical problems occur when certain corporations cannot do business at home, would try to enter other societies where ethical standards differ. At home, if it is difficult to follow the ethical standards, then such unsafe products (their countries doesn't permit) are sold where and there is demand in other countries and where ethical standards permit to use such products. Acceptable safety standards differ among nations and that honest differences of opinion exist among scientists and safety experts. There are some companies who have built factories in nations whose pollution control laws are less stringent than a particular country regulations. They are charged with **"exporting pollution"**.

What is thought to be ethically acceptable by one nation is considered unethical by another. The resultant ethical dilemmas can be difficult ones for business firms and their managers to solve.

Four groups to which business has a responsibility. Companies have a responsibility to:

- Society
- Employees
- **Customers** (Consumers)
- Investors

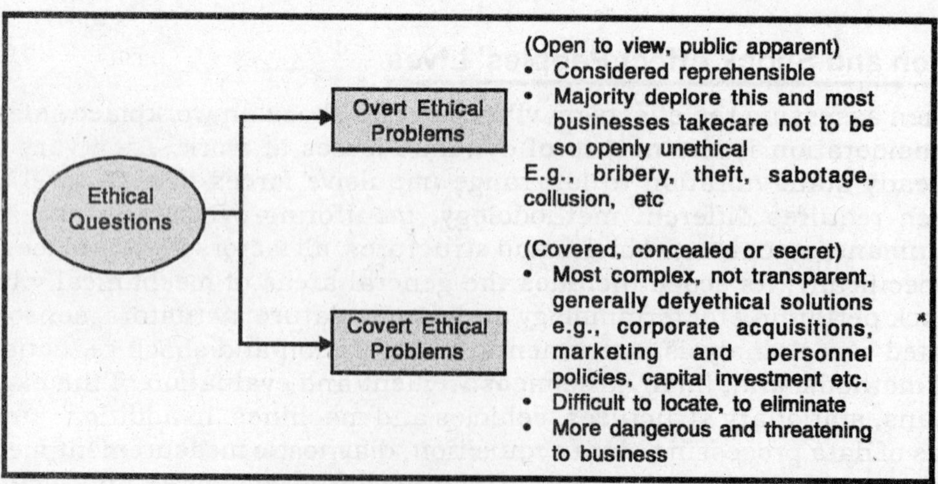

Fig. 5.21 Ethical Questions

Product Packaging and Labelling

Consumers need a certain amount of information to make rational choices. This information is not easily obtained. For example, A consumer examining a frozen apple pie in a sealed, opaque cardboard box. Without information on the label, consumers have no practical means for determining the size of the frozen pie, the ingredients used, the nutritional content, or the length of time the product was frozen etc. Health conscious consumer are disadvantaged by the welter of claims about low fat and salt content and the unregulated use of words such as light and healthy. The more information is provided, consumers can better protect themselves in the market place. There are acts like:

- **Fair packing and labeling Act** of 1966 to enable consumers to make meaningful value comparisons
- **Nutrition Labeling and Education Act** of 1990 (NLEA) states that the labels on packaged food products contain information about certain ingredients expressed by weight and as a percentage of the recommended daily diet in a standard serving size.

Manufacturers offer a number of reasons for not providing more information. These are often misunderstood by consumers who reject older products that are still good and packaging has to be designed with many considerations in mind. The objectives of the above mentioned acts, manufacturers argue, need to be balanced against a number of practical constraints.

(viii) Telecommunication Problem

(ix) Other Ethical Issues

Types of Corporate Crime

Business crimes cause serious financial losses. Further laws and ethics are not quite the same. Laws are similar to ethics because both are rules defining proper and improper behaviour. Illegal activities in business put great scars on business image. 55 per cent of the people said for a question in a public opinion in 1985 that most American corporate executives are not honest, 32 per cent said 'yes'. As long as this 'view is held by the public, business will have a difficult time being accepted as an ethical institution, even if the majority of business decisions and actions are entirely ethical. (See Fig. 5.23)

Crimes Against One's Own Company

Employees harm their own company by violating their duty of loyalty and fidelity to their employer by:

- Taking bribes
- Embezzle company funds
- Pad expense accounts

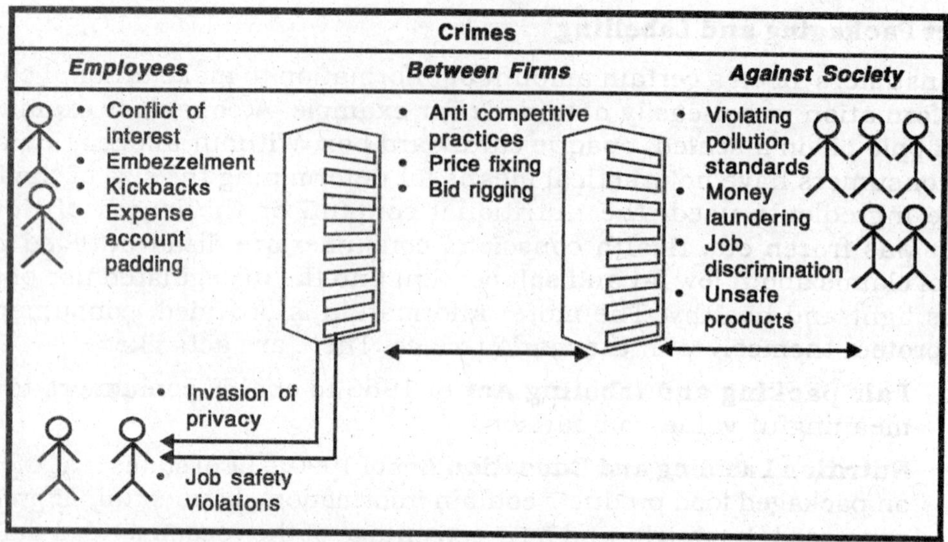

Fig. 5.22 Major Types of Corporate Crimes

- Engage in conflict of interest activities
  - Hiring unqualified family members
  - Channelling company business to outside firms in which they have a financial interest

Employees have enriched themselves unjustly at the employer's expense. Companies try to combat this by:

- Carefully screening prospective employees
- Installing surveillance techniques
- Establishing tight accounting controls
- Guidelines issuing in the form of code of ethics

Crimes Against Other Companies

Criminal actions are taken by one company against another for the purpose of financial or competitive gain.

E.g. If some service organisation (say electrical contractors) agree secretly to fix the prices of its services and to divide the available business among its members, their industrial customers will have to pay unfairly high prices These actions are forbidden by law. Inside training is another violation. It occurs when someone gets advance information about a potential change in the price of a company's stock and then proceeds to buy or sell the stock before others know about it.

Crimes Against Corporate Stock Holders and Public Interest

Dumping of dangerous waste by one corporation may harm people or the environment. When the corporation fails to comply with safety regulations intended to protect their employees, they are committing crimes against the general public or specific stake holder groups. Defective and dangerous manufacture of toys is also the same case. Society has acted through its legal system to forbid such harmful behaviour, so business has an obligation and an ethical duly to comply with the law.

Cheating the Investor

There are many ways to cheat investors, most fall into one of the two categories.

- Misrepresenting the potential of the investment
- Diverting the earnings or assets so that the investor's rightful return is reduced

Every year, tens of thousands of people are the victims of investment scams. In India, many firms are in deep trouble and they have not paid back their investment amount even after the maturity date (forget about the interest), Example: CRB, Madras Motors Finance and Guarantee Ltd., 20th century etc. like this thousands of companies several lakhs of invesotrs have been cheated. Some of the retired people who do not get pension or other benefits have gone to the streets.

A **'Ponzi scheme'** is a form of fraud in which money received from later investors is used to pay off the earlier investors. No real market existed for the fungus, and the scheme collapsed when the supply of new investors was exhausted. It is clearly illegal, but other ways of misrepresenting the potential of an investment fall within the law with a little 'creative' accounting. A business that is in deep financial trouble can be made to look reasonably good to all but the most astute, shrewed investors.

Business executives may also take advantage of the investors by using the company's earnings or resources for personal gain. There are many ways in which a manager can indirectly take money that rightfully belongs to the share holders. The most common approach is to cheat on the **expense account**. **Padding invoices** and then **splitting the overcharge** with the supplier is another common ploy. There is also the possibility of selling company secrets to competitors.

Shop Lifting

Shop lifting seems to be almost a fad or an 'in thing to do'. In USA some facts and figures are as under:

- USA retailers lose over $5 billion worth of goods annually from shop lifting.

- One out of every 15 shoppers leave the stores without paying for an item.
- A few of those caught go to trial.
- If all incidents of shop lifting were reported to the police, it would be the largest single crime in the USA.
- It has risen at a rate of 20 per cent a year since 1965.
- A typical store must sell about $5000 worth of merchandise for every $100 worth of merchandise stolen to make up the loss.
- In a New York city store, a study revealed: Out of 500 random shoppers, 1 out of 12 stole something; one study at the university of Massachusetts showed 75 of 100 students questioned are shoplifters. Out of which 50% said, they did it regularly. Some sororities (US female students society in university or college) and fraternities (US male students society) even make shoplifting item one of the entrance requirements.
- People shoplift for all kinds of reasons, inducing a best-the system game, poor customer service, lack of money, desire for the merchandise, and the thrill.
- Various reports also shows the people who shoplift are not 'professionals' but ordinary citizens with a variety of characteristics, social standing, education levels and incomes. Suspicion is on the youth segment of society. In New York, in a six week period two to three thousands of 4000 shoplifters caught were under 20. Out of which 36% were under 16. More and more are middle class, suburban and white. In 1968, 47.2% of the 1000 students at a Delaware high school has shoplifted at least once. In 1974, 33% of the student body at a New Jersey high school had shoplifted and 81% of these expected to do so again.
- Young people lead in shoplifting as per National Association of retail grocers.

  66% of shoplifters in supermarkets-less than 30 years old

  55% were under 18.

  9% were under 12.

Juvenile delinquency is observed (that is offences committed by people below age of legal responsibility).

Although Juveniles commit more thefts, they steal less.

- Juveniles - $2.47 per average theft.
- Adults - $5.73 per average theft.

42.6% of the adults apprehended are prosecuted.

25% of the Juveniles are turned over to the police.

Solutions to the Problems

Various solutions have been proposed

- People must be educated, should be taught shoplifting is a serious crime.
- Closed circuit TV, mirrors, sensitized tag systems, new alarm systems, more security people will reduce shoplifting.
- Increased store security.
- To prosecute more offenders and to publicise it.

The other view is:

- Convex mirrors help the shoplifters keep track of the store personnel.
- Closed circuit TV increases shoplifting if the cameras are visible.
- Warning signs act as a challenge to people who may never have thought of doing it.
- Prosecuting and punishing is a problem since the shoplifters subconsciously may want to be caught and punished.

The five year shoplifting trend is as given below:

Trend	*Number*	*Percentage*
Increase	41	50.0
Decrease	8	9.8
Constant	11	13.4
Uncertain	21	27.9
Total	82	100.0

As noted from the above shoplifting appears to be on the rise. Crimes are performed by outsiders who penetrate a computer system via. communication lines or by insiders who are authorised to use the computer system but are misusing their authorisation.

List Of Practices That Rose Frequent Problems For Managers Working Abroad:

Surveys of multinational firms consistently turn up list of practices that pose the most frequent problems for managers working overseas as shown:

- ***Small scale bribery:*** Payment of small sums of money to a foreign official to induce the latter to violate certain things and to speed up routine actions (grease payments, kickbacks, baksheesh).
- ***Large scale bribery:*** Significant payments made directly/indirectly to government or corporate officials to induce a violation of the law or to influence policy directly or indirectly (political contributions, agents commissions, party fund).
- ***Gifts, favours or entertainment:*** Lavish gifts, entertainment, call girls, expensive travel paid at the company expense.

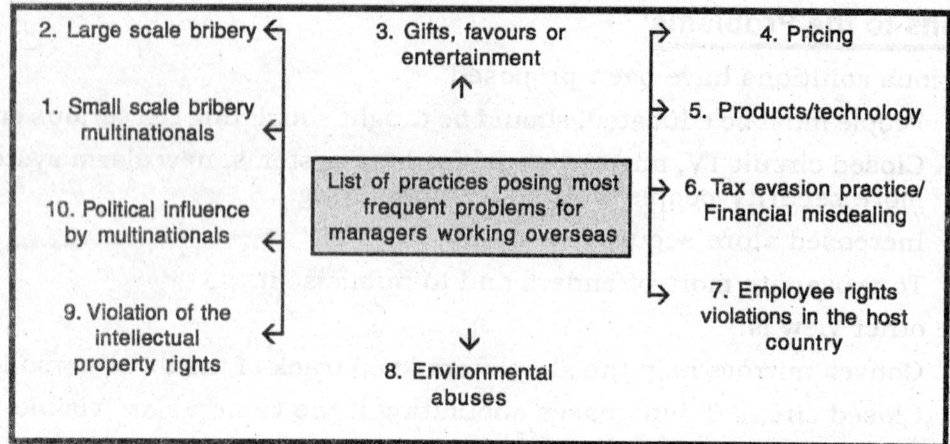

Fig. 5.23 Frequent Problems Faced by Managers Working Abroad

- ***Pricing:*** Practices favour selected customers, despotic or questionable invoicing, dumping products at prices well below those in the home country, legal/illegal price fixing, bid rigging.
- ***Products/technology:*** Export and sale of products or technologies banned for use in the home country may be legal in the host country (Unsuitable or inappropriate for use in the host country by their people).
- ***Tax evasion practices/Financial misdealing:*** Use of 'tax havens', evaluate forms or transfer pricing (prices or interest paid between applications and/or a parent company that are adjusted to minimise tax liabilities, transfer of currency against laws).
- ***Employed rights violation:*** Maintaining unsafe working conditions or participating in forms of racial, religious or sex discrimination prohibited by home country values and laws.
- ***Environmental abuses:*** Host nations reduced vigilance or legal standards to pollute the environment or to dispose of toxic wastes-advantages are taken.
- ***Violation of intellectual property rights:*** Involvement in toleration of product or technology copying in contexts where the protection of patents, trade names or trademarks not well enforced.
- ***Political influence by multinationals:*** Tampering with voting or other political processes, illegal technology transferring, involvement in marketing activities which both home/host country is at war/or under international controls.

India Ranks Among Most Corrupt Nations

India is one of the most corrupt countries and is ranked 66 out of 85 in the global corruption index prepared by the Germany based anti-corruption watchdog, Transparency International Central Vigilance Commissioner N.Vittal said here today.

India was also behind in social development ranking 132 out of 175 nations in human development index of the UN Development Programme, Mr.Vittal said in a lecture.

"Though our rank in the human development index this year is six places above the 1998 rank, still India is way below in this respect. When it comes to competitiveness on the global economic front, according to the world competitiveness index, we rank (a low) 50 out of 53 countries. Corruption flourishes in the country due to red tape, complicated rules, lack of transparency in decision making, legal loopholes favouring the corrupt and tribalism or biradari among the corrupt who protect one another", he said.

There was need for simplification of rules and procedures, he suggested, greater transparency in bureaucracy and severe punishment to those found guilty of corrupt acts.

He called for containing "political corruption" by building public opinion so that MPs and MLAs were required as public servants to give their annual property return to the speaker.

(**Source:** *Deccan Herald,* 17th Aug.1999)

5.4 Cross Cultural Issues

The cultural environment is made up of institutions and other forces that affect a society's basic values, perceptions, preferences and behaviours. People grow up in a particular society that shape their basic beliefs and values.

Managing Cross Cultures

Globalisation of the economy is a challenging task virtually for all employees in an organisation to become more internationally aware and adept. The companies who have to compete globally have to develop competitive advantage first and they have to accept challenges. In order to develop competitive advantage and to operate globally they should experience cross cultural arena. Many of the companies are forced to work with other companies abroad and they have to develop international relations with them may be dealing with foreign suppliers, customers, collaborators, financial institutions etc.

If General Motors of USA wants to make cars and sell it globally, it may work with a Japanese company for manufacture by providing its design. The assembly plant can be at Philippines and the marketing can be done by a Singapore firm. Together, all the four companies in different countries can work with virtual teams. While working like this, company teams may have to understand each other with different cultures. They may find difficulties in adjusting in cross cultures for a considerable period of time.

Employees bring their social culture to work with others in the form of customs and language.

Organisation culture is a byproduct of societal culture, in turn affects the individuals value/ethics, attitudes, assumptions and expectations.

Societal culture is shaped by various environmental factors:

- Economic/Technological setting
- Political/Legal setting
- Ethnic background
- Religion

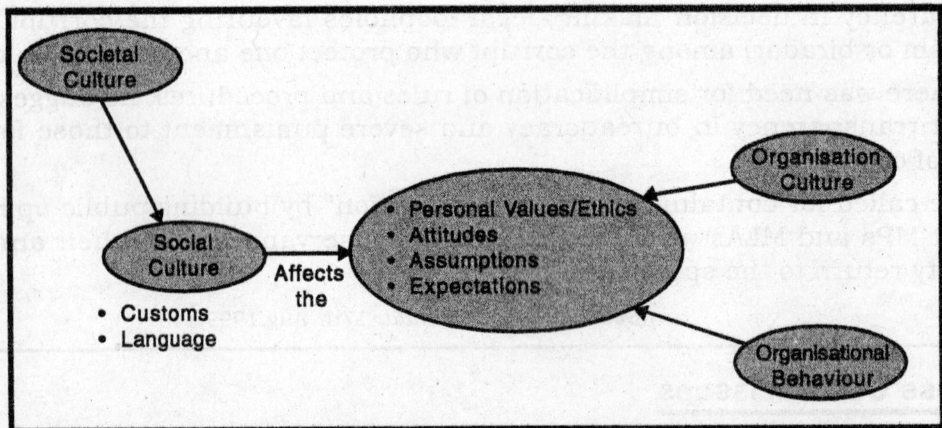

Fig. 5.24 Cultural Influences on Organisational Behaviour

Cultural Differences as Globalisation Advances

a) A comparison of this is given below between different countries

Details	USA	Asia *Japan, China, India*
(i) Business practices	Uniform everywhere	
(ii) Business Education	Same everywhere Ethics not monolithic, changed over time everywhere	
(iii) Managers approach to business	Similar	
(iv) Business Skills	Same worldwide	
(v) Fundamental values	same	

(vi) Ethics	Stubbornly Local
(vii) People's conception of ethical conduct	Rooted in particular culture
(viii) Cultural difference	Not confined to the problem of different standards that underlies the 'when in Rome' Question; Right and wrong varies from one culture to another; Different cultures pose a challenge for global business
(ix) Ethical issues: involves the use of concepts like: • Duty • Rights • Equality • Welfare • Freedom • Right	Meaning slightly different reflecting each country's culture and history. Meaning of these concepts have changed within our culture over course of time. Hence conception of rights is shared by people everywhere is not correct. Different cultures place different concepts. USA place to much stress on rights and too little on equality. USA says that human rights in China are understood differently in Asia and less important than the goal of improving peoples welfare.

b) Cultural differences that result in are:

— misunderstandings

— accusations

— misconduct

Eg. Japanese companies are blamed of showing favouritism to other Japanese firms (mistreating business potential foreign business partners). Japanese may defend that they are showing loyalty to companies in long established relationships. Whistle blowing is viewed negatively in Japan. In USA. it is considered a mark of integrity and moral courage. Hence, to conduct business globally, requires us to understand the ways in which cultural differences are reflected in people's moral outlook.

Broad generalisation about the ethics of any culture must be made cautiously.

c) Distinctive characteristics of different countries to the ethical outlook.

David Vogel calls this as an ethics gap which is shown below:

	USA	Europe	Japan
(i) Expectations for business	Very High	High	High
(ii) Regard the individual as the arbiter of right conduct	More to consult on their own values in deciding what is right or wrong	Normal (seek guidance from community and their own company) Impact of decision on the organisation is made	Normal (same as Europe) not inclined to navigate on their own 'personal moral compass'
(iii) Legalistic or rule oriented	More (Embodies business ethics in laws and rigorously enforced considers ethics as rules	Normal Rely more on informal mechanisms for securing ethical behaviours	Normal (Same as Europe)
(iv) Errant Managers than their counterparts abroad to face legal sanctions (like fines, imprisonment)	More in USA Rules regarded as universal prescriptions that apply impartially to everyone	-	View Moral obligations as arising from specific relationships
(v) Doing business in Asia	People are aware of the cultural differences in Asia to matters of ethics	Same as USA	Ethical outlook of Asians is different. Business managers to understand
(vi) Central role of long term relationship (Keiretsu)	-	-	More in Japan
(vii) Trust among parties	Not much	Not much	High level of trust among all parties In Korea, it is chacbol Reciprocating found.
(viii)	Japanese		
Practices are: - Kaizen (Continuous improvement) -JIT(Just in time) Just in time delivery, total quality control waste elimination - Statistical measures - Quality circles - Structured group activities	-	-	Started in Japan
- Keiretsu (Horizontal and vertical integration of firms) Relationships are conceived as a set of concentric circles. The inner circle is the family and the successive circles are looser ties(bondage)			Preference of cooperation over competition within the family. Fairness in competition
- Administration guidance (Two features it reflects in Japan) Ethical norms are situational and relative instead of being absolute and universal. Affairs in Japan are often described in terms of the iron triangle of (a) business (b) bureaucracy (c) politics.	In USA by pre use rules Mainly through courts If Americans come across of vague rules(since they are accustomed to clear and pre used rules) the need to obtain clarifications, raises suspicion of a 'rigged game'	same as USA	- By regulation - Powerful administrative bodies(Ministry of Finance, Industry etc.) regulate by making decisions, case by case process. But rules are vague, hence classifications are sought.

Ethical Relativism

The concept of relating any given decision about right or wrong, true or false to the specific situation at hand seemed appealing, as generated an approach which was the opposite of **absolutistic**. This kind of newer approach, a kind of **ethical relativism**, has been given many different labels, depending on the slightly different emphasis, various thinkers have made.

As already mentioned in para 3.1, two are most related to a discussion of business ethics are:

- Situation ethics
- Pragmatism

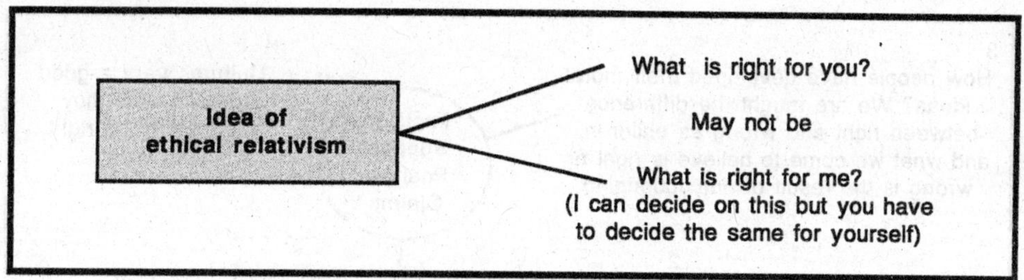

Fig. 5.25 Idea of Ethical Relativism

This idea if taken and formulated into a more systematic account, it seems to encompass.

- a negative claim (something it denies) - There are no universal moral norms;
- a positive claim (something it asserts) - No single standard for all human beings.

Here, one person takes a decision that it is right for him to tell a lie in certain circumstances; Another person takes a decision that it is wrong for him to tell a lie in exactly same circumstances. Both people could be right in their act.

This shows that the claim 'right and wrong are relative' means in part that there are no universal rights and wrongs. The positive claim of ethical relativism is comparatively to negative claim is difficult to formulate. In certain circumstances, ethical relativists seem to be asserting that the right and wrong are relative to the individual. Sometimes the assertion about right and wrong are relative to the society in which they leave.

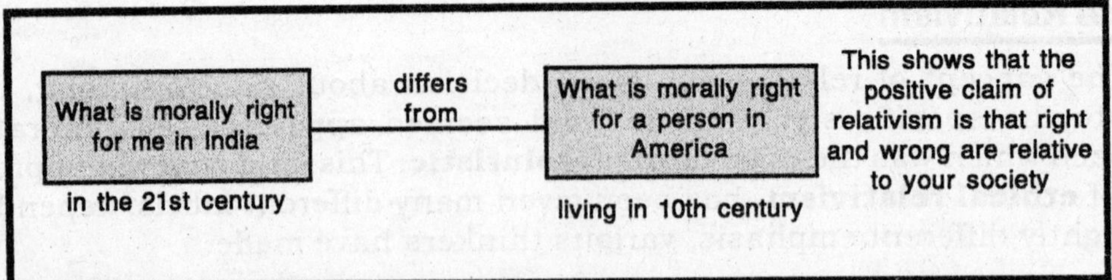

Fig. 5.26 Right and Wrong Relative to the Society

Ethical relativists explain a number of descriptive facts to support the positive claims.

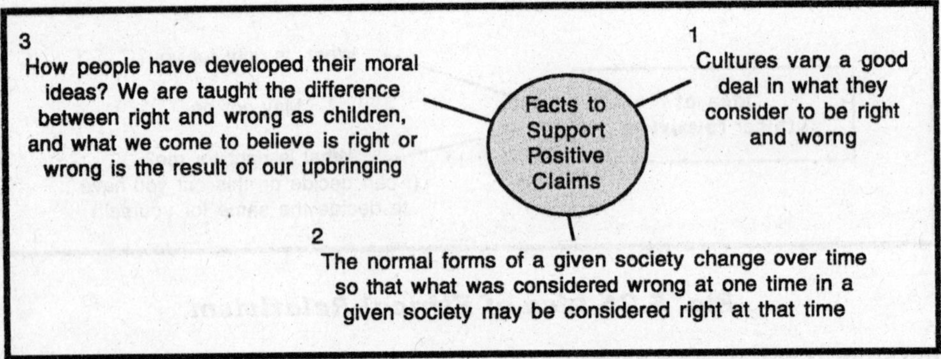

Fig. 5.27 Facts to Support Positive Claims

The examples for the above are:

- In Hindu society, married women wear Mangala Sutra and also bindis on their foreheads.
- In some societies, infanticide is acceptable where in other societies, it is considered wrong. For women to go out in public in some societies, it is considered wrong without their faces being covered. This is more so in Middle East countries.
- In some societies, women have to cover their heads with sarees. Saree wearing is a must in all festivals and religious functions.
- In Muslim communities, the burkas are used by women and in some of the countries, they cannot travel alone without accompanied by men.
- Polygamy is permissible in some cultures.
- Parents are not the only determinants of morality. A person develops more ideas from the experiences of he or she has in school, at work, with peers, and so on.
- Slavery was considered legal in many countries like India, USA at one time, but is now illegal and almost universally considered impermissible.

We have already made progress by clearly and systematically formulating the idea of ethical relativism-an idea you may have entertained or heard expressed, but never had a chance to examine carefully. We have been able to identify and articulate some reasons to support ethical relativism. The issues with the claims for these may be:

- There is and always has been a good deal of diversity of belief about right and wrong.
- Moral beliefs change over time within the society.
- Social environment shapes the moral ideas you have.

Questions arise about:

- Do these facts show that there are no universal moral rights or wrongs?
- Do they show that right and wrong are relative to the society?

It appears that the facts cited by ethical relativists do not support their claims. We can alternatively, without contradiction accept the facts and still deny ethical relativism. The facts do not necessitate that there are no universal moral standards or that ethics is relative.

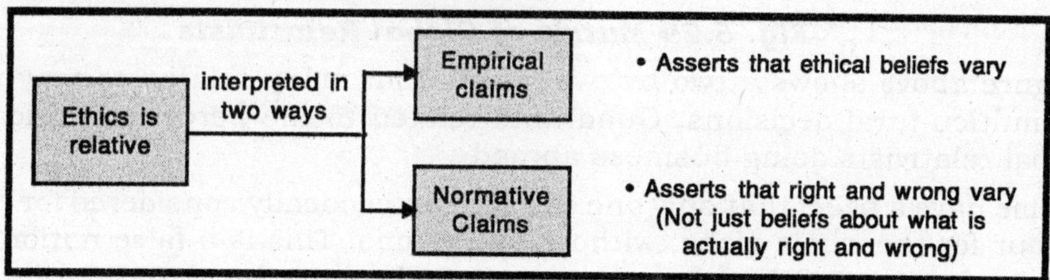

Fig. 5.28 Ethics Interpretation as Two Claims

Empirical Claim

If the claim 'ethics is relative' to be a description of human behaviour, then it does follow from the facts cited. Ethical beliefs vary. Individuals believe different things are right and wrong depending on how and by whom they have been raised and where and when they live.

Normative Claim

It is a claim asserting the negative and/or positive parts of ethical relativism, and it is not redundant. The facts do not support the claims.

The facts are compatible with the opposite conclusion as explained below:

- There is a possibility that a universal moral code applies to every one even though some or all fail to recognize it. eg. Long back, some people believed the earth was flat, others believed it as round. The earth's shape was not relative. Diversity of opinion on right and wrong does not tell us any thing about whether right and wrong are relative. The facts are compatible both (i) with the claim that there is no universal right and wrong and (ii) with the claim that there is a universal right and wrong.

- Our moral beliefs as we know are shaped by our social environment. This says nothing about the rightness or wrongness of what we believe.

e.g. Racism and sexisms are examples of moral attitudes we acquire from our environment, which turn out on reflection to be unjustifiable (bad) ideas.

Martrix for global relativists while making cross-cultural ethics decisions are as shown below:

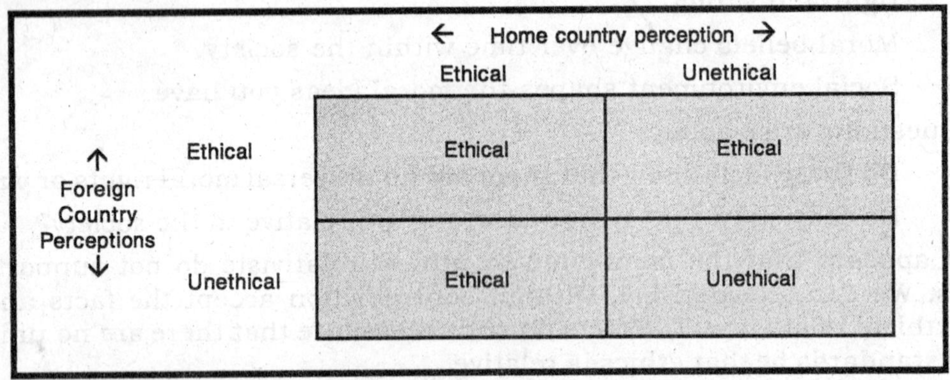

Fig. 5.29 Matrix of Global Relativists

Figure above shows a two by two matrix that many relativists may use to make multicultural decisions. Quadrants related to the perceived ethicalness for global relativists doing business abroad.

Some have a belief that only one culture can be ideally considered for ethical behaviour for the whole globe, without exceptions. This is a false notion since for the business relativist, there may be no relevant ethical standards. Some individuals may adjust to the ethics of a particular foreign culture or use their own culture as a defense of something unethical as perceived by the foreign firms in the foreign country. In his, they might be in conflict with their own individual moral standards and perhaps with their own culture's values and legal system. As business becomes more global and multinational corporations proliferate, the choices of ethical conflict increase.

Cultural Differences

As globalisation advances, business practices becomes increasingly uniform. Business education is same every where, Managers from diverse countries approach business in similar ways. Unlike business skills which are the same worldwide, people's conceptions of ethical conduct remain rooted in particular cultures. The importance of cultural differences is not confined to the problems of different standards. What is considered right and wrong varies as culture varies. Hence the difference in different cultures pose a challenge for global business.

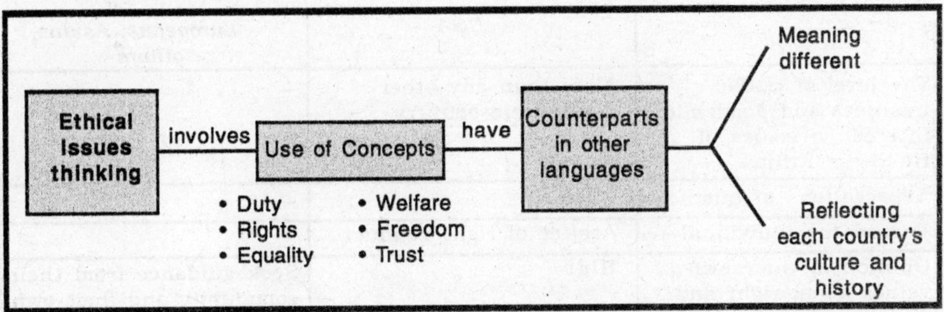

Fig. 5.30 Change of Concepts

The meanings of these concepts have changed within our own culture cover the course of time. Hence we cannot assume that our conception of rights, for example, is shared by people everywhere.

- Different cultures place different emphases on these concepts. E.g. Americans place too much stress on rights and lesson equality (High executive compensation).

Human rights are differently understand in Asia, but also less important than the goal of improving people's welfare.

- Cultural differences occasionally result in misunderstandings and accusations of misconduct.

E.g. Japanese companies sometimes show favouritism to other Japanese firms, mistreating potential foreign business partners. Japanese response is that they are showing loyalty to companies in long established relationship whereas foreign firms are criticised other way. Whistle blowing is viewed negatively in Japan vis a vis US, where it is often considered a mark of integrity and moral courage.

While conducting the business globally, it is essential to understand the ways in which the cultural differences are reflected in people's moral outlook. It is also seen how European and Asian Managers appreciate and view ethics as critical for successful interaction with them, as is a recognition of how America is distinctive. (Fig. 5.31)

Different cultures have different moral standards. The managers of some multinationals have adopted the theory of ethical relationism. this is a theory states that there are no ethical standards that are absolutely true and that apply or should be applied to the companies and people of all societies. It holds something right for the people or companies and people in one particular society if it accords with their societies (say Arab) e.g., it may hold that bribery is morally acceptable in Arab societies, and in USA it may be immoral.

	USA	*Europeans, Asians, others*
The level of public, business and academic interest in issues of Business Ethics	More than any other capitalistic country	–
Expectations of business	High	–
Regard the individual	Arbiter of right conduct	–
Opinion of their own values about right and wrong	High	Seek guidance from their community and their own business organisation
Ethical decisions	Themselves (Individual)	By a group (Specially in Europe)
Legalistic and rule oriented	More; Embody business ethics in laws rigorously enforce; Think ethics as a set of rules to be observed; voluntary codes	Rely more on informal mechanisms by securing ethical behaviour
Errant managers face legal actions	High (includes fines, imprisonment) Rules are universal prescriptions; Apply impartially to everyone	Low; view moral obligations as arising from specific relationships

Fig. 5.31 Distinctive Characteristics of Americans in Contrast to the Outlook of Europeans, Asians and Others

5.5 Cross Religion and Cross Racial issues

Religious discrimination is substantially different from discrimination based on race or sex. Religious discrimination are found plenty in which employees refuse to hire or promote individuals simply because of prejudice against members of certain religious groups such as Catholics and Jews. Most changes of religious discrimination in employment involve conflicts between the religious beliefs and practices of employees and work place rules and routines. Employees sometimes request revised work schedules for time off to observe religious holidays. Members of some religious groups have special dress or grooming requirements for Jeursh men and a turban and a beard for sick men. Some employees have religious objections to performing certain kind of work or to submitting to medical examinations. Others request prayer breaks and special foods in the company cafeteria. In India we find more religious activities and racial issues. People many a times hope from one religion to other religion to suit their convenience. Many a times the converted people are not given the same status from the people of the original religion in the society. This will also pose problems.

Religious discrimination involves the violation of right not to be adversely affected because of the religious beliefs and practices of employers or other employees. Aggressive proselytesizing of the job has occurred in many companies. There is a growing number. In Southeast Asian and certain far eastern countries, employees from particular ethnic backgrounds are not promoted. Female entrepreneurs in many countries may not be treated equally with male in offering credit,m and in starting a business and they face different legal system. Business women have become a rarity in middle Eastern countries.

Reducing discrimination helps:

— To decrease employee turn over (as people believe they are hired, promoted and treated according to their skills and abilities)

— With a diverse local work force, the companies enjoy the good will and support of the communities.

— Reduces the costs of hiring and training new employees.

— Receive favourable attention from stakeholder groups such as women's rights groups.

— Reputation of the firms and product brands enhances.

Questions

1. Define globalisation. Explain how ethics is considered important in global transactions?
2. Discuss ethical perceptions as applicable to international business.
3. What is global business? Which are the major questions about companies who go globally? How ethics plays a role in global business?
4. Explain the various factors influencing individual behaviour.
5. 'Ethical issues arise out of everyday business decision' Comment. If you agree, give an example.
6. Explain what is ethical convergence?
7. Compare and contrast the terms' Absolutism and Relativism with examples.
8. What is a multinational corporation?
9. How are the ethical decisions made? Which are the four factors involved? Give an example.
10. Explain the role of moral philosophies in decision making.
11. Mention a few suggestions for ethical decision making. Explain them.
12. 'People are generally moral agents in an ethical organisation' Substantiate.
13. Mention the ethical issues that arise for managers.
14. In spite of the positive benefits of good ethical practices, ethical problems do occur in business. Give reasons.
15. Comment on the guidelines to be followed by the corporate managers and employees needed in business. Discuss the various methods of ethical reasoning and how to use them?
16. Discuss on the three levels of decision making.

17. How do you decide on an ethical course of action during business decision making? Explain with suitable examples.
18. What are the arguments for and against business ethics?
19. Mention three objections of brining ethics into business.
21. Whar are your arguments in bringing ethics into business?
22. Do you think that new technologies will bring in host of ethical issues? If so, explain with examples.
23. Explain the relationship between business ethics and technology.
24. How is global business conducted? Explain. What are the difficulties experienced?
25. List down the main charges found against global corporations.
26. What do you mean by ethical convergence? Compare and contrast Absolutism and Relativism with examples?
27. Discuss on the foundational document for human rights.
28. Explain the ethics involved in Global business.
29. Explain the Model business principles issued by the US department of commerce (DOC) to codify the expectations of the US market in 1995 as guidelines for business conduct.
30. Explain the basic ethical ideals found in the caux principles.
31. Mention some of the international ethics standards for business.
32. Mention the grouping of the subject of caux principles.
33. Explain the Donald's suggestion for the fundamental rights as a moral minimum.
34. What are the guidelines offered by Richard DeGeorge about global companies?
35. "One kind of unfairness cited by critics is the often one sided division of the benefits from foreign investment. The gap between the rich and poor countries is an urgent moral concern. MNCs have much to offer." Comment.
36. Regarding wages and working conditions, give your views on the obstacles faced by developing countries.
37. Discuss on the justification for prohibiting foreign bribery.
38. What do you mean by the justified wages paid by the global companies?
39. Discuss on the ethics between East and West.
40. What are the distinctive characteristics of Americans noticed in contrast to the outlook of Europeans, Asians and others, while conducting the global business.
41. Write a note on cross religion and corss racial issues.
42. What do you mean by broader ethical issues in society?

43. What is corruption? How does it take place?
44. What is bribery? Explain giving an example.
45. What is black marketing and hoarding?
46. In India, corruption and bribery are taking place in most of the daily activities. Suggest some steps to eradicate or to control the same.
47. Discuss any one of the corruption cases you find interesting and give your views in the ethical context.
48. What are the results of the survey conducted by IIPO regarding corruption issues? What is the summary of the opinion survey?
49. What are the major types of corporate crimes? Explain them.
50. What is shop lifting? What is your opinion about shop lifting in India?
51. Explain the list of practices that pose frequent problems for managers working abroad.
52. 'India ranks among the most corrupted nations'. Give your views.
53. What is Tax haven?
54. 'The noise pollution is very high in India'. In this context, give your views on ethicality of this issue.
55. Write notes on 'Religious Morality'.
56. Explain lobbying. 'Lobbying is considered legitimate but a necessary activity in India' Do you agree? Comment.
57. What are the three different regimes that protect intellectual property rights?
58. What do you mean by intellectual property rights? Explain.
59. What is design? Explain.
60. Define design.
61. Define Trademark.
62. Define patents.
63. Define copyrights. Explain the brief history of copyright.
64. Make a comparison of trademarks, patents and copyrights.
65. Explain the central ethical issue involved in copyright.
66. What is trade secret?
67. Explain the copyrightable work. What is the protection provided for such acts?
68. 'Educational institutes deal mainly with copyright.' Substantiate this statement.
69. Explain plagiarism. What are its effects? How this could be prevented?
70. What do you mean by fair dealing?
71. 'India and other smaller/less developed nations and institutions fail to claim or register their IP rights, stand the risk of losing their rights to International Institutes.' Comment.

72. What do you mean by Digital Management of rights? Explain.
73. Explain ecological concerns which we are facing in India.
74. What is air pollution? What are its problems?
75. What is water pollution? What are its problems?
76. What is land pollution? What are its problems?
77. What is ecology? Mention any agencies in India which are fighting to maintain better ecological conditions and what are its activities.
78. 'Earth is warming due to human activity in the recent days.' What are your views?
79. Every day, we find animals suffering because of man's cruelty. What are your suggestions about this issue? Give your own examples.
80. "Many of the preventive techniques are used, but none of the techniques of shoplifting has been totally successful". Discuss.
81. Comment on work place hazards. How vibration and shock affects peoples lives? How hearing damages take place?

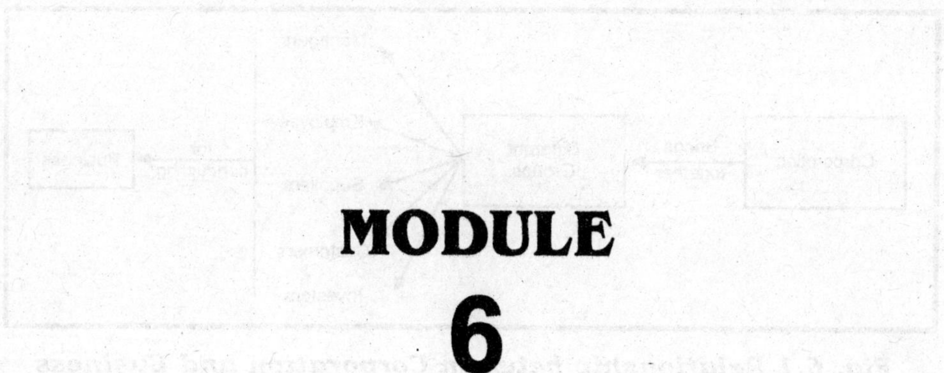

MODULE 6

Corporate Governance

6.1 Corporate Governance

The subject of corporate governance has been discussed in para 1.6.

Corporate means legally united into a body so as to act as an individual. **Governance** is control or direction. The two put together it gives a meaning that it brings together many different groups for the purpose of conducting business.

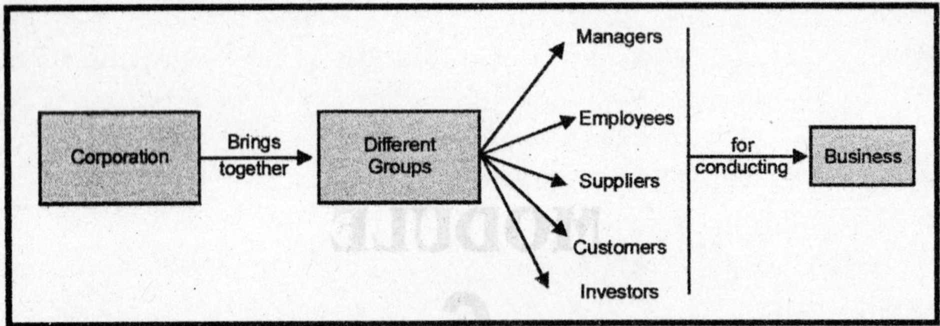

Fig. 6.1 Relationship between Corporation and Business

Main Elements of Corporate Governance

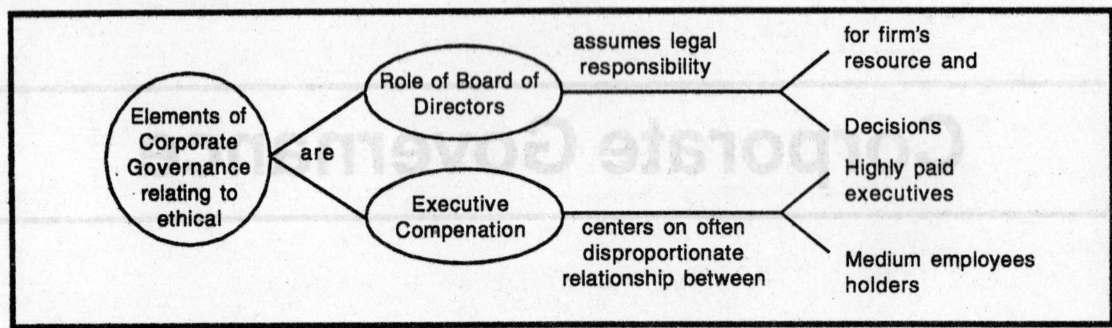

Fig. 6.2 CAUX Principles

The members of a public corporation's board of directors assume legal responsibility for the firm's resources and decisions.

Important issues related to corporate broad of directors are:

— Accountability

— Transpancy

— Independence

Board members appoint its top executive officers. They have a judiciary duty. This means that they have assumed a position of trust and confidence that entails central responsibilities, including acting in the best interest of those they serve. They are also responsible for appointing and setting the compensation for top executive officers.

The nature of the corporation is already explained in Chapter 1. The Caux principles is already explained in pages 283 & 285.

6.2 Accountability Issues

Buying a business makes sense when the benefit exceeds the cost. This means to find a seller who excepts too low a price, so that you can secure a benefit from acquisition by improving the targets performance.

Buyers of course, run into problems with competition law when their plans to improve a targets performance depends in the creation and use of monopoly power, they can actually be said to create wealth. They have to use the targets resources more efficiently than the seller or they exploit opportunities for synergy with existing business.

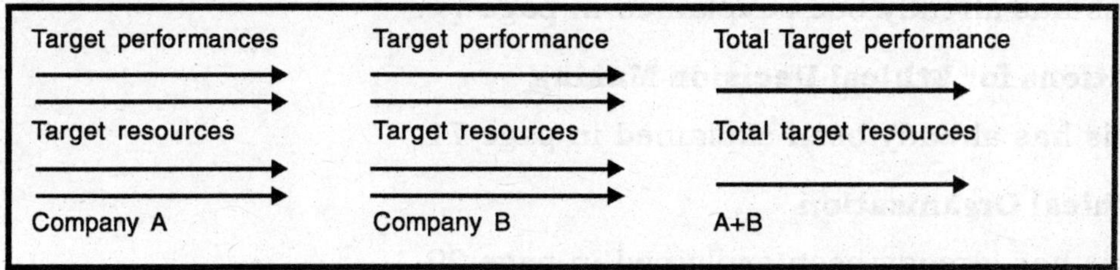

Fig. 6.3 Total Target Performances/Resources

The principal argument for a free acquisitions market is that it should allow business to gravitate towards the managers who can do the most with them. Buyers accounts often do not reflect real success and failure. There is therefore a danger that businesses will gravitate towards the most creative accountants than the best managers. The prospects of creating value from an acquisition arises whenever a potential target is poorly managed.

Two courses of action are open to a corporate buyer/buy out or buy in team.

- The target is well positioned in a market with a good future, then the buyer should aim to turn the business round.
- If the target is poorly positioned, perhaps in a stagnant market with poor products and people it makes more sense to strip the target. Most buyers other than management buy - out or buy-in teams have an existing business to which they can add an acquisition target. This existing business provides a further opportunity for a buyer to create from an acquisition through synergy (2+2=5). Two businesses can together achieve what is beyond their individual capabilities.

If the targets management is poor, little is lost by taking over the running of acquired business and forcing the pace on realising synergy gains. Alternatively, if it is good, such a takeover is likely to be damaging. The acquisition needs to be viewed as a merger and two business needs to be fused more gently. Negotiating a deal so that the extra value is not given away to the sellers also requires particular skill, where there are rival buyers.

Corporate issues are ethical questions raised about a particular organisation. These include questions about:

- The moralityu of the activity
- Policies
- Practices
- Organisational Structure of an individual Company (taken as a whole)

Ethical Decision Making, Ethical Decisions, How Are They Made?

This has already been explained in page 27.

The Role of Moral Philosophies in Decision Making

This has already been explained in page 71.

Suggestions for Ethical Decision Making

This has already been explained in page 71.

The Ethical Organisation

This has already been explained in page 29.

Ethical Issues that Arise for Managers and Difficulties in Decision Making

This has already been explained in page 32.

How to use Ethical Reasoning and Levels of Decision Making & Business Decision Making

This has already been explained in page 32.

The Corporate Governance issues are many. These issues normally involve stragic level decisions and actions taken by board of directors, business owners, top executives and other managers with high levels of authority and accountability.

These involve share holder rights, executive compensation, Board of directors composition and structure, auditing and control, risk management CEO selection and termination decisions, integrity of financial reporting, stakeholder participation input during decisions compliance with corporate governance reform, role of the CEO in board elections, organisational ethics programs etc.

Most companies have developed formal systems of accountability, oversight, and control-known as corporate governance to remove the opportunity for employees to make unethical decisions.

Examples of major corporate governance issues involved are: strategic-level decisions and actions taken by boards of directors, business owners, top executives and other managers with high levels of authority and accountability.

Issues of Corporate Governance

- Auditing of Corporate Governance
- Controlling of Corporate Governance

- Rights of Shareholders
- Compensation to the Executives
- Integrity in Financial Reports
- Input to decisions and participation of Stakeholders
- Ethical Programs in Organisation
- Board Decisions and the Role of the CEO
- Risk management
- Corporate Governance reforms with Compliance
- Decisions on Selection and Termination of CEO
- Structure of Board of Directors
- Composition of Board of Directors

Corporate Governance often been relatively free from scrutiny, risk and control, accountiability of resource, strategic direction, rights of stockholders, consumer activism, attention to government, scandals in ethics, change in technology, other factors have brought neww attention to such issues as transparency and other decisions made for the organisation.

Corporate governance has two perceptions of which we can view as a continuum. Classic economic precepts has the shareholder model in it which including the wealth maximization of both investors and owners. The stakeholder model which adopts the purpose of business that includes, satisfying the concerns from employees, other stakeholders, suppliers, special-interest groups and government regulators to communities.

The corporate governance has two major elements which relates to ethical decision making are the role of executive compensation and of the board of directors. Public corporation's board of directors and its members assume legal responsibility for the firm's decisions and resources. Very important issues related to corporate boards of directors which include independence, transparency and accountability etc. The board of directors are responsible for appointing and setting compensation to the top executive it is a controversial topic as well. The disproportionate relationship between the two i.e., the highest-paid executives and median employee wages in the organizations.

In accounting, fraud creates ethical issues related to how a company reports its financial position to interested stakeholders. Accounting field has dramatically changed in last few years. The public accountants who were certified as CPAs were not concerned about competition in the earlier days. The days have changed now. If CPAs are not concerned about the increasing competition, the whole company gets affected. All these have to cope up with the technological innovations which are taking place at a rapid rate. Pressures on accountants include the following:

- Time
- Reduced fees

- Client request to alter options (considering financial conditions) or lower tax payments.
- Increased competition.

Accountant has to stick on to the rules and data. He has to interprete all these correctly; He is involved with tremendous pressure as the ethical problems are on the rise. In view of these, accountants are to strictly adhere to code of ethics, which defines their responsibilities to their clients and the public interest. The code clearly defines the

- Concepts of integrity
- Objectivity
- Independence
- Due care

Apart from the standards, the code provides, the accounting industry has been the source of numerous fraud investigations in recent years. Act has been passed to address many of the issues that could conflicts of interest for accounting firms auditing public corporations. The law generally prohibits accounting firms from providing both auditing and consulting service to the same firm. Also it specifies that corporate boards of directors must have an external director from other firms or from the government with financial knowledge on the company's audit committee.

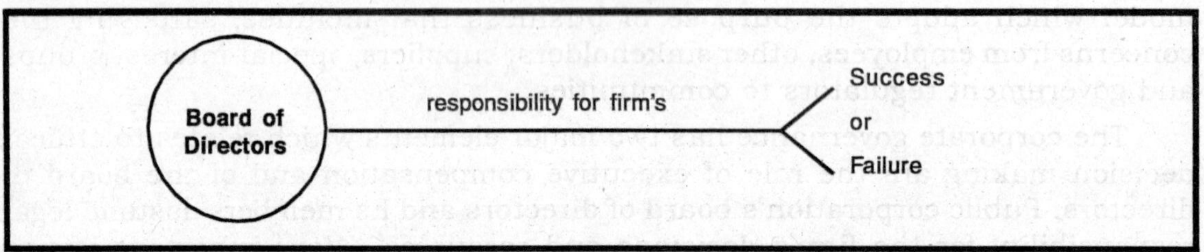

Fig. 6.4 Responsibility of Board of Directors

They assume legal responsibility for firm's resources and decision. They appoint its top executives; They have a fiduciary duty by assuming trust and confidence that entails certain responsibilities; They are not intended as a vehicle for personal gain. Stockholders and stakeholders demand greater accountability from board members in the recent days. If any untoward incident takes place in the company through accounting irregularities, the stockholders or stakeholders board members have to resign the company who had failed to prevent the same.

Board managers manage the corporation's business. Board meet a few times in a year which precludes them managing the business effectively. Daily attention by the directors are needed in many companies. Board of Directors are to monitor the decisions made by the executives on behalf of the company. They are the ultimate authority for the company's effective and subsequent performance. They should have sufficient qualification, experience and knowledge. Individual directors can represent multiple companies because of their reputation earned for going with top management at many places. Through this, they may foster a corporate culture that limits outside oversight of top management decisions. Board's independence is vital along with board quality, shareholder's accountability and corporate performance. Some companies have more external directors than internals to give them a strong sense of what is going on within the company. This provides an opportunity to address issues before they are converted as problems.

Consider the issues that must be addressed in developing the case for a right of privacy in accounting records and in formulating a company privacy protection plan for these accounting records. The issues are:

- The kind of accounting information that is collected
- The use to which the accounting information is put
- The persons within a company who have access to the accounting information
- The disclosure of the accounting information to persons outside the company
- The means used to gain the accounting information
- The steps taken to ensure the accuracy and completeness of the accounting information
- The access that employees have to information about themselves.

6.3 Disclosure to Outsiders

What is morally objectionable about an employees disclosing accounting information to an outside party. The outside party is not justified in having it so also the employee has no justification for giving it to out.

In a free market system, buyers bear the primary burden of informing themselves about the products offered for sale. Sellers are not obligated to provide complete information but only to avoid misrepresentation, although buyers are entitled to rely on any representations that are made and to make minimal assumptions about the quality of goods and their suitability. These are referred to in law as implied warranties of merchantability and fitness for use. Accounting also play a role in these along with marketing.

Board of Directors (BODs)

In the management, somewhere in between is the managing director, or general manager, with an integrated and balanced view point-a bird's eye view-taking is the whole scene at once. That at least is the theory. Yet all too often, despite promotion to general management, the former accountant, for example still remains an accountant. For one of the problems of any specialist in this context is learning how to stand back from his profession in order to look at the business objectively, as a whole, instead of from one side or the other.

The top or general management, all can be considered as being one and the same thing. These would normally include the board of directors, in particular the managing director, a general manager, and any other generalists of similar rank and responsibilities, whatever titles they might be given in real life.

To become a director is to get to the top, the BODs being in the key position from which to guide the activities of the business enterprise towards certain objectives. BODs can exert immense influence on the company's prospects. For the most past, we are concerned with public and perhaps private companies.

A public company offer its shares or debentures to the general public. A private company does not. We should bear in mind that there are other institutions, also concerned with management, where the governing body instead of being called a board of directors is given some title known as board of governors, councils, or committee of management. However, the general approach is same.

Theoretically, the directors are elected by the shareholders to run the business on their behalf in such a way that satisfactory (not necessarily maximum) profits are achieved. At one time, it was quite usual for a board to be dominated by one or more proprietary families which controlled the capital; but shares now tend to be widely spread over the communities. In the process many of our companies have grown considerably. Today's decisions seems to be much more difficult and complex.

The first election of director is normally carried out at the company's formation meeting, generally a personal selection from among the entrepreneurs and their supporters. Subsequent elections and reelections take place at statutory annual general meetings.

6.4 Board Objectives

This cannot be expected to perform all the fractions of top management though board is an important part of top management, unless it is entirely composed of executive directors. Much of the daily drive, initiative and business vitality should come from the Managing director and his team. If there is a part time (non-executive board) which of necessity has to leave most of the administrative duties to the executives.

The Director's role

(i) Approving or initiating the objectives, major policies, long-range planning and strategies in the light of the overall total environment.

(ii) Complying with all legal requirements.

(iii) Ensuring that sufficient capital is always available for effective operations.

(iv) Authorising large capital expenditures, including major contracts and other commitments; granting mandates, where appropriate to the executives; maintaining the physical assets.

(v) Engaging and selecting, top executives, including the managing director, and approving promotions of key managers and salary scales; ensuring management succession and effective executive development.

(vi) Maintaining a suitable organisational structure, and satisfactory relationships from the managing director downwards.

(vii) Providing leadership to the company as a whole, e.g., through the chairman, in liaison with the managing director.

(viii) Ensuring that the shareholders, whom they represent, are dealt with fairly with regard to dividend policy, changes in capital structure, and other matters affecting their financial interests.

(ix) Evaluating results achieved, and maintaining control with special reference to regular reports, and statements from the managing director, coupled with the technique of asking discerning questions.

(x) Initiating, depending or encouraging merger's and acquisitions, as appropriate, including take-over bids made or received, keeping the shareholders adequately advised of such developments.

(xi) Giving professional advice to executives, when consulted formally or informally.

In brief, the BODs has special responsibilities towards the shareholders, customers, employees, and the community at large. The board has to get the confidence of all the fair groups as above to exercise its full authority effectively.

The managing director, as the chief executive responsible to the board, must play his full part. But theoritically at least it is the chairman (also be the managing director) who actually leads the board. The right kind of chairman/managing director board room relationships is important.

1. The Governing Body

(a) Board of Directors, although elected by shareholders, is self-perpetuating.

(b) Familiarity with the companies acts and articles of association is important.

(c) Shareholders cannot easily control a board.

(d) A public company must have at least two directors.

(e) The board should be well balanced.

(f) The board may be organised as a two-tier structure.

(g) There may be divisional boards interlocking with the main board.

2. Types of Board

(a) Full-time directors are familiar with detailed operations.

(b) Part time directors bring in outside experience.

(c) A mixture of (a) and (b) provides the best of both worlds.

3. The Chairman

(a) The chairman must provide positive leadership.

(b) He must get on with managing director.

(c) He takes the chair at meetings and in responsible for the board in action.

4. Duties of the Board

(a) The board is concerned with objectives, major policies, long range planning and strategies.

(b) Board members must see that they are kept informed.

5. Board room procedure

(a) Board papers should be well prepared and circulated in advance.

(b) Agenda order is significant.

(c) Chairman allows full discussion but no time wasting.

(d) Managing director has an important role to play.

(e) Minutes of meeting should be translated into executive action.

A company can only be as good as its managing director; a managing director can only be as good as the board of directors will allow him to be; and a board can only be as good as its chairman.

The chairman can stimulate the board to have vision, new ideas and enthusiasm he is, in effect, putting a dead hand on the wheel and should accordingly be replaced. There should be a good relationship and working partnership, between the chairman and the managing director. The chairman, infact, be the managing director, as well. The chairman would be wise to ensure that there exists an effective organisational pyramid with a properly balanced board at the top, composed of directors specially selected for the valuable contributions they could be expected to make.

Achieving a proper balance is the most important thing. Whatever the type of director, there is no distinction in law, and all directors have the same fiduciary responsibilities.

In the large company, there will be many boards such as:

- Divisional and regional boards (broken into self contained divisions)
- Secondary boards (subsidiary operates on power generated by the main board)
- Interlocking boards.

6.5 Training and development of Directors

It is essential that meetings in the board room should be well planned and conducted. The main responsibility clearly lies with the chairman, while task is to see that the directors, individually and collectively discharge their duties efficiently. In small companies nominal meeting are often considered to be sufficient. But with growth, properly organsied meetings with full discussion are needed. A good chairman conducts his board as an orchestra and makes sure that every instrument comes in at the right time, and plays at the right volume and tempo. His job is to keep a sense of urgency and importance; stimulate creative thought and ensure that all new ideas are given a proper hearing; and refrain from importing prejudice by airing his own opinions before all present have had a chance to speak.

There will be sometimes confusion at the top. For example, a chairman, who is also the chief executive, with or without the support of one or more managing directors. Others will have a full-time or part-time chairman who is not an executive at all. The real power at the top can range from a one man dictatorship to group rule by committee. Such a directorship could be a chairman can chief executive, answerable only to the shareholders, or a strong managing director with a weak non-executive chairman and a 'rubber stamping' board. However, there should be unity at the top. Without this, there will be conflict and frustration.

The Managing Director Acts as a Focal Point

Between the board, and the executive, the MD is clearly at the apex of the staff/worker pyramid as their leader. He is also at the bottom of the reversed pyramid as the servant of the board the information should be processed upwards through the organisation into the board room. Taking of policy decisions, instructions are filtered downwards. Either way up or down, the focal point is the managing director, the words 'Focal point' being deliberately chosen. The responsibilities of MD are wide. The important ones are shown below:

(a) Making sure that the objectives, as laid down by the board, are kept well in mind by the whole organisation; recommending to the board revisions where necessary in those objectives to keep pace with change.

(b) Actively concerned with long-range planning and strategies based on a thorough understanding of the main trends in the dynamic environment of the firm. Supervising any changes e.g., in production considered necessary.

(c) Ensuring the financial soundness of the company as a whole.

(d) Maintaining an effective organisational structure, with the practical effects of growth. Building up a strong management team.

(e) Coordinating all activities.

(f) Being available, wherever possible to all important connections of the company e.g., principal shareholders, customers and suppliers.

(g) Keeping control over the business so that it conforms to the plans laid down.

(h) Providing a high standard of personal leadership and motivating all concerned to give continually of their best.

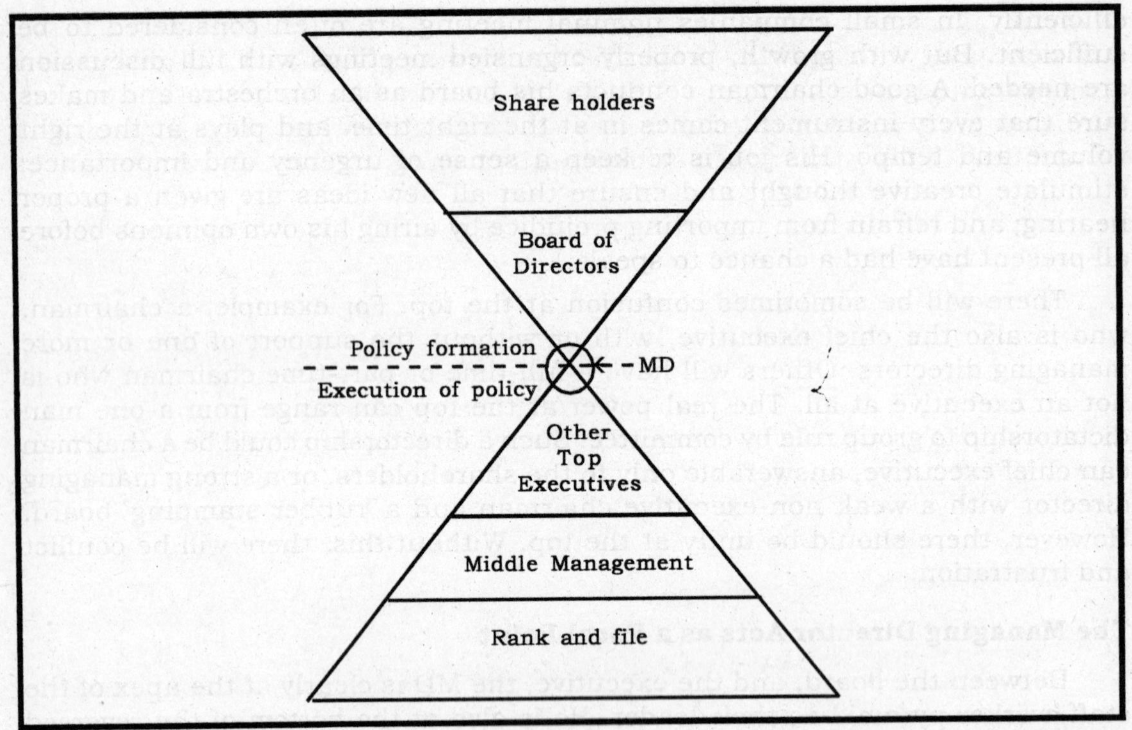

Fig. 6.5 The Managing Director as a Focal Point

The managing director must be a focal point; he must have right basic qualities; he has a wide range of executive responsibilities; his collaboration with the chairman is essential.

The directors and the role of managing director has been explained earlier. In view of this, the directors and the managing director has to take tremendous responsibilities in the work involved.

In order to have an effective board meeting, no wastage of time on irrelevant discussions should take place. For such a meeting in a large company, sufficient delegation with concentration on decision making rather than too much debate should be there on the part of directors. There are some directors who would like to dominate their presence and regard meetings as concert platforms for their own solo performance, who use each occasion to impress fellow board members with their expertise and experience, whether relevant to the item concerned or not. Some of the internal directors who are in large numbers can be trained and developed. Some of the directors are less loquacious and tend to take a back seat even though they have a great deal of value to contribute. Sometimes the MDs who are in the verge of retirement talk too much and waste time by seizing an opportunity to dwell on past glories. Tact from the chair is required here, as well as the handling of young upcoming directors with their sights set on the future, who are liable to become impotent with the restraining wisdom of their more experienced colleagues. Once again the emphasis must be on the achievement of a proper balance so that all concerned can make effective contributions to the end result. The training and development of directors to talk less and to be more effective in decision making is what is needed for the smooth going of the board activities. Decisions should evolve into actions. They must be in a position to translate the meeting's policy decision into everyday practice. All decisions taken at the board meeting are formally recorded in the minutes, generally by the company secretary.

Making the best use of Executive Time

This is possible with the following:

(a) The executive must find out in detail how his day is spent

(b) He can then attempt to regain initiative

(c) It is necessary to have the time available for constructive thought.

Executive Team in Action

(a) Sole command is fundamental

(b) The team must have a strong second line in support

(c) Regular meetings of top personnel help coordination

(d) An 'open-door' philosophy leads to good relationships with subordinates.

Board Structure

- A public company must have at least two directors.
- A private company should have at least one.
- The leading companies tend on average to have about twelve.
- Less number of directors on the board place a heavy burden on them individually fails to provide for emergencies and denies the company a wide enough range of experience and wisdom
- Too many directors, tends to slow down decisions through over-much debate. Time unnecessarily spent without constructive thought.
- Hence each company must work out its optimum size in the light of growth prospects, territory covered, and type of activity undertaken.
- The overall quality of the board is important. Instead of the old family director and the so called 'quinea-pig' director, the trend today is towards a mixture of subjective enterprise and objective wisdom.
- With too many internal directors results in a managing director dictatorship (If he is a CMD, Chairman cum Managing Director, the directors will restrict decision.)
- If non-executive are more in number, it leads, to a frustrated atmosphere, even though the nonexecutive board is good in theory in that it separates policy making from policy execution.

Ethics plays a vital role in all the above situations.

The Controversial Bullock Committee's Report on Industrial Democracy, 1977 proposed that the main boards of leading companies should consist of two groups, representing share holders and workers, with a smaller group of independent directors recruited jointly by both sides.

(a) **Supervisory Board:** Concerned with general policy and forward planning, but with power to appoint and dismiss executive directors, thereby exercising control on behalf of the share holders.

(b) **Executive Board:** With delegated authority to manage current performance within that general policy and planning laid down by the supervisory board.

6.6 Performance Evaluation of Board

Executive and nonexecutive directors each have offsetting advantages and disadvantages. The most successful type of board would appear to be a combination of both taking the best from each. Boards can have the right balance of ability, experience and range of view point, with perhaps the occasional rough diamond contributing an earthy wisdom and basic common sense to board room discussion. It is essential to take full advantage of all the qualities represented on the board in every way possible.

Whatever the type of director, no distinction exists in law, and all directors should be ethical in taking decisions and have the same fiduciary responsibilities.

Given the right selection, there in a valuable control element in the appointment of outside directors. Apart from acting as a check on the executive directors as body, likely to be influenced and led by the Managing Director, these can be complementary check on individuals. An enthusiastic marketing director, for instance, would be all the more effective if liable to be subjected at board meeting's to discerning questions from a non-executive director having special marketing skills and experience elsewhere.

Some attention has been given at various times to the concept of worker-directors, the essence of their participation being an increase in industrial efficiency. Some of these have no executive power, each would tend to become even more inhibited in the continual presence of higher authority, than executive directors. The danger is over course of time, they tend to get out of touch with the men.

Questions

1. Define corporate governance. Which are the main elements?
2. Discuss on the accountability issues.
3. Explain the role of board of directors.

4. What do you mean by disclosure to outsiders?
5. Discuss on the board objectives.
6. Explain the director's role involved in the organisation.
7. Mention the procedures involved in the board room.
8. Explain how to internal directors are trained and developed to involve fully in the board meetings?
9. 'The managing directors acts as a focal point in an organisation' Comment.
10. Discuss on the sailent points involved in board structure.
11. Explain how performance evaluation of board is conducted?

INDEX